Handbook of Demonstrations and Activities in the Teaching of Psychology

Volume II

Physiological-Comparative, Perception, Learning, Cognitive, and Developmental

edited by

Mark E. Ware
Creighton University

David E. Johnson
John Brown University

 LAWRENCE ERLBAUM ASSOCIATES, PUBLISHERS
1996   Mahwah, New Jersey

Lawrence Erlbaum Associates, Inc., Publishers
10 Industrial Avenue
Mahwah, New Jersey 07430

Library of Congress Cataloging-in-Publication Data

Handbook of demonstrations and activities in the teaching of psychology /
edited by Mark E. Ware, David E. Johnson.
    p. cm.
  Includes bibliographical references and index.
  Contents: v. 1. Introductory, statistics, research methods, and
history -- v. 2. Physiological-comparative, perception, learning, cognitive,
and developmental -- v. 3. Personality, abnormal, clinical-counseling, and social.
  ISBN 0-8058-1793-X (set : alk. paper). -- ISBN 0-8058-1790-5 (v. 1
: paper : alk paper). -- ISBN 0-8058-1791-3 (v. 2 : paper : alk.
paper). -- ISBN 0-8058-1792-1 (v. 3 : paper : alk. paper)
  1. Psychology--Study and teaching (Higher) 2. Psychology--Study
and teaching--Activity programs. 3. Psychology--Study and teaching-
-Simulation methods. 4. Psychology--Study and teaching--Audio
-visual methods. I. Ware, Mark E. II. Johnson, David E., 1953-
. III. Teaching of psychology (Columbia, MO)
BF77.H265 1996
150'.71'1--dc20   95-42447
                                                          CIP

Books published by Lawrence Erlbaum Associates are printed
on acid-free paper, and their bindings are chosen
for strength and durability.

Printed in the United States of America

10 9 8 7 6 5 4 3 2

Dedicated to

Charles L. Brewer

teacher, colleague, and friend

Table of Contents

4. Teaching Operant Conditioning

5. Teaching Biological Aspects of Learning

Section IV: Cognitive

Section V: Developmental - Child

1. Instigating Miscellaneous Techniques

2. Emphasizing Writing Assignments

3. Incorporating Field Experience

4. Instigating Miscellaneous Techniques

5. Using Videotapes

Preface

The history of teaching psychology is as old and as new as psychology in the United States. G. Stanley Hall, one of modern psychology's promoters, devoted considerable attention to the teaching-learning processes including the founding of the journal, *Pedagogical Seminary*, in 1891. In addition Hall (1905) examined the meaning of pedagogy and concluded that pedagogy aimed to "unfold all the powers of the individual to their maximal maturity and strength" (p. 375). In earlier writing about pedagogy, Hall (1881) commented that "reverence of knowledge for its own sake is superstitious. Ignorance is preferable to knowledge which does not affect life, and the object of discipline is to make it practical" (p. 321).

More recently, one committee at the National Conference on Enhancing the Quality of Undergraduate Education in Psychology discussed the use of pedagogical techniques authorities refer to as active learning. The committee's observation (Mathie, 1993) that pedagogy should "include strategies that foster critical thinking and problem-solving skills" (p. 184) seemed to reiterate and operationalize Hall's conclusion. Members of the committee also observed that "there is too much information being offered to students and too little attention being paid to the strategies for learning, inquiry, and problem solving" (p. 184). Thus for over 100 years, psychologists have recognized that effective teaching and learning consist of developing and applying students' skills. Because effective teaching strategies are never out of vogue, this book consists of a collection of tried and tested teaching demonstrations and activities.

Teaching of Psychology (ToP), the official journal of Division Two of the American Psychological Association, previously published all of the articles in this book. Since its inception in 1974, *ToP* has become increasingly respected as a journal devoted to improving teaching and learning at all educational levels. An article (Weimer, 1993) in an issue of *Change* featured three from among almost 50 pedagogical journals; *ToP* was one of those three. The year 1993 also marked the completion of two decades of publishing *ToP*. Those interested in a history of the journal will find the founding editor's (Daniel, 1992) personal account both stimulating and informative.

We organized 291 articles into three volumes. Volume 1 consists of 91 articles about teaching strategies for courses that make up the core of most psychology curricula; introductory psychology, statistics, research methods, and history of psychology. The topical headings in Volumes 2 and 3 reflect the order of topics in many introductory psychology texts. Volume 2 consists of 104 articles about teaching physiological-comparative, perception, learning, cognitive, and developmental psychology. Volume 3 consists of 96 articles about teaching personality, abnormal, clinical-counseling, and social psychology.

In general we assigned articles to courses in which authors developed the demonstration or activity. A table at the end of each volume identifies the primary course in which readers can use each demonstration. In many instances, we also identified other, secondary, courses in which readers might use demonstrations.

The percent of articles representing each of the 13 topical areas was about evenly distributed. Noteworthy exceptions with more than 10% of the total number of articles were developmental (14%), research methods (13%), and social (12%).

Curious readers might speculate about trends in publishing demonstrations and activities during each of *ToP*'s two decades. Inspection revealed that 62% of the total number of articles appeared during the second decade. The number of articles for developmental and social psychology showed the most dramatic increases. History and statistics were the only topics that showed a decrease in the number of articles. We can offer no unequivocal explanation for such trends.

We would like to acknowledge the assistance of several individuals who contributed to this book. Marianne Haindfield, Sergio deLourenco, and Paul Marchio from Creighton University and Beth Magallon and Blaine Hubbard from John Brown University provided dedicated and persistent assistance.

Mark E. Ware
David E. Johnson

References

Daniel, R. S. (1992). *Teaching of Psychology*, the journal. In A. E. Puente, J. R. Matthews, & C. L. Brewer (Eds.), *Teaching psychology in America: A history* (pp. 433-452). Washington, DC: American Psychological Association.

Hall, G. S. (1881). American and German methods of teaching. *The Harvard Register, 3*, 319-321.

Hall, G. S. (1905). What is pedagogy? *Pedagogical Seminary, 12*, 375-383.

Mathie, V. A. (with Beins, B., Benjamin, Jr., L. T., Ewing, M. M., Hall, C. C. I., Henderson, B., McAdam, D. W., & Smith, R A.). (1993). Promoting active learning in psychology courses. In T. V. McGovern (Ed.). *Handbook for enhancing undergraduate education in psychology* (pp. 183-214). Washington, DC: American Psychological Association.

Weimer, M. (1993, November-December). The disciplinary journals on pedagogy. *Change*, 44-51.

SECTION I
PHYSIOLOGICAL-COMPARATIVE

Preparing for Exams

James Ackil developed a game called PhysioPursuit to help students study for their physiological psychology final exam. Students formed teams that competed against one another. Similar to many popular board games, PhysioPursuit used a game board appropriately adorned with graphics of neurons and the brain.

Teaching Neuroanatomy, Neurophysiology, and Neuropharmacology

Craig Daniels gave his students 1.5 pounds of gray self-hardening clay with instructions for the construction of a complete hemisphere of the human brain. The instructions outlined procedures for molding the cerebral cortex, the cerebellum, and the brain stem. Additionally, students identified the major structures with stick-on labels and added neural pathways (e.g., the RAS) by attaching lengths of string. Students enthusiastically endorsed the activity which took approximately 75 minutes to complete.

Christopher Wilson and David Marcus modified Daniels' (1979) procedure of using clay to sculpt a brain. After standard laboratory dissections of the sheep brain, their students constructed a complete sheep brain layer by layer. The procedure focused on subcortical structures and gave the students a three-dimensional perspective of brain structures and an appreciation for the brain's evolutionary development.

Garbage bags, a bicycle pump, a cape, and a child's space gun served as props when Scott Hamilton and Thomas Knox demonstrated neuroanatomy and neurophysiology to a large class. Students volunteered to play roles such as dendrites, synaptic knobs, and neurotransmitters. The instructor cast the students in their roles and gave them directions for their activity. The entire process, from original stimulation of the afferent neuron to the contraction of a muscle, produced an entertaining and effective description of neural transmission.

Paul Solomon and his colleagues developed a series of computer simulations that demonstrated several principles of neuronal activity. The simulations showed ionic movement across the neuron membrane during an action potential, excitatory postsynaptic potential and inhibitory postsynaptic potential. The author developed the simulations for the Apple II+ and Macintosh computers.

Wolfgang Klosterhalfen described a skin conductance apparatus he developed for classroom use. The article included a schematic diagram that described the construction of the apparatus. The author included several suggestions for using the apparatus in the classroom.

Susan Schumacher gave her physiological psychology students first-hand experience in behavioral pharmacology. Using only behavioral tests, student teams attempted to determine the drug their laboratory rats had been given. Preparation for the activity required considerable research into the behavioral effects of 20 drugs from which the instructor chose. This laboratory exercise proved to be cost-effective and popular among the students.

Paul Wellman described a procedure he used in a physiological psychology laboratory that involved a simple procedure for students who were novices to surgery. Thermogenesis in brown adipose tissue provided a means of assessing the effects of drugs on several metabolic and neuropharmacological processes.

Teaching Hemispheric Laterality

Student interest in hemispheric laterality led Ernest Kemble and his colleagues to develop two experiments to demonstrate hemispheric specialization without requiring expensive equipment. The equipment consisted of children's wooden blocks with raised letters and numbers and several wooden dowels. One of the experiments required students to balance a dowel with their hand (preferred and nonpreferred) while performing a verbal task or while silent. Several outcomes of the experiments corresponded to predictions based on the left hemisphere's dominant role in language production.

Edward Morris simulated the behavioral and perceptual experiences of split-brain patients by asking two students to play the role of cerebral hemispheres. The students sat next to each other in an arrangement that required them to carry out tasks as if they were one person. The student on the left represented the left hemisphere and the student on the right represented the right hemisphere. They held their outside hands behind their backs and crossed their inside arms so that the right hand of the person on the left became the "patient's" right hand and vice versa for the person on the right. The instructor asked the students to perform a variety of tasks such as tying a shoe. Some tasks simulated the verbal and visual deficits observed in split-brain patients under specific conditions. Students responded enthusiastically to this demonstration.

Introducing Reaction Time as a Measure of Neural Activity

Rae Harcum devised a procedure for demonstrating the difference between a simple and disjunctive reaction time. Two groups of students responded to different instructions in a quiz about U.S. presidents. Members of the control group raised their left hands when the instructor mentioned the name of a president; members of the experimental group raised their right hands if the president served before Lincoln and raised their left hands if the president served after Lincoln. The remaining class members noted which group reacted faster. The control group was significantly faster than the experimental group. Subsequent discussion focused on the differential processing requirements of the groups. The author included several additional embellishments of the activity.

Based on procedures use by Helmholz, Paul Rozin and John Jonides designed several ingenious methods to demonstrate neuronal conduction speed with groups of students. One procedure required 10-20 students to link themselves in a chain by holding each other's shoulder. Students closed their eyes, and the instructor told them to squeeze the shoulder of the adjacent person when they felt their own shoulder squeezed. The instructor started the chain reaction and timed it. The class compared these times to those generated in a similar procedure in which they squeezed ankles, rather than shoulders. The neuronal conduction speed fell in the expected range. This article also presented demonstrations of mental processing speeds using memory sets and mental rotation methodologies.

Teaching Comparative Psychology

Robert Batsell's students played the role of rats in a classroom demonstration of timing and the internal clock. A modified peak procedure required students to estimate 20-and 40-s intervals and respond within a 4-s window at the end of the intervals to receive reinforcement. The instructor added blackout trials to demonstrate stopping and restarting the clock and interval shift trials to demonstrate the underlying timing mechanism. Data resembled those collected in timing studies with rats.

In his second article, Batsell modified transitive inference problems to simulate testing of nonverbal organisms. Students solved verbal transitivity problems with ease, but failed to understand how animals learned to respond correctly. By using pictures as stimuli, the instructor gave students a perspective that more closely approximated the experience of an animal. The procedure illustrated several transitivity-related issues and provided a basis to discuss theories of transitive inference in nonverbal organisms.

In a 2 × 2 factorial design, Robert Brown's students exposed albino and pigmented mice to both dim and bright light and recorded the resulting activity and defecation of the mice. Differential responses of the two strains of mice to the brightness manipulations facilitated the instructor's discussion of the interaction between genetics and environment. The experiment also gave students additional exposure to concepts such as operational definitions and interobserver reliability.

Ernest Kemble sought a less expensive alternative to traditional animal laboratory procedures and described his use of insects and rodents to illustrate several behavioral and physiological phenomena. The article also described the equipment and possible choices of rodents and insects.

1. PREPARING FOR EXAMS

PhysioPursuit: A Trivia-Type Game for the Classroom

James E. Ackil
Western Illinois University

A classroom game, based on a trivia-type game format, to help students prepare for the cumulative final exam in a physiological psychology course was designed. Details of game construction and play are described.

What are Schwann cells? Where are Merkel's disks located? Who was Karl Lashley's academic adviser? According to many students, studying for a final exam in any course, especially a course in physiological psychology, can be a dull and often anxiety-provoking task. Recently, however, I used a classroom game that seemed to make the task a little more pleasant. Based on a popular, trivia-type game format, the game came to be known as PhysioPursuit or TrivioPhysio.

Students were told about the game early in the course, but teams were not formed until a few weeks before the game was played during the last week of the semester. This gave me a chance to select the top students as team captains and assign players to balance the teams. In my class of 30 students, 5 teams of 6 students each were formed. To add to team spirit and competitiveness, team names such as The Limbic System, The Olfactory Bulbs, and The Basal Ganglia, were assigned. Prizes for the winning team were awarded as an incentive. These included individual certificates of achievement, members' names added to a permanent plaque hanging in my office, and a psychology textbook for each team member (culled from old editions cluttering my shelves). An additional incentive was the promise that a number of the questions asked during the game would appear on the final exam. This factor probably contributed to the almost perfect attendance and close attention on the last 2 days of the semester when the game was played.

I prepared short-answer questions for the game throughout the semester, storing them on 3 x 5" cards. All questions were taken from the textbook used in the course (Kalat, 1984). I tried to include a variety of easy and difficult questions. This pool of questions also came in handy in writing the final exam. A number (approximately 10%) of obscure or trivial questions were also included. These served several purposes. First, they prevented any one team from running away

with the contest. Second, the trivia questions provided some students with a chance to demonstrate knowledge that they were unaware they had. The student who knew that John B. Watson was Lashley's academic adviser was not one of the better students in the class. And, of course, these questions provided comic relief, occasionally in the form of groans.

The method of play was relatively simple and similar to many board games. A large gameboard was made of cardboard. A brain was drawn in the middle of the board. Four different colors of neurons, each color representing a collection of questions taken from a grouping of textbook chapters, formed a border around the edge of the board. Synapses connected these neurons, so that game pieces could be advanced from one neuron to the next. Corner neurons had axons that branched to form a synapse with the brain in the center of the board. To play, a team captain rolled a die, then moved from neuron to neuron around the board according to the number rolled. The team had to answer a question that corresponded to the neuron color on which it ended. The question came from the deck of 3 x 5" question cards I had prepared for each of the four chapter groupings. If the team answered the question correctly it rolled again and continued until it failed to answer a question. When a team answered two questions from each of the four decks, it had to land, by die roll, on the brain and answer one last question from the deck of its choice. The team that answered this final question won the game. Because no team made it to the brain before class time was up, the team that had answered the most questions was declared the winner. On the other hand, if a team had won too quickly, additional rounds could have been played.

Students seemed to enjoy playing the game. Some commented that it reminded them of spelling bees and other grade school competitions. One feature that made the game fun to play was that every student knew an answer that most others did not know. It was common for teammates and opponents to remark, "How did you know that?" Most students were surprised at how much they could recall. Students liked the challenge of playing, were made aware of their newly acquired knowledge, and appreciated clues to the enigmatic final exam. The large amount of factual information in the physiological psychology course makes it particularly suitable for the trivia game. Other courses and situations (e.g., history and systems course, Psi Chi activity) might also lend themselves to such a game. What year was it that Wundt established his first experimental psychology laboratory?

Reference

Kalat, J. W. (1984). *Biological psychology* (2nd ed.). Belmont, CA: Wadsworth.

2. TEACHING NEUROANATOMY, NEUROPHYSIOLOGY, AND NEUROPHARMACOLOGY

Should a Psychology Student Have a Brain of Clay?

Craig E. Daniels
University of Hartford

Ideally, teaching aids should motivate students and facilitate learning both in the classroom and later when the student studies the material on his own. A variety of teaching aids is often used when teaching brain structure to introductory psychology students, but few seem to meet all three criteria. For example, I have found demonstrations using actual human brains that students can handle if they wish (although relatively few wish to), are surefire "attention-grabbers." Along with slides and movies, such demonstrations pique a student's interest and can be quite useful classroom teaching aids but are of limited value to a student studying in his room for an exam. Diagrammatic handouts and topic outlines or summaries, on the other hand, are available for home study and can be very useful for already motivated students, but in my exeience do not themselves motivate students and in a few cases may even be a motivational handicap (the all-you-have-to-do-is-memorize-the–handouts syndrome).

Are there any inexpensive teaching aids that, in this area, meet all three criteria? My suggestion is to give your students 1.5 pounds of air-dry clay and have them model a three-dimensional hemi-section of the human brain. (The technique requires no more artistic talent on the part of either the instructor or the students than a paint-by-numbers set.)

I have used and refined the clay brain exercise over the past three semesters and informal and formal feedback suggests that introductory psychology students find the task "interesting" and "useful." Formal student evaluations are conducted each semester throughout the college and in response to an open-ended question on what the instructor has done especially well, each semester several students write comments such as the clay brains are "a great idea," "fun," "good study aid," "very helpful," "I enjoyed making it."

However, in order to more specifically assess student perception at the time when they would be maximally sensitive to the utility of the clay brain the following questions are asked anonymously of all students at the end of the course exam covering brain structure and function: "How helpful was making the clay brain in learning brain structures?" (options: very helpful, helpful, slightly helpful, not helpful); "Would you recommend that the clay brain be used next semester as part of this course?" (options: yes, no). More than 90%

of the students who made a clay brain indicated that it was "very helpful" or "helpful" and virtually 100% recommend that it be used the next semester.

The task requires approximately 75 minutes of class time, costs about 80¢ per student and As based on student feedback appears to be well worth the time, money and effort.

Procedure. At the class session prior to the one scheduled for the making of the models, students are given self-adhesive unprinted mailing labels together with a list of names of brain structures/areas. Students are instructed to cut each mailing label into smaller labels and write the name of the structures on these in pencil (ink smudges). The list of names indicates the approximate size for each label which range from approximately 3 x 6 mm for the pituitary and amygdala to

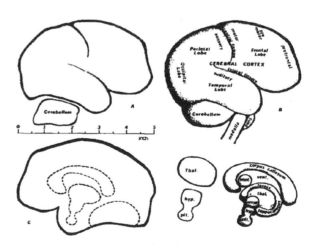

Figure 1. Student handout for construction of clay brain.

9 x 15 (mm) for the temporal lobe and cerebellum. It is much easier if the student removes the mailing label from the backing paper, cuts it into the desired number of small labels, and then resticks these small labels to the backing paper. This way the labels are easily removed in class and applied to the clay model as it is constructed.

When students arrive at the next class, they are given the following materials: a plastic bag containing approximately 1.5 pounds of grey self-hardening clay;

an old file folder or piece of plastic to use as a work surface; paper towels for clean-up; two printed diagrams as shown; a straight pin (colored head dressmakers pins are ideal), a sharpened pencil, a 4-inch piece of multistrand string, a 5-inch piece of colored yarn, and a plastic fork (optional).

Students begin by placing approximately 2/3 of their clay (1 pound) on the outline of the cerebral cortex (Diagram A). Using primarily the finger tips, they should mound up the clay (adding or subtracting clay if necessary) until it approximates the shape of the cerebral cortex. It is important that the final mound of clay conform to the outline on the sheet as closely as possible, and students should lift the edge of the clay from the diagram to check the outline periodically. Once the desired shape is achieved, the student should etch in the central and lateral fissures with the pencil and insert the appropriate label on the side of each fissure. To find the correct position for the central and lateral fissures, the student can lift the clay off the diagram slightly, and at this point the student should make sure the outline of the clay cortex corresponds to the outline on the diagram. Labels for the outside of the cerebral cortex can now be attached (frontal lobe, parietal lobe, motor area, auditory area, etc.), and random fissures marked in the clay between the labels.

Next the student should take a medium-sized ball of the remaining clay, and using the outline on the diagram, model the cerebellum in the same way as the cerebral cortex. The height of the cerebellum should approximate that of the cerebrum. The cerebellum can now be moved into position and attached to the cerebrum. Small pieces of plastic coffee stirrers or wooden matchsticks inserted halfway into each piece will give added structural rigidity—these pegs should be used when joining any two pieces of clay. In addition, the separate pieces must be firmly pressed together and the edges sealed with the side of the pencil tip so that the parts do not separate as the clay dries. Stria can now be made on the cerebellum using either the pencil or a plastic fork and the appropriate labels attached.

Similarly, the medulla and pons should be made by rolling and attaching a small cylinder and mound of clay respectively. Once these structures have been attached and labeled, the model should be carefully removed from the diagram, held gently in the hand (curved side down), and the flat surface (medial plane) smoothed. Using Diagram C as a template, the student should mark the position of the corpus callosum, the thalamus-hypothalamus-pituitary complex, and the boundary of the cerebellum by a series of pinholes through the dotted lines on the diagram into the clay (roughly cutting out Diagram C will aid in positioning the template but is not necessary). After removing the template (Diagram C), the outline of the corpus callosum and the cerebellum should be etched in with the pencil. (The thalamus-hypothalamus-pituitary complex should not be outlined—the pinholes are position guides.) The corpus callosum can then be stippled in with the tip of the pencil to make it stand out clearly

and the foliation of the cerebellum etched in (draw a diagram of the foliation on the blackboard). The hindbrain structures, corpus callosum, and areas of the cerebral cortex should now be labeled. Actually the model is not a true hemi-section but a medial sagittal section with attached contralateral thalamus and portions of the limbic system. Therefore, the student should refer to the handout for size and shape and make a small "pigeon egg" thalamus with attached hypothalamus and pituitary. (The infundibulum on the handout was exaggerated so that if modeled completely from clay the pituitary does not separate as the model dries; however, an alternative method would be to use a wood/plastic peg to simulate the infundibulum and attach the pituitary to the hypothalamus.) This complex should then be attached (with hidden pegs) in the proper position (pinholes in clay). At this point, the anterior end of the lateral ventricle can be added by making an indentation with the end of the pencil between the thalamus and the corpus callosum. The corpus callosum, lateral ventricle, thalamus, hypothalamus, and pituitary should now be labeled. Finally, the major portion of the limbic system (septal area/fornix, hippocampus, and amygdala) should be modeled by rolling a strip of clay into a "long worm," doubling the end back on itself, and pinching the clay at each end into a round ball, as shown on the diagram. This complex can then be fastened into position around the thalamus, and the septal and amygdaloid areas offset slightly. These structures should then be labeled, and at this point the basic model is complete.

Several additional systems/pathways, however, can easily be added. For example, the reticular activating system (RAS) can be represented by a piece of string as follows: Separate the string into individual strands; Knot the strands together about 1" from one end; Press the knot into the pons and fasten in place (a small U of wire is useful); Fan out the individual strands and, using the pencil tip, embed each strand in the clay cortex and cut off any excess string; Embed the short ends of the strands as a bundle into the medulla; Label the pontine nucleus of the RAS (knot) and the RAS.

The pyramidal system can also be easily represented by embedding one end of the piece of yarn in the motor cortex, tacking the center of the yarn in place with a wire U on the side of the thalamus, and embedding the other end in the posterior medulla.

Because the clay dries rapidly on exposure to air, students should be careful to keep the unused clay in the plastic bag until they are ready to use it. By the end of the 75-minute period, the clay will have begun to harden, and although it can be kept in plastic and finished at a later time, it is better to complete the model, including labeling, in one session. Left exposed to the air, the clay will dry in 1-2 days and will last indefinitely if handled carefully and not exposed to water.

Teaching Anatomy of the Sheep Brain:
A Laboratory Exercise With PlayDoh™

Christopher Wilson
David K. Marcus
Sam Houston State University

Undergraduates gain a three-dimensional view of the structures of the sheep brain, first by following a standard dissection procedure and then by constructing a model using PlayDoh™. Both methods demonstrate evolutionary trends in brain development. Students reported that the lab was helpful for learning about neuroanatomy, and they recommended its use in future semesters.

A typical procedure for learning basic neuroanatomy in a physiological psychology laboratory is to inspect, dissect, and identify various structures of a sheep brain. Laboratory manuals, such as Cooley and Vanderwolf (1979), Hart (1976), and Skinner (1971), provide detailed procedures for this task. Our undergraduate physiological psychology course enrolls about 25 upper level students (almost entirely juniors and seniors). It meets for 3 hr of lecture each week, with a 2-hr lab. One course goal is for students to gain a three-dimensional mental representation of the brain, so that they can identify structures and tracts from samples cut at both traditional and odd angles.

In the past, we had students inspect the outer surface of a sheep brain, locating the lobes and identifying the major gyri and sulci. They then dissected the brain, either with horizontal or coronal sections. They spent two lab periods (4 hr) dissecting the sheep brain. Over the years, we found that students could identify structures from traditional cuts they had made in lab, but they had problems identifying areas from cuts they had not seen before. This inability to recognize structures from nontraditional cuts seemed to indicate that the students did not have an adequate representation of the brain. After trying several approaches to help students develop more accurate and comprehensive representations of the brain, we added an exercise in which students construct brains out of PlayDoh™.

Constructing a PlayDoh Model

After two labs in which students dissected actual sheep brains, they then constructed models out of PlayDoh. The students used different colors of PlayDoh to demarcate various regions of the brain. Their directions were as follows: Roll out a spinal cord with an enlarged bulb representing the thalamus at one end (see Figure 1a). Add a pons wrapping around the spinal cord with a cerebellum attached to the dorsal extremities of the pons (i.e., the cerebral peduncles; see Figure 1b). On the ventral surface, just caudal to the pons, pinch midline tissue to represent the pyramids. Roll out a V to represent the cerebral peduncles, and attach it to the spinal cord just anterior to the pons (see Figure 1c). Inside the V, place two small pieces of clay representing the mammillary bodies, with a hole representing the infundibular recess just anterior to this. Place an X representing the optic chiasm, nerves, and tracts anterior to the recess (see Figure 1d).

Place four small pieces of clay at the posterior portion of the thalamus to form the inferior and superior colliculi (see Figure 2a). Construct two horned hippocampi, which join to form the fornix, and wrap this complex around the thalamus (see Figure 2b). Place two small pieces of clay representing the caudate nuclei on the dorsal and most rostral portions of the thalamus (see Figure 2c). Place some flattened clay, representing the internal capsule, around the lateral border of each caudate (see Figure 2d).

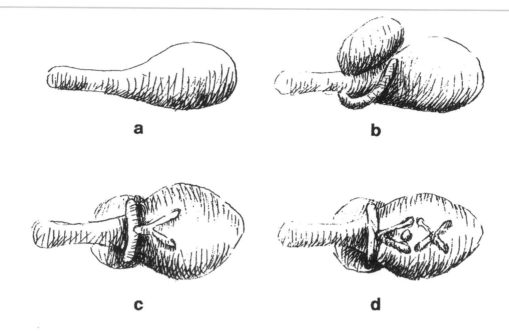

Figure 1. (a) Lateral view. (b) Lateral view. (c) Ventral view. (d) Ventral view.

Insert a pineal gland between superior parts of the superior colliculi. Lay a flattened piece of clay, to represent the corpus callosum, over the top of the area representing the caudate, hippocampus, fornix, and thalamus. Form the medullary core by intermixing the internal capsule with the extreme lateral portions of the corpus callosum (see Figure 3). Leave enough space under the corpus callosum to represent the lateral ventricles. Finally, lay a sheet of clay over the entire structure to represent the cortex.

By carefully manipulating the model, students could peer into the cisterna magna and the lateral ventricles and see the relative locations of the colliculi, fornix, hippocampi, caudate, and thalamus. Students could also view the fourth ventricle and, with a pencil point, insert a cerebral aqueduct. After being led through the process of building these models, students crushed them and built new models without directions from the lab instructor. The lab instructor examined these models and questioned the students about the different regions and structures they included. The entire modeling lab takes about 1.5 hr to complete.

Daniels (1979) also described a lab exercise in which students use clay models to learn neuroanatomy. Although both procedures use modeling, our procedures are complementary. Daniels had students construct a hemi-section of the human brain. The hemi-section provides the students with one particular cut, whereas our approach, which involves adding structures layer by layer, may give students more of a three-dimensional perspective. Because Daniels's

model is of a human brain, much more emphasis is placed on cortical structures. Our model of a sheep brain emphasizes subcortical structures. Finally, because we use a sheep brain, students can compare their models to the actual brains they dissected in class. Instructors may have students construct both models as a way to compare human and sheep neuroanatomy.

Student Evaluations

Twenty-five undergraduates (16 women and 9 men) enrolled in a physiological psychology course were asked to evaluate our procedure 2 weeks after they completed the lab. They used a 7-point scale, with 1 indicating the most negative view and 7 the most positive view. to respond to the: following: (a) I found the clay model lab to be a helpful way to learn about neuroanatomy, (b) I thought the clay model was (less at 1 to more at 7) interesting than a lecture on neuroanatomy, (c) I found that the clay model lab helped me to prepare for identifying neural areas, (d) I think the clay model lab should be used in future semesters, and (e) overall my feelings about the clay model lab were (very negative to very positive). Scores on each item ranged from 3 to 7, with a grand mean of 6.1. Thus, almost all the students evaluated the PlayDoh model lab quite positively.

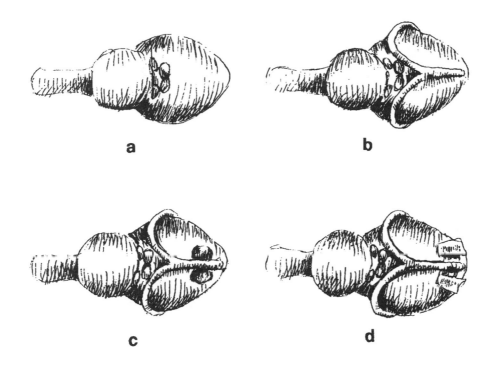

Figure 2. (a) Dorsal view. (b) Dorsal view. (c) Dorsal view. (d) Dorsal view.

Figure 3. Dorsal view.

Our procedure presents a few minor difficulties. Many students placed the hippocampi in backward, and lab instructors should watch for this common error. When asked to build the model on their own, students had difficulty constructing it to scale. For ex-ample, the caudate nuclei were consistently too large, and the cerebellum was consistently too small. After corrections from the instructor, most students pro-duced reasonable models. Considering the students' enthusiasm for the modeling lab and that this procedure probably allows students to develop three-dimensional images of brain structures, instructors may wish to consider using this exercise to supplement more traditional dissection labs.

References

Cooley, R. K., & Vanderwolf, C. H. (1979). *The sheep brain: A basic guide.* London, Canada: Kirby.

Daniels, C. E. (1979). Should a psychology student have a brain of clay? *Teaching of Psychology, 6,* 175-177.

Hart, B. L. (1976). *Experimental psychobiology: A laboratory manual.* San Francisco: Freeman.

Skinner, J. E. (1971). *Neuroscience: A laboratory manual.* Philadelphia: Saunders.

Notes

1. Portions of this article were reported at the Council of Teachers of Undergraduate Psychology at the Southwestern Psychological Association meeting, Austin, TX, April 1992.
2. We thank Carl Ashworth for producing the figures and three anonymous reviewers for their helpful comments.

The Colossal Neuron: Acting Out Physiological Psychology

Scott B. Hamilton
Thomas A. Knox
Colorado State University

Increasing enrollments in such survey courses as Introductory Psychology create special problems for the instructor interested in alternatives to traditional lecture methods. Although in-class demonstrations have been used to maintain student interest and increase the retention of information in large classroom environments, physiological psychology has been largely overlooked in terms of instructional innovation. This article provides detailed instructions concerning how to teach neuron anatomy and physiology via a ½-hour dramatic presentation involving 30 student volunteers. Data are presented to support the perceived educational and entertainment value of this active teaching method.

While university resources are diminishing, instructors are faced with increasingly large classes. This is especially true for those who teach such popular survey courses as Introductory Psychology where classes of 200, 500, or even 1,000 students are not uncommon. Thus, instructors must use limited educational resources to maximize an important learning experience for students.

The difficulties involved in effectively teaching large classes have been addressed by using a variety of approaches, including videotape (e.g., Rosenkoetter, 1984), dramatization (Older, 1979), and the creative use of teaching assistants (Silverstein, 1982). In addition, in-class demonstrations have been advocated to maintain student interest and enhance the retention of information by exploiting the relationship between course material and the everyday life experiences of students (Caudle, 1979; Rosenkoetter, 1984; Silverstein, 1982).

More specifically, demonstrations have been found to be beneficial in teaching such diverse content as cognitive psychology (Chaffin & Herrmann, 1983; Shaffer, 1982; Thieman, 1984), social psychology (Banziger, 1982; Smith, 1982), personality (Benjamin, 1983), learning (Gibb, 1983), sensation and perception (Beins, 1983), psychotherapy (Balch, 1983), and statistics (Levin, 1982). Brain structure (Daniels, 1979) and nerve impulse speed (Rozin & Jonides, 1977) have also been addressed, but demonstrations of neuron activity that are applicable to large introductory classes have not been presented in the teaching of psychology literature.

Therefore, the purpose of this article is to describe a demonstration concerning neuron anatomy and physiology that has been used as part of a large (i.e., 300 to 400 students) Introductory Psychology course at Colorado State University over the past 5 years. In addition, data from students will be provided to support its value as both a pragmatic aid to comprehension and as an entertaining educational technique.

PREDEMONSTRATION PREPARATION

The topic of physiological psychology is introduced with two 50-min lectures on the nervous system. These lectures are traditional in format and cover such basic information as types of neurons, glial cells, speed of neuronal transmission, neuron firing, the action potential, and neurotransmitter activity. At the close of the second lecture, students are informed that a demonstration will be presented during the next class period that will involve 30 students joining to construct a "functioning" colossal neuron.

Before the day of the demonstration, the instructor compiles what may, at first glance, appear to be a rather bizarre set of items. Table 1 presents the list of props to be used and the signs that will identify participants during the demonstration. Readers are encouraged to modify this list to suit their own resources and needs. Although the list may appear rather long, 15 min the night before should be sufficient time to procure the necessary props. The identification signs, made by printing on standard typing paper with a large felt-tipped marker, can be stored and reused each time the demonstration is conducted.

With the preparatory lectures accomplished and the equipment and identification signs collected, the instructor is ready for "Demonstration Day." The demonstration takes approximately 30 min, including the neuron review, casting, dress rehearsal, and demonstration proper.

Table 1. Props and Identification Signs Needed for the Colossal Neuron Demonstration

Props (generic)	Identification Signs	
Bicycle air pump (1)	Activating Stimulus (1)	Soma (2)
Child's space gun (1)	Dendrite (3)	Sodium Ion + (3)
Garbage bags (4)	Action Potential (1)	Synaptic Knob (4)
Cape (1)	"A" (2)	Neurotransmitter (3)
Lightning-bolt hat (1)	"X" (2)	Deactivating Enzyme (1)
	"O" (2)	Receptor Site (3)
	"N" (2)	Muscle (1)

Note. Numbers in parentheses indicate the quantity of each prop and identification sign needed. The preferred space gun emits noises that can be heard by all class members. The lightning-bolt hat is the soft plastic or cloth variety that can be obtained from most gag and department stores; worn by the runner, it helps in emphasizing the speed of neuronal transmission.

Neuron Review

The neuron review is accomplished in about 10 min and is used to consolidate information imparted over the previous two lectures as well as to link abstract content from the text with the concrete demonstration to follow. The knee-jerk reflex is used as the primary example because of its neurological simplicity, and an overhead transparency is used to point out such anatomical components as the receptor dendrites, the synapse in the spinal cord, and the motor neuron innervating the thigh muscle. A diagram illustrating the anatomy and physiology of an afferent and efferent neuron is also distributed (see Fig. 1).

After describing the knee-jerk reflex (with the aid of the first transparency), the instructor explains each step of the afferent-efferent diagram (which is also on a transparency), with reference to the knee-jerk reflex. For example, the students are shown how the activating stimulus is the same as the hammer that strikes the area below the kneecap, how the action potential is generated on stimulation of the dendrites, and how the action potential skips from node to node if the axon is myelinated. It is also emphasized that typically there is only one neurotransmitter in each neuron, and that a particular neurotransmitter fits into only one specific kind of receptor site. The roles of potassium and calcium ions are also reviewed, although they are eliminated from the diagram for the sake of simplicity. Once the neuron review is completed, casting begins.

Casting

The neuron review ends with the announcement that 30 volunteers will be needed for the "Colossal Neuron Demonstration." The call for volunteers (especially in classes of 300 or more students) is first met with silence, and then with whispers, giggles, and other uncooperative noises. To encourage participation, several sealed envelopes are held up as the instructor indicates that volunteers can have whatever is inside (usually they contain play money). Slowly, the first few volunteers come forward and are asked to stand near the stage in the front of the class while two "specialized" volunteers are sought. The students are first asked, "Who in the class is a track star or was a track star in high school?" If no one responds, the instructor asks, "Who has someone sitting near you who is a runner or a jogger?" (several are now pointing to a few students). A runner can now be fairly easily cajoled into joining the steadily-growing group of volunteers. Using the same technique, a weight-lifter/body-builder is added. By now there are a fairly large number of people milling about near the front of the class and the noise level is high throughout the room. Although for the moment it looks like pandemonium, the casting to form the colossal neuron is ready to proceed.

While Figure 1 is kept on the overhead projector, students are chosen to play each of the 30 parts and are arranged at the front of the room in the same position as in Figure 1. First the body builder is assigned to play the part of the muscle and is placed on the far right with the "MUSCLE" sign attached to the person's chest with cellophane tape. Four students are then chosen to play the efferent axon, and the appropriate signs are attached, lining them up so that they spell "AXON" when viewed by the rest of the class. A student is chosen to be the soma, then three males are selected to be receptor sites and three females to be neurotransmitters. A volunteer is now assigned the role of the deactivating enzyme and is given the space gun to hold. Next, the synaptic knobs are chosen, and then, the sodium ions. Each student is placed into position according to Figure 1, which remains projected overhead throughout the demonstration. The runner/jogger is assigned the role of the action potential, is given the lightning-bolt hat and cape to wear, and is placed into position. Four more students are chosen to be the afferent axon and are given plastic garbage bags to wear because of their myelinated status. Another student is assigned the role of the soma of the afferent neuron and is given the air pump to hold. Three males are chosen to be dendrites, and a female is assigned the part of the activating stimulus.

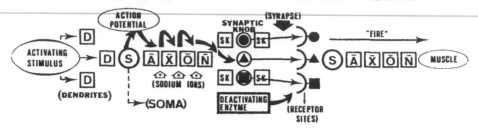

AFFERENT NEURON   EFFERENT NEURON

Figure 1. Diagram of neuron anatomy and physiology used during the colossal neuron demonstration. (The black circle, triangle, and square in the middle of the figure represent three different types of neurotransmitters.)

At this point, 30 students, some with props or costumes, and each wearing an identification sign, are arranged across the front of the room to match the overhead projection of Figure 1. Dress rehearsal for the activation of the colossal neuron can now begin.

DRESS REHEARSAL

The class is informed that the action of the nerve impulse will be performed in slow motion. First, a final check is made to ensure that everyone is in proper position and that the students comprising both axons are holding hands or locking arms in order to keep the sodium ions on the outside of the axon. The activating stimulus is then asked to "do whatever you would like to do to stimulate these dendrites." Although this instruction prompts various reactions from the audience, the instructor quickly directs the males playing the dendrites to "make the sound you usually make when stimulated." After the dendrites make noises, the soma is told to yell "fire," and immediately the runner/action potential, complete with lightning-bolt hat and cape, begins darting in and out along the axon between the myelinated students. As this action occurs, each student/axon in turn yells "fire" and drops hands, allowing each sodium ion to rush in sequentially. Thus, the permeability of the axon changes with respect to sodium ions, and depolarization takes place.

Depolarization is followed immediately by the soma "pumping" the sodium ions back out, via the action of the bicycle (sodium/potassium) pump. Meanwhile, the action potential bumps the neurotransmitters, which respond by moving across the synapse toward their respective receptor sites. Each neurotransmitter has either an "A," "B," or "C" on her sign, and each receptor site has the same on his sign. Thus, the "lock and key" specificity of neurotransmitters and receptor sites is again emphasized. (Students are reminded, however, that there would typically be only one neurotransmitter per neuron.) The receptor sites are told to hold their arms out in a receptive position and to "bind-on" (i.e., hug) their neurotransmitter as she arrives. Immediately, the deactivating enzyme shoots the neurotransmitters with the electronic space gun,

they collapse to the floor, and return on hands and knees to the area surrounded by synaptic knobs. Simultaneously, the efferent soma has yelled "fire" and the student/axons have each dropped hands and sequentially yelled "fire." Finally, as the last student yells "fire," the weight-lifter (muscle) is asked to strike a body-builder's pose, to the delight of all.

The class is then asked if they need one more dress rehearsal. Because they typically do, the performance is rehearsed in slow motion one more time, and then the announcement is made that it is time for "action."

DEMONSTRATION PROPER

The instructor moves to the back of the room and to the call of "ready . . . roll 'em," the sequence occurs with three consecutive repetitions. The instructor stands back and the audience watches as the activating stimulus "stimulates" the dendrites, the action potential starts running, the soma and subsequently each student/axon yell "fire," sodium rushes in and is quickly pumped back out, neurotransmitters migrate and then become deactivated, the muscle flexes, and the process begins again.

WRAP-UP

After the laughter subsides and a round of applause is given to the "Colossal Neuron Players," the instructor quickly retrieves all props and signs and responds to any questions and comments from the class. The role of sodium, potassium, and calcium ions is again emphasized. The transition from the molecular to the molar aspects of the nervous system is accomplished during the final 20 min of class. This traditional lecture content on the central and peripheral nervous systems provides an appropriate introduction to later lectures on cortical function and the endocrine system.

EVALUATION

During the past 5 years, it has been apparent that students have enjoyed the colossal neuron demonstration and have found it to be helpful. In order to obtain a more formal evaluation, data were collected via an anonymous 6-item questionnaire immediately following the fall, 1984 demonstration. Students were asked to rate on a 5-point Likert scale (0 = *not at all*; 4 = *extremely*) how helpful they found the 10-min neuron review, as well as the demonstration, in increasing their understanding of neuron anatomy and physiology. They were also asked to rate how entertaining they found the demonstration to be, and to indicate whether or not they thought the review and demonstration together would aid them in remembering neuronal content, whether the review should be retained as part of the course, and whether the demonstration itself should be retained. Comparisons were made between the responses of the 30 participants and the 311 nonparticipants.

RESULTS

The authors' impression that the demonstration appealed to students was supported by the finding that 99.1% of all students favored retention of the demonstration (100% of the participants and 99% of the observers). In addition, 99.7% indicated that both the review and demonstration assisted in their retention of the material, thus supporting the notion that the colossal neuron is not only entertaining but also educational.

Two-tailed t tests for independent samples indicated that there were no differences between participants and observers in terms of helpfulness of the review, helpfulness of the demonstration, and how entertaining the demonstration was (all $ps > .30$). These results suggested that participation was not necessary for self-reported benefits to occur and that participation did not interfere with perceived learning. The t tests for correlated measures suggested that students found the demonstration ($M = 3.37$; $SD = 0.64$) to be significantly more helpful in their understanding of neuron anatomy and operation than was the review ($M = 2.50$; $SD = 0.89$). Interestingly, however, 97.9% of all students favored retention of the review. These findings suggested that, although the demonstration was seen as being more helpful than the traditional lecture/review method, students perceived the educational relevance of the review in combination with the demonstration.

CONCLUDING COMMENTS

Recently, two business students who had taken Introductory Psychology 3 years earlier approached the first author to request assistance in setting up a demonstration for a management class using student participation. The gratifying nature of this encounter was that the students could recite the basic components and operation of the neuron by conjuring up an image of ". . . all those funny people running around on

stage," and that they were interested in applying this active teaching method to another field of study.

Although neither the preceding anecdote nor the subjective evaluations of students proves that the active demonstration method enhances learning and retention, the colossal neuron appears to have been well received by introductory students over the past 5 years. Because the anatomical and electrochemical aspects of neuronal activity are often seen as abstract and irrelevant to students' everyday experience, the colossal neuron combines the visual, auditory, and humorous aspects of live drama to allow difficult content to become anchored to concrete events. Although some instructors may prefer to spend less time on the molecular aspects of physiological psychology, the importance of neuronal activity in understanding such phenomena as schizophrenia, habituation, the effects of drugs, and other content areas, may justify the 2½ class periods devoted to this issue. Regardless of teacher preference, the colossal neuron may provide an effective alternative to the traditional presentation of physiological content in the large undergraduate classroom.

References

Balch, W. R. (1983). The use of role-playing in a classroom demonstration of client-centered therapy. *Teaching of Psychology, 10*, 173-174.

Banziger, G. (1982). Teaching about crowding: Students as an independent variable. *Teaching of Psychology, 9*, 241-242.

Beins, B. (1983). The light box: A simple way of generating complex color demonstrations. *Teaching of Psychology, 10*, 113-114.

Benjamin, L. T., Jr. (1983). A class exercise in personality and psychological assessment. *Teaching of Psychology, 10*, 94-95.

Caudle, F. M. (1979). Using "demonstrations, class experiments and the projection lantern" in the history of psychology course. *Teaching of Psychology, 6*, 7-11.

Chaffing R., & Herrmann, D. J. (1983). A classroom demonstration of depth of processing. *Teaching of Psychology, 10*, 105–107.

Daniels, C. E. (1979). Should a psychology student have a brain of clay? *Teaching of Psychology, 6*, 175-177.

Gibb, G. D. (1983). Making classical conditioning understandable through a demonstration technique. *Teaching of Psychology, 10*, 112–113

Levin, J. R. (1982). Modifications of a regression-toward-the-mean demonstration. *Teaching of Psychology, 9*, 237–238.

Older, J. (1979). Improving the introductory psychology course. *Teaching of Psychology, 6*, 75–77.

Rosenkoetter, J. S. (1984). Teaching psychology to large classes: Videotapes, PSI and lecturing. *Teaching of Psychology, 11*, 85–87.

Rozin, P., & Jonides, J. (1977). Mass reaction time: Measurement of the speed of the nerve impulse and the duration of mental processes in class. *Teaching of Psychology, 4*, 91–94.

Shaffer, L. S. (1982). Hamilton's marbles or Jevon's beans: A demonstration of Miller's magical number seven. *Teaching of Psychology, 9*, 116–117.

Silverstein, B. (1982). Teaching a large lecture course in psychology: Turning defeat into victory. *Teaching of Psychology, 9*, 150–155.

Smith, G . F. (1982). Introducing psychology majors to clinical bias through the adjective generation technique. *Teaching of Psychology, 9*, 238–239.

Thieman, T. J. (1984). A classroom demonstration of encoding specificity. *Teaching of Psychology, 11*, 101–102.

Computer Simulation of the Neuronal Action Potential

Paul R. Solomon
Scott Cooper
Dean Pomerleau
Williams College

A series of computer simulations of the neuronal resting and action potentials are described. These programs are designed to allow the user to observe the movement of ions across a neuronal membrane during: (a) an action potential, (b) a subthreshold excitatory postsynaptic potential (EPSP), (c) an inhibitory postsynaptic potential, and (d) a suprathreshold EPSP in the presence of the sodium channel blocker tetrodotoxin (TTX).

One of the most challenging tasks in teaching courses in behavioral neuroscience and physiological psychology is to present clearly the ionic basis of the resting and action potentials. Because an understanding of these principles of basic neuronal function serves as the building block for subsequent course material, this is one of the most important aspects of the course. One of the difficulties in presenting this material is that the action potential consists of a complex interaction of ionic events that occurs continuously. Using traditional techniques such as blackboard illustrations, handouts, and slides, it is only possible to illustrate these events at one (or perhaps a few) points in time. This article describes a computer simulation designed to help overcome this difficulty.

The Programs

The axon simulator programs (available in Apple Macintosh or Apple II versions) allow the user to observe the movement of ions across a membrane during: (a) an action potential, (b) a subthreshold excitatory postsynaptic potential (EPSP), (c) an inhibitory postsynaptic potential (IPSP), and (d) a suprathreshold EPSP in the presence of the sodium channel blocker tetrodotoxin (TTX). Each of these four neuronal events is depicted in a separate program.

Each program consists of a series of screens. Each screen depicts a patch of membrane showing potassium gates, sodium gates, chloride gates, lipid bilayer, and the sodium-potassium pump (see Figure 1). The intra- and extracellular fluids contain the appropriate ratios of protein anions (A), potassium (K), sodium (N), and chloride (C) ions. A scale on the bottom of each screen shows the potential (voltage) across the membrane (see Figure 1). The voltages accurately reflect the distribution of ions according to the Hodgkin-Huxley equations (see Kuffler & Nicholls, 1984).

The first screen of each program displays a neuron resting at a potential of −70mV. (A description of the ionic basis of the resting potential is included in the user's manual.) After a brief pause, the ions begin to move. For example, on Screen 1 of the Action Potential Program, sodium gates begin to open, producing an influx of sodium ions (represented by the letter N, see Figure 1), which then open additional voltage-dependent sodium gates. This movement is followed by a brief on-screen description of what has occurred. The user then signals the computer to switch to the next screen. This screen shows potassium gates beginning to open, leading to an efflux of potassium ions. After the action potential occurs, subsequent screens show the refractory period and the ionic balance being restored by the sodium-potassium pump. These events occur over the course of nine screens.

The movement of ions is consistent with the Hodgkin-Huxley equations. The voltage shown at the bottom of each screen continually changes to reflect the net potential across the membrane as the ions move. The movement of ions on each screen is slow enough to allow the user to appreciate the interaction of various moving ions in producing the membrane potential. At the conclusion of each screen, there is text that previews and explains what will occur on the next screen. Movement from screen-to-screen is controlled by the user.

We have been using these programs for 2 years in a sophomore-level course in brain and behavior. Specifically, the programs have been briefly demonstrated during a lecture on neural transmission. They have then been made available to students to use independently. To date, use has been optional. In order to monitor usage, students have been asked to sign out the diskettes. Approximately 30% of the 50 students per semester in the course have used the program. Of these, approximately 50% indicated that the programs significantly helped them understand the ionic basis of the resting potential, 30% indicated that the programs were of some help, and the remaining 20% indicated that the programs did not significantly help them. Because the programs are now available for the Apple Macintosh (a computer supported by the college and readily available to students), we plan to require all students to use them. We will then be able to obtain a more systematic analysis of the utility of the programs.

Axon Simulator Symbol Key

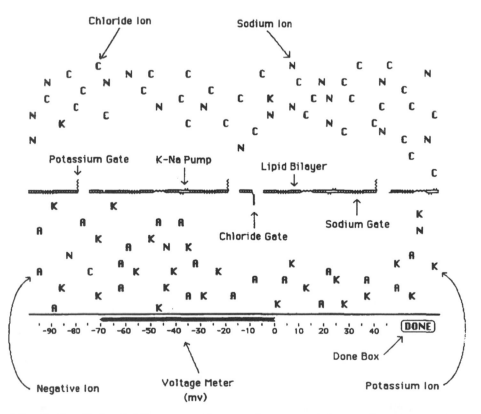

Figure 1. Screen 1 of the Action Potential Program. The membrane contains sodium, potassium, and chloride gates that open and close on various screens as a function of the voltage across the membrane. On this screen, the ions are distributed to produce a -70 mV resting potential. A constantly changing scale at the bottom of each screen shows the membrane potential. Ions move across the screen in accordance with the Hodgkin-Huxley equations. When ionic movement is completed the user signals the computer to switch to the next screen. Abbreviations: A = protein anions (A-), C = chloride (Cl-), K = potassium (K+), and Na = sodium (Na+)

Systems Requirements

The programs are easy to use and require only that the students insert a disk and select the program they wish to run. A user's manual describing the four programs and how to use them is available (see Note 1). The programs are available for Apple Macintosh systems with a minimum of 512 kilobytes of random access memory. One disk drive is sufficient. We also have a version suitable for the Apple II+ (48K of memory) system with one disk drive. The Macintosh program is written in Pascal. The Apple II+ program is written in BASIC and uses the DOS 3.3 operating system.

Reference

Kuffler, S. W., & Nicholls, J. G. (1984). *From neuron to brain* (2nd ed.). Sunderland, MA: Sinauer Associates.

Notes

1. The programs and supporting material can be obtained by writing to Paul R. Solomon, Department of Psychology, Bronfman Science Center, Williams College, Williamstown, MA 01267. Each package will include a diskette and user's manual. Users may make additional copies as needed. Requests should be accompanied by a blank diskette and a stamped return mailer.
2. This work was supported by a grant from the Sloan Foundation. We are grateful to S. Zottoli for his help throughout the project.
3. Scott Cooper is now at College of Physicians and Surgeons, Columbia University and Dean Pomerleau is now at Carnegie-Mellon University.

Teaching of Psychophysiology: Student Apparatus For Monitoring Skin Conductance

Wolfgang Klosterhalfen
University of Düsseldorf

Changes in skin resistance or conductance are well-suited for a demonstration of psychophysiological phenomena in the classroom. In small groups, the signal can be directly observed on a polygraph; in larger classes, additional video equipment is helpful. Although demonstrations of this kind are common, they involve several problems: (a) the equipment is expensive; (b) the polygraph uses high voltage; (c) only one student has the opportunity to compare his/her psychological and physiological responses; (d) quantification of responses is somewhat complicated and time-consuming; (e) data are from one person only; and (f) there are ethical problems in revealing hidden physiological responses to many spectators.

For our courses with medical students (groups of 24 students each), 12 units which monitor skin conductance responses (SCRs) were constructed.[1] Light-emitting diodes (LEDs) numbered from -5 to 10 (and arranged in a row across the control panel) indicate the slope of electrodermal activity on a ratio-scale. The LED's numbers are directly proportional to the steepness of the change (rather than absolute level) of skin conductance: LED 0 is turned on as long as no SCR occurs; during an accelerating increase in skin conductance the light moves to the right; a flat decrease is associated with LED -1, a steep decrease with LED -5. For an optimal resolution, the instrument's sensitivity can be adjusted individually over a

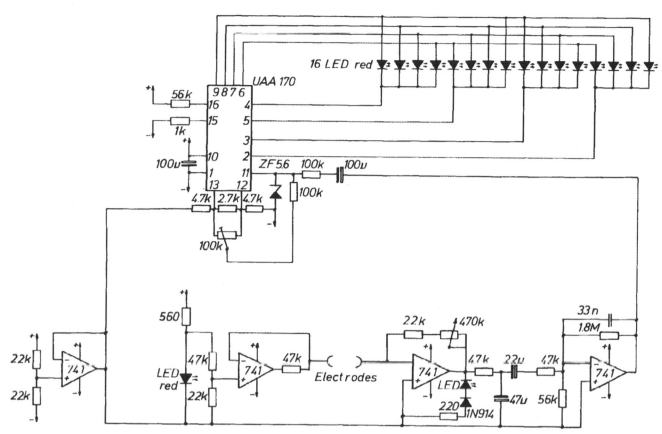

Figure 1. Circuit for one SCR unit.

Figure 1. Circuit for one SCR unit.

wide range. When an additional yellow LED (next to LED 10) signals overmodulation, sensitivity has to be reduced. Using nickel-plated brass fingerelectrodes with limpet clasps, electrode paste can usually be omitted.

Our units have so far been used by about 500 students. The system has worked reliably and either solved or substantially reduced the problems mentioned above: (a) parts for the construction of one unit (see Fig. 1) cost about $30; (b) Our lead-gel battery (7x2=14 Vdc) drives all units. Current consumption is about 0.5 watts per unit (a 12 V battery also proved to

be sufficient); (c) two students share one apparatus (they serve as subject and experimenter/record keeper alternately); (d) response maxima can easily be detected; (e) a median for the group can be obtained quickly by asking questions like "Who reached at least LED 5 in response to the first stimulus?" and (f) working together in pairs, students feel less exposed.

Note

[1] The SCR units were constructed by H. Tillmann.

An Alternative to the Traditional Physiological Psychology Laboratory: Identification of an Unknown Drug Through Behavioral Testing

Susan J. Schumacher
*North Carolina Agricultural and
Technical State University*

In many undergraduate psychology programs the students' exposure to the research process is limited to participation as a subject in studies conducted by graduate students or faculty members or to performance of some simple laboratory experiments, often computer simulated, as part of a course requirement in research methods. If the department offers no graduate program or if psychology faculty are not engaged in the type of research that can include participation of college students, some psychology majors may graduate without the experience of designing and conducting an actual investigation. The lack of equipment, teaching assistants, and funds also contribute to restricted opportunities for undergraduate research involvement.

In an attempt to provide an actual innovative research experience, to encourage interest in a physiological psychology class, and to increase familiarity with commonly abused drugs and their effects, a laboratory project was established in which students were to identify an unknown drug given to their laboratory animals by designing and conducting a series of behavioral tests.

Method. Physiological Psychology is one of a triad of three credit-hour courses, any two of which are required for the psychology major at North Carolina Agricultural and Technical State University, a minority university with 120 psychology majors. It is the only one of these three courses with a laboratory, which increases the contact hours required from three to four per week. This class consisted of three male and seven female psychology majors, eight of whom were seniors, with little or no research experience. Seven of the students enrolled had completed the Research Methods course in which experience in conducting simple experiments and handling laboratory animals (hooded rats) was obtained. One student dropped out of school during the semester, and his partner did not wish to proceed on his own or be assigned to another team. He was given an alternate related assignment for partial credit.

The class met twice a week for 1 hr. and 40 min. for 16 weeks, with the second weekly meeting being reserved for laboratory exercises. Evaluation comments from previous sections of the course had revealed a desire for laboratory experience that would not include animal surgery or dissection. Therefore, part of the laboratory activities were developed around a more applied problem—the effects of drugs on behavior. The class lecture and discussion the first meeting each week followed the traditional approach of chapter-by-chapter textbook coverage (Levinthal, 1979). The laboratory time was divided among three basic activities, all of which required the student to devote out-of-class time to complete. The first set of activities was designed to acquaint students with the various approaches to studying physiological psychology and their methodologies. This was accomplished through approximately four weeks of films, demonstrations, and selected slides from the slide series *Basic Principles of Neuroscience* (Pinsker, 1975), *Modular Lab Sessions in Physiological Psychology* (Perera, 1974), and *Introduction to Psychobiology* (Cox, 1979). The second activity was for student teams to identify an unknown drug their animal was receiving by designing and executing a series of behavioral tests for their animal in the drugged and undrugged state and comparing their results with the literature on the effects of various drugs. This problem was introduced during the third week of the course, and the literature search was begun immediately. Parts of ten laboratory periods were devoted to this project, along with a substantial amount of out-of-class time for the remainder of the semester. The details of this part of the laboratory follow. The third activity, occupying parts of approximately six laboratory periods and all of the last two, consisted of brief human demonstrations of perception, learning, and memory, and will eventually emphasize electrophysiological measures upon receipt of the appropriate equipment.

Students were paired in five teams of two so that at least one partner had completed the Psychological Research course and was familiar with the handling and care of the hooded rats, the Animal Room procedures and rules, and the basic experimental approach. This student was to instruct the partner in the handling and daily care of the hooded rat assigned to them. All rats were naive females approximately 150 days old at the onset of the study (180+ gr.) that had been obtained from a local pet store animal breeder. Rats were handled for approximately two weeks prior to assigning them to the students, who were then instructed to weigh and handle their animals daily as well as to routinely observe their behavior.

Students were familiarized with the use of the *Psychological Abstracts* and were given a list of books and journals containing material on drugs and animal drug studies, a list of 20 drugs from which all unknown drugs had been chosen, a handout on classification of drugs with examples of each of the subcategories, and a copy of a Rodent Emotionality Scale patterned after King and Meyer (1958). Each of the teams was to search the literature, discuss their findings, design four to six behavioral tests to be conducted with their animals in both drug and non-drug states or by using a control animal, and present their proposed methods to the instructor. Following approval of the instructor, they jointly submitted a detailed written procedural description with necessary apparatus for each test and began construction of any apparatus not available from the department.

The instructor selected five drugs from the list of twenty, based upon their availability in small quantities, price, and category, to represent major (chlorpromazine) and minor (chlordiazepoxide or Librium) tranquilizers, central nervous system stimulants (caffeine), and barbiturates and similar acting drugs (ethanol). The fifth drug (atropine sulfate) was never used because of lack of participation by one team of students. Each animal was given the appropriate dose intraperitoneally by the instructor approximately two hours prior to each testing session scheduled by the students. Doses were originally determined from Barnes and Eltherington (1973), *Handbook of Laboratory Animal Science* (Melby & Altman, 1976), and Kruckenberg's table in *The Laboratory Rat*, Vol. II (Kruckenberg, 1980, appendix 2). For two animals the dosages were adjusted on several occasions to produce observable behavioral changes without total inactivity or sleep.

Students were required to keep records of the daily weight of their animal and all laboratory operations. They were also encouraged to ask questions about the dose for each session, if the observed effects were typical, the most common method of administration, and the concentration, color, and other characteristics of the drug that would not automatically classify it as a stimulant, depressant, etc., but this information was not provided unless specifically requested. Students were supplied with a control animal upon request.

Some of the tests used by the students were the rate of food and water consumption, activity level, aggression (toward a control rat or inanimate object), grooming, exploratory behavior (nose poke, maze exploration, leaving their home or other cage in strange environments), a "free field" test, and shock sensitivity.

Following the initial meeting to approve the tests to be used, three progress reports were required. The first was to identify the general drug category (depressant, stimulant, etc.), with documentation from the literature and a description of the tests completed to date and their results, and this information was due four weeks after approval of the test to be used. Two weeks later, identification of the most specific category (minor tranquilizer, CNS stimulant, narcotic analgesic, etc.) of the unknown drug was due, along with the test results and supportive evidence from the literature to justify the choice of category. The following week the name of the drug was due with the rationale for that choice, based upon test results and literature findings. Feedback regarding accuracy was given following the first two reports, and correction of errors was accepted at any time.

Grading of the project was based upon the initial two progress reports, the number of different tests and references related to the correct drug (minimum requirements for each letter grade were specified in a handout), the suitability of the selected tests, the experimental procedures used, the completeness of the written descriptions of the results, and a 10 min. oral class presentation by each team to justify why the specific drug was selected as being the one their animal was probably receiving . The project was worth 300 of the 800 total possible points in the course.

Results. All four participating teams correctly identified the general category of their drug on the first attempt. Three out of four teams correctly identified the subcategory on the first attempt, and three out of the four teams identified accurately the actual drug their animal was receiving (Librium, caffeine, and ethanol). One team had identified their exact drug (Librium) at the time they submitted their general category, but no feedback concerning the accuracy of their choice of drug was given at that time, and these students were encouraged to continue their tests as planned. The fourth team missed both the subcategory and the exact drug (chlorpromazine), although their particular results also supported the drug they selected (Reserpine). Subjective reports by other faculty and the amount of time spent by most students on the project indicated a high level of enthusiasm for the project. Course evaluations indicated an improved overall rating for the course over the previous years, a positive attitude toward the part of the laboratory centered around the drug study and the suggestion that the course be increased to a four semester credit hour course, due to its time-consuming nature. One semester later, just prior to graduation, six of the seniors from the class contacted the instructor and expressed appreciation for that particular laboratory experience.

Discussion. The enthusiasm and interest of the students in the drug project along with the improvement in the quality of the written progress reports, the precision of their testing, and the accuracy of their results indicated that the unknown drug study was a very powerful learning experience. The low cost of the project (approximately $8.00 per student) makes it especially attractive for departments with limited resources. Equipment constructed by students was donated to the department for use by subsequent classes.

Information about dosage changes was apparently important for drug identification, especially in cases in which a tolerance to the drug seemed to develop. Designs to insure proper controls had to be carefully and repeatedly explained, and a laboratory assistant to monitor all out-of-class testing would have eliminated some procedural errors made by teams that the instructor did not detect until test completion.

In addition to becoming quite familiar with the effects of various drugs and drug categories and the experience of designing a miniature research study this project strengthened inductive and deductive reasoning skills and demonstrated an objective approach to problem solving that students had not experienced in other classes and that would be valuable in graduate study or in certain careers.

References

Barnes, C. D., & Eltherington, L. G. *Drug dosage in laboratory animals* (2nd ed.). Berkeley: University of California Press, 1973.

Cox, V. C. (Ed.). *Introduction to psychobiology.* Bayport, NJ: Life Sciences Associates, 1979.

King, F. A., & Meyer, P. M. Effects of amygdaloid lesions upon septal hyperemotionality in the rat. *Science*, 1958, *128*, 655-656.

Kruckenberg, S. M. Drugs and dosages. In H. J. Baker & J. R. Lindsey (Eds.), *The laboratory rat* (Vol. 2). New York: Academic Press, 1980.

Levinthal, C. F. *The physiological approach in psychology.* Englewood Cliffs, NJ: Prentice Hall, 1979.

Melby, C. E., Jr., & Altman, N. H. *Handbook of laboratory animal science* (*Vol.* 3). Cleveland, Ohio: CRC Press, 1976.

Perera, T. B. *Modular lab sessions* for *physiological psychology.* Englewood Cliffs, NJ: Prentice Hall, 1974.

Pinsker, H. M. (Ed.). *Basic principles of neuroscience.* Bayport, NY: Life Sciences Associates, 1975.

Brown Adipose Tissue Thermogenesis: A Simple and Inexpensive Laboratory Exercise in Physiological Psychology

Paul J. Wellman
Texas A & M University

Laboratory exercises in physiological psychology often involve considerable equipment investment, expense and faculty expertise, especially if these involve stereotaxic manipulation of the rat brain. The present paper describes a simple and inexpensive exercise in physiological psychology involving the measurement of temperature in a peripheral tissue, brown adipose, that is readily accessible in the laboratory rat. The advantages of this exercise are: (a) ease of surgical preparation and temperature recording; (b) robust experimental effects that are easily obtained by novice students; (c) a large variety of experimental treatments that will either increase or block the stimulation of brown adipose temperature; and (d) a laboratory experience that leads directly into a classroom discussion of the importance of metabolism within brown adipose for the regulation of body weight (i.e. the notion that obesity may result from deficient brown adipose metabolism).

By way of background, brown adipose tissue (BAT) is a form of adipose that, when stimulated by the sympathetic nervous system, liberates large quantities of heat. This tissue has been linked to non-shivering thermogenesis (i.e. the ability of mammals to maintain body temperature in extreme cold) and to thermogenesis induced by overconsumption of food. The latter effect, termed diet-induced thermogenesis, may serve to limit obesity when mammals overeat (cf. Rothwell & Stock, 1982).

A relatively large and accessible deposit (approximately 300-400 mg) of BAT is situated between the scapulae of the rat (interscapular BAT or IBAT). Brown adipose at this site consists of two paired lobes that lie on the midline (Foster, Depocas & Zuker, 1982). After anesthetization with urethane (Sigma Chemical; 1.2 grams/10 mls/kg, ip), the fur over the back is shaved and blunt scissors are used to expose the lobes of IBAT. Dissection to expose the lobes should always be in a longitudinal direction as a transverse dissection will damage BAT and minimize any thermogenic effects. Barbiturate anesthesia should be avoided because of complications arising from the action of this drug class on BAT thermogenesis. The rat is then placed in a foam-covered plastic half-cylinder to prevent heat loss through the ventral surface and a heat lamp is suspended over the dorsal surface .

Blunt tweezers are used to separate the lobes in preparation for insertion of the temperature probe. Upon positioning the tip of a thermometer probe well within the tissue, the incision is closed over the probe using 9 mm metal wound clips (suture or a hemostat work as well). To prevent the probe from moving during temperature recording, I attach the probe to a ringstand clamp by tape. Core body temperature is also monitored by positioning the tip of a second thermometer 4 cm into the rectum and is maintained within the normal range (36.5-37.0 degrees C) by adjusting the distance between the rat and a heat lamp.

Measurement of IBAT and rectal temperature is then carried out every minute for a 15 minute baseline period. Drug treatment is then given and temperature recorded for an additional 30 minute period. Drug injections should be given via a route that will not disturb the placement of the probes. I typically use intraperitoneal injections that are given via an aperture cut into the ventral surface of the plastic support base. The injection needle can be seen entering the peritoneum and the rat is not moved during injection. Temperature measurements may be made either with commercially available mercury thermometers or with electronic thermoprobes so long as the accuracy of the temperature measurements is 0.1 degree Centigrade.

Table 1 lists the variety of pharmacological and physiological manipulations that are known to activate or inhibit BAT thermogenesis. It should be noted that different techniques are used to evaluate thermogenesis. In vivo procedures comparable to those described herein are preceded by an asterisk. Other techniques (in vitro) involve treating the animal with a drug or hormone and then removing a chunk of BAT and measuring BAT oxygen consumption during maintenance in a tissue chamber. In general, drugs that stimulate the sympathetic nervous system (i.e. amphetamine) or that act directly on beta-adrenergic receptors (i.e. norepinephrine or isoproterenol) markedly stimulate BAT thermogenesis. The thermogenic response of BAT to such drugs is a stereotyped initial decline of .1 degree C (latency of 1-2 minutes) followed by a marked increase of some 1.0-1.5 degrees C over a 10-15 minute period. The parasympathetic nervous system apparently inhibits BAT thermogenesis in that blockade of parasympathetic receptors using atropine produces enhanced BAT thermogenesis. The importance of glucose metabolism is apparent in that 2-deoxy-d-glucose (2-dg), a glucose analogue that interferes with metabolism, reduces BAT thermogenesis. Finally, rats sustaining VMH lesions or that are spon-

Table 1. Influence of Various Pharmacological or Physiological Manipulations on BAT Thermogenesis.

Manipulation	Dose	Effect	Reference
* Norepinephrine	40 ug/100 g, ip	increase	Perkins et al (1981)
* Isoproterenol	1 mg/kg, ip	increase	Perkins et al (1981)
* Amphetamine	1-4 mg/kg ip	increase	Wellman (1983)
* Paredrine	4-16 mg/kg, ip	increase	Wellman & Watkins (1984)
Atropine	.5 mg/kg, ip	increase	Rothwell et al (1981)
2-dg	360 mg/kg, sc	decrease	Rothwell et al (1981)
* Propranolol	1.0 mg/kg, ip	decrease	Perkins et al (1981)
Estrogen	5 ug	increase	Kemnitz et al (1983)
* VMH stimulation	—	increase	Perkins et al (1981)
VMH lesions	—	decrease	Glick (1982)
Fatty Zucker rat	—	decrease	Glick (1982); Milam et al (1982)

Note: ip = intraperitoneal; sc = subcutaneous; a * denotes that the procedures are comparable to those described herein.

taneously obese (i.e. Zucker rats) display reduced BAT thermogenesis.

This exercise can be as simple as demonstrating the effect of isoproterenol injection on IBAT thermogenesis or can be modified for advanced undergraduate classes (e.g. what is the effect of amphetamine on BAT thermogenesis in rats that are tolerant or not to amphetamine?). Moreover, advanced students may be set to the task of verifying that the in vivo procedure described herein will yield the same results as those in vitro experiments listed in Table 1.

References

Foster, D. O., Depocas, F., & Zuker, M. Heterogeneity of the sympathetic innervation of rat interscapular brown adipose tissue via intercostal nerves. *Canadian Journal of Physiology and Pharmacology*, 1982, *60*, 747-754.

Glick Z. Inverse relationship between brown adipose thermogenesis and meal size: The thermostatic control of food intake revisited. *Physiology and Behavior*, 1982, *29*, 1137-1140.

Kemnitz, J. W., Glick, Z., & Bray, G. A. Ovarian hormones influence brown adipose tissue. *Pharmacology, Biochemistry and Behavior*, 1983, *18*, 563-566.

Milam, K. M., Stern, J. S., & Horwitz, D. A. Isoproterenol alters non-shivering thermogenesis in the

Zucker obese rat (fa/fa). *Pharmacology, Biochemistry and Behavior*, 1982, *16*, 627-630.

Perkins, M. N., Rothwell, N. J., Stock, M. J., & Stone, T. W. Activation of brown adipose tissue by the ventromedial hypothalamus. *Nature*, 1981, *289*, 401-402.

Rothwell, N. J., Saville, M. E., & Stock, M. J. Acute effects of food, 2-deoxy-d-glucose and noradrenaline on metabolic rate and brown adipose tissue in normal and atropinized lean and obese (fa/fa) Zucker rats. *Pflugers Archives*, 1981, *392*, 172-177.

Rothwell, N. J., & Stock, M. J. Neural regulation of thermogenesis. *Trends in Neurosciences*, April 1982, 124-126.

Wellman, P. J. Influence of amphetamine on brown adipose tissue thermogenesis. *Research Communications in Chemical Pathology and Pharmacology*, 1983, *41*, 173-176.

Wellman, P. J., & Watkins, P. A. Effects of 4-hydroxyamphetamine (4-OHAM) on in vivo brown adipose thermogenesis and food and water intake in the rat. *Behavioral Neuroscience*, (in press).

3. TEACHING HEMISPHERIC LATERALITY

Some Simple Classroom Experiments on Cerebral Lateralization

Ernest D. Kemble
Terri Filipi
Linda Gravlin
University of Minnesota, Morris

Two experiments designed to assess hemispheric specialization of function are described. The experiments require minimal equipment, can be rapidly conducted in the classroom, and yield substantial laterality effects. The ease of the experiments, combined with an extensive and varied literature and high student interest make this area an excellent introduction to research methodology for undergraduate students.

Hemispheric specialization of function is a popular research area that is prominently featured in many introductory texts (e.g., Ruch, 1984; Wortman, Loftus, & Marshall, 1981). We recently completed a series of experiments on this topic for our undergraduate research methods course and found them to be very useful. This article briefly outlines the instructional advantages of this topic and describes two simple experiments that can be conducted readily in classroom settings.

A prominent feature of this area is high student interest. Throughout the experiments our students actively participated in discussions of the readings and experiments; several students remained after each class to continue discussions. At quarter's end, the students were asked to rate the intellectual stimulation of the topic on a scale of 1 (*least*) to 5 (*most*) as part of a standardized course evaluation. Seventeen of 19 students were present for the evaluation and all rated this project as a 4 ($N = 9$) or 5 ($N = 8$). This interest was also translated into some of the most thoughtful and thoroughly prepared laboratory reports we have seen in recent years.

The rapid development and popularity of this area has also produced a large and diverse literature including popularized nontechnical accounts (e.g., Bakan, 1971; Gazzaniga, 1961; Kimura, 1973), which sometimes claim far-reaching significance for the topic (e.g., Bogen, 1975; Jaynes, 1976; Ornstein, 1978); extensive scholarly reviews (Corballis & Beale, 1983; Gazzaniga, 1970; Hellige, 1983; Springer & Deutsch, 1981); and an extensive primary research literature (see, e.g., Corballis & Beale, 1983; Kinsbourne, 1982;

Springer & Deutsch, 1981, for references). This extensive literature provides the instructor wide flexibility in both the range and depth of readings to be used. For more advanced students, the review of this area by Springer and Deutsch (1981) provides an excellent introduction. Finally, several approaches to hemispheric specialization are now available that are applicable to normal subjects and require only minimal equipment (see Springer & Deutsch, 1981, for review).

PRELIMINARY READINGS

Because most of our students were in their first or second year in college, we began with a series of nontechnical readings (Bakan, 1971; Gazzaniga, 1967; Sperry, 1964), some related supporting data (Geschwind & Levitsky, 1968; Wada & Rasmussen, 1960), and some suggested extensions of hemispheric asymmetry to other areas of human behavior (Bakan, 1971; Bogen, 1975; Ornstein, 1978; Witelson, 1977). These readings were supplemented by a brief overview of anatomical differences among sensory systems (particularly the pattern and degree of bilateral representation in the CNS) and discussions of major methodological issues raised by the readings (e.g., limitations of research on clinical populations, importance of stimulus and response variables, etc.). These assignments gave the students a brief overview of the area and some of its major methodological problems. Readings and discussion then focused on a number of experimental approaches to hemispheric specialization in normal subjects (Bakan, 1969; Kimura, 1961; Kinsbourne, 1972; Levy, 1969; Quinn, 1972). Because all sensory systems have at least some bilaterial representation in the CNS, considerable discussion was devoted to the techniques and experimental controls necessary to restrict stimuli, or stimulus configurations, to a single hemisphere. The importance of methodology in changing fundamental views about hemispheric function is particularly well illustrated by the development of the "Z lens" (see Springer & Deutsch, 1981, pp. 38-40) and was included in this section. One week was devoted to the initial material. The students then read a series of primary research reports directly related to the experiments they were conducting. Classroom discussion focused on the methodological details of both the readings and our experiments.

EXPERIMENT 1. TACTILE LETTER AND NUMBER IDENTIFICATION

Because their commissures are intact, it is critical to restrict, or in some way favor, the sensory input of normal subjects to one hemisphere. In many ways, the tactile system mediating light touch is well-suited for this purpose. Because this system projects primarily (approximately 95%) to the contralateral hemisphere, tactile stimulation can be largely restricted to right or left hemisphere by stimulating the contralateral side of the body only. Because the left hemisphere seems to be most heavily involved in language processes, it seemed reasonable to expect that tactile identification of language-related stimuli (letters) should be superior with the right hand, whereas no hand difference should be found with other stimuli (numbers). This experiment compared the latencies for correctly identifying single letters or digits by touch with the right and left hands.

Materials and Procedure

The apparatus consisted of a plywood box (20 x 45 x 20 cm) open at each end and outfitted with a cloth curtain suspended over one end extending to the apparatus floor. The stimuli were 18 children's wooden alphabet blocks consisting of nine single letters (C,D,F,L,P,R,S,U,Y) and nine single digits (0,1,2,3,4,5,6,7,9). In choosing stimuli, letter (e.g., O,I) and number (e.g., 0,1) pairs having similar geometric shapes were avoided. It is important that the outlines of the stimuli are sharp. If the letters and numbers are pressed rather than cut into the blocks, it may be necessary to increase their relief by carefully deepening their borders with a small electric drill. If the blocks contain a raised border, this should also be removed. Latencies for correct identification (multiple guesses were permitted) were timed by stopwatch.

Subjects were seated before the curtained end of the apparatus and the experimenter sat opposite the subject. Single blocks were placed on the floor of the apparatus and the subject was instructed to insert the right or left hand under the curtain, lightly trace the outlines of the stimulus with fingertips, and identify the stimulus. The stopwatch was started when the block was touched and stopped after a correct identification. Because this is a surprisingly difficult task, a cue card depicting all stimuli was placed before the subjects, who were always told whether the stimulus was a letter or a digit. Even so, identification latencies of 10-15 seconds were not uncommon. Because there are strong practice effects on this task, subjects were given eight warm-up trials (alternating hands, letters,

and digits) followed by 12 letter and 12 digit trials. Letters and digits and right and left hands were alternated. At the conclusion of testing, four mean identification latencies were calculated for each subject (right hand, letter; right hand, digit; left hand, letter; left hand, digit). These four means were employed for statistical analyses (t tests, analyses of variance) of data from 9 male and 22 female students.

Results

Initial comparisons revealed no overall difference in the performance of preferred and nonpreferred hand on warm-up trials and no systematic change in identification latencies for letters or digits in the course of the experiment. Thus, the results were not biased by overall superiority in the performance of the preferred hand at the outset of the experiment or by practice effects ($p>.10$). Comparisons of right- and left-hand performance revealed that female students identified letters more quickly with the right hand ($M = 8.74$ sec) than with the left ($M = 12.41$ sec., $p<.05$), but with no hand difference in digit identification (right, $M = 6.87$ sec; left, $M = 6.42$ sec., $p>10$). There were no hand differences among males in either letter (right, $M = 10.61$ sec; left, $M = 11.19$, sec., $p>.10$) or digit (right, $M = 6.09$ sec; left, $M = 6.41$, sec, $p>.10$) identification. Thus, the data support some left hemisphere specialization for language-related stimuli but also indicate that differences are sex-dependent under some testing conditions.

EXPERIMENT 2. VERBAL INTERFERENCE WITH A MANUAL TASK

A related experimental approach, which also seems to reflect hemispheric specialization, requires subjects to balance a wooden dowel rod on the forefinger of the right and left hand while engaged in a verbal task, or while remaining silent (Kinsbourne & Cook, 1971; Johnson & Kozma, 1977). These investigators found that balancing durations with the right, but not the left hand were shortened by a verbal task. They suggested that the massive and complex activity required of the left hemisphere by the verbal tasks competed with neural activity required for right-hand balancing. Since the right hemisphere is presumed to be less involved in language, the verbal task did not compete with left-hand balancing.

Materials and Procedure

This experiment requires only 4-6 wooden dowel rods (1.25 cm dia., 92 cm length), a stopwatch, and a list of verbal problems. Our verbal task consisted of a series of spelling problems (e.g., repeat the alphabet backwards, recite the alphabet forward giving every third letter, spell Afghanistan backwards). Because some subjects can balance the dowel for up to 600 sec. several pages of problems should be prepared.

The students were allowed to practice balancing the dowel for 5 min, alternating the right and left hands, and then received eight test trials (right hand = 4, left hand = 4). On each trial, the subject positioned the dowel on the right or left forefinger using the other hand. On command, the supporting hand was removed and the experimenter started a stopwatch, which was stopped when the dowel dropped or touched any other part of the subject's body. Half of the trials on each hand were conducted in silence and half with verbal tasks. The order in which conditions were presented was systematically varied across subjects. At the conclusion of testing, mean balancing durations for each hand under both silent and verbal conditions were calculated.

Results

The preferred hand (M = 64.72 sec) showed a marginally significant superiority in balancing duration to the nonpreferred hand (M = 49.57 sec. $.05 < p < .10$) during silent trials. The durations for males were also significantly longer than for females with both the right (male, M = 155.94 sec; female, M = 25.63 sec, $p<.02$) and left hands (male, M = 135.58 sec; female, M = 12.72 sec, $p <.05$). Comparisons of balancing durations under silent and verbal conditions revealed that the verbal task impaired performance in both the left (silent, M = 49.58 sec; verbal, M = 30.08 sec, $p <.002$) and right hands (silent, M = 64.72 sec; verbal, M = 32.2 sec., $p <.001$). Although these comparisons suggest no lateralized effect on balancing, examination of the data shows that the right hand (37.2% decline) was more severely impaired than the left (11.9% decline, $p <.05$) by the verbal task. There was no sex difference in this effect ($p >.10$). Thus, while the left hemisphere does seem to be more importantly involved in this task, both hemispheres seem to participate in more complex verbal tasks. Clearly, referring to the left hemisphere as "the language hemisphere" is an oversimplification.

DISCUSSION

In addition to the two experiments described here, we also completed a dichotic listening task similar to that reported by Kimura (1961). This experiment revealed right ear (left hemisphere) superiority in word recognition, which disappeared when subjects were instructed to pay attention to their right ear. Thus, demonstrations of hemispheric asymmetry may be partially dependent on the instructions given to subjects. These three experiments required less than 5 hours of laboratory time to complete and nicely illustrated the importance of a host of variables (e.g., sensory modality, task complexity, sex differences, measurement methods, and instructions) for research

in this area. In the course of the experiments it became quite obvious to our students that the hemispheres interact with each other in subtle ways rather than simply dividing major functions. Although the dichotic listening task requires somewhat elaborate equipment that may not be available in many labs, a number of additional simple measures have been described (e.g., Johnson & Kozma, 1977; Kinsbourne, 1972; Kinsbourne & McMurray, 1975; Levy & Reid, 1976), which may lend themselves to similar manipulations and further classroom projects. The simplicity of these experiments and the high student interest they engender make this an excellent way to introduce students to physiological psychology and research methodology.

References

Bakan, P. (1969). Hypnotizability, laterality of eye movements and functional brain asymmetry. *Perceptual and Motor Skills, 28*, 927-932.

Bakan, P. (1971, April). The eyes have it. *Psychology Today*, pp. 64-67, 96.

Bogen, J. E. (1975). The other side of the brain. VII: Some educational aspects of hemispheric specialization. *UCLA Educator, 17*, 24-32.

Corballis, M. C., & Beale, I. L. (1983). *The ambivalent mind: The neuropsychology of left and right.* Chicago: Nelson-Hall.

Gazzaniga, M. (1967). The split brain in man. *Scientific American, 217*, 24-29.

Gazzaniga, M. S. (1970). *The bissected brain.* New York: Appleton-Century-Crofts.

Geschwind, N., & Levitsky, W. (1968). Human brain: Left-right asymmetries in temporal speech region. *Science, 161*, 186-187.

Hellige, J. B. (Ed.). (1983). *Cerebral hemisphere asymmetry: Method, theory, and application.* New York: Praeger.

Jaynes, J. (1976). *The origin of consciousness in the breakdown of the bicameral mind.* Boston: Houghton Mifflin.

Johnson, O., & Kozma, A. (1977). Effects of concurrent verbal and musical tasks on a unimanual skill. *Cortex, 13*, 11- 16.

Kimura, D. (1961). Cerebral dominance and the perception of verbal stimuli. *Canadian Journal of Psychology, 15*, 166-171.

Kimura, D. (1973). The asymmetry of the human brain. *Scientific American, 228*, 70-78.

Kinsbourne, M. (1972). Eye and head turning indicates cerebral lateralization. *Science, 176*, 539-541.

Kinsbourne, M. (1982). Hemispheric specialization and the growth of human understanding. *American Psychologist, 37*, 411-420.

Kinsbourne, M., & Cook, J. (1971). Generalized and lateralized effects of concurrent verbalization on a unimanual skill. *Quarterly Journal of Experimental phychology, 23*, 341-345.

Kinsbourne, M., & McMurray, J. (1975). The effect of cerebral dominance of time sharing between speaking and tapping by preschool children. *Child Development, 46,* 240-242.

Levy, J. (1969). Possible basis for the evolution of lateral specialization of the human brain, *Nature, 224,* 614-615.

Levy, J., & Reid, M. L. (1976). Variations in writing posture and cerebral organization. *Science, 194,* 337.

Ornstein, R. (1978). The split and the whole brain. *Human Nature, 1,* 76-83.

Quinn, P. (1972). Stuttering: Cerebral dominance and the dichotic word test. *Medical Journal of Australia, 2,* 639-643.

Ruch, J. C. (1984). *Psychology: The personal science.* Belmont, CA: Wadsworth.

Sperry, R.1964). The great cerebral commissure. *Scientific American, 210,* 42-52.

Springer, S., & Deutsch, G. (1981). *Left brain, right brain.* San Francisco: Freeman.

Wada, J. A., & Rasmussen, T. (1960). Intracarotid injection of sodium amytal for the lateralization of cerebral speech dominance: Experimental and clinical observations. *Journal of Neurosurgery, 17,* 266-282.

Witelson, S. F. (1977). Developmental dyslexia: Two right hemispheres and none left. *Science, 195,* 309-311.

Wortman, C. B., Loftus, E. F., & Marshall, M. (1981). *Psychology.* New York: Knopf.

Classroom Demonstration of Behavioral Effects of the Split-Brain Operation

Edward J. Morris
Owensboro Community College

This article presents a method for simulating the behavior and perceptual deficits demonstrated by patients who have undergone the split-brain, or commissurotomy, surgical procedure. The volunteers sit next to each other in a manner that requires them to accomplish certain tasks as one person. Several easily staged activities, which require only readily available materials, show how split-brain patients illustrate certain lateralized cerebral hemispheric functions.

Various lab assignments and computer simulations illustrate the effects of the surgical procedure referred to as the commissurotomy. Most introductory psychology textbooks include descriptions of patients' behavior after the split-brain operation, but most of the examples are anecdotal. No demonstration exists to illustrate to students the potential subjective experiences of such patients.

The following demonstration allows students to participate in an activity designed to simulate the difficulty split-brain patients experience with certain perceptuomotor tasks soon after surgery (Nebes & Sperry, 1971). Participants experience the potential frustration patients feel as well as demonstrate for observers deficits in information processing that these patients may exhibit.

Method

Two volunteers sit at a desk; they should attempt to sit in one chair. The volunteer sitting on the left of the chair represents the brain's left hemisphere and the other represents the brain's right hemisphere. The instructor should ensure that both participants are right-handed in order to demonstrate the better dexterity of the right hand. The instructor may also vary the procedure to use two left-handed volunteers in order to demonstrate the possible differences among left-handers who have more dexterity in their left hands but who may be similar to right-handers in having their language dominance in the left hemisphere.

Each student places the outer hand (left hand for the left subject and right hand for right subject) behind his or her back. Subjects place their inner hands on the desk, one crossing over the other. The two hands on the desk represent the split-brain patient's left and right hands. The instructor directs the participant representing the left hand to refrain from talking from this point on.

Activity 1

Place a shoe with a lace on the desk in front of the subjects. Direct them to tie the lace. The participants must use only the designated hands. The volunteer using the right hand may talk. The instructor may ask the observing students why only the volunteer using the right hand may talk and may remind the students at this point that the left hemisphere is typically the dominant hemisphere and usually holds the language centers. This discussion gives students an opportunity to draw for themselves the conclusion that the left hemisphere is the only hemisphere able to communicate verbally its experiences. The instructor may then direct the discussion toward the data concerning left-handedness.

The instructor then discusses the difficulty with which the volunteers tied the shoe and how practice might affect their performance. The instructor describes the initial lack of spontaneous activity and numbness in the left side of the body and apparent "blindness" in the left visual field of split-brain patients (Gazzaniga, 1967, 1987).

Activity 2

In this demonstration, the instructor simulates the apparent visual deficits observed among split-brain patients. The instructor directs the volunteer representing the right hemisphere to look to the left and the representative of the left hemisphere to look to the right. The instructor may use a cardboard partition to separate the lines of sight and flashcards or actual objects to introduce a stimulus to the right visual field. The instructor should then ask the volunteer representing the right hand to name the stimulus and choose the correct stimulus object from a selection of objects. The volunteer should correctly name the object and choose the stimulus object correctly, demonstrating the link between the right visual field and the left hemisphere. The instructor then directs the volunteer representing the left hand to choose the presented object. The volunteer is likely to choose incorrectly or not at all, demonstrating the right hemisphere's lack of awareness of the right visual field.

The activity should be repeated with the stimulus presented to the left visual field. The left hand's ability to correctly choose from an array of objects containing the stimulus object demonstrates the connection between the right hemisphere and the left visual field. Next, the instructor should direct the volunteer representing the left hemisphere to name the stimulus object. The response will be incorrect, representing a guess by the left hemisphere.

In the discussion following this activity, the instructor may explain how this simulation demonstrates the apparent visual deficits observed in a specially contrived laboratory setting in which the gaze of the subject would be unnaturally restricted. In more normal settings, the subject would be able to scan both visual fields, allowing both hemispheres to receive the data presented to only one hemisphere in this demonstration.

Activity 3

The instructor blindfolds the volunteers and directs them to tie the shoe again. With visual cues absent, the volunteers are either unable to complete the task or find it very difficult. With each hemisphere attempting to complete the task independent of the other, the difficulty is soon apparent.

The instructor may ask students in the audience to speculate why the task is now more difficult. If the students do not spontaneously generate the idea that the volunteers could make the job more manageable by allowing the volunteer representing the right hand to talk the left hand through the task, then the instructor may direct the volunteers to do so. This activity helps the audience to infer that cooperation and coordination are possible, even when the subjects cannot see both hands.

Activity 4

While the subjects remain blindfolded, the instructor places a familiar object, such as a quarter, in the left hand. The instructor asks the left-hand volunteer if he or she can recognize the object, but the volunteer may respond only in a nonverbal manner. The instructor asks the speaker for the pair (i.e., the volunteer representing the right hand) to name the object. Very often the left-hand subjects will make a guess concerning the nature of the object. Given the circumstances, the guess may be accurate if the instructor selects an object readily available in the classroom setting.

During the ensuing discussion, the instructor may ask students how the left-hand volunteer's inability to name the object is similar to the experience of the split-brain patient. Again, the instructor elicits students' speculation about the relation between hemispheric language dominance and the experience of the split-brain patient.

Although the volunteer representing the left hand cannot communicate verbally, the instructor should encourage students to generate ideas concerning how the left hand might communicate its knowledge in other ways. For instance, the left-hand subject may pick the object from an array of objects placed in front of the volunteer pair upon removal of the blindfold.

Activity 5

For the final demonstration, the instructor places a retractable ball-point pen in the left hand and repeats the procedure for Activity 3. After the students speculate on the same conditions as in Activity 3, allow the left hand to retract the pen repeatedly. The instructor then encourages the volunteer using the right hand to try to name the object.

This activity allows students to generate hypotheses concerning the laterality of hearing. It also demonstrates the patient's reliance on all senses to make judgments and that the right hemisphere may be incapable of explaining the judgments. Consequently, the verbal hemisphere may not be capable of sufficiently explaining reactions or behavior, but may resort to rationalizations after the fact.

Instructors should encourage other students in the class to develop hypotheses concerning the behavior of the volunteers and suggest ways to test these hypotheses. The instructor would then be set to explain the laterality of the sensory organs.

Discussion

In these demonstrations, volunteers undergo the frustration split-brain patients may experience in a manner that loosely approximates actual conditions. When given time to practice, the volunteers learn to compensate for the handicaps involved with the condition. This learning process is similar to what split-brain patients experience after adaptation to the deficits. The restriction on the left-hand volunteer's speech makes the tasks more frustrating. This limitation simulates the split-brain patient's hemispheric dominance for language. Such insight into the subjective experience of the split-brain patient is impossible with computer simulations or textbook descriptions.

Before developing this demonstration, I used a class discussion and lecture to present the material and concepts involved in hemispheric dominance and the commissurotomy. This discussion preceded a computerized simulation that required students to conduct experiments with a simulated split-brain patient (Hay, 1985). After observing and participating in the classroom demonstration described in the present article, students report that the computer simulation is more understandable and meaningful.

Informal evaluation of the demonstration's effectiveness suggests that the students are more aware of brain functioning patterns demonstrated by the deficits resulting from the split-brain operation. Students ask more questions, and discussion is more spirited than in classes that do not see the demonstration, suggesting a greater level of interest.

In a survey of three introductory psychology classes, 85% of 131 students rated these demonstrations as either *helpful* or *very helpful* in understanding the information presented in class regarding the split-brain patient. More than 50% of the students rated the demonstrations as *more helpful* in understanding the related concepts than the computer simulation used in their laboratory assignments.

References

Gazzaniga, M. S. (1967). The split brain in man. *Scientific American, 217*, 24-29.

Gazzaniga, M. S. (1987). Perceptual and attentional processes following callosal section in humans. *Neuropsychologia, 25*, 119-133.

Hay, J. C. (1985). *Psychworld.* New York McGraw-Hill.

Nebes, R. D., & Sperry, R. W. (1971). Hemispheric deconnection syndrome with cerebral birth injury in the dominant arm area. *Neuropsychologia, 9*, 247-259.

Note

I thank Vickie S. Morris, Barbara St. John, and three anonymous reviewers for their critical reading of an earlier draft of this article.

4. INTRODUCING REACTION TIME AS A MEASURE OF NEURAL ACTIVITY

Reaction Time as a Behavioral Demonstration of Neural Mechanisms for a Large Introductory Psychology Class

E. Rae Harcum
The College of William and Mary

A straightforward and effective demonstration of the difference between simple and disjunctive reaction times (RTs) is provided. Several volunteers from a large class are assigned to a control group and instructed to raise their left hands upon hearing the name of a United States president. A comparable experimental group of subjects raise their left hands if the president served after Abraham Lincoln or their right hands if the president preceded Lincoln. Faster RTs to the name Ford *occur for subjects in the control group, indicating conduction over more neurons and synaptic delay when a choice of responses is required.*

Psychologists make inferences about the internal structure and states of an organism by studying the time required for subjects to make a specific response to a given stimulus under varying conditions (cf. Kantowitz, Roediger, & Elmes, 1988). This procedure, as Kantowitz et al. said, "gives psychologists a window into the mind" (p. 202).

The purpose of my demonstration is to illustrate for a large introductory psychology class the use of behavioral tests of RT to infer unobservable physiological mechanisms. The demonstration shows a delay in responding when the subject has more choices of responses (cf. Hyman, 1955). If one assumes that a more difficult choice of responses would involve more neurons and thus more synapses, then a RT requiring such a choice would be slower because of delays in crossing synapses plus the time for the spike potential to traverse individual neurons (Kalat, 1988).

As many students as is practical are recruited from the class and divided into two equal groups, with members of each group standing together at the front of the room. They are told that the instructor is going to say the name of a former United States president and that their task is to raise their hands as quickly as possible in response to the name. The subjects are then given additional written instructions according to their group, so that neither group knows the instructions given to the other. Members of the experimental group are told to raise their right hands if the president served before Abraham Lincoln and to raise their left hands if the president served after Lincoln. Members of the control group are told to raise their left hands when the instructor says the president's name.

The rest of the class is asked to note which group reacts faster. When each subject is ready, with each hand held next to the shoulder, the instructor says "Ready" and then "Ford." The control subjects, with the simple RT task, are clearly faster in raising their hands than the experimental subjects, as judged by the other students in the class, voting by a show of hands.

The hypothesis and design of the experiment are then explained to the class. The hypothesis is that more difficult tasks, requiring a choice among responses, involve longer neuronal paths and more synapses, both of which slow transmission of the neural signal. Therefore, it was predicted that the experimental group would be slower because their task required a choice. The class observations of the RTs clearly confirm the prediction and support the hypothesis. Therefore, a behavioral experiment has been used to test a physiological hypothesis.

As an exercise in scientific logic, it should be pointed out that the results of the demonstration were predicted on the basis of synaptic delay and additional numbers of neurons, but they also could have been predicted on the basis of slower neural conduction rates for the disjunctive situation. Until this alternative possibility can be discounted, this demonstration alone does not prove the existence of synaptic delay, although such synaptic delay has been demonstrated by physiological research.

One might use microswitches and timers for more elegance. The use of timers would, of course, permit quantitative comparison of less robust independent variables. For example, the RT to a less familiar presidential name, such as *Polk*, might be compared with the response to *Ford*. A more difficult task could be achieved by asking the subjects to discriminate between a word of more or fewer than six letters and could be made even more exotic by using homophones like *through* and *threw*.

Finally, the demonstration could be expanded to illustrate a way to determine the difficulty of discriminating among several stimuli (e.g., a method for sensory scaling of preferences). For example, the disparity in preference between two foods (e.g., potato and spinach) could be determined by the differences In the disjunctive RTs. The left-hand RTs for potato would give the degree of preference for potato over spinach. The shorter RTs would indicate an easier decision process, presumably reflecting a greater degree of preference for one stimulus over the other. Other related applications might include determinations of the semantic relatedness of words or their personal significance. For example, in the former case, the left-hand response would indicate if the comparison word was a mammal or, in the second case, if a comparison adjective represented a trait that applied to the subject. Although I have not actually developed and used these extensions of the demonstration, they should work if the proper stimuli are chosen. When the choices depend on personal preference or opinion, an independent measure of the differences could be correlated with the RT differences.

This demonstration has the additional benefit of illustrating an experiment with a meaningful outcome. The students enjoy the break from lecture and easily understand the teaching objective. Nevertheless, it requires just a few minutes of class time and entails little disruption of the class to set up and complete.

References

Hyman, R. (1955). Stimulus information as a determinant of reaction time. *Journal of Experimental Psychology*, *45*, 188-196.

Kalat, J. W. (1988). *Biological psychology* (3rd ed.). Belmont, CA: Wadsworth.

Kantowitz, B. H., Roediger, H. L., III, & Elmes, D. G. (1988). *Experimental psychology* (3rd ed.). St. Paul, MN: West.

Mass Reaction Time: Measurement of the Speed of the Nerve Impulse and the Duration of Mental Processes in Class

Paul Rozin
University of Pennsylvania
and John Jonides
University of Michigan

The "reaction time" subtraction technique is of both historical and current importance in psychology. It was used by Helmholtz in 1850 to demonstrate the speed of the nerve impulse, and it is a major tool of modern research in cognitive psychology. In-class or at-home reaction time demonstrations are typically difficult to arrange because they require use of reliable millisecond timers, and they require many trials in order to stabilize and reduce the variability of individual reaction times. We propose here two new variants of the reaction time technique which overcome these problems. They take advantage of the fact that summing over a series of reaction times, each less than a second, yields a time interval that can be measured easily with a stop watch or wristwatch. Because this total reaction time is summed over a large number of component times, the variability of the resulting value is lower than the variability of the individual times.

The basic procedure for in-class use is to chain a group of people (ideally 20 or so) together so that they must perform some task in sequence. When person n completes the task, he signals person n+1 who then completes the task, and so on. An alternative procedure that can be used in the student's home involves chaining tasks together (e.g. Neisser, 1963). In this way, instead of having to deal with the short times for a particular mental process, one can determine the time needed to complete this process n times.

Measurement of the Speed of the Nerve Impulse

In-class Form. The logic of this demonstration follows directly from Helmholtz's 1850 experiment. Simple reaction time to a pinch of the ankle is compared to simple reaction time to a pinch of the shoulder. The difference between these times should be an estimate of the time for the nerve impulse to traverse the equivalent of the distance between the ankle and the shoulder. Between ten and twenty students are needed for this experiment. Each student grasps the ankle of his neighbor (this can be arranged with a minimum of acrobatics if the person at the end of a row of seats links with the person in front of him). Subjects are instructed to close their eyes and to simply squeeze their neighbor's ankle as soon as their own ankle is squeezed. The last person in the series is instructed to yell "Stop" when he feels squeezed. The experimenter starts the series by tapping the ankle of the first subject with the starting pin of a stop watch, thus starting the stop watch and the squeeze simultaneously. The experimenter stops the watch on the agreed signal from the last person (i.e., the "Stop" signal). The same sequence of events must be then repeated several times, until the mass reaction time decreases and stabilizes. In our experience, six to ten trials suffice. Following this, the same procedure is repeated with shoulder squeezing. (These initial practice trials provide useful data from which the instructor can plot a learning curve [see Figure 1].) Two ankle and two shoulder trials can then be run in a counterbalanced order (e.g. ankle, shoulder, shoulder, ankle). Appropriate divisions and subtractions yield an ankle vs. shoulder mean time difference for a typical subject, which is divided into an estimate of the average ankle to shoulder distance for the subjects.

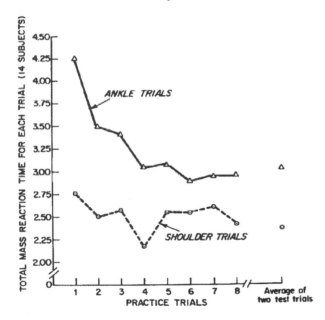

Figure 1. Total mass reaction time for shoulder and ankle trials during practice and test trials of the speed-of-nerve-impulse demonstration. The procedure included eight ankle practice trials followed by eight shoulder practice trials. Following this, test trials were run in the order ankle, shoulder, shoulder, ankle.

We have performed this experiment on eight separate occasions, resulting in values between 15 and 50 meters/second on each occasion (the expected range would be about 6 to 122 meters/second [Milner, 1970]). Figure 1 shows both the learning curves and

final test measurements of one such demonstration. It should be noted that because each measurement takes less than ten seconds to obtain, the total of 12-25 measurements needed does not take a great deal of class time.

At-home Form. The at-home version of this experiment requires only six students: five participants and one experimenter. The logic of the experiment is the same as that described above, but easily measurable time values are obtained by cycling four times around the five participants. That is, each participant grasps his neighbor's ankle or shoulder (depending on the type of trial), forming a circle. The squeezing is initiated by the experimenter, as in the in-class version. The fifth person in the cycle is instructed to signal "Stop" the fourth time he is squeezed. This procedure was used in an at-home experiment with a class of introductory psychology students and their roommates or other friends. Students were instructed to carry through a series of five practice trials and then to run four critical tests as described above. The mean estimate of nerve impulse speed for the fifteen participating groups was 32.7 meters/second (within the expected range) with a standard deviation of 17.4 meters/second. One group reported an unreasonably slow rate of below 6 meters/second (none were negative). On the high end, the maximum value was 83.2 meters/second, again within the normal range.

Measuring the Time for More Complex Mental Processes

In-class Form. The basic nerve-impulse-speed design can be extended to measure more complex mental processes with one modification. Many reaction time experiments of cognitive processes require subjects to choose between two (or sometimes more) response alternatives. To perform such experiments using the mass reaction time technique, one must provide each subject in the chain with a method of choosing between at least two alternative responses. We illustrate this technique with an experiment that measures the time it takes subjects to scan through a memorized list of target letters in order to determine if a probe stimulus letter is a member of that set (e.g., Sternberg, 1966). Before each trial, subjects are told two, three, or four randomly chosen target letters which they must hold in memory. They close their eyes, and a large stimulus letter is written on the blackboard in front of them. On a signal from his neighbor, a subject opens his eyes, determines whether the letter on the board is in the target set, and signals his neighbor in the following way: Each subject is instructed to hold his index and middle finger above the forearm of his neighbor, and to poke the neighbor's arm with his index finger if the stimulus is in the target set, or with his middle finger if it is not. Because the fingers are not actually touching the neighbor's skin before each trial, the neighbor has no way of knowing which decision his predecessor made when he is touched. The experimenter can observe the response which each subject makes and thus can ensure that no errors are made (subjects should be exhorted to make no errors, and trials with more than one error should be excluded). A trial is initiated by the experimenter who signals the first subject to open his eyes, and who simultaneously starts a timer. It ends when the last subject yells "Stop." This procedure, when used with ten to twenty subjects, results in an easily measurable time interval.

We performed this experiment in class with a group of twenty-one subjects in the chain. The critical test trials of the experiment were preceded by thirty practice trials, ten each with a different target set size. These practice trials were followed by twenty-five test trials; for fifteen of these (five for each memory set size), the stimulus letter was a member of the target set. For ten trials, it was not. These latter negative trials were discarded in the data analysis. The negative trials are needed minimally to keep the students honest—that is, to keep them from consistently responding with their index fingers. Once the fifteen critical positive mass reaction times are collected, they are divided into three groups, according to the size of the memory set. The five reaction times within each group are averaged and this average is then divided by the number of people in the chain. These overall means are graphed in Figure 2 below, as a function of memory set size. Clearly, there is an increase in mean reaction time as a function of number of items in the memory set. Furthermore, this increase appears to be

roughly linear, agreeing quite well with Sternberg's (1966) findings. We have calculated that the search rate in our experiment is approximately 52 msec. per item in the memory set (Sternberg's better controlled experiments give a typical value of 38 msec. per item).

Note that although a fair number of trials (55 in all) is required in this experiment, the actual time occupied by the experiment is not great. Each trial takes no more than 20 seconds so that the whole experiment can be completed in approximately 25 minutes.

At-home form. We have applied the same logic to at-home experiments of cognitive processes. In one case, we had our students replicate the Shepard and Metzler (1971) mental rotation experiment.[1] In this experiment, subjects are asked to judge whether two block figures are actually the same figure in different orientations, or whether they are two different figures. This task occupies some considerable time, and it is almost within the range of accurate timing on a wrist

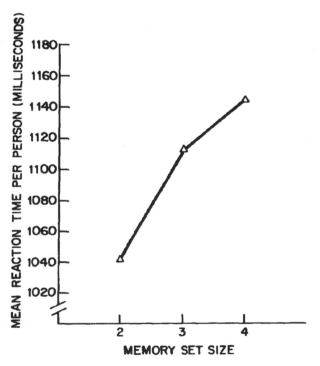

Figure 2. Mean reaction time as a function of memory set size for memory scanning demonstration.

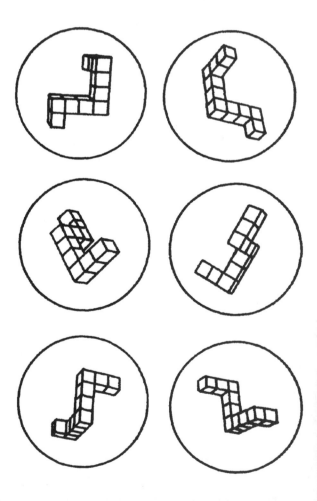

Figure 3. A typical triplet of pairs of block figures used in at-home demonstration of mental rotation effect. The members of each pair in this example are identical to one another, but differ by a rotation of 160°.

watch. However, to make it more appropriate for at home experimentation, we had subjects obtain mass reaction times from successive judgments about three pairs of block figures. Each subject was presented with a set of three pairs of figures on each page of a mimeographed handout (see Figure 3 for an example of a sheet of this handout). He was instructed to determine whether the members of each pair were identical (except for rotation) or whether they were different from one another. After making this determination for the first pair, the subject proceeded to the next pair, and then to the final pair of the three. At this point, he determined (with a wristwatch) how much time elapsed foray three decisions. He wrote down his responses for all three pairs, and then proceeded to the next triplet of pairs. Most of the triplets of pairs included in the task contained pairs all of which were identical, although subjects were not informed of this beforehand. As with the memory scanning experiment, negative instances (in this case, different pairs), were occasionally inserted to keep subjects honest, but the triplets which contained a different pair were not included in the data analysis. We constructed the all-identical triplets so that the disparity in rotation between the pairs in any triplet was the same: some triplets contained pairs which all differed by a 40° rotation, others by 80°, others by 120°, and finally, others by 160°. In all, there were eight such critical trials in the experiment, two at each of the four degrees of rotation.

Subjects performed all the calculations in this experiment based on instructions provided in a handout which they read after they produced the data. First they identified the eight triplets which contained pairs whose members were identical to one another. Then they determined whether their responses to these triplets were correct. Any triplet in which an incorrect response was made was excluded from data analysis. For any given degree of rotation, (40, 80, 120 or 160) subjects computed the average time taken to respond "identical" to a pair by adding together the reaction times for the two triplets representing that degree of rotation and dividing by six (the total number of pairs contained in both triplets).

One hundred-twenty-two subjects performed this experiment. Though there were many perturbations in the individual data, the group data for all subjects were quite interesting, as one can see by examining Table 1. Across subjects there is a roughly linear increase in time with degree of rotation. The slope of the linear function best fit to these data is 18.6 degrees per second, compared to the value of 55-60° that was re-

ported by Metzler and Shepard (1974). In view of the fact that so few trials were run in the present experiment, and that subjects were not pre-selected according to spatial ability (as were subjects used by Shepard & Metzler), this difference is not unreasonable.

Of the 122 individual data reports, 42 showed completely consistent data; that is, time increased as rotation degree increased across all three transitions (40–80, 80–120, 120–160). No subject showed the reverse pattern.

The mass reaction time technique here described thus appears to be a useful tool in demonstrating both measurement of the speed of the nerve impulse, and measurement of the durations of various cognitive processes.

Table 1
Mean Times for Mental Rotation
(Sec., Averaged Across 122 Subjects)

	40°	80°	120°	160°
Mean	6.42	8.92	10.73	12.98
S.D.	7.06	12.24	17.37	23.35

References

Metzler, J., & Shepard, R. N. Transformational studies of the internal representation of three-dimensional objects. In R. L. Solso (ed.). *Theories of cognitive psychology: The Loyola symposium.* Potomac, MD: Erlbaum Associates, 1974.

Milner, P. M. *Physiological psychology.* New York: Holt, Rinehart & Winston, 1970.

Neisser, U. Decision time without reaction time: Experiments in visual scanning. *American Journal of Psychology*, 1963, 76, 376-385 .

Shepard, R. N., & Metzler, J. Mental rotation of three-dimensional objects. *Science*, 1971, *171*, 701-703.

Sternberg, S. High-speed scanning in human memory. *Science*, 1966, *153*, 652-654.

Note

We thank Dr. Roger Shepard for supplying us with the stimulus materials used in his experiments.

5. TEACHING COMPARATIVE PSYCHOLOGY

Timing Like a Rat: A Classroom Demonstration of the Internal Clock

W. Robert Batsell, Jr.
Southern Methodist University

Students studying animal learning often have difficulty comprehending the procedures for studying timing and the properties of the internal clock if live animal models are not available. The following demonstration provides an alternative in which students respond for reinforcement using the peak procedure. The demonstration reveals various characteristics of the internal clock, including that it: (a) can be stopped and restarted within a trial, and (b) operates by timing up as opposed to timing down. This analog of the animal experiments helps students acquire a better understanding of the characteristics of the rat's internal clock and the methods needed to study cognitive abilities in nonverbal animals.

As the subject matter of animal learning becomes increasingly cognitive, experimental procedures and our understanding of an animal's abilities increase in complexity. Animal timing, for example, requires extensive training of the animal and complicated procedures to demonstrate the existence and properties of an organism's internal clock. These aspects of animal timing are sufficiently represented in numerous learning texts (e.g., Domjan & Burkhardt, 1986; Mazur, 1990; Roitblat, 1990); yet, it is often difficult for undergraduates to comprehend fully the experimental procedures and results without an adequate demonstration. Unfortunately, it is not practical for many learning instructors to train and maintain animals for demonstrations. This article describes a procedure using students as subjects to teach the properties of the internal clock.

Roberts (1981) introduced the peak procedure to study timing in the rat. The *peak procedure* is a modified discretetrials, fixed-interval (FI) procedure that uses standard and empty trials. In a standard trial, a brief light or tone signals the beginning of a trial in which reinforcement is provided for the first response made after a specified time (i.e., a 20-s or 40-s interval). After training, near the end of a signaled interval, typical FI scalloped responding occurs, with the peak of responding corresponding to the expected arrival of the reinforcer. An empty trial is also preceded by stimulus presentation, but no reinforcement is available. Also, these trials are considerably longer than the signaled interval. On empty trials, the animals' responses are similar to those on the standard trials; however, responding decreases shortly after the signaled interval. This drop in responding following completion of the signaled interval led Roberts to infer that rats discriminate by responding to these signaled intervals.

Using the peak procedure, Roberts determined that (a) rats can stop and restart their internal clock (see Roberts, 1981, Experiment 2), and (b) they use a *time-up* clock as opposed to a *time-down* clock (see Roberts, 1981, Experiment 5). To demonstrate the rat's ability to stop and restart the clock within a trial, blackout trials were used. On these blackout trials, the chamber lights were extinguished for a short period during a timing interval. This darkened period did not count toward the accumulation of time for that interval (i.e., a time-out period for the interval estimation). For instance, a tone signaling a 40-s interval started a trial. After 20 s of this interval, the lights were turned off for a 5-s period before being re-illuminated. Because of the blackout period, the rats responded 45 s after the start of the trial, not 40 s later. The animals always responded when the combined illuminated intervals equalled the signaled timing interval, regardless of the duration of the blackout or when it was inserted into the timing interval (Roberts, 1981; Roberts & Church, 1978). These results suggest that the rat can stop and restart its internal clock based on an estimation of the illuminated interval.

Using another variation of the peak procedure, Roberts (1981) examined whether the rat's internal clock times up or times down. After the rats learned the peak procedure, shift trials were introduced. A typical shift trial began with a stimulus, a light, signaling that reinforcement would be available a specific timing interval later (e.g., 20 s); however, before this interval had elapsed, a second stimulus, a tone, was presented. The tone signaled that reinforcement would not be available 20 s after the start, but would be available 40 s after the first stimulus. This second stimulus could be introduced at various delays (e.g., 5 s, 10 s, or 15 s) after the first stimulus. Regardless of whether the second stimulus, signaling the 40-s interval, was presented 5 s, 10 s, or 15 s after the first stimulus, the rats consistently responded 40 s after the start of the trial (see Roberts, 1981, Experiment 5), thus demonstrating their correct interpretation of the second stimulus.

A time-down clock is similar to a cooking timer in that it is set at the total timing interval (e.g., 20 s), and as time elapses, it approaches zero. If such a time-down clock was used, presentation of the second stimulus could result in one of two alternatives: (a) the rat could ignore the second stimulus and respond at 20 s, or (b) it could restart the time-down clock at the interval corresponding to the second stimulus. For example, if the tone was sounded 15 s after the light was presented, the rat would reset the clock to 40 s, begin timing again, and respond 55 s after the trial started. However, none of these possibilities agrees with the results of Roberts's (1981, Experiment 5) shift trials.

A time-up clock could involve two possible timing mechanisms. On the one hand, at the presentation of the tone, the rat might restart the time-up clock and respond 55 s after the start. This response would not distinguish it from the second proposed time-down timing mechanism. On the other hand, a time-up clock does not have to be reset when the tone is presented. Instead of stopping at the 20-s interval, the clock can continue to time until 40 s, and then the animal can respond. This time-up explanation is consistent with the shift trial results, which led Roberts (1981, Experiment 5) to conclude that rats time up. Again, these results are consistent with others (Roberts & Church, 1978) in suggesting that the internal clock starts at a zero value and times up, measuring elapsed time from the original signal at the start of the trial.

Procedure

The following demonstration is a modification of Roberts's designs to illustrate that (a) the internal clock can be stopped and restarted within a trial and (b) that it times up. First, students were familiarized with the internal clock and the peak procedure, but the results and logic of these studies were not explained until afterward. This enabled the class to compare the effectiveness of their own internal time-up or time-down clocks on shift trials. Students were asked to remove their watches and select partners. In each pair, students alternated being the experimenter and the subject. The subjects were instructed to turn their backs to the instructor, face their experimenters, and look only at their desks. Thus, only experimenters had an unobstructed view of the class instructor.

Next, the students were told how their procedure would resemble the peak procedure. The instructor explained that he would quickly make one of two sounds. One sound would signal a 20-s interval estimation trial, whereas the other sound would signal a 40-s interval estimation trial. Once either sound had occurred, the timing interval would begin. Reinforcement would be given if subjects responded by raising

their hands just after the signaled interval had elapsed. However, three stipulations were added: (a) to prevent continuous responding, subjects could only make one response; (b) responses made before completion of the timing interval would not be reinforced; and (c) reinforcement would be available for only 4 s following the completion of the interval. At this point, the instructor had half of the subjects approach the front of the room where they were discreetly instructed to use a time-down procedure. Then, the same procedure was repeated with the other half, but a time-up procedure was suggested to this group. Also, both groups had been informed that their timing method would result in more reinforcements. As a result, each group readily adopted its proposed timing method without question.

The experimenters were informed that once a trial began, the instructor would raise his hand when a timing interval was reached and lower it 4 s later. Thirty s after the instructor had lowered his hand, all students were informed that the trial was over. If a subject responded within the 4-s interval, the experimenter marked the response as correct and reinforced the subject with a piece of candy.

Before additional instructions for the blackout and shift trials were given, two standard trials were conducted—one at each interval. Then, students were instructed as follows about the modifications of the peak procedure to demonstrate the properties of the internal clock:

First, certain blackout periods will occur within a timing interval and these will *not* count for the total accumulation of that timing interval. These periods will be signaled by my turning off the overhead lights in the room. After a stimulus has signaled the beginning of a trial, for whatever period of time the overhead lights are off, this will *not* count for the total accumulation of timing, but whenever the lights are on, this will count toward the total amount of time.

Second, on some trials, one stimulus will start a trial, but the other stimulus may be presented *before* reinforcement is available. If so, reinforcement will be available at the *interval* signaled by the *second* stimulus; however, this interval was to be timed from the onset of the first stimulus, not by the second stimulus.

At this point, five trials were administered in random order: two blackout trials (a 20-s and a 40-s trial with a 10-s interval inserted 10 s into the trial) and three shift trials (two 20- to 40-s shifts and one 40- to 20-s shift). Once these trials were completed, the subject and experimenter changed roles and the entire procedure was repeated. These new subjects were members of the same group (time up or time down) as their partner.

Results

Forty-seven naive undergraduates were subjects: 30 were in the time-up group, and 17 were in the time-down group. Efforts were made to keep equal numbers in each group; however, once testing was over, 7 members of the time-down group revealed that they had switched to a time-up procedure to earn more reinforcements. Consequently, their responses were analyzed in the time-up group. Chi-square tests of independence were conducted using Response (correct vs. incorrect) and Type of Clock (time down vs. time up) as factors. Considering the relative ease all subjects had with the 20-s trials, only 40-s trials were included in the analyses. Separate tests were conducted over the 40-s standard trial, the 40-s blackout trial, and the two 20-s to 40-s shift trials.

Figure 1 presents the percentage of correct responses of the time-up and time-down groups over trials. It appears that the time-up group earned more reinforcements, yet analyses revealed that neither the time-up procedure nor the time-down procedure was significantly more effective on the 40-s standard trial, $\chi^2(1, N = 47) = 1.41, p > .05$, or on the 40-s blackout trial, $\chi^2(1, N = 47) = 1.23, p > .05$. These results are not surprising because these trials would not predict differences between the time-up and time-down methods. However, differences between the time-down and time-up procedures should be evident on the two 20-s to 40-s shift trials. Although the groups did not differ on the first shift trial, $\chi^2(1, N = 47) = 3.42, p > .05$, significant differences were observed on the second 20-s to 40-s shift trial, $\chi^2(1, N = 47) = 7.9, p < .01$. These results indicate that using a time-up timing method is more effective for responding correctly, at least on the second shift trial.

Discussion

The technique modified the peak procedure of studying timing in order to teach this design and its basic logic to students. After students were instructed in the methods and possible timing mechanisms, various trials were conducted. Results demonstrated that both time-down and time-up procedures were effective on basic timing intervals and blackout trials. However, only subjects using a time-up mechanism could successfully respond on shift trials. These results resemble those Roberts (1981) obtained using these procedures to study rat timing.

In addition to comparable results, other aspects of this demonstration should be emphasized. First, it effectively teaches the peak procedure and some of the considerations required for studying animal timing. The postdemonstration discussion centered on alternative explanations for the observed results and the difficulties of isolating timing as the sole mechanism of these results. Second, this technique is a good introduction to comparative cognition and to a discussion of the relation between humans and animals on other cognitive abilities. Finally, the most beneficial outcome is the demonstration of how only the time-up clock

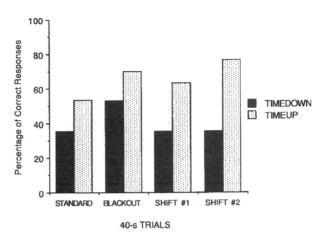

Figure 1. Percentage of correct responses by the time-down and time-up groups on the 40-s standard trial, the 40-s blackout trial with a 1 0-s insertion, and the two 20-s to 40-s shift trials.

could work on shift trials. In the past, students had struggled with the logical differences between the time-up and time-down procedures. However, this technique is successful not because it measures human timing, but because it forces the student to "time like a rat. " Using either a time-up or time-down method to solve the shift trials, students realize that only a time-up clock can account for Roberts's (1981) results. This human analog of Roberts's peak procedure is useful in teaching the basic methods of studying timing, generating discussion of the issues of studying cognitive abilities in other organisms, demonstrating that the internal clock times up and that it can be stopped and restarted within a trial, and providing fun!

References

Domjan, M., & Burkhardt, B. (1986). *The principles of learning & behavior* (2nd ed.). Monterey, CA: Brooks/Cole.

Mazur, J. E. (1990). *Learning and behavior* (2nd ed.). Englewood Cliffs, NJ: Prentice Hall.

Roberts, S. (1981). Isolation of an internal clock. *Journal of Experimental Psychology: Animal Behavior Processes, 7,* 242-268.

Roberts, S., & Church, R. M. (1978). Control of an internal clock. *Journal of Experimental Psychology Animal Behavior Processes, 4,* 318-337.

Roitblat, H. L. (1990). *Introduction to comparative cognition.* New York: Freeman.

Note

I thank the students in my learning and experimental psychology classes for their participation in this project. I also thank Michael R. Best, Ruth L. Ault, and the anonymous reviewers for their helpful comments on earlier drafts of this article.

A Classroom Simulation of Transitivity Problems in Animals

W. Robert Batsell, Jr.
Southern Methodist University

Transitive inference *involves the ability to infer a serial relation between ordered events that have been presented only in successive pairs. Successful completion of this task has been reported for humans, chimpanzees, monkeys, pigeons, and rats. Although students easily solve transitivity problems in a verbal format, they often have difficulty appreciating how nonhuman subjects might successfully solve these tasks. This article describes a classroom simulation modified from transitivity experiments with animals; its purpose is to familiarize students with the procedures and results from transitive inference studies with nonhuman subjects. Students enjoy this activity and report that it helped illustrate different perspectives of the transitive inference problem.*

Transitive inference is the ability to deduce relations among a series of items that were learned separately. After subjects learn about the relations between consecutive items, they can compare specific items or infer the underlying order of the series. Traditionally, transitivity problems have been studied with human subjects, and these tasks are presented in a verbal format (e.g., Riley & Trabasso, 1974; Thayer & Collier, 1978; Trabasso & Riley, 1975). In verbal (and symbolic) form, the transitive inference problem can be illustrated as follows:

1. If Mike is taller than Mary (A > B), and
2. If Mary is taller than Alan (B > C), then,
3. Who is taller, Mike or Alan (A vs. C)

Subjects successfully complete this problem when they infer that Mike (A) is taller than Alan (C).

Because a verbal format is obviously inadequate with animals, with nonhuman subjects the typical procedure presents two consecutive pairs from a five-item series, such as A > B, B > C, C > D, D > E. Subjects are reinforced for choosing the superior member of each pair. The inference test pits B against D, a novel pairing in which each element has equally signaled reinforcement or nonreinforcement during training. If subjects can infer the order of the series, they should select B. A number of nonhuman species, including squirrel monkeys (McGonigle & Chalmers, 1977), chimpanzees (Gillan, 1981), pigeons (Fersen, Wynne, Delius, & Staddon, 1991), and rats (Davis, 1992), apparently solve transitivity problems.

The critical issue that has arisen from the demonstration that various species can successfully solve transitivity tasks is whether the same strategy can explain the performance of all species. In other words, do these animals and humans use the same strategy to solve transitivity problems? Currently, researchers debate the various processes that animals may use to solve transitive inference tasks. In a simplistic form, some researchers have argued that reinforcement history is sufficient to explain performance (Couvillon & Bitterman, 1992; Fersen et al., 1991; Wynne, Fersen, & Staddon, 1992), whereas others advocate a more cognitive approach in which the subjects infer the order of the stimulus hierarchy (Davis, 1992).

My demonstration was not designed to convince students of the viability of one approach over another. Instead, it facilitates students' understanding that different species may use different strategies to solve the same problem. For instance, although students can easily solve a transitivity problem, they often report difficulty understanding why different theories may be necessary to explain similar performance by a nonhuman subject. To promote students' understanding of the processes involved when studying transitive inference with animals and various explanations of this result, this classroom demonstration allows students to participate in a five-item transitivity problem designed for nonhuman subjects.

Method

Apparatus

Any five discriminable stimuli that could be viewed by all members of the class would make suitable stimuli; however, the instructor should randomly determine the stimulus order, avoiding preexisting stimulus attributes such as size. For example, I have used a random ordering of 2 in. x 2 in. (5 cm x 5 cm) pictures of famous paintings as stimuli (e.g., Warhol's "Marilyn," Lichenstein's "M-Maybe," and Klee's "Marked Man").

Procedure

Although only one student volunteers as the subject, the other students are instructed to observe the subject's choices and reinforcements because they too will be tested. The instructions are kept to a minimum to illustrate the additional demands that are present when working with nonverbal subjects. The instructor states that the volunteer will be safe and can earn reinforcements (food, tokens, or points) for selecting the correct choice from each pair of stimuli. If the subject chooses the incorrect member of the pair, the instructor removes a reinforcement (if any are available). Although previous designs have not penalized the subject for incorrect choices, this experimental manipulation increases students' interest in the demonstration.

The instructor should vary the order of presenting the four pairs (A-B, B-C, C-D, and D-E) as well as the position of the correct choice. Six to eight exposures to each stimulus pair should ensure that the subject is responding correctly on most trials; however, more ambiguous stimuli will take more training trials. I wait until the subject has chosen the correct stimulus on all trials for two consecutive cycles through the stimulus pairs before testing. At this juncture, I have found that approximately half of the students can solve the problem. I prefer to stop at this point because it captures some students while they are still testing strategies. If the instructor wants to ensure that all of the students can successfully solve the transitivity tests, the instructor may want to delay testing until after the volunteer has completed three or more cycles through the stimuli.

For testing, all of the students are instructed to record their answers on a sheet of paper. I ask three questions to assess the students' ability to infer the underlying relation and to focus their attention on their problem-solving strategies. First, I present the standard transitive inference choice pair of B versus D and ask students to select the correct stimulus. Second, the students order the five stimuli from highest to lowest in terms of reinforcement value. Third, to facilitate understanding of the different processes that can solve the transitivity problem, I ask the students to write down the various strategies that they used.

The demonstration and testing take approximately 20 min. The instructor can reduce this time, however, by prefacing the demonstration with the information that the stimuli were chosen randomly and that the correct stimulus choice is not based on specific stimulus characteristics.

Evaluation and Discussion

In a recent Psychology of Learning class, 22 students participated in this simulation. On the first question (B vs. D), 68% of the students ($n = 15$) correctly picked B. On the second question, most of the students expressed surprise to learn that there was an underlying order to the stimuli; yet, over half of the students ($n = 12$) could accurately place the five stimuli in order. Although all of the students did not succeed at this second task, 86% ($n = 19$) had some knowledge of the underlying order because they were able to identify the terminal ends of the series (A and E). Also, all students reported that they enjoyed the simulation.

The follow-up discussion is the most important portion of this demonstration to promote understanding of transitivity performance in animals. After explaining the concept of transitive inference and providing the correct solution to the series, I asked the students to describe the strategies they tried on each trial. Each student could identify several strategies. Most of the students who could not solve the series attempted to isolate some stimulus characteristic that determined reinforcement. They remembered how some of these strategies produced short-term success but would fail on future trials.

Students who successfully ordered the five stimuli reported that they had abandoned their focus on stimulus attributes and, instead, centered on the relations between specific pairs. On the one hand, some of these students recalled that they were unaware that there was an underlying order to the stimuli, yet they were sensitive to the reinforcement value of the stimuli. For instance, these students recounted that they liked the stimulus that was always reinforced and hated the stimulus that always lost (i.e., A and E, respectively). A typical response was that one picture "was always reinforced, another never reinforced, and then some unspecified gradation of reinforcement" occurred between the other stimuli. The reports of these students were used to introduce the reinforcement explanation of transitivity results.

On the other hand, some students related that they became aware that there was an underlying order and that they "placed the stimuli in order based on this continuum." Their responses initiated a discussion of cognitive strategies that humans (and possibly animals) may apply to this task. Next, students discussed which strategy would produce the best results, and they concluded that each approach could effectively explain an animal's behavior. Following this discussion, all the students (including those who could not solve the transitivity problems) reported that they understood transitivity problems and how different approaches could successfully solve them.

To expand the consideration of transitivity problems, instructors could lecture on the following topics: (a) theories, such as the coordination models (e.g.,

Trabasso & Riley, 1975), the linear representation models (e.g., Riley & Trabasso, 1974; Trabasso & Riley, 1975), and the value transfer mechanism (Fersen et al., 1991; Wynne et al., 1992; also see Couvillon & Bitterman, 1992; Markovits & Dumas, 1992); (b) phenomena associated with the transitive inference design, such as positive and negative end effects, the serial position effect, and the symbolic distance effect (e.g., Bryant & Trabasso, 1971); and (c) the logic underlying why circular relations are difficult to solve using this method. (In this case, the instructor can repeat the demonstration but make the series of stimulus pairs circular [A > B, B > C, C > D, D > E, E > A]. Students, like past experimental subjects, will find this variation much more arduous to solve [e.g., Davis, 1992; Fersen et al., 1991] .)

The present simulation has been an effective classroom technique because it entertains and educates the students. Specifically, it illustrates a number of important concepts about studying transitive inference with nonhuman subjects. Also, by requiring human subjects to "act like an animal" to earn reinforcements, students can better understand how different approaches can successfully solve transitivity problems.

References

Bryant, P. E., & Trabasso, T. (1971). Transitive inferences and memory in young children. *Nature, 232,* 456-458.

Couvillon, P. A., & Bitterman, M. E. (1992). A conventional conditioning analysis of "transitive inference" in pigeons. *Journal of Experimental Psychology: Animal Behavior Processes, 18,* 308-310.

Davis, H. (1992). Transitive inference in rats (*Rattus norvegicus*) *Journal of Comparative Psychology, 106,* 342-349.

Fersen, L. von, Wynne, C.D.L., Delius, J. D., & Staddon, J.E.R. (1991). Transitive inference formation in pigeons. *Journal of Experimental Psychology: Animal Behavior Processes, 17,* 334–341.

Gillan, D. J. (1981). Reasoning in the chimpanzee: II. Transitive inferences and memory in young children. *Journal of Experimental Psychology: Animal Behavior Processes, 7,* 150-164.

Markovits, H., & Dumas, C. (1992). Can pigeons really make transitive inferences? *Journal of Experimental Psychology: Animal Behavior Processes, 18,* 311-312.

McGonigle, B. O., & Chalmers, M. (1977). Are monkeys logical? *Nature, 267,* 694-696.

Riley, C., & Trabasso, T. (1974). Comparatives, logical structures, and encoding in a transitive inference task. *Journal of Experimental Child Psychology, 17,* 187-203.

Thayer, E. S., & Collier, C. E. (1978). The development of transitive inference: A review of recent approaches. *Psychological Bulletin, 85,* 1327-1344.

Trabasso, T., & Riley, C. A. (1975). On the construction and use of representations involving linear order. In R. L. Solso (Ed.), *Information processing and cognition: The Loyola Symposium* (pp. 381-410). Hillsdale, NJ: Lawrence Erlbaum Associates, Inc.

Wynne, C.D.L., Fersen, L. von, & Staddon, J.E.R. (1992). Pigeons' inferences are transitive and the outcome of elementary conditioning principles: A response. *Journal of Experimental Psychology: Animal Behavior Processes, 18,* 313-315.

Notes

1. I thank students in my Comparative Cognition and Psychology of Learning classes for participating in this project. Also, I thank Ruth L. Ault and three anonymous reviewers for their helpful comments on a draft of this article.
2. Portions of this article were presented at the Southwest Regional Conference for Teachers of Psychology, Fort Worth, TX, November 1992.

Exercise Demonstrating a Genetic-Environment Interaction

Robert T. Brown
University of North Carolina at Wilmington

Using inexpensive equipment and a limited number of subjects, this exercise demonstrates, through a factorial design, an interaction between genetics and environment. It also provides experience in direct observation of behavior. Inbred albino and pigmented mice are individually observed in a bright or dim open field; students record activity and defecation. Under dim light, albino and pigmented mice both show high levels of activity; under bright light, the activity of albino mice is suppressed but that of pigmented mice is little affected. Albinos defecate more than pigmented under both lighting conditions. Significant results are usually obtained with as few as four mice in each of the four groups.

Teachers of laboratory courses frequently need experiments that are simple and inexpensive, can be conducted in a short period of time, and provide reliable results. Using a small number of mice and simple equipment, the experiment described in this article consistently yields significant results. It demonstrates the use of an independent variable (IV) × subject variable (SV) design to study genetic–environment relations. It also provides experience in observing behavior and determining interobserver reliability and produces data suitable for student analysis and written reports. The exercise takes about 2 hr and is appropriate for experimental psychology, developmental psychology, behavior genetics, and animal behavior courses.

The experiment is a simplified version of a study reported by DeFries, Hegmann, and Weir (1966). It was found that albino mice are frequently less active in bright than in dim light, whereas pigmented mice are active under both conditions and thus less affected by light. DeFries et al. (1966) suggested that albinos' behavior reflected a photophobia linked to the albinism gene. They crossed an inbred albino (BALB) with a pigmented (C57BL) strain, producing offspring that were albino or pigmented, but otherwise had a mixed genotype of the two parental strains. In tests of the albino and pigmented offspring in a brightly or dimly lighted open field, DeFries et al. (1966) found that for activity, pigmentation (genotype) interacted with lighting condition (environment): Pigmented mice were highly active under both dim and bright light, whereas albinos were less active under bright than dim light.

For defecation, the interaction was not significant; both strains defecated more in bright light than in dim. Because the low activity under bright light was carried along with the gene for albinism, DeFries et al. (1966) concluded that the gene for photophobia was linked to that for albinism, with the effects mediated by the visual system. Perhaps the best research context for DeFries et al. (1966) is *pleiotropism*, the term for multiple effects of a single gene. Plomin, DeFries, and McClearn (1980) provided a useful summary of DeFries et al. (1966) under the heading of *behavioral pleiotropism*.

Introducing the Experiment

Students should be familiar with the concepts of factorial designs, main effects, and interactions. Depending on the course, material on behavior genetics and genetic-environment interactions may be presented. In addition to DeFries et al.'s (1966) article, students are assigned to read Plomin et al.'s (1980) summary and a more general report of differences among strains of mice in open-field behavior (Abeelen, 1966). I also provide a handout summarizing the background information and methods of the experiment.

Conducting the Experiment

Design

The design is a 2 × 2 factorial with two levels of a true IV (bright vs. dim light) and two levels of an SV (albino vs. pigmented mice). Two dependent variables, activity and defecation, are recorded.

Subjects

The subjects are male albino and pigmented mice. The interaction between strain and lighting in activity will most likely be found with BALB and C57BL strains. Use of other strains may lead to different but still interesting patterns of results. We use male mice because they have low within-condition variability. Although four mice in each of the our conditions is generally satisfactory, six is recommended to increase reliability.

Apparatus

Testing is done in open fields. We use four fields to enable observation of several mice at once. The fields are relatively small, with 61 cm × 91.5 cm masonite floors divided into a 4 × 6 grid of 15.25 cm squares that serve as a guide for recording activity. The 41-cm high plexiglas walls are held in place by slotted wooden corner posts. The fields can be stored compactly when taken apart. Light is provided by a bulb in an aluminum reflector clip lamp attached to the top of one wall. Dim and bright light are provided by 7.5-W bulbs painted red and 150-W bulbs, respectively. The interaction in activity scores is more likely to occur with extreme differences between bright and dim light. The 150-W bulb is sufficient in our laboratory to suppress almost all activity in BALB mice. The room is unlighted except for an unobtrusive 7.5-W light next to the cages; this light enables the instructor to pick up the mice.

Procedure

At least three students are assigned to each field. On each trial, two students record activity; a third student times the trial length. Five-min trials provide reliable data. If multiple fields are used in the same room, mice cannot be run in both lighting conditions at the same time. We counterbalance across trials for lighting condition and test two albino and two pigmented mice on each trial.

General procedures are explained at the beginning of the lab session. I use this session to explain the use of operational definitions for recording specific behaviors, asking the students how they could record activity reliably (for this part of the exercise, the grids on the floors of the open fields are covered). I emphasize the need for objective and detailed definitions. We define *activity* as number of lines crossed by all four of the mouse's feet, recorded by tracing the mouse's path on a map of the field, and *defecation* as number of fecal pellets dropped during the trial. After each trial, fields are wiped with a sponge dipped in a mild disinfectant solution to remove fecal pellets and odors. After the last trial, students compile activity data by counting the number of tracings that cross the vertical and horizontal grids on their maps. Because "if a mouse can bite you, it will," instructors do all handling of the mice, placing them in the center of the field at the beginning of a trial and removing them at the end.

Interobserver reliability for activity can be calculated either by correlating all pairs of observers' scores or by calculating percentage agreement for each pair. We calculate percentage agreement by the formula: Percentage agreement = Number of agreements/Number of agreements + Number of disagreements, which is, for the two observers, the smaller number of lines recorded divided by the larger. Mean and median percentage agreement can be determined across all pairs of observers.

Typical Results

The study has been run several times with BALB and C57BL strains with consistent results. Activity scores show the interaction between strain and lighting condition re ported by DeFries et al. (1966): Albino and pigmented mice are both active under dim light, whereas albinos show very low and pigmented show high activity under bright light. Generally, both strain and lighting condition produce significant main effects, with higher activity overall for pigmented mice and under dim light. However, for defecation, only strain shows a significant effect; albinos defecate more than pigmented under both conditions, contrary to DeFries et al. (1966) .

Use of other albino and pigmented strains yields different, but interesting, patterns of results. For example, when testing A/J albino and DBA/2J pigmented mice, it was found that the A/Js were significantly more active than the DBA/2Js under both lighting conditions and activity was significantly higher for both strains under dim light; the interaction was not significant. When BALB albino and CXBK pigmented mice were used, it was found that the BALBs were more active in dim than bright light, as expected. This was also true of the CXBKs, which were somewhat but not significantly more active under both lighting conditions; the interaction was again not significant. The different patterns of results indicate that DeFries et al.'s (1966) suggestion that photophobia is linked to albinism may be limited to certain strains and give students the opportunity to study strain differences.

References

Abeelen, J. H. F. van. (1966). Effects of genotype on mouse behavior. *Animal Behavior, 14* , 218-224.

DeFries, J. C., Hegmann, J. P., & Weir, M. W. (1966). Openfield behavior in mice: Evidence for a major gene effect mediated by the visual system. *Science, 154*, 1577-1579.

Plomin, R., DeFries, J. C., & McClearn, G. E. (1980). *Behavioral genetics, a primer.* San Francisco: Freeman.

Note

I thank R. Dale McCall for supplying the mice used in this research.

Insect Predation by Rodents: Some Inexpensive Experiments in Comparative and Physiological Psychology

Ernest D. Kemble
University of Minnesota, Morris

The continuing erosion of financial support for undergraduate laboratories makes cost an increasingly important factor in the choice, if not survival, of undergraduate animal experiments. This article describes a number of projects employing insect predation by rodents which require minimal equipment, pose a number of interesting questions about animal behavior, and which my students have found to be interesting and challenging.

Equipment and Methods. Testing is conducted in glass aquarium fitted with hardware cloth or screen covers. For rats, a 10-20 gal. aquarium is large enough to permit observation of pursuit as well as attack and consumption of prey. Smaller rodents (e.g., mice, hamsters) are tested in 2-5 gal. aquaria. Since many insect species can readily climb the glass walls of aquaria (not only escaping the predator but often producing consternation among students) a thin film of Vaseline should be placed around the inside walls 4-8 cm wide, 6-12 cm above the floor. This provides an effective barrier to escape. Thorough habituation of rodents to the apparatus and human observers (4-8 thirty min periods) is very important, especially if observations are to be conducted in the classroom. Given adequate habituation, a high proportion (80-95%) of naive, undeprived rats (albino or hooded) will attack and consume insect prey within an initial 30 min trial. The initial predatory attack typically follows repeated physical contact between the insect and rat (especially vibrissae or tail), and consists of rapid pursuit and grasping movements with the forepaws, pinning or pouncing on the dorsal side of the insect with the forepaws, and a series of rapid bites to the head and/or anterior thorax. The insect is then picked up, the head bitten off and discarded, and all but the hardest parts of the exoskeleton consumed. This attack is very similar in form to that shown by the highly predatory northern grasshopper mouse (*Onychomys leucogaster*).

Crickets (*Acheta domestica*), mealworm larvae or adults (*Tenebrio monitor*), or american cockroaches (*Periplaneta americana*) are attacked and consumed by rats and are easily available from entomology laboratories, bait dealers, or scientific suppliers. These insects are also easily maintained in the laboratory. Large (2-4 cm) american cockroaches are particularly appropriate for instructional settings.[1] Their high level of activity tends to provoke rapid attack and their size permits observation of attack sites and details of prey consumption. If students, or instructors, are reluctant to pick up roaches, they may be captured in an empty baby food jar, capped, and dumped into the aquarium without touching them. If small insects are used with rats, attack is facilitated by placing several insects in the aquarium.

With repeated testing kill latencies rapidly decline (2-4 trials) to 30-120 sec. This is due primarily to a more rapid initiation of pursuit which requires fewer, then no, contacts between insect and rat.

Behavioral/Comparative Projects. The stereotyped pursuit, capture, and consumption of insects by rats with no previous predatory experience lends itself well to ethological analyses (e.g., releasing stimuli, etc.), discussions of genetic contributions to the behavior (what, if not genes, accounts for initial attack?), the evolutionary significance of predation in the widespread success of rodents as omnivores (e.g., Landry, 1970), and the behavioral deterioration which is presumed to have accompanied domestication in the rat (e.g., Blanchard & Blanchard, 1977; Lockard,1971). Insect predation also contrasts with muricide (still frequently employed as a measure of rat predatory behavior) in the high rate of spontaneous killing (e.g., Bandler & Moyer, 1970) and in the lack of agonistic components during attack (Blanchard & Blanchard, 1977). This, of course, raises interesting questions about the adequacy of muricide as a model of predatory behavior. The near-universal distribution and seasonal abundance of insects, or other nonmammalian forms (Bandler & Moyer, 1970), may provide more ecologically valid models.

If time permits repeated testing, the rapid improvement in predation also clearly reveals the importance of learning in the development of this behavior. Manipulations of antecedent experiences (e.g., opportunity for play, varied consummatory or manipulators experience) or of prey characteristics (e.g., activity levels, palatability, possession of defensive secretions or structures) might also be of interest for laboratory projects.

As mentioned previously, the form of the predatory attack by rats is similar to that of northern grasshopper mice. Grasshopper mice attack much more rapidly than rats during initial (1-30 sec) and subsequent (0.3-12.0 sec) trials. If grasshopper mice are available, species comparisons are easily conducted and yield marked quantitative differences. The golden hamster (*Mesocricetus auratus*) is an inexpensive and readily available rodent which also differs markedly from the rat in its predatory behavior. Although hamsters readily attack small insects and show decreased kill latencies with repeated exposures, the attack appears quite similar to defensive attack directed toward conspecifics (or the observer's hand). The insects are bitten and pushed away with the forepaws or buried repeatedly before consumption begins. In some cases I have observed hamsters to roll over on their backs while holding an insect, bite it several times, and push it away with their forepaws. Bites may be directed toward any part of the insect's body and consumption, during initial exposures, occurs only after numerous biting episodes which may be separated by appreciable delays. With the aid of a friendly field biologist most laboratories should also be able to extend these comparisons to other interesting rodent species.

Physiological Manipulations. Predatory behavior in both the rat and grasshopper mouse is susceptible to a number of simple physiological manipulations. Vibrissal amputation is a simple, reversible procedure requiring only ether and scissors but produces a dramatic disruption of predation in the grasshopper mouse. Although the location and pursuit of prey seems normal, they frequently fail to pin their prey or permit it to escape after grasping it. This phenomenon becomes even more accentuated if subcutaneous injections of the vibrissal pad with a local anesthetic are substituted for vibrissal amputation. Such differences may serve as the focus for discussions of the sensory control of this behavior. Since rapid and excited sniffing is a prominent behavior during the initial portions of insect predation, peripheral anosmia produced by intranasal zinc sulfate irrigation is yet another inexpensive procedure which might also be expected to disrupt this behavior. The sensitivity of predatory behavior to both sex differences (in the rat) and limbic damage (Kemble & Davies, 1981) also suggests that it should respond to hormonal and drug manipulations as well as brain lesions, stimulation, etc.

Summary. During the past two years 55 upper division comparative or physiological psychology students have participated in experiments involving insect predation. When asked to evaluate these projects all students have responded positively ("interesting," "valuable addition to the course," etc.) and have urged their continued use in the courses. In addition, five students have now completed independent research or tutorial projects on this topic and a sixth student is planning research for the coming year. Three of these projects are in preparation for publication. This level of interest combined with the contemporary relevance, openendedness, simplicity, and low cost of the research may make this a useful technique for other financially pressed instructors.

References

Bandler, R. J., & Moyer, K E. Animals spontaneously attacked by rats. *Communications in Behavioral Biology*, 1970, *5*, 177-182.

Blanchard, R J., & Blanchard, D. C. Aggressive behavior in the rat. *Behavioral Biology*, 1977, *21*, 197-224.

Kemble, E. D., & Davies, V. A. Effects of prior environmental enrichment and amygdaloid lesions on consumatory behavior, activity, predation, and shuttlebox avoidance in male and female rats. *Physiological Psychology.*, 1981, *9*, 340-346.

Landry, S. O. The rodentia as omnivores. *Quarterly Review of Biology*, 1970, *45*, 351-372.

Lockard, R. B. Reflections on the fall of comparative psychology: Is there a message for us all? *American Psychologist*, 1971, *26*, 168-179.

Note

A tropical cockroach species (*Leucophea madeira*) is also often available from entomology laboratories but is less readily attacked and consumed. The roach is quite inactive, is heavily armored about the head and has a distinctly unpleasant odor.

SECTION II
PERCEPTION

Acquiring Demonstrations

Ludy T. Benjamin suggested ways to develop inexpensive but effective equipment for demonstrating perceptual phenomena. Displacement goggles, the Pulfrich apparatus, and the trapezoidal window were among the pieces of equipment he described.

In a sensation and perception course, Walter Wagor asked students to construct and implement a demonstration of a sensory or perceptual phenomenon. Students donated their completed projects to the department for use in future courses. As a result, students learned more about a particular phenomenon and gained recognition for their work. The department acquired many useful demonstrations.

Teaching About Illusions

J. R. Corey described the construction of a three-dimensional figure that appeared to be solid but was actually hollow. The "cube," which was mounted and illuminated in a small box, provided viewers with compelling illusions of movement.

An overhead projector, black construction paper, and a razor blade constituted the materials required to demonstrate a variety of movement illusions in Thaddeus Cowan's classroom. Preparation for the demonstrations involved cutting out small patterns in two sheets of construction paper. The instructor presented illusions such as the phi phenomenon. The article also described how to develop more complex illusions.

Dale Klopfer and Michael Doherty outlined the procedures they used to modify an inexpensive plastic costume mask to demonstrate the Janus illusion. With minor modifications, the masks provided compelling demonstrations of several perceptual phenomena including binocular and monocular cues to depth. The authors included discussion topics for both introductory psychology and sensation and perception courses.

Mark Kunkel devised a simple demonstration requiring no equipment to illustrate proximal versus distal stimuli, retinal size, and other perceptual phenomena. Students imagined being outside on a clear night during the full moon. From a list of round items that ranged in size from a BB to a beach ball, they chose an object that would barely occlude the moon's image if held at arm's length. Most students grossly overestimated the size of the object required to occlude the image. The author also suggested uses for this versatile demonstration in units other than sensation and perception.

Paul Solomon and a philosophy colleague taught a course entitled Perception, Illusion, and Magic. The instructors used their skills as amateur magicians to illustrate a number of perceptual phenomena. The author provided a resource list for learning the magic tricks that can be used to demonstrate aspects of perceptual organization, perceptual set, and the effects of experience on perception.

E. W. Jacobs discussed several ways the mirror drawing apparatus can be used to illustrate psychological concepts in a variety of classes. For example, students in an educational psychology course gained a greater appreciation for the plight of learning disabled students after attempting to reproduce an image with the apparatus. The author discussed the use of the apparatus in introductory courses.

Teaching Color Vision

Donald Mershon solved the problem of demonstrating additive color mixture when only one slide projector was available. A prism created a duplicate projection of two colored dots mounted on a single slide. By manipulating the prism, the instructor mixed the colors by producing overlapping images of the dots. The author also presented tips for adapting this method to subtractive mixing.

Barney Beins designed a "light box" that proved to be an inexpensive and effective tool for demonstrating various color phenomena. The light box consisted of simple ceramic sockets connected to dimmers that controlled low-watt, colored light bulbs. Mounted in a small plywood box, the lights, in various combinations of intensity, illustrated several color-related topics including color blindness.

Teaching Sensation

Many demonstrations of sensory measurement and adaptation rely on visual and auditory modalities. J. Russell Mason devised a method to demonstrate psychophysical measurement techniques and the nature of sensory adaptation of olfaction. By using incrementally diluted solutions of butyl and propyl acetate, the author demonstrated the method of magnitude estimation for scaling odorant intensities with subjects who were in nonadapted, adapted, and crossadapted states.

With a signal generator, an oscilloscope, and a speaker, John Batson combined visual and auditory information to illustrate the properties of several auditory stimulus-sensation relations. Simultaneous presentation of wave patterns through the speaker and the oscilloscope allowed the students not only to hear the changes but to see them as well. In one exercise the author presented sine waves and square waves of the same frequency and amplitude and offered several possible explanations for perceived differences in the sound quality.

Teaching Various Concepts in Perception

C. James Goodwin enlisted students as "earphones" in a demonstration of selective attention. Two students sat on either side of a subject and read passages that represented typical dichotic listening stimuli while the subject attempted to shadow one of the messages. Data from the demonstration mirrored those collected using earphones. The advantage of this demonstration, however, was the ability of the entire class to experience and observe the stimulus presentation.

Gestalt principles of organization were brought to life in Frederick Kozub's introductory psychology class when he asked students to find examples from the "real world" and bring them to class. Students found many superb illustrations in advertisements and logos. Some students continued to bring examples to class two months later!

Ernest Lumsden used a sheet of plexiglas and several meter sticks to illustrate the relationship between projected size and distance. Meter sticks were placed at varying distances from a standard observation point. While viewing the meter sticks through the plexiglass, students traced the projection of the meter sticks on the plexiglass. Finally, the class plotted the distances of the meter sticks against the projections. The author presented several student comments that attested to the efficacy of this demonstration. (The author informed the editors that the formula, $b^3 = c^2 - a^2$, on page 106 should have read $b^2 = c^2 - a^2$)

Robert Terborg described the construction of a pair of displacement goggles that he used in classroom demonstrations of displaced vision. The goggles consisted of inexpensive Fresnel prisms attached to ordinary safety glasses. The goggles were easily constructed and provided displaced vision that was as effective as the bulkier, more expensive goggles.

1. ACQUIRING DEMONSTRATIONS

Perceptual Demonstrations—Or, What To Do With an Equipment Budget of $75

Ludy T. Benjamin, Jr.
Nebraska Wesleyan University

As a scientific enterprise, many areas of research in psychology require little or no expensive laboratory equipment. However, in some fields equipment can contribute significantly to the quality of instruction through class demonstrations and experiments. In truth, it may be redundant to attach the adjective "expensive" to laboratory equipment. Because of the high costs of these materials, even the less expensive items are beyond the equipment budgets of many undergraduate psychology programs. Fortunately, for the psychologist in this position there is a feasible alternative—build it yourself!

The present paper offers some ideas for equipment and visual materials for use in a course in perception, although their use is certainly not restricted to that course alone. These materials can be easily and inexpensively assembled, requiring no special skills. In a few cases however, minimal carpentry skills are helpful.

In addition to equipment ideas, this paper includes references which describe some of the experiments and/or demonstrations in which these materials can be used. These references are in no way meant to be exhaustive of the utility of the materials, rather they represent a starting point for ideas.

A course in perception should involve some real experience in perceiving, yet often the perceptual experiences come solely from diagrams in a textbook. Films can extend the reality of these experiences beyond the means of a textbook, but even films are not "real." Watching a trapezoidal window oscillate in a film does not provide the same kind of perceptual experience one gets from a live demonstration. These "live" demonstrations are indispensable in presenting the psychology of perception as an interesting and intriguing area of study. It is hoped that the ideas presented here will encourage that kind of course offering.

Displacement Goggles. Displacement goggles similar to those used in studies of perceptual adaptation to distorted vision can be made from welding safety goggles. These goggles are inexpensive (usually under $5) and are especially advantageous in that they permit the subject to wear prescription glasses when the goggles are in place. Select the kind of goggles with a rectangular faceplate and no center dividing bridge. Remove the safety glass lenses and replace them with a clear piece of one-eighth inch plexiglas. The triangular prisms (two) can be cut from one-inch plexiglas. Begin by measuring the dimensions of the exposed surface of the front side of the faceplate. Cut two pieces identical in size from the one-inch plexiglas and completely cover the exposed faceplate surface. Ideal prism angle should be between 20° and 30° (which provides 10° to 15° of actual visual displacement). Polish the two large faces of each prism and then cover those faces with masking tape. Spray the three exposed edges with a flat black paint to prevent light from entering those surfaces. Finally, after the paint is dry, remove the masking tape and attach the prisms to the plexiglas faceplate using a plexiglas glue such as ethylene dichloride. The prism bases should be mounted to the right or the left if vision is to be displaced in a lateral direction. In most welding goggles the faceplate is removable; thus the direction of the displacement can be reversed by reversing the faceplate. For other perceptual effects, the prisms can be mounted on the faceplate in a variety of orientations.

Harris, C. S. Perceptual adaptation to inverted, reversed, and displaced vision. *Psychological* Review 1965, *72*, 419-444.

Kohler, I. Experiments with goggles. *Scientific American*, May 1962, *206*, 62-72.

Weinstein, S., Sersen E. A., Fisher, L, & Weisinger, M. Is reafference necessary for visual adaptation? *Perceptual and Motor Skills*, 1964, *18*, 41-648.

Visual Cliff. A visual cliff for use with small animals such as rats and kittens can be constructed from masonite, plexiglas, and contact paper. The dimensions of the apparatus may vary depending upon the subjects you plan to use. A cliff that is 30 in. by 30 in. by 30 in. can be constructed from two sheets of one-fourth inch masonite (4' by 8'). The basic unit is a square box with floor and a center wall extending from the floor to within 6 in. of the top of the box. A section of masonite from the top edge of this center wall to one edge of the box forms the base of the shallow side of the cliff. The masonite should be used so that the smooth surface is always part of the interior of the box.

Handles for carrying the unit should be attached with screws from the inside and countersunk flush with the surface of the interior walls. The cliff can be painted in the traditional checkerboard pattern or a more convenient method is to use contact paper of a checkerboard design. This can usually be found in discount or department stores and has an adhesive backing for easy mounting. Line all exposed interior surfaces and the surface of the shallow side. A sheet of clear one-fourth inch plexiglas should be used to cover the shallow and deep sides of the box. This sheet should rest on the surface of the shallow side and on several plexiglas stops on the deep side walls for support. The center walkway in the cliff can be made from wood and either painted or covered with the contact paper. For the visual cliff described here, the walkway should be approximately six inches wide, with a height of two to three inches above the surface of the plexiglas.

Gibson, E. J., & Walk, R. D. The "visual cliff". *Scientific American*, April 1960, *202*, 64-71.

Somervill, J. W. Motion parallax in the visual cliff situation. *Perceptual and Motor Skills*, 1971, *32*, 43-53.

Walk, R. D., Gibson, E. J., & Tighe, T. J. Behavior of light-and dark-reared rats on a visual cliff. *Science* 1957, *126*, 80-81.

Walk, R. D., & Walters, C. P. Importance of texture-density preferences and motion parallax for visual depth discrimination by rats and chicks. *Journal of Comparative and Physiological Psychology*, 1974, *86*, 309-315.

Pulfrich Apparatus. The Pulfrich phenomenon is one of the most effective demonstrations in visual perception and one of the easiest to prepare. The subject views an object swinging back and forth at eye level in a plane perpendicular to the subject's line of vision. Viewing is binocular. However, one of the subject's eyes is covered with a sunglass lens (or some other form of light filter). The swinging object appears to be moving in an elliptical or circular orbit rather than in a straight line. The object will be seen to orbit in a clockwise or counterclockwise direction, dependent upon which eye is covered by the filter.

The simplest way to demonstrate the Pulfrich effect is to attach a string to the ceiling with a weight tied to the free end. The weight should be about the size of a flashlight battery or nine-volt transistor radio battery. (In fact either of those objects will work quite well.) The major problem with this technique is that you must continually restart the pendulum action when the arc begins to decrease. If motion of the object at a constant speed is important for your purposes (e.g., research) then you should consider attaching the pendulum to a motor. You could manufacture a motor and cam system that would supply the appropriate movement (an arc of 70° to 90°); however, that would be very difficult to construct. One solution is to find a motor which is designed for that kind of motion. For example, many motors that are used in window display advertising are often geared to moving an object back and forth. These motors are usually light duty so the shaft of the pendulum and the pendulum bob must be light in weight. A ping pong ball, painted some dark color so that it contrasts well with light colored walls, makes an excellent bob. The shaft can be made of some thin metal rod such as aluminum. It should be light enough not to induce undue strain on the motor, yet heavy enough to remain rigid in the pendulum motion. In demonstrating this phenomenon the background is a critical variable. There should be ample distance (six to ten feet) between the path of the swinging object and any adjacent walls, otherwise the magnitude of the effect will be diminished.

Diamond, A. L. Simultaneous contrast and the Pulfrich phenomenon. *Journal of Optical Society of America*, 1958, *48*, 887-890.

Lit, A. The magnitude of the Pulfrich stereophenomenon as a function *of* binocular differences of intensity at various levels of illumination. *American Journal of Psychology*, 1949, *62*, 159-181.

Rock, M. L., & Fox, B. H. Two aspects of the Pulfrich phenomenon. *American Journal of Psychology*, 1949, *62*, 279-284.

Standing, L. G., Dodwell, P. C., & Lang, D. Dark adaptation and the Pulfrich effect. *Perception and Psychophysics*, 1968, *4*, 118-120.

Distorted Room, Trapezoidal Window. A number of extremely effective demonstrations in perception originated with the Transactional group of psychologists at Princeton University. Undoubtedly the best known of these demonstrations are the distorted room and the trapezoidal window. The distorted room can be constructed in a range of sizes from one small enough to hold in your hands to one large enough to accommodate the presence of human adults. Cardboard can be used for the construction of the smaller models, while wood is required for the larger ones.

Similarly, the trapezoidal window can be made in a number of sizes and from a variety of materials including cardboard, wood, and sheet metal. The window should be mounted on a vertical shaft for rotation purposes. Rotation can be accomplished by motor or by a manual crank and gear system. The motor is usually the more desirable alternative as it provides a more constant rate of rotation.

Complete detailed construction plans for the distorted room and trapezoidal window (as well as eighteen other perceptual demonstrations) can be found in W. H. Ittelson's book, *The Ames demonstrations in perception. A guide to their construction and use* (Princeton University Press, 1952).

Epstein, W. A test of two interpretations of the apparent size effects in a distorted room. *Journal of Experimental Psychology*, 1962, *63*, 124-128.

Gerace, T. A., & Caldwell, W. E. Perceptual distortion as a function of stimulus objects, sex, naivete, and trials, using a portable model of the Ames distorted room. *Genetic Psychology Monographs*, 1971, *84*, 3-33.

Haber, R. N. Limited modification of the trapezoidal illusion with experience. *American Journal of Psychology*, 1965, *78*, 651-655.

Zegers, R. T. The reversal illusion of the Ames trapezoid. *Transactions of the New York Academy of Sciences*, 1964, *26*, 377-400.

Classical Psychophysics. A Müller-Lyer apparatus which consists of a stationary line and an adjustable line is particularly suited to the method of average error (method of adjustment). Plans for this apparatus which is made of wood and cardboard can be found on page 422 of the 1954 edition of *Experimental psychology* by R. S. Woodworth and H. Schlosberg (Holt, Rinehart, and Winston, Publishers).

A weight set for demonstrating the method of constant stimuli can be made from a collection of uniform containers. The small cannisters used for 35mm roll film are particularly well suited for this task. These containers are usually readily available at no charge from film processing shops, and may be filled with sand, small metal pellets, or similar heavy substances.

Engen, T. Psychophysics 1. Discrimination and detection. In Kling, J. W., & Riggs, L. A. (Eds.). *Woodworth and Schlosberg's experimental psychology* (third edition), New York: Holt, Rinehart, and Winston, 1971. (pp. 11-46)

Townsend, J. C. *Introduction to experimental method.* New York: McGraw-Hill, 1953. (pp. 69-83)

Overhead Transparencies and Slides. Numerous demonstrations and experiments in perception require only a projector and visual materials. These are especially desirable for presenting visual illusions, cues for depth perception, shapes, patterns, and words for recognition studies.

Any material which can be produced on paper can be converted to transparencies for overhead projection by means of a Thermo-Fax copier (or similar reproduction process). Slides (35mm) can be made in a similar manner. Material transferred to a transparency can be cut and mounted in cardboard slide mounts (which are commercially available) by sealing them with an ordinary clothes iron.

Attneave, F. Multistability in perception. *Scientific American*, December 1971, *225*, 62-71.

Gregory, R L. Visual illusions. *Scientific American*, November 1968, *219*, 66-76.

Gregory, R. L. *Eye and brain* (second edition). New York: McGraw-Hill, 1973.

Tolansky, S. *Optical illusions.* New York: Pergamon Press, 1964.

Using Student Projects to Acquire Demonstrations for the Classroom and Laboratory

Walter F. Wagor
Indiana University East

As part of the requirements for a Sensation and Perception course, students constructed and demonstrated a sensory or perceptual phenomenon. A special feature of this requirement was the request to donate the project to the Psychology Department for use in other classes. Students willingly complied with the request. Overall evaluation of the project was very positive.

Faculty at small institutions with limited budgets often have a difficult time obtaining adequate materials and equipment for demonstrating psychological phenomena in the classroom and laboratory. Although many resources, such as the journal *Teaching of Psychology*, textbook instructor's manuals, and teaching activities handbooks (e.g., Benjamin, Daniel, & Brewer, 1985; Benjamin & Lowman, 1981; Makosky,

Whittemore, & Rogers, 1988), present numerous ideas for inexpensive demonstrations, the time needed to construct such demonstrations often precludes their use. The demonstrations and classroom activities, therefore, remain locked on the pages of journals and books, existing only as dreams for too many faculty.

As part of the requirements for a Sensation and Perception course taught during the fall 1988 semester, students constructed a demonstration of a sensory or perceptual phenomenon, complete with a typed description of the phenomenon and all necessary instructions for conducting the demonstration. Students then demonstrated their projects during individual classroom presentations. The project was worth 15% of the course grade, and the class presentation was worth 5%. In order to facilitate the selection of appropriate projects, a sample list of project ideas was collected by the instructor from textbooks, instructor's manuals, activity handbooks, and journals, and these materials were placed on reserve in the library. Students were not, however, required to select a project from this list. Details about the project were provided during the first class meeting, and students were encouraged to review the library list and decide on a project as soon as possible. The instructor approved all projects before students were allowed to begin work. This procedure was intended to maximize the likelihood that students understood the project they had selected, to ensure that projects were of sufficient merit to meet the course requirements, and to avoid duplication of projects. Students could work alone or with a partner, but all chose to work individually. No deadlines, other than the semester's end, were specified. Students were encouraged, however, to complete projects close to the time in the semester that the class would be studying the particular phenomenon they were demonstrating.

In addition to these requirements, one new feature was added to this project. Most instructors have probably seen excellent projects taken home by students, only to be stuck in a closet or perhaps even discarded. In response to this problem, students were asked to donate their materials to the Psychology Department for use in future classes. Students were told that this was an attempt to have their hard work receive more permanent recognition and use than is usual. They were also told that their donations were important so that the benefit derived from each project would not be limited to those students in the current class, but would also be available to future students. All students willingly donated their work. Future users of each demonstration will be provided with a description of the phenomenon, instructions for using it, and the student donor's name accompanying the demonstration. The Psychology Department offered to reimburse students for the cost of materials, but no student requested reimbursement. There are, therefore, no data available about the cost of the projects.

Completed projects included a videotape of a student filmed in an otherwise darkened environment wearing strings of white Christmas lights to demonstrate biological movement (Johansson, 1975); materials for demonstrating illusions of movement with an overhead projector (Cowan, 1974); a set of special colored slides for demonstrating additive and subtractive color mixing with slide projectors (Mershon, 1980); a light box for demonstrating a variety of complex color phenomena (Beins, 1983); a collection of custom-drawn overhead transparencies of optical illusions, sensory organs, and brain structures selected by the instructor; and a plywood scale model of an Ames distorted room.

At the end of the semester, students answered a brief, anonymous questionnaire about the project. Overall evaluation of the project showed enthusiastic student reaction. All students reported that they liked the project concept and that it should be retained as a course requirement. Students were asked what they liked most about the project, and some representative comments included: "doing the project helped me to understand the aspect of perception [we were studying] by experiencing the phenomenon," "the project got us involved in our perceptions," and "it provided insight into how we perceive things and why." Students also agreed that the projects were of high quality. One wrote that "all of the projects ranked high in the categories of construction, complexity, practicality and usefulness." Another wrote, "On a scale from 1 to 10 an 8." Several students commented on the value of the projects, writing that the project "made me feel that our class was involved in helping future classes" and that they "were contributing to those who will come after us." Students were also asked to provide constructive criticism about the project, describing what they did not like and providing suggestions for improvement. Most students wanted deadlines for both selecting and presenting the project. One student thought that the "projects should be completed when their area of perception is being covered in class." Another wanted "a little more clear-cut direction." Finally, several students commented on their apprehension about doing the project, writing "I'm not really creative or handy" and "I think that I bit off more than I could chew with the project that I chose."

Evaluation by the instructor was also very positive, supporting the decision to retain the project when this course is offered again. Assignment of similar projects may be appropriate for other courses. However, student and instructor evaluations point to several changes. First, students need more direction in selecting their projects. Although such direction can probably be provided on an individual basis outside of class, a small amount of class time at the beginning of the semester would help. Second, more specific deadlines for project completion and presentation should be provided. I had hoped that students would have demonstrated their projects when that particular phenomenon was being covered in the course, but they usually failed to do so. Providing specific deadlines should overcome this problem. Third, working in pairs should be required or more strongly encouraged so that even better and more complex projects can be selected and completed. Although all students completed their projects, some thought that working with a partner would have been beneficial. For example, one student commented, "There were so many [projects] that I would like to have done, but didn't, because I was unsure of my ability to do them. A joint effort would have been nice under these circumstances." Fourth, to ensure quality control, more help and guidance from the instructor should be provided. After all, one purpose is to have a high-quality demonstration that will be used repeatedly. Poor projects fail to serve this important function.

References

Beins, B. (1983) . The light box: A simple way of generating complex color demonstrations. *Teaching of Psychology, 10,* 113-114.

Benjamin, L. T., Jr., Daniel, R. S., & Brewer, C. L. (Eds.). (1985). *Handbook for teaching introductory psychology.* Hillsdale, NJ: Lawrence Erlbaum Associates, Inc.

Benjamin, L. T., Jr., & Lowman, K. D. (Eds.). (1981). *Activities handbook for the teaching of psychology.* Washington, DC: American Psychological Association.

Cowan, T. M . (1974) . Creating illusions of movement by an overhead projector. *Teaching of Psychology, 1,* 80-82.

Johansson, G. (1975). Visual motion perception. *Scientific American, 232,* 76-88.

Makosky, V. P., Whittemore, L. G., & Rogers, A. M. (Eds.). (1988). *Activities handbook for the teaching of psychology* (Vol. 2). Washington, DC: American Psychological Association.

Mershon, D. H. (1980). Additive (and subtractive) color mixtures with a single slide projector. *Teaching of Psychology, 7,* 183-184.

Note

I thank Charles L. Brewer, David E. Johnson, and three anonymous reviewers for their comments on an earlier draft of this article.

2. TEACHING ABOUT ILLUSIONS

Constructing a Moving Cube Illusion

J. R. Corey
C. W. Post College

The construction of a moving cube illusion is described. Observers report a compelling illusion of movement of this stationary, three-dimensional object when it is viewed under proper conditions.

Under certain conditions, stationary, three-dimensional objects appear to move when an observer moves past them. Gregory (1970) reported, "When the inside of a mask appears as a normal face, it will swing to follow a moving observer . . ." (p. 128), and the same effect is seen when a three dimensional wire cube appears to be reversed. (The hollow mask and moving cube illusion both appear at the exhibit "Seeing the Light" at the IBM Exploratorium in San Francisco and the New York Hall of Science in Flushing Meadows, NY.) This phenomenon depends on an apparent reversal of distance cues in a three-dimensional object, which gives rise to a paradoxical reversal in motion parallax cues. Normally, points closer to an observer appear to move more than points farther away when an observer moves. Reversing this relationship produces a robust illusion of movement

In the hollow mask described by Gregory, the inversion of depth cues is produced by lighting from below. This has the effect of reversing normal light and shadow cues for depth, an effect first reported by Brewster (1844). In the wire cube, this reversal occurs spontaneously, just as it does in the two-dimensional Necker cube. This article describes an easily constructed three-dimensional figure, which appears to be a solid cube but is, in fact, a hollow figure. Perspective cues are distorted to enhance the illusion, and spotlighting from below further fosters the assumption that more distant features are closer (Ramachandran, 1988).

A display may be constructed for a classroom demonstration or permanent exhibit from the pattern in Figure 1. This pattern is cut out of heavy posterboard or matteboard. The dotted lines A-D and A-E are scored on the back of the pattern, and points B and C are folded forward. The edges A-C and A-B are glued together, resulting in a three-sided, three-dimensional figure that could be the inside corner of an empty cube.

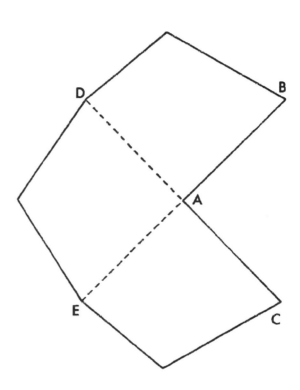

Figure 1. A pattern for producing a moving cube illusion.

The figure is mounted inside a display cabinet that conceals the inverted light source, a low (30 or so) wattage spotlight bulb. Low wattages are preferable because of safety considerations. The cabinet also serves to eliminate overhead illumination, which can destroy the illusion. The back of the cabinet is covered with black photographic drop cloth or paper, and careful adjustment of the spotlight eliminates distracting or counterproductive shadows. Mounting details, presented at the bottom of Figure 2, show a 5 cm finishing nail driven at a 45° angle into the back of the cabinet. A 2.6 cm section of drinking straw glued to the top of the inverted cube serves to house the nail. All dimensions are somewhat adjustable.

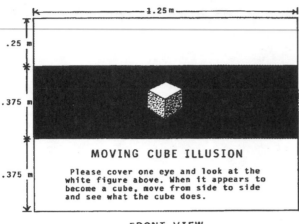

MOVING CUBE ILLUSION

Please cover one eye and look at the
white figure above. When it appears to
become a cube, move from side to side
and see what the cube does.

FRONT VIEW

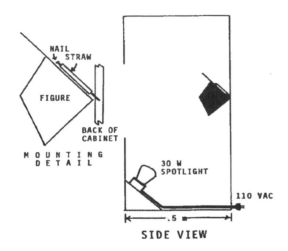

NAIL
STRAW

FIGURE

BACK OF
CABINET

MOUNTING
DETAIL

30 W
SPOTLIGHT

110 VAC

SIDE VIEW

Figure 2. Various views of a cabinet for displaying a moving cube illusion.

Instructions on the front of the cabinet read, "Please cover one eye and look at the white figure above. When it appears to be a cube, move from side to side and see what the cube does." The instructions for monocular viewing are designed to eliminate binocular disparity cues, which could reveal the cube's true shape.

Experimentations with other hollow surfaces, such as hemispheres, can produce other moving shapes that resemble rotating moons or eyes. These hemispherical constructs must be mounted flush on a flat forward surface. The moving cube illusion is simpler to construct and is more compelling.

This display has been installed near our departmental offices for more than 1 year and has provoked much student interest. Student inquiries provide the opportunity to explain the monocular cues for depth and the apparent movement produced by the inverted geometry of the cube. Some experienced observers report the illusion with binocular viewing. Few observers report difficulty in experiencing movement: One difficulty arose when an observer with poor vision in one eye covered up his good eye when viewing the display.

References

Brewster, D. (1844). On the conversion of relief by inverted vision. *Transactions of the Royal Society of Edinburg, 15*, 657-662.

Gregory, R. L. (1910). *The intelligent eye.* New York: McGraw-Hill.

Ramachandran, V. S. (1988). Perception of shape from shading. *Nature, 331*, 163-166.

Creating Illusions of Movement by an Overhead Projector

Thaddeus M. Cowan
Kansas State University

An overhead projector can be used to demonstrate illusions of movement by employing a principle incorporated by Michotte (1946, 1958) in his classical experiments on perceptual causality. Michotte made use of the fact that when a line is moved across a second stationary line with which it intersects, then the point of intersection will also move in a well defined direction and a determinable speed.[1] In Michotte's case the moving line was a painted line and the stationary line was a slit. In the descriptions presented here, both the moving line and the stationary line are slits or apertures. Specifically, if two opaque sheets containing different slit patterns are placed on an overhead projector, various movements of points of light are produced when one sheet is moved across the other.

There are a number of positive things that can be said about this procedure. For one, the equipment is simple and not costly. The items needed are an overhead projector, two pieces of construction paper, and a single edged razor blade. Furthermore, precision of construction need not be a concern, and the slit patterns can be made quickly so that spontaneous experimentation in the classroom is possible. Moreover, since these demonstrations appear in large scale on a projection screen, they can be shown to large audiences and are clearly visible to everyone.

What follows are the descriptions of eight visual effects of interest in a discussion of perception. Some illusions of movement are too complex to produce in a simple way. Yet with prior preparation even these can be shown by an overhead projector. The final description in this report describes one of these preparations.

Simple Constructions

Phi Phenomenon. Figure 1a shows how a simple phi phenomenon can be demonstrated. The stationary sheet has two holes placed at a reasonable distance apart. The sliding sheet has a slit cut as shown. The sliding sheet should have a stop placed appropriately on each slide to avoid over-shooting. Variations in the stimulus and inter-stimulus durations can be induced by changing the widths of the slit and the holes. Thus, Korte's laws can easily be demonstrated .

In Figure 1b, the moving slits are crossed, and the crossed slits are passed over a row of evenly spaced holes on the stationary sheet. If the movement is slow, the two end dots of light seem to move to the center then bounce apart. If the speed of the motion is increased the two end lights move to the center, then appear to pass through one another.

Michotte's Demonstrations. The patterns for Michotte's perceptual causality are shown in Figure 1c. The perceptual effect is one of A hitting B causing B to continue along A's path while A remains at B's initial location.

Figures 1d and 1e give the slot patterns for Michotte's "transporting" and "tunneling" effects. In the case of the former, A appears to meet B then carry it to the end of the path. With the latter, the spot of light disappears at B. then reappears at C giving the impression that it entered and emerged from a tunnel.

The Fujii and Johannson illusions. Fujii (1943) found that when a dot moves with constant velocity along a square path, then, depending on the speed, the dot appears to follow either a four-cusped hypocycloid path or a path which overshoots at the corners then quickly returns to the original line. A good de-

scription of these effects can be found in Festinger and Montague (1974).

Only half of the Fujii illusion can be shown in a simple way. A diagonal line passed over an L-shaped slit in the manner indicated in Figure 1f will produce an illusory distortion of the second line (the vertical line in Figure 1f) which the diagonal intersects.

Johannson's illusion (Johannson,1950; Kolers,1964) is created by orienting the moving diagonal slit in the opposite direction so that the point of first contact is either at the apex of the L-slit or the free ends of the vertical and horizontal lines (Figure 1g). A compound motion is established where the two dots move diagonally toward each other, while at the same time this pair of diagonally moving dots slides along the other diagonal. It should be noted that not everyone sees this compound motion (Kolers, 1964).

Cycloid Illusion. Any point on the rim of a wheel describes a cycloid curve as the wheel moves across a surface, and a light on the rim will be seen to trace a cycloid path. However, if a second light is placed at the hub, the rim light appears to move in a circular path around the hub and its cycloid characteristics are lost.[2]

This illusion is complex and cannot be produced in a simple way. However, a related effect can be created easily as shown in Figure 1h. A vertical slit is passed over a series of cycloid curves (here semicircles will do) which are bisected by a straight horizontal line. The effect one sees is an up and down motion of one point of light (on the rim line) passing through a second point of light moving horizontally along the hub line. The rim light in the absence of the hub light is seen to follow a cycloid (or semicircular) path. This effect has not been previously described in the literature, and it is similar to the compound motion of Johannson's illusion. Unlike the Johannson illusion, however, the compound motion produced in this way is readily seen.

Complex Constructions

A true cycloid illusion requires some preparation and polaroid filters are needed to produce it. In the preparation of this illusion these steps should be followed.

1. Construct a cycloid of at least two cycles See Riggs (1910) for a simple way of constructing this curve.

2. Bisect the cycloid horizontally with a hub line. Mark this line off in equal segments. Mark points on the cycloid by using each segment mark as a center and the radius of the generating circle (wheel) as a radius. Connect each cycloid point and its hub line segment mark with a straight line (see Figure 2a).

3. Place a piece of tracing paper over the figure so that the cycloid shows through at the bottom. Trace the first two points to the left which are connected by a

line. Move the tracing paper down some predetermined (arbitrary) distance, and mark the second two points connected by a line. Keep moving the paper

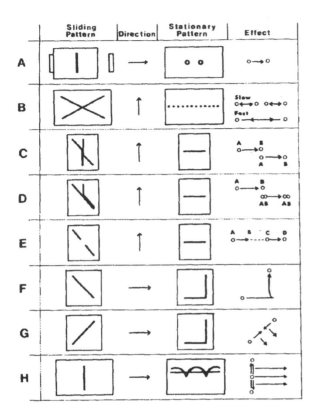

Figure 1. The two patterns, the direction of movement and the perceptual effects for the following phenomena: (a) Simple phi phenomenon (b) Complex phi phenomenon (c) Michotte's perceptual causality (d) Michotte's "transporting" effect (e) Michotte's "tunneling" effect (f) Fujii's illusion (partial) (g) Johannson's illusion (h) Modified cycloid illusion.

downward and perpendicularly across the cycloid at a constant distance each time and mark successive pairs of points until the last pair of points on the right has been traced (see Figure 2b). The two paths described by the points on the tracing paper should resemble the cycloid curve in Figure 2a; they will also appear slanted .

4. The two patterns shown in Figure 2b (the original and traced paths) are the figures that will be placed on the overhead projector. The projection figures can be made by placing thin strips of tape on two transparencies in the same pattern as the configuration of lines on the two sheets in Figure 2b. The transparencies are then spray-painted and the tape removed.

5. As one pattern is passed downward and perpendicularly across the other, four dots will appear. These are the hub line and cycloid line of the top pattern intersecting the hub and cycloid lines of the bottom pattern. It is necessary that only the intersection of the

two cycloid lines and the intersection of the two hub lines allow the passage of light. This is most easily accomplished by cross-polarization as shown in Figure 2c. Thin strips cut from polarized plastic sheets can be used here.

One figure is passed across the other with the same direction of movement used during the drawing of the patterns (see Figure 2b). The rim light is seen to describe a clear circular path around the hub light. If a polaroid strip of the right orientation is placed across either hub line to eliminate the hub light, the cycloid path described by the rim light can be observed. The effects are very realistic and startling in spite of the fact that the spots of light are rhomboid in shape. Interesting effects can be created by shifting the top sheet to the left or right before passing it across the bottom sheet; the rim light appears to roll like an oval rather than a circle.

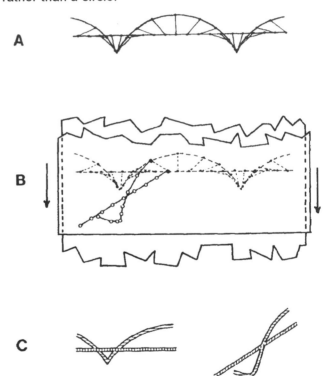

Figure 2. (a) Cycloid curve with points along the curve connected to the center of their generating circles. (b) The construction of the sliding pattern for the cycloid illusion. The broken line pattern is on the bottom sheet and shows through the tracing paper (the top sheet). The patterns formed by tracing appear in large open circles connected by solid lines. (c) Polarization of the slots in the sliding and stationary patterns for the cycloid illusion.

The more complicated constructions suffer from a loss of simplicity and ease with which the simpler effects can be made. Even with their complexities, however, they are far less bulky and less expensive than electronic equipment, and the advantage that these illusions can be shown to a large audience still remains.

Reference

Festinger L., & Montague, A. E. Inferences about the efferent system based on a perceptual illusion produced by eye movements. *Psychological Review*, 1974, *81*, 44-58.

Fujii, E. Forming a figure by movement of a luminous point. *Japanese Journal of Psychology*, 1943, *18*, 196-232.

Johannson, G. *Configurations in event perception*, Uppsala, Sweden: Almquist and Wicksell, 1950.

Kolers, P. The illusion of movement. *Scientific American*, October 1964, *211*, 98-108.

Michotte, A. *La perception de la causality*. Louvain Belgium: Editions "Erasme," Publications Universitaires De Louvain, 1946.

Michotte, A. Causality and Activity. In Beardsley and Wertheimer (Eds.) *Readings in perception*. Princeton: D. Van Nostrand Company, Inc., 1958.

Riggs, N. C. *Analytic geometry*, New York: Macmillan, 1910.

Von Fieandt, K. *The world of perception*. Homewood, Illinois: Homewood Press, 1966.

Notes

1. The fact that this is a degenerate case of a moire pattern should not go unnoted
2 It is said that Galileo was motivated to investigate the properties of the cycloid curve as a result of observing the paradoxes of this illusion (von Fieandt, 1966).

The Janus Illusion

Dale Klopfer
Michael E. Doherty
Bowling Green State University

A perceptual illusion, especially suitable for introductory psychology demonstrations, is described. The essence of the illusion is that an ordinary dime-store plastic mask, when facing 180° away from an observer, will nonetheless appear to face that observer. Moreover, as one moves left and right in the frontal plane, thereby changing the angle from which the mask is viewed, the mask generally appears to follow the moving observer. When the observer is stationary but the mask is rotated slowly, it will appear to oscillate. In addition to being fascinating in its own right, the illusion can be used to illustrate several important points, including that perception is still, as enunciated in the 19th century by Helmholtz, usefully conceptualized as hypothesis testing.

The Roman god Janus, having two faces, could look both forward and backward at the same time; whether one stood in front of or behind Janus, one was face-to-face with the god. In the Janus illusion, a mask appears to face the observer not only when it does, but also when it is placed at a 180° angle. The illusion was described by Gregory (1970, 1980), Gogel (1990), and Ramachandran (1988) and was recently investigated by Klopfer (1991). The Janus illusion is less well known than the Müller-Lyer, Ponzo, and moon illusions that commonly appear in introductory textbooks, but it nicely complements the more familiar static illusions. It is inexpensive to construct and provides a compelling demonstration.

Equipment

A reasonably rigid, plastic mask of a face, commonly sold in toy stores or in costume and novelty shops, is adequate. We have used opaque, smooth, white masks and translucent masks of smiling male and female faces, complete with laugh lines and forehead wrinkles. Guidelines for buying and preparing masks include:

1. Make sure that the mask is sufficiently rigid to withstand slow rotation without losing its shape. Grasp the chin of the mask between your thumb and forefinger and rotate the mask to the right and left. If the

mask wiggles or changes shape, then look for a sturdier one.

2. Make certain that the textures of the inner and outer surfaces of the mask are the same. This is not likely to be a problem with molded plastic masks; however, with some material, the inside may be smoother than the outside. The demonstrations may be less compelling if students can identify the inner and outer surfaces of the mask on the basis of surface differences.

3. If the mask is not already opaque, make sure that both surfaces of the mask can be painted; we spray painted ours a flat gray. If you show the illusion in a large room, a flat gray will make the features of the mask more readily discriminable from the back when the mask is of intermediate reflectance. With a black mask, features would be lost to the observer due to absorption of light; with a white mask, features would be lost due to excessive reflection.

4. Trim the edges of the mask, if necessary, to make the effects demonstrable at a wide variety of viewing angles. Consider the arc of the face from earhole to earhole to be 180°. Trim the mask so that it covers roughly 120° of arc. We trimmed the mask so that the edges were just behind the cheekbones of the mask, but not all masks will have cheekbones.

How you mount the mask will depend on the viewing situation. When the mask is static, a stand fashioned from a 1.25-cm diameter wooden dowel mounted perpendicular to a flat wooden base will suffice. The stand's height will depend on the classroom size. Make the stand sturdy enough to support the mask but small enough to carry. The mask can be attached to the dowel with a thumbtack or screw through the base of the chin. Be sure that the line of sight of the mounted mask is parallel to the ground plane, not tilted up or down.

For a rotating mask, mount the mask on the spindle of a LaFayette Model 14015 Illusionator, bolting it through a hole drilled in the base of the chin. Or you can use any variable speed motor with a vertical shaft on which to mount the mask, such as those used to demonstrate Ames's trapezoidal window illusion. You can also gear down an unused record player, so that it will spin at 2 or 3 rotations per minute (rpm).

In one of the viewing conditions described later, perceptions of the rotating mask are compared to those of an unfamiliar object.

One unfamiliar object could be the molded plastic packaging attached to cardboard that is often used for toys and that approximates the shape of one half of the enclosed toy. Make sure the molded plastic is sufficiently rigid to withstand rotation without undue deformation and it has a flat part that can be attached to the spindle of the variable speed motor. (See Figure 1 of Klopfer, 1991, for examples of unfamiliar objects.) As with the mask, we spray painted our unfamiliar objects gray.

Condition

Static Mask-Static Viewers

Instructors of fairly large introductory courses would most likely use this situation. Place the mask in the front of the room, as close to the center as possible, facing the students (the 0° position). Light the room normally, but provide more light coming from the back of the room. In a large (225-seat) classroom, turning off the overhead row of lights at the front of the room yielded quite satisfactory results. If you cannot create differential lighting or if your classroom is extremely deep, try dimming the room lights and focusing the light from a slide projector on the mask.

Have students close one eye and raise their hands if they think that the mask is looking in their direction. Then shield the mask from student view, move it 45° to the right, and repeat the request. Next shield the mask, move it 45° to the left of 0°, and ask for hands. Repeat with students using both eyes; the results should be the same as with one eye. The unremarkable result should be that students sitting in the center section of the class should raise their hands when the mask is set to face 0°, followed by those sitting on both sides.

Again shield the mask and set it at 180° (i.e., facing directly away from the students sitting in the center). Now nearly everyone should think that the mask is looking in their direction, regardless of where they are sitting. (Students at the extreme sides in the front row or two might not see the mask looking at them.)

Static Mask-Moving Viewers

This situation is best used in a standard classroom, but it could be adapted for a large lecture hall. Place the mask in the front of the room in the 0° orientation. Have students walk back and forth along the back of the classroom (i.e., in the frontal plane of the mask) and have them report the direction in which the mask faces as they walk. They should report that the mask maintains a constant orientation, facing toward the back of the room. Shield the mask, set it at 180°, and again have students walk back and forth in the frontal plane of the mask. They should report that the face follows them as they traverse the room, turning as they move from one side to the other. Some students may report that the mask appears to turn through a greater arc than that described by their path. For example, a student standing to the left of the mask may report that the mask appears to be looking over his or her left shoulder.

Rotating Mask-Static Viewers

In this situation, which is suitable for both standard classrooms and large lecture halls, the mask is rotated about its vertical axis. The procedures described later will enable students to compare perceptions of an unfamiliar rotating object with the perception of a rotating mask, but simply rotating the mask alone without a comparison object still provides a demonstration as stunning in its own way as Ames's trapezoidal window illusion.

Mount the unfamiliar object on the motor, and set it with the convex side facing the students. Tell the students that you will turn on a motor that will rotate the object slowly in one direction, and ask them to raise their hands if they see the object appear to change its direction of rotation. Rotate the object at 2 or 3 rpm for at least 1 min. A few students may see the unfamiliar object change direction, but the majority will see it rotate continuously in the same direction—the one in which it is in fact rotating. Then mount the mask on the spindle, so that the convex side faces the students (the 0° orientation). After a few complete rotations of the mask, nearly all students will see the mask oscillating twice during each complete physical rotation, changing its direction of rotation to maintain an apparent orientation facing the students. For the few who continue to see complete rotations even after 3 or 4 rotations, reduce the rotation rate to 1 or 2 rpm.

Videotape of a Rotating Mask

If a variable speed motor is not readily available but a VHS videocassette recorder and television or projection screen are, then the rotating mask can be shown from a videotape of the rotating objects used in Klopfer (1991). (For a copy of the videotape, send a blank ½-in. VHS tape to either author.) The experiences associated with the static situations can be reproduced via videotape, but not those associated with moving viewers or binocular vision.

Discussion

The phenomena described earlier allow students to ponder some issues in perception and to be exposed to some aspects of experimental methodology.

Discussion for Introductory Psychology

These demonstrations can be used, paradoxically, to argue that perception is normally highly veridical. Why else would illusions be so striking? This argument can be presented in a way to dispel the common notion that knowledge about the world is completely subjective. Although students are tricked in this unusual situation, they can see that their experience of something out of the ordinary is just that—out of the ordinary.

An important point to make is that the static, monocular retinal image is fundamentally ambiguous. Moreover, although viewing with two eyes often helps to disambiguate percepts, the retinal image cannot be completely disambiguated by binocular information; the Janus illusion would not be present with both eyes open. The retinal image cannot be completely disambiguated by motion information; mask rotation and observer motion would destroy the illusion.

Another important point is that past experience influences perception. We have millions of experiences with retinal images in which two eyes, a nose, and a mouth turn out to be a face. We have many fewer experiences with such objects turning out to be the inside of a mask. Consequently, we are likely to interpret the inside of a mask as a face. With an unfamiliar object, neither the inside nor the outside of the object is more familiar; hence, we tend to see the object in its true orientation.

The Janus illusion illustrates a general principle discussed in many introductory textbooks: Perception is not a simple, passive copying of external reality; rather, it is an active, constructive process that resembles hypothesis testing.

Discussion for Sensation and Perception

The static retinal image is inherently ambiguous; yet, when we look at the world, we experience a single arrangement of objects and surfaces; despite ambiguity in stimulation, our perceptions are generally unambiguous. Two general approaches offer explanations for the uniqueness of our experience. The first asserts that retinal information is insufficient to explain perception, so cognitive processes must aid the interpretation of sensory input. That is, our perceptual experience is based in part on what we think may have created our retinal image. This *constructivist* view, stated clearly by John Stuart Mill and by Hermann von Helmholtz over 100 years ago, has modern adherents (e.g., Gregory, 1980; Hochberg, 1986; Rock, 1983). It does not hold that we consciously weigh alternative interpretations of the retinal image, but that we make rapid unconscious inferences about reality.

The second approach holds that, under normal viewing conditions, stimulus information available to the viewer accounts fully for veridical perceptual experience (Gibson, 1966, 1979). This *ecological* approach holds that perception is not mediated by inferences, unconscious or otherwise, and that illusions result from artificial viewing conditions of the laboratory. In normal viewing, people are free to move about and look at objects with two eyes, thereby picking up a full complement of information from motion and binocular vision.

The Janus illusion allows the merits of both approaches to be explored. For the static mask, it is important for students to realize that no single experiment or set of experiments will adjudicate between the two general approaches, because aspects of both have merit. But the phenomena described earlier allow both approaches to be explored.

In the static mask–static viewer situation, when all students look at the 0° mask both monocularly and binocularly, only those sitting in the center of the room should indicate that the mask is facing them. The ecological view might claim that information about where the mask is facing is provided by shading, by texture, and, for those who are close enough, by accommodation. The same claim can be made when the mask is facing the left and right sides of the classroom. The constructivist view is that perceivers unconsciously infer that the object producing the retinal image is a mask facing the class. A similar argument applies when the mask faces the left and right sides of the room.

When the mask faces away from students, regardless of where they are sitting, they see the mask facing themselves. According to the ecological view, this should not happen, because information about where the mask is facing has been provided. The constructivist view can explain the illusion: The retinal image could have been created by a mask facing away, which looks like an inside-out face, or by a normal face looking at the perceiver. Because we are more likely to encounter normal faces than inside-out ones, we infer that the retinal image was created by a normal face, and that is what we see. The fact that the illusion persists when viewers use two eyes suggests that binocular depth information can be overpowered by our unconscious inferences.

In the static mask–moving viewer situation, with the mask at 0°, the mask is correctly seen to face the students. Here, motion parallax, which specifies depth relations among the parts of the mask, provides additional information for veridical perception. With the mask at 180°, however, the mask appears to face the viewer and to follow the viewer's movements. The inference that the mask faces the viewer seems to overpower the information specifying where the mask is actually facing, even to the point where a stationary object is seen as moving. The ecological view cannot readily account for this.

The rotating mask situations, both live and videotaped, yield a full complement of motion information specifying the mask's true orientation. If the object-based motion information allowed the viewer to see the mask in its true orientation, the mask should appear to rotate. Instead, it appears to oscillate, owing to the viewers' differential familiarity with normal and inside-out faces. With an unfamiliar object, differential familiarity does not apply, and the object is accurately seen as rotating.

We believe that the data favor a constructivist view of the nature of perception. Two interesting intellectual challenges are for students to produce this explanation themselves and to attack the constructivist explanation and reinterpret the data from an ecological perspective.

The Janus illusion demonstrations illustrate the intricacies of perception and show that perception is a proper field of investigation. Perhaps because perceptual experience is usually veridical, arising instantaneously and effortlessly, students naively believe there is nothing to study. They respond to the question "How do we see?" with an incredulous "We open our eyes and look, of course." As is true in many disciplines, teaching about perception requires disabusing students of their naive beliefs. Because visual illusions lack veridicality, students must confront their beliefs. Moreover, students can experience and explore compelling, theoretically relevant perceptual phenomena.

References

Gibson, J. J. (1966). *The senses considered as perceptual systems.* Boston: Houghton-Mifflin.

Gibson, J. J. (1979). *The ecological approach to visual perception.* Boston: Houghton-Mifflin.

Gogel, W. C. (1990). A theory of phenomenal geometry and its applications. *Perception and Psychophysics, 48*, 105-123.

Gregory, R. L. (1970). *The intelligent eye.* New York: McGraw-Hill.

Gregory, R. L. (1980). Perceptions as hypotheses. *Philosophical Transactions of the Royal Society of London, B 290*, 181-197.

Hochberg, J. (1986). Visual perception. In R. C. Atkinson, R. J. Hermstein, G. Lindsey, & R. D. Luce (Eds.), *Stevens' handbook of experimental psychology* (Vol. 1, pp. 195-276). New York: Wiley.

Klopfer, D. (1991). Apparent reversals of a rotating mask: A new demonstration of cognition in perception. *Perception and Psychophysics, 49*, 522-530.

Ramachandran, V. S. (1988). Perceiving shape from shading. *Scientific American, 259*(2), 76-83.

Rock, I. (1983). *The logic of perception.* Cambridge, MA: MIT Press.

A Teaching Demonstration Involving Perceived Lunar Size

Mark A. Kunkel
Texas Tech University

Lunar research in psychology is briefly reviewed. A teaching demonstration is described in which students are asked to mentally select an object that covers up the moon when held at arm's length. Possible applications are suggested of this demonstration to the general psychology topics of research methods, statistics, perception, and mental illness. Illustrative normative data for the demonstration are provided.

The moon has been the object of considerable research in psychology. Previous investigations have tended to cluster along two pathways: (a) sensory-perceptual, in which the moon illusion (see Plug, 1981) has figured prominently, and (b) lunar-behavior relations deriving from the historical concept of lunacy (cf. Rotton & Kelly, 1985). Research in the former domain has demonstrated the perceptual tendency to overestimate the size of the moon and to assume that lunar size varies with its height in the night sky. Many explanations have been advanced for these perceptual errors, including adaptation (Gilinsky, 1980), the nature of received external reality (Ariotti, 1973; Ross & George, 1976), loom–zoom phenomena (Hershenson, 1982), multimechanism (Coren & Aks, 1990; McCready, 1986), specific distance (Baird & Wagner, 1982), terrestrial passage (Reed, 1984), vestibular influences (Carter, 1977), visual accommodation and oculomotor adjustment (Iavecchia, Iavecchia, & Roscoe, 1983), visual angle (Baird, Wagner, & Fulk, 1990), and visual contrast (Enright, 1989; Smith, Smith, Geist, & Zimmerman, 1978; Tsai, 1987). Investigations of the relation between the moon and behavior have mostly sprung from folklore hypotheses of lunar influence on accidents and disasters (Kelly, Saklofske, & Culver, 1990), crime and other antisocial events (Frey, Rotten, & Barry, 1979; Little, Bowers, & Little, 1987; Tasso & Miller, 1976), substance use (Sharfman, 1980), suicide (Garth & Lester, 1978), and mental illness (Blackman & Catalina, 1973; Campbell & Beets, 1978; Stone, 1976; Templer & Veleber, 1980; Weiskott & Tipton, 1975).

The relative abundance of moon-related research and students' firsthand experience with these phenomena lend themselves well to a teaching demonstration involving estimates of perceived lunar size. The simple yet psychometrically sound demonstration described herein takes approximately 20 min and is easily understood by students. The demonstration may be applied, depending on its placement within the course and instructor preference, to various topics in general psychology. Presented early in the course, the primary application of the demonstration is to philosophy of science, research methods, schools of psychology, and basic statistics, in which students may better appreciate the underlying assumptions of research and the way results are interpreted and explained. The demonstration can also be integrated into later discussions of sensation, perception, and mental illness.

Student preparation for the demonstration varies with its placement in the course. Presented early as part of a discussion of science in psychology or research methods, the demonstration will be enhanced by student familiarity with schools in psychology and basic statistical concepts of reliability and validity. Later application to perception could benefit from student appreciation for concepts, such as proximal and distal stimuli, developmental influences on perception, and perceptual error. The demonstration also has been used to introduce various models of mental illness and the way in which the models influence scale construction, diagnostic terminology, and interpretation of findings.

Students receive a form (see Appendix) on which they are asked to imagine themselves outside on a clear evening with a bright full moon. They are then directed to mentally select from a group of items one that will occlude or cover up the full moon when held in the outstretched hand. The range of objects was chosen based on previous investigations of estimated lunar size (Coren & Aks, 1990).

Students' responses are compiled through asking for raised hands for each item choice. Alternatively, student responses may be written on small slips of paper and passed forward. A frequency histogram is constructed of students' estimates. Should the demonstration be used early in the course, the status of the demonstration as a scientific experiment may be evaluated within the context of philosophy of science and scientific methods. The concepts of experimental control, reliability, and validity can also be evaluated as they relate to students' participation in the demonstration. The demonstration can be used in conjunction with a history and systems overview to illustrate a structural approach to research in psychology. Analytical introspection and subject adequacy can also be demonstrated. Measures of dispersion (e.g., range) and central tendency (e.g., mean, median, and mode) can be computed and compared to existing norms (see Table 1) in a treatment of introductory statistics. The demonstration can also be used in a discussion of sensation and perception. The full moon occupies one degree (or 1/180th) of the night sky, irrespective of its altitude or the time of year, and can be occluded by a pea held at arm's length. As can be seen in Table 1, students tend to overestimate the size of objects required to occlude the moon; modal responses are between a quarter and a softball. The concepts of proximal versus distal stimuli, retinal size, contrast effects, and developmental influences of experience on perception can be brought to bear in interpreting the findings. Some of the references cited earlier are helpful in preparing such discussions, and students can be led to appreciate the fallacy of the "single right answer" in much of psychological inquiry. Another advantage is that students can easily verify their findings during the next full moon.

Table 1. Introductory Psychology Students' Estimations of Object Size Required to Occlude Full Moon When Held at Arm's Length

Object	Frequency	%
BB	2	.5
Pea	12	3.0
Dime	30	7.6
Penny	16	4.1
Nickel	30	7.6
Quarter	70	17.8
Golf ball	34	8.6
Baseball	26	6.6
Softball	56	14.2
Small salad plate	34	8.6
Large dinner plate	30	7.6
Frisbee	28	7.1
Basketball	12	3.0
Beach ball	14	3.6

Note. M estimation = 7.76, SD = 3.11. N = 394.

Finally, the demonstration can also contribute to a discussion of abnormal psychology, psychological disorders, or mental illness. Following an overview of the historical concept of lunacy and present folklore hypotheses about the influences of the full moon on human behavior, the instructor could present the demonstration as a test of lunacy or susceptibility to lunar influence. If the instructor argues, for example, that those who overestimate the moon's size are thought to be more subject to its influence, students will be led to appreciate how theories of abnormal psychology are grounded in prior assumptions. The notion of lunacy leads naturally to a discussion of a precedent for supernatural influences on behavior. If so inclined, the instructor can follow the thread of moon-behavior research into other investigations in which no significant effect has been found (Rotten & Kelly, 1985), perhaps also mentioning other areas (e.g., parapsychological phenomena) in which psychological perspectives differ from popular wisdom. In addition to being interesting for students, the demonstration has also been found to enhance their receptivity to other psychological findings that call into question their own experience.

References

Ariotti, P. (1973). Benedetto Castelli and George Berkeley as anticipations of recent findings on the moon illusion. *Journal of the History of the Behavioral Sciences, 9,* 328-332.

Baird, J. C., & Wagner, M. (1982). The moon illusion: I. How high is the sky? *Journal of Experimental Psychology: General, 111,* 296-303.

Baird, J. C., Wagner, M., & Fulk, K. (1990). A simple but powerful theory of the moon illusion. *Journal of Experimental Psychology: Human Perception and Performance, 16,* 675-677.

Blackman, S., & Catalina, D. (1973). The moon and the emergency room. *Perceptual and Motor Skills, 37,* 624-626.

Campbell, D. E., & Beets, J. L. (1978). Lunacy and the moon. *Psychological Bulletin, 85,* 1123-1129.

Carter, D. S. (1977); The moon illusion: A test of the vestibular hypothesis under monocular viewing conditions. *Perceptual and Motor Skills, 45,* 1127-1130.

Coren, S., & Aks, D. J. (1990). Moon illusion in pictures: A multimechanism approach. *Journal of Experimental Psychology: Human Perception and Performance, 16,* 365-380.

Enright, J. T. (1989). Manipulating stereopsis and vergence in an outdoor setting: Moon, sky and horizon. *Vision Research, 29,* 1815-1824.

Frey, J., Rotton, J., & Barry, T. (1979). The effects of the full moon on behavior: Yet another failure to replicate. *Journal of Psychology, 103,* 159-162.

Garth, J. M., & Lester, D. (1978). The moon and suicide. *Psychological Reports, 43,* 678.

Gilinsky, A. S. (1980). The paradoxical moon illusions. *Perceptual and Motor Skills, 50,* 271-283.

Hershenson, M. (1982). Moon illusion and spiral aftereffect: Illusions due to the loom-zoom system? *Journal of Experimental Psychology: General, 111,* 423-440.

Iavecchia, J. H., Iavecchia, H. P., & Roscoe, S. N. (1983). The moon illusion revisited. *Aviation, Space and Environmental Medicine, 54* (1), 39-46.

Kelly, I. W., Saklofske, D. H., & Culver, R. (1990). Aircraft accidents and disasters and the full moon: No relationship. *Psychology, 27*(2), 30-33.

Little, G. L., Bowers, R., & Little, L. H. (1987). Geophysical variables and behavior: II. Lack of relationship between moon phase and incidents of disruptive behavior in inmates with psychiatric problems. *Perceptual and Motor Skills, 64*, 1212.

McCready, D. (1986). Moon illusions redescribed. *Perception and Psychophysics, 39*(1), 64-72.

Plug, C. (1981). The moon illusion: Annotated bibliography. *Reports from the Psychology Department: University of South Africa, 6*, 1-42.

Reed, C. F. (1984). Terrestrial passage theory of the moon illusion. *Journal of Experimental Psychology: General, 113*, 489-500.

Ross, H. E., & George, M. (1976). Did Ptolemy understand the moon illusion? *Perception, 5*, 377-385.

Rotton, J., & Kelly, I. W. (1985). Much ado about the full moon: A meta-analysis of lunar-lunacy research. *Psychological Bulletin, 97*, 286-306.

Sharfman, M. (1980). Drug overdose and the full moon. *Perceptual and Motor Skills, 50*, 124-126.

Smith, O. W., Smith, P. C., Geist, C. C., & Zimmerman, R. R. (1978). Apparent size contrasts of retinal images and size constancy as determinants of the moon illusion. *Perceptual and Motor Skills, 46*, 803-808.

Stone, M. H. (1976). Madness and the moon revisited. *Psychiatric Annals, 6*, 170-176.

Tasso, J., & Miller, E. (1976). The effects of the full moon on human behavior. *Journal of Psychology, 93*(1), 81-83.

Templer, D. I., & Veleber, D. M. (1980). The moon and madness: A comprehensive perspective. *Journal of Clinical Psychology, 36*, 865-868.

Tsai, L. S. (1987). An enlarging hole on the palm illusion and a theory of the moon on the horizon. *Perceptual and Motor Skills, 65*, 816-818.

Weiskott, G. W., & Tipton, G. B. (1975). Moon phases and state hospital admissions. *Psychological Reports, 37*, 486.

Appendix

Imagine that you are outside on a clear night in which there are no clouds, and there is a bright full moon. Pretend that on a table in front of you are objects that range in size from a BB to a beach ball as follows:

1. BB
2. Pea
3. Dime
4. Penny
5. Nickol
6. Quarter
7. Golf ball
8. Baseball
9. Softball
10. Small salad plate
11. Large dinner plate
12. Frisbee
13. Basketball
14. Beach ball

Please pretend that you are going to pick one of these things that WHEN HELD AT ARM'S LENGTH JUST COVERS UP THE MOON. Imagine that you are picking one that when you hold it in your hand will JUST BARELY COVER UP THE MOON so that you can no longer see it.
____Put the number of the object you chose here.

Perception, Illusion, and Magic

Paul R. Solomon
Williams College

A little legerdemain can help you in teaching introductory, perception, and statistics courses, and you will be in good company.

The study of illusion has played a central role in psychology for over 100 years. The first psychological treatment of an illusion is usually credited to J. J. Oppel (1854) and since Oppel's paper there have been well over 1,000 articles published on the nature of illusion. It also seems likely that illusion played a role in prompting Wundt to study psychology as a discipline separate from physiology and physics (Coren & Girgus, 1978). The interest in illusion by psychologists still seems to be present. This is perhaps best indicated by the presence of sections on perception and illusion in virtually all introductory texts (Quereshi & Sackett, 1977).

Visual illusions have clearly attracted the most interest from researchers, although more recently psychologists have begun to examine auditory (e.g., Deutsch, 1975; Warren & Warren, 1970), tactile (Geldard, 1972) and gustatory (see McBurney, 1978) illusions. One class of illusions, relatively neglected by psychologists, however, is magical illusions. In this paper I will briefly argue that magical illusions are worthy of study and then describe how we have used magical illusions as a pedagogical tool for teaching the principles of sensation and perception.

The Psychology of Magical Illusions: A Brief History. The most comprehensive treatment of the psychology of magic by a psychologist was that of Triplett in 1900. In this paper entitled "The Psychology of Conjuring Illusions" Triplett first reviews the origins of conjuring (a term which he defines as "the performance of wonderful and miraculous deeds of any sort under the pretense of other than ordinary human agency") and then proceeds to make the case that conjuring tricks contain a good deal of material that is potentially valuable to the psychologist. In addition to cataloging several hundred magical illusions, Triplett discusses how certain phenomena such as attention, perception, association, and suggestion can be studied through the use of magical illusion.

Soon after the publication of Triplett's article, Jastrow (1901) published a similar paper called "The Psychology of Deception., Jastrow, of course, had published earlier papers on visual illusions (e.g., Jastrow, 1892) and in the 1901 paper he argued that magical illusions may be governed by many of the same rules as other types of "deception."

It is noteworthy that what appears to be the first treatment of magic by a psychologist was by Alfred Binet in 1894. Unfortunately, Binet's article, "The Psychology of Prestidigitation" has never been translated from French. Karelis (Note 1), however, has provided a summary which suggests that Binet makes many of the points subsequently raised by Triplett and Jastrow.

The German philosopher Dessoir (1893) was also well aware of the role of psychological factors in magical illusions and in his paper, "The Psychology of Legerdemain," Dessoir states "that which makes prestidigitation an art of deception is not its technical appliances, but its psychological kernel." Dessoir then discusses how memory (the past experiences of the observer), association, and expectations all play an important part in magic.

A more recent treatment of the psychology of magic was presented by Ceillier (1922). In this paper, Ceillier argued that there are two basic types of illusions, the psychological and the technical. Ceillier defines psychological illusions as those which rely on the "impressionability of the observer" whereas technical illusions are "rigorously undiscoverable by the senses."

Thus Ceillier seems to be making a distinction between sensory and cognitive illusions. It is interesting that in their recent treatment of visual illusions Coren and Girgus (1978) make a similar distinction.

Although psychologists have not written extensively on the subject of magic, others have. Magicians are prolific writers and almost all books on magic contain sections on the psychology of conjuring. Perhaps the most elegant treatment of the topic by a non-psychologist was by Robert-Houdin (from whom Houdini took his stage name). As Jastrow (1901) pointed out "Robert-Houdin, often termed the King of the conjurers, was a man of remarkable ingenuity and insight. His autobiography is throughout interesting and psychologically valuable, and his conjuring precepts abound in points of importance to the psychologist." This is still true nearly 80 years later.

Despite the sometimes elegant treatment of the psychology of magic by early psychologists, philosophers, and magicians, magic has been all but ignored by contemporary psychologists. Nevertheless it seems that magic may be worthy of study in its own right and, as the rest of this article will indicate, magic may be an interesting method for teaching the principles of sensation and perception.

Perception, Illusion and Magic: Course Description. The course was team taught by a psychologist and a philosopher. Both of us are amateur magicians with an interest in illusion. The course was offered during the Winter Study period during which students take one course for a four week period. There were 20 students in the class and we met four times a week for between two and two and one-half hours. Each class consisted of a one-hour lecture, usually on some aspects of illusion, followed by a workshop. During these workshops we helped students learn to perform magical illusions. My lectures covered various aspects of sensation and perception with special reference to illusion and magical illusion. Since a majority of the students had never taken a psychology course, these lectures were at the introductory level. The remaining lectures addressed the philosophical aspects of perceiving and knowing, again with special reference to magical illusion.

The main requirement of the course from the students' point of view was two-fold: first, to become familiar with the literature on illusion from several different perspectives (e.g., psychological, philosophical, historical, magical) and second, to become reasonably proficient at performing one illusion (this is not a task which is easily accomplished in one month's time). To demonstrate that they had accomplished this, each student was responsible for a presentation at the end of the month. During this presentation the student performed a magical illusion and then presented an analysis of the illusion in terms of the psychological principles involved. The students also tried to relate the magical illusions to other types of illusions. At the end of the course, each student submitted a paper based on their presentation.

The Use of Magical Illusions as a Pedagogical Tool.

Although magical illusions proved to be an interesting topic for a Winter Study course, it seems unlikely that most instructors could justify devoting an entire semester to this topic. Nevertheless, there are many aspects of magical illusion that can be incorporated into other courses. Courses in sensation and perception and the corresponding parts of the introductory course would be the most obvious settings, but with some ingenuity it seems that magic could be incorporated into several other areas (e.g., research methods and philosophy of science). To give an indication of how magical illusion can be used as a teaching method, I will describe several illusions that we presented in our course and their possible applications.

Past Experiences and the Basic Vanishes.

One of the basic tenets of virtually all models of perception is that present perception is built on past experience (see, e.g., McCleary, 1970). Although many phenomena such as sensory deprivation, visual stimuli present during development, and cultural influences may all fall under the category of past experience, magicians have simplified (perhaps oversimplified) matters somewhat by combining these factors under the heading: "We See What We Expect To See." Expectation, of course, can be influenced by any combination of the factors discussed above. There are many excellent examples of the role of expectation on perception that are non-magical in nature (e.g., Bruner's 1957 demonstration of perceptual readiness with a deck of playing cards), but there are also a number of magical illusions that nicely make this point.

The main asset of a good sleight of hand magician is mastery of the basic vanishes. There are literally dozens of vanishes but they all attempt to accomplish the same end: to give the illusion that an object has been passed, for example, from the left hand to the right hand when in fact the object is retained by the left hand. The magician will typically perform the move and then show the right hand empty, implying that the magician has vanished the object (Figure 1). All books on magic which teach vanishes stress the importance of the vanish appearing "natural" to the audience (Ganson, 1976). That is, all parts of the action of supposedly passing a ball, coin or other object from the left to the right hand must be the same as if the object were actually passed. The only difference is that the left hand actually retains (palms) the object. We would argue (as have many others) that this illusion works because the audience, based on past experience, expects the magician to pass the object from one hand to the other. This expectation is reinforced by the natural moves, and if this is practiced often enough (magicians often practice in front of a mirror), the de-

ceptive or guilty move of retaining the object is not detectable. The new magician can learn this move in a few hours (Tarr, 1976, 1978) and it makes an excellent classroom demonstration and starting point for discussion of the role of experience in perception and illusion.

Set and Perception and the Chinese Linking Rings.

There are a number of experiments which show the importance of cognitive set on perception (Murch, 1973) and there are many non-magical demonstrations of this phenomenon which are appropriate in the classroom Most of these rely upon perception of ambiguous figures (e.g., Leeper's, 1935, old woman/young woman drawing).

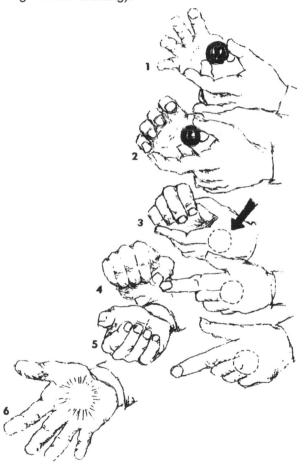

Figure 1. Basic Billiard Ball Vanish. The ball is held in the left hand (1). The right hand approaches the left (2) and while the right hand covers the ball, the ball is dropped into the left palm (3). The closed right hand, which is kept slightly puffed as if actually holding the ball, moves away from the left (4) and turns over (5). The magician then opens the left hand completing the vanish. As is the case with most vanishes, the move should be performed slowly.

There are several magical illusions which also rely on the principle of the effects of cognitive set on perception; perhaps the best example is the Chinese Linking Rings. In this illusion (actually a series of illusions which comprise a long routine), solid rings, which are passed out for inspection, are separated and linked together. The illusion is performed with eight rings and the key to its success is to convince the spectator that there are eight separate and solid rings. In fact, there are only two separate, solid rings. There is also a set of two permanently joined rings and a set of three permanently joined rings as well as a split (key) ring. The actual linking rings routine is too complex to detail in this paper (see Ganson, 1976, for an excellent discussion). But the beginning of the routine is germane to the idea of set and perception as it is here that the notion or cognitive set of eight solid and separate rings is established.

Briefly, the magician begins by holding all eight rings in one hand in a manner such that the closed hand conceals the linked parts of the permanently joined rings as well as the split in the key ring. The magician then passes out the two solid separate rings for inspection and thus establishes the cognitive set of solid, separate rings. The conjurer then asks a spectator to link the two rings. The person, of course, is not able to do this. While the spectator is still trying to link the two separate rings, the magician takes the two linked rings, carefully concealing the place where they are joined with his hand, and proceeds to apparently join them (usually by blowing on them). These are then passed out for inspection. The magician may then take one of the established solid, separate rings and join it to the key (split) ring. The routine can continue in this way for several minutes, but the key to its success is to continually pass out the solid and separate rings for inspection to maintain the cognitive set. Again, this is a fairly simple magical illusion to perform, and can be performed credibly in front of a class after a few hours of practice.

The Laws of Perceptual Organization and the "Popeye Pips." Another topic which is typically covered in courses in perception as well as introductory psychology is the principles of perceptual organization. Central to any discussion of these principles is the work of the Gestalt psychologists. Maas (1967) in his slide set for introductory psychology has summarized these principles by providing several examples. A magical illusion which we have used to demonstrate some of the Gestalt principles is the "Popeye Pips." This illusion is comprised of an oversized playing card with movable pips (diamonds) on both sides (Figure 2). Thus one side of the card (designated Front) may appear to be the One, Two or Three of Diamonds, whereas the back of the card can be anything from the Four to the Eight of Diamonds. There are a number

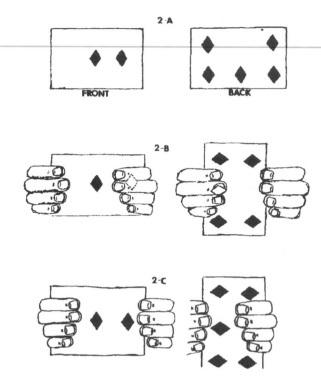

Figure 2. Popeye Pips. Figure 2A shows the playing card as it initially appears. The dotted lines in Figure 2B represent diamonds that are covered by the fingers. In Figure 2C the fingers actually cover the areas where diamonds would normally appear on a standard playing card.

of illusions that can be performed with this card, but it is the basic illusion that is best used to demonstrate the Gestalt principle of closure.

The magician begins with the configuration in Figure 2A. The conjurer then shows the front of the card to the class with the hands positioned as in Figure 2B-Front and says "This side is the One of Diamonds." The magician then reverses the card (Figure 2B-Back) and shows the Four of Diamonds on the back. Next, the magician turns the card back over (Figure 2C) and indicates that it is now the Three of Diamonds on the front (the spectators assume that the third diamond is under the hand) and then quickly turns the card over to show that it is now the Six of Diamonds on the back (Figure 2C). There are a number of variations of this illusion, but the basic deceptions all rely on the same principles.

It appears that this illusion takes advantage of several rules of perceptual organization which generally come under the heading of good figure (Koffka, 1935). For example, the principle of closure indicates that parts of a figure not present will be filled in by the observer in order to complete the picture. This appears to be one mechanism involved in the portion of the Pips shown in Figure 2C. We could also argue that illusion could not work if the spectators were not familiar with how playing cards are supposed to appear. Thus the role of past experience also enters into this illusion.

We have indicated to our students that the principle of closure may also be a factor in the linking rings. When the hand covers the split in the key ring, the audience assumes the key ring is complete. This, of course, is suggested by passing out solid rings for examination before showing the key ring. Other illusions that we have used to illustrate the principles of perceptual organization are rope illusions such as the Cut and Restored Rope and the Professor's Nightmare (see Resource List).

Auditory Illusions and the Multiple Coin Vanish. Most of the work on illusions, and sensation and perception in general, concerns visual phenomena Nevertheless, a number of investigators have recently begun to investigate auditory illusions and there are several magical illusions which rely, at least in part, on "deceiving" the auditory system. One example of this which can be performed with a minimum of practice is the multiple coin vanish (Tarr, 1976). In this illusion, four quarters are placed in the palm of the right hand. The right hand then appears to drop the coins into the left hand while actually retaining them in the right (Figure 3). The magician then holds the left hand in front of the body and drops the right hand to the side. The spectator assumes that the coins have been passed to the left hand (for the same reason that other vanishes work), but what makes the illusion particularly believable is when the magician shakes the left hand and the coins rattle. To accomplish this illusion the magician shakes the right hand (which is now out of view) simultaneously. This auditory deception works because the spectators are in front of the performer and have difficulty in localizing the source of the sound. This illusion is relatively easy to perform and provides an interesting starting off point for discussing sound localization and auditory illusions.

ESP and "Mental Magic." ESP is a topic which particularly interests students. Nevertheless it is a difficult topic to teach. This is probably because it is difficult to get the beginning student to appreciate some of the problems inherent in studying ESP (see McConnell, 1969, for a discussion). One of these problems is fraud. This particular problem is not attributable to researchers, who take great care to assure that fraud or subject cheating does not contribute to their results; rather, the problem is perpetuated by those who claim to be psychics, many of whom are well versed in mental magic (i.e., "mind reading" and predicting future events) and sleight of hand.

This problem has not gone unnoticed by scientists. In fact, interested scientists and philosophers have begun to debunk the claims of the psychics in a magazine called *The Zetetic* (Greek for skeptic). Similarly, Persi Diaconis (Diaconis, 1978), who is both

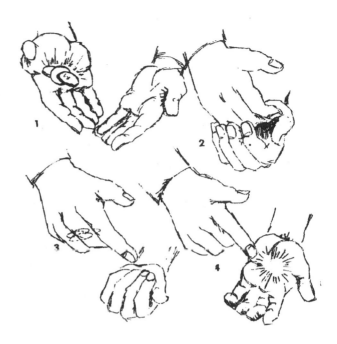

Figure 3. Multiple Coin Vanish. The right hand which contains 3 or 4 coins approaches the left (1). The right hand then turns over and appears to toss the coins into the left (2). Actually, the right hand catches the coins in the cupped fingertips, making a loud clanking noise. The right hand then palms the coins as the left hand closes (3). The magician can then drop the right hand to the side (out of sight) and shake both hands simultaneously, suggesting the coins are in the left hand (see text). The magician then opens the left hand completing the vanish (4).

a statistician and a magician, and who has been called on to debunk psychics including Ted Series and Uri Geller, has recently indicated how psychics have demonstrated their powers by using magical illusions and sleight of hand. Jastrow (1901) was also aware of this possibility, and one of his primary concerns in studying magic was to stop this sort of deception.

There are many magical illusions which can be used to demonstrate that magic can produce phenomena which can easily be mistaken for psychic events, but one which is particularly convincing is "Intuition" (Garcia & Schindler, 1975).

Prior to conducting this illusion we ask for a volunteer who does not believe he or she has any psychic powers. We then indicate to the person that we intend to show that they are wrong. We next ask the person to go through a deck of cards and select all the spades and hearts (actually any two suits can be used). The selected cards are thoroughly shuffled and then one by one the magician holds cards next to the forehead such that the back is to the volunteer and then asks the person to guess the suit of the card. The magician then places the card in one of two piles depending upon the volunteer's guess. The volunteer gets no feedback, but much to the person's disbelief, the conjurer constantly reassures them that they have guessed every card correctly. After the volunteer has made a guess for every card, the magician turns up both piles to show that the spades pile has all spades and the hearts pile has all hearts; that is, the subject had been correct on every card. After completing the illusion, we argue that the only explanation is clairvoyant powers and it is then relatively easy to get into some of the issues surrounding ESP research.[3]

Research and Magic. One final aspect of the use of magic in classroom situations seems worthy of mention. Triplett (1900) described an illusion in which the magician apparently throws a ball straight up in the air, only to have it vanish. This is a standard illusion, but what makes it notable is that Triplett used this illusion to conduct research on magic. In Triplett's experiment, in which 165 school children (no age was reported) served as subjects, the operator (magician) sat behind a teacher's desk, threw the ball 3 feet into the air, and then caught it and let the hands drop behind the desk. The second toss was 4 or 5 feet high and on return the hands were again dropped behind the desk. On the third throw, the hands went up with a regular throwing motion, but the ball was not tossed. The operator then waited for the ball to return.

Triplett reported that whereas 60% of the girls were deceived, that is, they reported seeing the ball go up on the third toss but not come down, only 40% of the boys reported seeing the illusion. Based on this observation, as well as previous work on non-magical illusions, he argued that there may be sex differences in regard to susceptibility to magical illusions. Triplett also reported that in other investigations of the same phenomena, he found the illusion to be more deceptive under dim illumination.

Using Triplett's early work as an example, we have encouraged students to begin to investigate what factors influence susceptibility to various magical illusions. We have pointed out that this has been a fruitful line of research in the study of visual illusion (e.g., Coren & Girgus, 1978), and suggested that it might be an interesting way to approach magical illusion.

Magical or More Traditional Illusions? I have described how we have used magical illusions as a framework for teaching some of the principles of sensation and perception. Because our institution has a Winter Term, we were given the luxury of devoting an entire four-week course to these topics; consequently, we were able to consider a variety of topics in detail. But as I have tried to indicate in this paper, the use of these techniques need not be limited to this type of situation. In addition to using magical illusion in the Winter Study Course, I have used these illusions as part of an introductory psychology lecture on perception. I have also used sleight of hand techniques in

order to produce some very unlikely events (e.g., selecting 4 aces, apparently at random, from a deck of cards; Garcia & Schindler, 1975) as a demonstration in my statistics course. This is quite useful in getting the class to discuss at what point are they unwilling to accept that something has occurred due to chance, and thereby leads to a discussion of the logic of the null and alternative hypothesis and Type I and Type II errors.

Clearly, there are other demonstrations which will accomplish similar ends, but it has been our experience that magical illusions not only convey material which is similar to that presented in more traditional demonstrations, but that they also have the advantage of creating a high degree of interest and enthusiasm among the students.

Table 1
Basic Illusions and the Principles They Can Be Used to Demonstrate

Principles	Illusions	Sources
Past Experience Perception	Billiard Ball Vanish	Tarr (1976, 1978)
	Sponge Ball Vanish	Ganson, Part II (1976) Tarr (1976)
Set and Perception	Chinese Linking Rings	Ganson, Part I (1976)
	Cups and Balls	Tarr (1976)
Perceptual Organization	Popeye Pips	See Tannen's Catalog
	Cut and Restored Rope	Tarr (1976)
	Professor's Nightmare	See Tannen's Catalog
	Multiplying Billiard Balls	Tarr (1976)
Auditory Illusion, Sound Localization	Multiple Coin Vanish	Tarr (1976)
	Hand to Hand Coins	Tarr (1976)
	Coin Box	Tarr (1978)
ESP	Intuition	Garcia and Schindler (1975)

List of Resources for Preparing Demonstrations

Tarr, W. *Now You See It Now You Don't.* New York: Vintage Press, 1976. A beginners guide to sleight of hand; this book describes the basic vanishes with coins and billiard balls. The illustrations are excellent.

Tarr, W. *The Second Now You See It Now You Don't.* New York: Vintage Press, 1978. Much like the first volume, but with an emphasis on cards and coins.

Garcia, F., and Schindler, G. *Magic With Cards.* New York: Reiss Graves, Inc., 1975. An excellent series of tricks on "mental magic" with cards; many of which are applicable to demonstrations of ESP.

Ganson, L. *Routined Manipulation* (Parts I and II). New York: Tannen, 1976. A sophisticated analysis of many illusions including the Chinese Linking Rings and basic billiard ball vanishes (available through Tannen's Catalog).

Tannen's Catalog. The official catalog of Louis Tannen's Magic Shop. The illusions discussed in this paper, as well as most other illusions are available from Tannen's Catalog.

References

Bruner, J. S. On perceptual readiness. *Psychological Review*, 1957, *64*, 123-152.

Ceillier, R. The psychological and technical problems of illusionism. *General Psychologique Bulletin*, 1922, No. 4-6, 1-42.

Coren, S., & Girgus, J. S. *Seeing is deceiving: The psychology of visual illusions.* Hillsdale, NJ: Erlbaum, 1978.

Deutsch, D. Musical illusions. *Scientific American*, Oct. 1975, *233*, 92-104.

Dessoir, M. The psychology of legerdemain. *The Open Court*, 1893, *12*, 3599-3634.

Diaconis, P. Statistical problems in ESP research. *Science*, 1978, *201*, 131-136.

Geldard, F. A. *The human senses* (2nd ed.). New York: Wiley, 1972.

Jastrow, J. On the judgment of angles and positions of lines. *American Journal of Psychology*, 1892, *5*, 214-221.

Jastrow, J. The psychology of deception, 1901. Reprinted in J. Jastrow (Ed.), *Fact and fable in psychology.* Freeport, NY: Books for Libraries Press, 1971.

Koffka, K. *The principles of Gestalt psychology.* New York: Harcourt, Brace, 1935.

Leeper, R. A study of a neglected portion of the field of learning. *Journal of Genetic Psychology*, 1935, *46*, 41-75.

Maas, J. B. *Slide group for general psychology.* New York: McGraw-Hill, 1967.

McBurney, D. A. Psychological dimensions and perceptual analysis of taste. In E. C. Carterette & M P. Friedman (Eds.), *Handbook of perception* (Vol. VI A). New York: Academic Press, 1978.

McCleary, R. A. *Genetic and experiential factors in perception.* Glenview IL: Scott Foresman 1970.

McConnell, R. A. ESP and credibility in science. *American Psychologist*, 1969, *24*, 531-538.

Murch, G. M. *Visual and auditory perception.* Indianapolis: Bobbs-Merrill, 1973.

Oppel, J. J. Ueber geometrisch-optische Tauschangen. *Jah resb richt des Frankfurter. Vereins*, 1854-1855, 37-47.

Quereshi, M. Y., & Sackett, P. R. An updated content analysis of introductory psychology textbooks. *Teaching of Psychology*, 1977, *4*, 25-30.

Triplett, N. The psychology of conjuring deceptions. *The American Journal of Psychology*, 1900, *11*, 439-510.

Warren R. M. & Warren, R. P. Auditory illusions and confusions. *Scientific American*, Dec. 1970, *223*, 30-36.

Notes

1. Karelis C. C. Personal Communication, May 1978.
2. I am grateful to Andrew Crider, Charles Karelis, David Morse and Richard O. Rouse for their helpful comments on an earlier version of this paper. I am especially grateful to Charles Karelis for providing copies of many of the papers discussed in the section on the history of magical illusions as well as for many provocative discussions on the psychology of magic. I would also like to thank Susan Marchant for drawing the figures.
3. Magicians generally subscribe to a code of ethics whereby they reveal the mechanisms of the illusions they perform only in trade publications. In this paper I have divulged the principles involved in several standard illusions. The illusion "Intuition," however, is a new illusion and it would be a breach of ethics to indicate how it works. Nevertheless, this information is available in Garcia and Schindler (1975).

The Versatile Mirror Drawing Apparatus

E. W. Jacobs
Presbyterian College

The mirror drawing apparatus (MDA) is presented as a versatile tool for providing an experiential activity to emphasize key points and generate discussion, and it serves to introduce laboratory equipment to the classroom. Three specific applications of the MDA for general psychology, educational psychology, and recruiting are described in detail. Introductory lecture material observed class reactions, and sample discussion topics are presented. Other potential uses for the MDA are also offered. Finally, some cautions are noted, and readers are urged not to be constrained by any equipment's designed purpose, but to seek creative applications.

Limited only by the imagination of the user, the mirror drawing apparatus (MDA) is an extremely versatile classroom learning device. Innovative applications can be used advantageously in generating discussion, emphasizing key points by providing students with a tangible experience and introducing laboratory equipment to the classroom. In particular, I have found the MDA to be a valuable experiential learning tool with specific applications in general psychology, educational psychology, and recruiting.

The MDA consists of three main parts, a drawing board, a mirror, and an opaque screen. The flat drawing board (31 cm x 33 cm) is placed on a table or desk in front of a seated subject. On the side opposite the subject, the mirror (20 cm x 25 cm) is attached at approximately a 90 degree angle to the board, and facing the subject. Finally, the opaque screen (23 cm x 25 cm), held in place by a supporting arm, is approximately 17 cm above the drawing board and slighly toward the subject. The screen is positioned in a manner that prevents the subject's direct view of the drawing surface, yet permits the reflection of the surface to be seen in the mirror. The typical use of the MDA is to place a sheet of paper on the drawing board, and to assign a subject some drawing task to complete while viewing only the reflection of the paper. The MDA is available from Layfayette Instrument Company, or other laboratory equipment vendors, for about $50.

In General Psychology classes I believe it is important to generate enthusiasm and curiosity initially.

Many texts present the assumptions of science in one of the first chapters and the MDA offers a simple demonstration of the viability of those assumptions. After lecturing on the general nature and value of assumptions, I focus on the assumption of order to demonstrate the validity of the scientific assumptions. I point out how much we rely on the world being ordered in our daily lives. As thought provokers I ask questions like "How would life be different if we couldn't always depend on gravity to pull things down?", and "How could we get to class if the landmarks we depended on yesterday were mysteriously moved during the night?" After some discussion, I inform the students that to find further answers regarding the validity of the assumption of order it is necessary to deviate from psychology and have an art lesson.

The art topic is the three-dimensional solid cube, which is a Necker Cube minus the internal lines. The purpose of the art lesson is to ensure that each student is able to draw a representation of a solid cube under normal conditions. The drawing procedures are explained and demonstrated on the board. Then the students are given an opportunity to practice drawing the cube. During this time I walk up and down the aisles of the classroom, providing encouragement or help as needed. When the students have mastered the cube, the MDA is presented as a device that violates the assumption of order. The students are divided into groups and directed to one of the MDAs. Paper is provided, the apparatus adjusted, and the assignment is given to draw the cube.

While the students are drawing the cube using the MDA, I have observed reactions ranging from nervous laughter to intense concentration. Occasionally a student will hastily tear the paper from the apparatus and crumple it up in frustration. As the students finish drawing the cube they are instructed to print their name at the bottom of the paper, again using the mirror. Printing their name is chosen because it is a familiar task, yet often no less difficult than drawing the cube.

A lively discussion usually follows the completion of the task, focusing on the nature of, and need for, valid assumptions. As a precursor of things to come, further discussions of student experiences, as participants and observers, are encouraged. A particular experience often mentioned is the sensation of arm paralysis that is felt when attempting to change the direction of drawing at the corners of the cube. The students are informed that this phenomenon, among others, will be studied later. By the end of the class period, students are aware of the importance of assumptions in science and their curiosity is piqued.

In my Educational Psychology course the MDA is used during the discussion of learning disabilities (LDs) to give the students an emotional experience analogous to that of LD children. After the basic definitions and classifications of learning disorders are presented, the MDA is introduced as a device that will simulate a perceptual learning disability. The same art lesson procedures described earlier are used in this course. The reactions observed and the liveliness of discussion are similar to those of the General Psychology class. The particular areas emphasized during discussion are the frustration and other emotional reactions that resulted from expending considerable energy on a task, only to achieve a less than satisfactory final product. Most students are awed by the experience, and by the end of the period, have a greater appreciation for the learning disabled. One point invariably mentioned by the class is that they now believe learning disabilities are real and are not merely expressions of laziness or cries for attention.

Finally, the use of the MDA is not limited to classroom settings. I have found it to be an effective recruiting tool. As with most schools, psychology majors are the lifeblood of our department. Attracting majors can be competitive, and without an audience, even the most persuasive arguments cannot influence the choice of a major. The MDA can attract an audience! I have taken it to high school career days, where many schools and companies are represented, and to college visitation days, where prospective students visit the campus to talk with the various departments. In both cases I set up the MDA at our department's table and display a poster entitled "Can you draw these simple shapes?" Under the title are drawings of the three-dimensional solid cube and the outline of a five-point star. Our table is often the busiest! I have prepared a brief explanation of the sensations experienced during the drawing process in terms of how individuals deal with conflicting input, in this case visual and tactile, and I emphasize that psychology is the field that investigates such phenomena. Although I have no data indicating the success of the MDA in attracting majors, I can state emphatically that our table draws a crowd.

The above examples, of course, do not exhaust the potential of the MDA. It can be adapted easily to many topics in general psychology, and to certain topics in learning, abnormal psychology, and social psychology. However, readers are cautioned against overuse. I have found that the greater exposure a particular student has to the MDA, the less its impact.

In summary, I have found the MDA to be an extremely versatile tool. Colleagues who have been introduced to its use, notably members of our special education department, have been equally enthusiastic. In closing, it is important to remember that the applicability of any equipment need not be constrained by its designed purpose. Equipment is only a tool, the uses must come from our own creativity. Readers having, or desiring, further information concerning the applications of the MDA are urged to correspond with the author.

3. TEACHING COLOR VISION

Additive (and Subtractive) Color Mixtures With A Single Slide Projector

Donald H. Mershon
North Carolina State University

The following suggestion is made under the assumption that both introductory and advanced discussions about perception can benefit from providing active demonstrations of perceptual processes. Reading about or hearing about various phenomena is fine but such information is much more meaningful if it can be associated with direct personal experience. Providing such experiences within a tightly limited (or non-existent) course budget is sometimes difficult. Although a 2 X 2 slide projector is basic, and is usually available, some demonstrations seem to demand two projectors. Additive color mixtures are such demonstrations. The following note describes hewn may accomplish good demonstrations of additive color mixing without having to find a second projector.

Additive mixtures of colors, of course, involve the new color experiences created by superimposing lights from two (or more) independent sources on the retina (or, equivalently, on a projection screen). Such a situation is standard in the experimental study of color mixture and understanding its basic rules is important for any appreciation of color vision. Unfortunately, the only type of color mixture with which a majority of students are familiar is subtractive mixture (the process involved in the mixture of paints). Even though it is possible to point out verbally that the rules for predicting additive and subtractive mixtures are different, and colored diagrams are shown in many textbooks to support the distinction, it is more effective to provide an immediate demonstration. It is necessary, therefore, to be able to superimpose at least two spots of projected light (one of each of the colors to be mixed).

The superimposition of two spots of light, say a red and a green, is simple with two projectors. Slides may be made using commercially available frames (with or without glass). A standard office hole punch and a small square of aluminum foil are used to create the "spot" for mounting in the slide frame. A piece of red (or green) filter material from the camera store, school supply house, or Edmund Scientific Co. (see Note 1) provides a well-saturated colored light.

Modifying the two-projector demonstration to a one projector demonstration requires that both spots be punched in a single piece of foil and that the red and green filters be mounted (one for each spot) in the same frame. For convenience, a vertical positioning of one spot above the other is helpful and will be assumed in the following directions. Finally, one needs a moderately large right-angle prism such as can be obtained from Edmund Scientific Co. for less than \$10.[1]

To demonstrate additive mixtures of the two chosen colors, project the slide as usual in a darkened room. The prism is now placed with its long axis perpendicular to the projection beam and slightly in front of, but below, the lens. By slowly raising the prism into the beam of light, some of the rays are captured by the prism and diverted to a new location on the screen, thus producing a double projection of each colored spot. By careful manipulation of the prism's orientation, the "extra" spots can be positioned to superimpose either of the original ones, creating the conditions for an additive mix. If a red spot is superimposed on a green, for example, a clearly yellow area appears. This is much more striking than being told that red plus green equals yellow.

The above demonstration has an additional advantage over any kind of static display of the same situation. The prism can be continuously adjusted, to show the result of changes in the relative proportions of red and green light. This manipulation is accomplished by slightly raising or lowering the prism in the projector beam, leaving the same two spots superimposed. As one lowers the prism, it intercepts less of the light and the "extra" image is reduced in intensity. As one raises the prism to intercept more of the beam, the extra image is enhanced while the contribution of the original fades. Thus, one can vary the "yellow" mixture from quite a green-yellow to a very strong orange. With a little practice at moving the prism, these manipulations are all readily accomplished.

Given the availability of the proper gelatin or acetate filters, one can proceed to prepare any two-color mixture one wishes. The red-green mix is recommended, however, because of the greater availability of suitable filters. (Any filters appearing to be pure green and pure red will do; one need not be concerned with the particular transmission characteristics.) It is usually good to note to the class that actual color vision experiments make use of monochromatic stimuli which the slides are definitely not.

For comparison of additive and subtractive mixtures, one can take small scraps of the same filters as were used to create the additive slide and bind them together in another mounting. One portion of each filter should be visible alone and another portion overlapped with the second filter. Some of the slide area should be left unfiltered to show how (in the subtractive situation) one or both filters remove portions of the original white light.

With a little imagination, a variety of color mixture effects can be produced in such a way that meaning is given to what are otherwise often confusing ideas to the new student of perception.

Note

We have used a "giant" silvered right-angle prism (base = 54 mm wide X 146 mm long; height of each face = 38 mm). Edmund Scientific Company (Edscorp Building, Barrington, N. J. 08007) lists such a prism as No. 800. If other prisms are available, they might be tried first since the basic requirement is simply the sufficient control of a secondary image to allow the spots to be superimposed. (Edmund Scientific also sells a variety of colored filters).

The Light Box: A Simple Way of Generating Complex Color Demonstrations

Barney Beins
Thomas More College

Most undergraduates find the process of color vision interesting, but hard to comprehend without concrete examples. Further, unless one is equipped with demonstrational apparatus, examples of color phenomena are severely limited. In order to enhance the discussion of color vision in our Sensation and Perception course at a reasonable cost, we generated an independent project for one of our undergraduates to construct a "light box" that would provide color demonstrations. Under faculty supervision, he assembled the necessary components, wired the electrical apparatus and constructed the wood housing. In the classroom, it generated some surprising and interesting color effects.

Apparatus. The rationale for building the light box was to design something that could, with minimal expense, generate several different effects. Consequently, we wired the equipment to hold four light bulbs of different colors, each controlled by a dimmer switch that would allow adjustment of illumination level for various demonstrations.

The design of the equipment was relatively simple. It consisted of four ceramic sockets to be used for holding three different General Electric colored party bulbs and one regular white bulb. General Electric manufactures four differently colored bulbs: red, green, blue and yellow They come in two varieties, clear and frosted. Depending on the stimuli to be used with the lights, different bulbs will be preferred. We chose the clear red and blue and the frosted yellow bulbs.[1]

We wired four ceramic bulb sockets in parallel, each attached to its own dimmer switch, in order to control brightness independently. Dimmer switches with the so called infinite level controls are preferable to the two or three position dimmers. Care should also be taken not to exceed to voltage limitations specified for each dimmer; in general, the 25-watt party bulbs pose no problems.

In addition to wiring the apparatus, we constructed the housing, which measured 5" x 8" x 24". A single 4' x 4' piece of quarter-inch plywood was cut to the appropriate dimensions. The top was hinged; the rest of the body was constructed with screws.

A 1½ inch hole cutter can be affixed to a power drill to make holes in order to attach the sockets to the top of the housing; the dimmer switches can also be attached to the housing after a hole for the body of the dimmer is made. The hinged top allows periodic examination of the wiring should any contacts loosen. Electrical tape can be used to connect the wires although shrink tubing can be a convenient substitution on some connections. (It should be mentioned that some knowledge of electricity is required to make the box, and that an electrician should inspect the apparatus to attest to its safety.) The total cost was less than $35.00.

Demonstrations. In order to illustrate the fact that colored surfaces absorb most wavelengths, the colored lights can be turned on individually and students can be induced to guess the color of a stimulus placed next to the light. One striking effect is that a green object appears jet black under red illumination.

In addition, we used artist's colors and felt-tipped markers to draw individual letters on large (175 x 300 mm) pieces of cardboard. Under illumination by different bulbs, the same letter changes appearance. This apparent variability seemed to capture students' interest effectively.

Through the use of stimuli like pseudo-isochromatic plates (i.e., hidden figures) in which, for example, green colored dots form a pattern among red colored dots, color anomalies or color blindness can be illustrated. By viewing these figures under a single colored light, the student can be rendered temporarily "color blind" or "color anomalous."

To show that color is a function of intensity as well as of wavelength, students can view objects of a given color under slowly increasing illumination. We have found that a yellow stimulus will go through a broad range of phenomenal colors by turning on yellow light (the stimulus appears white) and then slowly adding red light (to produce orange). When red is at maximums turn yellow off and slowly begin to add blue lights at which time the stimulus will become successively blue and then green (with these bulbs). This demonstration can be used to explain color additivity.

Demonstration of rod versus cone vision is relatively easy to simulate although with even a 25-watt white bulbs any object within ten to fifteen feet is sufficiently illuminated as to activate the cones. With distance viewing, the falloff in brightness permits achromatic vision. Within closer range the dimmest settings of red permit essentially achromatic viewing although the color shift with longer wavelengths distorts the brightness of many objects with normally short wavelength coloration.

Evaluation. After the segment on color vision had been completed students filled out an open-ended questionnaire concerning the apparatus. Of the 18 respondents, all were positive in responding to the question "Are there any advantages to using the light box for learning about color vision?" In spite of this leading question, the students later made favorable comments about their impressions of the sessions. Typical comments (14 of 18 students) suggested that the demonstrations made the abstractions more concrete, thus easier to understand. An extreme but consistent

statement by one of the students was that "by using the light box, we are forced into believing what you have said. Without it (the light box), it would be hard to believe that something yellow could look white." Many of the students often specifically asserted surprise that a single stimulus could change color as they watched (10 of 18 students). They were much more impressed with the effects under red illuminations presumably because of its narrower spectrum relative to blue. In facts there were 32 general comments concerning the effectiveness of the apparatus: 27 were positive and four of the remaining five negative comments mentioned the less dramatic appearance changes under blue illumination.

In order to see whether students actually became more aware of the mechanisms of color additivity, I administered a pre-test and an identical post-test to the students asking them to name the "real" color of the letters held up before them. For illumination under red light, students improved significantly from pre-test to post-test, $t(16) = 2.36$, $p < .05$. It is also true that students experienced less compelling color shifts under blue illumination, as evidenced by a lack of change in their accuracy in pre- and post-test situations, $t(16) = -0.61$, $p > .05$.

With red illuminations the initial guesses of the students seemed to be just that guesses. On the 15-item pre-tests students initially averaged over six guesses of either blacks white or gray. This dropped to just over three guesses on the identical post-test after they had been exposed to the light box demonstrations, $t(16) = 7.06$, $p < .001$. (There were actually two white stimuli among the others.) The increase in student accuracy is actually more impressive than the mean number correct suggests because in many cases, students responded that an item was blue when it was actually green; green and blue appeared very similar when viewed under red lights.

The students were initially wrong often enough to convince us that the demonstrations did not introduce trivial effects but actually illustrated more complex psychological phenomena. From the comments on the questionnaires and from the reactions in class, the students seemed not only to learn about color processes but also to enjoy the experience .

Notes

1. The spectral ranges for our bulbs are as follows: clear red bulbs 587-685 nm; clear yellow bulb, 487-662 nm, frosted yellow, 526-652 nm; clear blue bulb, 425-562 nm. A spokesperson for General Electric noted that different bulbs will show somewhat different ranges
2. I would like to thank Jack Wells of the Thomas More Physics Department for his assistance in measuring the spectra of the various bulbs.

4. TEACHING SENSATION

A Novel Experiment for Introductory Psychology Courses: Psychophysical Assessment of Olfactory Adaptation

J. Russell Mason
Monell Chemical Senses Center

Experimental psychology courses often include laboratory exercises in human psychophysics. These exercises tend to stress psychophysical methods such as the method of limits, the method of constant stimuli and the method of adjustment, at the expense of other newer methods such as the method of magnitude estimation. Also, visual or auditory stimuli typically are used instead of olfactory or gustatory stimuli. The exclusive use of visual or auditory stimuli is unfortunate given recent and increasing professional interest in olfaction and gustation and the inexpensiveness of generating olfactory and gustatory stimuli as compared to common methods of generating visual or auditory stimuli. The present report describes a simple experiment using the method of magnitude estimation to scale odorant intensities: (a) when the subject is in a non-adapted state; (b) when the subject is in an adapted state; and (c) when the subject is in a cross-adapted state. In addition to becoming familiar with the useful psychophysical technique of magnitude estimation, the student is introduced to the phenomenon of adaptation which is believed to reveal something about the nature of the olfactory stimulus and the olfactory receptor (Cain, 1970; Moncrieff, 1957).

The results of this experiment are likely to be robust even when collected in crowded classroom settings and can be interpreted by students with no special background in statistics All of the materials necessary to perform the experiment are usually accessible in a chemistry storeroom.

Adaptation, i.e., reduced sensitivity as the result of prior stimulation, is a well-known sensory phenomenon which reliably occurs when the olfactory system is exposed to stimulation (Berglund, Berglund, & Lindvall, 1978; Cheesman & Mayne, 1953). It generally is believed to reflect changes at the receptor level rather than changes in more central neural locations and is relatively stimulus-specific. Adaptation to one odorant does not necessarily hamper the perception of another odorant. To explain this specificity, one may assume that there are a number of different and relatively independent receptor mechanisms whose sensitivity can be influenced separately or at least to a different degree by adaptation to different stimuli (Cain, 1970).

Olfactory self-adaptation, that is, the reduction in sensitivity to an odorant as the result of previous stimulation by that odorant, and cross-adaptation, that is, the reduction in sensitivity to one odorant as the result of previous stimulation by another odorant, are believed to result from stimulation of the same receptor mechanisms by both odorant presentations. This belief has led to groupings of odorants on the basis of common influence (i.e., the extent of self- and cross-adaptation) on the same receptor mechanisms (Moncrieff, 1956).

Method. The stimuli are five concentrations of butyl acetate and five concentrations of propyl acetate diluted with propylene glycol. Each succeeding concentration should be ten times as dilute as the previous concentration. A convenient set of dilutions might begin with 1 ml of pure butyl acetate (Eastman Kodak, AR grade) or propyl acetate (Eastman Kodak, AR grade) diluted with 9 ml of propylene glycol (Mallinckrodt, AR grade). Subsequent dilutions can be produced by adding 9 ml quantities of propylene glycol. These odorant dilutions are easily kept over long periods in small glass test tubes or glass vials stoppered with teflon plugs (Kimble). Teflon plugs are preferable to rubber or cork plugs since the latter have slight odors

Non-adapted intensity estimates. Initially, the subjects will make magnitude estimates of the perceived intensities of the five concentrations of butyl acetate and the five concentrations of propyl acetate using one three-second sniff of the headspace above each odorant concentration in its container. The subject may assign any number to represent the perceived intensity of the odorant vapor (for discussion of the method of magnitude estimation, see Engen, 1972, pp. 73-79) The inter-trial interval should be at least 90 seconds to permit full recovery of olfactory sensitivity and to minimize the effects of initial trials on subsequent ones.

The first odorant concentration presented to subjects should be the middle (i.e., third) concentration. Subjects may assign whatever number they deem appropriate to this intermediate concentration. Then, subjects should be presented with the other odorant concentrations in a random order and asked to judge the intensity of each in relation to the perceived intensity of the intermediate concentration

Self-adapted intensity estimates. First, subjects should make a non-adapted intensity estimate of the intermediate concentration of butyl acetate; this intensity estimate will serve as a standard for subsequent trials Then subjects should make magnitude estimates of the perceived intensities of the five butyl acetate concentrations after self-adaptation. Each self-adaptation trial should consist of sniffing the high (or low) concentration of butyl acetate followed immediately by sniffing one of the five butyl acetate concentrations. The subject should make a magnitude estimate of the second of the pair of stimuli in relation to the perceived intensity of the standard stimulus. A ninety second interval should be allowed before the next trial to permit full recovery of olfactory sensitivity and to minimize the effects of initial trials on subsequent ones. Different concentrations of butyl acetate should be presented on successive self-adaptation trials.

Cross-adapted intensity estimates. First, subjects should make a non-adapted estimate of the intermediate concentration of butyl acetate; as previously, this intensity estimate will serve as a standard. Then subjects should make magnitude estimates of the perceived intensities of the five butyl acetate concentrations after cross-adaptation. Each cross–adaptation trial should consist of sniffing the high (or low) concentration of propyl acetate followed immediately by sniffing one of the five butyl acetate concentrations. The subject should make a magnitude estimate of the second pair of stimuli in relation to the perceived intensity of the standard stimulus. A ninety second interval should be allowed before the next trial to permit full recovery of olfactory sensitivity and to minimize the effects of initial trials on subsequent ones. Different concentrations of butyl acetate should be presented on successive trials.

Results and Discussion. For each sort of intensity estimate (i.e., non-adapted, self-adapted, cross-adapted), the subject's estimates should be transformed to a scale of ten. This will permit comparisons among all of the sorts of intensity estimate using the same scale. Thus, for example, if the subject assigned "50" as the intensity of the middle concentration of butyl acetate in the self-adapted series, all magnitude estimates in that series would be multiplied by "0.2". If the subject had assigned "1" to the middle concentration, all magnitude estimates would be multiplied by " 10.0" (Cain, 1970).

The geometric mean for intensity estimates for each concentration of butyl acetate in each series (i.e. non-adapted, self-adapted, cross-adapted) should be calculated. This descriptive statistic is commonly used in olfactory psychophysics because it is less sensitive to extreme scores than is the arithmetic mean. In addition, the geometric mean is commonly used with the method of magnitude estimation because magnitude estimation has a true zero point, unlike some other psychophysical methods (See Engen, 1972, pp. 73-79)

The medians of the geometric means for the entire class (i.e., all subjects) can be used to summarize the data. For example, medians could be plotted and the plots readily compared with figures in a variety of current research journals usually available in college collections. Also, differences between medians of the geometric means of magnitude estimates in each condition can be assessed using a simple modification of the sign test (Lehmann, 1975, pp. 162-163). Figure 1 shows sample results of the present experiment collected by college students during a laboratory exercise. Differences between medians of the geometric

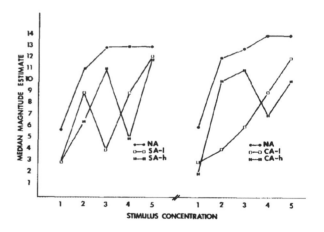

Figure 1. Medians of geometric means of magnitude estimates during non-adaptation (NA), self-adaptation with a low concentration of adapting stimulus (SA-l), self-adaptation with a high concentration of adapting stimulus (SA-h), cross-adaptation with a low concentration of adapting stimulus (CA-l), and cross-adaptation with a high concentration of adapting stimulus (CA-h)

means of magnitude estimates were assessed using the sign test ($p<.05$). Magnitude estimates of butyl acetate increased reliably with higher stimulus concentrations regardless of the adaptation condition. Also, both self-adaptation with butyl acetate and cross-adaptation with propyl acetate decreased magnitude estimates relative to estimates collected in the non-adapted condition. Within the self-adapted condition, both high and low concentrations of adapting stimulus produced about the same decrement in magnitude estimates. Within the cross-adapted condition, high or low concentrations of adapting stimulus produced different decrements in magnitude estimates. These decrements were dependent upon the concentration of butyl acetate to be judged. These sample findings are readily comparable with findings published by others (e.g., Cain, 1970; Engen, 1963) and are representative of the findings typically obtained using the present design.

References

Berglund, B. Berglund, B. & Lindvall, T. Olfactory self- and cross-adaptation: Effects of time of adaptation on perceived odor intensity. *Sensory Processes*, 1978, 2, 191-197.

Cain, W. S. Odor intensity after self-adaptation and cross-adaptation. *Perception and Psychophysics*, 1970, 7, 271-275.

Cheesman, G. H., & Mayne, S. The influence of adaptation on absolute threshold measurements of olfactory stimuli. *Quarterly Journal of Experimental Psychology*, 1953, 5, 22-30.

Engen, T Cross-adaptation to the aliphatic alcohols. *American Journal of Psychology*, 1963, 76, 96-102.

Engen, T. Psychophysics II: Scaling methods. In: J. W Kling & L. A. Riggs (Eds.), *Experimental psychology.* New York: Holt, Rinehart & Winston, 1972, pp. 73-79.

Lehmann, E. L. *Nonparametrics: Statistical methods based on ranks.* San Francisco: Holden-Day, 1975. pp. 162-163.

Moncrieff, R. W. Olfactory adaptation and odor likeness. *Journal of Physiology*, 1956, 133, 301-315.

Moncrieff, R. W. Olfactory adaptation and odor intensity. *American Journal of Psychology*, 1957, 70, 1-20.

Demonstrations of Auditory Stimulus-Sensation Relations

John D. Batson
Furman University

This article describes several ways to demonstrate the relation between various aspects of auditory stimulation and sensation. Simple equipment, including an oscilloscope and a sound generator is required to hear and visualize simultaneously a variety of auditory signals. These demonstrations allow students to learn more about auditory function in particular and sensory processing in general.

The relations between physical stimulation and the perceived sensory experiences of such stimulation are integral components of several traditional psychology courses. Such lessons are typically included in introductory courses as well as in courses in sensation and perception and physiological psychology. This article suggests several ways to demonstrate selected stimulus-sensation relations in the auditory system.

To appreciate these demonstrations, students need to know that simple auditory signals are defined by two independent parameters, amplitude and frequency, and that sound energy is, as McConnell (1989) described it, "vibrations of the molecules in the air" (p. 92). Although students readily memorize these facts,

the facts become more meaningful when the vibrations are actually demonstrated.

Some easy demonstrations use the equipment shown in Figure 1. The output from an adjustable sine wave generator is routed through an audio amplifier to a loudspeaker and an oscilloscope. Although many people see an oscilloscope as an exceedingly difficult instrument to use, only the simplest settings are required for these demonstrations. With just a little assistance from someone with expertise, any instructor can quickly learn enough for these demonstrations. If the oscilloscope's settings are properly adjusted, its screen will "freeze" an image of the sine wave appearing at the loudspeaker and the ear. As the properties of the sine wave are changed, so too are the images of the signal on the oscilloscope's screen. Thus, if the tone generator allows for independent and continuous control of frequency and amplitude, each of these parameters may be changed independently and students can "watch" the change as they hear it. One of the first demonstrations I perform shows that at a set frequency, changes in amplitude do not noticeably affect pitch. I then change frequency without changing amplitude to show that frequency is the primary determinant of pitch.

To demonstrate that sound is nothing more than vibrations of air molecules, students observe that the speaker cone moves back and forth as the sound is produced. These movements are more obvious (visually) when very low frequencies (e.g., 10 Hz to 30 Hz) are generated from a large speaker, such as one that is 6 x 9 in. or larger. With such low frequencies, it is tempting to increase the amplitude of the signal substantially so that students can actually see the movement of the speaker without hearing the sound it produces. However, care should be exercised while increasing sound amplitude because it is very easy to damage the speaker or other equipment—or at least to blow a fuse—with high amplitude signals, especially with sounds that cannot be monitored with the ear.

Demonstrating Differential Sensitivities

Any discussion of sensory systems must necessarily indicate that our sensory transducers are capable of detecting only a limited range of stimuli. Thus, absolute and terminal thresholds for sound frequencies may also be demonstrated. If the sound generator can produce sounds below 20 Hz and above 20,000 Hz, then students can "see" sounds outside their normal frequency range of hearing. Unfortunately, many amplifiers and speakers distort sounds at low and high frequencies, and some speakers cannot reproduce sounds above 15,000 Hz to 18,000 Hz. Hence, demonstrations of absolute and terminal frequency thresholds may be difficult or impossible with an inexpensive speaker.

Demonstrating the limits of sensitivity to amplitude is not recommended for several reasons. These thresholds will depend greatly on ambient noise levels. Moreover, very loud noises are painful and can damage ears and sound production equipment. Nevertheless, students should appreciate that, at least by some measure, the range of detectable amplitudes seems to be much greater than the range of detectable frequencies. To illustrate, for frequency detection, the lowest and highest detectable energies differ by a factor of approximately one thousand. The analogous amplitude factor is close to one million. The sensitivity of the ear to amplitude is truly remarkable because, for at least some frequencies, movement of the eardrum by as little as a fraction of the diameter of a hydrogen atom can produce an auditory sensation (von Békésy, 1957).

Although it is tempting to imply a one-to-one correspondence between stimulus characteristics and sensations, instructors should emphasize that the auditory system, like other sensory systems, does not accurately (linearly) represent all changes in stimulation. Some of these distortions are easily demonstrated. One often overlooked distortion con- cerns humans' enhanced sensitivity to signals between approximately

1,000 Hz and 4,000 Hz. Perhaps because we normally teach that loudness is determined by stimulus amplitude, it surprises many students to learn—and hear and "see"—that frequency" parameters can also affect perceived loudness. To perform this demonstration, I keep the amplitude of the signal generator at a relatively low level while slowly increasing the frequency of the signal from approximately 200 Hz to 10,000 Hz. Although students see that amplitude does not change, they invariably perceive the signals in the 1,000 Hz to 4,000 Hz range as louder than other signals.

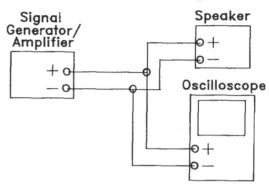

Figure 1. Equipment needed for demonstrations.

What explanation can we offer for this effect? One explanation suggests that the shape of the ear canal and other physical properties of the outer and middle ear are responsible for the enhanced sensitivity to sounds in the 1,000 Hz to 4,000 Hz range (Thompson, 1967; von Békésy & Rosenblith, 1951). Another explanation suggests that the human auditory system and the vocalization system evolved together, exerting mutual influences on their individual functions so that maximum sensitivity is to frequencies close to those characterizing human speech. In fact, the frequency range of most human speech is between approximately 100 Hz and 2,000 Hz and closely coincides with the range of frequencies to which the auditory system is most sensitive (Licklider & Miller, 1951; Stevens & Warshofsky, 1965). Other interesting examples of auditory coevolution come from comparative psychology. Many insects, for example, are extremely sensitive to frequencies of sound emitted by their predators (see Alcock, 1989, especially chapter 5).

Amplitude can also affect pitch perception, particularly frequencies near the absolute and terminal thresholds (Licklider, 1951; Wever, 1949). However, these effects are usually less obvious and more difficult to demonstrate than the effects of frequency on loudness.

Comparing Different Waveforms

The sound generator I use (similar to the combined audio signal generator/amplifier made by Lafayette, Model 15010) permits square wave as well as sine wave outputs. Frequency and amplitude may be changed with predictable changes in pitch and loudness. However, the sound quality of a square wave is very different from that of a sine wave of the same frequency. A dramatic difference between sine and square waves of identical frequency and amplitude is that the square wave sounds much louder than the sine wave. What causes this difference? Two factors seem responsible. First, square waves generate greater volumes of air disturbance through time. When compared graphically, square waves cover more area than sine waves. Second, square waves cause the air pressure to change more abruptly than sine waves. One might say that square waves have a "sharper edge." Because other sensory systems are demonstrably more sensitive to changes in stimulation than they are to steady stimuli, I assume that the auditory system has its own mechanisms for "enhancing" the neural response to stimuli that change rapidly. A possible analog in the visual system is lateral inhibition (Hartline & Ratliff, 1958; Kalat, 1988), a mechanism that enhances neural responses to edges of light, thereby facilitating our ability to detect visual contours. Regardless of the reasons for this auditory phenomenon, students hearing both sine and square waves learn that characteristics of the signal determine the sound sensation.

Demonstrating Real-World Sounds

The demonstrations just described are best accomplished with simple sound signals such as sine or square waves. However, students should recognize that their worlds are filled with sounds that are much more complex for at least two reasons. First, at any given moment audible sounds arise simultaneously from several sources. Second, individual natural sounds contain a fundamental frequency plus overtones or harmonics (consisting of different frequencies and amplitudes), thus creating different timbres. The C notes on an oboe and a piano may both have identical fundamental frequencies, but we distinguish the two by their overtones.

The differences in frequency responses of musical instruments provide an interesting way to talk about "real-world" sounds. Musically astute students can add much to discussions of overtones and the way sounds are produced in woodwind, brass, string, and percussion instruments. A comparison of woodwind instruments and the human vocal tract can also be enlightening. Both systems generate sound with air pressure disturbances in an air column or resonance chamber. But the vocal system can produce a much greater variety of harmonics because the spatial volume and shape of its resonance chamber—the oral cavity—can be changed in far more complex ways than a woodwind's chamber (Backus, 1977). When discussing music, it is also worth mentioning that the fundamental frequencies of orchestral instruments are considerably below 4,500 Hz and that most instruments generate few or no overtones above 10,000 Hz

(Backus, 1977). Because human hearing is most sensitive in the 1,000 Hz to 4,000 Hz range, students should be reminded that our enjoyment of music depends on the capabilities and limitations of the auditory system. Students may also be interested in comparing the fundamental frequency capabilities of orchestral instruments (Pierce, 1983).

One simple way to demonstrate everyday sounds is by substituting a small radio or cassette player for the sine wave generator. The leads of the radio speaker (or the leads from an earphone jack) can easily be connected to the two inputs to the oscilloscope. Some adjustments of the oscilloscope may be required, but students can readily see that radio sounds are combinations of many waveforms. I perform this demonstration last in my classes, and students always enjoy "seeing" signals from different types of radio broadcasts. The wave forms produced by rock music are noticeably different from those produced by classical music or by an announcer reading news items or commercials. Indeed, my students usually want to tune in to and "watch" different stations, such as classical, country, and rock music; they always laugh at the differences they see in the signals.

An FM radio is also useful for demonstrating white noise. The signal between stations approximates white noise, and the oscilloscope signals clearly indicate desynchronized sound waves. An additional benefit of discussing white noise is the opportunity to remind students why such noise is called white (compared with white light).

To increase student participation in these demonstrations, I have occasionally solicited volunteers to speak into a microphone that is connected to the oscilloscope. Although this procedure involves students more actively, it is considerably less valuable than playing different radio stations because the human voice is less variable than different types of music. However, more variety in human sound production can be observed by asking volunteers to whistle in different pitches or by comparing soprano and bass voices. After examining these individual sounds, simultaneous combinations of them should yield more complex visible signals.

Discussion

With equipment that is often readily available and easy to use, instructors can perform a number of different procedures to demonstrate a variety of stimulus-sensation relations in the auditory system. I use these demonstrations in my Physiological Psychology and General Psychology classes, but they can also be used in sensation and perception courses. The goal, of course, is to provide examples of the relation between physical and mental events. The demonstrations help students think about sensory transduction and neuronal/synaptic processes. They are also useful for distinguishing between sensation and perception and can help students appreciate the mind-body issue that remains critically important in psychology.

Although I have never verified their pedagogical value systematically, informal feedback has convinced me that these demonstrations are highly effective in teaching students several important lessons about sensory processing in general and the auditory system in particular. For example, students routinely tell me how much they enjoy the demonstrations. On end-of-term evaluations, students typically comment that these activities were highly memorable and especially helpful in understanding the material.

References

Alcock, J. (1989). *Animal behavior: An evolutionary approach* (4th ed.). Sunderland, MA: Sinauer Associates.

Backus, J. (1977). *The acoustical foundations of music* (2nd ed.). New York: Norton.

Hartline, H. K., & Ratliff, F. (1958). Spatial summation of inhibitory influences in the eye of limulus, and the mutual interaction of receptor units. *Journal of General Physiology, 41*, 1049-1066.

Kalat, J. W. (1988). *Biological psychology* (3rd ed.). Belmont, CA: Wadsworth.

Licklider, J. D. R. (1951). Basic correlates of the auditory stimulus. In S. S. Stevens (Ed.), *Handbook of experimental psychology* (pp. 985-1039). New York: Wiley.

Licklider, J. D. R., & Miller, G. A. (1951). The perception of speech. In S. S. Stevens (Ed.), *Handbook of experimental psychology* (pp. 1040-1074). New York: Wiley.

McConnell, J. V. (1989). *Understanding human behavior* (6th ed.). New York: Holt, Rinehart & Winston.

Pierce, J. R. (1983). *The science of musical sound.* New York: Freeman.

Stevens, S. S., & Warshofsky, F. (1965). *Sound and hearing.* New York: Time.

Thompson, R. F. (1967). *Foundations of physiological psychology.* New York: Harper & Row.

von Békésy, G. (1957, August). The ear. *Scientific American*, pp. 66-78.

von Békésy, G., & Rosenblith, W. A. (1951). The mechanical properties of the ear. In S. S. Stevens (Ed.,), *Handbook of experimental psychology.* (pp. 1075-1115). New York: Wiley.

Wever, E. G. (1949). *Theory of hearing.* New York: Dover.

Notes

1. Detailed information concerning the equipment, including costs and suppliers for a variety of signal generators and amplifiers, is available from the author. Colleagues in physics departments can also provide help in acquiring and operating the equipment.

2. I thank Charles L. Brewer and three anonymous reviewers for their valuable comments on an earlier version of this article.

5. TEACHING VARIOUS CONCEPTS IN PERCEPTION

Selective Attention With Human Earphones

C. James Goodwin
Wheeling College

A method to conduct dichotic listening tasks in the classroom for demonstration purposes is described. It involves substituting humans for earphones, thereby allowing direct student observation of various selective attention phenomena.

Selective attention is a standard topic in the beginning cognitive psychology course. Students typically begin by learning about Broadbent's (1957) filter model and then progress to more contemporary capacity models (e.g., Johnston & Heinz, 1978). They also learn about classic experiments that involve shadowing and dichotic listening procedures. Students easily understand the problem of attending to two messages simultaneously, and they may be reminded of that difficulty with a simple demonstration such as the one described by Reed (1988): Two students stand in front of the class and simultaneously read passages from a text, and the other students are asked to comprehend both messages. The technique described here goes one step further and effectively demonstrates some of the classic research findings using the dichotic listening paradigm.

The essence of the method is to substitute humans for earphones. Six or seven student volunteers are needed. Two serve as earphones throughout the demonstration, and the others are tested individually as subjects. The earphone volunteers should be the same gender, and their voices should be similar in tone, loudness, and pace. They should be recruited the day before the demonstration and must practice reading simultaneously.

Before starting the demonstration, the subjects are sent out of the classroom for a few minutes while the students in the class are told what to expect. Subjects are then brought in, one at a time, for testing. A subject sits in a chair facing the class, and the two human earphones sit immediately to the subject's left and right, facing the subject. The distance between an earphone's mouth and the subject's ear should be no more than 2 ft.

The session begins with a subject receiving some practice in the shadowing procedure, using a message from a textbook which is read aloud by one of the earphones. Next, the subject is given standard dichotic listening instructions to shadow one message while another message is being presented to the other ear. While one earphone reads the message to be shadowed, the other earphone reads a second message, which differs slightly for each subject. For the first subject, this second message is just another passage from the text. For the second subject, the message begins in the same way, but changes pitch when the earphone switches from a low to a high register. For the third subject, the distracting message has an embedded word repeated after every fifth word of text. For the fourth subject, the embedded word is the subject's first name. If the instructor happens to have a bilingual earphone, the message in the nonattended channel could switch in midsentence from English to some other language. As a final example, the message could be identical to the one being shadowed, but several words ahead or behind it.

After shadowing for a period of about 2 min. each subject is asked to recall information that has been presented to the nonattended ear. Standard results (e.g., Reed, 1988) are surprisingly consistent, considering the crudeness of the task and the occasional audience interruptions. Subjects generally fail to report the semantic content of the nonattended information, unless the content contains what Norman (1968) referred to as pertinent or meaningful information (e.g., their names). Also, subjects notice when the physical dimensions (e.g., pitch) of the nonattended message change, and they generally fail to report the meaning of irrelevant messages (e.g., a repeated word).

Although replication of classic research is interesting in itself, the real value of the demonstration is that students experience these attention phenomena, which would not be possible if the subjects were wearing real earphones. The class can appreciate the difficulty of the task, for example, by being told, before the subject enters the room, to listen to the repeated words that will be embedded in the message to the nonattended ear. To hear subjects subsequently express total ignorance of the repetition is a much more convincing illustration of selective attention than if students simply read about Moray's (1959) experiment in the text.

I recommend that the demonstration be used before students are taught about selective attention. When the topic is covered in detail, reference back to the demonstration can serve to clarify difficult points. For instance, by asking how the subjects were able to detect that their names were embedded in a nonattended message, students will learn that information is processed for meaning even if it is not in the immediate focus of attention.

In summary, although the procedure is not sophisticated and lacks the precision of a demonstration with real earphones and taped messages, it has pedagogical benefits that make it superior to the standard dichotic listening task. This demonstration offers an excellent way for a class to experience the phenomena of selective attention.

References

Broadbent, D. E. (1957). A mechanical model for human attention and immediate memory. *Psychological Review, 64,* 205-215.

Johnston, W. A. & Heinz, S. P. (1978). Flexibility and capacity demands of attention. *Journal of Experimental Psychology: General, 107,* 420-435.

Moray, N. (1959). Attention in dichotic listening: Affective cues and the influence of instructions. *Quarterly Journal of Experimental Psychology: 11,* 56-60.

Norman, D. A. (1968). Toward a theory of memory and attention. *Psychological Review, 75,* 522-536.

Reed, S. K. (1988). *Cognition: Theory and applications* (2nd ed.). Pacific Grove, CA: Brooks/Cole.

Oh Say, Can You See?

Frederick J. Kozub
University of Richmond

Introductory psychology textbooks often illustrate Gestalt organizing principles in visual perception by means of lines, dots, and squiggles. An exercise for discovering the use of these principles in readily available contemporary formats (advertisements, posters, and t-shirts) is described.

Many introductory psychology textbooks (e.g., Carlson, 1990; Morris, 1990; Rathus, 1990) present information about Gestalt psychology's principles of visual perception by using lines, dots, and squiggles. Although these are appropriate abstractions, I neither "see" the world nor assume that my students see the world in that fashion. Rather, we are bombarded with images from catalogs, magazines, posters, and t-shirts that compete for our attention. I wondered if I could take advantage of these readily available sources of visual stimulation to help my Introductory Psychology students understand the application of Gestalt principles involved in visual perception.

After an in-class discussion of the principles involved using the standard lines, dots, and squiggles, I showed slides, transparencies, and posters of every-day advertisements taken from a wide range of sources. I used advertisements from popular magazines, record jackets, posters from the school bookstore, and catalogs from mail-order houses and major department stores. We discussed each example with respect to the use of changes in luminosity and hue that define edges and contours; the use of proximity and similarity of size, shape, and color; and the use of the law of Pragnanz, including symmetry and closure. Where possible, I either used a transparent overlay or drew directly on the item to abstract and highlight the basic principle. A line drawn through some items separated them into symmetrical components. For others, simple measurements of the angle of limbs in human figures showed similarities of bends (e.g., forearm-upper arm and thigh-lower leg). For still others, repetition of images was shown, as was similarity in the use of color and meaning.

Students were asked to locate and bring to class examples of these organizing principles from their own visual worlds. They were told that several organizing principles could be operating in the same advertisement but to pick the best one they could find to illustrate each principle. They were required to highlight (via an overlay, tracing, or sketch) the principle involved and to describe it. They were told not to damage any item that was not theirs and that should they desire it, items would be returned to them (e.g., record jackets, t-shirts, buttons, posters, etc.).

I was delighted with the quality and range of the students' submissions. All were good examples; many were superb. The materials included sew-on patches, pins, t-shirts, student-produced photographs, reproductions of favorite paintings and/or posters, and a wide range of advertisements.

I offer student comments and some examples about the efficacy of this exercise. Some comments were, "I never realized that this was going on"; "I look at ads a bit differently now"; "Gosh, ads are more complicated than I thought"; and "Maybe that's why I like that painting so much. "

The students appeared excited about some of their discoveries. For example, in the painting *American Gothic* by Grant Wood, the repetition of the three-prong design in the pitchfork, cactus, seams on the overalls, and the male face (outer edge of face and chin cleft) were noted; symmetry was expressed in corporate graphic symbols (e.g., Chrysler and Chase Manhattan Bank); mirror image symmetry was noted in advertisements for cameras, shirts, and jewelry. One student presented an advertisement for woolen clothing that showed a hat, scarf, and sweater in warm shades of brown, orange, and yellow worn by a female model holding an orange and brown tabby cat. The student used two copies of the advertisement, the original and one in which she painted the cat black

with sleek fur. She commented that the use of the orange and brown cat conveyed warmth, softness, and fuzziness (like wool), whereas the black sleek cat did not appear to convey the same meaning as the intended selling points for the use of wool.

In one unusual submission, a student took photographs of a television commercial in which the image was black and white but the product was in color. This example was a good illustration of a figure-ground relationship.

Several students kept bringing new material 2 or 3 months later when they found better examples. Students' reactions are not hard evidence, but it seems fair to conclude that the exercise achieved its goal of using contemporary materials to illustrate Gestalt principles of organization in visual perception.

References

Carlson, N. R. (1990). *Psychology: The science of behavior* (3rd ed.). Boston: Allyn & Bacon.

Morris, C. G. (1990). *Psychology: An introduction* (7th ed.). Englewood Cliffs, NJ: Prentice Hall.

Rathus, S.A. (1990). *Psychology* (4th ed.). Fort Worth: Holt, Rinehart & Winston.

Note

This exercise was developed as part of the exercise/experiment component of the Introductory Psychology course.

A Laboratory Exercise Demonstrating the Relation of Projected Size to Distance

Ernest A. Lumsden
University of North Carolina at Greensboro

This exercise demonstrates the idea which Leonardo da Vinci reportedly utilized in one of the first systematic studies of linear perspective. The basic notion is that by viewing the environment through a transparent frontal parallel plane, one can study the relationship of projected size to distance. In this manner, many other cues to distance based on this geometric

relationship can be appreciated as well. The instructions are:

1. Clamp a large piece of plexiglas (or framed glass) in a vertical position with the top edge at a height of 5 feet from the floor. The transparent material should be at least 16 inches in width and 12 inches in height.

2. In order to assure that the observer's head will remain relatively stationary throughout the experiment, one can either require that the observer view through a very small hole in a reduction screen or place his head in a head holder. We successfully utilized a reduction screen with a hole 3/8" in diameter. This screen should be secured in place by clamps in a fronto-parallel position 14 inches from the vertical Plexiglas with the center of the viewing hole at a height of 5 feet from the floor, even with the top of the plexiglas. This point in space at which the observer's eye is to be located is hereafter referred to as the point of observation.

3. Several meter sticks (yard sticks or any other objects of uniform length could be utilized) should be placed on the floor at equal intervals from the point of observation. The first meter stick should be placed in a fronto-parallel position to the observer at a distance of 6 feet from the observation point. Because the distance from the observation point to the floor directly beneath it is 5 feet, the distance from this point on the floor to the first meter stick is 3.32 feet. The Pythagorean theory was utilized in the determination of the distances on the floor that will effect equal increments of 4 feet from the observation point. Specifically, the first distance was determined by considering the 6-foot distance from the observation point to the first meter stick as the hypotenuse of a right triangle, "c," the height of the observation point from the ground as the altitude of that right triangle, "a," and the distance on the ground to the first meter stick can be considered as the base of the right triangle, "b." For any viewing distance, c, the floor distance, b, can be determined in the following manner: $b^3 = c^2 - a^2$, with the altitude of the right triangle, a, remaining equal to 5 feet throughout the experiment. In this way, the distances on the ground producing distances from the observation point of 6 feet with increments of 4 feet were determined and are provided in Table 1. The meter sticks should be aligned in a fronto-parallel position to the observer, as are the plexiglas and reduction screen.

4. While holding the head very still and using only one eye, the observer traces the projection of the me-

ter sticks onto the surface of the plexiglas with a black grease pencil. In order to ascertain that the viewing eye is at the same precise point in space when all the edges are being traced, the observer should always check to assure that the lines that have already been traced on the plexiglas overlap perfectly with those meter sticks in the visual field before proceeding to trace any additional edges. The observer proceeds in this manner until all of the meter sticks are traced.

5. Remove the plexiglas and measure very carefully the horizontal length of the projection of each of the meter sticks on the plexiglas. Prepare a data sheet, writing this measurement beside the distance from which it was viewed (6 feet, 10 feet, 14 feet, etc.).

6. Plot a graph showing the projected horizontal length (dependent variable) of each meter stick as a function of the distance (independent variable) from which it was viewed.

The function in Figure 1 was obtained by plotting the means from 18 students, although each of the individual curves (as called for in step 6) approximated this figure very closely.

This demonstration permits the students to study the stimulus information in the retinal projection that corresponds to increased distance. It was very gratifying to hear the comments of the students relating how surprised they were to find that the decrease in projected size is as drastic as it is, particularly over the first 10-15 feet. At the conclusion of the semester, in the context of course evaluation, I solicited anonymous comments on the various demonstrations that had been utilized during the course. The following comments are some of those that were volunteered regarding this particular demonstration as described here:

"The experiment done in lab on projected visual angle was, in my opinion, a very negative way of demonstrating what had previously seemed an almost impossible notion (naive realist here!). Seeing and trying to comprehend this idea through the use of graphs and verbal explanations can't possibly be as effective as demonstrating it for one's self, as was done in lab. Not only were we able to "draw" these different projections, but also took the measurements and made our own graphs—comparisons made of these graphs we did ourselves and those studied earlier made believers out of more than a few of us."

"I felt the use of the plexiglas was very important. It was very surprising to see how the lines got so small as you drew them on the surface I felt it had a great impact and should be used more extensively."

"I found it very helpful to transfer the 3-D to the 2-D In taking the meter sticks out of the visual background and examining them in isolation was helpful."

Table 1
Variable Dimensions Related to Viewing Six Meter Sticks from an Observation Point 5 feet Above Floor Level

Distance from Observation Point to Successive Meter Sticks	Distance from point on floor directly below observation point	Horizontal length of projection on plexiglass of successive meter sticks
6'	3.32'	7.95"
10'	8.66'	3.88"
14'	13.08'	2.57"
18'	17.29'	1.98"
22'	21.42'	1.64"
26'	25.51'	1.35"

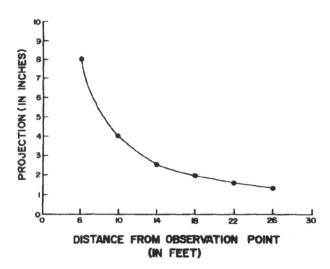

Figure 1. Projected length as a function of object distance.

"It was more easily understood, to me, after having drawn the images on plexiglas than when explained to me on the board. It is easier to understand because the finished product eliminates other cues."

"Enjoyed the plexiglas experiment. Helped me to understand constancy—excellent visual aid to point out how extreme the differences are between what is there and how I perceive it."

My own experience with this exercise and such student comments as these convince me that use of this exercise permits an appreciation of the size-distance relationship well beyond that afforded by the more traditional expository approaches alone.

With no further modification in the procedure described, one can also measure and plot the decrease in the vertical distance between the projection of the successive meter sticks on the plexiglas. I have found this relationship to be a decreasing negatively-accelerated function of distance also but asymptoting at a distance slightly less than does the function relating horizontal projection to distance. This method also, of course, permits the study of the relationship of distance to linear perspective, relative size, texture gradient, as well as the vertical position of the visual field just alluded to. Furthermore, the same basic procedure can readily be modified for the study of motion parallax and binocular disparity.

The phenomenon of size constancy can be discussed more meaningfully following this demonstration of the size distance relationship. The data generated in Figure 1 reflect a decreasing, negatively-accelerated projection of increased distance. Needless to say, size constancy is not phenomenologically in accord with this decreased projection.

An Improved Device for Studying Adaptation to Displaced Vision

Robert H. Terborg
Calvin College

For years psychologists studying or demonstrating the effects of adaptation to displaced vision have used thick, bulky prisms mounted on welder's goggles or eyeglass frames to produce displaced vision. A new method is presented here for creating lightweight compact eyeglasses that displace one's vision. These eyeglasses can be constructed to displace vision horizontally, vertically, or both. The necessary materials can be obtained from many optical suppliers for a reasonable price. The eyeglasses are easy to use for classroom demonstrations or for student research projects.

The study of adaptation to displaced vision began more than a century ago. Harris (1965), Kohler (1962), and Rock (1975) provided interesting and informative materials on he subject. Using a device that displaces vision, one can perform a variety of interesting demonstrations in the introductory psychology course or courses in sensation and perception. One can demonstrate adaptation and readaptation to displaced vision. Such adaptation involves motor adaptation, and it can easily be shown that such motor adaptation does not transfer from the right arm to the left arm or vice versa. Benjamin (1981) and Kling (1987) presented several examples of demonstrations using activities that involve pointing at objects, hitting a target with one's index finger, or throwing objects (e.g., balls, darts, or marbles) at a target or into a cardboard box.

Benjamin (1981) and Kling (1987) described economical ways of constructing such a device. Usually this involves buying or making prisms that can be inserted into eyeglass frames or attached to the faceplate of welder's safety goggles. Although the results of such methods are fairly satisfactory, the production of such devices can be time-consuming, and the finished product is somewhat bulky.

Using Fresnel Prisms

Fresnel prisms provide an economical solution to the inconveniences just mentioned. Most Fresnel prisms consist of concentric circles that allow visual material to be focused through them so that an image of the visual material can be displayed on a screen. If you look closely at the faceplate of an overhead projector, you will notice that it is made up of many fine-lined concentric circles. These are Fresnel prisms. Fresnel prisms that consist of virtually parallel lines, rather than concentric circles, are now available. These prisms are fairly flat and unlike other prisms, which may be as much as 1-in. (2.54-cm) thick.

Signet Armorlite Corporation distributes a type of Fresnel prism called 3M Press-on® optics.[1] The Press-on® optics come in blanks, which are approximately 2.5 in. (6.35 cm) in diameter. The self-adherent blanks can be cut to match the size of a standard lens in a pair of eyeglasses and attached to the inside surface of the lens. The prisms can be ordered in various angles, but the most common for demonstration purposes is a 30° angle. It is not necessary to be concerned with other variables (e.g., number of lines per inch) that affect the quality of Fresnel prisms because the manufacturer of the Press-on® prisms has chosen values that allow for the best visual acuity. Select a prism with an angle twice that of the desired visual displacement because the actual visual displacement of the prisms is about one half of the angle of the prism (e.g., a 30° prism provides actual visual displacement of about 15°[2]).

The special eyeglasses for distorting vision can be worn like any other pair of eyeglasses. The prisms can be mounted so that both lenses distort to the right, left, up, or down. The prisms can also be mounted so that they distort on an angle. For example, they could be

rotated 45° from the horizontal so that they distort to the left and downward at the same time. (This would result in an actual distortion of about 11° to the left and 11° downward.) Kohler (1962) reported that interesting stereoscopic effects can be studied by having the lenses distort in opposite directions (i. e., both lenses distorting inward or outward). Some of these stereoscopic effects involve color distortion.

Construction Instructions

The prism blanks can be purchased for about $10 each from local optical suppliers. Plastic safety glasses worn inmany natural science laboratories and in woodworking shops should be obtained. These are often available in college bookstores. Plastic safety glasses are ideal because they: (a) have larger lenses; (b) come equipped with side shields, which prevent the wearer from observing side movements of the hands and arms; and (c) can usually be worn over existing corrective lenses with the help of an elastic strap. There are several different styles of plastic safety glasses. Those with separate lenses, rather than a continuous lens across the front, are preferable because separate lenses help to guide the placement of each Fresnel prism.[3]

Attach the prisms to the inside surface of each lens by carefully pressing the smooth side of the blank against the inside surface of the lens. To ensure that the prism in one lens is parallel to the prism in the other lens, you may want to attach the prisms while working over a sheet of lined paper. By looking through the prisms as you are mounting them in the glasses, you can align each prism so that the lines in each lens fall directly on top of the same line or are parallel to the same line on the paper underneath. If you want to apply the prisms so that they are rotated a specific number of degrees away from a vertical or horizontal position, all you need to do is rotate the paper underneath the glasses so that the lines of the paper are the required number of degrees away from the vertical or horizontal. Do your best to avoid touching the smooth surface of the prism blank. Use a razor blade or sharp scalpel to trim away any portions of the blank that extend beyond the edges of the lenses or the molded edges of the plastic safety glasses. Remove the sideguards from the plastic safety glasses and spray paint them a flat black. You may wish to paint other portions of the plastic safety glasses. (I have not found it necessary to paint anything other than the sideguards of the plastic safety glasses in attempting to eliminate peripheral vision and other distractions.) Be careful not to get paint on the prism material.

---

[1]Press-on® is the registered trademark of the 3M Corporation. Press-on® optics are designed and manufactured by Vision Care/3M, St. Paul, MN 55144. They are distributed by Signet Armorlite, 101 Armorlite Drive, San Marcos, CA 92069. Many optical suppliers (listed in the "yellow pages" of the telephone directory under the heading "Optical Goods—Whol. & Mfrs.") stock them or will be able to obtain them for you.

[2]Optical suppliers often refer to 30° prisms as 30 diopter prisms.

---

[3]Willson Safety Products, 2nd and Washington Streets, Reading, PA 19601, produces "visitors glasses" that work very well for this purpose. The model number is VS7B Clear.

One caution should be mentioned in the application of the prisms. It is best to apply the prisms under conditions of low humidity. They will adhere better to the surface of the lens and reduce the chance of getting air bubbles between the lens and the prism. A few small air bubbles will not affect your use of the lenses. Construction of distorting eyeglasses using the methods and materials described in this article has allowed me to replace thick bulky prisms with lightweight, compact eyeglasses. They are economical to construct, easy to store, and easier to use for classroom demonstrations.

These distorting eyeglasses are as effective as previous devices in performing the demonstrations described by Benjamin (1981) and Kling (1987). When performing these demonstrations, keep in mind Benjamin's (1981) advice that the subject's "arm motion must be rapid and must start from outside of the subject's field of view" (p. 52). This procedure prevents the subject from correcting a response once it has begun and restricts the effects of peripheral vision.

References

Benjamin, L. T., Jr. (1981). Adaptation to displaced vision. In L. T. Benjamin, Jr. & K. D. Lowman (Eds.), *Activities handbook for the teaching of psychology* (pp. 51-53). Washington, DC: American Psychological Association.

Harris, C. S. (1965). Perceptual adaptation to inverted, reversed, and displaced vision. *Psychological Review, 72,* 419-444.

Kling, J. W. (1987). Adaptation of the hand-eye system. In V. P. Makosky, L. G. Whittemore, & A. M. Rogers (Eds.), *Activities handbook for the teaching of psychology* (Vol. 2, pp. 37-40). Washington, DC: American Psychological Association.

Kohler, I. (1962). Experiments with goggles. *Scientific American, 206,* 62-72.

Rock, I. (1975). *An introduction to perception.* New York: Macmillan.

Notes

1. An earlier version of this article was presented at the annual convention of American Psychological Association, New Orleans, August 1989.
2. I thank Joseph Palladino and three anonymous reviewers for comments on an earlier draft of this article.
3. A copy of a graph showing the amount of vertical and horizontal distortion achieved when the prisms are rotated through various angles is available from the author.

SECTION III
LEARNING

Introducing Learning

Lance Olsen avoided an overly simplistic presentation of the relationship between stimuli and responses by emphasizing the continuous nature of the S-R relationship. By asking several questions about a specific stimulus and response, the instructor de-emphasized the simple notion that the stimulus is "out there" and the response is "in here."

Thomas Rocklin attempted to avoid the tendency of students merely to memorize definitions from their textbook. In a psychology of learning class, students read a list of 10 events. Some of the events clearly represented learning and some clearly did not represent learning. A third group depicted events that were ambiguous. Students discussed the events prior to developing a standard definition for learning. The class applied the definition to each of the 10 events. Judgments about whether the events represented learning were clear-cut except in the cases that involved computers. A computer simulation developed by the author served as a follow-up exercise.

Using Animals to Teach Learning

Michael Owren and Dana Scheuneman developed a laboratory exercise using planaria that gave students hands-on experience with concepts such as dishabituation, spontaneous recovery and short- versus long-term habituation processes. The entire laboratory exercise required a few eyedroppers, petri dishes, water, and planaria. Students expelled drops of water on the planaria from eyedroppers and estimated contraction response. Students produced significant habituation.

Karl Hunt and Rosalie Shields outlined their use of gerbils in an operant conditioning laboratory. They listed the pros and cons of using gerbils versus rats.

Glass gallon pickle jars from restaurants served as operant conditioning chambers in Larry Plant's introductory psychology class. The instructor modified the jars by adding a food magazine and water container. Each student took home a jar and a gerbil and completed an operant conditioning assignment. Low cost and the availability of materials make an animal conditioning experience available to departments with limited equipment budgets.

Paul Solomon and David Morse developed a way to involve students in a unique operant conditioning exercise. Students trained rats to compete with each other in an olympic-like sporting atmosphere. Rats competed in competitions such as the highest number of bar-presses, best discrimination, and longest behavioral chain. Student response to the exercise was very positive.

Gary Nallan and D. Mark Bentley designed a classical conditioning component for their learning course that used existing operant conditioning equipment. Students conditioned increases in rearing and orienting toward the food magazine in rats by pairing a light with food presentation. Successful acquisition, extinction, and reaquisition resulted from the procedure.

After mentioning some problems with using rats, James Ackil and Eric Ward described why and how they used chickens in an operant conditioning laboratory. Chicks are less expensive, their behavior can be shaped very quickly in cardboard chambers, which students can build in 30 min. and data from experiments with chicks are almost identical to data produced by rats and pigeons in more complicated equipment. More kinds of discrimination problems can be studied with chicks because they have color vision. Chicks are less "nervous" and distractible than rats. The authors have never had a student who required a tetanus shot because of a chick bite. Teachers with limited facilities and budgets might consider a chick lab.

Prompted by Ackil and Ward's report, David Rowland and his colleagues described their use of chicks in an upper-level animal learning course. Although agreeing that chicks offered several advantages compared to rats, the authors encountered some unexpected problems. For example, certain varieties of chicks possessed unacceptable growth rates.

Teaching Classical Conditioning

Dennis and Rosemary Cogan used sweetened lemonade powder as an unconditioned stimulus in a classroom demonstration of classical conditioning. The instructors presented the name "Pavlov" and a visual cue after which the students administered the powder, placing a small amount on the tips of their tongues. Test trials interspersed throughout a 50 min class period generated strong salivary conditioning.

Gerald Gibb demonstrated classical conditioning in class by associating a lemon with a loud noise and recording the resulting GSR. After 10-15 trials, he elicited strong GSR responses to the presentation of the lemon. Presentation of additional common objects such as a lime, a tennis ball, and a cucumber illustrated discrimination and generalization. Spontaneous recovery resulted from presentation of the lemon in a subsequent class period.

The Conditioner resulted from John Sparrow and Peter Fernald's attempt to devise an apparatus that demonstrated classical conditioning. The Conditioner consisted of a variable light source, a buzzer, and a loud siren mounted in a small wooden box. Startle reactions proved easy to condition to the previously neutral light stimulus because of the intensity of the siren. As with many of the other classical conditioning articles in this section, this one included demonstrations of extinction, spontaneous recovery, generalization, and discrimination.

Mark Vernoy relied on an old magician's trick to illustrate classical conditioning. Most people flinch or blink, a classically conditioned response, when in the vicinity of a balloon that someone is about to prick with a needle. The instructor demonstrated this response by walking around the classroom and by breaking several balloons he had distributed to students. Eventually, he implemented the trick by sticking the needle into a balloon that did not burst. Students flinched and blinked in the absence of the unconditioned stimulus. This exercise led to spirited discussion of the parameters of classical conditioning.

Art Kohn and James Kalat also broke balloons in a demonstration of classical conditioning. Their approach differed from the previous one by using a muscle tensing response rather than a flinching response. The authors outlined several advantages to their procedure including demonstration of a CR that was significantly different from the UR.

Teaching Operant Conditioning

Joan Chrisler asked her students to condition one of her classroom behaviors as part of a major project in a learning course. Students selected the behavior, chose the contingencies, and proceeded to implement the study in an ABAB design. A thorough debriefing followed the exercise, and students wrote manuscripts in APA style describing the project.

To modify the students' participation rates, Gordon Hodge and Nancy Nelson developed and implemented operant conditioning contingencies in an introductory laboratory. The technique modified student behavior, and participants learned useful information about altering behavior in applied settings.

Robert Tauber gave students a quiz to assess their knowledge of negative reinforcement. He found considerable misunderstanding about the concept. For example, students could not provide another word or concept that meant the same thing as negative reinforcement. The article listed several strategies for allaying the misconceptions.

Teaching Biological Aspects of Learning

Ernest Kemble and Kathleen Phillips avoided some of the ethical complications of demonstrating the effect of biological constraints on learning in rats. Rather than administer toxic substances or electric shock, the instructors developed a procedure to reinforce the biologically important behavior of rearing or the less important lever-pressing behavior. After obtaining lever-pressing and rearing baselines, different groups of rats were reinforced for either lever-pressing or rearing. As expected, rats in the rearing response group responded at a higher level than those in the lever-pressing group.

J. W. Kling outlined several procedures for demonstrating learned taste aversions in rats. The procedures were safe and effective in illustrating several conditioning principles such as preparedness, learned safety, and latent inhibition.

I. INTRODUCING LEARNING

On the Nature of Stimulus and Response

Lance A. Olsen
College of Great Falls

We do not teach psychology in a vacuum. Our students come to us from other courses and leave us for other courses, every day. Sooner or later, in our own classes or elsewhere. they hear someone articulate the view that scientific psychology is "reductionistic." One model of behavior, the stimulus-response model, long taught by psychologists, is particularly vulnerable to this charge. Students quickly learn to criticize this model, and they find reward for that criticism from faculty who refer to the S-R model as "simplistic" or reductionistic. I challenge that contention in my courses.

The relationship between stimulus and response is usually taught (and written about, in texts) so as to make their relationship appear to be discontinuous, dichotomous. That is, the stimulus is "out there," in the environment, whereas the response is "in here" in the organism. To show my students how S-R relationships are typically taught, I draw on the chalkboard a profile of a human head, with eye, and a few feet away I draw a light bulb. I ask my students to imagine that the person drawn on the board is in a darkened room, and that the light has just come on. I draw lines emanating from the light bulb to suggest the emitted light, and tell my students that the person has blinked. In this case, it would certainly appear that there is a stimulus and a response, and that one is out there in the environment while the other is in here in the organism. Since I seldom teach introductory psychology, I am therefore in the position of explaining the basics of S-R theory to students who already know: they nod patiently, wishing I'd move on. I don't.

I tell my students that we'll linger on S-R for awhile, to look at it from another perspective, in order to examine a larger issue: so-called scientific reductionism. What I then do is to ask a series of rhetorical questions, beginning with "What is 'the stimulus' in this example?" Is the stimulus the light bulb? Is it the light between the bulb and the person's pupil? Is it the light between the pupil and the retina? Is it the photochemical reaction in the receptors? Is it the reaction of the bipolars or the ganglia, or the impulses coursing up the optic nerve, or the lateral geniculate body, or the optic projection area? Is it the reaction of the motor areas of the brain which control the muscles of the eyelid/pupil? Is it, I finally ask, the eyeblink or the closure of the pupil? Is, indeed, the response the stimulus? At this point, some students blink in response.

So far, none of my students has walked away from this example ready to label light as a response or an eyeblink (in this example) a stimulus. They do grasp, however, that the relationship between stimulus and response is a *continuous* one, and not the simplistic or reductionistic one they'd been led to believe by critical faculty or, alas, their psychology textbooks. They do also grasp that, just because some of us teach simplistic *models* of behavior, that the behavior is itself not necessarily simplistic. In this example, they readily see that a whole series of complex phenomena are involved, including retinal photochemistry and neuroanatomy. This example is one I've used profitably in discussions of perception, brain functions, and learning theory. It has "holistic" aspects which appeal to students inclined toward humanistic approaches, and seems to be somewhat useful in rapproachement of S-R and holistic approaches.

Next I tell my students that the discontinuity of organism and environment is equivalent to the discontinuity of stimulus and response: apparent but not real. I stress that organism and environment are as continuous with each other as are stimulus and response. To demonstrate this point, I revive Andras Angyal's (1941, pp. 88-92) critique of the traditional model of organism-environment relations. I ask my students to recall what they had for breakfast or lunch and point out to them that the food they had on their fork was, at that time *environment*. I ask them whether it was still environment after they'd put it in their mouths, to chew it. Is food in a mouth still part of the environment? Is it part of the environment when it's being drawn down the esophagus? Is it still environment when in the stomach? the intestine? When drawn through the wall of the intestine, into the bloodstream? Is it still environment when, distributed by the bloodstream, it becomes flesh, bone, brain fuel? And what about the eventually resultant urine and feces? When is urine environment? When it splashes into the toilet bowl? When it lies waiting in the bladder!?

I tell students that with stimulus and response and with organism and environment we have cases of a *flow of energy* and a *transformation of energy.* I stress that one language they can employ to conceive of the relationship qua relationship between stimulus and response/organism and environment is that of *continuity*, not discontinuity. To give them an alternative language, and to reinforce the same basic notion, I quote from John Dewey's (1896) classic critique of the reflex arc in which he wrote that, ". . .the older dualism of body and soul finds a distinct echo in the current dualism of stimulus and response" (p. 358). I then hasten to add the notion of continuity is not just an historical artifact from the days of John Dewey and Andras Angyal, but is also a current event, and can be found expressed in the continuity pointed out by F. J. McGuigan's (1978) discussion of "cognitive psychophysiology," a discussion which is a refusal to reduce consciousness to the domain of the brain alone. All of this review and critique of S-R, then, leads to a critique of so-called reductionism in psychology. I think the

time I take to linger where texts typically speed by, in order to critique the charge of reductionism for my students, is well worth it.

References

Angyal, A. *Foundations for a science of personality.* Cambridge: Harvard University Press, 1941.

Dewey, J. The reflex arc concept in psychology. *Psychological Review* III (July, 1896), pp. 357-370.

McGuigan, F. J. *Cognitive psychophysiology. Principles of covert behavior.* Englewood Cliffs, NJ: Prentice-Hall, 1978.

Defining Learning: Two Classroom Activities

Thomas Rocklin
University of Iowa

This article describes two activities designed to help students evaluate potential definitions of learning and arrive at a useful one. The first activity involves discussion of 10 events, ranging from clear cases of learning, through ambiguous cases, to cases that are clearly not learning. The second activity involves interacting with a computer program that simulates problem solving and appears to fit most published definitions of learning. The two activities seem to help students evaluate proposed definitions of learning.

One of the first topics addressed in a course on learning is the definition of learning. Defining learning is more difficult than might be expected for two reasons. First, students have an intuitive notion of what learning is, and they use the term frequently in its vernacular sense. Therefore, they do not immediately see the need for a technical definition. The second reason is intrinsic to the term itself. Hergenhahn (1982) devoted an entire chapter of his textbook attempting to define the term, and Hilgard and Bower (1975) spent nine pages characterizing and defining learning. Two classroom activities were developed to help students

in an upper-division course in learning theories with the task of defining learning.

Activity No. 1: Food for Thought

On the first day of class, students were handed a list of 10 events (see Table 1) and were asked to decide which were examples of learning and which were not. Some of the listed events were clear cases of learning; some were clearly not cases of learning; some were ambiguous. The students discussed the events on the list and generated a fair amount of disagreement on several of the events, particularly those involving computers. In order to defend their assertions that a particular event either was or was not an example of learning, students were asked to propose their own definitions of learning.

At the next class meeting, I presented Hilgard and Bower's (1975) definition of learning:

Learning refers to the change in a subject's behavior to a given situation brought about by his repeated experiences in that situation, provided that due behavior change cannot be explained on the basis of native re-

116

sponse tendencies, maturation, or temporary states of the subject (e.g., fatigue, drugs, etc.). (p. 17)

For our purposes, Hilgard and Bower's definition has two key elements. First, it focuses attention on overt behavior, and for students not familiar with behaviorism, the reasons for focusing on overt behavior must be explained. Second, the definition is (as Hilgard and Bower observed), "peculiar," because it defines learning by exclusion. That is, learning is a change in behavior that cannot be accounted for by other explanations.

Applying the definition to the 10 events yielded fairly clear-cut decisions on most of the examples, but the examples concerning computers generated disagreement. Probably the most common argument against the possibility of a computer demonstrating

Table 1. Events Used in Initial Discussions of the Definition of Learning

1. The cessation of thumb sucking by an infant.
2. The acquisition of language in children.
3. A computer program generates random opening moves for its first 100 chess games and tabulates the outcomes of those games. Starting with the 101st game, the computer uses those tabulations to influence its choice of opening moves.
4. A worm is placed in a T maze. The left arm of the maze is brightly lit and dry; the right arm is dim and moist. On the first 10 trials, the worm turns right 7 times. On the next 10 trials, the worm turns right all 10 times.
5. Ethel stays up late the night before the October GRE administration and consumes large quantities of licit and illicit pharmacological agents. Her combined (verbal plus quantitative) score is 410. The night before the December GRE administration, she goes to bed early after a wholesome dinner and a glass of milk. Her score increases to 1210. Is the change in scores due to learning? Is the change in pretest regimen due to learning?
6. A previously psychotic patient is given Dr. K's patented phrenological surgery and no longer exhibits any psychotic behaviors.
7. A lanky zinnia plant is pinched back and begins to grow denser foliage and flowers.
8. MYCIN is a computer program that does a rather good job of diagnosing human infections by consulting a large data base of rules it has been given. If we add another rule to the data base, has MYCIN learned something?
9. After pondering over a difficult puzzle for hours, Jane finally figures it out. From that point on, she can solve all similar puzzles in the time it takes her to read them.
10. After 30 years of smoking two packs a day, Zeb throws away his cigarettes and never smokes again.

learning was that "a computer does only what it is programmed to do."

Activity No. 2:
A Computer Program That Learns?

The lack of consensus concerning the possibility of a computer learning suggested a second activity. I wrote a computer program that seems to learn, although most people would not attribute much intelligence to it. The program is designed to solve a single class of problems, which can be described in terms of a guessing game. One player thinks of a formula describing Y as some function of χ (e.g., $Y = 4 + 3\chi$). The other player supplies values for χ and requests the corresponding value for Y. When the guesser knows the formula, he or she tries to "guess" the value of Y for a particular value of χ. If three guesses in a row are correct, the game is over and the guesser has accomplished the goal, presumably by deducing the formula. The computer program uses multiple regression to solve the problem and can reliably "figure out" any formula that can be reduced to the form:

$$Y = b_0 + b_1\chi + b_2\chi^2 + b_3\chi^3 + b_4 \operatorname{sqrt}(\chi)$$

After giving a sequence of three correct responses, the program reports the formula.

One class period was devoted to demonstrating the program and providing students with an opportunity to use it. Before the demonstration, I handed out a brief description of the game and an explanation of the computer's claim to learning. The claim seems clearest by analogy. A worm that makes more turns to the right in a T maze after being reinforced in the right arm of the maze is clearly demonstrating learning. Repeated trials that lead the computer to make more correct responses should serve as evidence that the computer has learned.

During the class period, students took turns playing the game against the computer and each other. The students generally used formulas of the form $Y = b_0 + b_1\chi$ and the computer responded appropriately. This formula has two coefficients to solve for; the computer solved the problem in two attempts and then went on to give three correct responses in sequence, for a total of five responses. This performance is similar to the performance of the students in the class whose mean was 5.29 ($SD = 1.57$) responses. One student stumped the computer twice: once with the formula $Y = \chi^{-1}$ and once with the formula $Y = 2^X$. The first of these formulas can be solved by the algorithm used in the program, but it had not been anticipated. The second formula cannot be solved by the regression algorithm used because it is not a linear function.

The exercise took the entire 50-min period (for a class of 17 students) and there was insufficient time for all students to play against the computer. The students left class arguing with one another about whether or not the computer had learned. We spent a portion of the next class meeting following up the activity with further discussion.

Evaluation

The goals of these activities are to help students evaluate their proposed definitions of learning and to arrive at and understand a useful definition of the term. Students often approach definitions uncritically and simply memorize them. Although no formal evaluation was completed, these two activities seem to have been effective in accomplishing these goals. The enthusiasm with which students discussed the definition of learning (during and outside of class and with the instructor and among themselves) suggests that the activities engaged their interest. Students' responses to a short essay question on the midterm exam concerning the meaning of learning were uniformly impressive.

The major drawback to the activities is the time consumed. The activities can be streamlined somewhat by managing the discussion more closely and, if a computer lab is available, assigning the computer exercise to be completed outside of class. The value of devoting a moderately large amount of time to these activities during the first days of class goes beyond the immediate goals of the activities. Because a great deal of controversy was generated, many of the students participated in the discussion, which encouraged active participation in class for the rest of the term.

References

Hergenhahn, B. R. (1982). *An introduction to theories of learning* (2nd ed.). Englewood Cliffs, NJ: Prentice-Hall.

Hilgard, E. R., & Bower, G. H. (1975). *Theories of learning* (4th ed.). Englewood Cliffs, NJ: Prentice-Hall.

2. USING ANIMALS TO TEACH LEARNING

An Inexpensive Habituation and Sensitization Learning Laboratory Exercise Using Planarians

Michael J. Owren
Dana L. Scheuneman
University of Colorado at Denver

We describe an inexpensive laboratory exercise that uses planarians to demonstrate habituation and sensitization. Students drop water from an eyedropper onto a planarian's anterior region and observe its contraction responses. Initially, students practice the procedure until attaining high interobserver reliability in scoring the degree of contraction. Subsequently, they measure the decline in responsivity that occurs over repeated stimulus presentations. Following habituation, the planarian is drawn in and out of the eyedropper several times, resulting in sensitization and dishabituation of the contractile response in accordance with dual-process theory (Groves & Thompson, 1970). This procedure can also be used to demonstrate spontaneous recovery and short-versus long-term habituation processes.

Difficulties associated with demonstrating fundamental learning processes to large groups of students without large costs have inspired many ingenious laboratory exercises requiring simple equipment. One successful approach uses planarians (e.g., *Dugesia dorotocephala*) as experimental subjects. As Katz (1978) noted, planarians occupy a unique position in evolutionary history as the earliest bilaterally symmetric animals. These simple, aquatic, invertebrate flatworms evince synaptic nerve conduction and are capable of learning. Planarians are small (1 to 2 cm long), non-threatening to students, inexpensive, and easy to care for (see Kenk, 1967). Descriptions of planarian anatomy (e.g., Pearse, Pearse, Buchsbaum, & Buchsbaum, 1987; Stachowitsch, 1992) and behavioral biology (e.g., Jenkins, 1967) are readily available. These animals exhibit habituation, classical conditioning, and instrumental conditioning (reviewed by Corning & Kelly, 1973). Descriptions of planarian based laboratory exercises for educational settings are available for classical and instrumental conditioning (e.g., Abramson, 1990; Katz, 1978) but not for habituation and sensitization. The latter phenomena can be shown using other invertebrates (e.g., Abramson, 1990), but the specialized equipment required may make such exercises impracticable with large groups of students.

This article extends the literature concerning the use of planarians in the undergraduate learning laboratory to include the processes of habituation and sensitization. As defined by Groves and Thompson (1970), *habituation* refers to the decrease in responsiveness to a stimulus that can occur as a result of repeated exposure to that stimulus. Conversely, sensitization refers to an increase in responsiveness as a result of stimulation. Groves and Thompson's dual-process theory proposed that habituation is the simplest form of true learning, resulting from experience-based changes in a specific stimulus-response system. Sensitization, in contrast, was hypothesized to result from state changes in a central arousal system that does not reflect a learning process.

A planarian swimming in a Petri dish initially exhibits a reflexive contraction response when a water droplet is released onto or near its anterior region (hereafter referred to as its head). This response declines in magnitude over repeated trials but shows partial or full recovery following moderate physical agitation. We have used this simple, inexpensive preparation in the habituation/sensitization component of an upper division laboratory course in animal learning that has an enrollment of approximately 30 students. Due to limitations in available resources and concerns about the use of more complex vertebrate subjects in the psychology curriculum, the laboratory uses invertebrates as much as possible. Students taking the course must also be enrolled in the corresponding junior-level lecture section, but introductory psychology is the only prerequisite. Laboratory exercises are designed not only to be inexpensive and practicable but also to be appropriate for students who have little or no scientific experience.

Procedure

Planarians can be readily obtained from a biological supply company, as can plastic Petri dishes and eyedroppers. Purchase three or four of these subjects for each individual student or small group. The planarians will probably arrive in a few small water-filled containers, each of which will house many animals. However, individual planarians can easily be transferred to a Petri dish using an eyedropper.

Planarians can easily live for months in a laboratory setting if they are fed regularly and kept at room temperature. If they are to be kept for less than 1 week or so, no care is required other than to leave the top of the shipping container unsealed, thereby oxygenating the water. Otherwise, transfer the planarians to approximately beaker-sized containers filled with nonchlorinated water. These animals are carnivorous and can be maintained indefinitely on raw beef liver. They should be fed as often as every other day and can be safely disposed of in a sink or toilet or released into a spring or stream.

Table 1. A Scale for Scoring the Planarian Contraction Response

Score	Description
0	No response. The planarian remains in extended swimming position.
1	Simple flinch. The planarian responds but without visible shortening of its body.
2	Head retraction. Visible widening of the planarian's body and a concomitant decrease in the head–body distinction.
3	Full contraction. Near or complete loss of the head–body distinction.

Teams of up to three students can work together effectively in the exercise, for instance, by taking turns as experimenter, observer, and data recorder. Each group prepares a Petri dish with enough nonchlorinated water to completely cover the bottom (up to approximately 5 mm) but not so much that the planarian can avoid the impact of a falling water droplet. A planarian is then transferred into the Petri dish.

When fully extended, a planarian can readily be characterized as consisting of head and body sections. When fully contracted, a planarian appears to be an undifferentiated, roughly circular blob. For each trial in the habituation procedure, the experimenter expels one drop of water from the eyedropper onto the planarian's head from approximately 1 cm above the water's surface. There is little or no danger of harming the animal by dropping the water from greater distances, but this height appears sufficient to elicit an unambiguous response. The planarian should be gliding through the water in an extended position away from the side of the Petri dish when the stimulus is delivered. The observer judges the planarian's response on each trial, using a scoring scale like that shown in Table 1. The data recorder transcribes scores and performs interval-timing chores.

Students should establish interobserver reliability using a "practice" planarian before beginning the exercise proper. One might, for instance, require group members to agree on at least 90% of their ratings over at least 10 habituation trials (see Lehner, 1979). Students should also practice drawing the planarian into and expelling it from the eyedropper, the action used to produce sensitization. Although this maneuver is neither particularly difficult nor typically harmful, it can damage the planarian through carelessness or malicious force. The experimenter should also draw a substantial amount of water into the eyedropper along with the planarian; otherwise, the animal may cling to the eyedropper's inside surface and be difficult to expel.

Habituation trials can be conducted at variable or constant intervals, but an interval of at least 10 sec allows time both for the planarian to resume its gliding motion and for the students to prepare for a new trial. As shown in Figure 1, significant habituation can occur in 10 trials. Nonetheless, it may be useful to conduct as many as 50 trials to demonstrate asymptotic short-term habituation. Following these trials, the planarian is sensitized by drawing it into and expelling it from the eyedropper three to five times in rapid succession. This number of sensitizing trials typically produces the effect without much risk of injury to the subject.

Results and Discussion

Data in Figure 1 reflect the responses of 10 planarians tested by student groups in the learning laboratory class. Trials 1 through 11 represent presensitization habituation training and resulted in a statistically significant decline in responsiveness. A repeated measures t test showed a significant difference between the mean contraction scores on Trials 1 and 11, $t(9) = 2.91$, $p < .05$. The planarians were then sensitized, and results from subsequent habituation training appear as Trials 12 through 20. A dishabituation effect occurred on Trial 12, where mean responsiveness increased significantly relative to Trial 11, $t(9) = 3.67$, $p < .05$, but was indistinguishable from Trial 1 scores, $t(9) = .43$, $p > .05$.

Depending on the amount of time available for this exercise, a pause can be inserted following a series of habituation trials to demonstrate spontaneous recovery of the habituated response. Between-groups or within-subjects designs (in which both a pause and the sensitization maneuver occur) can be used. In the latter case, the issue of possible order effects can be raised and examined by counterbalancing the pause and sensitization sequence across student groups and comparing their respective results. A minimum interval of at least 5 to 10 min is suggested for the pause.

Spontaneous recovery following intervals of 1 or more days can be demonstrated if the planarians are kept over a longer period of time. Repeated testing over several days can demonstrate short- versus long-term habituation processes (e.g., Whitlow & Wagner, 1984). Finally, if many subjects are tested, it may be possible to demonstrate the initial sensitization effect that sometimes precedes subsequent habituation to a potent stimulus. This effect is indicated in Figure 1 by a short-lived increase in mean contraction on Trials 3 and 4, but this increase was not statistically significant, $t(9) = 1.96$, $p > .05$.

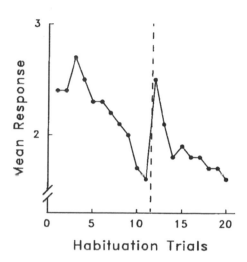

Figure 1. **Mean contraction responses shown by 10 planarians over a series of 20 habituation trials. The sensitizing stimulation occurred between Trials 11 and 12.**

Because our laboratory course does not require exams, we cannot report any quantitative data concerning the pedagogical value of this exercise for understanding the phenomena of habituation and sensitization. Individual laboratory activities are not evaluated, so a formal comparison to other exercises we have used is also impossible. However, this particular exercise appears to be our most successful "canned" experiment. Informally at least, it receives very favorable ratings from students, who deem the experience to be educational and enjoyable. Because our department has no animal facility, we cannot routinely provide students with opportunities to conduct experiments with nonhuman subjects. However, this planarian-based exercise appears to provide a practicable and successful hands-on exercise for the animal learning laboratory.

References

Abramson, C. I. (1990). *Invertebrate teaming: A laboratory manual and source book.* Washington, DC: American Psychological Association.

Coming, W. C., & Kelly, S. (1973). Platyhelminthes: The tubellarians. In W. C. Corning, J. A. Dyal, & A. O. D. Willows (Eds.), *Invertebrate learning: Vol. 1. Protozoans through annelids* (pp. 171-224). New York: Plenum.

Groves, P. M., & Thompson, R. F. (1970). Habituation: A dualprocess theory. *Psychological Review, 77,* 419-450.

Jenkins, M. M. (1967). Aspects of planarian biology and behavior. In W. C. Corning & S. C. Ratner (Eds.), *Chemistry of learning: Invertebrate research* (pp. 116-143). New York: Plenum.

Katz, A. N. (1978) Inexpensive animal learning exercises for huge introductory laboratory classes. *Teaching of Psychology, 5,* 91-93.

Kenk, R. (1967). Species differentiation and ecological relations of planarians. In W. C. Corning & S. C. Ratner (Eds.), *Chemistry of learning: Invertebrate research* (pp. 67-72). New York: Plenum.

Lehner, P. (1979). *Handbook of ethological methods.* New York: Garland STPM Press.

Pearse, V., Pearse, J., Buchsbaum, M., & Buchsbaum, R. (1987). *Living invertebrates.* Palo Alto, CA: Blackwell Scientific.

Stachowitsch, M. (1992). *The invertebrates: An illustrated glossary.* New York: Wiley-Liss.

Whitlow, J. W., Jr., & Wagner, A. R. (1984). Memory and habituation. In H. V. S. Peeke & L. Petrinovich (Eds.), *Habituation, sensitization, and behavior* (pp. 103-153). New York: Academic.

Note

We thank Ruth L. Ault and three anonymous reviewers for numerous helpful comments concerning this article.

Using Gerbils in the Undergraduate Operant Laboratory

Karl Hunt
Rosalie Shields

Many psychology instructors know that conditioning an animal under controlled laboratory conditions is one of the best ways for students to learn basic operant principles. While typically the animal to be conditioned is the albino rat, other animals could be used if there were reasons to do so. We feel that there are reasons to use the Mongolian gerbil (Meriones unguiculatus), and would like to present some of them here. Also, we will mention a few of the unique characteristics of gerbils relevant to conditioning, so that the path may be made easier for those who wish to follow.

Our original motivation for using gerbils was humanitarian. Although we had a well-equipped animal laboratory, we lacked the facilities for keeping animals after they were no longer naive. So they had to be sacrificed. Not wishing to kill the animals, nor to give up the operant laboratory exercises, we decided to try gerbils. We felt that it would be relatively easy to find homes for the gerbils after the students were through with them; not only do individuals keep them in private homes as pets, kindergarten and elementary school teachers like to have them in classrooms .

The lack of aversiveness which makes finding homes for gerbils a feasible proposition also helps in teaching students to handle and work with them. Gerbils are more easily obtained than rats, either at pet stores or from people who have (intentionally or otherwise) bred them at home. This, in turn, allows universities and colleges with limited funds and laboratory facilities to lessen the cost and burden of a student operant lab by using gerbils. If the students buy their own animals and take care of them, the greatest proportion of the cost is eliminated. If necessary, cages and other equipment can be purchased at a local pet store. This is, in effect, asking the students to pay a laboratory fee, just as they might in another course. The cost per student should not exceed seven to ten dollars, if they work in small groups of two or three and split the cost.

There is one disadvantage to gerbils as compared to the usual albino rats, as well as some other important differences. The disadvantage is that gerbils take somewhat longer to condition. Thus, students will usually complete a set of exercises including initial barpress training, extinction, and stimulus discrimination, but will not be able to go on to such things as chaining and intermittent reinforcement as they might with rats. However, we don't feel that this is a total loss by any means, because the students are uniformly successful, and the difficulties encountered are typical of most "real life" applications of operant conditioning.

A major and obvious difference between gerbils and rats is the smaller size of the former. We have found that gerbils are too small for one to successfully employ the usual method of increasing an animal's hunger by systematically depriving it of food until it reaches 80% of its normal weight. The result is that many of the animals become sluggish and often ill, and take an inordinate amount of time to accomplish even magazine training. The alternative method we use is that of feeding the animal for an hour at the same time every day for two to three weeks. Then, once the operant exercises have begun, the animal is not fed at all except for the pellets obtained in the operant chamber and the food provided for the weekends.

Another result of the gerbil's small size is that most ordinary rat-sized operant chambers cannot be used without modification. Of course, if one is starting out with new equipment, smaller, more appropriate chambers can be purchased. However, if one has equipment designed for rats, two changes may have to be made. By far the most extensive change is that of either lowering the bar or replacing it with a more easily pressed bar. The second change is much easier but just as important; a solid floor should be placed in the chamber, as gerbils have a difficult time keeping their footing otherwise. We have used a heavy cardboard mat cut so that it fits snugly against the sides of the chamber.

Gerbils exhibit a number of behaviors which affect their conditioning. During the early stages, i.e., magazine training and shaping the barpress, they will often pause to explore the chamber or engage in chewing or digging. This occurs regardless of their state of deprivation. If an animal doesn't perform whatever act is currently being conditioned within five minutes, we have the students return it to its cage for another 24 hours of deprivation; provided that this doesn't happen more than two days in a row and that the to-be-conditioned behavior has a fairly high probability of occurring.

The chewing and digging often appear when an animal seems to be in state of frustration, as during extinction. There are occasions when students simply have to wait out the digging, as when the animal digs in the food trough in an apparent attempt to get at the source of the food. However, when a gerbil digs at the bar rather than simply pressing it, we have the students engage in some response differentiation in order to eliminate or reduce the frequency of the digging. We like to point out the analogy between the problem of temper tantrums in a child and inappropriate digging in a gerbil. (Digging, of course, is a high-frequency behavior for gerbils, as they are naturally burrowing animals.)

While the foregoing should help anyone interested in using gerbils as operant subjects, there is much more information that we haven't been able to cover here. We have written an instructor's manual (Hunt & Shields, 1977) which goes into more detail, including care and handling.

Reference

Hunt, K., & Shields, R. Instructors manual for the use of Mongolian gerbils (*Meriones Unguiculatus*) in an undergraduate operant laboratory. *JSAS Catalog of Selected Documents in Psychology*, 1977, 7, 97. (Ms. No. 1573)

The Gerbil Jar: A Basic Home Experience in Operant Conditioing

Larry Plant
Niagara County Community College

For several years I have sought a method of making the experience of the fundamental techniques of operant conditioning accessible to large numbers of students taking classes in Introductory psychology. Of high priority in thinking about this objective, is that the system must be: (a) interesting and educationally beneficial to students; (b) relatively inexpensive; and (c) something the students are able to do on their own time.

The advantages of using Mongolian Gerbils in the undergraduate operant laboratory have been detailed elsewhere (Hunt & Shields, 1978). In my classes at Niagara County Community College, students are introduced to conditioning concepts through standard textbook assignments and class lecture presentations. As an optional experience students elect to view a videotaped demonstration of shaping a gerbil to perform various simple operant tasks, i.e., lever pressing or bell ringing, (the videotape is placed on closed reserve at the Library Learning Center). They are then given a gerbil and an operant conditioning chamber to take home to explore these processes on their own.

The operant chamber is a modified glass gallon pickle or olive jar (plastic containers are unsatisfactory as gnawing gerbils will quickly chew an escape). The large jars are readily available from local restaurants who seem willing to save them upon request. The essential process in the rather simple modification of the jar is the capacity to drill various holes in the side for installation of a food magazine, water, and ventilation. This is accomplished with a carbide drill bit specifically designed for drilling glass. Because the gerbils are so small, conventional rat chambers are unsatisfactory and would have to be modified. A gallon pickle jar is an ideal substitute in terms of size, visibility, convenience and cost.

Shelled raw sunflower seed is the reinforcer of choice in my experience with gerbils. The standard beginning exercise is for students to train the gerbil to ring a bell which is suspended on a string from the top of the jar.

Shaping, extinction, generalization, discrimination and various schedules of reinforcement are all explorable on an independent (home) study basis. The student is provided with a mimeographed handout which explains these concepts as well as deprivation schedules, and gives further details and hints as to their specific application. Enthusiastic students have advanced to more difficult operant tasks for their gerbils such as back flips and lifting and carrying various small objects. Coupled with selected readings on behavior modification, the introductory student through his experiences with the "gerbil jar" achieves a firm experiential understanding of both the process and relevance of operant conditioning. Feedback from students indicates that the gerbil training experience is positively reinforcing for them as well as the gerbil.

The costs are insignificant especially when compared to commercial operant chambers which range from sixty to several hundred dollars. Large numbers of "gerbil jars" can be prepared in a few hours for pennies each. To provide a continuous supply of naive gerbils at NCCC, we maintain a small breeding colony at a total cost of approximately $300 per year. For those colleges without the facilities to maintain a gerbil colony, students might be encouraged to purchase a gerbil from a local pet store.

Specific jar modification details are available upon request.

Reference

Hunt, K., & Shields, R., Using gerbils in the undergraduate operant laboratory. *Teaching of Psychology*, 1978, *5*, 210-211

Teaching the Principles of Operant Conditioning Through Laboratory Experience: The Rat Olympics

Paul R. Solomon
Williams College

David L. Morse
State University College, New Paltz

Somewhere in the program of an undergraduate psychology major, most students have the opportunity to gain first hand experience in operant conditioning (see Maas & Kleiber, 1976; Siegel, 1975). In many instances, this takes the form of shaping a rat to perform several tasks (see Michael, 1963; Reese, 1964). Although advanced students generally appreciate the important role operant conditioning has played in understanding behavior, it is often difficult to convey this to the beginning student. Consequently, it has been our experience that when students are first asked to operantly condition a rat, they do not always approach the task enthusiastically. But once students begin to apply the principles of operant conditioning, their interest grows considerably. We have used "The Rat Olympics" technique over the past eight years to help students overcome initial reluctance.

The Rat Olympics. Although the rat olympics could be incorporated into a number of courses we have always used it in the context of a course in the Psychology of Learning. As part of the course requirements, each student conducts a laboratory project carried out during the second half of the semester after exposure to some of the subject matter. Prior to conducting the project, each student meets with the instructor to design the experiment or demonstration. The projects

have ranged from demonstrations of classical eyelid conditioning in rabbits to studies on memory for text in humans. In lieu of conducting traditional experiments, we also offer the students the opportunity to compete in the rat olympics. The proportion of students who have opted for it during any one semester has ranged from 30-50 percent.

The rat olympics consists of a competition between student-rat teams. At the beginning of the olympics we specify a number of behaviors ("events") which can be shaped using operant conditioning techniques and which rats can perform with varying degrees of proficiency. Although the responses to be shaped vary from semester to semester, we typically include highest number of bar presses during a two minute period, best discrimination, and longest behavioral chain. Each student or group of students who participates enters one animal in each of two events. (Because some behaviors require large blocks of time, we encourage students to work in groups of two or three.) In this way we have three to five students in each of three events.

We indicate to the students that they may use any techniques to condition their animals as long as it follows humane guidelines (we review APA and NIH guidelines for use of animals). We also indicate the kinds of assistance that we will provide. For example, a student can always ask for references about any topic To facilitate this we distribute an annotated bibliography. The students may also request any form of technical help. We do not, however, answer very broad questions such as what schedule of reinforcement produces the highest number of responses during extinction, or how do I train my rat to discriminate. In response to this type of question we refer the student to the pertinent references. Once the student has identified and read the important papers, we are happy to discuss the details and give advice so he or she can implement the procedures.

The students are given the last six weeks of the semester to train their animals. At the end of this time the rat olympics are held.

Responses of Rats and Students. During the eight years that we have been conducting the rat olympics we have seen a wide range of methods used by students to shape their animals. Some have been remarkably innovative and successful. Others have had their difficulties. In this section we will briefly define the events and present some of the methodologies and techniques that the students have used.

Highest Number of Bar Presses. The procedure for this task is straightforward. The animal is placed in the operant chamber and permitted to make 10 bar press responses. If necessary, the students are permitted to use a shaping procedure during this stage. After the tenth response, we time a two minute period and record the number of bar presses the rat makes.

One common training tactic that we have seen students use, at least initially, is the commonsense approach of overtraining the animal. They train their animals daily and often twice a day on a continuous reinforcement schedule. But as they quickly discover, the animals reach asymptotic levels which are not very high (they also have problems with satiating the animal). Better informed students have taken the more successful approach of using different schedules of reinforcement. Many students do thorough literature surveys to determine optimal parameters for training. We have seen all varieties of fixed and variable ratio schedules and even a few attempts at compound schedules. Perhaps the most industrious attempts involve physiological techniques. For example, one group of students implanted electrodes in the medial forebrain bundle, a brain area which produces high rates of self stimulation (see Phillips & Mogensen, 1978, for a review), and trained their animals to bar press for brain stimulation. It is noteworthy that these students had no prior experience with stereotaxic surgery or brain stimulation. Another group of students took this one step further. They discovered through their literature search that increased brain catecholamine levels facilitated bar pressing for brain stimulation (e.g., Stein & Wise, 1969). Consequently, they gave their animals d-amphetamine prior to the animal's bar pressing for brain stimulation.

Best Discrimination. This event consists of four one-minute periods. During the first and third minutes a cue light is on, and each bar press produces a reinforcer. During the second and fourth minutes the light is off and a bar press does not produce a reinforcer. To determine the success of the animal we divide the number of responses when the light is on by the total number of responses. The object is to have the animal with highest ratio. As was the case with the first task, the rat is given a ten-response warm-up period prior to the first minute.

Students (like researchers) have tried a number of ways to produce sharp generalization gradients. Some students simply overtrained their animals on the reinforced stimulus. As many studies have shown, this is not the most efficacious method (see Moore, 1972). A somewhat more successful approach involved discrimination training. Other students have increased the rate of responding to the reinforced stimulus by using partial reinforcement schedules. But the most successful, and in our opinion also the most innovative, approach we have seen to date was conducted by a group of students who trained their rats using an errorless discrimination procedure (see Terrace, 1963). This procedure produced virtually flawless discrimination at the olympics.

Longest Behavioral Chain. This is the task which attracts the greatest attention. It is also our impression that it entails the most work. The evaluation of performance in this task is somewhat less objective than in the previous two. We not only consider the number of discrete acts the animal completes, but we also attempt to evaluate how difficult each behavior was to shape

During any semester we see chains which involve only a few responses such as pulling a string to turn on a light which serves as a discriminative stimulus for bar pressing for a reinforcer, to rather complex chains involving many behaviors. Perhaps the most elaborate chain, and one which gives an idea of how much work some students carry out, is the following:[1] the rat climbed over a wooden block which gave it access to an inverted cup; picked up the cup to uncover a small bell; picked up the bell and actually rang it; that produced a loop which dropped from the ceiling; the rat pulled the loop down and jumped through it; this produced a house light which served as the discriminative stimulus for bar pressing. The final link of the chain was for the animal to press the bar for a food pellet.

Evaluating Student Performance. During the six weeks in which the students are training their animals we ask them to keep a log. This indicates how much time they spent with their animals each day, what they did, and how successful they were. The log is quite important in certain instances because a rat may "freeze" during the olympics. If so, the log can show that the students had devoted a good deal of time and energy to their project despite their rat's poor performance. We are, of course, much more interested in what each student has learned during the course of the project than in the rat's performance, although it is sometimes difficult to convince the students of this.

At the end of the semester, each student submits a modified laboratory report, including their literature survey. The methods section indicates the techniques they used, and the results and discussion sections are an evaluation of the success of each method as well I as suggestions for improvement

In addition to having the log, laboratory report, and performance in the rat olympics to give us an idea of the effort of each student, we attempt to monitor weekly progress by simply observing students working with their animals. This usually takes little initiative on our part since there seems to be a constant influx of students who want to show us what their rat is doing (or not doing).

References

Maas, J. B. & Kleiber, D. *A Directory of teaching innovations in psychology.* Washington, DC: American Psychological Association, 1976.

Michael, J. *Laboratory studies in operant behavior.* New York: McGraw-Hill, 1963.

Moore, J. W. Stimulus control: Studies of auditory generalization in rabbits, In A. H. Black and W. F. Prokasy (Eds.) *Classical conditioning II: Current theory and research.* New York: Appleton-Century-Crofts, 1972.

Phillips, A. G., & Mogenson, G. J. Brain stimulation and reward: Current issues and future prospects. *Canadian Journal of Psychology/Review of Canadian Psychology,* 1978, *32,* 124-128.

Reese, E. *Experiments in operant behavior.* New York: Appleton Century-Crofts, 1964.

Siegel, M. H. Symposium: Teaching the experimental psychology course. *Teaching of Psychology,* 1975, *4,* 162-163.

Stein, L. & Wise, C. D. Release of norepinephrine from hypothalamus and amygdala by rewarding stimulation and amphetamine. *Journal of Comparative and Physiological Psychology,* 1969, *67,* 189-198.

Terrace, H. S. Discrimination learning with and without "errors." *Journal of the Experimental Analysis of Behavior,* 1963, *6,* 1–27.

Note

This animal was trained by Heather Laird, Anne Ricketson, and Carl Tippit.

A Classical Conditioning Laboratory for the Psychology of Learning Course

Gary B. Nallan
D. Mark Bentley
University of North Carolina at Asheville

Laboratory exercises in the psychology of learning course can help students understand the principles of conditioning, learning, and memory. This article describes a classical conditioning lab project that involves rats and operant conditioning equipment. The conditioned stimulus (CS) is a light, the unconditioned stimulus (UCS) is food, and the conditioned responses (CRs) are rearing (standing on the hind legs) and magazine (standing motionless in front of the food magazine with nose or head in the magazine). Students observe the rats and record these behaviors. The lab exercises described in this article can be accomplished in 4 to 5 weeks. Additional exercises could expand the lab to a full semester.

Many courses in the psychology of learning include laboratories. Such labs typically involve a series of operant conditioning exercises with rats, including shaping of the lever-press response, simple schedules of reinforcement, generalization and discrimination, and chaining a series of behaviors. Manufacturers of operant equipment (e.g., BRS/LVE and Lafayette) offer student operant boxes designed for such labs. We have had a lab option in our department for several years. Students in our learning course may choose this lab or a traditional term paper. (Students who elect the lab also write up their project.) Students enjoy the lab and report that it makes the lecture and textbook material on operant conditioning "come alive" for them.

We think that it is also important for students to have the opportunity to learn about classical (Pavlovian) conditioning in the laboratory. As Rescorla (1988) pointed out, classical conditioning is one of the most frequently studied psychological phenomena, but it is often misunderstood and misrepresented.

We developed a classical conditioning lab as another option for our learning course. This lab uses rats and the same conditioning chamber as the operant conditioning lab. The classical conditioning lab is derived from the work of Holland and his associates (Holland, 1977, 1980; Holland & Ross, 1981). Holland found that when a light (CS) was paired with the presentation of a food pellet (UCS), rats exhibited two distinct CRs. One CR was rearing, which was standing on the hind legs with both front paws off the floor. This occasionally included stretching to the full extent. The other CR was magazine, which was the act of standing motionless in front of the food magazine with nose or head in the magazine.

We offered our classical conditioning lab for the first time in the fall of 1989. The lab was limited to four students who worked in pairs. Each student was assigned a laboratory rat, and the students and the animals had several get-acquainted sessions. As in our operant lab, the students learned to care for their animal, including daily weighing, watering, and controlled feedings. (The animals were free-fed for several weeks before the lab. Students calculated the target 80% weight and used the controlled feedings to reduce the rats' weight to target weight.) The students were also taught to operate the lab equipment during the get-acquainted sessions .

The chamber used was manufactured by BRS/LVE. Both sides of the box were clear plastic. The interior dimensions were 31.1 x 24.1 x 25.4 cm. One end panel contained two operant conditioning levers (nonfunctional for the classical conditioning lab). The food cup was centered on this end panel, 2.5 cm above the floor. Three lights were equally spaced on this panel, 15.2 cm above the floor. Only the center light was used in the classical conditioning lab. The chamber was located in a room with an observational one-way mirror. Students used electromechanical switching circuitry, located in a room on the other side of this mirror, to present the light alone, a food pellet alone, or to pair the light with delivery of a food pellet.

Lab sessions lasted approximately 1 hr (i.e., ½ hr per subject). Students used the first sessions to magazine train the rats. They were cautioned to avoid any accidental operant reinforcement of specific behaviors. Magazine training took 2 or 3 sessions and ended when the rat consistently approached and ate food pellets. Students observed and recorded behaviors, including rearing, magazine, freezing, and sleeping. Throughout the lab sessions, the pairs of students took turns operating the equipment and observing behaviors.

After magazine training, students conducted five sessions pairing the light with food (acquisition). There were 10 trials in each session. The light presentations were 10 s. The intertrial intervals were randomly selected from 1, 1.5, and 2 min. chosen about equally often (the three intervals appeared at least three times in each session). Students observed the rats for the critical CRs (rearing and magazine) during the 10-s light presentations and during the 10 s before the trials. During acquisition, all four rats displayed clear increases in rearing and magazine during the 10-s light presentations, but not in the 10 s before the light presentations

Next, students conducted five sessions identical to acquisition, but with no food delivery (extinction). All four rats yielded clear extinction curves by Day 3.

Last, students conducted five sessions identical to acquisition (reacquisition). By Day 3, clear reacquisition curves were obtained in both rearing and magazine CRs, and these occurred at the same levels attained in Days 4 and 5 of acquisition. The rats' performance stabilized across Days 3 to 5 of reacquisition, indicating asymptotic performance.

Each student submitted a 10- to 12-page paper based on this project. The papers contained: (a) an introduction, including background information from Holland (1977); (b) a procedure and observations section, including discussion of all procedures and findings as well as tables or graphs; and (c) a summary and conclusions section, including discussion of principles learned and insights gained during the lab experience. The papers were quite good and a pleasure to read. Each paper ended with comments, and we obtained permission from the students to mention their reactions.

All four students were enthusiastic about the lab and said that they learned a lot about the classical conditioning process. Students found it more meaningful to observe classical conditioning than just to hear or read about it. One of the students, an animal rights advocate, complimented us on our ethical treatment of the animals, and she was glad that we used food rather than shock as the UCS.

This lab could be developed into a semester-long series of exercises. Holland (1977) reported that a tone paired with food leads to different CRs (startle and head jerk) than a light paired with food. With the lab described in this article plus the use of tone as an additional CS, exercises demonstrating generalization, discrimination, spontaneous recovery, overshadowing, and blocking could be developed.

Another popular operant conditioning procedure uses pigeons trained to peck an illuminated disk for grain reinforcement. Teachers with this lab arrangement could also develop a classical conditioning lab for the learning course. Brown and Jenkins (1968) reported that pairing an illuminated disk (CS) with presentation of grain (UCS) led to approach and pecking CRs. They labeled this procedure *autoshaping.* Interested readers should see the monograph by Hearst and Jenkins (1974), which includes many references to the autoshaping literature. More recently, autoshaping has had substantial impact on theoretical conceptualizations of classical conditioning (see Rescorla, 1988).

Some people who teach the learning course have time, space, and equipment limitations that preclude laboratories. Under these circumstances, classroom demonstrations of conditioning are recommended. The same rat or pigeon equipment can be used to demonstrate both classical and operant conditioning in the classroom.

References

Brown, P. L., & Jenkins, H. M. (1968). Auto-shaping of the pigeons key-peck. *Journal of the Experimental Analysis of Behavior, 11*, 1-8.

Hearst, E., & Jenkins, H. M. (1974). *Sign tracking: The stimulus-reinforcer relation and directed action.* Austin, TX: Psychonomic Society.

Holland, P. C. (1977). Conditioned stimulus as a determinant of the form of the Pavlovian conditioned response. *Journal of Experimental Psychology: Animal Behavior Processes, 3*, 77-104.

Holland, P. C. (1980). Second-order conditioning with and without unconditioned stimulus presentation. *Journal of Experimental Psychology: Animal Behavior Processes, 6*, 238-250.

Holland, P. C., & Ross, R. T. (1981). Within-compound associations in serial compound conditioning. *Journal of Experimental Psychology: Animal Behavior Processes, 7*, 228-241.

Rescorla, R. A.(1988). Pavlovian conditioning: It's not what you think it is. *American Psychologist, 43*, 151-160.

Note

We thank the four students who participated in the classical conditioning laboratory: Christy Hollingsworth, Lisa Jackson, Allison Smith, and Teri Thomas. We gratefully acknowledge the helpful comments on an earlier version of this article by Charles L. Brewer, Kathleen A. Nallan, and three anonymous reviewers.

Chickens in the Classroom: Introductory Laboratory Courses in Experimental Psychology

James E. Ackil
Eric F. Ward
Western Illinois University

Most psychology departments offer and many require their undergraduate majors to complete an introductory laboratory course in experimental psychology. In common with students in other psychology courses, students in the experimental course are introduced to research methods in psychology by having them read and discuss scientific methodology and research design. The unique aspect of this course is that the students also are required to conduct experiments during the class. This requirement is intended to give the students first hand experience in a variety of research activities including searching the literature, formulating a hypothesis, designing a study, conducting an experiment, analyzing and interpreting data, and writing a research report. Such activities are designed to provide an appreciation and understanding of scientific psychology as well as help in the acquisition of research skills.

In our laboratory course in experimental psychology at Western Illinois University, students conduct research in a variety of areas such as human memory and cognition, psychophysics, personality, social psychology, animal behavior, and animal learning. As is common in many laboratory courses, the animal behavior and animal learning portions of this course have traditionally used rats as subjects. Although the animal section of the course constitutes only a few weeks out of the semester, the course is often labeled "rat lab" by the students.

The use of animal subjects in the introductory experimental course is attractive because it leads to appreciation of the advantages and problems associated with animal studies. For the instructor the use of animals offers increased control of scheduling and organization of laboratory exercises.

Rats have been used with some success as subjects for these exercises, but their use has not been free of problems. One of the problems is the expense involved. The primary expense is the initial cost and shipping. In our location, sexually mature male rats cost approximately $4.00 each, including shipping. If younger rats are ordered the cost of maintaining them until they are of a useful age offsets any lower initial cost. General maintenance of rats is also expensive as it involves the cost of caretakers, bedding material, and food. An additional expense is the equipment needed for conducting experiments. Because rats are inveterate chewers, equipment must be made of heavy materials, preferably metal. A final expense is the humane disposal of rats once the animal portion of the course is completed. Because of their varied experiences in the laboratory course these animals can seldom be used in other experiments and so are usually sacrificed, costing in staff time and drug expense.

Another problem presented by the use of rats as subjects is the time necessary in pretraining the animals for experimentation This pretraining includes handling (gentling), magazine training, and shaping of instrumental responses. Pretraining activities usually take students a minimum of three to four sessions. Using three or four class sessions for pretraining takes time away from actual experimentation, either stealing time from animal experiments or from other portions of the course. In addition, the deprivation level of rats must be carefully controlled and this requires additional staff time either to take care of the deprivation or to supervise the students in such care.

A final problem in using rats has been in the actual handling of the animals. On rare occasions students have been bitten. While this does not pose a serious health or safety problem it does contribute to the apprehension many students feel when asked to handle rats Some students exhibit a phobic reaction and are unable to work with rats at all. Also, allergic reactions to rats are fairly common among students and instructors.

The Use of Chicks. Our solution to the problems arising from the use of rats as subjects in the experimental psychology laboratory course has been to use 2-4 week old chickens. It has been our experience that the use of chicks as subjects eliminates the problems encountered when using rats and even provides some additional benefits.

In terms of cost, chickens are very inexpensive. When we first began using them in 1973, they were approximately two cents each, less than the cost of an egg. Presently, day-old white Leghorn cockerels cost about fifteen cents each and are available in all parts of the country from poultry farms. We have found that conditioning chambers made of cardboard boxes are adequate for work with chicks, and, of course, are a negligible expense. Disposal of chicks at the end of the experiments is not a problem as area farmers are not only happy to get a supply of 4-6 week old chicks, but are willing to pick them up from the laboratory. During one term we used Cornish game birds. They worked equally well and were disposed of at the end of the experiment even more easily than were Leghorns.

Using chicks also leads to considerable savings in time. Unlike rats, chicks require virtually no gentling and very little adaptation time. In fact they can be adapted to a conditioning chamber and shaped to keypeck for food by most students in a single 30 minute session. We have yet to have a student fail to shape the keypeck response by the end of the second session. This kind of success is rare with rats. Another saving in staff time is gained because chicks this young are voracious eaters and will perform well for food with a minimum of deprivation. Because there is virtually no time spent in adapting the chicks, and because they can acquire an operant response so quickly, much more time is available for carrying out experiments.

In contrast to rats, handling chicks has presented no problems. Of course, no student has yet been injured by a chick. The students are not afraid of the chicks, and most find them "cute" and fun to handle. In addition no students or staff have yet shown an allergic reaction to them.

In addition to providing a solution to the problems we experienced with rats, we have found that using chicks offers additional benefits. One benefit is that each student can quickly build a conditioning chamber, allowing all students to have individual chambers and subjects instead of having to share. Constructing a conditioning chamber for chicks takes only 20-30 minutes and can easily be done at home by the students.[1] Chicks quickly show the effects of reinforcement schedules, quality of reinforcement, and other effects, as well as the initial operant. Data from these student-run experiments are almost indistinguishable from data produced in automated laboratories using pigeons or rats. The fact that chicks possess color vision adds greatly to the variety of discrimination problems that can be studied. Indeed, the students seem to understand the logic of color discrimination experiments better than they understand the logic of brightness or pattern discrimination.

A final attribute of chicks, one which may be responsible for many of the advantages already cited, is the lack of "nervousness" inherent in the birds. Rats are often frightened by noises, but the chicks seem impervious to this sort of distraction. This characteristic allows the instructor to interact while experiments are being conducted without disturbing the performance of the animals.

In sum, we have been very pleased with the results of several years experience with using chickens in the introductory undergraduate laboratory course in experimental psychology We think you and your budget will appreciate them as well.

Note

Various sizes and types of chambers have been constructed by our students over the years, but all have had one or more one inch diameter holes in a wall behind which a stimulus can be displayed. For stimulus display, a cardboard wheel pinned to the wall behind the key peck hole is positioned so that turning the wheel exposes a new stimulus. This simple system works very nicely. The chambers also all contain a food tray which can be slid into the box beneath the pecking key(s) for delivery of reinforcement. For reinforcement we use a poultry starter which is used as the home cage diet as well. A good source for ideas about constructing chambers and for uses of birds in the experimental laboratory course is Reese, Ellen P. *Experiments in operant behavior*, 1964: Appleton, Century, Crofts. N. Y.

On the Use of Chicks as Experimental Laboratory Subjects

David L. Rowland,
Emily K. Jordan and
Mark Olson
Valparaiso University

In a recent article in this journal, Ackil and Ward (1982) reported on the use of chicks as experimental subjects for an introductory laboratory course in psychology. Stimulated by that report, we decided to use chicks in an upper level laboratory course on animal learning. This particular course had traditionally relied on rats as experimental subjects; however, because rats serve as subjects in all of our other animal laboratory courses, we felt that exposure of students to the behavior of a different species might have pedagogical value as well as the practical value indicated by Ackil and Ward (1982). Indeed, as these authors have suggested, chicks do offer several advantages over rats; however, in our case, the transition from a rat lab to a chick lab was hampered by our lack of specific knowledge regarding the physical and behavioral characteristics of chickens. In the following paragraphs, we offer suggestions designed to supplement the information provided by Ackil and Ward, suggestions that might be helpful to other instructors considering the use of chicks for a lab course in psychology. In addition, we gathered student feedback on the chick laboratory through a short survey, the results of which are presented below.

Subjects. The greatest restriction on the use of chicks in our area is their availability. Hatcheries in our northwest Indiana locale do not hatch chicks during the winter months, the date of the earliest availability being the first week of March, the latest being about mid-September. Thus, a conditioning experiment that was planned for implementation in January had to be postponed until after spring break in March.

Size and rate of growth are also important considerations. The local hatchery supplied us with 2-week old Cornish-White Rock hybrids, fryer-type birds. These chicks are bred for rapid growth, standing over 6 in. tall at the time of purchase and nearly full grown by the end of a 3-week experiment. Such factors have important implications for the design and construction of housing and experimental chambers. We have since learned that egg-laying varieties of chickens (e.g., Rhode Island Reds) are slower-growing birds and therefore would be more suitable for an experiment lasting more than a week or two.

Despite the above limitations, in most respects chicks did afford a significant advantage over rats. Two week old chicks are inexpensive ($0.95 each), locally available, easily tamed, and readily disposed. An area farm, for example, was quite eager to take all of the chickens at the end of the experiment.

Housing. Housing arrangements were fairly simple once we learned the basic rules for warmth, food, and water. We acquired a metal chick housing unit from our university's biology department; but any cages that are about 12 in. high with an open metal grid floor would have sufficed. The five=tiered communal compartments on our unit contained 60-watt red light bulbs to maintain a temperature of about 85°F, a necessity for chicks of less than 2-3 weeks in age. Inexpensive water fonts ($0.85 each) were obtained from the hatchery. These fonts screwed onto inverted Mason jars and were placed directly into the housing compartments. Food arrangements might be more problematic, particularly if converted rodent cages are being used to house the chicks. Our unit came equipped with feeder trays lying outside of, but attached to, the living compartments. Wire grating prevented the chicks from stepping over the trays and out of the cages. The outside placement of the feeder trays is essential to keep the food clean, dry, and free of droppings. Before we realized we would have access to chick cages, we had considered cutting openings in our rodent cages and attaching butter tray lids (upside down) to the outside for feeder trays.

Chicks being hearty eaters, we used 50 lbs. of starter feed for a dozen chicks over a three week period. Fortunately, the started feed was inexpensive ($6.00 for 50 lbs.), eliminated the need for grit, and was available from the hatchery or local grain feed store. On the other hand, it was necessary to change the litter every 2nd or 3rd day in order to keep the odor at a tolerable level, even in a well-ventilated area. Our chicks were housed four to a cage making individual identification necessary; this can be accomplished by marking the head or back of the animal with felt pens of different colors (Stokes, 1975).

Conditioning Apparatus and Procedure. Several different approaches have been taken toward the construction of experiment conditioning chambers (Ackil & Ward, 1982; Reese, 1964). Unlike the temporary, disposable test boxes described in these reports, we wanted to construct chambers that would combine durability for long term use with minimal effort and cost. We converted four manual operant chambers originally designed for rats (9½ X 8½ X 8 in.) into chicken chambers for less than $100 each. By removing one end of the chamber and replacing it with a template designed to accommodate an illuminated pecking key and manual grain feeder (both available from Tech-Serv, Inc.), we were able to construct experimental chambers usable for continuous reinforcement, intermittent reinforcement, and discrimination learning. In keeping with Reese's (1964) suggestions for pigeons, the food aperture of the chamber was

2-in. square; the pecking key was located 6-8 in. above the floor of the box.

Within a period of nine 40-min. sessions (distributed over three weeks), inexperienced students were able to shape the chicks, bring them to a VR 10 or FR 10 schedule of reinforcement, and train them on a color discrimination task. We found that 3 hours of food deprivation, although not essential, facilitated the conditioning process. Specifically, by following a slightly modified version of Reese's (1964) procedure for training pigeons, chicks were hopper-trained and shaped in two sessions, had reached a ratio schedule of reinforcement by about the sixth session, and had learned color discrimination by the ninth. Indeed, this fast pace was not only desirable from the standpoint of efficient use of laboratory time, but it was necessitated by the rapid growth rate of the chicks which were outgrowing the experiment chambers. After having worked with rats in a similar capacity for five years, we were surprised by the exceptional visual discrimination learning ability of the chick. Although establishment of a VR 10 did pose some problems for our chicks (one subject never learned the task), their performance was certainly comparable to that demonstrated by rats.

Student Reactions. At the end of the 3 week experiment, student reaction to the use of chicks was assessed with a survey. All 17 students in the lab had been exposed to rats earlier in the semester in an experiment on motivation and frustration, and, therefore, they had some basis for evaluating the use of chicks in comparison with rats. The results of the survey (Table 1) indicate that the students responded favorably to our conditioning lab using chicks (Items 1, 2, & 3). In comparison with rats, however, there was no definitive preference for chicks (Items 4 & 5); and, in fact, there was a clear problem in handling the chicks as they

Table 1. Student Reaction to the Use of Chicks as Experimental Animals

Item	Mean (N = 17)	SD
Learning experience	2.53	1.59
Demonstrated principles associated with the experiment	2.19	1.17
Demonstrated value of particular species in conditioning behavior	2.06	1.03
Rats would have demonstrated principles as well	3.30	1.50
Less fear of chicks than rats	3.82	1.91
Easier to handle than rats	5.47	1.94
No problem in handling chicks as they grew in size	5.94	1.48
With no prior lab experience, would prefer chicks to rats	5.16	1.73
Recommend experimental use of chicks to other students	3.24	1.72

Note. Reaction scale was 1 to 7 where 1 = strongly agree and 7 = strongly disagree.

full maturity (Items 6 & 7). Students felt that were it a choice between one or the other species for a novice lab student, rats would be preferred (Item 8).

Our overall reaction to the use of chicks in our course on animal learning was positive. With respect to economy and convenience, we can only reiterate the benefits mentioned by Ackil and Ward (1982). From a pedagogical standpoint, chicks were conditioned easily, they demonstrated various principles of operant learning well, and they exposed students to the behavior of a different species. From the students' viewpoint, the reaction to the use of chicks varied. The major problem stemmed from the difficulty experienced in handling older chickens, but this problem could be remedied by using younger or slower-growing chicks.

References

Ackil, J. E., & Ward, E. F. Chickens in the classroom: Introductory laboratory courses in experimental psychology. *Teaching of Psychology*, 1982, *9*, 107-108.

Reese, E. P. *Experiments in operant behavior.* New York: Appleton-Century-Crofts, 1964.

Stokes, A. W. Social organization and courtship behavior in chickens. In E. O. Price & A. W. Stokes (Eds.), *Animal behavior in laboratory and field.* San Francisco: Freeman, 1975.

3. TEACHING CLASSICAL CONDITIONING

Classical Salivary Conditioning: An Easy Demonstration

Dennis Cogan and Rosemary Cogan
Texas Tech University

Most creatures learn, but the direct experience of learning often seems to bear little resemblance to the principles of learning which we teach in our introductory courses and our courses in the psychology of learning. The principles of acquisition, extinction, spontaneous recovery, and generalization displayed so neatly on gradually changing curves in our textbooks seem for most students far removed from the insightful grasping of new material that students readily recognize as learning. No amount of lecturing, giving of examples, or drawing of graphs can serve to replace the immediate understanding produced by direct experience (Dewey, 1967).

Over the years, we have tried several techniques for illustrating fundamental learning principles in the classroom, concentrating particularly on simple classically conditioned responses (Pavlov, 1928). We have carried out defensive conditioning of the eyeblink response and found this difficult for students to observe. We have demonstrated conditioning of the patellar tendon reflex which is more obvious to the observing student, but lacks immediacy of experience and relevance to everyday life. Gibb (1983) has described a relatively straight-forward demonstration of GSR conditioning which, in addition to the usual objections, also requires considerable instrumentation. We have developed a demonstration of classical conditioning which can be experienced by every member of a large group in a single one-hour class period with minimal outlay for equipment. In addition, it has relevance to daily living and is enjoyable by all but the most jaded participant. The purpose of this presentation is to describe the demonstration and what it can achieve pedagogically.

Method. The equipment necessary for this demonstration consists of one can of sweetened lemonade powder (e.g., Minute Maid) and a sufficient number of small cups so that each member of the group has his or her own (the cups used for mustard or ketchup in the university cafeteria are convenient and economical). The demonstration is usually carried out early in the semester, after an explanation of the place Pavlov holds in the history of psychology, and a discussion of the principles of the Pavlovian method (i.e., definitions of CS, UCS, CR, & UCR and their relationship to each other).

After each student has been given the lemonade powder, we choose some neutral stimulus to serve as a CS. Usually the students have no suggestions and we choose the word "Pavlov." The instructions consist of telling the students to moisten the tip of the index finger of their preferred hand and to watch the instructor for the signal to "dip" the moistened finger into the lemonade powder and transfer a small amount to the tip of their tongues. The signal for the transfer should be some easily discernable sign, such as the raising of the instructor's hand or arm The CS is given (the name Pavlov spoken by the instructor), and, after some small delay (usually .5 to 1.5 seconds), the visual signal for transfer of the lemonade powder is given Through trial and error we have discovered that most of our students are not able to detect an anticipatory salivary response in the optimal CS-UCS interval of 5 to 1.5 seconds. In order for them to experience the conditioned salivary response, we introduced the idea of test trials. During the instructions the students are told that every so often the instructor will say the words "test trial" instead of giving the signal for putting the lemonade powder on the tongue. On such a trial the student is to refrain from applying the CS and concentrate on observing their own experience. Before continuing on to the next conditioning trial we usually ask for a show of hands of those who salivated on the test trial. Trials are given at ten to fifteen second intervals, and test trials given after every 5 to 15 conditioning trials. The more frequently one gives test trials, the slower acquisition tends to be. Test trials every 10 conditioning trials works well in fifty minute classes.

These data were taken with the students' eyes open, so it is possible that suggestion may have affected the data. On several other occasions, we have asked the students to keep their eyes closed while reporting salivation, and the results have been virtually identical.

When most or all of the students have demonstrated conditioning, extinction is begun, using the same test trial procedure. Extinction should be completed during the same class period. During the next class period (usually two days later) it is possible to demonstrate spontaneous recovery, reacquisition, and stimulus generalization.

The presence of conditioned responses is tracked by the show of hands method. These data may be plotted in the usual fashion as either number or percent CRs as a function of number of test trials or number of conditioning trials (see Fig. 1 for an example from our own classes). In addition to the data on the number of conditioned responses, we have also found it valuable and interesting to pass out a brief questionnaire evaluating the nature and details of the experience as well as its perceived value. We ask the students if they experienced such things as a lemon taste, "puckering," the graininess of the lemonade crystals, etc. In general, most of the students have experienced a salivary response which is strong for some (41%) and moderate for most (52%). Other aspects of the salivary response often experienced include the taste of lemon flavor crystals (44%), and a "puckering" feeling (41%). Most of the students (96%) reported enjoying the demonstration and the same proportion felt the demonstration to be helpful or very helpful in facilitating their understanding of conditioning phenomena.

In addition to the very positive student response, the events occurring during the demonstration (we usually plotted the data from the test trials on the board as they were obtained) provoke a great deal of interaction and questions. Most of the reactions can be guided into further elaboration of the points to be made concerning the principles of learning and how they apply to real life problems. Because of the clear educational and practical advantages of this demonstration, we can heartily recommend its use. Also, if you wind up buying your own lemonade powder (as we do), it's deductible (and you may drink the leftovers).

References

Dewey, J. *The early works, 1882-1889. Vol. 2: 1887. Psychology.* Carbondale, IL: Southern Illinois University, 1967.

Gibb, G. D. Making classical conditioning understandable through a demonstration technique. *Teaching of Psychology*, 1983, *10*, 112-113.

Pavlov, I.P. *Conditioned reflexes* (Translated by W. H. Gantt). New York: International, 1928.

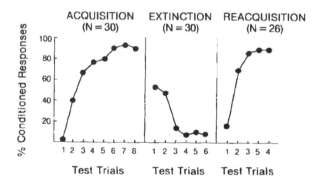

Figure 1. Typical Class Results of the Conditioning Demonstration.

Making Classical Conditioning Understandable Through A Demonstration Technique

Gerald D. Gibb
Eastern Illinois University

An inevitable part of all introduction to psychology courses are the principles of classical conditioning (Pavlov, 1927). Students often display a wide variety of symptoms of confusion ranging from repeatedly asking for clarification of the material, to showing a wide eyed look of bewilderment on their faces. Typically the concepts of acquisition, generalization, discrimination, spontaneous recovery, and extinction, of classically conditioned behaviors are introduced via Pavlov's dogs and their lust for meat powder. The purpose of this article is to give instructors of psychology a more innovative and enjoyable approach in presenting this material to students. The approach described is also advantageous in that it relates classical conditioning to human behavior.

Method. One lemon (as the CS), an assortment of other fruits and vegetables (apple, orange, lime, banana, cucumber, etc.), a tennis ball, and a Galvanic Skin Response (GSR) meter to provide a measurable CR are needed. A GSR meter manufactured by Lafayette Electronics Corp., model number 77026, is especially useful because the front and rear coverings are made with a clear plastic, enabling an instructor to project the GSR readings on a screen by using an overhead projector. A block of wood or a small hammer, and a hard surface such as a table top, will also be required to create a sharp noise to serve as the UCS.

Explain the function of the GSR meter and the activity it measures. Students also find it interesting to know that GSR is one of the measures used as part of a polygraph test. Invite a student to participate in the demonstration, assuring the student repeatedly that there is no pain or electric shock involved. This is critical, as anticipation of shock will cause increased GSR from the volunteer. The volunteer should sit comfortably in a chair while facing the class, taking care to instruct them that normal breathing and little movement is important to the success of the demonstration. After attaching the volunteer's fingers to the electrodes of the apparatus, instruct the students to remain silent, and allow at least 3 minutes to establish a baseline GSR reading for the volunteer.

After the GSR reading has become stabilized, present the lemon at eye level to the volunteer for a period of 1 second. The GSR meter may register some upward activity at this point. Repeat this process for 3 or 4 additional trials until the volunteer does not react to the presence of the lemon. With the volunteer still facing the class, create a loud noise (UCS) behind them using a hammer, or block of wood, and the surface of a table. A startle reaction and a dramatic increase in GSR will result if the UCS is of sufficient strength. While waiting for the volunteer's GSR to again stabilize to baseline, inform the students of other unconditioned responses in humans (leg flexion, salivary response, finger retraction, pupil dilation). It is also useful to have students record the GSR reading after each trial from this point on. A good practice to use is to have the students record the highest level of GSR activity after a trial.

To begin conditioning, present the CS, lemon, at eye level for about 1 sec., followed by the UCS, sound delivered behind the volunteer. It is crucial that the volunteer can not see, nor anticipate, the start of each conditioning trial. Repeat this procedure for 10 to 15 trials allowing a 15 to 20 second interval between trials.

To demonstrate the classically conditioned response of GSR to the newly conditioned stimulus (lemon), present the lemon alone for 6 trials using a 15 second interval between trials. The first 2 trials will show a dramatic increase in GSR, and the remaining trials will clearly demonstrate the concept of extinction, as the GSR readings will steadily decline.

In demonstrating the concepts of discrimination and generalization, repeat pairing the lemon and the loud noise as before for an additional 6 trials. On the seventh and eighth trials try using one of the other objects as a new stimulus. Stimuli such as the tennis ball and the lime will invariably cause a high GSR activity because of their relative similarity with the original conditioned stimulus. In order to try a variety of new stimuli the instructor will have to reestablish the conditioned response to the lemon over the course of an additional 6 trials.

On the following class day demonstrate spontaneous recovery by once again attaching the same volunteer to the GSR apparatus and presenting the lemon alone. The first two trials will usually reveal some spontaneous recovery of the galvanic skin response, after which extinction will again occur.

The concepts of time interval effects and stimulus order may also be explored by using the same procedure with new volunteers. By increasing the time interval to 2 seconds and 5 seconds it can be easily demonstrated how important a role temporal variations play in classical conditioning.

Evaluation. The effectiveness of the technique was measured by comparing exam scores from a semester using the standard lecture format to cover the material, with exam scores from a semester using the new classical conditioning demonstration technique. For the purpose of this evaluation, only exam items which pertained directly to classical conditioning were considered. During the Fall 1981 semester in which the standard lecture format was used, 20 multiple choice items met this criteria. The demonstration technique was introduced in the Spring 1982 semester, and again, only 20 multiple choice test items met this criteria and were used for the analysis. The test items from each semester were comparable and the instructor, course, and classroom were held constant. For each semester, the first 100 scores of alphabetically listed students who were administered the exam at its regularly scheduled time were used for the analysis.

The means were 74.40 and 68.75, for demonstration technique format and lecture format, respectively. An analysis of variance between the exam scores of the two groups yielded an $F=8.32$, (df 1, 198) which is significant beyond the .005 level.

Reference

Pavlov, I. P. *Conditioned reflexes* (Translated by G. V. Anrep), London: Oxford University Press, 1927.

Teaching and Demonstrating Classical Conditioning

John Sparrow
Peter Fernald
University of New Hampshire

Problems relating to classroom demonstrations of classical conditioning, especially tendencies to misrepresent Pavlov's procedures, are discussed. The design and construction of the Conditioner, *an apparatus used for demonstrating classical conditioning, and guidelines for its use in presenting principles faithful to Pavlov's original demonstration are described. Students experience the process of conditioning as well as the processes of generalization, extinction, discrimination, and spontaneous recovery.*

Few concepts and principles are more central to both the discipline of psychology and the introductory course than those of classical conditioning. However, presenting classical conditioning in a manner that captures students' interest and remains faithful to Pavlov's procedures is not an easy task. In one demonstration of a conditioned salivary response, for example, students placed dental rolls in their mouths during the presentation of a smell-of-cooking-hamburger stimulus. The roll was weighed and compared with the weight of a dental roll students had placed in their mouths during the presentation of a neutral stimulus. Student responses were highly variable, not to mention soggy and messy, and use of the demonstration was discontinued (J. A. Nevin, personal communication, 1987). Another demonstration of classical salivary conditioning involved the use of sweetened lemon powder. Students were instructed to "watch the instructor for the signal to "dip" a moistened finger into lemonade powder and transfer a small amount to the tip of their tongues" (D. Cogan & R. Cogan, 1984, p. 170). A major difficulty, however, was that the unconditioned stimulus (US) was administered by the students themselves. The conditioned stimulus (CS) probably was not the signal "dip, " but rather the act of dipping and/or moving the dipped finger toward the tongue. Moreover, the neutral stimulus (NS) and US were produced by the subject, not the experimenter, an arrangement that differs substantially from Pavlov's procedures.

One imaginative classroom demonstration of a classically conditioned startle reaction involves popping balloons with a foot-long magician's needle as the CS. When deeply inserted near the knot or nipple of the balloon, where the rubber is relatively thick, the balloon does not pop, yet the students flinch (startle). The demonstration is fun, dramatic, easily conducted, and inexpensive (Vernoy, 1987), but it has a serious drawback. Because most students have experienced balloons being popped by sharp objects, the demonstration involves an already-conditioned response, not the process of conditioning.

In another classroom demonstration of a classically conditioned startle reaction, the unconditioned response (UR) is the galvanic skin response (GSR), the CS is the presentation (sight) of a lemon, and the US is the sound of a hammer striking a hard surface immediately behind a subject who sits facing the class (Gibb, 1983). The subject's GSR is recorded and projected onto a screen to be viewed by the entire class. An advantage of this arrangement is the comparatively precise measurement of the UR and conditioned response (CR), at least in comparison to the salivary response and to the more complex, multifaceted startle reaction. A drawback is that only one student experiences the conditioning process.

To demonstrate classical conditioning as a process, the instructor must use both an appropriate conditioning apparatus and teaching procedures that carefully and precisely spell out Pavlov's paradigm of how a NS becomes a CS. We use an apparatus, known as the Conditioner, that allows every student in the class to experience the process of classical conditioning. We also present instructional guidelines for teaching classical conditioning and related processes in a manner similar to that outlined by Pavlov (1927).

The Conditioner

All electrical components of the Conditioner are housed in a wooden box (54 x 34 x 24 cm) made of pine shelving and plywood available from any local lumber yard (Figure 1). The light source is a standard 100 W household incandescent bulb located in a ceramic receptacle situated between an aluminum reflector and a frosted-glass octagonal window in the front of the wooden box. Serving initially as the NS and subsequently as the CS, the bulb is capable of a wide range of luminance. Luminance is controlled by a household rotary dimming switch located in the Conditioner's remote control unit. A luminance scale is calibrated in jnds by noting those points alongside the perimeter of the dial at which 50% of the class notices a luminance change. This calibration procedure, however, is not a critical aspect of the demonstration.

The source of the US, the siren, is an automobile burglar alarm system horn (Radio Shack Model #49-525) that operates on 12 VDC. Two sound options, warble and steady, may be selected by a switch located on top of the box. A small buzzer, placed in the box, can be used to demonstrate higher order conditioning. Both the siren and the buzzer, activated from the unit's remote control, require the use of a 12 VDC power supply. The model chosen for our apparatus (available from Jameco Electronics, Model #PS 9335) is a switching power supply capable of delivering a clean, well regulated 1.5 A flow of current. The only disadvantage of this particular power supply was the noisy circuitry needed for power regulation. To quiet the circuitry and, more important, to eliminate extraneous conditioning cues, a dummy load of power resistors is necessary. When the power switch is turned on, a ventilation fan prevents the power supply

and other components from overheating. To ensure safety, the power supply has an easily replaceable fuse. Total cost of the Conditioner, excluding labor, was $180.00.

Procedure

Before describing the four procedural steps of the demonstration, an important caveat must be mentioned. Because some students may have a low tolerance for loud noise, instructors should carefully check the noise level, especially directly in front of the Conditioner where the sound is loudest. As an additional precaution, we make sure that no student sits directly in front of and close to the Conditioner.

Table 1. Four Steps in Demonstrating Classical Conditioning

	Stimuli	Response	Purpose
Step 1	NS ⟶ (light)	No Response	Demonstrate NS
Step 2	US ⟶ (loud noise)	UR (startle reaction)	Demonstrate US
Step 3	NS and US →	UR	Pairing of US and NS
Step 4	CS ⟶	CR (partial startle reaction)	Demonstrate CS

The process of classical conditioning is properly demonstrated by following the four steps outlined by Pavlov (1927): demonstrate the NS, demonstrate the US, pair the NS and US, and demonstrate the CS. The demonstration is conducted as the instructor lectures on classical conditioning, using the Conditioner to illustrate each step. The first step consists of demonstrating that the light is a NS by turning on the light at midrange luminance several times before beginning the conditioning process. Each time the light is presented, the instructor points out that it is a NS that produces no unusual reactions other than possible minor pupillary contractions.

The US is then demonstrated by sounding the horn 2 or 3 times. The instructor should indicate that the identifying feature of an US in its elicitation of an UR. In the present case, the UR is the startle pattern in which the mouth widens, the eyes bulge, and the head jerks; there are increases in heart rate, respiration, skin conductance, and muscle tension. It is important to emphasize that the loud sound is considered a US because it automatically elicits a UR, the startle reaction. The stimulus-response sequence, loud noise followed by startle reaction, is a "wired in," inborn reflex.

After demonstrating the NS (Step 1) and US (Step 2), the instructor pairs the NS and US (Step 3), thus demonstrating the actual conditioning process. After about 10 pairings of the NS and US, the instructor immediately demonstrates the CR (Step 4) by presenting

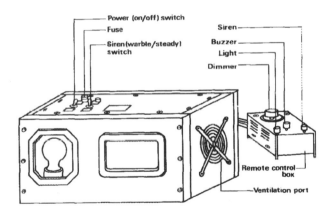

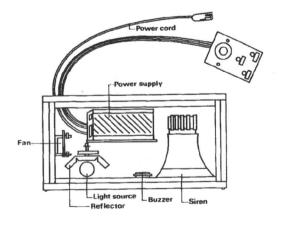

Figure 1. The Conditioner. Two perspectives are shown, outside view (top) and inside view (bottom).

the light alone for several trials. When asked to describe their reactions to the light flash, most students report that they experienced either the startle response or involuntary tenseness in anticipation of the loud sound. Their reports suggest that classical conditioning occurred because the light, previously a NS, became a CS. It is important to tell students that the CS typically elicits a diminished (not a full) startle reaction, which indicates the CS is not as effective as the US. The four steps of the demonstration may be diagrammed on the chalkboard as shown in Table 1.

The conditioning procedure may be carried out more effectively with a bit of deception. One instructor informed the class that it was the first time he had used the apparatus and that he had not received any instructions on how to use it. While "fumbling about," he proceeded through the four conditioning steps. This procedure may help reduce demand characteristics and students' proclivities to be good, faithful, apprehensive, or bad subjects (Adair, 1973; Fillenbaum, 1966; Orne, 1962).

Measuring the Response

Measurement of the UR and CR involves self-report with its attendant difficulties. Some students, realizing that the demonstration involves conditioning and wishing to be "good" subjects, may report a startle reaction when none occurred. Mention of this possibility provides an opportunity to discuss experimenter demand characteristics. Also, there may be peer demand for students influenced by the startle reaction reports of other students.

Rigor is added to the demonstration by recruiting a few student confederates to act as observers. Each observer watches and records one student's reactions. Observers typically report no unusual reactions during the preconditioning trials, indicating (a) that the light initially was neutral; (b) a startle response (UR) during the pairings of the light and the sound; and (c) signs of at least the anticipation of a startle response, if not the full response (CR), for one or more trials immediately following the pairings. It is important to point out to the class, however, that the observers are subject to two biases: (a) experimenter (observer) expectancy, because they either have been informed about or have figured out the anticipated outcome; and (b) experimenter (instructor) demand, if they feel obliged to please the instructor (and possibly their classmates) with their observations.

One way to circumvent experimenter demand effects is to measure the GSR component of the startle reaction. Although this procedure cannot be used with all students, GSR recordings can be made on a single subject, and the recordings are readily projected on a screen by means of an overhead projector (Gibb, 1983). This arrangement incorporates the experience of the conditioning process for all students and the observation and precise measurement of an UR and CR in a single subject.

Related Concepts and Principles

Generalization is readily demonstrated by presenting the light at lower and higher brightness levels. Most students report at least a partial startle reaction upon initial presentation of these different stimuli. However, because the CR tends to decrease (become extinguished) through the various presentations of light intensities in the generalization demonstration, it is best to re-pair the original light and sound for a number of trials before proceeding. *Extinction* is demonstrated by presenting the original light stimulus alone 10 to 15 times. Students typically report either no CR or a greatly diminished CR following extinction trials.

Following extinction, the instructor returns to lecturing; several minutes later the original light stimulus is presented again. The students are asked to report their reactions, and many report a partial startle reaction, suggesting *spontaneous recovery.* It is important to mention that spontaneous recovery occurs only if the CR after the time interval is greater than the CR before the time interval.

To demonstrate *discrimination*, the light is presented randomly at three different intensities (low, medium, and high) and the sound is paired only with the medium intensity. After each light intensity has been presented about 10 times, the instructor indicates to the students that the light will be presented 6 more times and that they should pay close attention to their reactions. Each light intensity is presented twice in a random sequence, and the students are asked to describe their responses, if any, to the three stimuli. Most students report little or no startle reaction to low and high light intensities and at least a partial startle reaction to the medium intensity.

The Conditioner also readily lends itself to demonstrating the relationship of the NS-US time interval to speed of conditioning. Our informal experiments suggest the optimal interval to be about 1 s. We have not demonstrated in the classroom the difficulties of producing a CR through simultaneous and reversed (backward) presentation of the NS and US or with a comparatively long (2 or 3 s) NS-US time interval. However, it seems reasonable that this aspect of the conditioning process could be readily demonstrated with the Conditioner, especially if the NS-CS time interval was monitored by an adjustable, automatic timing device. Not surprisingly, we have not been able to demonstrate higher order conditioning with the Conditioner. However, once the light has become a CS, the process whereby higher order conditioning might be achieved is readily demonstrated and explained by pairing the light with the sound of the buzzer.

We have observed that the startle reaction appears to attenuate over trials, possibly due to adaptation and/or an incompatible bracing response. In attempting to diminish the startle response, some students seem to resist its occurrence. The bracing response can be used to illustrate the concepts of operant, avoidance, and two-factor conditioning.

Conclusion

Because the concepts and principles relating to conditioning are complex, many introductory students find them difficult to learn. An overly simplified description and demonstration of classical conditioning that does not closely simulate Pavlov's experimental conditions often leaves students misinformed or confused. Such a presentation does not do justice to this important topic. Use of the Conditioner and the teaching procedures described here provide assistance to the introductory psychology instructor striving for more success in this difficult teaching task.

References

Adair, J. G. (1973). *The human subject: The social psychology of the psychological experiment.* Boston: Little, Brown.

Cogan, D., & Cogan, R. (1984). Classical salivary conditioning: An easy demonstration. *Teaching of Psychology, 11,* 170-171.

Fillenbaum, S. (1966). Prior deception and subsequent experimental performance: The "faithful" subject. *Journal of Personality and Social Psychology, 4,* 532-537.

Gibb, G. D. (1983). Making classical conditioning understandable through a demonstration technique. *Teaching of Psychology, 10,* 112-113.

Orne, M. T. (1962). On the social psychology of the psychological experiment: With particular reference to demand characteristics and their implications. *American Psychologist, 17,* 776-783.

Pavlov, I. P. (1927). *Conditioned reflexes.* New York: Dover

Vernoy, M. W. (1987). Demonstrating classical conditioning in introductory psychology: Needles do not always make balloons pop! *Teaching of Psychology, 14,* 176-177.

Demonstrating Classical Conditioning in Introductory Psychology: Needles Do Not Always Make Balloons Pop!

Mark W. Vernoy
Palomar College

Explaining classical conditioning to introductory psychology classes is sometimes difficult. This article describes a demonstration of a classically conditioned response that occurs when a needle pierces, but does not pop, a balloon.

When introducing students to psychology, I am constantly striving to make each topic come alive for them. One of the topics that is not only easy to demonstrate but is also capable of sparking a good deal of enthusiasm in students is classical conditioning. In my introductory psychology classes, I have tried several types of classical conditioning demonstrations. I have demonstrated the conditioned eyeblink, which never worked very well and was hard for the students in the back row to see. I have taught students how to condition their dogs to salivate to a tone (Pavlov, 1927), and

brought my pet basset hound into class as living proof that dogs really can be taught to drool on command. (Most of my students thought this was disgusting, so I never did it again.) I even considered duplicating John B. Watson and Rosalie Rayner's (1920) Little Albert experiment, but the college child care center pointed out that the California child abuse laws specifically prohibit its replication. After several such failures and near misses, I finally found a classical conditioning demonstration that is effective, sanitary, and legal. This article describes that demonstration, which has proven to be not only effective but also fun for me and my students.

The premise of the demonstration is that nearly all of us have been classically conditioned to flinch or blink when we watch someone stab a balloon with a needle. In this conditioning situation, the neutral stimulus is the needle, the unconditioned stimulus is the noise produced by the popping balloon, and the unconditioned response is the startle response (a flinch or blink) produced by the loud noise. Eventually, the needle becomes the conditioned stimulus that produces the startle response when it is brought in contact with balloon. In this way, we have learned that needles always pop balloons. Or do they?

The equipment needed for this demonstration includes about 20 to 30 good quality, round balloons and a needle. Any sharp sewing needle will do, but for dramatic effect I use a foot-long needle that I borrow from a colleague who is an amateur magician. You can acquire these large needles at any good magic shop.

Before class, blow up about 30 balloons and transport them to the classroom in a large trash bag. When you are ready to begin the demonstration, randomly distribute 10 to 15 balloons to students in the classroom, then bring out the needle and pop about half of the balloons. (When popping the balloons, make sure students hold them away from their faces and the faces of other students.) Then, begin a discussion of classical conditioning and ask students to identify the unconditioned stimulus, the unconditioned response, and so on. Make sure to ask the students what makes them jump when the balloon pops, and persist until they produce the obvious answer: noise. Then, pop the remaining balloons.

Now the fun begins. Pick up one of the balloons from the trash bag and stick the needle into the balloon without popping it. As you might have guessed, there is a trick to this part of the demonstration. Piercing a balloon without popping it does not require a special balloon or a special needle; all that is neces-

sary is to know where to stick the needle. In a blown-up balloon, there are usually two places where the rubber is relatively thick because of the small amount of tension on the skin of the balloon: the nipple and near the knot. Thus, if you pierce the balloon with a sharp needle in the thick area of the nipple, the balloon should not pop; if you pierce it with a foot-long needle, you should be able to insert it through the nipple and pull it out through the thick area near the knot, without popping the balloon.

After having been conditioned to the popping of balloons at the beginning of the demonstration, the students can be expected to flinch or blink when you insert the needle in the balloon. But the balloon does not pop. There is no unconditioned stimulus, but the students flinch anyhow. This generates a real enthusiasm for joining in on a discussion of the classical conditioning processes at work. In this discussion, encourage students to use classical conditioning terminology. (By the way, after the balloon is pierced, it loses air and soon becomes flat. You can let it go flat to show that you did indeed pierce it, or if you have a long needle you can run the needle through the balloon to show it was pierced, then end your act by throwing the balloon up into the air and popping it.)

References

Pavlov, I. P. (1927). *Conditioned reflexes.* New York: Dover.

Watson, J. B., & Rayner, R. (1920). Conditioned emotional reactions. *Journal of Experimental Psychology, 3,* 1-14.

Preparing for an Important Event: Demonstrating the Modern View of Classical Conditioning

Art Kohn
North Carolina Central University

James W. Kalat
North Carolina State University

A simple classroom demonstration can dramatically illustrate the process of classical conditioning. This demonstration differs from others because it elicits a conditioned response that differs significantly from the unconditioned response. As a result, this demonstration provides an effective introduction to the contemporary notion that the function of classical conditioning is to help an organism prepare itself for an important, upcoming event. The demonstration requires very little preparation and only a few minutes of class time. Data indicated that the procedure produced a conditioned response and that other processes, such as habituation, cannot explain the results.

Are your students less impressed by classical conditioning than they should be? As instructors, we know that classical conditioning can profoundly shape our emotional and motivational lives. Despite our enthusiasm, however, many students remain unimpressed and wonder why we make a fuss about a dog learning to salivate to a bell.

One reason that students underestimate classical conditioning is that the conditioned response (CR) and unconditioned response (UR) are very similar in most of our classroom examples. This similarity may cause students to overlook the fact that the CR and UR serve different adaptive functions. For example, the CR and UR were identical in each of the creative demonstrations described in *Teaching of Psychology* (Cogan & Cogan, 1984; Gibb, 1983; Sparrow & Fernald, 1989, Vernoy, 1987). Cogan and Cogan (1984), for instance, signaled the students (the conditioned stimulus, CS) to place lemon powder (the unconditioned stimulus, US) in their mouths; in this demonstration, both the CR and UR were salivation. In Sparrow and Fernald's (1989) demonstration, the instructor flashed a light (the CS) and shortly after that produced a loud noise (the US); both the CR and the UR were a startle reaction. Likewise, the CR and the UR are similar in most of our standard textbook examples, including the salivary reflex, the eye blink response, and the Little Albert story.

Although these examples illustrate the essential procedures of classical conditioning, they suggest to students two conclusions that are not entirely correct: (a) the CR and UR are necessarily similar, and (b) the function of classical conditioning is simply to expedite a response so that it occurs before the US begins.

These notions are clearly inconsistent with the emerging view of classical conditioning that (a) the CR can be very different from the UR, and (b) the function of classical conditioning is to elicit a preparatory response (CR) that enables the subject to cope better with an impending event (Holland, 1984; Hollis, 1984; Rescorla, 1988; Zener, 1937). In this emerging view, the CR is a preparation for the US, whereas the UR is a reaction to it.

Several lines of research illustrate how the CR and UR can be quite different. For example, in the signaled-shock procedure, the rat's UR to a shock is to run around and squeal; its CR, however, is to freeze (Bindra & Palfai, 1967). The difference between the CR and UR is also apparent in Siegel's (1977, 1983) classical conditioning explanation of drug tolerance. In this procedure, the UR to an anesthetic drug is a reduced sensitivity to pain; the CR, however, involves mobilizing the body against the effects of the drug.

The following demonstration can help students better understand the contemporary view of classical conditioning. The demonstration can be performed quickly, requires little preparation or equipment, and conditions almost everyone in the classroom. Finally, the CR and UR are different, highlighting the preparatory nature of the CR.

The Demonstration

Before class, tape 5 to 10 balloons to a wall or to a table in front of the class. You should inflate them fully so that they produce a loud noise when they burst. Explain to the class that you are going to demonstrate classical conditioning and that, for the next few minutes, you want everyone to observe their own reactions closely.

Take a long needle, dart, or pin, show it to the class, loudly count "One, two, three," and break the first balloon. Wait a few seconds, and then repeat this procedure with the next balloon and with two or more additional balloons. Be sure to vary the amount of time between balloon bursts so that you do not inadvertently induce temporal conditioning. (You may notice that students flinch less and less with each successive balloon.) When you get to the fifth or sixth balloon, say "One, two, three," lower the needle toward the balloon, but miss it. The balloon does not burst. How do the students react?

When we first tried this demonstration, we expected the students to flinch as a CR. In fact, nearly all of the students sat unmoved and expressionless. Had the demonstration failed?

Not at all. Wait a few seconds, perhaps pass the time by feigning your confusion over their lack of response, and discreetly slip the needle down to your side; then, without providing the "One, two, three" warning, burst a balloon. The students jump visibly; indeed, they will jump more than they had to any of the previous balloon bursts.

Following the demonstration, while everybody settles down, draw a graph on the board and label the x-axis *Trial Numbers* and the y-axis *Mean Size Startle Reaction*. Next, ask the students to recall the extent of their startle reaction on each trial including the ones when you did not pop the balloon and when you popped it without warning. In turn, plot the class's mean reaction on the chart. Results will show a steady decline in responding across trials, except that the last trial—the one with the unwarned burst—will involve the largest response of all.

Now, challenge your students to identify the CS, US, CR, and UR. Ordinarily, they have no trouble identifying the bang as the US and their flinching as the UR. Likewise, they will recognize that the CS is some combination of your counting "One, two, three" and the movement of your hand. However, they may have a bit of trouble identifying the CR; initially, some students may guess that the CR was also flinching, but point out that this cannot be the case because few students flinched when the CS was presented alone. If they continue to have trouble, point out that the CR is the response elicited by the CS. Ask them "What did you do when you heard me counting?" After a bit of introspection, they quickly realize that when they experienced the CS, their CR was not flinching; instead, it consisted of tightening their muscles in order to inhibit a flinch. To reinforce this interpretation, refer to your graph and point out that (a) across trials, their flinching decreased as they were better able to emit the preparatory muscle-clenching response; (b) they did not jump at all when they heard "One, two, three" alone; and (c) they jumped their highest during the last trial because, when you gave no warning, they had no chance to emit the preparatory CR.

Evaluation

To evaluate the validity of our observations, we recently conducted this demonstration in our class and carefully monitored the students' responses with a video camera.

Method

We performed the demonstration for 55 students in Introductory Psychology. Before the demonstration, we arranged a video camera facing the students which provided a clear record of their activities. The students appeared to habituate to the camera very quickly, and it seemed to have no effect on their subsequent behavior. With the camera rolling, the instructor popped five balloons, faked the popping of the sixth one, and after a brief delay, popped the last balloon without giving the "One, two, three" warning.

Later, two judges watched the tape and rated the extent of the class's startle reaction for each trial. Judges rated startle reactions on a scale ranging from *no reaction* (0) to *large reaction* (4). Both judges were blind to the purpose of the demonstration.

Results

As Figure 1 shows, the extent of the startle reactions was consistent with our expectations. The students emitted an intermediate-size startle reaction in Trials 1 and 2, a somewhat reduced reaction during Trials 3 and 4, and no reaction on Trial 5. Likewise during Trial 6, when only the CS was presented, subjects again showed no startle reaction. Finally, during Trial 7, when the US was presented without the CS, the subjects emitted the largest response. In rating the tape, the two judges showed a high interrater reliability, with a mean correlation of .853 and a Spearman-Brown correlation of .917.

Discussion

After completing the demonstration and emphasizing the preparatory role of the CR, you may wish to discuss alternative explanations of the results. The simplest alternative is that no conditioning occurred during the procedure and that the CS "One, two, three" had acquired its aversiveness before the demonstration. This seems unlikely, however, because the CS evoked little flinch inhibiting on Trial 1 and much more on successive trials, suggesting that some form of learning took place. Another explanation is that the subjects habituated to the loud noise during Trials 1 through 5; however, habituation cannot account for the very large startle response on the last trial.

A third explanation involves operant, rather than classical, conditioning. According to this interpretation, in the presence of the discriminative stimulus "One, two, three," the students began to emit the operant response of tensing their muscles. In turn, this tensing response may have been reinforced by minimizing their startle response. We find it difficult to determine whether the tensing response is operant, classical, or a mixture of both; in class, therefore, we emphasize that operant and classical conditioning frequently overlap and are capable of evoking similar responses. Furthermore, we point out that, in some cases, such as autoshaping (Williams & Williams, 1969), both types of conditioning work together to sustain a pattern of behavior.

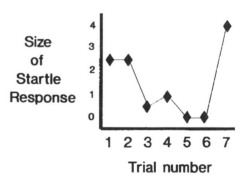

Figure 1. Mean startle reaction on successive trials of balloon popping. On Trial 6, we faked popping the balloon; on Trial 7, we popped the balloon without the "One, two, three" warning.

Finally, it also may be instructive to contrast the results of this demonstration with one described by Vernoy (1987). Vernoy used a long needle to pop a balloon held by the students themselves. The ensuing pop produced a noticeable startle reaction that was the UR. After popping 5 to 8 balloons, however, Vernoy held the balloon himself and inserted the needle in such a way that it did not pop the balloon; although there was no US, Vernoy reported that the students still showed a startle reaction, which was the CR. Why did the students startle in his demonstration and not in ours?

One explanation for the differing results is that the students in Vernoy's demonstration did not emit the flinching responses that Vernoy reported. We recently made several attempts to replicate Vernoy's procedure using a panel of judges to rate the extent of the students' startle responses. In each case, the judges reported no startle reaction when the balloon did not pop.

A second explanation for the difference is that the students in Vernoy's procedure may have experienced pseudoconditioning. In pseudo-conditioning, successive presentations of the US, especially of an aversive US, sensitizes subjects and thereby increases the probability of their emitting the UR following a neutral stimulus (Staddon & Ettinger, 1989). As Wickens and Wickens (1942) put it,

> if a series of fairly strong unconditioned stimuli is presented alone and that series is followed by a previously neutral timulus, it is found that this previously neutral stimulus now reduces a response similar to the one given to the unconditioned stimulus. (p. 518)

Thus, in Vernoy's procedure, the bangs may have sensitized the subjects such that the movement of the instructor's arm produced a startle reaction.

A more intriguing explanation for the differing results concerns the preparatory nature of classical conditioning. In Vernoy's procedure, the balloon was close to the students' faces. Perhaps the students learned the natural preparatory action (CR) of pulling back from the balloon as the needle approached it. In our demonstration, however, the students were seated farther away from the balloon; for them, the natural preparatory response (CR) may be to inhibit an embarrassing startle reaction.

The modern understanding of classical conditioning emphasizes that this primitive form of learning is broader and more intriguing than previously thought. Classical conditioning not only can produce anticipatory salivation, but also can evoke a range of adaptive responses that help people and animals prepare for important events. We believe that this modern view of classical conditioning will earn from students the respect it deserves.

References

Bindra, I., & Palfai, T. (1967). Nature of positive and negative incentive motivational effects on general activity. *Journal of Comparative and Physiological Psychology, 63*, 288-297.

Cogan, D., & Cogan, R. (1984). Classical salivary conditioning An easy demonstration. *Teaching of Psychology, 11*, 170-171.

Gibb, G. D. (1983). Making classical conditioning understandable through a demonstration technique. *Teaching of Psychology, 10*, 112-113.

Holland, P. (1984). Origins of behavior in Pavlovian conditioning. *Psychology of Learning and Motivation, 18*, 129-174.

Hollis, K. L. (1984). The biological function of Pavlovian conditioning: The best defense is a good offense. *Journal of Experimental Psychology: Animal Learning and Behavior, 10*, 413-425.

Rescorla, R. A. (1988). Pavlovian conditioning: It's not what you think it is. *American Psychologist, 44*, 151-160.

Siegel, S. (1977). Morphine tolerance as an associative process. *Journal of Experimental Psychology: Animal Behavior Processes, 3*, 1-13.

Siegel, S. (1983). Classical conditioning, drug tolerance and drug dependence. *Research Advances In Alcohol and Drug Problems, 7*, 207-246.

Sparrow, J., & Fernald, P. (1989). Teaching and demonstrating classical conditioning. *Teaching of Psychology, 16*, 204-206.

Staddon, J. E. R., & Ettinger, R. H. (1989). *Learning: An introduction to the principles of adaptive behavior.* San Diego: Harcourt Brace Jovanovich.

Vernoy, M. W. (1987). Demonstrating classical conditioning in introductory psychology: Needles do not always make balloons pop! *Teaching of Psychology, 14*, 176-177.

Wickens, D. D., & Wickens, C. D. (1942). Some factors related to pseudoconditioning. *Journal of Experimental Psychology, 31*, 518–526.

Williams, D. R., & Williams, H. (1969). Auto-maintenance in the pigeon: Sustained pecking despite contingent nonreinforcement. *Journal of the Experimental Analysis of Behavior, 12*, 511–520.

Zener, K. (1937). The significance of behavior accompanying conditioned salivary secretions for theories of the conditioned response. *American Journal of Psychology, 50*, 384-403.

Note

We thank Neal Womack and Wendy Howard for helping to collect the data reported herein. We also thank Greg Kimble for his perceptive comments on a draft of this article and Wendy Kohn and Ruth Ault for their editorial assistance.

4. TEACHING OPERANT CONDITIONING

Conditioning the Instructor's Behavior: A Class Project in Psychology of Learning

Joan C. Chrisler
Connecticut College

A project in conditioning for a Psychology of Learning class is described. Students work as a group to select a target behavior and implement conditioning procedures using an ABAB design. The instructor serves as the subject of the experiment. Each student describes the experiment in an APA–style paper, which counts for 25% of the course grade. The project is popular with students; their experiments are often successful and fun.

Learning by doing has long been a desirable technique for any level of instruction. In a Psychology of Learning course, where practice can follow precept, engaging students actively is particularly valuable.

Anecdotes about groups of students conditioning their professors as a practical joke are legion. Many of us have heard and probably retold the stories of the class that increased the frequency of their professor's facial tic and of the professor who was shaped by the class to stand only in the left-hand corner of the classroom. My classes have enjoyed the stories of students conditioning professors, thus it seemed appropriate to suggest that they try it themselves.

Method

On the first day of class, students are informed about the project and given an approximate date of completion. However, the date is flexible and may be altered at the students' request. The instructor must remember that this is the students' project; they control it and they make all decisions about its form and content.

Students are advised to observe the instructor's behavior during the first 2 weeks of the semester and look for a behavior that they would like to change. They are asked to choose a behavior that they would like the instructor either to increase or decrease. Students are told that it is easier, under the circumstances, to increase a behavior than to decrease one and are advised to be very specific in defining their target behavior. I ask them not to choose anything obscene or embarrassing, but to choose a behavior that will improve my teaching and/or be helpful to me.

During the next 2 weeks, the lectures include information about operant conditioning procedures that the students will need to plan their project. I introduce the concept of shaping and the use of rewards and punishments, describe simple experiments, discuss the importance of taking a baseline, and explain how to record and graph data. I also discuss the concept of interrater reliability and suggest that two students, who do not sit near each other, record the data daily. Students are given class time (usually about 30 min) to set up their experiment. I review what they must accomplish and facilitate the election of a project coordinator who receives extra credit for moderating discussion and for the daily collection of data. I then retreat to my office until a student calls me to return and resume conducting the class. The experiment starts with the next class meeting.

The experiment uses an ABAB design, and students are given the following instructions: (a) take a baseline—approximately 1 week, (b) apply conditioning procedures—approximately 2 or 3 weeks, (c) stop conditioning and return to baseline—approx-imately 1 week, (d) apply conditioning procedures–approx-imately 2 weeks. Times are approximate to allow students the flexibility to conduct their own study and to ensure that the instructor is never aware of the exact phase of the experiment. Students decide how long each phase of the experiment should last. They often lengthen the phases to compensate for holidays or to make up for class periods in which the instructor's plans make it impossible for them to work on their project. Occasionally problems arise that require more class time to discuss and solve. I make it clear that I will gladly leave the room so that the students will have time to discuss changes; I encourage them to ask for time as soon as a problem arises.

About 6 weeks into the project, I ask the students to give me a date by which they expect to finish. I also spend a class session discussing the APA format and teaching them how to organize and write each section. Students are encouraged to begin work immediately on the Introduction and Method sections. The paper counts for 25% of their course grade, replacing a more traditional term paper.

At the project's end, the students debrief their subject and a lively discussion of the project ensues. I am always surprised to find out what has been going on, even when the class has been successful at changing my behavior. My surprise provides a nice illustration of the fact that behavior can change without conscious awareness. Students explain the reasons behind their choice of target behavior and describe their methodology. I offer feedback on their methods and suggest some points to cover in their papers.

Students' Reactions

Students enjoy this assignment, particularly when they are successful. Some students report that it makes them feel powerful to have control over the planning and timing of a major assignment, and to have some influence on the instructor's behavior! On course evaluations, many students write that this project and other brief in-class experiments and demonstrations were very helpful in making clear the concepts described in their texts. A few students have announced a desire to become behavior therapists.

When the experiment is unsuccessful, the students, although disappointed, are still able to recognize the value of the experience. Often, they realize what went wrong too late in the semester to correct it. They learn about the value of shaping, and that it is not as easy as it seems. Students have also frequently learned important lessons about group interactions; often their discussions mention processes like diffusion of responsibility, social loafing, conformity, groupthink, and polarization. Some students conclude that they are so used to working under specific instructions from their professors that they were unsure of how to go about designing a project.

Some successful projects my students have carried out include conditioning me to make eye contact with all members of the class, to move about the classroom more frequently, to give more examples from my personal life and experience to illustrate concepts, and to write on the blackboard more often. When the students told me about the blackboard project, they were delighted by my sudden realization that the learning had generalized; I had been using the blackboard more often in all my courses that semester. Powerful reinforcers applied by the students include eye contact, smiling, note taking, nodding, and class participation.

Obstacles to Success

Class size seems to be an important factor; students in larger classes work together less well. Small classes have the greatest success with this project, which works best with groups of 25 or less. The one time I assigned this project to a class of 50, social loafing and poor communication were major problems. The project coordinator complained about students who were absent on the days they were assigned to record data or who never delivered reinforcers. These students' papers contained information different from that used by the rest of the group.

Only once has the project been a disaster. The students chose the unworkable plan of trying to stop me from sipping water while lecturing (I was battling a severe cold and sore throat) and they became bored and depressed when they could accomplish nothing. I also became bored and depressed because I received no reinforcement from the class. Attendance dropped, and I didn't feel like going to class either. Course evaluations were conducted before the project was completed, and I was called to the department chair's office to explain what was happening. The debriefing discussion in this class was particularly good as we figured out what had gone wrong and shared how we felt about it. The importance of reinforcement in social relationships was particularly well illustrated by this situation. To prevent future disasters, I tell students about this experience and urge them to stop and reevaluate an experiment that is not working well.

The subject in this experiment may feel self-conscious early on when the students are scrutinizing the teacher's behavior to choose a target. Once the project is underway, I don't think too much about it as there are plenty of other details to occupy my time. If a class discussion goes particularly well, however, I suspect that their experiment is working out.

Conclusion

After assigning this project to six classes (nearly 200 students) at two colleges, I can recommend it for its benefits to students and instructor. Working on the project increases students' involvement in the course, gives them firsthand experience with conditioning techniques, provides practice in writing an APA-style paper, and models the importance of learning by doing. The instructor benefits with each successful experiment as the students shape their subject's teaching behavior to increased effectiveness.

Demonstrating Differential Reinforcement by Shaping Classroom Participation

Gordon K. Hodge
Nancy H. Nelson
University of New Mexico

A classroom demonstration using differential reinforcement was devised to shape classroom participation of 14 students in an introductory psychology lab. Based on our observations and student comments, the technique was useful for illustrating how reinforcers shape behavior. The demonstration facilitated students' understanding of operant conditioning procedures and seemed to encourage a more equitable distribution of classroom participation for all students.

Principles of operant conditioning are easily presented in classroom demonstrations. For example, descriptions of students operantly shaping their instructors' behaviors have been reported (Chrisler, 1988; Melvin, 1988). As a variation on this theme, we devised a demonstration in which the instructor shapes the students' level of class participation using a differential reinforcement procedure.

In our experience, uneven distribution of student participation in the classroom is common. In large lecture sections of 400 to 600 students, opportunities for participation are sometimes limited by time constraints and the intimidating atmosphere. But in small classes, such as seminars, labs, or discussion sections, the ideal scenario is one in which all students contribute, and discussions dominated by the assertive few are minimized.

We strive to foster creative exchange and discussion of ideas in the introductory psychology labs. As stated in the syllabus, students receive a grade for class participation. They are encouraged and, presumably, motivated to take part in discussions; still, many students do not participate.

In one lab section, we noted that three students overly participated in discussions at the expense of other students who rarely spoke. We believed it would be advantageous to foster more equitable interactions. We also saw an opportunity to implement an educationally valuable demonstration that would enhance previously learned class material.

Method

Subjects

Subjects were 8 women and 6 men enrolled in an introductory psychology lab at the University of New Mexico.

Materials

Two weeks before the actual demonstration, students circled the value on a 7-point scale that best indicated their own level of class participation. The scale ranged from *I never participate* (1) to *I always participate* (7). These ratings provided a baseline level of self-perceived participation for each student.

After the demonstration and before debriefing, each student completed an anonymous questionnaire consisting of the following three items:

1. In your own words, describe the demonstration implemented during today's class. Include whether or not you believe the demonstration influenced your level of class participation.
2. Was the demonstration useful in illustrating how reinforcers may be used in an operant conditioning procedure? Explain how the demonstration was useful and possible ways it may be changed and/or improved.
3. Any additional thoughts concerning this demonstration.

Design and Procedure

One week after the lecture on learning, the lab instructor distributed the scale assessing each student's perceived level of class participation. To avoid biasing the demonstration, students were not told the reason for filling out the questionnaire. The scale was used to assist the instructor in determining the appropriate differential reinforcement schedule to be implemented during the demonstration.

153

The demonstration using differential reinforcement to shape classroom participation was implemented 2 weeks after the rating scales were distributed. Each student's initials were placed on the top of the chalkboard at the front of the class. The reinforcer consisted of a plus mark placed underneath a student's name whenever the desired behavior (increased or decreased participation) was emitted. The instructor determined before the demonstration which students would receive a reinforcer for either participating or not participating, based on the rating scales and familiarity with class dynamics.

Among the 14 students, 3 were judged as overparticipators; they were reinforced only when they did not participate or interrupt or when specifically called on by the instructor after raising their hands. The 5 students who rarely participated were reinforced for making even the slightest effort to participate; for example, hand raising, saying anything (correct or not) when called on, and, in one instance, making eye contact with the instructor. These students were then reinforced less frequently as they began to emit more responses according to general shaping procedures (Gordon, 1989). The remaining 6 students normally participated in a moderate fashion and were reinforced on a variable ratio schedule to maintain their active participation.

Following the demonstration and before debriefing, a short questionnaire was given to assess whether the students caught on to the demonstration and to get their feedback and suggestions. Debriefing consisted of discussing the items on the questionnaire in a classroom forum and reemphasizing the principles of operant conditioning, shaping, and differential reinforcement.

Results

Student responses on the rating scale reflected the instructor's perceptions of participation levels. Only one student, rated by the instructor as a 1 (I never participate), placed a rating of 2 on his scale. The scales, therefore, appeared to complement the ratings made independently by the instructor, providing a reasonably reliable tool for devising a differential reinforcement schedule for each student.

Based on the instructor's subjective observation, class participation seemed noticeably more balanced after the technique was implemented. Overparticipators contributed much less; underparticipators contributed more often and enthusiastically. Only one of the identified underparticipators remained reticent. This balance in participation was noticed by 5 of the students on their questionnaires. One wrote that "people like an upbeat situation and are encouraged to join in," and another student noted that "students that [sic] don't normally contribute began to participate."

Based on the responses to the first item on the questionnaire, 12 of 14 students identified the demonstration as an example of operant conditioning or the use of a shaping procedure or both. One student identified it as a motivational study (the demonstration was implemented during a lecture on motivation), and one students did not answer the question.

In response to the second part of Item 1 (whether or nor the demonstration influenced their level of class participation—either increasing or decreasing it), 10 of 14 students believed that the demonstration affected their class participation. One student stated "I think some people talked a lot more than usual," and another stated "many students gave input that usually do not." The other 4 students did not believe the demonstration affected their participation.

In response to Item 2, 12 of the 14 students found the demonstration useful in illustrating the role of reinforcers in an operant conditioning procedure, noting that the demonstration was "closely related to our computer assignment" (which dealt with shaping) and better "integrated our lecture notes." Four students mentioned that they would prefer a more potent reinforcer, such as extra credit, rather than "just a plus mark."

Discussion

The demonstration was a valuable and worthwhile way to illustrate differential reinforcement in shaping classroom participation. The usefulness of the demonstration, based on responses to the questionnaire, is evident, although there are obvious limitations. The demonstration is limited to a small class size (approximately 20 students) in order for the instructor to implement an effective differential reinforcement procedure tailored for each student. With larger groups, it would be difficult to keep track of the target responses and dispense reinforcers in a timely fashion.

Of some concern was how students, particularly overparticipators, perceived the fairness of the procedure. For example, overparticipators might have wondered why others received plus marks and they did not. On the questionnaires, two students expressed frustration for not receiving reinforcement of their active participation. One student wrote that the activity was "quite frustrating, considering that I didn't get a plus until the latter portion of the demonstration after participating considerably." That overparticipators experienced frustration when their normally high participation levels went unrewarded was not surprising. In general, overparticipators seem frustrated whenever the instructor fails to call on them or limits their comments. The concern is whether frustration elicited by the demonstration was notably different from feelings ordinarily elicited during routine classroom management.

Some frustration was probably due to initial misperceptions that the goal was to increase everyone's participation equally, rather than differentially. As the demonstration progressed, however, overparticipators responded by curtailing their behavior in order to earn plus marks. One student's strategy provided insight into the process: "I initially increased participation to ascertain whether I would receive points. This attempt was to no avail so I proceeded to lessen my degree or amount of participation" (for which the student was then reinforced). Although frustration occurred, there were no indications from questionnaire responses or discussions during debriefing that overparticipators thought the experience was unfair. Both students who expressed initial frustration reported that the demonstration was interesting and useful. Nevertheless, instructors should be alert for signs of unusual discomfort or frustration and be ready to end the demonstration and initiate debriefing as necessary.

In discussing the demonstration with students, it is worthwhile to point out that the changes in participation frequencies probably reflected a real-life application of an operant conditioning procedure. Moreover, even though students became aware of the purpose of the demonstration while it was ongoing, their behavior nevertheless changed in response to the procedures (cf. Blanchard & Johnson, 1982). Discussion could then focus on students' ideas of how similar procedures could be applied in other situations (e.g., encouraging more balanced communication in a personal relationship).

Although not quantified, some positive effects on class participation appeared to remain throughout the semester. This pleasant residual effect may have occurred because students and instructor were now more aware of their class behavior. Students who normally did not participate may have felt more comfortable about contributing after their first experience in speaking, or, possibly, the class dynamics became less threatening and more comfortable to these students.

Ways to improve this demonstration include developing a more objective, less intrusive assessment of class participation in addition to the questionnaire. One possibility would be to use a hidden tape recorder or video camera to record a baseline session before the demonstration, record the demonstration, and then have an objective third party score the tape(s).

The demonstration is a useful technique for illustrating differential reinforcement and for encouraging more equitable participation in small classes.

References

Blanchard, K., & Johnson, S. (1982). *The one minute manager.* New York: Berkley.

Chrisler, J. C. (1988). Conditioning the instructor's behavior: A class project in psychology of learning. *Teaching of Psychology, 15*, 135-137.

Gordon, W. C. (1989). *Learning and memory.* Pacific Grove CA: Brooks/Cole.

Melvin, K. B. (1988). Rating class participation: The prof/peer method. *Teaching of Psychology, 15*, 137-139.

Note

We thank Frank A. Logan, Charles L. Brewer, and the anonymous reviewers for their helpful comments.

Overcoming Misunderstanding About the Concept of Negative Reinforcement

Robert T. Tauber
Division of Humanities and Social Sciences
Pennsylvania State University

Negative reinforcement is a misunderstood concept. This article describes a quiz that helps students ascertain whether they understand the concept. Six remedies for alleviating their misunderstanding are also described. The first three remedies pertain to teaching the concept of negative reinforcement. The remaining remedies alert students to the problems associated with the connotative meaning of the word negative *and to the relative paucity of literature citations and textbook coverage of negative reinforcement.*

When applying operant conditioning principles, the goal is to increase or decrease behaviors by providing appropriate consequences. Although there are many examples of simple consequences, all fit into four main categories defined by whether one applies or removes a reward or an aversive stimulus. These four consequences are known as positive reinforcement, time-out, punishment, and negative reinforcement. None of these consequences is more understood than negative reinforcement. By using a negative reinforcement quiz to highlight the misunderstanding and then applying the following six remedies, this misunderstanding can be overcome.

Evidence of Misunderstanding

Before teaching the concept of negative reinforcement, ask students to take a quiz similar to the one discussed next. The quiz forces students to acknowledge what they know or don't know about the concept and, as a result, makes them more receptive to instruction.

When two colleagues and I administered this quiz to 140 Introductory Psychology students, the quiz results revealed much misunderstanding of the concept. The first question asked students to provide another word that meant the same thing as negative reinforcement. Only 16% gave a correct answer; 37% responded incorrectly by answering *punishment.* One percent responded with words that meant the same thing as punishment, such as *yell* and *embarrass,* and 46% gave answers that were too general to be easily categorized.

On the second question, 73% of the students incorrectly answered that negative reinforcement is used to decrease behavior. Only 26% correctly said negative reinforcement increases behavior; 1% percent had no response.

The third question asked whether people usually look forward to negative reinforcement. Seventy-six percent of the respondents said "No"; 26% said "Yes." A few respondents answered "Yes" and "No," causing the total to be 102%. These results further indicate that the students confused negative reinforcement and punishment.

Two final questions showed that 92% would regularly use positive reinforcement in the future and 66% would regularly use negative reinforcement. The majority justified their future use of negative reinforcement by saying that people had to be punished to be motivated. Again, punishment and negative reinforcement were regarded as synonyms.

Alleviating the Misunderstanding

Presenting a 2 x 2 consequence-grid matrix is one remedy that can alleviate misunderstanding. A matrix will demonstrate that one can only apply or remove (column headings) consequences, and that consequences can only be categorized as something desired or something dreaded (row headings). Challenge students to think of other combinations of actions and consequences that could not be described by the consequence grid. None exist. The four quadrants of the matrix can then be labeled by students, with each quadrant having a unique label. Students realize that the quadrant labeled *negative reinforcement* cannot, at the same time, be labeled *punishment.*

A second remedy is to present several examples to illustrate that trying to distinguish instances of punishment and negative reinforcement sometimes results in ambiguous situations. For instance, "Because you talked back, you will have to stay after school," and "You will have to stay after school until you clean your desk," represent punishment and negative reinforcement statements, respectively. In the first statement, an aversive stimulus (staying after school) is being applied in order to decrease an unwanted behavior. In the second statement, an aversive stimulus (staying after school) is being removed in order to increase a desired behavior.

As a third remedy, distribute teacher-prepared examples of each consequence. Ask students to label each consequence by identifying whether something desired or dreaded is being applied or removed. After students have mastered this activity, have them create their own examples, exchange them, and then evaluate each other's work.

The remaining three remedies do not deal directly with teaching the concept of negative reinforcement. However, they do call attention to problems that interfere with learning the concept of negative reinforcement.

As a fourth remedy, indicate that part of the confusion over negative reinforcement concerns the connotative meaning of the word *negative.* Too often people forget that the word *negative* in negative reinforcement simply indicates an action, not a value judgment. Positive refers to supplying something; negative refers to removing something. Students overlook the fact that both positive reinforcement and negative reinforcement contain the key word *reinforcement*—something to which most people look forward.

How far we go to avoid dealing with anything negative, including negative numbers, is highlighted in the familiar example of Scholastic Aptitude Test (SAT) scores. In reality, SAT scores are simply z-scores with a mean of zero, a standard deviation of 1, and a range from -3 to $+3$. Imagine the panic if students earned SAT scores of $-.3$, $-.5$, or -1.6. Of course, when the negative sign and the decimal are removed by multiplying by 100 and then adding 500, one obtains the more recognizable and less threatening scores of 470, 450, and 340, respectively.

Mention to students the relatively infrequent appearance of negative reinforcement in the literature as the basis for a fifth remedy. To demonstrate that they have fewer opportunities to learn about this concept, you might have students review three common indexes, *Psychological Abstracts,* the Educational Resources Information Center's (ERIC) *Resources in Education (RIE),* and *Current Index to Journals in Education (CIJE).* Have them count the number of citations for negative reinforcement, positive reinforcement, time-out, and punishment. A citation is any entry that includes the term in the title of the article.

A hand search of *Psychological Abstracts* (1980-1985) revealed twice as many articles about positive reinforcement (180) and four times as many articles about punishment (362) than articles about negative reinforcement (80). An on-line DIALOG search (1966-1987) revealed only 9 articles on negative reinforcement in *CIJE* and 3 in *RIE,* compared to 41 and 15, respectively, on positive reinforcement and 205 and 70, respectively, on punishment. Time–out citations, another misunderstood consequence, were not tallied.

A sixth (and related) remedy is to show that textbooks shortchange the treatment of negative reinforcement. My review of the indexes of 20 randomly sampled introductory psychology and educational psychology textbooks (1975 or later) revealed a total of 38 pages devoted to negative reinforcement, 63 to positive reinforcement, and 111 to punishment. Students could conduct a similar review. If students' first exposure to negative reinforcement is a class lecture supplemented by assigned textbook readings, it is not surprising that negative reinforcement is so poorly understood.

Summary

Administering the negative reinforcement quiz demonstrates misunderstanding about the definition and use of negative reinforcement and prompts students to begin learning the concept. Specific remedies, including using the consequence-grid matrix, presenting examples of negative reinforcement and punishment, and having students devise, analyze, and evaluate their own examples, enhance this learning. Indicating the connotation of the word *negative* helps prevent the temptation to stereotype negative reinforcement as something inherently bad. Finally, mentioning the infrequent appearance of negative reinforcement in the literature and in textbooks alerts students to the extra attention required to learn the concept.

It is important for psychology students to understand the concept of negative reinforcement and to use it correctly. Without this understanding, only three behavior consequence categories in operant conditioning will be available for use. The suggestions presented in this article will help students overcome their misunderstanding of negative reinforcement.

Note

I thank Tonya Beater for her library research.

5. TEACHING BIOLOGICAL ASPECTS OF LEARNING

Constraints on Learning: A Useful Undergraduate Experiment

Ernest D. Kemble and
Kathleen M. Phillips
University of Minnesota, Morris

Although the topic of biological constraints on learning is attracting increased attention in psychology texts, the selection of experiments in this area that are appropriate for undergraduate participation poses a number of problems. The classic demonstrations of constraints may require the administration of toxic substances (often traumatic for student and subject alike), considerable experimental sophistication, prolonged testing, or somewhat elaborate instrumentation. We would like to describe an experiment that is simple to instrument, can be conducted within a single week, yields highly reliable results, and raises a number of interesting theoretical and methodological issues.

Since Shettleworth (1972) has demonstrated that responses are one important source of constraints on learning, we chose to compare the acquisition rate of a food reinforced lever press response to that of a rearing response. Rearing is an extremely common behavior of many rodent species in both the laboratory and field that apparently has considerable adaptive significance. It might be expected then that the ease of acquisition of such a response would differ substantially from the presumably less "natural" lever-press response.

Apparatus and Procedure. The testing apparatus was a 29 x 29 x 11 cm chamber constructed of clear Plexiglas with a floor of 0.5 cm diameter steel rods spaced 1.6 cm apart. A 3.0 cm^2 food cup was placed in the center of one wall, and a 4.0 x 2.0 cm lever requiring 19 g pressure and approximately 0.5 cm excursion was placed 20 cm from the food cup along one of the side walls. The hole through which the lever projected was sufficiently large to allow 1.0–2.0 cm adjustment of the lever toward or away from the food cup. A photoelectric system (Veritas, Model V-942) was mounted outside the end walls of the testing chamber with the photobeam 23 cm above the floor. The photocell units were suspended on threaded steel rods that were inserted through small Plexiglas platforms extending beyond each end of the apparatus at roof level. The rods were secured by wing nuts that permitted continuous adjustment of photobeam height. Both lever and photobeam relays were connected to separate banks of four Sodeco counters and a recycling 5-min timer. Toggle switches allowed the activation of a pellet dispenser by either rearing or lever pressing, or bypassed the dispenser entirely for recording of operant (baseline) rates of the two responses. The testing compartment was housed in a sound attenuating chamber with all programming equipment located in an adjacent cubicle. Observations were carried out through a one-way vision screen.

Prior to the experiment, the rate of both unreinforced rearing and lever pressing was recorded for eight pilot rats. During these sessions, the height of the photobeam and position of the lever were adjusted until (a) the operant rates of the two responses were similar and (b) the manipulanda (lever and photobeam) were equidistant from the food cup. (We assumed that nonreinforced rears, on the average, would occur at the midpoint of the chamber.) A photobeam height of 23.0 cm and a 20 cm lever to food cup distance produced the desired results. The experimenters were 19 undergraduate students enrolled in an introductory course in research methods. They had little or no previous animal research experience. The subjects for the experiment proper were 19 female albino rats (Holtzman Company) weighing 273-322 g. Prior to student assignment, the rats were habituated to the chamber for 20 minutes, were food deprived (23.5 hrs), and then received five consecutive daily periods of magazine training. Forty 45 mg Noyes food pellets were delivered during each session with care being taken never to reinforce either rearing or lever pressing. After habituation and magazine training, each experimenter was assigned one rat that was weighed and food deprived on the first day of the experiment.

On the following day, each rat was placed into the apparatus and the number of unreinforced rears and lever presses was recorded for a single 20-min session. The baseline response levels were then used to assign rats to either rearing (N = 10) or lever pressing (N = 9) groups which were virtually identical (M = 55.0 and 57.2, respectively) in the unreinforced rates of their assigned operant responses. The rats then received nine daily 20-min acquisition sessions during which the designated operant response was reinforced on a CR schedule. No shaping was necessary for either response. Body weights were maintained at 80-90% of *ad libitum* values by limited feeding after each session.

Results. The results are summarized in Figure 1. It can be seen that while the operant (baseline) levels of the two responses were nearly identical, striking group differences emerged during the first day of acquisition [$U(9, 10) = 20$, $p = .05$] and that the rearing group responded at a higher level throughout acquisition [$F(1,17) = 6.75$, $p < .025$]. It should be noted that these group differences occurred despite the considerable inter-subject variability which was due in part to the use of multiple experimenters. Although acquisition was continued for nine days, it can also be seen that response rates were asymtotic and group differences clearly established within five days [$F(1, 17) = 7.70$, $p < .025$]. Even with this brief period of training, the experiment seems to provide a clear demonstration of constraints on learning with most potentially confounding variables reasonably well controlled.

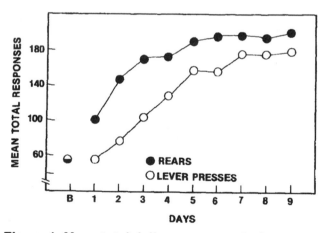

Figure 1. Mean total daily responses during baseline testing (B) and acquisition.

The immediacy of group differences in acquisition, however, may well cause more able or advanced students to be skeptical. It is possible, for example, that the similarities in baseline responding during the 20-min test masked group differences in the temporal patterning of the responses. If rearing responses were emitted rapidly early in the session but decreased below a steady rate of lever pressing, then the rearing response would be favored early in acquisition. To examine this possibility, we compared the intrasession baseline responding of the two groups. Although the response levels declined steadily during this session [$F(3, 51) = 7.53$, $p < .001$], there was neither a reliable group difference nor a groups by intervals interaction

($Fs<1.0$). Thus, temporal patterning of baseline responding does not seem to account for the overall group difference. In contrast, group comparisons of intra-session responding during the first day of acquisition reveal significantly higher response rates by the Rearing Group during the first 5 min of training [$U(9, 10) = 17$, $p < .05$] and throughout this session [$F(1, 17) = 4.43$, $p < .05$]. There were no changes over intervals nor groups by intervals interaction ($Fs<1.10$).

Comparison of intrasession responding on these two days is presented in Figure 2. It can be seen that while the Rearing Group exceeded its own baseline throughout the first day of acquisition, this did not occur until the final 5 min for the Lever-Press Group. Although the rearing response did seem to be more rapidly acquired, the group differences were exaggerated by the initial depression of lever-pressing. Why did the introduction of food reinforcement inhibit lever-pressing? Observations suggest that the design of the apparatus required the rats that lever pressed

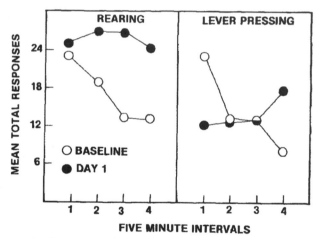

Figure 2. A comparison of intrasession baseline and first day of acquisition responding by rearing and lever pressing rats.

(but not those that reared) to turn away from the food cup to make the operant response. In essence, we may have presented the rats that lever pressed with an umweg problem described many years ago by gestalt psychologists (Köhler, 1925).

If that feature of the experiment were removed by minor apparatus alteration, this seemingly clear demonstration of constraints might disappear. Inasmuch as this experiment can be conducted within a single week, suitable follow-up experiments could easily be conducted in more advanced courses. In any case, the experiment certainly highlights some of the methodological problems in investigating constraints on learning. This feature, combined with relative simplicity and robustness of the effect, suggests that the experiment would be a useful undergraduate laboratory project.

References

Köhler, W. *The mentality of apes.* New York: Harcourt, Brace, 1925.

Shettleworth, S. J. Constraints on learning. In Lehrman, D. S., Hinde, R. A., & Shaw, E. *Advances in the study of behavior* (Vol. 4). Academic Press: New York, 1972, pp. 1-68.

Note

The authors would like to thank Dr. W. Miles Cox for his helpful comments on an earlier version of this report.

Demonstration Experiments In Learned Taste Aversions

J. W. Kling
Brown University

Demonstration experiments or laboratory exercises for undergraduate courses should produce robust effects with relatively simple apparatus and procedures. Furthermore, they should not involve methods that cause physical or emotional distress for the students or the subjects. There are many examples of operant conditioning that fit these requirements, but few suitable demonstrations of classical conditioning seem to be available for undergraduate courses. At various times, we have tried conditioning human eyelid closure, finger withdrawal, and knee jerk. None of these produced consistently successful and orderly results. We have avoided conditioned suppression procedures with rats or pigeons on the grounds that strong aversive stimulation raises too many ethical and safety problems to warrant its use in lower-level undergraduate courses.

Fortunately, learned taste aversions provide a simple and convenient way to demonstrate principles of classical conditioning. In addition, this topic encourages the experimental study of such interesting problems as biological constraints and preparedness, neophobia, learned safety, and the relations between conditioning and physiological variables. The existence of annotated bibliographies (e.g., Riley & Clarke, 1977) related to learned taste aversion publications is a major asset for the instructor.

The learned taste aversion procedure usually involves the creation of some degree of gastrointestinal upset in the experimental subject. Ionizing radiation, or introduction of toxins through esophageal intubation or intraperitoneal injection, are the common ways of producing such illness in the laboratory. Each of these methods has obvious drawbacks for use by beginners.

This report describes a convenient and completely safe way to produce mild malaise and generate robust and reliable conditioned taste aversions without producing noticeable distress in the animal. The technique relies upon the relative inability of animals to distinguish the taste of safe sodium chloride (NaCl) from that of poisonous lithium chloride (LiCl). To illustrate the procedure, one experiment done in an undergraduate course will be described. (Some practical suggestions for organizing and implementing the conduct of such experiments are offered in the Appendix.) In this experiment, the students were led (on the basis of readings and class discussions) to ask whether familiarization and novelty effects had their expected consequences when a complex taste substance was encountered. Typically, flavors that have been met previously will be approached more readily than novel flavors, illustrating the decline in neophobia (Barnett, 1958). If a familiar food is poisoned, rats that recover tend to return to it more readily than if the food has been novel (Rzoska, 1953). If novel and familiar foods are both present and illness occurs, conditioned taste aversions are more likely to occur to the novel food (Revusky & Berdarf, 1967). But what would happen if the food that immediately precedes the onset of the illness is a unique combination of flavors that includes one or more familiar elements? As one student described the problem, "If a person has always enjoyed hot dogs, but becomes ill after his very first chili dog, will he later have an aversion to chili but continue to eat hot dogs?"

In the experiment designed to examine this problem, NaCl was the familiar flavor; NaCl in sodium saccharin (NaSacc) solution was the new compound taste for the Control Group, and LiCl in NaSacc was the new compound for the Experimental Group. Later, each rat would be tested with NaCl, NaSacc, and the mixture of the two.

Method. Twenty male albino rats of the Charles River CD strain were used. They had previously served in several operant conditioning experiments in the undergraduate laboratory, and had been mildly food deprived. Prior to starting the present experiment, they were kept on ad lib. food and water for 10 days. The rats were housed in a small room within the undergraduate lab area. The lights were off from 10 pm to 8 am.

Water bottles were removed from the cages, and 24 hrs later the food was removed. The rat in his individual cage was carried to an adjacent test area where a drinking opportunity was provided. After drinking, the rat in his cage was returned to the cage rack. After 10-20 min. water bottles were placed on each cage for a 20-min supplemental drink. The bottles then were removed, and the food returned to the cages. During preconditioning and conditioning sessions, the drinking opportunity lasted 10 min; during post-conditioning testing, each of the three test solutions was presented for 5 min.

All rats were given water in the drinking situation on the first two days, and then were given 0.15 M NaCl solutions for the next six days. On Day 9, a mixture of 0.15M NaCl in 0.01 M NaSacc was presented to the Control Group rats; the Experimental Group animals received 0.15 M LiCl in 0.01 M NaSacc. On the next two days, the rats remained on the cage rack and received 30 min of "supplemental" watering. On Day 12, each rat was offered 0.15 M NaCl, 0.01 M NaSacc, or the compound of the two. A 5-min pause was inserted between each test taste, and midway in the pause the rat was allowed to take about 10 laps from the spout of a water bottle (to "rinse the mouth").

Drinking tests were conducted by sliding the rat's cage up to a stainless steel drinking spout inserted into a 50 ml burette, and the resulting intake was measured to the nearest 0.1 ml. Supplemental drinking was measured by weighing the water bottles to the nearest 1.0 g before and after use. All solutions were mixed from reagent grade chemicals and distilled water, and were presented at room temperature.

Animals were ranked according to their intakes of NaCl on Days 6-8 and one of each adjacent pair was assigned at random to the Experimental Group. The order of presentation of the test solutions was varied across pairs of rats. Spouts and burettes were used for one solution only, and were thoroughly cleansed between animals.

Results. Preconditioning intakes of NaCl were vigorous, as would be expected from the finding (Ernits & Corbit, 1973) that 0.15 M is the preferred concentration for mildly thirsty rats. On the last 3 days of NaCl familiarization, the mean intake was 15.2 ml (SD = 1.0 ml). On the Conditioning Day, the rats had their first exposure to the compound containing saccharin. The mean intake in 10 min. was 12.2 ml (SD = 5.8 ml) for the Control Group and 5.36 ml (SD = 3.6) for the Experimental Group. For Control Group rats, the change from NaCl (on Day 8) to NaCl + NaSacc (on Day 9) produced a small decrease in drinking ("neophobia") that was not statistically significant (p <.10); for the Experimental Group rats, the change from NaCl to LiCl + NaSacc was significant (p <.001, t for paired measures, one-tailed).

Most rats in the Experimental Group drank rapidly for 2-3 min; a few continued for 5 min. but none drank throughout the 10 min period. No rat displayed the overt symptoms (cf. Barker, Smith & Suarez, 1977) of severe lithium poisoning (complete inaction, gagging, diarrhea); all rats drank as soon as the water bottles were placed on the cages.

On the Test Day, rats in the Control Group took approximately equal amounts of each of the three solutions. Rats in the Experimental Group drank large amounts of the familiar NaCl, but took very little NaSacc and NaSacc + NaCl compound. ANOVA revealed significant effects for illness, for test solution, and for their interaction (all p <.01). The results are summarized in Figure 1.

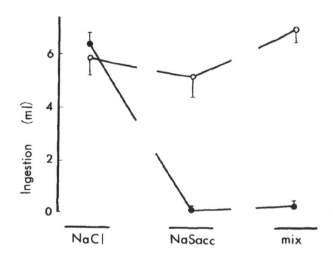

Figure 1. Amount ingested on test day. Filled circles: Experimental Group. Open circles: Control Group. Vertical lines = 1 Standard Error

Discussion. The results illustrate several well-established phenomena of learned taste aversions that have important implications for classical conditioning. For example, preconditioning familiarization with a stimulus decreases the strength

164

of the conditioning to that stimulus. This effect hasbeen ascribed to such processes as habituation of the novel-stimulus reaction (Carlton & Vogel, 1967); to learned safety (Kalat & Rozin, 1973); and to latent inhibition (Lubow, 1965; Best, 1975).

Next, the data show the conditioning of a strong aversion to a novel taste stimulus (the compound) on the basis of a single experience. Such results are typical in learned taste aversions, and are one of the reasons for the widespread acceptance of such principles as "preparedness" (Seligman & Hager, 1972) and "stimulus relevance" (McFarland, 1973). The view that only relative differences exist between taste aversion learning and other examples of conditioning (i.e., "general process theory") has been explored in papers by Krane and Wagner (1975) and Bitterman (1975), among others.

Finally, the data also show that the rat responds to the saccharin taste as if it were a novel element that had been included within the compound, suggesting that taste mixtures can be analyzed by the rat into their taste elements (cf. Rescorla & Cunningham, 1978). But note that the experimental design does not allow us to reject the possibility that a new taste (like the NaSacc) presented for the first time after an illness, might be avoided even if it had not been present on the conditioning day. (Based on experimental analysis of nonassociative novelty effects by Best and Batson, 1977, it would seem unlikely that so strong a reaction to NaSacc would be seen, but an appropriate control group would have strengthened our confidence that the aversion to NaSacc is a conditioned one.)

Human learned taste aversions are thought to be frequent, durable, and based on specific experiences early in life (Garb & Stunkard, 1974). Loss of appetite by cancer patients that continues long after the immediate effects of chemotherapy have subsided, seem to be due, in at least some proportion of the instances, to learned taste aversions (Bernstein, 1978). And it has been suggested (Garcia, 1979) that anorexia nervosa might have its origins in learned taste aversions in some cases. For many students, the potential for dealing with such practical problems validates the efforts invested in animal behavior investigations and provides a useful bridge between the discussions of basic research and applied technology.

Appendix. Animals need not be handled by students. If each rat already is housed in an individual cage, it is convenient to remove the cage and place it on a flat board or small tray for ease of carrying. (The plastic trays measuring 27 x 35 cm that are used by lunch counters and fast-food outlets are an ideal size.) Place a paper towel on the tray to minimize clean-up problems. The open top of the individual cage requires a lid: a piece of 1/4 inch plywood with L-shaped molding glued around 3 edges slides on the cage and

provides a secure closure. In the drinking situation, the calibrated tube is positioned so that the drinking spout will be approximately 3 cm above the floor of the cage, and when ready, the tray and cage can be moved forward until the spout passes through the cage mesh and is within reach of the rat. At the end of the interval, sliding the tray and cage away from the spout stops drinking without incurring spillage.

Supplemental drinking is monitored to insure an adequate daily fluid supply. Weighing the animal's water bottle to the nearest 1 g before and after the supplemental drinking provides adequate accuracy. Food should be absent during all drinking opportunities to eliminate prandial drinking. When fluid is available once a day while food is absent, rats lose about 5% of their body weights over the first day or two, but they recover quickly and start slow weight gains again.

During drinking tests, measurements of intake should be accurate to at least 0.5 ml. Weighing fluid containers ordinarily is unsatisfactory because of spillage. Volumetric readings are convenient, and some calibrated containers can be obtained at relatively little cost. Burettes allow measurement to the nearest 0.1 ml but are expensive. In undergraduate chemistry labs, 50 ml burettes broken at the stopcock end are fairly common. Ask your chemistry colleagues to save these for you, have the glassblower cut off that end, and use a 00 rubber stopper to seal the open end. A standard stainless steel drinking spout will fit snugly into the newly cut end if a piece of gum rubber tubing is used instead of a stopper. This arrangement places the numbers on the burette in the upright position for easy reading. Be sure to borrow a burette brush for convenience in cleansing the tubes. Burette clamps that fit on ringstands also provide convenient and stable mounts for the tubes. If burettes are not available, calibrated centrifuge tubes or graduated cylinders may be substituted, or plastic syringes can be adapted to this purpose (Robbins, 1977). On the test day, each solution must be pre-loaded in a tube. Color coding the tubes and stoppers helps minimize errors and avoid taste contaminations. Standard stainless steel drinking spouts vary considerably in the size of aperture; for drinking tests, select spouts that are of uniform size.

Most of the taste aversion literature specifies taste solutions in percent-by-weight terms, while most studies of taste sensitivity use molar concentration specifications. There are some advantages to the latter, not the least of which is that the instructor does not appear to be ignorant of physical science techniques. Dispensing fluids when students are milling about can be messy: a neat way of filling burettes is provided by a gallon jug (ask your colleagues to save their empties) equipped with a siphoning tube ending in a hose clamp and a short pipette (as a nozzle). These work as well as the more expensive Lister Bottles that can be had from apparatus supply sources. In mixing compounds, the aim is to maintain the concentration of each of the elements. For example, 0.15 M NaCl requires 8.76 g of salt plus enough water to bring the solution to one liter; 0.01 M NaSacc requires 2.41 g plus the water; a compound of NaCl + NaSacc would be made with 8.76 g NaCl plus 2.41 g NaSacc plus enough water to total one liter. To the human observer, each of the tastes is present, although careful analysis suggests that each is somewhat weakened or "compressed" in its intensity by the mixture (Bartoshuk, 1977).

The apparatus and procedures are those that have worked well for rats, but they probably could be adapted for the use with mice (Kimmeldorf, Garcia, & Rudadeau, 1960; Robbins, 1979) guinea pigs (Bravemen, 1974), or other animals that are readily available.

References

Barker, L. M., Smith, J. C., & Suarez, E. M. "Sickness" and the backward conditioning of taste aversions. In L. M. Barker, M. R. Best, and M. Domjan (Eds.), *Learning mechanisms in food selection.* Waco, TX: Baylor University Press, 1977

Barnett, S. A. Experiments on "neophobia" in wild and laboratory rats. *British Journal of Psychology,* 1958, *49*, 195-201.

Bartoshuk, L. M. Psychophysical studies of taste mixtures. In J. LeMagnen & P. MacLeod (Eds.), *Olfaction and taste VI.* London: Information Retrieval, 1977.

Bernstein, I. L. Learned taste aversions in children receiving chemotherapy. *Science,* 1978, *200,* 1302-1303.

Best, M. R. Conditioned and latent inhibition in taste-aversion learning: Clarifying the role of learned safety. *Journal of Experimental Psychology: Animal Behavior Processes ,* 1975, *1,* 97-113.

Best, M. R., & Batson, J. D. Enhancing the expression of flavor neophobia: Some effects of the ingestion-illness contingency. *Journal of Experimental Psychology: Animal Behavior Processes,* 1977, *3,* 132-143.

Bitterman, M. E. The comparative analysis of learning: Are the laws of learning the same in all animals? *Science,* 1975, *188,* 699-709

Bravemen, N. S. Poison-based avoidance learning with flavored or colored water in guinea pigs. *Learning and Motivation,* 1974, *5,* 182-194.

Carlton, P. L., & Vogel, J. R. Habituation and conditioning. *Journal of Comparative and Physiological Psychology,* 1967, *63,* 348-351.

Ernits, T., & Corbit, J. D. Taste as a dipsogenic stimulus. *Journal of Comparative and Physiological Psychology,* 1973, *83,* 27-31

Garb, J. L., & Stunkard, A. J. Taste aversions in man. *American Journal of Psychiatry,* 1974, *131,* 1204-1207.

Garcia, J. Discussion. In M. B. Kare & O. Maller (Eds.), *The chemical senses and nutrition.* New York: Academic Press, 1979, p. 290.

Kalat, J. W., & Rozin, P. "Learned safety" as a mechanism in long-delay taste-aversion learning in rats. *Journal of Comparative and Physiological Psychology,* 1973, *83,* 198-207

Kimmeldorf, D. J., Garcia, J., & Rudadeau, D. O. Radiation-induced conditioned avoidance behavior in rats, mice, and cats. *Radiation Research,* 1960, *12,* 710-718.

Krane, R. V., & Wagner, A. R. Taste aversion learning with a delayed shock US: Implications for the "generality of the laws of learning." *Journal of Comparative and Physiological Psychology,* 1975, *88,* 882-889 .

Lubow, R. E. Latent inhibition: Effects of frequency of nonreinforced preexposure of the CS. Journal of *Comparative and Physiological Psychology,* 1965, *60,* 454-459.

McFarland, D. J. Stimulus relevance and homeostasis. In R. Hinde & J. Stevenson-Hinde (Eds.), *Constraints on Learning.* London: Academic Press, 1973, 141-155.

Rescorla, R. A., & Cunningham, C. L. Within-compound flavor associations. *Journal of Experimental Psychology: Animal Behavior Processes,* 1978, *4,* 267-275

Revusky, S., & Bedarf, E. W. Association of illness with ingestion of novel foods. *Science,* 1967, *155,* 219-220.

Riley, A. L. & Clarke, C. M. Conditoned taste aversions: A bibliography. In L. M. Barker, M. R. Best and M. Domjan (Eds), *Learning Mechanisms in Food Selection.* Waco, TX: Baylor University Press, 1977.

Robbins, R. J. An accurate, inexpensive, calibrated drinking tube. *Laboratory Animal Science,* 1977, *27,* 1038-1039

Robbins, R. J. The effect of flavor preexposure upon the acquisition and retention of poison-based taste aversions in deer mice: Latent inhibition or partial reinforcement? *Behavioral and Neural Biology,* 1979, *25,* 387-397.

Rzoska, J. Bait shyness: A study in rat behavior. *The British Journal of Animal Behavior,* 1953, *1,* 128-135.

Seligman, M. E. P, & Hager, J. L. *Biological boundaries of learning.* New York: Appleton-Century-Crofts, 1972.

SECTION IV
COGNITIVE

In an effort to increase students' understanding about psychologists' versus philosophers' use of the term *mind* Lance Olsen developed a metaphor of internal combustion for mind. In addition to defining mind as a physical process, the author used the metaphor to point out the interdependency among independent variables.

Frank Hassebrock asked students in his cognitive psychology course to scan selected journals' tables of contents, from the last 40 years. Students judged whether each article represented a cognitive or behavioral framework. This activity helped the students compare the two frameworks, gave them an appreciation for the historical development of cognitive explanations, and introduced them to research issues in contemporary cognitive psychology.

To reduce some students' resistance to a computer model for human information processing, Leigh Shaffer adapted Jevon's classic demonstration. The equipment consisted of pennies and a cardboard box. Without counting, students estimated the number of pennies, and the instructor plotted the number of correct responses as a function of the number of pennies. The author reported that the demonstration was an extremely robust one. A variation of the demonstration for groups uses flash cards with varying numbers of dots.

W. Scott Terry described student use of a forgetting journal. Students recorded instances of forgetting, such as forgetting names, tip-of-the-tongue phenomena, inability to correctly place a person, forgetting appointments, and the like. Instructions directed students to describe the event, report factors they thought were relevant to the forgetting, and try to explain why forgetting occurred. Advantages of the journal included using the events to illustrate concepts in the course, suggesting remedies for forgetting problems, and pointing out the advantages and disadvantages of a case-study approach.

Scott Gronlund and Stephan Lewandowsky instructed students in an introductory cognitive course to make TV commercials using principles learned in class. The commercials illustrated the cognitive principles of chunking, primacy and regency, repetition, rehearsal, depth of processing, and cue dependence. Favorable course evaluations and the high quality of students' productions led the authors to conclude that the project was successful.

Marianne Miserandino described a teaching demonstration in which the names of the Seven Dwarfs introduced and explained basic memory processes. The authors contrasted recall and recognition to develop an understanding of important memory principles such as organization by sound, letter, and/or meaning, the tip-of-the-tongue phenomenon, long-term memory, and short-term memory. Students reported that the demonstration was effective in helping them master the basic principles of memory.

Conventional wisdom asserts and some researchers conclude that repeating verbal material facilitates transfer into long-term memory and thus improves memory. Roger Chaffin and Douglas Herrmann developed a demonstration whose conditions produced the paradoxical results of poorer memory for students who repeated the information than for those who did not. The authors described a procedure that illustrated the role of depth of processing. The article also identified three features of the procedure that maximized the demonstration's effectiveness.

To demonstrate the effect of attention on learning Janet Larsen presented students with stimulus cards of different colors, each of which had a word and a number on it. The instructor asked students to remember either the words, the numbers, or the colors of the cards. As expected the highest recall was for stimuli to which the students paid attention.

Thomas Thieman developed a simple and effective method to illustrate the relation between cues given during the study and testing phases of a verbal learning task. The procedure illustrated the effect of cue concordance between encoding and retrieval that is a prominent feature of the encoding specificity hypothesis.

Name mnemonics can provide a powerful technique for remembering names. Steven Smith's classroom demonstration taught students how to construct and use name mnemonics. Working in small groups of 2 to 4 individuals, students created mnemonics for each other. Students also described their name mnemonics to the class. In addition to teaching mnemonics, the exercise gave students an experience with group problem solving and ensured that members of the class would know nearly every Class member's name.

Albert Katz described a low tech, paper-and-pencil test for producing reliable reaction-time data suitable for an instructional laboratory. Although the article described the procedure applied to semantic memory, instructors can apply the technique to other topics in Cognitive psychology. The author concluded by suggesting that the demonstration can keep students up to date about techniques, theories, and experimentation in the literature.

Lawrence Schoen developed a computer demonstration of the word fragment completion effect to enhance students' comprehension of an experimental paradigm used in cognitive psychology. The robust word fragment completion effect introduced students to the implicit memory paradigm and illustrated the advantages inherent in such a procedure. The author Concluded that the demonstration was a useful tool for comparing and contrasting experimental procedures and as a starting point for discussing multiple memory models.

An Introductory Model of Mind

Lance A. Olsen
College of Great Falls

Students in introductory psychology courses may experience disappointment and surprise when they learn that psychology has become a "science of behavior." My experience is that they expect psychology to be the "science of mind," Students anticipate that from the psychology course they will learn something about the "mystery of the human mind," or "how the mind works." Consequently, they seem interested in learning how "mind" became a discredited subject in psychologists' own "minds." They listen sympathetically (albeit not fully convinced) when I explain how psychologists came to prefer the study of behavior Briefly, I tell them that "mind" had an ineffable, metaphysical quality. No "mind-stuff" could be found. Mind could not be measured. No one had ever obtained a cubic centimeter of it or had plucked it from the brain to set it upon a scale. In fact, no one had ever seen "mind." There is not and never has been any form of direct access to "mind." Thus, there was no way to demonstrate publicly that it actually existed, although "publicness" is crucial to science. Obviously, if psychology were to be scientific discipline, I tell them, it could not have continued to make "mind" its subject matter. So when I tell my students that, on the other hand, behavior is directly observable, and when I give them examples of how behavior can be measured, they see why psychologists have come to prefer the study of behavior to the search for the elusive mind. Of course, not all students are impressed. Some are highly skeptical, apparently believing that psychologists have merely dodged the issue. Some have said as much.

The mind-body problem and the problem of student response to psychologists' shift to the study of behavior comes up again in an advanced course I teach: brain functions. This course seems to remind students of the notion of "mind" which they may have discarded earlier, in emulation of their skeptical psychology faculty. Especially because so many texts for courses on brain functions explicitly revive the language of "mind," the issue raises its troublesome head as much in this advanced course as in the introductory course.

I have developed a paradigm of mind that appears to free students of the older metaphysical paradigm at both ends of the curriculum. Although I retain the language of mind, it seems that the paradigm helps them to discard successfully any metaphysical annotations of that terminology. In fact, my use of the paradigm is for the purpose of *debunking* the metaphysical construct. Once that is done, students seem agreeable to more appropriate terminology.

I tell my students that mind is analogous to internal combustion. I tell them that internal combustion can not be set upon a scale, to be weighed. I tell them that no one has ever put a cubic centimeter of internal combustion out on a dissecting tray, held it in hand for scrutiny, or put it under a microscope. Internal combustion, like "mind," is not a thing or an object: it is not tangible in the usual sense. Internal combustion can not be plucked from the engine for scientific analysis It is not a product, as is an engine or brain, and yet it is not *metaphysical.* Internal combustion, like mind, is a physical *process*.

The so-called mind is brain-in-process, not simply brain per se, reminding them that internal combustion is not engine per se, but engine-in-process. Then, having said that, I add a caveat regarding use of the term "in," saying that mind is not "in" the brain any more than internal combustion is "in" the engine. Rather, mind is the processor the brain, as internal combustion is the process of the engine. So stated, "mind" begins to be less "mysterious" to students. Those who were skeptical and wary lean forward to make a note or two in their notebooks. Some have voluntarily made mention of the "internal combustion model of mind" in later class discussion.

Having defined mind as a physical process, I next remark on how it works. In so doing, I think that students get an insight into fallacies of determinism and distortions in the interpretation of relationships between "independent" and "dependent" variables, and into the nature of "systems." I say that spark plugs are "singly sufficiently powerful" variables in the engine system so that tinkering with them will indeed impair the process of internal combustion. I add that if psychologists studied the behavior of engines, they would conclude that, "Presence or absence of spark plugs is significantly correlated with internal combustion, but causal relations are not demonstrated." To help students see the limits of the lexicon of experimental research, I tell them that the behavior of the engine would be a dependent variable manipulable by tinkering with the spark system, a variable which could be construed as an "independent" variable in this case. To make a point about systems theory and science, I cite a recent remark by a group of psychologists who point out that, " . . . variables of interest to psychologists are rarely, if ever, independent." (The Laboratory of Comparative Human Cognition, 1979, p. 827.) My students have already got the point when I remind them that the same thing applies to the relations between carburetors and spark plugs and pistons, the various variables of significance to internal combustion. In systems such as brains and engines, all components are *interdependent,* and each of the components may be "singly-sufficiently powerful variables" to affect the processes of that system.

This originally outrageous-appearing paradigm seems useful in moving my students (in both introductory and advanced courses) past a spurious dichotomy which has resisted demise over the entirety of psychology's history: the mind-body or metaphysical-physical division. I refer to differences between anatomy and physiology, and in order to further weld the product-process relations of brain-mind, it seems useful to labor my point a bit, by referring to the difference between the "anatomy and physiology" of the engine, and to the difference between the engine's structures and its functions As an incidental point I like to raise about the bashful nature of psychology as a science, I point out that the absence of "internal combustion stuff" did not embarrass automotive engineers into avoidance of studying internal combustion, whereas psychologists

(evidently more timid souls) have been fleeing "mind" in droves. This observation earns some knowing smiles.

The internal combustion model of mind seems to have utility in demonstrating that just because psychologists do not accept a metaphysical model of mind, the field of psychology is not thereby "mechanistic," or "reductionistic," as students have no doubt been told by a faculty member in some other discipline during their varied day This model of mind seems to help them move away from the language of "mind" altogether, toward more appropriate brain-process concepts such as 'cognitive psychophysiology" or "covert behavior" terms thoroughly and skillfully developed by McGuigan (1978). At least students are likely to have an alternative to metaphysics "in mind" when they hear the term, "mind."

References

McGuigan F. J. *Cognitive psychophysiology: Principles of covert behavior.* Englewood Cliffs, NJ: Prentice-Hall, 1978.

The Laboratory of Comparative Human Cognition. Cross-cultural psychology's challenges to our ideas of children and development. *American Psychologist,* 1979, *34,* 827-833.

Tracing the Cognitive Revolution Through a Literature Search

Frank Hassebrock
Denison University

Using a literature search, undergraduates in a cognitive psychology course examine the tables of contents in volumes of selected journals published during the last 4 decades. Students judge whether each article's topic and terminology represent a behavioral or cognitive framework. This assignment is used to: (a) compare how topics of learning and memory are approached from behavioral versus cognitive frameworks, (b) demonstrate the historical and dynamic nature of conceptual frameworks in psychology, and (c) introduce concepts and research topics in contemporary cognitive psychology.

Proliferation of research, textbooks, and courses associated with cognitive psychology has occurred in the past decade (Chodorow & Manning, 1983). Most undergraduate cognitive psychology textbooks provide an overview of the theoretical and empirical background from which the cognitive approach emerged. Many authors suggest that the cognitive approach is an example of a "revolutionary change" in the shared framework or metatheoretical position of psychologists (e.g., Baars, 1986; Lachman, Lachman, & Butterfield, 1979). Development of cognitive psychology is also reflected in changes of focus and content of research studies published in psychology journals since the emergence of contemporary cognitive psychology in the late 1950s (Mandler, 1985). Although most psychologists probably have a historical perspective on the paradigmatic development of psychological thought, many undergraduate students do not (Henderson, 1988; Schilling, 1983).

To help my students understand the "cognitive revolution," I developed a literature search task assigned after the course's second lecture. Students examine the terms or topics contained in titles of articles selected from a sample of journals published during the last 4 decades. They then judge whether a research article represents either a behavioral (or nonbehavioral) framework or a cognitive approach. By examining the research published in a specific journal over a period of time, students can trace conceptual changes associated with the study of learning and cognition and thus better understand these trends described later in lectures and readings. This assignment helps students: (a) become familiar with the terminology and topics of contemporary cognitive research, (b) recognize distinctions between theoretical and research approaches of cognition and behaviorism (or neobehaviorism), and (c) appreciate the development and change of scientific frameworks or paradigms.

Students in this course have typically completed three or four psychology courses, and most have some familiarity with behaviorism and cognitive psychology. This exercise is most effective when assigned after introductory lectures that highlight the content and history of cognitive psychology, distinguish behavioral and cognitive approaches, and describe the role of scientific paradigms (Kuhn, 1970) and frameworks (Baars, 1986). Thus, the initial lectures and readings provide students with materials to which they can refer as they make their judgments.

Following a brief explanation of the assignment's goals, each student is assigned a particular journal such as Journal of Memory and Language (previously published as Journal of Verbal Learning and Verbal Behavior), Journal of Experimental Psychology (and specifically for recent volumes, JEP: Learning, Memory, and Cognition), Quarterly Journal of Experimental Psychology (for recent volumes, QJEP: Human Experimental Psychology), Psychological Review, Child Development, and Journal of Experimental Child Psychology. I include Psychological Review because its articles typically compare theoretical perspectives on a variety of research topics. By examining the developmental psychology journals, students can observe the impact of the cognitive approach on a distinct field of psychology.

After locating an assigned journal in the university's library (a valuable learning activity in itself), students photocopy one issue's table of contents from each volume published in the 1950s, 1960s, 1970s, and 1980s, depending on the publication history of specific journals. Then, based solely on the title, they judge whether each research article represents a behavioral or a cognitive approach. The students write their judgment next to the title and underline specific words in the title that support their judgment. They are forewarned that some research may appear to represent other conceptual frameworks and, in such cases, the article should not be categorized.

A later class period is conducted in a seminar format, allowing the students to discuss the results of the literature search. Students present examples of article titles and justify their judgment by identifying and then briefly explaining the concepts that correspond to the underlined words in a title. During the discussion, I point out the significance of specific research studies or topics and respond to students' misconceptions. Students also compute percentages of titles in the behavioral and cognitive categories for each issue over the different decades. Typically, the class finds that the majority of articles published between the 1950s and 1965 represent behaviorism, whereas those published between 1965 and 1975 provide nearly equivalent percentages. Articles published after 1975 clearly represent a cognitive approach. The move away from a neobehavioral, verbal learning approach was demonstrated by one student who reported that 8 of 10 articles published in the first issue of Journal of Verbal Learning and Verbal Behavior (1962) studied paired-associate learning or word associations, but these topics were not evident in any titles of articles published in the February 1986 issue of Journal of Memory and Language.

Although the shift in conceptual frameworks appears to be a robust finding from this task, I thought a more formal evaluation of the students' judgments would provide additional information on the general reliability of the exercise. First, I compared the students' judgments with my own and found an agreement of 79%, thus the students' responses were sufficiently reliable for the purposes of this exercise. Second, following the most recent use of this exercise, a behaviorally oriented colleague and I independently judged the set of titles submitted by the students. We reached agreement on 403 of 467 titles (86.3%). Most disagreements occurred when one of us decided an article did not fit either approach and the other included it in one of the categories. Third, using only the agreed on titles, the percentages of articles representing a behavioral or cognitive approach, respectively, by decade were as follows: 1950—90% and 10%, 1960—69% and 31%, 1970—32% and 68%, and 1980—9% and 91%.

Evaluative ratings and written comments have consistently shown that students believe the task contributes to their awareness of significant issues and research topics associated with the development of cognitive psychology. Having used this exercise several times, I believe that the literature search and ensuing discussion provide a salient demonstration of how psychological research topics are grounded within conceptual frameworks that undergo change or revision over time. Furthermore, this initial assignment reveals gaps in students' knowledge of both behavioral and cognitive constructs and provides information that promotes understanding of later lectures and assignments.

The literature search can easily be modified by assigning other journals that publish research on learning and cognition, including those associated with a behavioral perspective. Alternatively, the impact of the cognitive framework can be traced in journals associated with other specialties, such as social psychology, personality, and clinical psychology. Finally, the general procedure of this literature search can be used to trace conceptual changes in psychological terminology and research topics for fields other than cognitive psychology.

References

Baars, B. J. (1986). *The cognitive revolution in psychology.* New York: Guilford.

Chodorow, M. S., & Manning, S. K. (1983). Cognition and memory: A bibliographic essay on the history and issues. *Teaching of Psychology, 10,* 163-167.

Henderson, B. B. (1988). What students know about the history of psychology before taking the course. *Teaching of Psychology, 15,* 204-205.

Kuhn, T. S. (1970). *The structure of scientific revolutions* (2nd ed.). Chicago: University of Chicago Press.

Lachman, R., Lachman, J. L., & Butterfield, E. C. (1979). *Cognitive psychology and information processing: An introduction.* Hillsdale, NJ: Lawrence Erlbaum Associates, Inc.

Mandler, G. (1985) . *Cognitive psychology: An essay in cognitive science.* Hillsdale, NJ: Lawrence Erlbaum Associates, Inc.

Schilling, K. L. (1983) . Teaching psychological issues in context: A library exercise. *Teaching of Psychology, 10,* 57.

Note

I thank Rita Snyder for her assistance in evaluating the reliability of this exercise and for reading earlier versions of this article. I also thank Charles L. Brewer and two anonymous reviewers for their helpful comments and suggestions.

Hamilton's Marbles or Jevon's Beans: A Demonstration of Miller's Magical Number Seven

Leigh S. Shaffer
West Chester State College

The widespread acceptance and influence of cognitive psychology has resulted in the formal consideration of that perspective in introductory psychology textbooks. It is now the task of pedagogy to assess which features of the perspective would be heuristic to teach to an introductory class. Textbooks have frequently started with the computer as a metaphor for human information processing (see, for example, Hilgard, Atkinson & Atkinson, 1979; Lindzey & Norman, 1977). There are two problems with the metaphor that I have repeatedly encountered. First, students do not know much about a computer, especially its mathematical character; for example, Weizenbaum (1976) has cataloged many of the common misconceptions of the computer's ability to process natural language. Second, the computer metaphor suggests to the students such a mechanistic view of humans that using the metaphor risks alienating a large number of humanistically-oriented students before they can appreciate the insights of the cognitive approach. Therefore I found myself searching for a means of introducing cognitive psychology that would be less likely to invoke the cultural misperceptions or apprehensions that students often bring to an introductory course. I found what I consider to be such an approach in considering two "classic" papers by George Miller (Miller, 1956a, 1956b).

Many textbooks (for example McNeil & Rubin, 1977) introduce information processing by explicating Miller's famous "magical number seven" concept of the limitation of sensory capacity for processing information (Miller,1956a). I discovered that the intellectual predecessors of Miller's work were William Hamilton and William Stanley Jevons, who described the results of primitive experiments (with marbles and beans, respectively) that demonstrated the limits of visual information processing; these demonstrations are reported in Miller (1956a) and more extensively in Woodworth's (1938) *Experimental Psychology.* Hamilton asserted that after throwing marbles on the floor, an observer would find it difficult to view more than "six, or seven at the most, without confusion" (quoted in Miller, 1956a). Woodworth (1938) noted that Hamilton's data were taken informally and probably never recorded, but indicated that Jevons carefully performed a similar experiment on himself in 1871 by throwing beans into a box, and Woodworth's edition reports Jevons' procedures and data (Woodworth, 1938, pp. 685-687). Jevons reported that without counting he could determine that there were three or four beans without mistake, that he was sometimes wrong if the number was five, that he was accurate only 43% of the time when the number was ten, and was wrong on 82% of the trials when the number reached 15. Being somewhat literal-minded myself, I found a box, pitched various numbers of pennies into the box, and roughly verified those findings.

It occurred to me that reviving Hamilton's marbles or Jevons' beans would make for an excellent classroom demonstration of a concept which I had previously covered too abstractly for most of my students to follow. Instead of trying to define information, the value of a bit, the notion of channel capacity, and so forth, I took my box and my pennies to the classroom. My only "refinements" were done in an effort to facilitate the demonstration and avoid some obvious "demand characteristics."

I used a table of random numbers to prepare in advance an order for the number of coins used on each trial. I chose a student confederate to play the role of experimenter and "pitch pennies" for each subject. I chose a box with a lid so that the experimenter could exercise some control over the viewing time by using the lid as a shutter. I set a two second exposure as a reasonable exposure time that would preclude obvious counting and allowed the experimenter to estimate the interval of exposure. Finally, I had the experimenter instruct the subject to try to determine the number of pennies in the box "only by observation," and instructed the subject to

"avoid counting" the pennies. The demonstration was then conducted by having the experimenter follow the predetermined sequence in putting pennies into the box for each trial, allowing the subject to look into the box for approximately two seconds, having the subjects report the number of pennies they thought they saw, and having another confederate record the responses and privately record "correct or incorrect" for each trial (subjects were not given any feedback about the accuracy of the judgments).

When several subjects had attempted the task, the results were tabulated and presented to the class on the chalkboard as a frequency distribution of the number of correct responses as a function of the number of pennies viewed. The results each time I have performed the demonstration have clearly followed the predicted pattern, as would be expected of such a robust phenomenon. I have never seen an error for as many as four pennies, I have seen occasional errors at five pennies, the plotted curve most often decelerates with eight pennies, and with ten or more pennies the frequency of correct responses is so low as to easily be attributed to guessing. (Indeed, to minimize spuriously high frequencies of correct guesses, I have avoided telling subjects the maximum number of pennies to expect.)

I have found this demonstration to be extremely useful. It is based on a robust phenomenon, so it is unlikely to go awry. It is easy to comprehend the limits to information processing in this demonstration, and it focuses on a *human* phenomenon which will be congenial even to students with a bias against mechanistic views of behavior. It is also, of course, highly portable so that it can be used impromptu— even at a playground marble game or on the floor of a country store! It is also adaptable for use with large groups, with some technological support. I have prepared flash cards with varying numbers of dots on them; these need only to be randomly ordered prior to their use, and then everyone in a lecture class can be a subject. A cleaner version of the latter approach merely involves the advance preparation and ordering of the same stimuli to be presented as slides by a carousel projector, especially a projector with a tachistoscopic mechanism But whether it is done with technological sophistication or not, I highly recommend the use of this demonstration that was first performed over a century ago. It represents a simple, interesting, and non-threatening introduction to cognitive psychology.

References

Hilgard, E. R., Atkinson, R. L, & Atkinson, R. C. *Introduction to psychology* (7th ed.). New York: Harcourt, Brace, Jovanovich, 1979.

Lindzey, P. H. & Norman, D. A. *Human information processing: An introduction to psychology* (2nd ed.). New York: Academic Press, 1977.

McNeil, E. B. & Rubin, Z. *The psychology of being human* (2nd ed.). San Francisco: Canfield Press, 1977.

Miller, G. A. Information and memory. *Scientific American*, 1956, *195*, 2-6. (a)

Miller, G. A. The magical number seven, plus or minus two: Some limits on our capacity for information processing. *Psychological Review*, 1956, *63*, 81-97. (b)

Weizenbaum, J. *Computer power and human reason: From judgement to calculation.* San Francisco: Freeman, 1976.

Woodworth, R. S. *Experimental psychology.* New York: Holt, 1938.

A "Forgetting Journal" for Memory Courses

W. Scott Terry
University of North Carolina

An instructional technique that many have found to be valuable is the student journal (see Hettich, 1976 for a description). This note will describe an application to courses that include instruction on human memory. The basic idea is for the students to keep a diary of instances of forgetting during the semester. These examples can then be used for analysis by the individual, the instructor, or the class.

The intent of the project is to have the students apply their course material on learning and memory outside of the class. This should help them generalize the theories and findings learned in class or from the text, from the (typically) laboratory situations to real world settings. The exercise gives the students concrete examples to work with, and allows them to be analytical about their own behavior.

The procedure is to instruct the students to begin keeping a journal of instances where they realize they have forgotten something. They are to write down the situation involved, to record any factors they think are relevant to the forgetting (such as the stimuli present, their emotional state, other activities they were engaged in), and to try to explain why the forgetting occurred. They also record whether the forgotten material was later recalled, and the situations surrounding this event.

(Calling the diary a "forgetting" journal may be something of a self-fulfilling prophecy. The first thing the students have to learn to remember is to keep up with their journals.)

I also suggest that unusual instances of remembering can be just as informative. For example, the sudden remembrance of something they thought they had forgotten. Again, the student should try to describe the conditions leading to this sudden memory retrieval.

The journals are collected periodically by the course instructor. I usually make comments in the books about alternative sources of the forgettings and rememberings, and examples from the journals are presented in class for discussion.

In the introductory lecture to the journal project, I suggest some of the kinds of everyday forgettings the students might look for. Reed (1979) gives a partial listing of "Everyday anomalies of recall and recognition," such as forgetting names, not being able to correctly place a person, repetitive checking behaviors, déjà vu, and the feeling of knowing. In addition, one might mention the tip-of-the-tongue phenomenon, forgetting of intentions or plans, forgetting places and routes, forgetting of dreams or childhood experiences, and examples of motivated forgettings (see chapters in Kihlstrom & Evans, 1979, for discussion of some of these). The students may also want to consider mistakes in their behavior which occur as a result of false retrieval or retrieval failure (Norman, 1981). Two additional sources concerning everyday forgetting are Freud's *Psychopathology of Everyday Life* (1901/1966), and Neisser's *Memory Observed* (1982).

Little need be said here concerning the instructor's analysis of the forgettings. After collecting only a few journals, there will be examples of nearly every concept presented in a learning and memory course. One could also use the course material to suggest remedies for the forgetting problems.

There are other advantages to this project. The material is intrinsically interesting to the student. One can illustrate research methodology, and point out the strengths and weaknesses of case-study and field research. Finally, the instructor will certainly get to know the students in reading about their lives outside of the class.

References

Freud, S. *The psychopathology of everyday life.* London: Ernest Benn, 1966. (Originally published, 1901.)

Hettich, P. The journal: An autobiographical approach to learning. *Teaching of Psychology,* 1976, *3,* 60-63.

Kihlstrom, J. F., & Evans, F. J. *Functional disorders of memory.* Hillsdale, NJ: Erlbaum, 1979.

Neisser, U. *Memory observed: Remembering in natural contexts.* San Francisco: W. H. Freeman, 1982.

Norman, D. A. Categorization of action slips. *Psychological Review,* 1981, *88,* 1-15.

Reed, G. Everyday anomalies of recall and recognition. In J.F. Kihlstrom, & F. J. Evans, (Eds.), *Functional disorders of memory.* Hillsdale, NJ: Erlbaum, 1979.

Making TV Commercials as a Teaching Aid for Cognitive Psychology

Scott D. Gronlund
Stephan Lewandowsky
University of Oklahoma

Many students approach psychology in general, and cognitive psychology in particular, with serious misconceptions about the scientific nature of the discipline. In order to address this problem and bring laboratory findings in cognitive psychology into a real world context, we asked students in an introductory cognitive course to make TV commercials using principles learned in class. The success of the approach became evident from analysis of course evaluation forms and the generally high quality of students' productions.

One of the problems facing teachers of experimental psychology is not that they must teach a science to nonmajors but, paradoxically, that they have to teach a science to majors. Students preparing to major in chemistry, physics, or any other hard science know to take plenty of math and science courses in high school and expect to continue taking these courses in college. Unfortunately, there is a widespread misconception that psychology, although acknowledged to be a science, relies less on computer literacy, quantitative skills, or methodological sophistication than do other fields. In reality, many areas of psychology require training as a scientist in much the same way as does chemistry or physics.

Psychology instructors have to contend with majors who are intimidated by introductory statistics courses and see little connection between abstract laboratory experiments and their daily experiences. We have found that the latter problem can be addressed by getting students involved in the design and production of TV commercials.

Parallels to our approach can be found in Stahl's (1991) call for increased involvement of undergraduates in the subject matter of a discipline and, more specifically, in Labianca's (1991) use of TV in the teaching of toxicology to nonscience majors. Labianca used detective shows to enhance students' interest in toxicology. For example, in an episode of "Murder, She Wrote," atropine is used as a chemical weapon. Throughout the episode, students learn about the symptoms of atropine poisoning and its treatment. By requiring the creation of an episode from scratch, our use of TV commercials takes student involvement one step further.

Background

We are cognitive psychologists responsible for a junior level introductory course in human memory and cognition. Not satisfied with past attempts to motivate our students with the current set of cognitive textbooks, and reluctant to cover the standard set of laboratory-based findings in a lecture format, we tried to increase student interest and participation by asking our students to produce TV commercials using principles learned in lecture and in the textbook.

Preparation of Commercials

The major project in the course was to design, script, film, and defend orally a 2- to 3-min TV commercial for some fictitious product or service. Students worked in small groups of approximately 4 to 5, randomly formed at the beginning of the semester. Each of the 12 groups met with the instructor two or more times during the semester to discuss ideas for the commercial, the cognitive principles to be illustrated, and other relevant details.

Students met outside of class to film their commercials. Although camcorders could have been made available through the university, each group had access to its own recording device. With the prevalence of camcorders today, lack of equipment or facilities is unlikely to restrict use of this teaching tool.

Toward the end of the semester, on two special "commercial days," each group screened its commercial, followed by an oral cognitive analysis. The instructors and an additional faculty member not familiar with these students served as judges, conferring special recognition for best production, best actor/actress, best sound effects, best illustration of a cognitive principle, and so forth. Half the grade points for all students in a given group were based on the judgments by faculty, and the remaining grade points for an individual were assigned anonymously by the other group members, thus giving equal weighting to group and individual performance. Although grading by peers is known to identify students who did not fully participate in a group project (Michaelsen, Watson, & Shrader, 1985), among our 12 groups only 1 such student was identified. Overall, the commercial accounted for 20% of the course grade.

Evaluation by Students

We augmented the standard end-of-semester course evaluations with 10 additional questions that students rated on a scale ranging from *strongly agree* (1) to *strongly disagree* (5). Three of these questions concerned the commercials. Most students (86%) strongly agreed with "I enjoyed watching the commercials," 80% strongly agreed or agreed with "I enjoyed making my commercial," and 46% strongly agreed or agreed with "Making my commercial helped me better understand the course material."

A comparison with the remaining items, which questioned the utility of other teaching tools, helps put the role of the TV commercial in perspective. Students had to (a) keep a journal of everyday experiences relevant to the course material, (b) complete a library project to become more familiar with various literature-research tools (*Psychological Abstracts, Social Sciences Citation Index,* etc.), and (c) read classic articles from the literature to supplement the text. Table 1 shows the distribution of responses to the

Table 1. Percentage of Responses to Questions Concerning Better Understanding of Course Material

Response	Teaching Tool			
	TV Commercial	Library Project	Journal	Readings
Strongly agree	20	10	0	6
Agree	26	23	30	13
Neutral	36	16	26	20
Disagree	6	10	23	33
Strongly disagree	10	40	20	26

question "Doing . . . helped me better understand the course material" for each of these teaching tools.

It is apparent from Table 1 that students considered the TV commercial to be a superior teaching tool in comparison to the other components of this course: Only 16% of the respondents disagreed with the assertion that the commercial was helpful, whereas 43% of respondents disagreed with the utility of the journals. This is noteworthy because journals form part of the standard repertory of teaching devices (e.g., Svinicki & Dixon, 1987). Similarly, 59% of the students did not feel that the inclusion of classic articles from the literature in their reading list was beneficial, and 50% saw little merit in the library project.

Another way of summarizing these data is by comparing the mean response across teaching tools. The commercial ($M = 2.65$) is distinguishable from the library project (3.32), the journal (3.26), and the extra readings (3.55). A one-way within-subjects analysis of variance for the 31 respondents confirmed that the differences between those means were significant, $F(3, 90) = 4.05$, $p < .01$. A Newman-Keuls multiple comparison test (at the .05 level) established that the TV commercial was judged more favorable than the other three teaching tools, which did not differ from each other.

Although these results demonstrate that students held the commercials in higher regard than the other projects, the questionnaire cannot reveal the extent of learning or the potential gain in knowledge resulting from the commercials. One way to assess these potential gains is by analyzing the oral presentations that accompanied each commercial.

Evaluation by Instructors

The instructors and the third faculty member present at the commercial screenings recorded the cognitive principles that students included in their oral presentations. Principles are included in the following list only if students explained them correctly and if they were indeed used in the commercial. That way we do not include principles that students used accidentally, simply by copying features of actual commercials.

Chunking

Virtually every commercial relied heavily on chunking (Miller, 1957) to make phone numbers and the like more memorable (e.g., 1-800-CHEATIN).

Primacy and Recency

All groups placed important parts of the message at the beginning and end of the commercial, thus maximizing the probability of retention by exploiting primacy and recency effects (e.g., Glanzer, 1972). In addition, most commercials ended on a spoken repetition (as opposed to visual display) of the product name or the key message, in line with the fact that recency is greater with auditory than visual presentation (e.g., Crowder, 1972).

Repetition

Important parts of the commercials' messages were usually repeated, and most groups took into account the spacing effect (e.g., Hintzman, 1974), which shows that repetitions are most effective in improving memory when they are spaced apart with other material intervening. Thus, one group interspersed pricing information and further product details between repetitions of a telephone number.

Rehearsal

One group intended to induce rehearsal of the key message, which remained ambiguous for most of the commercial. The commercial featured several people who described recent predicaments in their lives (e.g., unemployment and delayed child-support payments), always concluding their sad story by sighing, "we'll see." In the end, this commercial turned out to advertise the services of one Will C. Gates, attorney.

Depth of Processing

Several commercials attempted to induce deep or elaborative processing of the message (Craik & Lockhart, 1972). Thus, one commercial engaged the viewer in disambiguating a homophone during presentation (e.g., *waste* vs. *waist*) that later formed part of a phone number (1-800-NO-WAIST).

Cue-Dependence

To encourage memory of the product name, several groups presented it with potentially effective retrieval cues (e.g., the title music of the film *Ghostbusters* or some of Strauss's music from *2001*). The groups claimed that this technique would later help reinstate awareness of their product when the viewer heard the corresponding music.

Experimentation

One commercial, produced by a single individual, was pretested by true experimentation. The commercial advertised a children's soup, and the subjects were elementary school children who had to memorize and then pronounce various potential product names. The results pointed to "Mutant Ninja Turtle Soup" as the optimal name for the product, and the commercial then consisted of a series of these children walking up to the camera, trying to pronounce the product name as quickly as possible.

Conclusion

The consensus among the attending faculty members was that the quality of students' productions generally was very high. Numerous reasons for this apparent success can be cited. First, all the commercials were humorous, which not only made the productions fun to watch but no doubt also fun to produce, thus ensuring active participation by all group members. Second, because nearly everyone is an expert on commercials, having seen thousands, all students can offer ideas for design and scripting. Third, as shown by the analysis of oral presentations, students could extract principles from a typical textbook and apply them to the production of commercials. Although some of the cognitive aspects outlined earlier may not survive empirical scrutiny (e.g., if memorability were compared to an explicitly noncognitive commercial), there is little doubt that students were able to apply textbook knowledge to a practical problem in a creative fashion.

References

Craik, F. I. M., & Lockhart, R. S. (1972). Levels of processing: A framework for memory research. *Journal of Verbal Learning and Verbal Behavior, 11,* 671-684.

Crowder, R. G. (1972). Visual and auditory memory. In J. F. Kavanaugh & I. G. Mattingly (Eds.), *Language by ear and by eye: The relationships between speech and reading* (pp. 251-276). Cambridge, MA: MIT Press.

Glanzer, M. (1972). Storage mechanisms in recall. In G. H. Bower & J. T. Spence (Eds.), *The psychology of learning and motivation* (Vol. 5, pp. 129-193). New York: Academic.

Hintzman, D. L. (1974). Theoretical implications of the spacing effect. In R. L. Solso (Ed.), *Theories in cognitive psychology: The Loyola symposium* (pp. 77-99). Hillsdale, NJ: Lawrence Erlbaum Associates, Inc.

Labianca, D. A. (1991). Toxicology for nonscience majors: Using TV. *College Teaching, 39,* 100-104.

Michaelsen, L. K., Watson, W. E., & Shrader, C. B. (1985). Informative testing: A practical approach for tutoring with groups. *The Organizational Behavior Teaching Review, 9,* 18-33.

Miller, G. A. (1957). The magical number seven plus or minus two: Some limits on our capacity for processing information. *Psychological Review, 63,* 81-97.

Stahl, F. A. (1991). Research and teaching: Partnership, not paradox. *College Teaching, 39,* 97-99.

Svinicki, M. D., & Dixon, N. M. (1987). The Kolb model modified for classroom activities. *College Teaching, 35,* 141-146.

Memory and the Seven Dwarfs

Marianne Miserandino
Hobart and William Smith Colleges

This article describes a teaching demonstration in which the names of the seven dwarfs are used to introduce and explain basic processes of memory for an introductory psychology or cognition class. Recall and recognition are contrasted in order to develop an understanding of other important memory principles: organization by sound, letter, and/or meaning; the tip-of-the-tongue phenomenon; long-term memory; and short-term memory. Empirical verifications of this teaching method found it to be effective in helping students master the principles of memory.

Name the seven dwarfs. This deceptively simple task can be an engaging and effective way to illustrate basic principles of memory for students in introductory psychology or cognition classes. The task is appropriate for any class size and can be easily adapted to the level and interest of the class. This demonstration has been used in three different classes of introductory psychology at a small liberal arts college and at a community college. The entire demonstration takes approximately 15 to 20 min.

Theoretical Background

This demonstration is based on Meyer and Hilterbrand's (1984) study of recall and recognition of the names of the seven dwarfs. They found that subjects were more likely to recall the five rhyming names and to recall them in a cluster. They also found that recognition facilitated subjects' memory, indicating that the names were "available but not accessible" in memory (p. 54). These authors suggested that the results of their study can be used as a classroom demonstration of basic memory processes.

Part 1: Free Recall of the Seven Dwarfs

Instructions

Explain to the class that an interesting and effective way to learn about principles of memory is to examine their own thought processes as they perform a memory task. Instruct them to take out a blank sheet of paper and to write down all responses that come into their minds in the order they recall them. Because an important part of the demonstration is the process of recall, emphasize that their incorrect responses are just as important as their correct responses in illustrating how memory is organized. Their task is to name the seven dwarfs.

Discussion

Discuss the following topics with the class, cautioning them to limit their discussion to responses that they know are clearly wrong. Do not reveal correct dwarf names during this initial discussion. Students' responses will suggest many questions and ideas. Lead the discussion in the direction that best suits the class.

Difficulty or ease of the task. How difficult or easy did students find the task? Why? Many students claim that they were unable to name all seven dwarfs because of the lack of recent practice or the culture-bound nature of the task. Others, such as

Disney or trivia buffs, may have been more familiar with the dwarfs and found the task easy. Still others will claim that distractions, such as the weather or disruptions, precluded their success.

In an introductory class, 12 of 66 students correctly named all seven dwarfs. Four students did not correctly name any. Two of these students had not grown up in American culture: One was from Honduras, and the other was from Sri Lanka. There were 152 wrong guesses of 84 different names.

Tip-of-the-tongue phenomenon. Did students have the feeling that they knew a name but were unable to articulate it, like it was "on the tip-of-their-tongues"? If students volunteer that they did have this experience, ask them to describe as much as they can about the word: How many syllables does it have (six of the seven dwarf names have two syllables)?; What letter does it start with (*s* and *d* occur most frequently)?; What meaning or connotation does the word have (most of the names are vivid, state adjectives)? Generally, students will be quite accurate. Explain that this is called the *tip-of-the-tongue* (TOT) phenomenon, which occurs when the generation process does not produce a complete response but produces parts that must then be constructed into a whole (Glass & Holyoak, 1986).

Organization of memory by sound, letter, and meaning. Instruct students to study carefully the order in which they recalled the names, looking for any patterns. Memory is usually organized by sound, letter, or meaning, and this is illustrated by people's wrong answers in two ways. First, many of their wrong answers will be similar in sound, letter, and/or meaning to correct dwarf names. For example, 91% of the class's wrong guesses were two-syllabled names ending in a *y-sound*; 5 of the 7 correct names end in *y* and have two syllables.

Similarly, *s* and *d* each occurs as the initial letter of correct names twice. Wrong guesses beginning with the letter *s* occurred the most frequently (in 22% of the wrong guesses), and 14% began with the letter *d*.

Students also recalled words similar in meaning to actual dwarf names, such as Lazy (13.8%), Clumsy (12.3%), Droopy (7.7%), or Grouchy (6.1%). Also, many people recalled names from the correct superordinate category but named characters other than dwarfs—Snoopy (6%), Pokey (6%), Moe (5%), Curly (3%), and Charlie (1%)—and two other Disney characters—Goofy (9%) and Thumper (1%).

Second, organization by sound, letter, and meaning will typically cause subjects to recall names in a run or pattern of similar names. Runs occur when the generation of one correct item acts as a cue that facilitates recall of other items with similar sounds or meanings (Bousfield & Wicklund, 1969; Meyer & Hilterbrand, 1984). Virtually all of the students demonstrated runs in their recall of dwarf names. These runs occurred for both correct and incorrect names and varied in length from 2 to 15 names.

Recall versus recognition. Ask the class if they would be able to remember more names if this was a recognition task. Recall involves a two-step process: generation of possible targets and identification of genuine ones. Recognition is generally easier because the first step is given as part of the question; subjects need only decide if the given information is correct (Glass & Holyoak, 1986). Because the task is easier, the majority of students say they would prefer and do better on a recognition task.

Part 2: Recognition of the Seven Dwarfs

Instructions

Prepare a handout for the class by listing the following correct dwarf names and distracters on a page: Grouchy, Gabby, Fearful, Sleepy, Smiley, Jumpy, Hopeful, Shy, Droopy, Dopey, Sniffy, Wishful, Puffy, Dumpy, Sneezy, Lazy, Pop, Grumpy, Bashful, Cheerful, Teach, Shorty, Nifty, Happy, Doc, Wheezy, and Stubby. Instruct students to circle the names they recognize as correct dwarf names, cross out the ones they know are incorrect, and leave the others alone.

Discussion

Ask students if they were able to remember more of the dwarfs on this task and to explain why. Did they find this recognition task easier than the recall task? Some students may have found that the discussion of wrong answers cued the correct names or that the names on the paper itself cued their recall.

In the introductory class, the 12 students who correctly named all seven dwarfs in the recall task also correctly recognized all seven. Omitting these students, 91% of the others did better on the recognition task than they did on the recall task, 6% did the same, and 4% did worse.

Finally, give the class a list of the seven dwarfs. In order from most to least likely to be recalled, according to Meyer and Hilterbrand (1984), they are: Sleepy, Dopey, Grumpy, Sneezy, Happy, Doc, and Bashful. Meyer and Hilterbrand (1984) found that college students were more likely to recall the five rhyming names and to recall them in a run, an example of organization by sound. The subjects were least likely to remember Bashful, an example of organization—or absence of—by meaning.

Short-term memory (STM) and long-term memory (LTM). STM is transient memory that can hold information for only a few moments. It is often called *working memory,* because it holds information that is currently in use. LTM can hold information for a greater time—hours, days, and years (Anderson, 1985). Many experiments have been conducted to determine the capacity of STM. Despite much debate about how to measure the capacity of STM, most psychologists agree that it is approximately seven pieces of information, plus or minus two (Miller, 1956)—the same as the number of dwarfs. Through the use of chunking or other organizing schemata, however, the actual number of items recalled can be greater than 5 to 9. For many students, the recall task was a test of recall from LTM—assuming that the names were encoded there to begin with, raising more issues for discussion. But now, if they have been following the discussion, the names should be in STM.

Discussion of other memory processes. Many other issues can be discussed, depending on the level and interest of the class:

1. Choice of distracters for multiple-choice and other tests. The distracters used here came from the subject's wrong guesses in the Meyer and Hilterbrand study.
2. Judgment tasks. Have students classify their responses as positive hits, negative hits, false positives, and false negatives.
3. Measurement of the capacity of STM and LTM.
4. Iconic memory, echoic memory, and memory for other senses. Do they exist? Are they different? Do they have different capacities?

Part 3: Posttest Recall of The Seven Dwarfs

Complete the demonstration by having students turn the sheets over and recall the names of the seven dwarfs. Now everyone theoretically should be able to name all seven dwarfs—plus or minus two. Indeed, 95% of the students named 5 to 7 dwarfs this time, including 3 of the 4 students who were unable to name any the first time.

Student Evaluations

Students in the introductory psychology class were enthusiastic about this demonstration. On a scale ranging from *no, not at all* (1) to *yes, very much* (7), students gave a mean rating of 5.79 (*SD* = 1.15) to their enjoyment of the activity. An overwhelming 94% of the students rated the demonstration as a 5 or higher in helping them to understand the difference between recall and recognition (*M* = 5.96; *SD* = .99) and in illustrating the basic principles of memory (*M* = 5.73; *SD* = .92), and 75% rated it as a 5 or higher in helping them to understand how items are organized in memory (*M* = 5.22; *SD* = 1.23). Finally, 91% of the students found that, overall, it was useful or very useful (*M* = 5.69; *SD* = .95).

References

Anderson, J. R. (1985). *Cognitive psychology and its implications.* San Francisco: Freeman.

Bousfield, W. A., & Wicklund, D. A. (1969). Rhyme as a determinant of clustering. *Psychonomic Science, 16,* 183-184.

Glass, A. L., & Holyoak, K. J. (1986). *Cognition.* New York: Random House.

Meyer, G. E., & Hilterbrand, K (1984). Does it pay to be "Bashful"? The seven dwarfs and long-term memory. *American Journal of Psychology, 97,* 47-55.

Miller, G. A. (1956). The magical number seven, plus or minus two: Some limits on our capacity for processing information. *Psychological Review, 63,* 81-96.

Note

I thank Raymond J. Folven for piloting the demonstration with his Introductory Psychology students so that their data could be used in my analyses. I also thank Joseph J. Palladino, the reviewers, and Mary Murray for comments and suggestions on this article.

A Classroom Demonstration of Depth of Processing

Roger Chaffin
Trenton State College
and Douglas J. Herrmann
Hamilton College

When people have to memorize something they often repeat the material to themselves as a way of remembering it. The common sense view that long-term retention is aided by repetition of the material found expression in the late 1960s in what will be referred to as the "standard view" of memory (Shiffrin & Atkinson, 1969; Waugh & Norman, 1965). The standard view still provides the framework used to introduce students to the topic of memory in most textbooks. According to the standard view, repeating information both maintains the information in short-term memory (STM) and increases the chances that the information will be transferred to long-term memory (LTM).

In the demonstration to be described below students find that when they can repeat material their memories are, paradoxically, poorer than when they are prevented from repeating the material. The paradox is explained by the depth of processing approach to memory which maintains that long-term retention depends on how elaborately the information is processed (Craik & Lockhart, 1972; Craik & Watkins, 1973; Glanzer, 1978; Jacoby, 1973). According to this view, simply repeating information, although it maintains information in an acoustic form, will not improve long-term retention .

The standard position was initially supported by studies that demonstrated a relationship between the number of times a word was rehearsed and the probability of later recall (e.g., Rundus, 1971). Later studies showed that the nature of the rehearsal was critical. Thinking about the meaning of a word improved its long-term retention, but merely repeating it did not, as maintained by the depth of processing position (Jacoby, 1973; Lichtenstein, Note 1; Meunier, Ritz & Meunier, 1972; Modigliani & Seamon, 1974) .

The present demonstration, which is derived from these studies, is an elaborate one that lays one paradox on another while illustrating many of the main concepts covered in an introductory unit on human memory.

Five-word lists are read to the class. After each list one of two interpolated tasks is performed and is followed by an immediate recall test. The interpolated tasks are to repeat the list rapidly over and over, or to say "hello" rapidly for 15 seconds. When all the lists have been presented, an unexpected delayed recall test is given, followed by a recognition test. Immediate recall is, of course, better for the repeat than for the hello lists. The first paradox comes with the delayed recall. Common sense, the standard position, and the results for immediate recall lead the student to expect better recall for the "repeat" lists. Instead recall is better for the "hello" lists (Lichtenstein, Note 1). The students now expect the same result for the recognition test. Again they are surprised; for recognition there is no difference. The results can be explained in terms of the distinctions between short and long-term memory maintenance and elaborative rehearsals recall and recognition.

The procedure has been used as a demonstration in learning and as a class experiment in lab courses. As a demonstration the data are collected by a show of hands, the recognition test is omitted, and the procedure requires 30 minutes. As a lab 75 minutes are needed to complete the tabulation of the data. The equipment needed includes a tape recorders a tape of the instructions and stimulus lists, copies of the stimulus lists recognition test and key for each student and 14 file cards. Numerous variations in the procedure have been used; the version described below was used recently in an experimental lab section at Trenton State College. A copy of the tapes stimulus lists recognition test and key can be obtained from the first author.

Procedure. Twelve lists of 5 words were selected from among 110 high frequency, high imagability words selected from the Paivio, Yuille, and Madigan (1968) norms. Two lists were used for practice ten for the experimental lists. The remaining 50 words served as new items on the recognition test.

Instructions and word lists were presented on a tape recorder. The procedure was described to the class; to overcome self-consciousness the students practiced covering their ears while doing the hello and repeat interpolated tasks with two practice lists. Individuals were coached as necessary to ignore other class members, and to speak audibly but quietly. Additional coaching was giving during the two warm-up trials. The instructions emphasized that, although it was hard to recall 5 words after saying "hello" for 15 seconds, it was possible, and it was up to the students to devise a mnemonic strategy to do it.

Words were read at a 2-second rate. At the end of each list the class was instructed to "repeat" or to "say hello." The two tasks were alternated. After 15 seconds of this interpolated task the class was instructed to write down the five words. Fifteen seconds were allowed for this and then the class was told to prepare for the next list and reminded of the task to be done after the list. While each list was read, the instructor held up a card listing the five words and the task to be done. After all of the lists had been presented the class was instructed to turn over the paper on which they had been writing and to relax. After one minute the class was asked to write down all the words they could recall from all of the lists When everyone had finished writing (about 5 minutes), a recognition test was distributed. The 50 words from the experimental lists were randomly interspersed with the 50 words not presented. The students were instructed to check those words that had been on the lists. Finally each student was given the stimulus lists and a key for the recognition test and asked to score the number of words correct from the repeat and hello lists for immediate recall, delayed recall, and recognition. Warm-up lists were not included. There were 15 students in the class.

Results. The mean scores are given in Table 1 as percentages. Immediate recall was higher for repeat than for hello lists, $t(14)=2.99$, $p,<.05$; this is predicted by both the standard and the depth of processing views. For delayed recall, performance was better for the hello than for the repeat lists, $t(14)=5.10$, $p<.01$. This result supports the depth of processing position and is inconsistent with the standard view. On the recognition test there was no difference between the two conditions, $t(14)=.24$. (The results for the recognition test are reported in terms of correct recognitions as there were only 3 incorrect recognitions.)

Table 1. Mean Recall and Correct Recognitions as Percentages for the Repeat and Hello Conditions.

Retention Type	Condition	
	Repeat	Hello
Immediate Recall	95.5	86.4
Delayed Recall	21.3	43.2
Recognition	76.4	75.6

Discussion. For the immediate recall test performance for the repeat lists was almost perfect; mere unthinking repetition was effective in maintaining acoustic information for immediate recall. Immediate recall was poorer for the hello lists because STM storage was impaired by the hello task. In order to recall the list it was necessary to create an elaborated representation an image or story—involving the five concepts, as they were presented. This elaborative rehearsal had transferred much of the information from STM to LTM. As a result delayed recall was better for the hello lists than for the repeat lists. For the repeat lists little information had been transferred to LTM. Maintenance rehearsal of the acoustic information had been adequate for the immediate task, but produced poor delayed recall. Recognition in contrast was not affected by the level of processing. Recognition requires only the knowledge that a word has been heard recently. This information was equally available for words from the hello and repeat lists, because the memory representation for both sets of words had been activated when the words were presented (Glenberg, Smith, & Green, 1977). Although retrieval was improved by more elaborate processing, recognition was not (Jacoby, 1973).

The effects are robust. The direction of the differences is always the same. The size of the effect for delayed recall is sensitive to subject strategies and sometimes fails to reach significance. Three aspects of the procedure are important for maximizing the effect. First, the instructions should make clear that the students must devise a way to do well on immediate recall for the hello lists and that this will require some ingenuity on their part. If the students are not familiar with standard mnemonic strategies explicit suggestions should be made. Seconds practice trials with each task must be given to overcome self-consciousness and allow the development of effective strategies. Thirds the lists should follow one another without delay to prevent boredom and thus discourage elaborative rehearsal of the repeat lists.

The appeal of the procedure for classroom use comes from the apparent conflict between the results obtained for the three measures of memory. After the commonsensical result has been obtained for immediate recall, each of the succeeding results for delayed recall and then recognition becomes paradoxical The unfolding of the results can be made very dramatic. The procedure requires a considerable investment of class time but it presents in concrete and memorable form some of the main Concepts that must be conveyed in an introduction to human memory.

References

Craik. F. I. M., & Lockhart, R. S. Levels of processing: A framework for memory research. *Journal of Verbal Learning and Verbal Behavior,* 1972, *11,* 671-684.

Craik, F. I. M., & Watkins, M. J. The role of rehearsal in short-term memory. *Journal of Verbal Learning and Verbal Behavior,* 1973, *12,* 599-607.

Glanzer. M. Commentary on "Storage mechanisms in recall." In G. M. Bower, (Ed), *Human Memory Basic Processes.* New York: Academic Press, 1978.

Glenberg, A., Smith, S. M., & Green, C. Type I rehearsal: Maintenance and more. *Journal of Verbal Learning and Verbal Behavior,* 1977, *16,* 339-352.

Jacoby, L. L. Encoding processes, rehearsal, and recall requirements. *Journal of Verbal Learning and Verbal Behavior,* 1973, *12,* 302-310

Meunier, G. F., Ritz, D., & Meunier, J. A. Rehearsal of individual items in short-term memory. *Journal of Experimental Psychology,* 1972, *95,* 465-467.

Modigiani, V., & Seaman, J. G. Transfer of information from short to long-term memory. *Journal of Experimental Psychology,* 1974, *102,* 768-772.

Paivio, A., Yuille, J. C. & Madigan, S. H. Concreteness imagery, and meaningfulness values for 925 nouns. *Journal of Experimental Psychology,* Monograph Supplement, 1968, *76,* (No. 1, Part 2), 1-25.

Rundus, D. Analysis of rehearsal processes in free recall. *Journal of Experimental Psychology,* 1971, *89,* 63-77.

Shiffrin, R. M., & Atkinson, R. C. Storage and retrieval processes in long-term memory. *Psychological Review,* 1969, *76,* 179-193.

Waugh, M. C., & Norman, D. A. Primary memory. *Psychological Review,* 1965, *72,* 89-104

Note

Lichtenstein, E. K. Effects of central and peripheral rehearsal on sentence memory. Unpublished manuscript, University of Illinois, 1972.

Pay Attention! Demonstrating the Role of Attention in Learning

Janet D. Larsen
John Carroll University

In this demonstration, students receive one of three different sets of directions regarding what to learn about a set of stimulus cards. How attention affects memory is shown by students' tendency to recall best the characteristic they were told to remember.

This demonstration can be used on the first day of an introductory psychology class to illustrate the importance of knowing what you are supposed to learn before you begin studying. It can also be used to show the basic elements of a scientific experiment.

Preparing the Materials

You will need six large cards of different colors and the instruction booklets described later. In large letters on one side of each card, print the name of an animal. I use three letter words: *dog, cat, pig, rat, cow,* and *hen.* Write a single digit number below each word. Arrange the cards so that these numbers do not correspond with their positions in the stack.

The instruction booklets contain a cover page, an instructions page, and three data collection sheets. The cover page states "Demonstration 1, Please do not open until instructed to do so," to keep students from prematurely reading the next page. The second page gives one of three sets of the instructions: "You will be shown a series of cards. Try to remember the (words on) (numbers on) (colors of) the cards in the order they are shown."

Each sheet can be ¼ of a regular sized sheet of paper. The three data collection pages and the cover page can all by typed on one 8½ x 11 in. sheet of paper. The three different sets of instructions can be printed on another page. Each data collection sheet contains six lines, numbered 1 to 6, and instructions to remember the (words on) (numbers on) (colors of) the cards in the order they were presented. For those instructed to "remember the word," data collection sheets should be arranged as follows: (a) recall words, (b) recall numbers, and (c) recall colors. For the "remember the number" group, the order is: (a) recall numbers, (b) recall words, and (c) recall colors. Finally, for those told to "remember the colors" the order is: (a) recall colors, (b) recall words, and (c) recall numbers.

Take one of each type of booklet, randomly arrange them in a stack; take another three (one of each type), randomly arrange them and add them to the stack; and so on. This random ordering of the booklets and students' selection of where they will sit determine their assignment to the three conditions. You assure identical treatment of the groups because you show them the cards in the same way and at the same time.

Conducting the Demonstration

When all students have their booklets, ask them to open the booklet and read only the first page. Next, show the six cards for about 5 s each. Be sure to show each card for the same length of time by counting silently to the same number at a regular rate. After showing the cards, tell students to turn to the next page, follow the instructions, and continue through the booklet until they are finished. After the students have written as many items as they can recall, show them the cards again and have them score their own responses. Ask them to write on the cover page the number of words, numbers, and colors they got correct. Then ask them to assemble in groups according to what they were instructed to remember and to find the group mean for each of the three kinds of information.

The main point of the activity is to demonstrate that, on the average, each group will have remembered more items in the category they were asked to remember. Only those asked to remember the colors of the cards get many of the colors correct. The same basic effect occurs in the other two groups, but to a lesser degree. Those with the "number" instructions usually remember more numbers than the other groups, and those with the "word" instructions tend to remember more words than the other groups. I conducted a 3 x 3 (Instructions x Recall Category)

analysis of variance on the data from 30 students who participated in this demonstration. There was no main effect for instructions, $F(2, 27) < 1$, and no main effect for recall category, $F(2, 54) = 2.08$, ns, but there was a significant interaction, $F(2, 54) = 17.70$, $p < .01$. The means and standard deviations for this sample are shown in Table 1.

Table 1. Means and Standard Deviations of Items Recalled Out of Six Items in Each Category by Groups With Different Instructions[a]

| | Items Recalled | | | | | |
| | Color | | Word | | Number | |
Instructions	M	SD	M	SD	M	SD
Remember color	5.1	1.9	2.3	1.8	1.6	2.0
Remember word	1.7	1.3	4.1	1.9	3.2	2.0
Remember number	0.7	1.3	3.4	1.5	4.4	1.6

[a]n = 10 per condition.

What Does it Show?

Some important elements of conducting an experiment are illustrated by the procedure. Subjects were randomly assigned to conditions, and all other variables were kept constant.

A discussion of what the students were expecting can yield interesting information. Usually a couple of people figure out the experiment and remember the colors even though they were not instructed to do so. This fact can be used to illustrate that subjects in experiments often act as problem solvers.

As the statistical analysis shows, students usually recall about the same number of items regardless of the instructions, and no one category is more memorable than any other. However, each group remembers best the category they were told to remember. I use the fact that attention increases memory to emphasize the importance of looking at chapter outlines or lists of learning objectives in the textbook before studying. Pay attention!

A Classroom Demonstration of Encoding Specificity

Thomas J. Thieman
The College of St. Catherine

Historically, theories of verbal learning have focused on mechanisms such as decay, erasure, displacement, and interference to account for forgetting. Countless paired–associate experiments were designed to investigate the details of Osgood's transfer surface and the "fate" of first-list associations due to unlearning, response competition, and the like. Collectively, these approaches have been referred to as trace-dependent forgetting, with the loss of information viewed as a function of the actual change or erosion of memory traces.

More recently, the concept of cue-dependent forgetting, with information loss attributed to retrieval failure, has become very popular. Major support for this view has come from Tulving's demonstrations of the encoding specificity principle (Thomson & Tulving, 1970; Tulving & Osler, 1968; Tulving & Thomson, 1973). The principle asserts that a retrieval cue will be effective if, and only if, the to-be-remembered (TBR) item was specifically encoded with respect to that cue during input. Accordingly, forgetting results from an item being misplaced or functionally lost (technically speaking, inaccessible even though available), for want of an effective retrieval cue to remind the learner of how the item was first entered into memory.

Considerable debate has centered on the strength or generality of the encoding specificity principle (e.g., Postman, 1975; Tulving, 1983), but the phenomenon of recall differences based on cue concordance between encoding and retrieval (study and test) remains a strong and compelling one. This article describes a simple classroom experiment that can provide an opportunity to demonstrate the encoding specificity phenomenon, note its limitations, and discuss its cause and importance. It avoids the tenuous distinction between strong versus weak associate cues based on group norms, and distinguishes instead between study-test cue pairs that are either semantically related or unrelated with respect to the sense of the TBR item that was initially encoded.

Method. The design for this experiment is an extension of one suggested in the Instructor's Manual to *Human Information Processing* (Lindsay & Norman, 1972), and attributed to Endel Tulving's musings in an English pub. The materials, listed in Table 1, include 39 target words that are to be recalled by the subjects. Three groups of 13 words each are distinguished by the brief descriptive cues associated with them at presentation and test. Cues for the control condition, the first item in each triad in Table 1, are the same at the time of study and test. Cues for the meaning-preserving condition, the second item of each triad, differ from study to test but both refer to the same meaning of the TBR target word. Cues for the meaning-shifting condition, the third item of each triad, also differ from study to test and refer to different meanings of the homographic TBR target words.

The 24 members of my Learning and Memory laboratory course served as subjects. Students were told that they were going to learn a long list of words. Before each word was read, however, it would be preceded by a short phrase or cue that would help them think about the word. At the time of test, another set of cues would be read. These cues may be exactly the same as those read at presentation, or they may be different, but in every case they would be related to the target words. The list was then read with a 2 sec pause between cues and target words and a 3 sec pause between cue-target word pairs. Following presentation, the instructor gave a standard lecture for 15 min before reading the second set of cues at a 5 sec rate and requesting recall. Initial presentation order was blocked, with 13 randomly ordered triads of words, one from each of the three cueing conditions. At test, the cues were also arranged in triads, but in different combinations and random orders than those used at presentation.

After cued recall, students were given a scoring sheet listing each target word and its first and second cue, divided into three conditions. Students scored their own data and reported the number correctly recalled out of 13 for each cueing condition.

Results and Discussion. The mean number of target words correctly recalled in the repeated, meaning-preserving, and meaning-shifting cue conditions was 11.04, 9.88, and 3.71, respectively. An overall repeated measures ANOVA yielded a significant main effect for cue condition, $F(2, 46) = 196.29$, $p < .01$, and all three pairwise t-tests between condition means were also significant (repeated vs meaning-preserving, $t(23) = 3.98$; meaning-preserving vs meaning-shifting, $t(23) = 15.16$; and repeated vs meaning-shifting, $t(23) = 15.51$; all $p < .01$).

The strictest version of the encoding specificity hypothesis would have predicted the meaning-preserving and meaning-shifting cueing conditions to have produced equally poor levels of recall compared to the repeated cue condition since in both cases the original cue was absent at test. Obviously, this was not the case, as the meaning-preserving cues supported a high level of recall. However, even though the originally-encoded meanings of the target words were accessible by these cues, recall was not as effective as with the repeated cues.

For the homographs that had a second meaning referred to by the test cue, recall was significantly reduced but not equal to zero. Some subjects reported recognizing at presentation that these words had

multiple meanings and anticipated the connections with the new test cues. In these cases, the meaning-shifting cues were beneficial because both meanings of the words had been encoded and stored in the subjects' event or episodic memories. Other subjects reported remembering certain target words, in the sense of their originally cued and encoded meanings, but hesitated recalling them because their connections to the revised cues did not become immediately evident to them. This occurred to a lesser degree with the different but meaningpreserving cues. Occasionally, as subjects worked out these relationships during the test period, they emitted the self-satisfied "Aha" of an insight experience. Finally, other subjects lost track altogether of the target words that were prompted with the meaning-shifting cues. These cases most directly demonstrate the encoding specificity phenomenon.

This lab has provoked considerable discussion of cuedependent forgetting phenomena and reinforced students' personal insights that memory failure is often the result of an unsuccessful search or lack of an appropriate hint of what to retrieve rather than a true indication that the information is simply no longer in memory. It also offers an opportunity to discuss the usefulness of Tulving's (1972) distinction between episodic and semantic memory, and the difference between encoding specificity as a principle of the relationship between the properties of the memory trace of an event and the effectiveness of retrieval cues, and encoding specificity as an empirically verifiable phenomenon.

Table 1. Materials for Encoding Specificity Experiment

Cue Provided at Presentation	Target Word	Cue Provided at Recall
A day of the week	Thursday	—
A government leader	king	A member of royalty
A type of bird	cardinal	A clergyman
A famous psychologist	Thorndike	—
A menu item	wine	An alcoholic beverage
A personality trait	charm	A small trinket
A vegetable	cabbage	—
Associated with heat	stove	A kitchen appliance
A round object	ball	A social event
Found in the jungle	leopard	—
A crime	rape	A type of assault
A baseball position	pitcher	An article of pottery
Associated with cold	north	—
Song accompaniment	banjo	A musical instrument
Taken to a birthday party	present	A grammatical tense
A girl's name	Susan	—
A type of footgear	boots	Needed in snow
A manmade structure	bridge	A card game
A weapon	cannon	—
A sweet food	banana	A fruit
An indication of possession	mine	Associated with coal
A large city	Tokyo	—
A sign of happiness	smile	A facial expression
A student	pupil	Found in the eye
A long word	notwithstanding	—
Has four wheels	Chevrolet	A type of car
A part of a bird	bill	A monthly reminder
A member of the family	grandfather	—
A favorite time of the year	Christmas	A holiday
A part of a word	letter	A form of communication
A tool	wrench	—
Found next to a highway	motel	A vacation reststop
A type of sports equipment	racket	A type of noise
Part of a building	chimney	—
Made of leather	saddle	Associated with horse
A tropical plant	palm	Part of the hand
A synonym for big	colossal	—
Associated with lunch	noon	A time of day
Part of the intestine	colon	A punctuation mark

References

Lindsay, P. H., & Norman, D. A. *Human information processing.* New York: Academic Press, 1972.

Postman, L. Tests of the generality of the principle of encoding specificity. *Memory & Cognition,* 1975, *3,* 663-672.

Thomson, D. M., & Tulving, E. Associative encoding and retrieval: Weak and strong cues. *Journal of Experimental Psychology,* 1970, *86,* 255-262.

Tulving, E. Episodic and semantic memory. In E. Tulving & W. Donaldson (Eds.) *Organization of memory.* New York: Academic Press, 1972.

Tulving, E. *Elements of episodic memory.* New York: Oxford University Press, 1983.

Tulving, E., & Osler, S. Effectiveness of retrieval cues in memory for words. *Journal of Experimental Psychology,* 1968, 77, 593-601.

Tulving, E., & Thomson, D. M. Encoding specificity and retrieval processes in episodic memory. *Psychological Review,* 1973, *80,* 352-373.

A Method for Teaching Name Mnemonics

Steven M. Smith
Texas A&M University

Name mnemonics provide a powerful technique for remembering names. This classroom demonstration teaches students how to construct and use name mnemonics. Students create mnemonics for each other in small groups. Students then describe their name mnemonics to the class. The exercise teaches mnemonics, gives students an experience with group creative problem solving, and ensures that nearly every class member's name will be known to all others in the class.

When people meet me for the first time, they can't help noticing my bushy *beard*. This may remind them of the man with the beard on packages of *Smith* Brothers cough drops. Now, if you need cough drops for your cough or cold, you may also have a stuffy nose; if so, you should remember that in an emergency, one's *sleeve* may be substituted for a missing handkerchief. Because sleeve rhymes with *Steve,* you can remember my entire name simply by seeing me, face to (bearded) face: The *beard* leads to *Smith* brothers cough drops, which leads to *sleeve,* which rhymes with *Steve.*

This is an example of a name mnemonic, a mental device for remembering names that works surprisingly well, even for novices. The mnemonic associates a person's appearance and name, using imagery and rhymes. Teaching name mnemonics on the first day of class in introductory psychology, cognition, memory, or experimental psychology can demonstrate the power of cognition via a firsthand experience. Within a short period of time, not only can it be demonstrated that "psychology really works," but students will be impressed with their own untapped mental abilities. The exercise teaches about mnemonics, the use of interacting imagery and rhymes to achieve useful associations in memory (see Shimamura, 1984). Students will also get experience with group creative problem solving as small groups try to think divergently in order to create name mnemonics for each group member. Finally, and perhaps most important, the exercise helps to ensure that everyone in the class (including the teacher) will know everyone else's name, a situation likely to facilitate any class where frequent and open discussions are encouraged.

METHOD

The exercise should begin with a brief discussion on the importance of knowing others' names in a variety of social and professional situations. Students can be given the opportunity at this time to testify as to how difficult it is for them to remember names, and how that difficulty may have caused some of them considerable embarrassment.

At this time the teacher should come to the rescue with the name mnemonic, which one can use either to remember others' names, or to ensure that others will remember one's own name. The name mnemonic technique could be described (see Bellezza, 1982) with the aid of the teacher's own name mnemonic as an example. Briefly, a mnemonic is a mental device that helps memory, often creating associations via the creation of interacting mental images that link or integrate the items to be associated, or creating associations via acoustic properties (such as rhymes) which the to-be-associated items have in common. Generally, names are needed when the person in question is seen; hence, the name mnemonic should begin with an image of the person's appearance (or with some real or imagined component of the person's appearance), and should link that image with an image related to the sound of the person's name (or related to the sound of part of the name).

The teacher might throw out a few other examples of both good and poor name mnemonics. For a good example, my burly former teaching assistant named Rodney Flanary could be easily imagined as a football player who had a knee injury; hence the *rod* in his *knee—Rodney.* Benched for the injury, he kept warm by wearing *flannel—Flanary.* This example makes use of a physical cue (burliness) that immediately evokes an image, and the components of the image are acoustically related to the name. Mnemonics that fail to use a physical appearance cue or imagery associations, or that use obscure personal characteristics unknown to the learner (e.g., "I like to read science fiction") are typically less memorable.

At this time the teacher should inform the students that their task for the next few minutes will be to convene in small groups (2 to 4 students per group) and create name mnemonics for each member of the group. Students will ultimately be responsible for their own name mnemonic, but the groups greatly facilitate this creative process. Assign students to the small groups, and recommend that they first appoint a secretary to write down the name of each member of the group. Also, recommend that each student try to come up with a mnemonic for at least one of their names, but preferably for both names.

Briefly monitor the groups, one at a time. Ask about current progress and make a few suggestions to groups that seem to be totally stuck. Encourage them to be as creative and free-wheeling as possible, as it will help them get ideas. Teachers familiar with brainstorming or other group techniques devoted to divergent thinking should make suggestions along those lines. Briefly, brainstorming has four basic rules: (a) avoid criticism of ideas, at all costs; (b) the wilder the idea, the better; (c) the more ideas, the better; and (d) combine and modify ideas. For a further discussion of brainstorming, see Osborn (1957).

After 5 or 10 minutes, have the students reassemble into the original large group. One at a time, each student should go to the chalkboard, legibly print his or her name, speak the name aloud, clearly enough to satisfy everyone in the room, and give the mnemonic for his or her name. It is also helpful if, while at the chalkboard, students briefly mention a bit of personal data, such as where they are from, why they are taking the course, or what their hobbies are. Such information helps to enrich and elaborate learning, making it more memorable. After giving all information, each student should erase his or her name before returning to be seated. If names are left on the board, confusion about which name belongs to which student is bound to result.

Finally, when all the name mnemonics have been given, the teacher should call on two "volunteers" from the class to recite every name in the class. Students are rarely impressed with a psychology teacher who can use mnemonics, but they are greatly impressed when they can use the mnemonics successfully. The volunteer should select students in any order he or she wishes, looking at each one for a visual cue, and recalling each name aloud. When a volunteer falters on a name, the class should prompt the student with a hint about the mnemonic in question. After the first student has finished, a second volunteer should say the names again. This procedure will assure that nearly everyone will know nearly everyone's name in the class.

Once students' names have been learned with this mnemonic, there is likely to be a considerable amount of repetition of names throughout the semester and names are not likely to be forgotten. Even without such repetition, however, the instructor can demonstrate later in the semester that the mnemonics can endure the test of time by giving a pop quiz over the names of class members. Performance should remain at a high level.

This method for teaching name mnemonics may be limited by class size, but possibly not so much as one might think. The largest class for which I have used this technique had 64 students, and both student volunteers got more than 50 names correct even without prompts from class members.

Another limitation that may concern teachers is the anticipated difficulty with very unusual or "foreign" names. My experience has been that such names are no harder than more common "American" names and occasionally such names are easier than others because of their distinctiveness. Memorable examples are "Bahardoust," who said her name might be "the hardest," or "Sinha," who had us imagine that he looked like a "sinner."

Should the learner be advised to use bizarre imagery rather than more common images? There is no clear consensus on this question, as the relative usefulness of bizarreness appears to depend on such factors as number of learning trials, type of test (free or cued recall), and delay between learning and testing (see O'Brien & Wolford, 1982; Wollen & Cox, 1981).

One final problem may be in the mnemonic "decoding" stage. That is, sometimes learners recall the mnemonic device, but cannot remember the correct name that goes with it. For example, Rodney Flanary (rod-knee-flannel) might be remembered as Rodney Flannigan, or Steve Smith (sleeve-cough drops) might be remembered as Steve Vicks. The remedy for such difficulty is fairly simple; one or two practice trials will usually solve the entire decoding problem.

References

Bellezza, F. S. (1982). *Improve your memory skills.* Englewood Cliffs, NJ: Prentice-Hall.

O'Brien, E. J., & Wolford, C. R. (1982). Effect of delay in testing on retention of plausible versus bizarre mental images. *Journal of Experimental Psychology: Learning, Memory, and Cognition, 8,* 148-152.

Osborn, A. (1957). *Applied imagination.* New York: Charles Scribner's.

Shimamura, A. P. (1984). A guide for teaching mnemonic skills. *Teaching of Psychology, 11,* 162-166.

Wollen, K. A., & Cox, S. D. (1981). Sentence cuing and the effectiveness of bizarre imagery. *Journal of Experimental Psychology: Human Learning and Memory, 7,* 386-392.

Demonstrating Semantic Memory in the Teaching Laboratory with a Paper-and-Pencil Task

Albert N. Katz
University of Western Ontario

Although reaction-time procedures and data have assumed prominent importance in the study of cognitive processes, the individual testing and need for sophisticated (and expensive) equipment required to produce reliable reaction-times has made it difficult to use this technique in the teaching laboratory. The present report describes a paper-and-pencil method for producing reliable reactiontime data suitable for group situations and, as such, can be considered a variant of techniques originally outlined by Rozin and Jonides (1977). In the present exposition the technique was specially constructed to contrast the two traditional theoretical approaches to semantic memory, although the technique itself can be directly applied to other questions of interest to cognitive psychology.

The technique itself only needs the use of prepared test booklets and a stop-watch. The critical component is in the construction of the booklet. Each page of the booklet consists of a homogeneous set of problems or questions. Participants can indicate their answers in several ways. For example, if the problem involves judging or choosing between paired alternatives, they can check the member of each pair which they prefer. Alternatively, if the problem involves solving for truth-value of a statement, the participant can circle a T (for True) or F (for False) printed beside each statement. The task itself is also simple. The participants are given orienting instructions. When a signal is given they turn to the first page of the booklet and go down the page responding to as many of the problems as they can. When a second signal occurs they turn to the next page and repeat on those problems. The logic of this procedure is that one can estimate the time taken to respond to each homogeneous problem-set page by determining the number of items from each homogeneous set (page) which was answered in a set time by the formula:

$$RT = \frac{\text{Time Allocated to page}}{\text{Number of Correct Responses}}$$

Thus, if on one page a person correctly responded to 15 questions in a 20 second period, the average reaction-time would be 20 seconds/15 responses or an average of 1333 milliseconds per response.

In order to examine alternative models of cognitive processes or to demonstrate basic phenomena, one need only vary the relationship found from page to page in the booklet. Consider, for instance, the so-called "symbolic distance effect" in which people respond more quickly to items which are symbolically distant than to those more close. Using Moyer and Landauer's (1967) initial demonstration of this phenomenon as an example, one would transcribe their individual technique to a group procedure useful for the classroom by constructing booklets as follows. One page would consist of a set of paired digits that differed in value only by one digit (i.e., pairs such as 5 4; 8 9). Another page would consist of pairs differing by 3 digits (5 8; 6 9), and a third page would consist of pairs differing by, let's say, 5 digits in value. Naturally one would ensure that the larger digit appeared equally often on the right and left, and that the order in which the pages appeared in the booklet were counterbalanced. In the task itself, the participants would, on signal, start at the first page of their booklet and, within a given amount of time on each page, choose the digit with the larger value. To replicate the classic findings of Moyer and Landauer (1967) one would expect that the average RT should be fastest for the page in which the pairs differed by 5, and slowest for items differing only by 1 digit.

One could apply the basic technique to many other phenomena of interest. For example, mental rotation (e.g., Shepard & Metzler, 1971) could be demonstrated by presenting booklets in which pairs of figures are presented. The manipulation here would be to vary the degree to which the objects differ in rotation (e.g., 20°, 40°, 60°) from page to page in the booklet. Similarly, differences in processing sentences with varying grammatical meaning (e.g., Clark & Chase, 1972) could be demonstrated by presenting simple pictures and beside each picture a descriptive phrase. In this case each page of the booklet would differ in the nature of the phrase employed (for example, whether the phrase is in positive or negative form such as "star is above cross" or "cross is not above cross"). Responding here could be indexed by having participants choose a T if the phrase was a true description of the picture or an F if otherwise.

A detailed example of the technique, and some data on its comparability to data obtained by the typical individual testing technique is provided below. The technique was specially constructed to contrast two influential models of semantic memory. In very recent years (e.g., Collins & Loftus, 1975) data based distinctions between these two models have narrowed. Nonetheless, I find that detailing the earlier distinctions, and the data that were brought to bear on these distinctions, make current models much easier to understand. The comparability of the group data to the original individual based data will be examined by three independent indicators: the pattern of reaction-time across different conditions, error data, and absolute reaction-time values.

Models of Semantic Memory and Reaction Time Data. Semantic memory is assumed to embody the knowledge we have about the world. It can be considered a mental thesaurus wherein knowledge about words, concepts, their meanings and relationships, and rules for their manipulation is stored. Historically, two broad classes of theories have proven most successful in describing the structure of semantic memory. One such class is the network model and is best exemplified by the work of Collins and Quillian (1969). This model assumes that the elements of knowledge are organized in an hierarchical arranged network. Moreover the *time* it takes to answer a semantic memory question is assumed to reflect the network structure. Thus to answer the question "is a collie an animal?" requires progression through the inferences, a collie is a dog, a dog is a mammal, a mammal is an animal. Thus three steps are required, whereas to answer, "is a collie a dog?" requires only one step. The prediction of this model is very clear: it should take less time to answer the second question (which involves the time required for one step) than the first (three step) question. Collins and Quillian (1969) provided impressive experimental support for this prediction.

The second class of theories, and best exemplified by the work of Rips, Shoben and Smith (1973), assume that concepts consist of a set of distinctive attributes of features and that one concept can share no, some, or many attributes with another concept. According to these models, people evaluate whether or not two or more semantic concepts belong together by comparing the degree to which they share features in common. Presumably if two concepts share many defining features in common it will be easier (and hence quicker) to decide they belong together. For positive answers, this model makes the same prediction as a network model since items closely related also tend to share more defining features in common.

The two models do make an additional, differentiating prediction however. Consider the following two questions: Is a fish a mammal? Is a fish a chair? According to the network models, items close in the network (fish-mammal) should require fewer steps to find the relevant information and hence should be associated with faster decision times to negate than are more distant items (fish-chair). Set theoretic models make the complete opposite prediction. Since items such as fish and mammal share more features in common than do fish and chair it should be more difficult (and hence take longer) to decide they don't belong together. Experiments which test the different predictions have favored the set-theoretic over the basic network approach (Schaeffer & Wallace, 1970; Rips, et al., 1973) although recent network models have been modified to overcome this shortcoming. The paper-and-pencil technique described below was constructed to contrast the basic network and feature models.

The Group Procedure. Booklets were constructed. On each page of the booklet was a series of 25 statements of the form: A_____is a(n)_____. For example, two such relationships would be: (1) A shark is a piano; (2) A dog is an animal . Beside each statement were the letters "T" (for True) and "F" (for False). The booklets consisted of four pages. On each page there were 5 items meant to keep the subject "honest." These distracter items will be described in more detail later. The 20 non-distractor items were of four types, with each type defining a different page of the booklet. Two pages consisted of relationships for which the correct answer was TRUE. One such page consisted of items in which the semantic relationship was close (e.g., a dog is a mammal) whereas in the other page the relationship is more distant (e.g., a dog is a living thing). The other two pages consisted of items for which the correct answer was FALSE. Again, one of these pages consisted of semantically close relationships (e.g., a shark is a mammal) with the other page consisting of more distant relationships (e.g., a shark is a piano). The criteria for designating a relationship as either close or distant were as follows. For true relationships distance was determined by position in a superordinate hierarchy. Thus, given "dog" as the subject of the sentence, the concepts 'mammal', "animal" and "living thing" would represent systematically more distant true relationships. For false relationship, semantic distance was manipulated by violating the animate-inanimate distinction, a technique successfully employed by Rips, et al. (1973). For example, the distance involved in the sentence "A robin is a fish," in which both the subject and object are animate, is considered smaller than the distance involved in the sentence "A robin is a bed room."

In order to keep subjects honest, five distracter relationships were interspersed on each page (in lines 3, 7, 8, 13, 18). For the true-close and true-remote pages, the distractors consisted of items which were false, and for the two "false" question pages, the distracters were true statements. The exact same distractors, placed in the same positions were employed for the two positive sheets. The two negative sheets were similarly treated. The order of the pages in the booklet were randomly assigned, thus eliminating order effects.

The 32 members of my second year laboratory course in Cognition served as subjects. They were instructed to turn to the first page of their booklet and, when a signal was given, to go down the page sequentially and answer as many of the questions as possible. Both speed and accuracy were stressed. When a second signal was given they were instructed to turn to the next page and repeat the procedure. The students were given 20 seconds on each page.

Results and Discussion. These results were evaluated with respect to three criteria. First, in accordance with predictions concerning the pattern of reaction-times, it was quicker to confirm (by 650 msec.) true-close than true-remote relationships, $t(31)$ = 5.66, $p<.01$. Thus, as predicted by both network and feature models, people, on the average, correctly answered statements such as "a robin is a bird" more quickly than more remote questions of the form "a robin is an animal." Moreover, consistent again with the literature (e.g., Rips, *et al.*, 1973), people were faster (by 160 msec.) at disconfirming remote statements (of the form "a robin is a bedroom") than those less remote (e.g., "a robin is a fish"), $t(31)$ = 2.38, $p<.025$. Thus, the group procedure exactly replicated the expected pattern of result obtained initially by individual testing on sophisticated equipment.

Second, the examination of my error data was completely in line with data obtained with the single subject technique. Our overall error rate of 6.7% was comparable, for example, to the 5.8% errors observed by Schaeffer and Wallace (1970) or the 8% observed by Collins and Quillian (1969). The examination of error data is an important extension of Rozin and Jonides (1977) technique for two reasons. It permits examination of issues critical to the interpretation of reaction-time data. With respect to one such aspect of the present data, error rate increased with reaction-time, confirming that the present findings did not reflect a trade-off between speed and accuracy. Also, with the Rozin and Jonides technique an error trial disrupts performance, at least when the RT chain is of an insufficient length. The present technique does not have this problem. Finally, the absolute value of the observed reaction-time for false statements (from 1540 msec. to 1700 msec.) is comparable to the 1308-1582 msecs. range reported by Rips, et al.

(1973). Similarly, for true statements, my observed values (of 1414 - 2058 msec.) although larger than those reported earlier (Collins & Quillian, 1969: 1180 - 1240 msec.; Rips, et al. 1973: 1315 - 1373) are still relatively similar. Rozin and Jonides also examined absolute RT; the present validation extends this comparison to more complex cognitive activities.

Concluding Remarks. One of our responsibilities as teachers should be to keep our students abreast of techniques, theories and experimentation current in the literature. The present technique affords the student all of these experiences. I have used the group procedure discussed above to introduce the logic of reaction time as a dependent measure, weaknesses in such a usage, and its application to the study of cognitive processes. With respect to semantic memory, it has permitted me to introduce basic models and empirical phenomena. One assigned "thinking" task which directly follows from these labs has been to attempt to modify the basic network model to try to incorporate the apparently inconsistent data. This assignment has proven to be a most useful means of introducing current models, such as that proposed by Collins and Loftus (1975) and, in a more general sense, has sharpened the students' appreciation of the role of experimentation in theory building.

References

Clark, H., & Chase, W. On the process of comparing sentences against pictures. *Cognitive Psychology,* 1972, *3*, 472-517.

Collins, A., & Loftus, E. A. spreading-activation theory of semantic processing. *Psychological Review*, 1975, *82*, 407-428.

Collins, A., & Quillian, M. Retrieval time from semantic memory. *Journal of Verbal Learning and Verbal Behavior,* 1969, *8*, 240-248.

Moyer, R. S., & Landauer, T. K. Time required for judgments of numerical inequality. *Nature*, 1967, *215*, 1519-1520.

Rips, L., Shoben, E., & Smith, E. Semantic distance and the verification of semantic relations. *Journal of Verbal Learning and Verbal Behavior*, 1973, *12*, 1-20.

Rozin, P., & Jonides, J. Mass reaction time: Measurement of the speed of the nerve impulse and the duration of mental processes in class. *Teaching of Psychology*, 1977, *4*, 91-94.

Schaeffer, B., & Wallace, R. The comparison of word meanings. *Journal of Experimental Psychology,* 1970, *86*, 144-152.

Shepard, R., & Metzler, J. Mental rotation of three-dimensional objects. *Science*, 1971, *171*, 701-703.

The Word Fragment Completion Effect: A Computer-Assisted Classroom Exercise

Lawrence M. Schoen
New College of the University of South Florida

A computer demonstration of the word fragment completion effect was developed to enhance students' comprehension of an experimental paradigm used in cognitive psychology. The robust word fragment completion effect is used to introduce students to the implicit memory paradigm and to illustrate the advantages inherent in such a procedure. The demonstration is a useful tool for comparing and contrasting experimental procedures; it also provides a starting point for a discussion of multiple memory models.

A course in cognitive psychology or information processing typically includes discussion of memory, involving both recognition and recall. Psychologists have long used these measures in their experiments, and such procedures lend themselves quite easily to class demonstrations. However, newer procedures that permit researchers to explore other aspects of memory also occur in the literature. The new procedures have not appeared in many textbooks or classrooms. One such procedure involves implicit memory and can be demonstrated with the word fragment completion task. In this task, subjects attempt to complete words that have various letters missing (e.g., C_A_P_G_E). The task begins by exposing subjects to a list of words, some of which will be presented later as fragments to be completed. After viewing the words, subjects are given the word fragments, some of which were primed in the first word list. Completion of the unprimed word fragments can be a difficult task and often cannot be accomplished within the time allowed. However, the primed fragments are typically completed in a few seconds, even if the subjects realize they have seen the words before.

Method

Effective use of the demonstration program involves three parts: (a) a lecture introducing the implicit memory paradigm in general, and word fragment completion studies in particular; (b) running the demonstration program and allowing the students to participate as subjects in an experiment; and (c) a classroom discussion focusing on the students' performance, the function of the implicit memory task in the demonstration, and a comparison of this paradigm with other more common experimental procedures.

The demonstration program is written in Basic, using the DOS 3.3 operating system and requires an Apple II microcomputer with a minimum of 64K memory, a 5¼ disk drive, and a display monitor. The program may be used by students individually or as a classroom exercise, if the monitor is large enough to allow students to read normal size (40 column) text from their seats. If the class is too large, multiple monitors connected to the single computer can be used. No programming knowledge or specialized computer skill is required by either the students or the instructor.

Lecture

The demonstration begins with a lecture about the implicit memory task, the assumptions of the paradigm, and some examples of its use in research (e.g., word-stem completion). One point to cover is the influence of the type of task on memory. Lindsay and Norman (1977) distinguished between *data-driven* and *conceptually-driven* tasks, noting that both the physical characteristics of the stimuli (e.g., the shape of letters) and the format of the experiment (e.g., generating synonyms of materials) can dictate the manner in which information is encoded. Another relevant topic is the differences between implicit memory tasks and more traditional recall and recognition techniques that seem to focus on explicit memory (Graf & Schacter, 1985). In recall and recognition studies, subjects are asked to actively search their memory—a deliberate and conscious process. In contrast, implicit memory tasks do not depend on intentional recollection, but assess memory performance in a more indirect manner. This subtle method of assessment is illustrated in the present demonstration. An introductory lecture of this nature will permit students to appreciate the demonstration not merely as an impressive psychological phenomenon, but also as a tangible and understandable example of some of these concepts.

Demonstration

At the outset, the program permits the user to select the presentation rates. In the course of the demonstration, the program displays 45 words on the monitor, 1 word at a time. After the entire list of words has been presented, the program clears the screen, and prompts the user to proceed to the next phase. (Although fixed in the actual demonstration, the presentation order was determined randomly after assigning distracters to both the beginning and end of the list.)

Numbered answer sheets can be distributed for the students to use during the fragment completion phase. Students are directed to work on completing a fragment, only so long as it stays on the screen, and not to go back to earlier, uncompleted items. This stipulation ensures that students are completing the fragments in the specified time and not using time allotted to other fragments.

The program lets the user set the display duration of the fragments. After the user makes a selection, the program again displays words on the screen, this time omitting some of the letters of each word (e.g., MA_G_R_T_). As each fragment appears, students will have the selected duration in which to complete the word and write it on their answer sheets. At the end of the chosen duration, each fragment is automatically replaced by the next item; this continues until all the fragments have been displayed.

After all of the fragments have been presented, the program will request the instructor to input the number of students in the class and the number who successfully completed each item. A show of hands should supply these data. The program then displays class percentages for each item and indicates whether the item was novel or primed. The program also presents the total number of completed and uncompleted fragments for both novel and primed words.

Class Discussion

An excellent way to begin discussion is to examine the effects of priming on completion of the fragments. The completion effect is robust, and a clear difference between the two groups of primed and unprimed words should be evident. The earlier discussion distinguishing data-driven tasks from conceptually-driven tasks can be reintroduced, illustrating that fragment completion depends more heavily on the appearance of the primed words (i.e., is data driven) than the meaning of the words (i.e., is not conceptually driven).

Studies (Graf & Mandler, 1984; Jacoby & Dallas, 1981) have demonstrated that manipulating the conceptual aspects of a task has large effects on tests of explicit memory (e.g., recognition and recall tasks), but produces little, if any, effect on implicit tasks such as the word fragment completion effect. Likewise, another study (Graf, Shimamura, & Squire, 1985) has shown that, when perceptual characteristics of the stimuli are manipulated, little or no effect appears in explicit memory tasks, whereas tests of implicit memory show sizable effects.

Summary

Implicit memory tasks now enjoy great popularity in cognitive research and are an ongoing theoretical and empirical concern. Implicit tasks like the word fragment completion are not often included in cognitive psychology and information processing texts. Although it is reasonable to assume that this lack will be rectified in upcoming revisions and newer books, we now have little material available for lecture or demonstration. This computer exercise was developed to fill this void, providing instructors of cognitive psychology and information processing courses a useful tool with which to integrate several complex concepts in a single demonstration. The fragment completion effect is powerful and easy to obtain; it provides a captivating introduction to discussions of experimental procedures, several different memory models, and current research interests.

References

Graf, P., & Mandler, G. (1984). Activation makes words more accessible, but not necessarily more retrievable. *Journal of Verbal Learning and Verbal Behavior, 23*, 553-568.

Graf P. & Schacter, D. L. (1985). Implicit and explicit memory for new associations in normal and amnesic subjects. *Journal of Experimental Psychology: Learning, Memory, and Cognition, 11*, 501-518.

Graf, P. Shimamura, A., & Squire, L. R. (1985). Priming across modalities and priming across category levels: Extending the domain of preserved function in amnesia. *Journal of Experimental Psychology: Learning, Memory, and Cognition, 11*, 386-396

Jacoby, L. L., & Dallas, M. (1981). On the relationship between autobiographical memory and perceptual learning. *Journal of Experimental Psychology: General, 111*, 306-340.

Lindsay, P.H., & Norman, D. A. (1977). *Human information processing.* New York: Academic

Notes

1. The words and word fragments in the demonstration program are taken from a master's thesis by

Mary Susan Weldon and are used with with her permission.

2. A copy of the demonstration program is available from the author at the address above. Please include $1.50 for the cost of a diskette and postage. All necessary documentation is included on the diskette.

SECTION V
DEVELOPMENTAL – CHILD

Instigating Miscellaneous Techniques

Douglas Hardwick adapted a technique in which on the first day of class he asked students to write a question they had about child and adolescent development but that they "were afraid to ask." The instructor arranged the questions according to sections of the course and used the questions to organize specific lecture topics. The article summarized the most frequently asked questions. The author concluded that this technique was particularly helpful in large lecture classes in which the instructor may have difficulty getting to know what students want to know.

David Miller had found that explaining the complex interrelationship between genes and experience in the development of organic structure and behavior was very difficult. He described his use of a cooking metaphor as a means of conceptualizing the nature-nurture problem. This metaphor allowed the author to illustrate several important developmental principles.

Stephen Dollinger and Dale Brown developed a simulation technique for students in their child psychology class. Students arranged themselves into triads consisting of a parent, child, and observer. The context for the interaction was Christmas shopping in a department store. The authors' manipulation of conditions associated with the simulation illustrated a factorial design. The majority of students rated the simulation favorably. The instructors' concerns about students' reluctance to participate in the simulation proved unfounded.

William Balch had undergraduate volunteers test children ages 3 to 10 years on a standardized set of developmental exercises. The sessions could be videotaped and shown later in class or performed in the classroom. Students reported that the exercises promoted understanding of developmental concepts and considered them a worthwhile teaching tool.

Students in Natividad Allen's child psychology classes experienced mini-labs in a university's child care center. The mini-lab required two college students to observe the same subject for 40 min. From students' responses to a rating scale and essay question, the author concluded that the mini-lab broadened students' views of child behavior and clarified the use of the paired-observation method.

Judith Sugar and Marilyn Livosky described a journal option in which students spent 2 hr each week throughout the term as volunteers at a preschool. Students were to make weekly journal entries that integrated lecture and text material with practical experience. Students' evaluations indicated that the project was enjoyable as well as educational. Moreo-

ver, local preschools eagerly participated in exchange for the volunteers.

Incorporating Piagetian Concepts

Gregory Harper designed a demonstration to help young adults experience an infant's intellectual development by learning about a novel object. The instructor presented an invisible novel object, described its weight and size, and explained that one would have to plug in the object and allow it to warm up. The instructor answered students' relevant questions about the object using previously prepared answers. A test of students' knowledge about the object suggested that they could experience an infant's development of a cognitive schema.

Jane Ewens (née Jane Holbrook) described two classroom demonstrations, Piaget's standard water conversion task and an adult conservation-like task too difficult for most students to solve. The author analyzed students' approaches to the adult task in terms of centration, irreversibility, and concreteness. The author concluded that students gained an appreciation of preoperational thought. Students may also earn how one can get stuck on irrelevant details, see new approaches to a problem, and gain fresh insight into the need to relinquish a particular viewpoint for a larger comprehension.

Jeanne Ormrod and Kyle Carter viewed Piaget's logical problems and clinical method as important concepts for developmental and educational psychology courses. The authors described their experiences giving students hands-on opportunities for administering Piagetian clinical interviews. Because data indicated that undergraduate students could not be easily trained to conduct a thorough or systematic interview, the authors developed flowcharts for Piagetian tasks. The flow charts provided a technique by which undergraduate students could conduct substantive interviews.

Promoting the Study of Exceptional Children

Robert Fox and his colleagues set out to establish an empirical basis for the impact of volunteer experience on undergraduates' understanding and attitudes toward special needs children. Students volunteered for a minimum of 10 hr with 1 of 11 agencies serving exceptional children. Some students provided routine care, others offered early intervention or day care services, and still others worked as teaching assistants or classroom aids. Although most students initially reported feeling anxious, by the end of the experience, many students reported wanting to do more volunteer work.

Nicholas Vacc and Ann Pace designed a technique to provide information and produce more open-minded attitudes toward exceptional children. The authors assigned students self-study materials consisting of abridged didactic information and written exercises aimed at fostering accepting attitudes. Pre- and post test evaluations revealed significant increases in achievement scores, however attitudes toward exceptional children remained open and non-fearful.

Because of limitations associated with field trips to and internships with special needs children, L. W. McCallum designed a technique to develop students' empathic understanding for such children. Working in groups of four or five, students were responsible for developing experience sessions involving members of the class. The seven content areas were mental retardation, visual disabilities, auditory disabilities, physical disabilities, learning disabilities, behavior disorders, and gifted children. Student evaluations of the experiences were very favorable.

Using Videotapes

Polly Trnavsky and Diane Willey provided students with visible examples of infants' behavior by getting friends' permission to videotape their infants during the first 18 months. The results were five 15 to 20 min tapes with each tape illustrating a different facet of development. The authors identified difficulties they encountered in making the tapes.

John Silvestro developed five 30 min videotapes of children 3, 4, 6, 7, and 8 years of age. The children performed tasks related to cognitive, social, language, motor, and affective development. A handout describing the tapes accompanied each tape. Although ratings of the tapes varied, students generally rated the tapes very favorably. The author made suggestions far readers who would like to develop their own tapes.

Debra Poole asserted that multipurpose demonstrations of child development were easy to produce by videotaping children while they interacted with parents, siblings, or friends. Unlike commercial films, videotapes without narration allowed students to formulate and test their own research questions. This article also described how to use unedited videotapes for laboratories in children's language and infants' motor, cognitive, and social development.

1. INSTIGATING MISCELLANEOUS TECHNIQUES

On the Value of Asking Students What They Want to Know About Child Development

Douglas A. Hardwick
Illinois State University

For several years now I have taught an introductory level course on the psychology of child and adolescent development. This course is taught as a service for nonmajors. As a result, it draws a fairly representative sample of the 19,000 students who attend Illinois State University. As a teacher, I have always attempted to keep the course lively, despite its large, lecture section format. In addition, I have always tried to keep the course relevant to the students who are enrolled without sacrificing my academic integrity as a developmental psychologist. Toward these ends, I have instituted a variety of classroom activities. One of the simplest of these activities has proved to be among the most effective in terms of both student and instructor goals for the course.

For the last three years, I have begun the first class by asking students to think for a moment and then write out a question that they have had about child and adolescent development, but "were afraid to ask." Following a suggestion by Pyke (1976), the questions are submitted on standard mimeographed forms which ask the students to give themselves a pen name: "something phoney, funny, or crazy" (e.g., Roseanne Rosanna Danna). After the initial class meeting, the questions are sorted into topical categories. In subsequent meetings selected questions are read to the class as organizing questions for specific lecture topics. When several similar questions on the same topic are submitted, a representative question is used.

What Students Ask. Summarized below by categories, are the questions asked by 557 students during a six semester period from 1979-1982 in terms of percentage of total questions.

Basic Concepts. Prenatal development (10.41%): hereditary influences (9.16%); self concep/self esteem (6.64%); sex roles (6.10%); language & cognition (5.56%); concept of normalcy (5.21%); growth & motor development (3.41%); sensory processes (2.87%); research/ethics (2.51%)

The Family. Working mothers (8.80%); single parents (8.08%); discipline (5.56%); birth order/spacing (3.05%)

Special Topics. Obesity (2.87%); death (2.33%); television (3.33%); competitive sports (1.08%)

Teacher Training Issues (2.69%)

Freudian Topics (1.79%)

Other Topics (9.61%)

Inspection of these data reveals several interesting facts. First, the authors and publishers of traditional child development textbooks can take heart. More than 50% of the questions asked by students concerned topics routinely covered by those texts. Indeed, the questions grouped under Basic Concepts would comprise a fairly adequate table of contents for most textbooks. Because my course is a service course, and typically attracts more female than male students, it is not surprising that questions about prenatal development constituted the largest single group of questions. Notice, however, the category labeled "concept of normalcy." It is my impression (subject to correction) that many textbooks do not make an effort to deal explicitly with this concept. Instead, the concept of normalcy is allowed to unfold over the course of an entire book. Although this seems to be a reasonable strategy, the questions I have received have prompted me to address explicitly, both early and often, the concept of normalcy.

Consider next the second large category of questions shown in the list—the family. The questions comprising this category clearly indicate an interest among students in the practical aspects of child-rearing and the impact of changing family structures on child development As a result, I now make a special effort to show how the selective use of empirical research might provide the answers to some very practical concerns.

Consider finally, the remaining categories shown. The questions comprising these categories are important, for they tend to suggest lectures on new or unusual topics, or topics outside the mainstream of developmental psychology. To illustrate, about 1% of the questions I have received have asked about the effects of competitive sports on young children. Although such questions were few in number, they were all received within the last two semesters. As a result, I am currently trying to construct a coherent lecture on children and sports. Generally speaking, however, the relative proportion of questions comprising each of the last four categories serves as a check on my own unbridled enthusiasm for certain lecture topics For example, television and its effects on children has not been a major topic of interest to my students. Thus, if the textbook I am using gives adequate coverage on this topic, I do not attempt to present additional information.

Although the questions comprising the last four categories of the table are important, note that they constitute less than 25% of all the questions asked. Again, this suggests that nonmajors want a relatively traditional course that answers very basic questions about child development. Certainly, the overall pattern of questions I have received do not argue in favor of a "pop psychology" approach to child and adolescent development.

Value of the Exercise. I cannot claim that this exercise takes the "ho hum out of the first two days of developmental psychology" (Walls, 1978). but it clearly pays long-term dividends to both student and instructor. First, student generated questions help keep the course fresh by pointing out new or overlooked lecture topics. Second, reading aloud the questions and identifying pen names tends to grab the students' attention and lighten the typical lecture hall atmosphere. Moreover, because the questions are written in an informal style, they tend to keep resulting lectures from becoming overly stuffy and sterile. Third, it is my impression that the prepared questions stimulate additional, spontaneous questions from the floor. Fourth, using student-generated questions to open a lecture provides an excellent vehicle for demonstrating to nonmajors the problems and procedures involved in satisfactorily answering the everyday questions people ask about children and child development. This, in turn, enables the students to more easily grasp the relationship between empirical research and the real world of growing children. Finally, responding to student-generated questions appears to promote a more positive attitude toward the course. Students seem to feel that the lectures are more personalized than they might have been without the exercise Inspection of the open-ended course evaluations given at the end of each semester reveals a number of spontaneous student comments praising this aspect of the course.

Conclusions. An experienced instructor always seems to sense what students need to know. However, in a large lecture section course the instructor may not be able to sense what students *want* to know. Alternatively, the instructor may simply feel that what students want to know is secondary to what they need to know. In either case, unless interrupted by questions from the floor, an instructor may appear to lecture "at" the students and thereby compound the feelings of impersonalization that can arise from sitting in a room with one hundred, or more, students. The simple exercise described here helps to overcome these problems and seems to promote a positive attitude toward a lecture course. In addition, the exercise clearly shows that the wants and needs of students enrolled in a child development course are not mutually exclusive. Using this exercise, instructors can be responsive to what students want to know without sacrificing the academic integrity of their courses.

References

Pyke, S. W. Participatory devices in large lectures. In I. Kusyszyn (Ed.), *Teaching, learning process seminars* (Vol.1) Toronto: York University, 1976.

Walls, R. E. Taking the "ho hum" out of the first two days of developmental psychology. *Teaching of Psychology*, 1978, *5*, 158-159.

The Nature-Nurture Issue: Lessons From the Pillsbury Doughboy

David B. Miller
*Department of Psychology and Center for the
Ecological Study of Perception and
Action University of Connecticut*

*One of the most difficult concepts to explain in the
classroom is the complex interrelationship between
genes and experience in the development of organic
structure and behavior. This article describes the use
of a cooking metaphor as a means of conceptualizing
the nature-nurture problem.*

One of the most difficult concepts to teach is the
intricate transaction that takes place between genes
and experience throughout development. This is
hardly surprising, given that the nature-nurture problem has engrossed the minds of scientists for centu-
ries. Recent literature is replete with claims for
innateness (e.g., Herzog & Hopf, 1984; Marler & Pickert, 1984), *genetic programs* (e.g., Mayr, 1982; Moltz,
1984), and attempts to assess how much of a given
trait is influenced by genes and how much by the environment (e.g., Marler & Sherman, 1985; Owens &
Owens, 1984). The problem with claims of innateness
and genetic programs is that they merely label rather
than explain the developmental process. The problem
with attempting to assess the extent to which a given
behavior is caused by genes and how much by the
environment relegates the developmental process to a
simplistic interaction between two entities (i.e., genes
and environment), neither of which seems capable of
affecting the other (see Hebb's, 1953, critique of this
point of view). It is, therefore, no wonder that students
share the confusion expressed by their teachers and
textbooks.

During the last several years, I have tried to explain
the intricate transaction (i.e., a complex interaction in
which the interactants are inseparable and constantly
changing-see Miller, 1988) of genes and experience by
using the metaphor of cooking, which is a microcosm
of development. In this metaphor, flour is analogous to
genes. Genes, of course, have their own environments
that will influence their activity throughout development. Genetic activity is also influenced by (and influences) other components unique to any organism.
Such is the case with flour in the cooking process.

As I explain the analogy to my students, I take four
different food items (i.e., developmental outcomes)
that use flour as a base (i.e., genetic factors), but that
also have other ingredients that will interact with the
flour in unique ways (i.e., yielding different developmental trajectories). Also, different cooking methods
(i.e., experiential factors) influence these developmental trajectories and yield different developmental outcomes.

In the first case, FLOUR + SALT + WATER fried in
shortening "develop" into a FLOUR TORTILLA. In the
second case, we take precisely the same ingredients
and provide them with a "baking" experience (without
shortening). The developmental outcome is entirely
different as a function of this alteration in experience,
for now these ingredients yield a MATZO. In the third
case, we keep these three ingredients and add YEAST
to them. While baking, these develop into BREAD.
Finally, we retain the FLOUR and SALT, but add to
them BUTTER, COCOA, and SUGAR. Again, bake
them, and the result is a BROWNIE.

I have tried two different methods of presenting this
metaphor to my classes, each with equal impact (as
far as I could judge). The less dramatic method involves preparing and showing a sequence of slides of:
(a) the ingredients, (b) the frying or baking process
(i.e., the ingredients, still boxed, sitting in a frying pan
atop a stove or in a baking dish inside an open oven),
and (c) the developmental outcomes. The more dramatic method is rather messy and requires a bit of
theatrics; specifically, bring the ingredients to class
and mix them on paper plates before the students,
explaining what the developmental process will entail
(either frying or baking). Then, pull out of a paper bag
the developmental outcome of each. Students in both
large and small classrooms have found the latter
demonstration particularly informative (if not amusing).
I prefer it because it enables me to have the ingredients and the outcomes laid out on the table as I continue to explain the metaphor with behavioral
development (discussed next). (Flour, when tossed
exuberantly on small paper plates in a fashion that
would rival that of Julia Child, can make quite a mess.
I caution that students may find this amusing, but most
janitors do not!)

The growing literature showing dramatic effects of
different developmental contexts on the expression of

201

behavioral as well as morphological outcomes provides a good example of this cooking metaphor. For example, it has often been assumed that physical variations within a species are due solely to genetic variation. However, James (1983) transplanted red-winged blackbird eggs between nests located hundreds of miles apart and found that nestlings were, in some respects, more similar in physical appearance to their foster parents than to their biological parents. Thus, common ingredients (i.e., shared genes between parent and offspring) yielded different developmental outcomes due to different cooking methods (i.e., different environments). With respect to behavior, I have shown how rearing and observing domestic mallards in a species-typical environment (i.e., a natural pond) results in the expression of species-typical social courtship displays (Miller, 1977). Prior to this research, it had been believed that these behaviors were genetically altered or entirely bred out of domestic breeds (Lorenz, 1974). Rather, my study showed that such behaviors are inhibited due to the unfavorable species-atypical environments (e.g., barnyards) in which domestic animals are reared. Again, the developmental outcome is primarily a function of the cooking process.

This cooking metaphor illustrates several important developmental principles. First is the concept of developmental constraints. That is, there is a range of possible outcomes constrained by nature of the ingredients and the types of developmental interactions that take place. For example, in no way will the ingredients described before yield vanilla pudding or duck à l'orange. Accordingly, genetic and environmental factors that develop into some form of primate cannot give rise to amphibians. Second, flour does not "code" for any specific outcome, nor do genes code or contain programs for developmental outcomes. The developmental outcome is a complex transaction involving the flour (genes), other ingredients, and the nature of the developmental process (cooking method). Altering the environment yields very different outcomes, even with the same set of ingredients (e.g., flour tortilla vs. matzo as a function of frying vs. baking the same three ingredients). Third, as development proceeds (or, as you get further along in the cooking process), the organism (or food item) achieves greater form, more closely approximating the developmental outcome (see Oyama, 1985). Fourth, one cannot partition a developmental outcome into heritable and environmental components. It would be entirely arbitrary to quantify the degree to which bread is a function of flour (i.e., heritability) as opposed to baking (i.e., environment). Accordingly, heritability quotients and assertions about environmental variance are highly arbitrary estimates and yield little information about the development and expression of behavior. Finally, when you have reached the developmental "endpoint" or outcome, you cannot easily identify the earlier constituent elements. That is, you cannot look at the brownie and see the individual ingredients or the nature of the transactions of those ingredients that occurred

throughout the brownie's ontogeny. The same is true of behavioral and morphological development. If the individual factors leading up to the developmental outcome were apparent, developmental psychologists, psychobiologists, and ethologists would have rather boring jobs and little to quarrel about.

References

Hebb, D. O. (1953). Heredity and environment in mammalian behavior. *British Journal of Animal Behavior, 1*, 43-47.

Herzog, M., & Hopf, S. (1984). Behavioral responses to species-specific warning calls in infant squirrel monkeys reared in social isolation. *American Journal of Primatology, 7*, 99-106.

James, F. C. (1983). Environmental component of morphological differentiation in birds. *Science, 221*, 184-186.

Lorenz, K. (1974). *Civilized man's eight deadly sins.* New York: Harcourt Brace Jovanovich.

Marler, P., & Pickert, R. (1984). Species-universal microstructure in the learned song of the swamp sparrow (*Melospiza melodia*). *Animal Behavior, 32*, 673-689.

Marler, P., & Sherman, V. (1985). Innate differences in singing behavior of sparrows reared in isolation from adult nonspecific song. *Animal Behavior, 33*, 57-71.

Mayr, E. (1982). *The growth of biological thought.* Cambridge, MA: Belknap.

Miller, D. B. (1977). Social displays of mallard ducks (*Anas platyrhynchos*): Effects of domestication. *Journal of Comparative and Physiological Psychology, 91*, 221-232.

Miller, D. B. (1988). The development of instinctive behavior: An epigenetic and ecological approach. In E. M. Blass (Ed.), *Handbook of behavioral neurobiology: Vol. 9. Developmental psychobiology and behavioral ecology* (pp. 415-444). New York: Plenum.

Moltz, H. (1984). Why rat young respond to the maternal pheromone. In G. Greenberg & E. Tobach (Eds.), *Behavioral evolution and integrative levels* (pp. 277-288). Hillsdale, NJ: Lawrence Erlbaum Associates, Inc.

Owens, M., & Owens, D. (1984). *Cry of the Kalahari.* Boston: Houghton Mifflin.

Oyama, S. (1985). *The ontogeny of information: Developmental systems and evolution.* New York: Cambridge University Press.

Note

I thank Charles F. Blaich and Gloria Hicinbothom for many fruitful discussions about behavioral development. Devising this exercise depended on a re-evaluation of past and present developmental theories, which came about largely through their insights. I also thank the editor and three reviewers for helpful suggestions. One of the reviewers suggested the point about heritability quotients and I am grateful for that insight.

Simulated Parent-Child Interaction in an Undergraduate Child Psychology Course

Stephen J. Dollinger
Dale F. Brown
Southern Illinois University

Simulation can be a useful technique in teaching undergraduate child psychology courses. Recently we used simulated parent-child interactions in a unit on child behavior management and discipline. Our objectives involved (a) illustrating the types of discipline used, and (b) integrating the students' everyday knowledge (or "implicit psychology") of children with research and theory. As a secondary benefit, the simulation illustrated the concept of factorial design in experiments.

Because the simulation took place in December, the context selected for the parent-child interaction was Christmas shopping in a department store. The child's demands for an expensive toy provided the conflict situation that the students role-played.

The 45 students were asked to arrange themselves into triads, consisting of a parent, child, and observer. Each participant received an instruction sheet describing the context, their role, and some suggestions for how they might respond. "Parents" received suggestions for a wide variety of disciplinary practices and were urged to "see what works with your child." In addition, half of the "parents" were given a reminder that they felt embarrassed by the child's behavior, wanted to avoid "creating a scene," and had a long shopping list to get through. These additional instructions were given to lower their tolerance of the "child's" disruptiveness.

Students playing the role of the child were given suggestions on a variety of manipulative techniques to persuade their "parent." Instructions for half of the children also suggested that they "back down" if it seemed that their parent was getting angry or "if it seems that parent no longer loves you." These instructions established the "good child" group. By way of contrast, the other half of the "children" were given egocentric instructions which emphasized (a) that their sense of being loved depended on whether the parent bought the toy for them; and (b) that they could use this in the interaction (e.g. "you never loved me").

Observers were instructed to keep notes on the interaction. It was also suggested that the observers watch for four types of parenting statements: reason-oriented discipline (explaining why he/she would not buy the toy); power assertion (pulling rank); guilt-inducing discipline (making the child feel naughty or guilty); and evasive discipline (avoiding the issue).

The two types of parent and child instructions were combined to make four types of triads: tolerant parent-good child; tolerant parent-egocentric child; intolerant parent-good child; and intolerant parent-egocentric child. With 45 students participating, there were 15 triads, 3 of the first types and 4 of the other types.

The interaction in all groups began with the "child's" request for the parent to buy an expensive toys followed by the "parent's" refusal. Following this, the students improvised for 5-10 minutes. At the end of the interactions the "parent" and "child" answered questions on their instruction form, and the observer briefly interviewed them about their feelings. Then the observers reported to the class on how their interaction went and what types of discipline were used. Also, the "parent" and "child" ratings were collected and the results were presented in the next class period.

While the results were not amenable to statistical analyses there were some interesting trends which in many cases parallel what likely would be found in the "real world." First, all groups used reason-oriented discipline (generally this was tried first). Power-assertion was most likely within the intolerant parent-good child groups (3 of the 4 groups), but was never used within the tolerant parent-egocentric child groups. Guilt-inducing discipline was only used within the intolerant parent-egocentric child groups (2 of the 4 groups), and evasive discipline was used most in the two egocentric child groups (6 of the 8 egocentric groups vs. 3 of 7 non-egocentric groups). In none of the groups did the "parent" resort to spankings a result partly attributable to the instruction that "parents" should say "now I would spank you" rathert han actually use punishment. Ratings of satisfaction with the outcome of the interaction showed that the "parents" were more satisfied when their "child" was good rather than egocentric and "children" were more satisfied when their "parents" were tolerant rather than intolerant. Additionally "parents" overall were more satisfied than "children," a result which is not surprising since the "child" received the toy in only 1 of the 15 groups.

The results suggest that, much as in the "real world the "parents" accommodated their discipline to the special characteristics of their "children," and "children" accommodated to their "parents." The findings which are suspect in this regard are the high frequency of reason-oriented discipline (100%) the low frequency of physical punishment (0%), and the low frequency of cases where the "child" was successful in getting the toy (7%). However, these results might be expected within the context of a group of university students who have elected a course in child psychology most of whom are not yet parents.

On teacher evaluation questionnaires completed at the end of the semesters the students were given an opportunity to comment on the usefulness of the simulation and to give ratings from 0 to 9. Forty-five percent gave a rating of 8 or 9 indicating very favorable attitudes 23% had mildly favorable attitudes (ratings of 6 or 7), 16% had neutral ratings (4 or 5), and 16% had mildly unfavorable ratings (2 or 3). Comments generally reflected attitudes expressed in the ratings: "fun!" "it was great!" "thought it was worthless" and "good idea." Other students suggested that there be more use of simulations in class. Negative comments generally addressed the issue of people being "too shy" to participate.

When ratings were grouped according to the students' major courses of study, it appeared that the most favorable ratings came from students in psychology, social welfare, and special education. Since students in these majors have probably had more opportunities for role-playing in class, they may have felt fewer reservations about participating.

Several concerns prior to using the simulation were that students would have difficulty taking the "child" role, that most students would be reluctant to participate and that the contrived nature of the simulation would have no relationship to the "real world." These concerns appear to have been unfounded. In summary, the use of simulated parent-child interaction has promise as an instructional and motivational aid in teaching undergraduate child psychology.

The Use of Student-Performed Developmental Exercises in the Classroom

William R. Balch
The Pennsylvania State University, Altoona

Using this technique, undergraduate volunteers test children 3 to 10 years old on a standardized set of developmental exercises. The sessions may be videotaped and shown later in class, or performed "live" in the classroom. The exercises promote understanding of developmental concepts; students consider them a worthwhile teaching tool.

Undergraduate psychology students generally respond with enthusiasm to exercises that require their direct participation in class. For instance, having groups of them play roles in front of their classmates can produce an active and creative learning experience, for those directly involved and for those watching (Balch, 1983; Benjamin, 1981; Brooks, 1985). Brooks reported using teams of students in a history of psychology course to create and perform plays that illustrate the interaction of famous figures (Locke, Wundt, Skinner, etc.). In Balch's (1983) exercise, students improvised dialogue in a client-centered therapy scenario given to them by the instructor.

The technique reported here combines student participation with the presentation of research methodology and results. With this technique, student volunteers perform research exercises that are viewed by the entire class. I have used the method in my introductory and child psychology classes to demonstrate developmental trends. Each student participant is responsible for testing one child on a set of exercises that I describe in a handout at the beginning of the semester. To keep the number of involved students manageable, I make the exercises optional, and give a small amount of extra credit for participation. In classes that average about 80 students, the number of participants has varied from 5 to 12.

I recommend that each student's session with a child be videotaped, and that the recording be shown later in class. A suitable alternative, however, is to have the students perform the sessions directly in front of the class. In this case, it is important to instruct the class in advance in order to avoid reactions from the students that might bias, discomfort, or distract the child.

The Exercises

The best results are achieved by preparing a standard set of exercises. I have used adaptations of three well-known demonstrations that are easy to perform and for which the age effects are robust and clear in implication. The recommended age range for these exercises is 3 to 10 years. I describe them briefly here.

1. Acting out sentences. Adapting a technique used by Bever (1970), the student performing the exercises asks the child to act out several sentences—using the verb *bump*—with three toy dolls: a girl, a boy, and a dog. A standard set of sentences should be included in the handout and used for each child. Half should be active (e.g., "The dog bumps the boy") and half passive (e.g., "The dog is bumped by the girl"). I used four sentences in the order: active-passive-passive-active.

The children have no difficulty acting out active sentences. However, those who are less than 5 years old usually misinterpret at least one passive sentence, treating it like an active one. For example, a younger child might make the dog bump the girl in the passive sentence mentioned above.

2. Conservation. Each child is tested on liquid conservation, according to the familiar method of Piaget (1965). Water is poured into two identical glasses until the child agrees that the glasses contain equal amounts. After the water from one glass is poured into a taller, thinner glass, the child is asked to compare the amount in the new glass with that in the remaining original one. An explanation of the child's response is then requested. Children who are younger than 7 years old almost always judge the amounts to be unequal, and usually say that the taller, thinner container has more water. Most older children recognize that the two glasses still have equal amounts of water.

Children who pass the liquid conservation test are given a simple adaptation of Piaget's weight conservation exercise, which is often not passed by children who are younger than 9 or 10 years old (Ginsburg &

Opper, 1979; Piaget & Inhelder, 1974). In this version, the child first agrees that two balls of Pla-doh® are equally heavy. (Rather than using a balance beam, as Piaget did, I have found that simply letting children hold one ball in each hand, and judge themselves, is a satisfactory method that is easier for videotaping purposes.) One of the balls is then transformed into a sausage shape. The child is asked, without being permitted to hold the balls again, whether they are still equally heavy. The interesting feature of this demonstration is that many 7- to 8-year-old children pass the liquid conservation test, but then fail to pass the weight conservation test. This phenomenon exemplifies Piaget's notion of the "horizontal decalage" or "gap" (Flavell, 1963), which refers to the child's acquisition of two different forms of the same concept at different ages.

3. Moral judgment. In this exercise, the child is asked to identify which of two hypothetical children is "the naughty one." Two pictures from the instructional handout are shown. In the first picture, a little girl is standing by a desk with a tipped over bottle and a large puddle of ink on it. The child in the exercise is told that this little girl accidentally spilled a lot of ink on her father's desk. In the second picture, the same girl, bottle, and desk appear, but there is just a small amount of ink on the desk. It is explained to the child that this girl only spilled a little ink on her father's desk, but that she did it on purpose.

This demonstration is based on a well-known series of stories used by Piaget (1932), but here pictures are used and the accompanying verbal accounts are made as simple as possible. This procedure makes the results of the exercise clearer when shown on videotape to the class.

Piaget (1932) found that up to age 8 or 9 years, children based their evaluations on an objective criterion, identifying wrongdoing with the amount of damage done. However, older children judged on a subjective basis, so that the child with the harmful intention is more to blame. In my version of the exercise, the objective answer is that the girl who spilled more ink accidentally is the naughtier and the subjective answer is the girl who spilled less ink on purpose.

Using the Exercises as a Teaching Tool

One key to the success of this demonstration is the detailed handout, which is distributed at the beginning of the course. This handout should include (a) instructions on how to perform each exercise; (b) necessary materials, such as the sentences to be used in the acting out of the sentences exercise and the pictures to be shown to the children in the moral judgment exercise; (c) a discussion of Piaget's clinical interview method, which emphasizes not only adherence to the specific procedures, but also interacting with the children and eliciting from them justifications of their answers; and (d) a slip for parents to sign indicating their permission for the child to participate in the exercise.

In my classes the student volunteers find children for the demonstration with little difficulty. Occasionally, someone will want to participate in the exercises, but will not know of an available subject. I can usually solve this problem by asking the class if anybody can suggest a possible child.

It is important to meet with the volunteers before the student-child sessions are conducted. In addition to providing instruction and answering questions, I can check on the ages of the children who will take part. Generally, I have obtained an adequate variety of age groups without special planning. Occasionally, I have had students seek children of a particular age, in order to have a representative set.

If possible, the student-child sessions should be videotaped. In-class performance of these sessions is feasible, but younger children tend to be more anxious in a large class. When videotaping is to be done, the instructor should make arrangements in advance with the audiovisual facility. Each session takes only about 15 to 20 min to tape, and the resulting footage lasts only about 5 min. Though most of the children appear to find the sessions intrinsically rewarding, an extrinsic reward (e.g., candy or perhaps a small, colorful certificate issued for the purpose) is a good way of expressing appreciation to the children.

Participants should state their names at the beginning of the tape, along with the child's first name and age. It should be stressed to students that they are responsible for keeping their appointments, being well prepared to conduct the exercises, and providing the necessary props (toys, glasses, etc.). I have had few problems with students along these lines. (My students provide their own conservation glasses, Pla-doh®, and toy dolls so that I do not have to keep track of this equipment. Additional standardization could be achieved by using the same props over and over again.)

Interesting methodological and theoretical points arise when presenting and discussing the sessions in class. For example, a child commented during the liquid conservation test that the tall glass was bigger than the shorter original one. The student performing the exercise alertly pointed out that she was asking about the amount of water, not the glass size. A frequent issue concerns whether all children, especially young ones, fully understand the questions or instructions. Even when great care is taken to help the child understand the task, the results are usually predictable from the child's age.

Generally, the results of the class exercises support established age trends (e.g., Gardner, 1982) for conservation (achieved at around 7 years) and comprehension of passive sentences (around 5 years). To this end, it is useful for the instructor and/or students to keep a running record of the key results in the exercise, and to tabulate them according to age. For instance, out of 20 children taped over the last 2 years,

5 of the 8 children who were at least 7 years old passed liquid conservation, and 10 of those 12 children under 7 years of age did not. However, our classroom results on moral judgment show much earlier emergence of subjective moral judgment than age 8 or 9, as Piaget (1932) found. All but two of the 15 children 5 years of age or older gave the subjective answer, and even two of the five 3- to 4-year-olds answered in this way. One reason for the earlier emergence of subjective moral judgments in my task may be the shortened verbal explanations and the reliance on pictures.

Evaluation

One criterion for evaluating this exercise is its effect on an objective measure of students' understanding of developmental concepts. To test their comprehension of the main points related to the demonstration, I included the following three items in a five-question pop quiz.

1. Describe a difference between the sentence comprehension of a 4-year-old and that of a 6-year-old.
2. Describe a way in which a 5-year-old's understanding of quantity differs from that of an 8-year-old who has achieved concrete operations.
3. How would a very young child morally evaluate a situation in which a little boy accidentally knocked over a heavy lamp on a dog and broke the animal's leg? How would the older child be likely to evaluate the same situation?

In the next scheduled class, the quiz was given to one section of general psychology in which the demonstration was used. In addition, the quiz was given to another section in which the demonstration was not used. In the latter section, the material necessary for correctly answering the three critical items on the pop-quiz was covered as part of the lecture, in the class prior to the one in which the popquiz was taken.

I scored the items correct (1) or incorrect (0) without knowing from which section the students' quiz papers came. Only those students who had attended the preceding class, and had thus been present at the demonstration or at the lecture where the relevant material was covered, were included in the analysis. The mean score (out of 3) on the items was 2.24 for the class ($n = 58$) in which the demonstration was employed, and 1.84 for the class ($n = 54$) in which it was not used. The better performance of the former class was significant, $t(110) = 2.11$, $p < .05$. Therefore, the demonstration is helpful in teaching those developmental principles that are illustrated in the exercises.

Some students rated the demonstration on a 5-point scale ranging from *not at all worthwhile* (1) to *very worthwhile* (5). Based on 60 respondents (from a developmental psychology class not included in the analysis just reported), the mean rating was 4.34 (4.60 for the 12 who reported being participants and 4.28 for the others). In addition, they rated whether they would prefer watching the demonstrations done by their classmates, or the same demonstrations done on a psychology series film on a 5-point scale ranging from *definitely prefer film* (1) to *definitely prefer videotape exercises* (5). The mean rating for this question was 4.20.

Their preference for the demonstration over a film is noteworthy, because films might convey the same information with comparable effectiveness. Student involvement appears to provide motivation and perhaps a sense of reality, as well as instruction. Those who participate are reinforced by the recognition they receive as "television stars" performing in front of their classmates. Even those who do not actually perform the demonstration often say that the exercises are interesting and real to them because people they know are testing children from the local area. This impression of reality is bolstered by spontaneous and sometimes humorous moments on the videotapes: for instance, a 3-year-old helping himself to a drink of water from one of the conservation test glasses; or a 6-year-old bumping two dolls together with such enthusiasm that the head of one drops onto the floor. I recommend this videotaping technique as enjoyable and informative for undergraduate psychology classes.

References

Balch, W. R. (1983). The use of role-playing in a classroom demonstration of client-centered therapy. *Teaching of Psychology, 10*, 173-174.

Benjamin, L. T., Jr. (1981). *Teaching history of psychology: A handbook.* New York: Academic.

Bever, T. G. (1970). The cognitive basis for linguistic structures. In J. R. Hayes (Ed.), *Cognition and the development of language* (pp. 279-362). New York: Wiley.

Brooks, C. I. (1985). A role-playing exercise for the history of psychology course. *Teaching of Psychology, 12*, 84-85.

Flavell, J. H. (1963). *The developmental psychology of Jean Piaget.* New York: Van Nostrand.

Gardner, H. (1982). *Developmental psychology.* Boston: Little, Brown.

Ginsburg, H., & Opper, S. (1979). *Piaget's theory of intellectual development.* Englewood Cliffs, NJ: Prentice-Hall.

Piaget, J. (1932). *The moral Judgment of the child.* New York: Harcourt, Brace.

Piaget, J. (1965). *The child's conception of number.* New York: Norton.

Piaget, J., & Inhelder, B. (1974). *The child's construction of quantities: Conservation and atomism.* New York: Basic Books.

Note

I thank Drew McGhee for his cooperation in videotaping many sessions of students' exercises.

Enriching Child Psychology Through the Mini-Lab

Natividad Macaranas Allen
Eastern New Mexico University

Much of the research in child psychology has relied on the use of human observers, typically college undergraduates, to collect the necessary data (Wildman & Erickson, 1975). The focus is on the minimization of observational errors and the necessity for an objective means of recording behaviors occurring in the natural environment (Arrington, 1932; Wildman & Erickson, 1975). Some investigators (Mash & McElwee, 1974; Johnson & Bolstad, 1973) emphasize the importance of observer accuracy, and others (O'Leary & Kent, 1973; Romanczyk, Kent, Diament & O'Leary, 1973) identify factors influencing observer reliability, including complexity of observed behavior (Reid, 1970) and effects of prior information (Mash & Makohoniuk, 1975). The emphasis is on the accurate collection of data to provide a basis for the understanding of preschool children's behavior. Research has not focused on enriching course content and experience by actively involving students in learning about the observational method as opposed to telling about it in lecture form. It is this lack that prompted the author to include the mini-lab as one of the requirements for the undergraduate course, Child Psychology.

The mini-lab is an educational-psychological method which can be used with practically no special equipment or laboratory facilities. Mini-labs can be carried out in any Child Care Center with a minimal disruption of the on going activities of the child being observed. It has been reported by preschool workers that children go about their activities without paying much attention to observers. Habituation to adult strangers occurs almost instantaneously.

Description. The mini-lab is a form of observation that lasts for a total of forty minutes. The paired-observation method is used in which two students (Observer₁ and Observer₂) observe the same subject at the same time. One twenty minute period is for free observation, and the other is a direct recording of the child's behavior in terms of behavior units (BU).

The free observation is a free-hand written record of the subject's activities. For four 5-minute periods, everything the observer hears and sees about the subject is recorded: what the subject is doing to what, or what is being done to the subject and by whom.

The direct recording of behavior units is a check-mark record of the subject's activities. A rating sheet is provided. For four five-minute periods each observer independently records with a check mark a new behavior unit. This division of the behavior into units, and the rating of the units for dependency or aggression, is to be done while observing. No verbal description of the behavior sequence is made. The two observers start a new 5-minute interval at the same time.

The students in the Child Psychology class in which the mini-lab was first tried agreed upon the observation of dependent and aggressive behaviors of preschool children rather than other behavioral patterns such as sexual behavior, leadership styles, or play activities. Dependent behavior is characterized by attention-seeking in which the subject invites cooperative activity or praise by disruption, defiance, or oppositional behavior. The subject seeks reassurance, comfort, and protection through such actions as asking permission unnecessarily, touching, holding, or seeking to be near another child, group of children, or teacher. Aggressive behavior is characterized by attack in which the subject makes a physical or verbal attack on another child or object. The behavior may be aimed directly at another person, or it may be deflected through objects or activity. A subject may try to get others to attack or punish someone or may talk about future aggression toward others.

After completing the forty-minute observation, the observers score the free observation record in terms of BUs independent of each other. There are three ways in which the relationship between the behavior and the environment of a subject may change, creating new BUs: (a) There is a change in S's behavior following an observable change in the environment (e.g., S cries after being hit by another child). (b) There is a change in S's behavior with no observable change in S's environment (e.g., S cries without provocation or observable stimulus). (c) There is no change in S's behavior following an observable change in S's environment (e.g., S continues playing after being attacked by another child). After dividing the record into BUs, each observer examines his or her own record to see if each unit included either dependent or aggressive behavior performed by the subject.

Observers and Subjects. The student observers are given careful and detailed instructions on the proper use of the paired-observation method. Usually, three or four lecture periods are spent for this purpose. In addition, a graduate assistant is available to answer specific questions about the mini-lab. Each student selects a partner, and they study again the directions to make sure that they understand all facets of the assignment. Before going to observe, they sign up on a schedule sheet for the date and time best suited for them. This scheduling insures only the three pairs of observers that the Center can accommodate during a forty-minute period.

The subjects are children aged three to five years who are enrolled at the Child Development Center. The observers choose their subject in accordance with their own criteria. The information needed about the subject are age and sex. For ethical considerations, the subject's family background is not obtained.

Analysis. The percent agreement in scoring the behavior between O_1 and O_2 is computed by multiplying the number of agreed upon BUs by two and dividing by the total number of O_1 plus O_2 BUs. This computation is used for the total number of units recorded, and for the ratings of the units in terms of dependency and aggression.

Summary scores for data are obtained as follows: (a) Average number of BUs observed for each of the observation tasks (free observation and direct BU observation) by both observers; (b) Average number of aggressive responses, and the average number of dependent responses are computed in the same way; (c) Relative frequency of the responses: average number of aggressive responses/average number of BUs.

To illustrate the analysis of data, a sample summary score and observer agreement are seen in Tables 1 and 2. Table 1 shows the summary score and percent agreement of a pair of observers. The data show high degrees of agreement between them for all

Table 1
Sample Summary Score and Percent Agreement

Behavior Unit	Free Observation					Direct Recording				
	1	2	3	4	Total	1	2	3	4	Total
Observed by O_1	10	8	10	10	38	10	10	14	13	47
Observed by O_2	11	12	12	11	46	11	10	14	13	48
Agreed upon	10	8	10	10	38	10	10	14	13	47
% Agreement					90					98
Dependent by O_1	1	3	1	2	7	3	3	4	2	12
Dependent by O_2	2	6	3	3	14	5	6	4	6	21
Agreed upon	1	3	1	2	7	3	3	4	2	12
% Agreement					67					73
Aggressive by O_1	1	0	4	1	6	2	1	2	1	6
Aggressive by O_2	2	0	3	2	7	3	1	3	2	9
Agreed upon	1	0	3	1	5	2	1	2	1	6
% Agreement					77					80

Table 2
Averages and Relative Frequencies of Dependent and Aggressive BUs

BUs	Free Observation	Direct Recording
Total	42	48
Dependent	10.5 (25%)	16.5 (34%)
Aggressive	6.5 (15%)	7.5 (16%)

categories of behavior units and for both free observation and direct recording procedures. The direct recording technique seems to yield a higher percentage of agreement than the free observation technique.

These findings are typical of most pairs of observers. The factors that may contribute to this result are the intensive training sessions with the instructor, the personal tutoring by the trained graduate assistant, and the study done by both observers to the point of mastery before their actual mini-lab.

Table 2 shows the averages and relative frequencies of dependent BUs and aggressive BUs. The averages represent a composite score for the two observers. The relative frequencies of dependent or aggressive behavior units are based on these composite scores. The relative frequencies of dependent BUs for the free observation and direct recording sessions are similar (25% and 34% respectively). The relative frequencies for aggressive BUs (15%—16%) are practically the same for the two methods. The essential agreement for the two techniques is more or less the same for all observers.

An examination of Table 2 further reveals that for this particular subject the averages and relative frequencies for dependent BUs are higher than those for aggressive BUs. This finding seems to be typical of the preschoolers at our Child Development Center.

Evaluation. A total of 110 students in two classes was used to assess the mini-labs. Each observer was asked to evaluate in terms of goals and personal benefit. Anonymity was preserved by not requiring names on the evaluation form. The goals were description of behavior units during a specified period of time (i.e. forty minutes), learning through participation, objective observation of children in their natural environment, and enrichment of course content. The personal benefit was in terms of how beneficial each goal was to the observer. This part of the evaluation was included to elicit a numerical measure of the subjective comments of the student toward the mini-lab portion of the course. Very often, a student would say, "I really enjoyed observing children," or "It was a most beneficial experience for me as a mother of a three-year old." There were two parts of the mini-lab evaluation: (a) a rating scale for the attainment of goals and personal benefit, and (b) an essay question that asked whether or not the assignment was effective or ineffective in enriching course content for broader participation and learning. In responding to the questionnaire, the observer was asked to encircle the number on the continuum that best approximated his or her judgment of goal attainment or non-attainment and personal benefit or non-benefit, and the scale was arranged from 0 (poorest) to 5 (best). To the question "Was the goal of *description* of behavior attained?" the mean rating was 4.9; for "How beneficial was this goal to you?" it was 3.8; for "Was the goal of learning through participation attained?" it was 4.6; and for "How beneficial was this goal to you?" the mean was 4.2.

The essay question allowed the observer to write freely about experiences during the mini-lab in terms of enriching course content—"Was the assignment effective or ineffective in the attainment of the goal of enriching course content? Why?" The respondents rated this assignment 81% effective and 19% ineffective. The 89 students (81%) who rated the mini-lab as effective in enriching course content gave the following as the most frequent responses: Brief but enriching in terms of observing behavior units in preschool children; Something different and fun added to the Child Psychology curriculum; The observational mode generalizes to other children in gaining an understanding of their behavior; No testing involved, and therefore a relaxing assignment; Get to discuss with partner and become friends. The 21 students (19%) who rated the assignment as ineffective gave the following reasons: Difficulty in finding a partner; Partner not responsible in showing up during the scheduled time to observe; A waste of time—the lecture method is better than the actual doing in regard to time saved.

Discussion. The mini-lab has been a requirement in the investigator's undergraduate class in Child Psychology for ten years. A personal evaluation of this assignment by the author is that it broadens the students' view of child behavior through actual observation, and clarifies the use of the paired-observation method in a 40-minute lab. Students also develop observational skills which generalize into other situations involving children. Student evaluations over the ten-year period support the author's evaluation.

Before the observers actually did their mini-lab, they were trained to the point of mastery of the free observation and the direct recording techniques. Research on individual differences in the attainment of this mastery is needed.

References

Arrington, R. E. Interrelations in the behavior of young children. *Child Development Monographs*, Monograph No. 8. New York: Teachers College, Columbia University, 1932.

Johnson, S. M., & Bolstad O. D. Methodological issues in naturalistic observation: Some problems and solutions for field research. In L. Hamerlynck, L. C. Handy, & E. J. Mash (Eds.), *Behavior change: Methodology, excerpts, and practice.* Champaign, IL: Research Press, 1973.

Mash, E. J., & McElwee, J. D. Situational effects on observer accuracy: Behavioral predictability, prior experience, and complexity of coded categories, *Child Development*, 1974, *45*, 366-377.

Mash, E. J., & Makohoniuk, G. The effects of prior information and behavioral predictability on observer accuracy. *Child Development*, 1975, *46*, 613-519.

O'Leary, K. D., & Kent, R. Behavior modification for social action: Research tactics and problems. In L. A. Hamerlynck, L. C. Handy, & E. L. Mash (Eds.), *Behavior change: Methodology, concepts and practice.* Champaign, IL: Research Press, 1973.

Reid, J. B. Reliability assessment of observation data: A possible methodological problem. *Child Development*, 1970, *41*, 1143-1150.

Romanczyk, H. G., Kent, R. N., Diament, C., & O'Leary, K. D. Measuring the reliability of observational data: A reactive process. *Journal of Applied Behavior Analysis*, 1973, *6*, 175-184.

Wildman, B. G., & Erickson, M. T. The effects of two training procedures on observer agreement and variability of behavior ratings. *Child Development*, 1975, *46*, 520-524.

Note

The author gratefully acknowledges Dr. Harold Stevenson for introducing her to the mini-lab concept.

Enriching Child Psychology Courses With a Preschool Journal Option

Judith Sugar
Marilyn Livosky
Colorado State University

This article describes a preschool journal option for child psychology classes. The option requires students to spend 2 hr each week throughout the term as volunteers at a preschool. Weekly journal entries must integrate lecture and text material with practical experience. Participating students earn extra credit, commensurate with their performance, toward their final course grade. Students' evaluations indicate that the project is enjoyable as well as educational. Furthermore, local preschools are eager to participate in exchange for the volunteers.

Various techniques for enriching the education of undergraduates through practical experience have been reported; some involve entire courses (e.g., Fernald et al., 1982; Sherman, 1982), whereas others have been more limited in scope (e.g., Fox, Lopuch, & Fisher, 1984; Saxon & Holt, 1974). The consensus is that fieldwork is a valuable addition to a student's education. In psychology courses, and particularly child psychology courses, nothing can take the place of direct experience with the subject matter. Unfortunately, large classes and a shortage of resources often preclude even the occasional live demonstration of some aspect of child development. This article describes a method that provides students with the opportunity to interact with preschoolers and to integrate that experience with course material. In addition, the structure of the option minimizes the amount of time needed to administer it.

Students choosing the "preschool journal option" are required to spend 2 hr a week in day care centers and to keep a journal of their experiences throughout the term. The primary goals of the preschool journal option are (a) to make students aware of the relationship between course material and a practical application and (b) to help students develop a sensitivity to the range of behaviors characteristic of preschoolers. The option is not intended to train students as naturalistic observers, which would require a separate class or many training sessions. Instead, the option provides an opportunity for students who have had little or no contact with preschoolers to see firsthand some of the concepts discussed in the course. Students are directed to look for behaviors consistent with the topics being covered in class—including motor, social, sex-role, perceptual, memory, cognitive, and language development. Evaluations and informal feedback indicate that these goals are met. Students report that they are "able to make the connection between the agency experience and lecture" and that "actually working with children helped [to] really see certain behaviors, theories, concepts." Furthermore, the journal itself is an important aspect of the option because it requires students to integrate their practical experiences with the lecture and text material. The students often appreciate this fact, as indicated by the following representative comment: "I thought keeping a journal was helpful in that it made me think about my experience [at the preschool] and made me relate it to the text."

Two aspects of the option make it practicable for a large class. First, students deciding to participate in the project are required to make their own arrangements with approved preschools whose directors have agreed to monitor students' participation in exchange for a regular pool of volunteers. Second, the project is optional and requires additional effort on the part of students for extra grade credits; consequently, not all students choose to do it.

Although the availability of day care settings for student volunteers may vary, even in a town of 80,000 our students have no difficulty finding a placement; in fact, day care directors often ask for more students than we can provide. The agencies have accommodated from 1 to 12 students at a time ($M = 4$). In any one term, 11% to 19% of the students have chosen the option.

Many students choose not to participate. The typical reasons are an unwillingness to commit to the extra hours of work or a lack of interest in the preschool age group. Neither final course evaluations nor informal comments from these students reveal any resentment toward those who choose the option.

Structure of the Option

The Agencies

Before the start of the term, a graduate teaching assistant (GTA) calls local preschool directors to explain the project and obtain their consent to participate. The GTA makes periodic follow-up calls throughout the term to check on students' progress. Preschool directors are asked to provide an enriching range of opportunities for the students and to ensure that students fulfill participation requirements.

Requirements

The course syllabus describes the optional project and lists the names, addresses, and phone numbers of participating preschools. During the first 2 weeks of class, students decide if they want to participate in the project; those interested contact preschool directors to arrange a mutually convenient 2-hr time slot for the remaining weeks of the term.

Participating students keep a journal of their experiences with the children, which must include one entry for each 2-hr session. Journal entries should describe developmental processes rather than just list the day's activities. Strong emphasis is placed on integrating lecture and text material with practical experience. For example, when lectures and readings concern motor development, students' journal entries focus on that aspect of development. All students electing to participate are provided with a handout of guidelines for keeping a journal. Sample journals from previous classes are available for review.

Grading

Students receive feedback on their performance at least three times during the term. After the first 2 weeks of participation, students submit their journals to the GTA who checks them for content and provides written comments, helpful suggestions, and questions. Midway through the term, students again submit their journals and receive an estimated final grade based on maintaining their current performance. Students dissatisfied with their estimated grade have ample time remaining in the term to demonstrate improvement. Journals are returned during a meeting arranged between the GTA and the student. Additional feedback is provided at this time, and students may ask questions or express concerns about the project in general. During the last week of the term, students submit (a) their journal for final grading, (b) a note from the preschool director confirming the required participation, and (c) a one-page description of their specific duties and responsibilities at the preschool, along with their assessment of the experience.

Students who complete the option are awarded a bonus percentage that is added to their term grade. If they do A work on the project, they receive a bonus of 5%; B work earns a bonus of 4%; and C work earns a bonus of 3%. Failure to complete the project, or D work, results in a 10% reduction, and a substantial lack of work on the project, or F work, results in a 20% reduction. The possibility of a D or F grade on the option discourages less serious students from participating and allows us to maintain good relationships with the preschool directors.

Preschool directors have not complained about any students participating in the option. It is likely that the lack of complaints is due to two aspects of the option's structure which ensure that only dedicated students participate: the time commitment and the potential grade penalty for poor performance. Over five terms, 107 students have chosen the option; only 2 students requested a withdrawal from the option because they did not enjoy the experience. In consultation with the preschool director, the decision was made that it would be better for all parties concerned, including the children, if the students withdrew. However, due to the requirements of the option and their potential negative effects on grades, the students were required to replace their day care commitment with weekly one-page critiques of selected journal articles covering a range of course topics.

Evaluation of the Option

Data from 669 students over five semesters showed a significant difference in final course grades between those choosing the option ($n = 107$) and those not ($n = 562$), $\chi^2(4, n = 669) = 16.62$, $p < .002$. Almost half of the students electing the option ($n = 49$) increased their overall course grade by successfully completing the option. The largest number of grade improvements was due to students improving from a B to an A ($n = 22$). Furthermore, 91% of the students taking the option obtained a final course grade of C or better, compared to 84% of students not taking the option. Thus, the option seems to be effective in recruiting students who are interested in the opportunity to integrate practical experience with classroom work, and does not simply recruit poor students who are only interested in improving their grades.

The structure of the option encourages good performance; only one student has received a D and one an F on the project (both for failing to complete the project). Of the seven students who chose the option and received a final course grade of D, five did not achieve grades high enough for the extra option credit to help them, one increased her grade from an F, and the other had his course grade lowered from a C for not completing the project. The three students who chose the option and received a final course grade of F had failed their tests, and, thus, the extra credits were not enough to redeem them.

Liability and Ethical Issues

To protect the anonymity of the children and the agencies, students use only the children's first names and do not include the name of the agency in their journals. The handout given to participating students at the beginning of the term emphasizes that information gathered on individual children and situations should be treated confidentially and with respect. Furthermore, students are informed that it is unprofessional and unethical to discuss information they acquire at the day care centers in social conversations.

With reports of abuse in day care centers, liability has become an increasingly important issue. Instructors will need to check on the prevailing conditions in their area (e.g., some day care centers carry insurance that covers volunteers, universities and colleges may have insurance coverage for students doing fieldwork as part of a course, and students in state schools may be covered by state insurance). Furthermore, the students are not substitutes for employees—they are always supervised.

In summary, improved grades and students' feedback demonstrate that the preschool journal option is a valuable contribution to the undergraduate child psychology course. Students enjoy the experience, the community benefits, and instructors are not unduly burdened with administering the option. Teachers are encouraged to consider such an option to enhance the educational experiences of undergraduates.

References

Fernald, C. D., Tedeschi, R. G., Siegfried, W. D., Gilmore, D. C., Grimsley, D. L., & Chipley, B. (1982). Designing and managing an undergraduate practicum course in psychology. *Teaching of Psychology*, *9*, 155-160.

Fox, R. A., Lopuch, W. R., & Fisher, E. (1984). Using volunteer work to teach undergraduates about exceptional children. *Teaching of Psychology*, *11*, 113-115.

Saxon, S. A., & Holt, M. M. (1974). Field placements as an adjunct experience for developmental psychology students. *Teaching of Psychology*, *1*, 82-83.

Sherman, A. R. (1982). Psychology fieldwork: A catalyst for advancing knowledge and academic skills. *Teaching of Psychology*, *9*, 82-85.

Note

We thank Gerry Benson, who originated the preschool option, and Ralph W. Richards, who modified and refined the project.

2. INCORPORATING PIAGETIAN CONCEPTS

Introducing Piagetian Concepts Through the Use of Familiar and Novel Illustrations

Gregory F. Harper
State University of New York, College at Fredonia

One of the many vexing problems encountered in the teaching of child development or child psychology courses occurs in the discussion of Piagetian terms as they apply to early childhood or infancy. This discussion typically presents two sources of difficulty from the pedagogical point of view: (a) the terms themselves; assimilation, accommodation, equilibration, schema are either entirely alien as applied to intellectual development or are confused with everyday usage of the terms; (b) it is difficult for the older adolescents typically found in these courses to relate to the developmental tasks faced by the infant. Students tend to find it difficult to see how these processes operate in the case of the infant and perhaps more problematically how they operate in their own experience.

In an attempt to overcome these difficulties, it is helpful to provide illustrations, or examples, which encourage students to actually experience intellectual development in the sense this is applied to infants. A schema, when applied to infant (sensorimotor) development, refers to a primitive behavior or pattern of behaviors (Piaget, 1969). Few of these remain intact but, rather, are accommodated into larger schemas. In a lecture device called "gloquex and lollipops" students are invited to rediscover some basic schemas and to relive the exciting prospect of learning about (trying to make sense of; i.e., equilibrate) a novel object.

In the lollipop segment, each student is given a lollipop (herein defined as hard candy on a stick) and encouraged to ingest it. Lollipops of courses tend to elicit the most basic of schemas, sucking a fact that is loudly apparent. Such osculation, it can be pointed out, likely represents a tertiary circular reaction. It is also noted that the variations in the lollipop sucking schema for example, rolling the lollipop on the tongue, biting, chewing, etc., represent elaborations on that schema. Students often note that the sucking schema may be applied to a variety of other objects (contents)—for example, beer bottles, cigarettes—with some adaptive modifications. These adaptions, of course, are the essence of intelligent behavior.

In the gloquex (pronounced glocks) segment, students are introduced to a completely novel object. This allows them to recreate the basic discovery processes used by young children. The gloquex itself is invisible (to avoid premature labeling), and it is usually introduced by removing it from a large, preferably black, box and placing it upon a table before the class. To guide instructors using this device, it may be noted that gloquexes weigh approximately 10 kilograms and are about 60 mm x 30 mm x 30 mm. It is important to plug the gloquex in and allow a brief warm-up period. Since the name "gloquex" is never mentioned, students upon recovering their composure, usually begin to ask relevant questions regarding the object before them. Instructors may encounter the following questions regarding the gloquex (sample responses are provided).

1. What is it called?—Gloquex.
2. What does it do?—The gloquex counteracts negative electromagnetic waves (i. e., bad vibes) often encountered in the college classroom.
3. How does it work—An inversely reciprocating frimfram bollixes any waves entering the aperture
4. What is it made of?—hyperventilated case hardened mallox.
5. Why can't I see it?—You can't? (followed by an incredulous look).

After the question period, students are tested regarding their knowledge of gloquex. This testing should focus upon the students' understanding of the workings of the gloquex, the principles upon which it operates, etc. Usually students' responses suggest a level of knowledge commensurate with that of a young child; they know the name of the object, its ostensible purpose, perhaps its composition, and that it belongs to the general class of machines. It can then be suggested that students have little understanding of the abstract qualities of "gloquexness" and, because, presumably, the gloquex fits into no previously existing schemes, their attempts to describe it or talk about it rely on terms such as: "it's like a. . .," "it's similar to a . . .," "it's sort of like something I saw once on 'Star Trek,'" etc. Most of these definitions are enactive (as are a young child's) and clearly reflect attempts to fit a novel object into previously existing schemas (assimilation) or perhaps to modify schemas (accommodation).

The gloquex presents an excellent starting point for discussions on the nature of concepts and how they are constructed, in most cases, by exposure to a variety of objects belonging to that class. An eighteen-year-old learning about a gloquex is faced with a task not dissimilar to an eighteen-month-old learning about a dog.

In summary gloquex and lollipops are an attempt to allow students to see first hand how cognitive schemas are developed and elaborated. It may also permit them to remember the wonder and excitement with which a young child would, and perhaps we all should, approach each new learning opportunity.

Reference

Piaget, J., & Inhelder, B. *The psychology of the child.* New York: Basic Books, 1969.

Bringing Piaget's Preoperational Thought to the Minds of Adults: A Classroom Demonstration

Jane Ewens Holbrook
University of Wisconsin Center-Waukesha

Two classroom demonstrations, Piaget's water conservation and an adult conservation-like task too difficult for most students to solve, are described. Students' approaches to the adult task are analyzed in terms of centration, irreversibility, and concreteness. Students gain an appreciation of preoperational thought and are encouraged to examine their own thinking. They may learn how one can get stuck on irrelevant details, see new approaches to a problem, and gain fresh insight into the need to relinquish a particular viewpoint for a larger comprehension.

Students who study Piaget are often captivated by his descriptions of children's reasoning, learning that children do not simply know less than adults but actually think differently. Many instructors demonstrate conservation tasks because they draw students into the child's world. Students begin to appreciate the complexities of the child's reasoning and view of reality. In addition, these demonstrations can sometimes strengthen the conviction that adults are clearly more reasonable than children. To indicate that adult thinking is not always reasonable and that inability to solve a conservation task is not unique to childhood, two tasks are demonstrated. The first is a standard conservation task (water pouring). The second is a conservation-like task too difficult for many students to solve. Students analyze their ways of problem solving by applying the same Piagetian concepts used to understand the nonconserving child; they are thus encouraged to ponder their own thinking.

For the water conservation task, place two identical glasses, each filled to the same point, in front of a 5 year old. Ask, "Do these two glasses contain the same amount of water?" When the child agrees, pour all the water from one glass into a taller, thinner glass. Now ask, "Do these two glasses contain the same amount of water, or does one glass have more?" The typical 5 year old will answer that the taller glass has more water. Ask the child to explain why. This demonstration can be made more elaborate by having the child do the pouring and by varying the wording and asking more questions.

According to Piaget (1952), the nonconserving child's reasoning can be explained by referring to the characteristics of preoperational thought. *Centration* describes the child's tendency to focus on only one aspect (height of water). *Irreversibility* describes the child's inability to imagine reversing the physical action; in this case, it is the pouring process that would return the water to its original glass. The preoperational child is said to be *concrete* and *perceptually bound*, reaching conclusions by how the world looks rather than by systematic reasoning; perceptual cues supercede logical principles.

Students are usually surprised by the child's first response to the task; they are even more surprised that, after repeating demonstrations and explanations of water pouring, the typical 5 year old will hold firm to the belief that the taller glass contains more water. For many students, the child's refusal to see what seems obvious is strong evidence that children do not reason like adults.

The second demonstration should be used after students are familiar with Piaget's stages. In addition, familiarity with some of the questions about the validity of the conservation tasks (e.g., the effect of the wording of the questions) would be useful background for the second part of the demonstration. Introduce the second task as a conservation-like problem for adults. Place two identical jars on a table, explaining that one jar contains exactly 200 red jelly beans and that the other contains exactly 200 black jelly beans. The scoop on the table will hold exactly 15 jelly beans. Tell the students that you are going to fill the scoop with 15 red jelly beans and pour them into the jar containing the black jelly beans. Then, you are going to shake that jar to mix the jelly beans. You will then scoop 15 jelly beans (any 15) from the jar containing the black jelly beans and pour them into the jar containing the red jelly beans. (The description of this process should probably be repeated so students are sure of the procedure.) Then ask, "Will the number of red jelly beans in the jar that initially contained only black jelly beans be the same as the number of black jelly beans in the jar that originally contained only red jelly beans?" Some students will immediately realize that the answer to the question must be "the same," but most students, like children, will examine the demonstration as a new problem.

If you are interested in keeping track of students' initial responses, distribute a questionnaire, including a place to check "yes" or "no," and a space to explain their answers. Begin the discussion after collecting their responses. Most students will argue that there will not be the same number of black beans in the jar that initially contained only red jelly beans as there are red beans in the jar that originally contained only black jelly beans; some students will answer "yes" but give an incorrect reason. Because most people do not enjoy being wrong, it is important to comment that the reason some people get the wrong answer is because they have too much information rather than too little. To let the students know that failure is usual, but temporary, it is helpful to discuss the research that suggests that 40% to 60% of college students have difficulty solving formal operations problems (Neimark, 1975) and that children and adults think more reasonably about familiar tasks (Chi, 1978; Siegler, 1986). Use the list of reasons given by the students who answered incorrectly to begin the discussion of how sensible thought patterns can lead to incorrect answers. To dramatize the solution, repeat the actual scooping-mixing-scooping process several times to demonstrate that the answer is indeed always "the same."

Of 54 students in two introductory psychology classes, 6 answered correctly after the first presentation of the problem. After the discussion accompanied by the actual pouring of jelly beans, 11 students still answered "no." They could see that the numbers remained the same but could not reason why. For weeks after the demonstration, students reported on how their friends responded to the problem and continued to argue among themselves about how to understand the demonstration. They also suggested more dramatic ways of setting up the demonstration (e.g., using crates of easter eggs or giant cookie jars).

Why do college students have such difficulty solving this problem? How does their difficulty help them understand Piaget's theories about preoperational children Centration is a useful concept; people focus on one aspect of the task and lose sight of the whole context. Typical student comments are "But the probability of getting the same number of red jelly beans the second time is very low," "If you've mixed them up, you just can't end up with the same number," "The chances of getting the same number might be 1 in 10 million." By centering on the mixing of the red and black beans, students turn the task into a probability problem. Focused on the probability of scooping exactly the same numbers of red and black beans, they cannot see that the actual numbers are irrelevant. Other examples of centering include focusing (a) on the colors, (b) on certain words like mix or same, and (c) on the process of scooping or pouring or mixing. Like the children who are sure that the height of the water proves their point, these adults are sure that the detail they have selected is the key to the solution. In the child, the centration is perceptual; in the adult, the centration is conceptual. Some may argue, however, that the first step for those adults who turn the task into a probability problem is to focus on color or number cues. These are perceptual cues, the concept of probability is what the adult applies to these cues. The adult subject is more likely to be misled by the conceptual cues, but the way in which the concept misleads the adult is analogous to the way in which the percept misleads the child. Only by decentering, by giving up the focus on the chosen detail, can the solution be seen.

Irreversibility also illustrates reasoning that leads to an incorrect solution. A person who cannot imagine reversing the scooping process (by which any single jelly bean must be replaced by a jelly bean from the other jar) often fails to see that the two jars together provide the whole context simultaneously. The person who sees the solution understands that it does not matter how many jelly beans of each color are removed each time as long as the total number in the scoop is the same. Moving the jelly beans (and pouring the water) could be repeated endlessly without changing the answer.

The person worried about the mixing, the colors, and the probability of coming up with equal numbers of red and black jelly beans can also be described as being concrete, or perceptually bound. Like the child who is perceptually caught by the height of the water, the adult is trapped by the significance of the colors and particular words. These detailed aspects of the demonstration are distracting enough to prevent the observer from seeing the larger context.

The process of solving the problem can be very instructive. Students may learn how one can get stuck on irrelevant details, see new approaches to a problem, and gain fresh insight into the need to relinquish a particular viewpoint for greater comprehension. It is difficult to predict what will cause the decentering process. Students' descriptions of their decentering process suggest that it involves attention shifts similar to those that Gelman and Baillargeon (1983) taught to promote conservation in preoperational children. The catalyst to decentering may be a verbal suggestion, for example, "It's a spatial, not a probability problem," or watching the actual scooping and mixing of the jelly beans. Many students who watch the process will acknowledge that the final numbers are the same, but they remain mystified about why. They are like the child who pours the water back into the shorter glass and declares that magic accounts for the result. For students struggling with the problem, the decentering process is often gradual, taking several days. Once they understand, they are amazed at how they missed the obvious. If time permits, the experience of coming to understand the jelly bean task can be tied to discussions of critical thinking, general problem-solving techniques, and functional fixedness.

Some students claim that they have a new appreciation for children's thinking and a new interest in thinking about their own thinking. In the long run, being wrong may encourage students to examine their certainties and to listen to other perspectives before reaching conclusions. These demonstrations are simple and short but bring important puzzles to the classroom. Both use a straightforward question with a single correct answer to raise questions about answers, show how language may hinder and help reasoning, and suggest that a comprehensive focus entails letting go of limited points of view.

References

Chi, M. R. H. (1978). Knowledge structures and memory development. In R. Siegler (Ed.), *Children's thinking: What develops?* (pp. 73-95). Hillsdale, NJ: Lawrence Erlbaum Associates, Inc.

Gelman, R. & Baillargeon, R. (1983). A review of some Piagetian concepts. In J. H. Flavell & E. M. Markman (Eds.), *Handbook of child psychology: Vol. 3. Cognitive development* (pp. 167-230). New York: Wiley.

Neimark, E. D. (1975). Longitudinal development of formal operational thought. *Genetic Psychology Monographs, 91*, 171-225.

Piaget, J. (l952). *The child's conception of number.* London: Routledge & Kegan Paul.

Siegler, R. S. (1986). Unities across domains in children's strategy choices. In M. Perlmutter (Ed.), *Perspectives on intellectual development. The Minnesota symposia on child psychology* (Vol. 19, pp. 1-48). Hillsdale, NJ: Lawrence Erlbaum Associates, Inc.

Systematizing the Piagetian Clinical Interview for Classroom Use

Jeanne Ellis Ormrod
Kyle R. Carter
University of Northern Colorado

Piaget's logical problems and clinical method are proposed to be important components of coursework in developmental and educational psychology. The authors describe their experiences with giving undergraduate educational psychology students hands-on opportunities for administering Piagetian clinical interviews. Their experiences have indicated that undergraduate students cannot easily be trained to conduct a thorough or systematic interview. To facilitate the training process, the authors have developed flowcharts for Piagetian tasks, including instructions, checklists for student responses, and alternative procedures to be followed dependent on a child's responses. Flowcharts have provided a means by which substantive interviews can be conducted by undergraduate students.

A discussion of Jean Piaget's theory of cognitive development is frequently included in courses in developmental and educational psychology. Briefly, Piaget has described development as a progression through four stages, each characterized by qualitatively different thought processes. Although concerns have been cited regarding the validity of some of his theoretical propositions (Modgil & Modgil, 1982), Piaget's theory has nevertheless had a major impact on how we observe and conceptualize children's behavior.

There are at least two aspects of Piaget's work that we believe are important parts of any course dealing with children's learning and development: the logical problems developed by Piaget to demonstrate children's thinking processes and the clinical method used to administer these problems. The logical problems involve either concrete objects or verbal information, and yield different responses from children at various stages of development. An example of such a problem is conservation of displaced volume. In this task, two identical glasses containing approximately equal amounts of liquid and two balls of clay of approximately equal size are presented to the child. The child is asked to modify the amounts of liquid and clay, until both glasses are judged to contain the same amount of liquid and both balls of clay are judged to be the same size. The interviewer places one ball of clay into one of the glasses of liquid, and the child sees the water level rise. The interviewer then slices the other ball of clay into two pieces. The child shown both glasses and the sliced ball of clay, is asked to predict the level to which the liquid in the second glass will rise once the clay has been immersed in it. The child who predicts that the liquid will rise to the same level as the liquid in the first glass is believed to be reasoning at least at the advanced stage of concrete operations. A child who predicts a level different from that of the first glass demonstrates reasoning characteristic of an earlier level of thought.

The reason for the child's decision is as important in determining the stage of development as the decision itself. For example, a child who correctly predicts the level of the liquid but is unable to explain the solution is judged to reason at a lower level than a child who answers correctly and explains that the sliced ball has the same volume as the intact ball and, for that reason, should displace the same amount of liquid. Other examples of Piaget's logical problems may be found in texts by Bybee and Sund (1982), Flavell (1963), and Wadsworth (1979).

Piaget's clinical method allows insight into a child's logical thought processes in a one-on-one interview. The interviewer presents a logical problem, and the child solves the problem while also describing the rationale used in problem solution. The interviewer then asks a series of follow-up questions, tailored to the responses given by the child, until the interviewer has determined not only what conclusions the child has reached about the problem presented, but also the logic behind those conclusions. The clinical method was used extensively by Piaget as a way of collecting observations about children's approaches to a particular task, observations which then led to hypotheses that could be tested through more traditional experimental methods (Flavell, 1963). The clinical method can also be useful as a means of gaining insight into an individual child's idiosyncratic ways of conceptualizing the world.

TEACHING THE CLINICAL METHOD

Because we believe that Piaget's logical problems and clinical method are valuable tools for anyone working with children, we wanted to provide hands-on experiences with the problems and method within the context of our educational psychology classes. We identified seven Piagetian tasks to assess concrete and formal operations: reverse seriation, conservation of substance, conservation of area, conservation of displaced volume, combinatorial logic, separation and control of variables, and proportional reasoning (all described by Bybee & Sund, 1982). Tasks were designed in such a way that we could obtain or create materials easily and inexpensively. For example, for the conservation of area task, in which wooden blocks are typically used to mark out a certain area, sugar cubes were used instead of blocks.

After presenting 4 class hours of lecture on Piaget's theory and stage characteristics, we trained students for 2 hours in the basic techniques of the clinical interview. Students were given a manual describing the specific procedures to be followed and the instructions to be presented to the child. During the training sessions, students practiced administering the tasks to each other, using the manual as a guide. As instructors, we critiqued the students' performance and answered all questions that arose during training.

Children enrolled in the university's summer program for gifted and talented children, ranging in age from 8 to 14 years, participated in the project. The children were tested in the laboratory school cafeteria, with separate interviews being conducted at each end of the long cafeteria tables. The undergraduate students worked in pairs in conducting the interviews, with each pair interviewing three or four children. The children differed in age by 3 or more years so that students administering the interviews could work with children at different levels of logical thought. One member of each pair presented the task while the other recorded observations; they alternated roles for successive children. Sessions with each child lasted approximately 20 min.

Student responses to the experience were overwhelmingly positive: Students reported that the interview had been beneficial in understanding the Piagetian approach and complemented the class lectures very well. In that sense, the project had been successful. Unfortunately, when we looked at the reports the students wrote based on our manuals, it was clear that the students had not conducted appropriate interviews: Questions were not asked, responses were not recorded, and vague responses were not followed by the necessary probing questions. We began to question what the students had really learned from the experience. Despite the procedures manual and training sessions we had provided, the students had simply not known what to look for when conducting the interviews.

Materials: 2 glasses containing equal amounts of water; glass containing extra water; 2 balls of clay equal in size; small amount of extra clay; 2 rubber bands; 1 plastic knife.

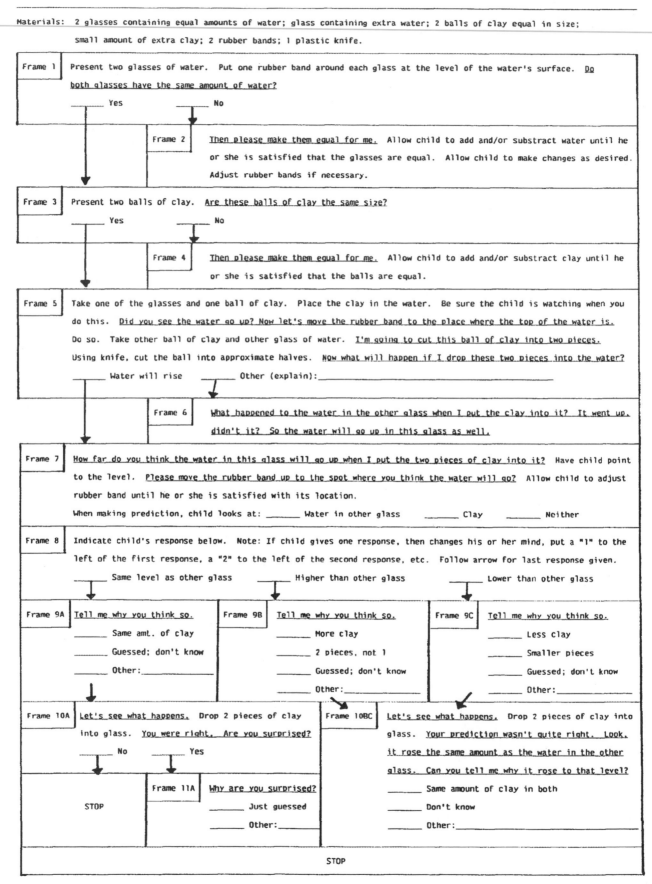

Frame 1 Present two glasses of water. Put one rubber band around each glass at the level of the water's surface. <u>Do both glasses have the same amount of water?</u>

_____ Yes   _____ No

Frame 2 <u>Then please make them equal for me.</u> Allow child to add and/or substract water until he or she is satisfied that the glasses are equal. Allow child to make changes as desired. Adjust rubber bands if necessary.

Frame 3 Present two balls of clay. <u>Are these balls of clay the same size?</u>

_____ Yes   _____ No

Frame 4 <u>Then please make them equal for me.</u> Allow child to add and/or substract clay until he or she is satisfied that the balls are equal.

Frame 5 Take one of the glasses and one ball of clay. Place the clay in the water. Be sure the child is watching when you do this. <u>Did you see the water go up? Now let's move the rubber band to the place where the top of the water is.</u> Do so. Take other ball of clay and other glass of water. <u>I'm going to cut this ball of clay into two pieces.</u> Using knife, cut the ball into approximate halves. <u>Now what will happen if I drop these two pieces into the water?</u>

_____ Water will rise   _____ Other (explain):_____

Frame 6 <u>What happened to the water in the other glass when I put the clay into it? It went up, didn't it? So the water will go up in this glass as well.</u>

Frame 7 <u>How far do you think the water in this glass will go up when I put the two pieces of clay into it?</u> Have child point to the level. <u>Please move the rubber band up to the spot where you think the water will go?</u> Allow child to adjust rubber band until he or she is satisfied with its location.

When making prediction, child looks at: _____ Water in other glass _____ Clay _____ Neither

Frame 8 Indicate child's response below. Note: If child gives one response, then changes his or her mind, put a "1" to the left of the first response, a "2" to the left of the second response, etc. Follow arrow for last response given.

_____ Same level as other glass   _____ Higher than other glass   _____ Lower than other glass

Frame 9A <u>Tell me why you think so.</u>

_____ Same amt. of clay

_____ Guessed; don't know

_____ Other:_____

Frame 9B <u>Tell me why you think so.</u>

_____ More clay

_____ 2 pieces, not 1

_____ Guessed; don't know

_____ Other:_____

Frame 9C <u>Tell me why you think so.</u>

_____ Less clay

_____ Smaller pieces

_____ Guessed; don't know

_____ Other:_____

Frame 10A <u>Let's see what happens.</u> Drop 2 pieces of clay into glass. <u>You were right. Are you surprised?</u>

_____ No   _____ Yes

STOP

Frame 11A <u>Why are you surprised?</u>

_____ Just guessed

_____ Other:_____

Frame 10BC <u>Let's see what happens.</u> Drop 2 pieces of clay into glass. <u>Your prediction wasn't quite right. Look, it rose the same amount as the water in the other glass. Can you tell me why it rose to that level?</u>

_____ Same amount of clay in both

_____ Don't know

_____ Other:_____

STOP

Figure 1. Flowchart for conservation of displaced volume.

Table 1. Sample Scoring Methods for the Displacement of Volume Task

Child's Prediction	Reason	Classification Point Method	Method
1. Any incorrect response.	Cannot give a reason.	Preoperational	10
2. Higher or lower, shows surprise.	Explanation unrelated to concept of conservation.	Concrete I	15
3. Higher or lower.	After observing solution, explains correctly using identity or reversibility. Doesn't identify specific variable (e.g., weight, mass).	Concrete II	20
4. Says "same," then changes mind.	Same reason as #3.	Transitional I	23
5. Says "same."	Explains correctly, but uses wrong variable (e.g., weight).	Transitional II	25
6. Says "same."	Explains in terms of density.	Early Formal	30

Table 2. Sample Questions for Research and Measurement Assignments

Sample Question	Statistic
1. What is the average age for successful performance on conservation of substance?	Mean
2. Which task shows the greatest variability for girls? For boys?	Standard deviation
3. Can you predict a child's overall performance if you know the age?	Correlation coefficient
4. Are there sex differences on any of the tasks?	Mean, standard deviation, t test

Student reports concerning the experience were so positive, however, that we were determined to continue to provide hands-on experience with the clinical interview. The solution appeared to lie in structuring the procedures manual in such a way that administration errors would be minimized and the observations recorded in a fashion easily interpreted by anyone reading the report. What evolved was a flowchart that included instructions for each task, checklists in which a child's responses would be indicated, and alternative follow-up instructions dependent on a child's response.

To illustrate the flowchart approach, we present the conservation of displaced volume task shown in Figure 1. The following two principles must be applied in its use:

1. Text with no underscore indicates procedures to be followed by the interviewer; underscored text indicates instructions or questions to be presented to the child.
2. Progression from one frame to the next is always *down the page*, unless otherwise indicated by arrows.

On several occasions, we have had undergraduate classes use the flowcharts in assessing cognitive level. Training in the administration of the tasks, including use of the flowcharts, is never more extensive than one or two 50-min sessions, often conducted outside of class. The extra instructional time appears to be well worth the cost. Students' motivation to learn and interpret Piaget's theory is increased over what we observe when we use lectures and reading assignments alone. In addition, students regard the interviews as valuable learning experiences, because they observe firsthand how children at various stages of development approach and respond to problems designed to illustrate Piaget's theory.

SCORING METHODS AND THEIR USE IN CLASSROOM DISCUSSION

Scoring of the flowcharts may be done in either of two ways. One way is simply to classify each child's performance on each task as being preoperational, concrete operational, formal operational, or transitional between two of these stages. Another approach is to a assign 10 points for preoperational performance, 20 points for concrete operational performance, and 30 points for formal operational performance, with intermediate scores also being possible. These point values are referenced against specific behavioral criteria that are characteristic of the successful and unsuccessful approaches to each task. To illustrate, scoring criteria for the displacement of volume task are shown in Table 1. If desired, scores on the different tasks can then be added together for a total score.

Although the validity of combining task scores into a composite is questionable on statistical grounds (Gronlund, 1976), the numerical scoring system does have practical instructional uses. For example, the second author of this paper has used the flowchart and numerical scoring system as a vehicle to make research and measurement concepts more meaningful

221

to students. After the class has completed its unit on Piaget, including administering the flowchart interviews, data from the interviews are analyzed and discussed within the context of a unit on research and measurement. First, students are required to score the protocols using a scoring system like the one shown in Table 1. The scoring system is used to provide a frame of reference for general measurement concepts such as standardization procedures, interrater reliability, and methods for increasing reliability and validity. Next, results are compiled into data sheets listing subject variables (e.g., age, sex) and Piagetian interview scores for each task. The students use these data to answer questions that require the use of basic statistical concepts.

Sample questions are shown in Table 2. Each question requires the calculation of a specific statistic. Students complete the assignments in small groups outside of class. When the assignments are discussed in class, the instructor uses the students' computations to introduce basic research concepts. For example, the data may suggest that one sex performed better than the other on a task. Discussion of results such as these can easily lead the class to the discovery of such concepts as sampling, equivalence of groups prior to assessment, and random assignment. This method of introducing research and measurement to undergraduate students has proven effective: Students develop an understanding of the concepts through hands-on experience with them.

ALTERNATIVE USES OF THE FLOWCHART

In our case, we are fortunate to have access to a large number of children through our university laboratory school. Therefore, it is possible for all of our undergraduates to have experience with several children. In settings where children are not so easily available, other uses of the flowchart are possible. Interviews between the class instructor (or a student) and several children at different cognitive levels may be presented in front of a class and possibly videotaped for later use. Students who are observing should be given copies of the flowchart so that they can follow along while the demonstration proceeds. As an alternative, students can be asked to find their own children to interview (after securing parental permission, of course); it has been our experience in other situations that students often know willing children either in the university community or in their hometowns.

However the flowchart-directed interview is integrated into one's course, we encourage its use in undergraduate classes. Students will find the experience motivational as well as instructional.

References

Bybee, R. W., & Sund, R. B. (1982). *Piaget for educators* (2nd ed.). Columbus, OH: Charles E. Merrill.

Flavell, J. H. (1963). *The developmental psychology of Jean Piaget.* New York: Van Nostrand Reinhold.

Gronlund, N. E. (1976). *Measurement and evaluation in teaching* (3rd ed.). New York: Macmillan.

Modgil, S., & Modgil, C. (Eds.). (1982). *Jean Piaget: Consensus and controversy.* New York: Praeger.

Wadsworth, B. J. (1979). *Piaget's theory of cognitive development* (2nd ed.). New York: Longman.

Note

The authors thank Kathy Atkinson for her assistance in the early stages of this project.

3. PROMOTING THE STUDY OF EXCEPTIONAL CHILDREN

Using Volunteer Work To Teach Undergraduates About Exceptional Children

Robert A. Fox
Wanda R. Lopuch
Marquette University
and Eve Fisher
Ohio State University

Most universities and colleges offer a course on the psychology and education of exceptional children. For many undergraduate students, such a course may be their first and possibly only formal exposure to this special population of children. Therefore it is important that instructors structure an experience for these students that will enhance their understanding and appreciation of exceptional children. McCallum (1979) provided classroom activities to foster an "empathetic" rather than a "sympathetic" understanding of the problems of such children. Many instructors teaching a course in this area include a practicum or volunteer experience to provide direct student contact with exceptional children, but the impact of these experiences occurring outside of the classroom had been minimally reported in the literature. For example, Stainback and Stainback (1982) found that undergraduates exposed to severely retarded individuals had more positive attitudes about integrating these handicapped students with their nonhandicapped peers than did a control group of undergraduates. Clearly more studies of this nature are needed.

The purpose of this study was to begin to establish an empirical base concerning the impact of volunteer experiences on the undergraduate student in terms of their understanding and attitudes toward children with special needs. During a fall quarter at Ohio State University, the first author taught a course entitled the Psychology of Developmental Disabilities. Six male and 32 female undergraduate students agreed to volunteer for a minimum of ten hours with an agency serving exceptional children. The majority of these students were juniors and seniors (N = 34) with a mean age of 21.3 years (SD=1.3). Students represented a variety of different disciplines including psychology, nursing, social work, physical therapy, speech, home economics, and others. Psychology was the most frequent major (N=17). Twelve students reported having at least two years of previous experience with exceptional individuals; five students had one to two years of previous experience; nine students had less than one year of experience and twelve students had no previous experience with exceptional people.

Eleven different agencies or programs serving exceptional individuals provided the volunteer experiences. Students were given a choice of settings in which to volunteer. They reported engaging in a variety of experiences that were unique to each volunteer setting. Some students chose to volunteer at a large residential public institution for severely and profoundly retarded children and adults. These students functioned as aides providing routine care (e.g., dressing, feeding, toileting) and as assistants to a staff psychologist who was developing and implementing programs on the institutional wards. Four of the volunteer settings offered early intervention or day care services for children with developmental disabilities between the ages of two and five. Students reported that these settings served a variety of children including those who were mentally retarded, autistic-like, physically handicapped (cerebral palsy, blind), epileptic and environmentally disadvantaged. They worked as teaching assistants and became involved in implementing various objectives of the childrens' Individual Educational Plan such as developing self-help skills, teaching basic knowledge and improving social interaction. These early childhood settings were very popular among the students. Another group of students also worked as teaching assistants but with older mildly and moderately retarded children in the public schools. A school for the blind also interested some students who functioned primarily as classroom aides. A few students became therapy assistants in an established play therapy program for developmentally disabled children. These students met weekly with a doctoral student for the play therapy session. They also attended a weekly group session with the supervising professor of psychology. The remainder of students volunteered in programs serving the adult retarded. These adult experiences included participation in recreational programs (e.g., dances, bowling), helping out in a group home, and assisting in an obesity research project. Ten hours of volunteer work was required, but the majority of students exceeded this minimum.

Near the end of the quarter students completed an anonymous questionnaire regarding their volunteer experience. In addition to describing the content of their work, they responded to a number of Likert type scale items that assessed their perceptions about various aspects of the experience. Students also retrospectively completed the Adjective Generation Technique (AGT, Allen & Potkay, in press). The AGT required that the students write down five adjectives that would best describe them when they first learned they would be doing volunteer work with exceptional children and again following their volunteer experience. Finally the questionnaire included general questions where the students could provide narrative comments regarding their feelings about exceptional individuals before and after their volunteer experience.

Several of the questionnaire responses that could be quantified were subjected to a simple correlation analysis. Students rated their respective volunteer settings using a one (very negative) to seven point scale (very positive) on a number of characteristics including the general atmosphere of the setting, how well the volunteer experience was organized for them and the helpfulness of the supervision provided. They also rated the degree to which they felt personally involved while volunteering (one = very limited, to seven = highly involved) and how they felt their attitudes had changed toward exceptional children (one = not at all to seven = very significantly). The three ratings for the volunteer setting (i.e., atmosphere, organization and supervision helpfulness) were combined, resulting in one overall rating. This overall rating was found to correlate significantly with the degree that students became involved in the volunteer experience ($r(36) = .45$, $p < .01$); but not with attitude change toward exceptional people. Also a significant correlation was found between years of previous student experience with exceptional individuals and perceived attitude change toward this population ($r(36) = -.70$, $p < .01$). Surprisingly, previous experience did not correlate significantly with the degree of student involvement.

The AGT was scored using available norms (Allen & Potkay, in press) on a favorability and an anxiety dimension. *T* tests for related measures for AGT scores prior to and following the volunteer experience, reported retrospectively, showed a significant reduction on the anxiety dimension ($t(37) = 9.48$, $p < .001$) and an increase on the favorability dimension ($t(37) = 5.38$, $p < .001$).

Student responses to the questions requiring narrative comments were categorized according to common themes. Sixty-three percent of them ($N=24$) felt that the volunteer experience changed their perceptions about exceptional children. Comments such as "I now know how to work with a cerebral palsied child and what kinds of activities can be done to help them." "I was surprised at the wide range of abilities." "I'm more

aware of the need for early intervention." "I now know that in most cases the handicapped individuals are very similar to the nonhandicapped person in attitude, emotions, etc." were typical of this theme. Thirteen students also reported personal changes (e.g., "I'm much more sensitive to this population." "The first day I was there I just stared at them and felt so sorry for them; now I know I can work with them and I'm more sure of myself." "I now feel more comfortable with myself knowing the problems of others." "It gave me some more confidence"). Fourteen students mentioned that they were encouraged to do more volunteer work and several actually continued to volunteer at their settings during the following quarter. Seventeen students also reported that the experience will help them with some future decisions they will be making (e.g. "Now I know I don't want to work with the mentally retarded and I do want to do more volunteer work with other populations." "It reinforced my desire to work with mentally handicapped people and has helped me to choose a minor in special education." "Confirmed which age range of developmentally delayed population I want to work with—infants and preschoolers").

In summary, most students initially reported being anxious about working with exceptional children. However, with some initial encouragement from the instructor to get involved, students entered the volunteer experience and reported reduced levels of anxiety and increased levels of favorability following volunteering. Many reported wanting to do more volunteer work in the future and some continued volunteering within their chosen setting even after the course was over. Students were more likely to increase their personal involvement in an agency or setting if it was well-organized, had a positive atmosphere and provided good supervision. It also appears that students with little or no previous experience with exceptional populations were likely to change their attitudes in a positive direction as a result of volunteering and taking a course on the topic. Although these findings are preliminary, they do suggest that including some direct contact with exceptional populations as part of a didactic course on the topic may enhance the impact of this experience for undergraduate students.

References

Allen. B. P., & Potkay, C. R. *Adjective Generation Technique (AGT): Research and applications.* New York: Irvington Press, in press.

McCallum, L. W. Experiences for understanding exceptional children. *Teaching of Psychology*, 1979, *6*, 118-119.

Stainback, S., & Stainback, W. Influencing the attitudes of regular class teachers about the education of severely retarded students. *Education and Training of the Mentally Retarded*, 1982, *17*, 88-92.

Use of Attitudinal Exercises and Abridged Didactic Materials for Fostering Understanding of Exceptional Children

Nicholas A. Vacc
University of North Carolina at Greensboro
and Ann J. Pace
University of Delaware

Since the passage of Public Law 94-142, The Education for All Handicapped Children Act, preparing pre-service teacher education students to work with exceptional children in the classroom has become an increasing concern. A study by Vacc (1978) of the training of classroom teachers regarding exceptionalities indicated that only 34 percent of the elementary education and 24 percent of the secondary education teacher training programs surveyed required a specific course such as "Psychology of Exceptional Children." When these specific courses are not required, information concerning exceptional children may be included in existing courses, such as those in educational psychology or the psychological foundations of education.

Typically, instructors teaching about exceptionalities concentrate on the acceptance of persons with disabilities. To promote greater understanding and acceptance of exceptional individuals, field trips to agencies providing services for handicapped children are arranged, or students are requiem red to provide direct services for such children. Unfortunately, although these activities are worthwhile, they are time consuming and difficult to schedule effectively as part of a psychological foundations course that encompasses multiple dimensions of psychology related to teaching. The more topics included in an educational psychology course, the less time is available for adequate coverage of any one of them.

Instructional Method. Our solution to the dual problems of providing information about exceptionalities and helping to develop more open-minded attitudes toward handicapped students within such constraints was to assign students self-study materials consisting of abridged didactic information concerning basic aspects of exceptionalities, accompanied by written exercises aimed at fostering accepting attitudes toward exceptional children. The use of these two types of self-instructional materials provided pre-service teachers with insight and information concerning exceptionalities without allocating large blocks of course time or

making major changes in the curriculum. Examples of the selected abridged materials are: *Exceptional Children in Focus* by Payne, Kaufman, Brown, and DeMott; and *The Exceptional Child: A Primer*, by Schwartz. Such didactic material provided sufficient information for the students to become involved in the attitudinal exercises. Limited class time could then be centered on the affective concerns rather than on the presentation of background information. The importance of such an attitudinal focus was illustrated by Vacc and Kirst (1977), who stressed the need for classroom teachers to gain additional training for working with handicapped children and more open-minded attitudes toward them.

Presented below are two of the nine attitudinal exercises included in the course. The first was included in the introductory section on exceptionalities and the second was part of the section concerning hearing disabled children.

Introduction to Exceptionalities

1. Identify the most important person, event, and future goal in your life.
2. List two disabilities that you would least want to experience.
3. Write a brief passage concerning each disability indicated in item 2, discussing why you would find the disability particularly difficult.
4. Take the most undesirable disability selected for item 2 and list four ways in which it would affect your life concerning the person, the event, and the goal listed for item 1.
5. List five things that would be most helpful to you in working with your disability in order to be an active member of the community.

Hearing Disabled Children:

Please read the following information and then respond to the questions.

You have been contacted by the local chapter of an organization of hearing disabled individuals and asked if you would like to be a member to explore problems between hearing disabled and non-disabled persons.

1. List three elements which you would like to have as part of your discussion.
2. Do you foresee any difficult issues for you when addressing the group—please indicate two of them.
3. Comment briefly on how you might more effectively approach the issues indicated in item 2.

Evaluation Procedure. To measure the effectiveness of the above instructional format, an achievement test and an attitude questionnaire were employed with two groups of juniors enrolled in four undergraduate sections of a course in the psychological foundations of education. One group of students (N = 33) received a course curriculum that included the abridged didactic information concerning handicapping conditions, as well as the self-enrichment attitudinal exercises. The control group (N=27) did not use the self-study materials, but were assigned readings and experienced a more traditional class lecture and discussion approach. Achievement and attitudinal pretests were given to the group using the self-study exercises during the spring semester, prior to beginning the unit on exceptionalities. Posttests were administered at the conclusion of the unit. The traditional discussion group was assessed with the same measures, although these students were enrolled in the course during the following fall semester. The basic research design followed was that of a modified separate-sample pretest-posttest control (Campbell & Stanley, 1963).

Instrumentation. The achievement test, developed by the instructor, was a 55-item multiple-choice measure which assessed basic knowledge of the incidence and characteristics of exceptional children.

Because the instructor was also concerned about student attitudes toward disabled children, a 24-item attitude questionnaire was developed to (a) measure the extent to which a student perceived exceptionalities as fearful and (b) assess student preference toward educating handicapped children. Six of the 24 items on this instrument comprised a pathophobic scale that measured fearful or negative responses to exceptional children. Another set of six items assessed students' attitudes toward educating handicapped children. The remaining 12 items concerned other aspects of educational practice regarding exceptional individuals.

Results. Two-tailed t-tests were used to measure differences between the pre- and posttest scores on the achievement tests. Such differences were found to be significant (t= 4.51, df = 64, p < .05) for the self-study group, but not significant (t = .56, df = 54, p > .05) for the traditional discussion group. Mean pre- and posttests scores, respectively, were 29.18 and 35.27 for the former group and 29.03 and 30.22 for the latter.

Responses of the two groups on the pathophobic scale of the attitude questionnaire indicated minimal fear of children with exceptionalities, both on the pre- and post-assessments. An item which questioned whether a handicapped person could become a good president of the United States reflected some change in the attitudes of both groups toward less fear, although mean responses were initially highly accepting. On the other hand, a question which asked students whether they found the behavior of handicapped children upsetting" showed an increase in negative responses by the self-study group (22 percent to 27 percent agreement from pre- to post-assessment) .

Responses on the items concerning attitudes toward educating handicapped children indicated that the students in both groups viewed the public school system as responsible for providing for exceptional children. Students viewed the placement of exceptional children in regular classrooms as beneficial to both handicapped and non-handicapped children. There was little change in the students' responses from pre- to post-assessment with the exception of two items. The traditional discussion group revealed an increase in agreement that provisions in the regular classroom can be as adequate as those in the special classroom, and the attitudinal exercise group showed greater agreement that placing handicapped children in regular classes with non-handicapped children would be beneficial to the handicapped children. Overall, the post-assessment responses of the attitudinal self-study exercise group were slightly more favorable toward handicapped students than were the responses of the traditional discussion group.

To evaluate the reactions of students using the self-instructional materials to this approach, they were asked at the end of the semester to judge separately the value of the attitudinal exercises and the abridged didactic reading materials related to exceptionalities. On a Likert scale which ranged from one for excellent to four for poor, the mean rating of the material was 1.68. The following are examples of the written comments accompanying the evaluations: "I have become more sensitive and aware of the abilities and problems of exceptional persons."; 'It has helped me to understand the causes of exceptional children and to accept them."; and "This study has made me more aware of these persons and their needs."

The original goal of finding a way to include content relative to exceptionalities that would require a minimum amount of class time in a general educational psychology course was met. Achievement scores improved significantly with the self-study group, whereas attitudes toward exceptional children remained open and non-fearful for both groups. The approach of using abridged didactic materials and attitudinal exercises within a comprehensive educational psychology course seems to offer a relatively simple, instructionally effective, and time efficient way to enhance undergraduate students' achievement scores concerning exceptionalities.

References

Campbell, D. T., & Stanley, J. C. *Experimental and quasi-experimental designs for research.* Chicago: Rand McNally, 1963.

Vacc, N. A. Preservice programs deficient in special education courses. *Journal of Teacher Education*, 1978, *19*, 42-43.

Vacc, N. A., & Kirst, N. Emotionally disturbed children and regular classroom teachers. *Elementary School Journal,* 1977, 77, 309-317.

Experiences for Understanding Exceptional Children

L. W. McCallum
Augustana College

At most colleges and universities a course is offered which deals with the psychology and education of exceptional children. In addition to the standard textbook and lecture material, it has been this author's experience that most such courses also provide for the student some contact with the children under study. Such contact ranges from field trips to various agencies providing care and/or educational services for these children, to a short term internship where the student interacts directly with one or more of these exceptional children. The goal of these experiences has generally been to allow the student to see "in action" many of the principles discussed in the course. Although such experiences often meet that goal, I became convinced that it is very difficult to gain an effective understanding of the needs of these children without first gaining some empathy for their problems. It is one thing to say that the dyslexic child experiences frustration because of his inability to sort out incoming visual stimuli, and quite another to have experienced such problems. During the first two years that I taught an exceptional child course, several options were tried in an attempt to give the students some exposure to exceptional children. The general result of these experiences appeared to be a "sympathetic" rather than an "empathetic" understanding of the problems of such children.

These concerns led me to initiate, during the third year, a course requirement which attempts to provide some of the "empathetic" understanding desired. At the beginning of the course the seven content topics of the course are described, those being: (a) mental retardation; (b) visual disabilities; (c) auditory disabilities; (d) physical disabilities; (e) learning disabilities; (f) behavior disorders; and (g) gifted children. The students are told that each of them, along with three or four other students (depending on class size), will be responsible for leading one "experience session" following one of the course topics. The students are then given a chance to sign up for one of the topics. Priority is given to student preferences where possible, but ultimately the class is divided into seven groups as equal sized as possible. During the class period following the end of the coverage of each of the units, the group associated with that topic then takes one 50 minute class period to lead their experience session .

The following guidelines are suggested for each session: (a) devise three or more separate "experiences" for the class, corresponding to subtopics discussed in class (e.g., social aspects of the disability, academic aspects of the disability, and motor aspects of the disability); (b) divide the class into the same number of groups as there are subtopics, and rotate these groups among different experiences; (c) avoid situations where some small part of the group participates and the others watch (e.g., try to keep each class member busy at all times); (d) work on timing of the experiences so that they take the same amount of time in order to avoid waiting between rotations; (e) try all of the experiences on the other members of the group to help insure that the experience has the desired effect; (f) allow time at the end of each subsection to explain the purpose of the experience and allow the participants to discuss their experiences, and (g) be sure each student knows that he may decline to participate in any one section or all parts of the experience session. At the end of the class period the instructor passes out evaluation sheets to the students. They are to evaluate the session on the following criteria: (a) appropriateness of the experiences to the topic; (b) effectiveness of the experiences in accomplishing the goals as stated by the group; and (c) overall. The students are told that if they give less than full credit, they are to specify the reasons for their evaluation. The class mean rating is then averaged with that of the instructor. The scores are assigned equally to all members of the group unless they request to be evaluated individually. Leading the experience session generally accounts for about one fifth of the student's course grade.

The following is an example of a typical set of experiences associated with the unit on learning disabilities. After dividing the class into three groups, a member or members of the experience session leaders takes one third of the class into one room, another member or members takes another one-third of the class into another room, and the remaining one-third of the class stays with a member or members of the leaders in the regular classroom. In this way, three separate experiences can be occurring simultaneously. In the first room, one group will be dealing with the social aspects of a learning disability. The leader of this group announces that he/she will take the role of a learning disabled child, and the members of the class will be assigned the role of mother, father, teacher, etc. The leader then poses such questions as "I know I'm not dumb, but I can't seem to learn. Why?" The class members then have to try to explain such problems as if they were talking to a learning disabled child. After these questions are posed and answers are attempted, discussion will focus on the difficulty a family has in interacting with a learning disabled child.

In the second room a group will be dealing with academic problems of the learning disabled child, specifically the dyslexic child. Each person will be handed a Xerox copy of a short paragraph in which letters have been reversed, phonemes substituted or omitted, letter sequences rearranged, etc. The students will, in turn, be asked to read aloud part of the passage. Discussion will then center on the academic as well as the social problems associated with such a reading disability.

In the third room a group will be dealing with motor problems. To illustrate the fine motor skills problems of a learning disabled child, the students will be asked to trace a star with their preferred hand, but while using a mirror tracer. To illustrate gross motor skills problems, each student will be spun around about ten times with his eyes closed, and then following the rotations will be asked to skip across the room. Following these exercises discussion will focus on the academic and social difficulties of a child who has "nonspecific motor awkwardness." When each subsection is completed, the groups will be rotated so that each class member participates in each experience. After all of the sessions, the class members return to the classroom to evaluate the experience.

At the end of each quarter as a part of a general class evaluation, the students are asked to judge the value of the experience sessions. On a Likert type scale ranging from 1 (poor) to 5 (excellent), the mean rating of the experience sessions over the past four years has been 4.76. In the written comments associated with the evaluations only three students out of nearly 400 have said that the experience sessions should be dropped from the course. The remaining positive comments have generally focused on three aspects of the experiences: (a) the sessions allow the leaders to get some in depth experience and content in one given area of the course; (b) participating in the experiences has allowed the students to gain some insights into the feelings and problems of each type of disability; and (c) participating in the sessions has allowed the class members to get to know one another through some "shared experiences."

The experience sessions, particularly when supplemented by first hand experiences with some of the exceptional children being served by community agencies, seem to provide the students with some insights not otherwise available. Although genuine "empathy" may not be possible, the students do report some movement away from sympathy and toward understanding. Since many of the students who take the course will eventually be dealing directly with such children (e.g., in speech therapy), such experiences seem to be a valuable asset to their understanding.

4 . USING VIDEOTAPES

Developing Instructional Videotapes

Polly Trnavsky
Appalachian State University
and Diane L. Willey
Kennesaw College

As a beginning teacher of undergraduate courses in developmental psychology and child psychology, the first author became frustrated because of difficulties encountered in trying to expose students to examples of developing behaviors in infants. There was a shortage of movies or videotapes. Attempts to provide students with opportunities to visit nurseries were only partially successful (too many students, too few available infants); finally, infants brought into the classroom could be relied upon only to sleep or cry.

Not willing to give up attempts to provide students with visible examples, the first author persuaded friends to permit periodic videotaping of their soon-to-be-born infant during the first 18 months of life. The second author joined the project shortly thereafter.

We conducted ten different videotaping sessions, beginning when the infant was 18 days old and ending when he was 16.5 months old. Before each session, we listed the various behaviors we would attempt to elicit that day, hoping to capture behaviors pertaining to several areas of development. We also expected that the infant would produce a variety of spontaneous behaviors, because all of the sessions were conducted in his home, after his mid-day nap.

All videotaping was in color, using a low-light camera fixed on a tripod. When the infant's state suggested the likelihood of maximum cooperation, we began taping while one of us (Trnavsky) attempted to elicit behaviors of interest. The other (Willey) stood by the camera operator to direct the focus to the critical aspects of each scene. For example, when we elicited a reach for an object, the camera would be directed to the infant's hand, arm, and upper torso.

The mother was present for all sessions and participated by occasionally presenting various tasks and, when the infant was old enough, by seating him in her lap at a table. In order to preserve the infant's anonymity, the mother withheld permission for her face to be shown; thus the framing of scenes was often restricted. For observations of gross motor development, the infant was placed on a table or on the floor; when he began to locomote, the camera tracked his movements to the extent possible.

As each session proceeded, we paced the presentations of various stimuli and tasks according to the infant's state. The length of sessions varied from 20 to 90 minutes, depending upon the infant's degree of cooperation and the number of different events we wished to record.

After the ten videotaping sessions were completed, the first author developed scripts to be used to guide the production of classroom videotapes. A professional narrator, working with a sound technician, then recorded the narration for each scene on audiocassettes.

Finally, classroom videotapes were assembled, scene by scene, copying from the original session videotapes to master tapes and then adding narration to the masters. The results are five videotapes of from 15 to 20 minutes duration. Each tape pertains to only one aspect of development. The title of the series is *Observations during Infancy.* Individual videotapes are: *Sensorimotor Thinking, Gross Motor Development, Fine Motor Development, Social Development,* and *Early Language.* Each tape begins with a comment about the purpose of the project and then presents a brief discussion of theoretical problems and explanations concerning the source of developmental change in the behaviors depicted in the tape. Then the development of the behaviors in question is shown. Each tape ends with a summary of the material just presented.

The first three tapes listed above have been well-received by students and colleagues. The latter two are somewhat boring, partly because we could not include the mother's face in the finished product; one sees only one-half of social exchanges or "conversations." In addition, the language tape suffers because the quality of the sound on the original session tapes is poor (because of poor acoustics in the infant's home).

What began as a simple idea (let's show students how behaviors develop during infancy) ended some three years later as a major project. Had we known anything about the technical aspects of audiovisual production at the outset, the results would be more polished. A major problem ensued from the task itself; the original taping sessions did not take place under studio conditions. However, one audiovisual expert who viewed the tapes commented that he could produce a technically perfect tape but that it would lack content. Our goal was to stress content. We believe we have been at least partially successful and that the project represents a viable marriage of developmental psychology with educational media.

Should any reader like to know more about the technical aspects of the project, the nature of the agreements among the people and the two institutions which were involved, the financial arrangements, or the particular content of any tape, we would be happy to provide those details.

Neither of the two participating institutions has a university press, so the videotapes are not being marketed. However, copies of the tapes are available to interested persons for a small charge to cover the cost of copying. Inquiries should be directed to the first author.

Notes

1. This project began while the first author was at Kennesaw College, which supported the ten original videotaping sessions. The project received partial financial support from the Southern Regional Education Board and from the Center for Instructional Development at Appalachian State University.
2. We would like to express our appreciation to the following people: Morris Borenstein, Aaron Camp, and C. H. Pattishall (camera and sound; Media Center, Kennesaw College); Kevin Balling and Diannah Pennington (post production; A. V. Services, Appalachian State University); Mary M. Dunlap (narration); Ellen Arnold (project coordinator, Center for Instructional Development, Appalachian State University); and our subject and his parents.
3. A brief report of this project and one of the classroom videotapes was presented to the annual meeting of the Georgia Educational Research Association in Atlanta, GA on Nov. 19, 1982. One of the videotapes was presented to the biennial meeting of the Society for Research in Child Development, Detroit, MI on April 24, 1983.

Use of Video-Cassette Summaries of Childhood In Teaching Developmental Psychology

John R. Silvestro
State University of New York
College at Fredonia

One of the major problems in teaching an undergraduate course in developmental psychology (with a definite child–adolescent orientation) is the difficulty in providing students with real-life observations of the principles and content presented in the course. An ideal solution to this problem would be to simply put the undergraduates on a bus, find the target population of children under study, and point out the salient examples of development related to previous class discussions. However, being a realist, I am aware of the logistical problems inherent in arranging for the field study of children. In an effort to satisfy the need for direct observation of children, I decided that a system of video cassettes of children at varying developmental levels would be in order.

With the assistance of a locally developed Faculty Mini-Grant for the Improvement of Instruction, the organization and development of the video-cassette system became a reality. This paper is an attempt to explain the goals, methods, and results of the video-cassette system.

The primary intent of the video-cassette project was to achieve the following goals: (a) to improve comprehension of the principles of developmental psychology by providing greater exposure to observations of children; (b) to increase the number and variety of observations of children in order to demonstrate the principle of individual differences in rates of development in children; (c) to demonstrate the orderly, but non-linear process of developmental change from the preschool period into middle childhood; and (d) to provide developmental psychology students with an opportunity to observe the parents of young children, and parental interpretations of child development patterns.

Method. The project director developed five 30-minute video-cassettes of children 3, 4, 6, 7, and 8 years of age. During the Summer of 1977, the five children were selected from towns adjacent to the State University College in Fredonia, New York. All children selected were in the normal range of development, with none demonstrating any notable physical, mental, or emotional handicap. Children were also selected for their ability to relate well with the child interviewer (project director) and to sustain their attention for a 30-minute period. The children selected were each given a five-dollar honorarium for their participation.

Each child and his or her mother were taped in a child observation room using a video camera hidden behind a one-way mirror so as not to distract the participant. Generally, the child was taped for approximately 25 minutes performing tasks related to cognitive, social, language, motor, and affective development. Included among the tasks for some of the children were Piagetian conservation activities, *Minnesota Preschool Scale* items, measures of sex role stereotyping, attitude toward school surveys, moral development dilemmas, and a variety of other structured and unstructured tasks. During the last five minutes, the mother of each child was interviewed concerning such topics as the child's past health, early childhood experiences, relationships with siblings, adjustment to school, and temperamental style.

All five tapes were then edited with the assistance of the College's Instructional Resources Center and were transferred onto 30-minute video-cassettes for final use. In addition, the project director developed five 4-page study guides for the completed cassettes. The study guides were developed to assist students in interpreting the cassettes and to require them to integrate class lecture and assigned readings with the child observations.

The five video-cassettes were available for student viewing during the last third of the Fall 1977 and Spring 1978 semesters. Each cassette was shown for a one-week period, with 10 showings per week. The showings were conducted in a room reserved by the project director for the entire academic year, with a seating capacity of 15 students. Students could earn up to two points for viewing each cassette, with one point for viewing and one point for satisfactorily completing the study guide. The students were given a ditto sheet describing the entire video-cassette system prior to the initial showing. The students were told that they could view all, some, or none of the cassettes and that regularly scheduled examinations would not include material presented in the cassettes.

Results. In analyzing the results, the project director conducted separate analyses for the two semesters. The results were based on a Video-cassette Evaluation Form which was distributed to all students at the time of their final examination. Since there was 100% attendance at these examinations, it proved to be an optimal time for student feedback. Students were instructed to complete their form anonymously and pass it in after completing their examination.

Concerning the extent of student participation in the video-cassette project for the undergraduate developmental psychology students, 79% of the 103 Fall students and 86% of the 91 Spring students viewed one or more of the cassettes. In order to assess the content quality of each of the five cassettes, the students were asked to rate each of the cassettes which they had viewed on a scale of "5" to "1," with "5" indicating an excellent rating and "1" indicating a poor rating.

In addition, each student who viewed at least one cassette was asked to answer three questions concerning the value of the cassette program, once again on a five-point rating scale. The results of both these rating scales are presented in Table 1 and Table 2.

As can be seen from Table 1, the ratings of cassette content quality were generally quite high, with the majority of all ratings falling in the "5" or "4" range. Overall, the content ratings were slightly lower in the Spring semester than in the Fall semester.

Concerning the perceived value of the cassette program, mean ratings are shown in Table 2. Data

Table 1
Ratings of Video-cassette Content Quality
for Students Viewing One or More Cassettes

Video-cassette Designation	n	Percentage Responding				
		Excellent 5	4	3	2	Poor 1
Fall Semester, 1977						
A	56	13%	43%	32%	11%	1%
B	60	18	57	23	2	
C	68	46	44	10		
D	57	32	54	14		
E	57	28	56	16		
Spring Semester, 1978						
A	62	13%	45%	29%	6%	6%
B	72	4	56	36	1	3
C	74	32	44	22	1	1
D	66	12	45	41		2
E	63	19	51	27	1	1

Table 2
Ratings of Value of Video-Cassettes
for Instruction

Item	Mean Score on Scale[a]	
	Fall Semester[b]	Spring Semester[c]
Helped in my understanding of course content	4.33	4.19
Increased my interest in the course	3.96	3.70
They should be made a course requirement	3.05	2.55

[a]Scale from 1 to 5, with 5 being "strongly agree"
[b]N = 81
[c]N = 78

showed 91% of the Fall students and 89% of the Spring students either agreed or strongly agreed with the statement that the cassettes helped in their understanding of the course content. A total of 73% of the Fall students and 64% of the Spring students either agreed or strongly agreed with the statement that the cassettes increased their interest in developmental psychology.

Concerning the statement about making the cassettes a course requirement, the data generally indicate much less approval of this idea. Perhaps since students, could earn extra credit for viewing the cassettes, they wanted to maintain the concept of reward for those students who possessed the motivation to do additional work. Or the data could simply be interpreted as a preference for freedom of choice over coercion.

Discussion. It appears that the response of the developmental psychology students to the video-cassette system is highly favorable. Students are apparently helped in their understanding of the course content and also increase their interest in developmental psychology. The project director plans to continue using the video-cassette system with some minor modifications. A cassette based on an adolescent will be produced and it will replace the cassette of the seven-year-old child. This should result in greater variety in the developmental sequence of cassettes. In addition, a major revision of the study guides will be undertaken in order to introduce more discussion questions and also to elaborate on some of the tasks demonstrated in the cassettes.

For those who teach courses in developmental psychology and would like to make use of the materials or procedures described herein, there are several options available. All or any of the video-cassettes may be duplicated from the original cassette. This can be accomplished by sending the author one UCA 30 video-cassette for each cassette desired plus $10.00, payable to the author to cover duplication and shipping costs. The video-cassettes could be shipped to interested parties within 20 days of initial request.

For those who would prefer to develop their own videocassettes, and I strongly recommend this alternative, a few suggestions are offered. First, it is incumbent upon developers to consult with their representative in charge of audio-visual or technical services in order to determine if the project is technically feasible. One can also obtain from this person an accurate estimate of the total cost involved. Second, an outline of the entire project should be developed, including plans for the number of video-cassettes, the ages of the children involved, a tentative calendar for taping and editing, and a plan for instituting the instructional technique into one's course. Third, developers should present the project outline to their administrative supervisor for review, coupled with a plea for some form of financial assistance. From this author's experience, a set of five video-cassettes can be produced for about $200.00. Fourth, once administrative approval and support is obtained, the project developer can proceed with the process of production. In this regard, it is recommended that one video-cassette be produced from start to final edited product, in order to appreciate the integration of details which the project necessitates and to detect possible bugs in the production process. Finally, the project developer should incorporate all of the videocassettes in his or her series into their appropriate course. It is best to accomplish this by introducing the video-cassette series at the very beginning of the course in the course syllabus, in order that students may be apprised, in advance, of how the cassettes contribute to the course and how they may profit (e.g. extra credit, greater knowledge) by viewing them .

It is hoped that the above suggestions provide interested readers with some practical advice for adopting the videocassette system in their courses. The author would be most pleased to communicate further with readers to assist them in their efforts in video-cassette production.

Note

This article is based on a paper presented at the convention of the American Psychological Association, Toronto, Ontario, 1978.

Laboratories and Demonstrations in Child Development With Unedited Videotapes

Debra Ann Poole
Beloit College

Multipurpose demonstrations of child development are easy to produce by videotaping children while they interact with parents, siblings, or friends. Unlike commercial films, videotapes without narration allow students to formulate and test their own research questions. This article describes how to use unedited videotapes for laboratories in language development and a demonstration of infant development.

Psychology teachers often supplement lectures and discussions with opportunities to observe psychological phenomena. Classroom demonstrations, films, and research projects conducted outside of class are valuable activities in many courses. However, most teachers of developmental psychology do not provide opportunities for students to work directly with children because of the difficulties in arranging and supervising contact with children on a regular basis.

When I began teaching child development, I was frustrated by not having a variety of laboratory experiences for my students. Although films were useful for illustrating research techniques and findings, they did not provide extended samples of behavior, and the structured narration did not allow students to analyze behavior on their own.

During the past 4 years, I have been experimenting with a variety of demonstrations and laboratory projects using videotapes of children from birth to 6 years of age. Children are brought into our laboratory by a parent and filmed while they engage in an activity for approximately 20 min. The segments are easy to produce, are not usually edited, and are not narrated. The videotapes are more realistic than most commercial films and can be used for a variety of purposes (see Trnavsky & Willey, 1984, for a discussion of edited and professionally narrated videotapes).

Laboratories in Language Development

I produce laboratories in language development by videotaping children while they interact with their parents. The filming takes place in a room that is equipped with a chalkboard, a chair or table that the children can stand on, an unplugged telephone, and a variety of books and games. I instruct parents to talk with their children and to elicit as much language as possible. The parents select activities during the filming because they usually have the most knowledge about their children's vocabulary and interests. To increase the chance that every child will be alert and cooperative, I schedule each appointment for a time when the child is usually playful, and all children are encouraged to explore the room and equipment for 10 min before the filming. When a child shows hesitation about being filmed, I encourage the child to view a videotape of another boy or girl.

These videotapes have a variety of uses. One project that has been successful in my classes is to have students analyze three 10-min segments of children who are between 18 months and 6 years of age. Students begin by watching the videotapes in a laboratory and then returning to class with a detailed transcription of each. Although transcribing is somewhat time-consuming, the students become very familiar with the content of each segment and often cite examples from the videotapes during classroom discussions. I then assign three reports that require analyses of various aspects of language development. Although I assign general topics for these reports, each student selects specific questions to explore based on lectures, discussions, and assigned readings. The format for these reports appears on the course syllabus as follows:

Short videotapes of the linguistic performance of three children are available in the Social Science Laboratory. These tapes illustrate the issues we will be discussing in class and provide an opportunity for you to participate in linguistic research. You will write three reports on data you collect from these videotapes. The topics of the three reports are: (a) phonological development, (b) vocabulary growth and syntactic development, and (c) dyadic interaction and pragmatic

Each report should include (a) an introduction that summarizes the issues you wish to consider, the relevant background literature, and your method of coding the data; (b) a summary of the data, including graphs and tables where appropriate; and (c) your conclusions, including the relationships between your data and the existing literature, the limitations of your analyses, and suggestions for future research.

I supplement these guidelines with a class discussion on how to develop a paper topic. For example, I might ask the class how they would investigate changes in the total amount of linguistic output of children between 18 months and 6 years of age. The class must first decide how to define *linguistic output*: Should we count words, morphemes, or all distinct utterances, including sighs and cries? Should we code the proportion of time that the children are emitting sounds, or the number of utterances in a fixed time period? Once the class has defined a variable, I ask them for a hypothesis concerning changes in that variable across development. I then ask the class how they could present their data verbally and in a graph. Although most of my students have taken a required course in research methods, students without a methods class have no difficulty understanding these instructions.

After the class understands the general format for their reports, each student generates research questions for three independent papers. The first report is a phonetic analysis of the children's speech. Most students begin by documenting the vowel and consonant sounds that the children produced, which motivates many students to use phonetic transcription. The number and types of production errors (e.g., deletion of a final consonant, cluster reduction, and substitution) that occur at each age illustrate phonological development (see de Villiers & de Villiers, 1978, for a brief discussion of common phonological mistakes).

The second report documents the development of vocabulary and syntax. I provide the class with several suggestions for analyzing developmental trends, such as changes in the proportion of words falling under the various parts of speech, changes in mean length of utterance (MLU), and evidence of grammatical rules (e.g., the consistent use of word order, the presence of overgeneralization, and the use of tag questions).

The final report deals with the pragmatics of speech; that is, the functional uses of language and the interactions between the children and their parents. Students can analyze the function of each utterance (e.g., to assert or to request), look for simplification in the speech of parents with young children, or look for violations of adult conversational rules (see Bruner, 1983, for a brief view of language development emphasizing pragmatics). For each report, I advise students to state clearly what questions they are exploring, to explain how they coded the data, and to use figures or tables that present their results clearly.

In my experience, students who actively participate in analyzing language are better prepared to deal critically with questions raised in class, such as, "Can we really separate semantics, syntax, and pragmatics?" or "When should researchers use context to interpret children's speech?" Advanced students can

also plan their own videotape projects, such as comparing speech directed to adults with speech directed to younger siblings, or examining referential communication skills.

Students are generally enthusiastic about conducting their own research. In response to the question, "What did you like best about this course or instructor?", students wrote, for example, "The language labs reinforced and applied information in the text and articles. I really felt I learned a great deal from transcribing the tapes and writing on the three areas," and, "The best part of the course was the analysis which we did on the three children. I really enjoyed writing those papers. I learned a lot not only about the language problems of these three children but also about some little children in my own family." The only negative feedback I have received is an occasional complaint about not being able to understand the children, or not having an adequate data base to write the reports. Often, students with these criticisms are not selecting appropriate research questions. These frustrations, when brought out in class, provide an opportunity to discuss the difficulties of linguistic research and the differences between idealized films and natural observation.

Infancy Demonstration

Students' comments about a 45 min videotape of infant development were so positive that I plan to develop additional demonstrations for future classes. The purpose of this first videotape was to illustrate infant motor, cognitive, and social development. I filmed my son at approximately 2-month intervals during his 1st year, and at 6-month intervals during his 2nd year. During each filming, I demonstrated his motor abilities and engaged him in games appropriate to his age level. Before showing the videotape, I provided students with a handout of infant developmental norms and asked them to circle each achievement when they observed it. Although my son did not always cooperate, and there was a home-movie quality to the final product, students unanimously felt that it was useful to see a natural example of development during the first 2 years of life. Obviously, a comparable videotape could be produced quickly by using a cross-sectional sample of infants.

Additional Suggestions

Although some people might think that it would be preferable to have professional videotapes, I have been encouraged by students' responses to unedited demonstrations. The major advantage of videotapes without narration is that students are able to observe and analyze behavior themselves rather than have explanations and conclusions provided for them. Short demonstrations can illustrate many topics in development, such as play development and peer interaction in early childhood, problem solving in middle childhood, and moral reasoning in adolescence. Often a single videotape depicts more than one aspect of development. For example, pairs of children could cooperate on a task such as drawing a picture together or Creating one building with blocks. Students can then analyze the children's verbal skills, describe how children of various ages cooperate, or look for individual differences in social behaviors, such as aggression or leadership. Although many textbooks tend to present a fragmented view of development, viewing videotapes provides an opportunity to discuss the relationships among motor, cognitive, and social development.

In my experience, parents are eager to volunteer their youngsters for filming, provided that the children's moods and wishes are respected. Although I frequently film the children of friends and neighbors, I have also recruited parents and their children through notices on local nursery school bulletin boards. Unfortunately, I have not obtained parental permission to duplicate videotapes. However, I plan to ask parents for permission to distribute videotapes in the future, and would like to hear from other faculty members who are interested in sharing demonstrations.

References

Bruner, J. (1983). *Child's talk: Learning to use language.* New York: Norton.

de Villiers, J. G., & de Villiers, P. A. (1978). *Language acquisition.* Cambridge, MA: Harvard University Press.

Trnavsky, P., & Willey, D. L. (1984). Developing instructional videotapes. *Teaching of Psychology, 11,* 169-170.

SECTION VI
DEVELOPMENTAL – ADOLESCENT

Because he sensed a loss of touch with the youth scene, Raymond Wlodkowski developed a technique to relate his course to current problems and issues. The author asked three adolescents to serve as consultants to the course by gathering material and media resources that were indicative of the current adolescent population, by attending all class meetings, by participating in class activities, and the like. Responses by members of the class were favorable to the presence of the youth.

Paula Schwanenflugel described an interview method for teaching adolescent psychology. Each student interviewed an adolescent on the topic to be covered the following week and wrote a report on that interview. The interviews constituted the basis for classroom discussion. This technique encouraged students to examine the topic before class and highlighted the relevance of psychological research for understanding adolescent behavior.

John McManus reported on a variation of the case study method. Students composed hypothetical cases, proposed solutions to problems, and surveyed other groups regarding case dilemmas and adolescent issues. The method appeared to help students integrate concepts covered in the course and to increase their motivation.

John Charlesworth and John Slate developed a small-group exercise to promote students' discussion of affective and cognitive aspects of puberty. Students wrote a group letter to their fictitious male and female children explaining the changes each child would encounter during puberty. Pretest-posttest results showed that students' knowledge about pubertal issues increased. In addition, students reported feeling more comfortable in discussing puberty with members of both sexes.

John McManus designed a case study and journal record technique in which college students met weekly with teenagers and recorded their observations and interpretations that pertained to topics in the course. Narrative findings revealed benefits to both the college students and their teenage participants. The author also discussed suggestions for future research.

In addition to classroom lectures on textbook material, Ignatius Toner developed a teaching technique in which students produced a videotaped drama that paralleled issues in the text. One production consisted of a situation involving an interracial teenage couple who endured parental rebuke, job discrimination, an unwanted pregnancy, and the like. Students rated the technique very highly.

Thomas Ward assigned a project that required students to observe a medium (e.g., television) and determine the extent to which particular themes occurred. Critical features of the project were that students (a) considered some aspect of the medium that was relevant to a portion of the course, (b) set up clearly defined categories, and (c) counted the number of observed instances in those categories. The authors identified advantages and disadvantages of various approaches to the project.

Putting The Youth Back Into Adolescent Psychology

Raymond J. Wlodkowski
University of Wisconsin

I am pleased to share with readers of ToP a positive change which I have incorporated in my teaching of a basic adolescent psychology course at the University of Wisconsin-Milwaukee.

I have had, for the last four years, the responsibility of teaching this course in the School of Education. About two years ago, I became discontented with the process of the course experience itself. There appeared to be three reasons for my dissatisfaction:

1. students who demonstrated mastery of cognitive learning showed very little attitudinal or behavioral change;
2. the multiplicity of views regarding current adolescent behavior generally confused rather than enlightened discussion within the class; and
3. I was beginning to feel a loss of touch with the current youth scene.

As I deliberated my concern for the course, I began to realize that I had a strong feeling that it was too adult oriented. Adults took it. Adults taught it. Adults wrote the textbooks. Adults did the research. The only way to get to an adolescent was through an adult. Access to young people was always indirect. Adults did the interpreting (and maybe the confusing, too). My respect for phenomenology supported my awareness that I was not providing my students with direct contact with the adolescent life-space. Also, most professional problems for my students came in the areas of methodology and communication. The course I was teaching was not helping to resolve this.

Getting in touch with these feelings led to the logical conclusion: "Get some young people into the course." But how? Doing what? With whom? And the biggest question of all—How will this make me look?—was answered.

I began by refocusing the course toward principles of adolescent development and behavior which relate to current problems and issues. This focus was to be given as often as possible in both the adolescent and adult perspective with the longer range goal of increasing empathetic regard for each other. Thus, the class would concern itself with how both generations perceive and respond to aggression, drugs, alienation, sexuality, peers, insecurity, feminism, identity, decision making, etc. In order to incorporate the youth component, I asked three adolescents to serve as youth consultants to the course and gathered as much material and media resources as possible which were composed by or directly indicative of the current adolescent population.

The socioeconomic make-up of the three consultants was: one white lower-class 15 year old male, one black lower-class 16 year old female, and one white middle-class 17 year old female. The responsibilities of the three consultants were mutually arrived at and included:

1. attendance at all class meetings and reading of textual material
2. participation in any appropriate class activity i.e., discussion, role playing, and communication exercises,
3. biweekly planning sessions to structure course content and classroom procedure,
4. assistance to students for class projects,
5. presentation of course material where appropriate i.e., student rights, drug usage, etc.,
6. liaison to resources outside of class, i.e., underground newspapers, radical groups, etc., and
7. evaluation of instructor's presentation for credibility and insight.

The presence of young people in the class significantly affected the classroom climate. The young people often brought friends and this further reduced the adult-youth ratio. The atmosphere was open, but adults (including myself) were more careful in making broad generalizations and way-out implications about adolescents. Credibility and insight on various issues were facilitated because we could immediately supplement theory with the opinion of our consultants. Adults and youth became more positive in their regard for one another. Role playing and communication exercises were much more effective and influencing because of the young persons' participation. Abstract philosophizing reduced itself and concrete practicality asserted itself more often. The young people put me in touch with things happening outside of the university such as certain radical groups and underground papers of which I had no awareness. Their feedback facilitated the relevancy of my lectures and presentation. They constantly reinforced the viewpoint that although adolescents are in a particular stage of development, they are unique human beings about which few generalizations can be made. I felt I was having a team teaching experience from which I could learn and grow.

In order to determine the attitude and reaction of students in the course to its youth orientation (youth consultants and *youth* perspective) a questionnaire was administered at the end of the semester to which students could respond anonymously. Rather than include the entire questionnaire, I have chosen three questions which I feel most accurately indicate student reaction in a meaningful context. The questions and percentage of student responses for each item are found below. There were 31 students in the class.

1. Did you feel the effect of a youth orientation in this course? Strongly 39%, Significantly 45%, Barely 16%, Insignificant 0%.
2. Which term best describes your general attitude toward the youth orientation in the adolescent psychology course? Highly Favorable 45%, Favorable 36%, Neutral 13%, Unfavorable 6%, Highly Unfavorable 0%.
3. Would you recommend that the youth orientation of this course continue? Strongly recommend 62%, Recommend 32%, Doesn't Matter 3%, Advise Against 3%.

Thus, most students significantly felt the presence of a youth viewpoint and were favorable in their attitude toward it as well as encouraging its continuation. I realize that this is not very hard data and that I must further research the effects of youth participation. However, I desire to present an idea at this point rather than specific evidence. I am currently teaching the same course in a similar manner and my students and I remain enthusiastic. I only regret that I waited so long to discover such a valuable resource for the teaching of adolescent psychology—adolescents themselves!

An Interview Method for Teaching Adolescent Psychology

Paula J. Schwanenflugel
University of Georgia

This article describes an interview method for teaching adolescent psychology. Each student interviews an adolescent on the topic to be covered the following week and writes a report of that interview. The interviews are then used as the basis of classroom discussion. This technique is useful in encouraging students to consider the topic before class and in highlighting the relevance of psychological research for understanding the adolescent.

A common problem for the instructor of adolescent psychology is that the typical student in such a course has very little, if any, background in psychology. The students often have only a minimal understanding of the scientific method used in psychology. Yet, it is often impractical to impose prerequisites. For example, many states require prospective high school teachers to take an adolescent psychology course to receive certification, but leave little room in the student's schedule for additional psychology courses. This article presents an effective method for dealing with these problems. I describe how I use the interview technique, student comments regarding its effectiveness, and some of its unexpected benefits.

The Interview Method

One of the main goals of the interview technique is to encourage students to think about the topics they will be covering in class before they come to class. To initiate productive thought about the topics, I give students a list of recommended interview questions before covering the topic in class. These questions consist of items that are either adopted from journal articles on the topic or designed by me. The students are given instructions concerning how they should conduct the interview so that there will be some standardized practices across students. However, they are also told that they can deviate somewhat from the list of questions if (a) they see that more accurate information will be gained by rephrasing the question or asking further questions or (b) the interviewee seems hesitant about answering any particular question(s). Students are told that parental permission must be obtained before they interview an adolescent. An interview rarely requires more than 20 min.

When the interview is completed, the student prepares a written report, which includes the gender and age of the interviewee (but not the name). The report also includes an interpretation of the adolescent's responses, with comments about how the interviewer might have answered the questions and inferences concerning implications that the answers have for adolescence in general. Students are told that their interpretations can be uniquely their own or that they might integrate the adolescent's answers with what appears in the readings for the week's topic. The interviews are graded mainly on the quality and the effort evident in the interpretation portion of the reports.

Lectures and class discussions focus on the interviews. As we address individual topics, the relevant questions from the interview are discussed. Students volunteer information from their interviews, recurring points are noted on the board, and I describe the pertinent research from the psychological literature. We then discuss the degree to which the data collected from the interviews are consistent with the concepts described in the literature. From this procedure, students learn to appreciate how psychologists derive conclusions about typical adolescents from the data collected; they also learn about the range of answers that are supplied by adolescents of similar ages. Further, students become aware of developmental changes that emerge when younger adolescents are compared with older ones. Consequently, the students indirectly learn about the scientific method and how to look at adolescents as a psychologist does.

The interviews cover the following aspects of adolescent psychology: cognitive development, social cognition, political and religious reasoning, moral reasoning, parent-child relationships, peer relations, and historical perspectives. Two representative examples of the interviews used in my class are presented here. (A set of all the interviews may be obtained upon request.)

Historical Perspectives on Adolescence

This interview is designed to establish the point that concepts of adolescence vary as a function of historical time (Elder, 1980):

Next week, we will be examining historical views of adolescence. However, it turns out that we don't have to go very far to find a real "history" of adolescence. For this interview, I want you to interview someone who is over 70 years old. Find out what their adolescence was like and how it differed from the typical American adolescent of today. Here is a list of suggested questions (but you may develop some of your own):

— Did you attend high school? Did you want to? What kinds of subjects did you study? What kind of homework did you get? Did most of the adolescents in your neighborhood go to high school?

— How many hours per week did you work (not including school-related work)? How much did you contribute to the family income? Did you want to go to work?

— Did you get along with your parents when you were a teenager? What kinds of restrictions or rules did your parents place on your behavior?

— What were your clothes like? Were you concerned about fashion?

— Did you date in high school? At what age were you allowed to date? What did you typically do on a date?

— How did you and your friends spend your free time?

— What was your most nagging problem as a teenager?

— What do you see as the main difference between the teenagers of today and yourself as a teenager? What do you think of today's teenagers?

Adolescent's Relationship With His or Her Peers

This interview is designed to show that the person's concepts of friendship are changing throughout adolescence (Dunphy, 1963; Selman, 1980):

Next week, we will be examining the characteristics and concepts of adolescent friendships. For this interview, I want you to interview a person between age 10 and 19. Here is a list of suggested questions:

— What makes a friend different from an acquaintance?

— What happens when you and your friend have a fight? Is that person still your friend? How do you try to resolve the problem that caused the fight?

— List the names of the people in your group of friends. Whom do you typically hang out with after school? Whom do you typically hang out with on weekends? Whom do you typically invite to your parties?

— Who is the most popular person in your group? What is that person like? Why do you think that person is popular?

Evaluation of Effectiveness

All 19 students who used this method were professional teachers pursuing a graduate degree in education. Following the final exam, they were asked to write a short, anonymous evaluation of the effectiveness of the method as an instructional tool. These evaluations were overwhelmingly positive. In describing their attitudes toward this method, 26% of the students used moderately positive adjectives such as "good," "informative," or "interesting"; 37% used strongly positive descriptors such as "very good," "very useful," or "very effective"; and 32% used the very highly positive terms "excellent" or "extremely useful." A large number of students (74%) spontaneously noted that the technique helped them to focus on concepts mentioned in the reading assignments or class discussions. There were very few negative comments about the procedure. However, several students (16%) said that too much class time was spent discussing the interviews. This problem might be remedied by having small groups of students compile the information and by then discussing the general trends in class. On the whole, students liked and thought that they benefited intellectually from having the class conducted in this manner.

Several unexpected benefits occurred as a byproduct of this procedure. For example, an observation described in the literature was sometimes either not robust enough to transcend minor differences in research technique or had become outdated. Thus, this method provides a continual evaluation of the suitability of the topics covered. Another benefit was that the students were very likely to view the course as relevant to their concerns as classroom teachers because they were able to see for themselves that adolescents actually behave in a manner described in the psychological literature. Consequently, I have found this technique to be a highly effective pedagogical tool for informing professional teachers of the value of psychological research in understanding the adolescent.

The effectiveness of this method is not limited to this particular group of students. Undergraduate and graduate students in other disciplines may also benefit from this kind of instruction. Similarly, the method should also be effective for teaching other developmental courses, such as the psychology of aging. However, two limitations of the method should be noted. First, it cannot be used when the verbal capacity of the target population is too limited to provide meaningful interviews (e.g., with very young children). Second, the method would not be useful in situations where the students do not have ready access to the necessary population. Without these limitations, this method can be truly effective for teaching basic concepts of development.

References

Dunphy, D. C. (1963). The social structure of urban adolescent peer groups. *Society, 26,* 230-246.

Elder, G. (1980). Adolescence in historical perspective. In J. Adelson (Ed.), *Handbook of adolescent psychology* (pp. 3-46). New York: Wiley.

Selman, R. L. (1980). *The growth of interpersonal understanding: Developmental and clinical analyses.* New York: Academic.

Student Composed Case Study in Adolescent Psychology

John L. McManus
Eastern Michigan University

A variation of the case study method is described. Students in Adolescent Psychology composed hypothetical cases, proposed solutions to problems, and surveyed other groups regarding case dilemmas and adolescent issues. The method appeared to help students integrate concepts covered in the course and to increase students' motivation.

The case study method has been used successfully in a number of courses to improve student learning and motivation. Positive learner outcomes have been noted elsewhere (see McManus, this issue). This article describes a slight variation of the usual case study approach. College students compose their own cases in an Adolescent Psychology course.

Method

During the first week of class, the case study method is described. Case formats are discussed, focusing on short incident, issue, and vignette (Hoover, 1980). The short incident is a case study that involves a brief sketch (100-200 words) of an incident dealing with a conflict situation between two or more persons. An issue case centers around one or more problems (issues) and presents background material to help understand the setting for the case. A vignette is a short portrayal of some human experience with no completion of story plot or resolution of problems among characters. Students choose from a number of alternative solutions to solve dilemmas presented in the case. Focusing on common problems for particular groups of persons helps students to appreciate individual differences and integrate course concepts.

Students are given an assignment to develop their own case studies according to the following guidelines:

1. Form small groups of four to seven students.
2. Select a topic of interest for case study development (e.g., delinquency, drug involvement, values conflicts, sexual dilemmas, communication problems with parents, educational crises, and peer relationships).
3. Focus on just one central problem or adolescent dilemma and agree on your case study format—incident, issue, or vignette.
4. Compose your case study, making it interesting and consistent with information presented in the text and class.
5. As a group, generate as many potential solutions as you can for the problem you have described.
6. Rank your group's solution from most to least favorable.
7. Decide on a few different target groups to interview concerning the case (e.g., teenager, parents of teenagers, clergy, males/females, young/old, persons from various race or socioeconomic statuses).
8. Each group member interviews a small sample from one target group. Show them your written case and ask for their preferred solution(s) to the dilemma presented. Then ask them to rank your group's potential solutions.
9. Reconvene to discuss and integrate the findings from your own solutions and the survey results from the various target groups. Write a summary.
10. Present your case study and findings to the class.

Results and Discussion

Two classes involving 11 student groups participated in this variation of the case study method. Case problems covered the gamut of adolescent developmental issues and areas of concern. In their interviews, most students focus on age differences concerning problem resolutions. For example, in one case, a 14-year-old female, Cindy, lives at home with her divorced mother; her father lives in another state. She is pressured to pose nude by her mother's photographer boyfriend. He tells Cindy she will be paid well and that her mother could really use some of the extra money. Cindy's dilemma involves a serious values conflict. This group of students constructed a questionnaire and administered it to persons from 13 to 65 years old. Even with a small sample, clear differences were noted across ages. Persons under 20 years old thought that Cindy should run away or seek help from peers. Those 20 to 50 years old recommended community agencies to provide help for Cindy (e.g., schools [counselors], mental health facilities, or police departments). Individuals over 50 years old suggested that help for Cindy's problem should come directly from her own family—mother, father, or a close relative.

Many of the student groups included a wide range of questions in their surveys, going beyond the specific dilemma of the case. This helped to broaden issues under consideration in the case. For example, in a case describing the dilemma of teen pregnancy, the group's survey included questions not only on potential resolution of the teenager's problem, but also on viewpoints regarding issues such as sex education in the schools, parental responsibilities, and the role of societal agencies in family planning. In a case describing a chronic adolescent shoplifter, the survey asked teenage respondents anonymously to report the frequency of their own shoplifting behavior. These surveys stimulated much discussion during the group's class presentation.

Students reported several beneficial outcomes of this case study format. Composing their own case studies stimulated creativity. Investigating potential case problem resolutions among various groups increased student motivation and interest in the course. Analyzing results of their approach to the case dilemma, along with those of the various groups surveyed, helped to integrate course concepts. Finally, the method fostered class discussion and interaction, which encouraged sharing diverse viewpoints. Student composed case studies tended to highlight the complexity of adolescent development.

Conclusion

Using student composed case studies has been helpful in an Adolescent Psychology class. My informal assessment (based on survey data, student course evaluations, and remarks from students) suggests several beneficial outcomes for students in motivation, creativity, interest, and integration of course concepts. I will continue to use this case study approach in Adolescent Psychology classes and encourage others to employ similar strategies.

References

Hoover, K. A. (1980). Analyzing reality: The case method. In K. A. Hoover (Ed.), *College teaching today: A handbook for postsecondary instruction* (pp. 199-223). Boston: Allyn & Bacon.

McManus, J. L. (1986). "Live" case study/journal record in adolescent psychology. *Teaching of Psychology, 13,* 70-74.

Teaching About Puberty: Learning to Talk About Sensitive Topics

John R. Charlesworth, Jr.
John R. Slate
Western Carolina University

A small-group exercise was developed to allow students to discuss affective and cognitive aspects of puberty. Students were requested to write a group letter to a male and female child explaining the changes each child would encounter during puberty. Pretest-posttest results showed that students' knowledge about pubertal issues increased. In addition, students reported feeling more comfortable in discussing puberty with members of both sexes. This teaching exercise could be helpful to persons teaching courses in developmental psychology.

College students and other adults seldom have a complete understanding of the physical and psychological changes encountered by their own sex during puberty, and they are even less likely to have a complete understanding of the pubertal changes experienced by the opposite sex. Because of the taboos associated with discussing such topics, particularly with members of the opposite sex, ignorance and misconceptions about such topics remain (Taylor, 1981). McCreary-Juhasz (1967), for example, reported that 40% of a sample of college women did not know the basic facts of menstruation. More recently, Adams and Gullotta (1983) noted that menarche, a major sign of adult sexual status, is infrequently written about in our society. Moreover, they concluded from their review of the literature that boys receive little or no preparation for physical changes that occur during puberty. Another effect of our inability to discuss pubertal changes is that we fail to develop a sense of cross-sex empathy about the affective changes that accompany puberty.

In most academic courses, the issue of puberty is handled in an antiseptic way with the focus on cognitive objectives, namely, acquiring knowledge of the physical changes that accompany puberty. What is left out is an emphasis on affective objectives such as the need to develop an empathic understanding of the different emotions adolescents experience in puberty, and the need to increase comfort in discussing such topics. Becoming more comfortable with such an emotionally laden experience may be related to an individual's level of personal adjustment. Sharing feelings about pubertal changes should enable an individual to comprehend and support others undergoing puberty. Parents and teachers who are both comfortable and knowledgeable about these topics are more likely to educate and help adolescents understand and cope with puberty than parents and teachers who are less comfortable and knowledgeable about the experience.

The purpose of our research was to ascertain whether an innovative classroom exercise would: (a) decrease the discomfort associated with discussing pubertal topics, (b) decrease the belief that the education about pubertal changes should be the sole responsibility of the same-sex parent, (c) provide an appropriate model to use when discussing these changes with children about to enter puberty, and (d) increase knowledge about the physical and sexual changes that occur during puberty.

The first author developed a small-group exercise that was designed to meet affective as well as cognitive objectives. Initially, the following exercise was administered to 24 graduate students (18 females, 6 males), ranging in age from 24 to 55 years, enrolled in Adolescent Psychology at a southeastern university. The class met for 4 hr, one night a week for 10 consecutive weeks. One week before the classroom exercise, class members were instructed to read the chapter on puberty in the required text (Adams & Gullotta, 1983). Other than the assigned reading, the class had not been given any advanced preparation for the exercise. At the beginning of the class period, students were asked to rate their passage through puberty as early, average, or late relative to their peer group at that time. Students then discussed the relative advantages and disadvantages of early, average, and late maturation for each sex. Class discussion centered around how class members had first learned of the changes they would experience during adolescence. Almost all students indicated that they wished they had been better prepared for these changes. Discussion also confirmed that most of these students had received little or no preparation for these changes from their parents.

The students were then orally instructed to divide into six groups of four people each, with one male in each group, and given the following scenario:

> Each of you has two children, a boy and a girl, about to enter adolescence. At the present time, you are a long distance from your children and tomorrow you will be leaving on a long journey that will prevent you from having contact with either child for the next 10 years. Tonight is your last opportunity to inform your children of the changes they will experience during puberty, so you need to use this chance to tell your children what you consider important to help them better deal with these changes. The only form of communication available to you is the mail. Each of you is to assist your group in writing two letters, one to your daughter and one to your son. As a group you must decide what to put in your letters. The choice is yours except that in the letter to your daughter you must discuss the menarche, and in the letter to your son you must discuss nocturnal emissions and spontaneous erections. You are to write these letters using a vocabulary that will be understood by these children and that will give them a positive attitude toward the changes they will experience. Each group must decide which letter it is going to write first. When the letters are completed, each group will be asked to read its letters, and the students from the other groups will be asked to comment on what they liked about each group's letters such as content, phrasing, degree of positiveness, and so forth.

After 90 min the students were still vigorously working to complete their letters and requested more time. They were given an additional 15 min. A representative from each of two groups was then asked to read their groups' letter addressed to their female adolescent. Following the reading of each letter, the letters were critiqued by the class members with the instructor providing feedback. The remaining groups were then asked to contribute any additional phrases or topics from their letters that they considered significantly better or different from the letters already presented. Again, these contributions were critiqued with the instructor providing feedback. The same procedure was used to evaluate the groups' letters to the male adolescents. Students were then asked to evaluate the worth of the exercise. Approximately 30 to 45 min were required for the letters to be read and critiqued and the exercise evaluated.

Students' responses about the exercise were extremely favorable. Although class members agreed that initially they were uncomfortable discussing such topics, they stated that they became much more comfortable as the exercise continued. Several of the students expressed a desire to have copies of the letters so they could use them as a guide for discussing these topics with their children. Many participants expressed an increased sense of confidence in their ability to discuss these changes with their children. Informally, it appeared that the degree of comfort in discussing pubertal changes increased for these students.

Because of the perceived success of this exercise with graduate students, we decided to use it in an undergraduate class to collect empirical evidence regarding its effectiveness. The subjects were 18 undergraduate students (3 male, 15 female), ranging in age from 20 to 35 years (M = 25 years), enrolled in a course titled Child and Adolescent Development. The class met 2 hr each day for 5 consecutive weeks. The procedure was similar to that used with the graduate class with a few exceptions because of time constraints. At the beginning of the class, the students were given a pretest which consisted of three parts: (a) degree of comfort in discussing pubertal topics, (b) parental responsibility for explaining pubertal changes, and (c) cognitive knowledge about changes that occur during puberty.

Here is an example of an item for each of the three sections.

1. Degree of comfort in discussing pubertal topics: "Rate how comfortable you would feel discussing menstruation with an adult friend of the opposite sex."
2. Parental responsibility for explaining pubertal changes: "Rate your agreement with the statement that the father alone should explain to his son(s) the changes that occur during puberty."
3. Cognitive knowledge about changes that occur during puberty: "List as many of the specific physical and sexual changes that occur during puberty as you can."

After completing the questionnaire, students were divided into small groups. Each group consisted of either 4 or 5 females and 1 male. Each group member was given a handout describing the exercise. The instructions were very similar to those given orally to the graduate class except that the groups were not required to read their letters aloud and each group's letters were not critiqued by the other groups. The class activity lasted for 75 min. At the end of class, the groups turned in the letters they had written to each child. The subjects were administered a posttest during the following class period. The posttest was the same as the pretest. Feedback was then provided to the students concerning the appropriateness of their letters.

A multivariate analysis of variance (MANOVA) with repeated measures was performed on the pre- and posttests. Significant differences were obtained between total scores on the pre- and posttest measures in affective and cognitive areas, $F(1, 15) = 6.89$, $p < .01$. As expected, students had significantly more knowledge of physical and psychological changes after the exercise. Following the overall analysis, the affective survey items were divided into two categories: parental responsibility for explaining changes and the degree of comfort in discussing pubertal changes (e.g., menstruation, nocturnal emissions, and spontaneous erections). Although no difference was obtained with regard to the parent who is responsible for explaining pubertal changes, $F < 1.00$, a significant difference was found for the degree of comfort in discussing these changes, $F(1, 15) = 7.50$, $p < .01$. Students reported that they felt less discomfort in talking about pubertal changes after the exercise.

Following this exercise, both the graduate and undergraduate students reported feeling more comfortable discussing issues related to puberty. This increased level of comfort may permit these individuals to better discuss changes involved in puberty with their own children, particularly if they have a "crutch," such as a copy of their group's letter(s) to lean on. Further research is needed to determine if the change in attitude brought about by this exercise is maintained over time.

This exercise did not, however, bring about a significant change in the attitude of the subjects about the responsibility for one or both parents to educate their children about pubertal changes. This lack of change may be partially due to the rather liberal view of these subjects that both parents have a shared responsibility to educate their children, regardless of the sex of the child. The limited number of subjects involved in this exercise may have also contributed to the lack of significant difference in attitude change. It would be interesting to determine if this exercise would have an impact on individuals with more restrictive attitudes about which parent is to take responsibility for the sexual education of children. This is particularly important because of the increasingly large number of children being raised in single-parent families.

Because of the lack of a control group, the findings could be attributable to attendance in the course and reading the assigned material. Future research with a control group is needed to determine the effects of this teaching activity.

This exercise could be extended or modified in several ways. Copies of each group's letters could be given to each individual in the class. Then individuals could be asked to develop two letters (one for a daughter and one for a son) combining or using what they considered to be the strong points of the group letters. Another modification might ask each group, with the aid of copies of other groups' letters, to write two final revisions. Copies of the final revisions could then be provided for each class member.

In conclusion, our results suggest that it may be possible not only to "cover the material" about puberty but also to increase individuals' degree of comfort in discussing pubertal changes. In relation to topics such as this, affective objectives are critically important, especially when ignorance and misconceptions are quite strong. This small group exercise may be helpful to individuals who teach a developmental psychology course.

References

Adams, G., & Gullotta, T. (1983). *Adolescent life experiences.* Monterey, CA: Brooks/Cole.

McCreary-Juhasz, A. (1967). How accurate are student evaluations of the extent of their knowledge of human sexuality. *Journal of School Health, 37*, 409-412.

Taylor, C. J. (1981). Teaching more than the facts of menstruation: Exercises to stimulate dialogue about a taboo topic. *Teaching of Psychology, 8*, 105-106.

Note

We thank two anonymous reviewers and Bruce B. Henderson for their helpful comments and suggestions on an earlier draft of this article.

"Live" Case Study/Journal Record in Adolescent Psychology

John L. McManus
Eastern Michigan University

Case study and journal record methods are described and positive outcomes for learners are noted. A "live" case, along with journal records, was used in teaching adolescent psychology. Evaluation indicates benefits to both college students and involved teenagers. Suggestions for future research are discussed.

Hoover (1980) described the case study as an account of a realistic problem or situation experienced by an individual or a group. Included in the case method were a statement of the problem and a description of perceptions and attitudes of those facing it. Hoover said that cases may be either fictitious accounts of realistic situations or recordings of events that have actually happened.

The case study as a teaching tool was first used at Harvard Law School in 1870. The method has since been applied in many different courses, including business, social studies, speech communication, home economics, science, technology, theology, and human relations. Gilliland (1982) and Vande Kemp (1980) provided examples of using the case method in psychology courses.

Hoover (1980) described seven case study formats, ranging from short incidents to lengthy novels. Cases usually focus on one or more problems that students attempt to resolve. The problem-solving process results in many benefits to student learning. Graham and Cline (1980) described positive outcomes of the case study method as follows:

1. Decision-making skills are developed in students.
2. Course concepts are integrated better as students evaluate, make inferences, and see relationships through a case study.
3. Indirect experiences of students are made more real.
4. Abstract, theoretical information becomes concrete and easier to understand.
5. Course concepts become internalized as students solving case problems go beyond mere intellectual understanding or memorization of isolated facts.
6. Conceptual information becomes personal-ized as students apply concepts directly to themselves.
7. Students' experiences are broadened.
8. Students see different points of view through various resolutions of case problems. They test alternative hypotheses and examine exceptions to the norm. Students come to appreciate individual differences.

Beckman (1972) suggested that case studies also increase student motivation and aid longer retention of course information. Graham and Cline (1980) noted two disadvantages of the case method. First, a case study includes limited coverage of course material. The typical case may only relate to one or a few course concepts. Second, as many case studies are fictional, they may not present life as it really is.

The journal record is similar to a diary. The diary is a chronological record of personal or historical events (Christensen, 1981). A diary records the contents of a person's life (Nelson, 1978). A journal, on the other hand, describes the meaning one derives from life events. The journal is a place where one's inner relationship to the contents of life is worked out.

The journal has also been used as a teaching tool in a variety of courses from preschool through college. Hettich (1976,1980) discussed the journal method in college psychology courses, including general, learning, cognition, consumer, industrial, physiological, experimental, and statistics.

Similar to the case method, the journal record promotes many positive outcomes in student learning. For example, academic skill development has been facilitated in written language (Staton, 1980), in integration of course concepts (Lott, 1978), and in helping students to identify and clarify their strengths and weaknesses (Indrisano, 1976). Hart (1972) noted increased motivation for learning through journal techniques. Hettich (1976, 1980) described four benefits of the journal record: (a) it stimulates critical thinking abilities, (b) it aids self-directed learning, (c) it helps students connect course concepts to their everyday experiences, and (d) it provides feedback about student learning processes, which helps the teacher evaluate the course.

Journal records also foster self-understanding and personal growth. For example, Miller (1979) described instances of values clarification, creativity, and catharsis resulting from the journal method. Other authors who described the journal as a personal growth method include Baldwin (1977), Jung (1965), Milner (1967), Nin (1969-1981), Progoff (1975), and Rainer (1978).

This article describes a teaching method that combines case study and journal record techniques in a college adolescent psychology course. Its purpose is to foster the many advantages of both techniques. The method attempts to overcome the two disadvantages of the traditional case study by using a "live" case. College students interacted with an actual teenager and studied all aspects of adolescent development through that person.

Method

Design of Project

The course, Psychology of Adolescence, includes lecture, discussion, and simulation experiences. The course text, Dacey (1982), covers 13 topics: definition of adolescence, identity formation, physical growth, cognitive style, moral development, family interactions, peer relationships, love and sex, educational influences, substance abuse, emotional disturbance, delinquency, and values. Fall and winter semesters extend 14 weeks so course topic areas fit generally into a weekly period. Spring semester is condensed into 7 weeks.

During the first class meeting, students are given a choice of participating in one of two class projects—teen teacher or research activity. Students who choose the teen teacher activity are instructed to meet the adolescent they will be working with by the second week of class and turn in a Parent Consent Form at that time. The consent form describes the project for parents and asks permission for their child's involvement. Examples of activities the college student and teenager will be engaging in, the confidential nature of the journal record, and benefits to the teenage volunteer are mentioned in the form.

College students meet with their teenager at least once a week. Based on their interviews, observations, and interactions, they keep a journal record describing their impressions of the teenager's development in the course topic areas. This information from a "live" teenager, along with class lectures and discussions, role plays, and simulations, helps the student to integrate the various sources of data about adolescence. The student is required to observe or participate in at least two common teenage activities (e.g., sports, recreation, school, cruising). The instructor checks student journals several times during the semester and provides appropriate feedback. Students are encouraged to share their experiences and learning from the project during class discussions. This approach helps them to relate textbook material to contemporary teenagers. Students write a summary of their experience at the end of the semester and also complete an evaluative survey. The survey asks students to rate the value of the experience as a learning tool on a 5-point scale ranging from *excellent* (5) to *terrible* (1) (a score of 3 is average), and complete several short questions about the project. Teenage volunteers also complete a similar survey.

Teenagers come from local junior and senior high schools. The instructor makes brief class presentations at several nearby schools before the semester begins. Teenagers agreeing to participate complete personal information cards so the college students can contact them. After an initial phone call, the student goes to the teenager's home and explains the project thoroughly to the teenager and parents. Parents then read the sign the consent form. Some commuting students choose teen volunteers in their own communities.

At first many of the college students express nervousness about this project and say they are not really sure how to interact with a teenager. In order to reduce anxiety, the first few classes focus on communication, particularly listening and interviewing skills. The instructor role-plays different simulated interactions involving teenagers. Case study and journal record formats are discussed. Students are encouraged to reinforce teenagers for volunteering to participate in the project.

Toward the end of the semester, about eight of the project teenagers are invited to attend a college class and serve on a "teen teacher panel of experts." They are chosen as a representative sample by age and sex. During their visit, the teen panel reacts to issues raised by the class and instructor. This activity helps to integrate all the course concepts.

Students choosing the research activity decide on an adolescent topic to explore by the second week of class. They turn in to the instructor at least two written abstracts per week, reviewing research articles or book sections read. A summary paper is submitted at the end of the semester.

Interest Areas Investigated

Eight areas of interest were examined:

1. How would the college students and teenagers rate the overall experience on a 5-point Likert-type scale ranging from *excellent* (5) to *terrible* (1)?
2. Would course grade attainment differ significantly between students in the teen teacher activity and students in the research activity?
3. Would the positive outcomes previously noted in the case study/journal record literature be achieved for college student participants?
4. Would the combined case study/journal record method provide feedback about student learning processes and help the instructor evaluate the course?
5. Would using a "live" case, along with the journal record, help to overcome the two disadvantages of the traditional case study method?

6. What positive outcomes would be observed for teenage participants in the project?

7. Would there be any incidental outcomes not previously noted for students or teenagers?

8. What suggestions would college students and teenagers make for improving the project?

Results and Evaluation

Evaluation was performed through survey results, comparison of course grade attainment between the two project groups (teen teacher or research activity), and perusal of journal records by the instructor. The major focus was on individual rather than group data.

A total of 91 college students, along with 91 teenagers, participated in the teen teacher project during four semesters. The research activity was chosen by 41 students.

Question 1 of the surveys for college students and teenagers requested an overall rating of the project from *excellent* (5) to *terrible* (1); a score of 3 is *average*. In the college sample, 87% rated the experience above average and only 4% rated it below average. In the teenage group, 83% rated the experience above average and none rated it below average. These findings suggest that most of the students and teenagers evaluated the project in a positive fashion.

As noted in Table 1, regarding course grade attainment for the total group of students, there was no significant difference between the teen teacher group (M = 4.05) and the research project group (M = 3.83), $t(134)$ = .51, p > .05. There was one exception; during the Fall semester, the research project group (M = 3.54) did receive significantly higher course grades than the teen teacher group (M = 5.03), $t(51)$ = 2.47, p < .05. In general, participation in either group did not influence course grades.

Evidence of positive outcomes was noted in the case study/journal record literature for college student teen teacher participants in 11 areas. Following is a listing of those outcomes, along with one exemplary comment in each area:

1. Through evaluation, drawing of inferences, and perceiving relationships among concepts, students were better able to integrate course concepts. "Through the teen teacher experience, I was able to put into better perspective both the lectures and the textbook material. Each week it was almost like watching a movie unfold by comparing L. with the many concepts on adolescence that we focused on in class. In almost every aspect discussed, I would try to associate it in some way with L.—her behaviors, attitudes, and ideas; it helped me make the theoretical real and continuously put more and more together as my association and knowledge of L. progressed."

2. By focusing on contemporary youth, the curriculum was made more relevant. "Although I am now only 8 years older than my teen, I had forgotten about the many pressures a teenager, then and now,

must encounter—plus I really liked learning about the many different concerns of teenagers today."

3. Studying the development of one teenager helped make abstract/theoretical course material more

Table 1. Mean Scores for Course Grades (A = 1 to D = 10) for Both Groups of Subjects—Teen Teacher Activity (1) and Research Activity (2)

Semester	n	Group	M	SD	t
Fall	29	1	5.03	1.97	2.47*
	22	2	3.54	2.36	
Spring	12	1	2.16	1.89	1.58
	4	2	4.00	2.44	
Winter	28	1	4.03	2.58	.52
	7	2	4.57	2.22	
Spring	22	1	3.81	2.15	.10
	10	2	3.90	2.51	
Total	91	1	4.05	2.35	.51
Group	43	2	3.83	2.32	

*p < .05.

concrete and easier to understand. "From the text readings and classroom experiences, I was able to connect the feelings expressed by my teen with an actual title and then better understand why things were happening the way they were during adolescence in a real, concrete way."

4. Students were able to internalize broad course concepts and go beyond a simple intellectual understanding. "The teen teacher experience was so innovative—it gave me a chance to express my own viewpoints in my journal writing, to make my own hypotheses, always in relation to the combined information I was deriving from the text, from talking with H., and from my own self, then and now."

5. Conceptual information became personalized as students applied concepts observed in the teenagers to themselves. "After this project, I now see clearly that most of the conflicts I experienced during my teens were very similar to my teen teacher's and at the time I really thought I was the only one who had them."

6. The curricular experience became broadened to include both cognitive and affective domains. "The experience really stirred past memories—by talking with my teen, it made me remember a lot of experiences and the intense feelings that went with them; it sort of made dry reading of terms in the text come alive with my own past."

7. Motivation for learning was increased in the teen teacher group as they observed concepts in their "live" teenagers. "This was my very first psychology course ever where I was able to apply my accumulated knowledge through observation, interaction, and practical application . . . it kept me going with interest every day of the semester, I just wish every course could be like this one where you can really learn hands-on."

8. Although there were no measurable differences between the two groups of students in retention of course material, there were some suggestions that the teen teacher group would remember information longer. "Whenever I do a research paper, there is always last minute reading, writing, typing, and then I forget it all. But with this experience, I was able to do it more at my leisure and more frequently on a weekly basis, so it flowed smoothly and gradually, allowing me to absorb much more over time so now I'll remember it much longer and in considerably more depth."

9. The "live" case study/journal record method promoted self-understanding and personal growth. "This experience helped me to learn so much more about myself also—I now realize that my problems as a teenager were quite normal, and I shall continue to learn."

10. By observing student learning processes through journal records and class discussions related to case studies, the instructor was aided in course evaluation. "I didn't really understand the concept of the 'imaginary audience' when it was discussed in class until I saw it in my teen—everywhere we go, she is convinced everybody is staring just at her."

11. Using a "live" case did appear to overcome the two disadvantages of the traditional case study method—a limited coverage of course content and not presenting life as it really is. "The teen teacher experience was so thoroughly activity oriented, it was like a TV script where I could see A.'s life as a teenager unfolding more and more each day as the semester went along; in most courses, you learn a concept one day and then forget it the next when you move on to new ones, but with this, I had to keep putting the concepts all together by putting A. together—I guess it was sort of like a puzzle that I kept adding to every day until it became one complete whole." "The teen teacher project gave me real-life experiences to compare continuously with what I was reading in the book."

Positive outcomes were also observed in teenage participants. Abstract concepts were made more concrete and easy to understand, and interacting with a college student in a teaching role facilitated self-understanding in the adolescents. For example: "Each week we would go over the chapter discussed in class and see how it fit my life; that way, I learned all about the scientific steps to development that I never knew existed—now I know some of the real reasons for my behaviors, why I do the things I do, and now I can attach the right label to them"; "hearing what my college student was studying about teenagers, all teenagers, made me realize that my problems are not such a big deal, and that they will go away in time and that most teenagers go through this same type of thing I am experiencing, the whole thing simply gave me a much better awareness of myself by having to explain it all to the college student."

There were several positive incidental outcomes for both college students and teenagers. The experience facilitated a focus on a life span developmental perspective. For example, students and teenagers noted that they both were working on many of the same developmental issues. Other incidental outcomes for both groups were increases in self-esteem, improved communication skills, formation of friendships, and development of career interests in working with youth.

There were several suggestions for improving the teen teacher experience. Both college students and teenagers thought that there should be more than two required activities during the semester and a few group activities, such as picnics. That way, both students and teenagers could share their individual activities, make comparisons, and stimulate creative approaches to the project. Concerning how best to interact with the teenager, college students offered varied viewpoints. For example, many students thought it was important for the college student to remain spontaneous and flexible, allowing teens to follow their own agenda; but an equal number stressed rigid organization, the college students always having a written agenda for any interaction that was to take place. Both students and teenagers emphasized promptness for meetings and the importance of using good listening skills. College students thought the 7-week Spring semester did not allow enough time for this type of experience.

Discussion

Results of the "live" case study/journal record method in adolescent psychology suggest many beneficial outcomes for student learning. Survey and journal record data support the method as a valuable addition to standard curricular approaches. Using a "live" case appears to connect all course concepts to contemporary developmental issues in a realistic fashion. College students, mostly young adults, were able to review their own adolescence objectively by focusing on current teenagers. The experience also appeared very beneficial to teenage participants; by discussing adolescent issues with an interested young adult, they were able to gain insights into their own development.

Future research on the "live" case study/journal record approach might explore several different areas. Course grade outcomes and retention of information could be examined by studying comparable groups of students. In this study, there was no attempt to match the two groups, teen teacher or research activity, on variables such as age, sex, prior grade point average, and so on. As noted, there were no overall grade attainment differences between the two groups; perhaps self-selection contributed to the research activity group's attaining higher grades for the one semester. Of course, further research may determine that neither method alone contributes significantly to final course grades. Follow-up studies over varying time periods could assess long-term retention effects. All the outcome variables noted in the foregoing could be explored systematically in controlled studies. Modifying the "teen teacher" variable, the method might be evaluated for other psychology courses and elsewhere. For example, students taking child psychology could meet with a child for the semester and students in abnormal psychology could meet with someone in a particular diagnostic category. Last, more evaluation could occur regarding teenage participants. A few considerations might be: (a) different ways to get volunteers, (b) characteristics of teenagers who volunteer for such a project, and (c) positive outcomes for teenagers if they also kept journal records.

Summary

As supplementary pedagogical techniques, the case study and journal record may facilitate student learning. Positive outcomes have been observed in such areas as course relevance, student motivation, integration of course concepts, applying conceptual information to the self through internalization and personalization, making abstract material more concrete, personal growth through self-understanding, and affective learning.

Using a "live" case appears to connect course concepts in a comprehensive and realistic fashion and to promote incidental outcomes, such as increased self-esteem, improved communication, and the formation of friendships. Teenagers also appear to experience many positive outcomes by being teen teachers. It was suggested that controlled studies on the "live" case study/journal record approach be conducted in a variety of courses.

References

Baldwin, C. (1977). *One to one: Self-understanding through journal writing.* New York: M. Evans.

Beckman, M. D. (1972). Evaluating the case method. *Educational Forum, 36,* 489-497.

Christensen, R. S. (1981). "Dear diary": A learning tool for adults. *Lifelong Learning: The Adult Years,* pp. 4, 5, 31.

Dacey, J. S. (1982). *Adolescents today* (2nd ed.). Glenview, IL: Scott, Foresman.

Gilliland, K. (1982). Use of drama students as "clients" in teaching abnormal psychology. *Teaching of Psychology, 9,* 120-121.

Graham, P. T., & Cline, P. C. (1980). The case method: A basic teaching approach. *Theory Into Practice, 19,* 112-116.

Hart, N. I. (1972). Using the personal journal in literature teaching. *Reading Improvement, 9,* 87-89.

Hettich, P. (1976). The journal: An autobiographical approach to learning. *Teaching of Psychology, 3,* 60-63.

Hettich, P. (1980). The journal revisited. *Teaching of Psychology, 7,* 105-106.

Hoover, K. A. (1980). Analyzing reality: The case method. In Hoover, K. A. (Ed.), *College teaching today: A handbook for postsecondary instruction* (pp. 199-223). Boston: Allyn & Bacon.

Indrisano, R. (1976). The journey inwards. *Instructor, 85,* 59-60.

Jung, C. C. (1965). *Memories, dreams, reflections.* New York: Random House.

Lott, J. (1978). Improving reading in the social studies: Classroom journals. *Social Education,* 15-17.

Miller, S. U. (1979). Keeping a psychological journal. *Gifted Child Quarterly, 23,* 168-175.

Milner, M. (1967). *On not being able to paint.* New York: International Universities Press.

Nelson, G. L. (1978). Learning from within: Ira Progoff and the power of personal writing. *Media and Methods,* pp. 48, 49, 50, 111, 112, 113.

Nin, A. (1969-1981). *The diary* (Vols. I-VII). New York: Harcourt Brace Jovanovich.

Progoff I. (1975). *At a journal workshop.* New York: Dialogue House Library.

Rainer, T. (1978). *The new diary.* Los Angeles: J. P. Tarcher.

Staton, J. (1980). Writing and counseling: Using a dialogue journal. *Language Arts, 57,* 514-519.

Vande Kemp, H. (1980). Teaching psychology through the case study method. *Teaching of Psychology, 7,* 38-41.

A "Dramatic" Approach to the Teaching of Adolescent Psychology

Ignatius J. Toner
University of North Carolina

Empirical data on how adolescents think and act are remarkably scarce. Even though the adolescent years comprise more than 10 percent of the average life span, this period is the object of less than two percent of all psychological articles since 1942. Before 1942, less than one percent of articles in psychology were devoted to adolescence (L'Abate, 1971). What has been written of the adolescent years usually has taken the form of attitude surveys and behavioral frequency counts that describe adolescents rather than clarify the processes that influence their development. With such a dearth of valuable empirical data, the instructor of adolescent psychology often finds that he can learn as much from his students as he can teach them. College students are relative experts on that period of life that they have recently experienced. Therefore, a teaching technique designed to augment the mastery of a body of scientific knowledge of this age period with significant input provided by class members may provide a means of improving the traditional teaching methods prevalent in adolescent psychology courses.

In two summer sessions, my sophomore level classes in adolescent psychology were offered the opportunity to produce a video taped drama that paralleled the issues raised in an assigned textbook (Conger, 1973) instead of receiving lectures during the class periods. In addition, the class would be regularly tested on material from the text throughout the semester in order that they be exposed to a comprehensive body of knowledge on adolescent psychology.

During the first classes of the semester, each class developed a general setting for their drama (e.g., a formalized presentation; a talk-show, a soap opera, etc.). With the format agreed upon, each class was then divided into three-person groups to write one scene each based on issues raised in selected chapters from the assigned text. During class periods, groups presented to the class the scenes they had written and each contribution was modified to fit into a consistent presentation. When all scenes had been reviewed by the class, several general revisions were made and, with the final script now available, class members were cast in the roles created by the writers.

After several rehearsals, the class members executed the entire production in various campus locations before video tape cameras. What resulted from this effort was a dramatic presentation that, to a considerable degree, reflected the major issues discussed in the textbook.

In the most recent execution of this technique, a class wrote and performed a "soap opera" production that involved an inter-racial teenage couple who endured, among other things, (a) parental rebuke, (b) rejection by former friends, (c) poor advice from a 'hip" counselor, (d) job discrimination, (e) conflicts over sexuality, (f) an unwanted pregnancy, (g) drug abuse and a resultant death, and (h) total alienation from society. The story was narrated by a five foot tall white rat.

Grading in each of the classes using the dramatic technique was based on each student's performance on three tests from the assigned textbook. If the student decided to be involved in the dramatic production, beyond assisting in writing a scene (which was a course requirement), the final course grade would be raised. There was no penalty for non-participation in the production.

Class members rated the technique very highly at the end of the semester with 86% of class members describing the course as "good" or "very good" on an anonymous course evaluation and only 1% rated the course as "poor" or "very poor."

Together with traditional testing on textbook material, the dramatic technique is offered as a means of increasing student participation and input into an adolescent psychology course as well as a means of teaching the instructor how today's students view the adolescent years.

References

Conger, J. J. *Adolescence and youth: Psychological development in a changing world.* New York: Harper and Row, 1973.

L'Abate, L. The status of adolescent psychology. *Developmental Psychology*, 1971, 4, 201-205.

The Media Project: Enhancing Student Interest in the Psychology of Adolescence

Thomas B. Ward
Texas A&M University

One difficulty in teaching service courses such as Psychology of Adolescence is maintaining the interest of nonmajors without sacrificing course-relevant content. A course project that is helpful in overcoming this problem is described. The project requires students to observe some type of media (e.g., television) and determine the extent to which particular themes occur. The three crucial features of each project are that the students: (a) consider an aspect of the media that is relevant to some portion of the course material, (b) set up clearly defined categories, and (c) count the number of observed instances of those categories. There are pitfalls to consider, as well as advantages and disadvantages of various approaches to the project.

One general difficulty encountered in teaching broad, survey-type courses is that the students in these courses have widely disparate backgrounds and levels of interest in the material. This situation is particularly characteristic of service courses that consistently attract high proportions of nonmajors. As an example, the Department of Psychology at Texas A&M University offers Psychology of Adolescence as a service course. Other departments, in particular Health and Physical Education, require their majors to take the course. What this means is that the Adolescence course enrollment includes at least 50% physical education majors. While some PE majors are intensely interested in the topics relevant to a psychology course, most seem less interested. In fact, the most common response to the question of why students are taking the course is "Because it's required." A critical problem in teaching such a course is to increase the students' level of interest without sacrificing the psychologically relevant course content. An approach that has helped me in this regard is to get the students more involved in the material by way of a course project. Although the project will be discussed specifically in terms of this Adolescence course, the general approach could be adapted quite readily to a wide variety of other courses.

The project that I assign requires the students to take a careful, objective look at some medium to which adolescents are exposed and then to speculate, based on what they observe, on the likely impact of that medium on the developing adolescent. For example, a student might examine the way that love is depicted in contemporary music, and consider the impact of such messages in relation to the development of the adolescent's first romantic attachments. The student might use the number of songs that fall into categories such as committed emotional love, committed physical love, uncommitted sexual relations, and so forth, as a way of characterizing the music.

Although the projects vary in terms of the media studied and the issues examined, they share three crucial features. First, the projects must focus on an issue or question of relevance to some phase of the adolescent's life as described in the course material. Second, they require students to construct a set of *clearly defined* categories that allow them to classify instances from the media that they observe. Third, they require students to quantify their observations rather than cite just a few examples.

The first requirement, that the project relate to some aspect of the course material, is often the easiest to convey. A class period devoted to examples of good projects that tie in with course material is useful here. Students have had good success with the following topics, but this is by no means an exhaustive list. (a) Because adolescents are forming ideas for their occupational choices, a project examining the occupational roles of males and females on TV relates to that aspect of the course. How many female doctors are shown on TV? How many male homemakers? (b) Because adolescents are forming their first romantic attachments, an assessment of how romance is depicted in rock or country music is in order. What percentage of songs contain the themes of committed love versus casual sexual encounters? (c) The presence of prosocial versus antisocial themes on Music Television (MTV) ties in nicely with the topics of development in moral and social reasoning. (d) The depiction of violence on TV (who are the perpetrators and who are the victims?) relates to the development of attitudes and stereotypes. (e) The depiction of beauty (flawless skin, straight and white teeth, blue eyes, shiny hair, absence of fat bulges, etc.) in magazines can be related to the developing adolescents' self-image and struggle to accept their bodies. (f) The relative emphasis on weight loss in magazines now as compared to 10 years ago can be studied in relation to increases in the incidence of anorexia. (g) The presence of "unhealthy" influences such as alcohol and tobacco advertisements in sports magazines can be related to the adolescent's struggle with the decisions to use or avoid those substances.

The second and third requirements are often the most difficult ones for students, who are accustomed to making subjective evaluations of media and finding examples to "prove" that the media are a certain way. The problem of converting their subjective impressions into an objective set of criteria, and then using those criteria to count instances often seems insurmountable. I have found that taking one or two class periods to illustrate the need for objective criteria and the process of constructing those criteria is beneficial.

A good way to illustrate the need for objective criteria is to bring examples from the media (a rock song, a magazine advertisement, a short clip from a TV show, etc.) to class. Present those examples and ask the students to write down the major theme presented. Generate a class discussion about the themes they have written down. Almost certainly you will find many different subjective interpretations of the media example. These can then lead to a class discussion of the need to set clear criteria and to a class exercise generating those criteria. This exercise could even be done as part of a unit on experimental design in which the issue of operational definitions is considered. In effect, the project asks students to develop operational definitions of their categories.

Some hints that help students in constructing these operational definitions are as follows. First, the students should specify their definitions clearly enough so that a total stranger could take their definitions, observe the media, and know how to categorize each instance. (This hint could also be used as a way of illustrating the concept and the importance of reliability checks.) Second, they should focus on concrete, observable actions rather than dictionary definitions of terms. What exactly do characters in a TV program have to do for their behavior to be classified as an instance of sex? Walk into a bedroom? Hold hands? Kiss or hug?

A surprising number of students have problems in determining ways to tabulate their findings and then convert them to percentages or averages. A brief example or two of constructing tally sheets and using simple mathematics (e.g., calculating percentages) can be helpful here.

In addition to these requirements, I suggest to students that they incorporate some "creative twist" or meaningful comparison into their projects. As an example, rather than simply looking at the relative proportion of emotional and physical love songs in contemporary music, students could note whether the singer is male or female. Does contemporary music reflect the stereotype that males are more concerned with the physical and females are more concerned with the emotional aspects of love? As with the project in general, the "creative twist" or comparison should be uniquely related to some aspect of the course material.

Obviously, many other types of projects could be assigned, but the media project has distinct advantages over other types. First, it capitalizes on activities in which students are normally engaged (e.g., watching television, listening to the radio). Second, because students are not asked to study adolescents themselves it avoids the difficulties of projects in which students must gain access to a population of adolescents to study. Finally, the project forces the students to become more aware of the world around them.

This last advantage ties in with a more general goal of the Adolescence course, which is to make the students more aware of the forces in the world that influence adolescents. I try to make them realize that they are part of the adolescent's world and, therefore, they must be sensitive to the adolescent's needs and aware of their own impact. I also try to get them to be more sensitive to the effects of media upon developing individuals.

I require both a written report and an oral presentation of the projects. In both, the student is asked to specify the issue studied, the method used, the results obtained, and the suspected impact on the developing adolescent. The oral reports are extremely valuable for two reasons. First, they allow all students to benefit from their peers' projects. Second, they provoke interesting discussions concerning the importance of precise definitions when people who have done fairly similar projects get widely discrepant results.

The instructor must decide on two issues: whether to allow groups to work together or to require individual projects, and whether to assign particular projects or allow students to develop their own. There are advantages and disadvantages to the various approaches. I have tried the different possibilities and now use a group project-assigned topic approach.

Working in groups the students seem less fearful and more interested in the task. They have an opportunity to brainstorm and use teamwork. Group projects also allow students to check the reliability of their coding schemes. An additional advantage is that it is more efficient for me as an instructor to meet with 10 groups of about six people than with 60 individuals to discuss the details of their projects. Group projects do introduce the possibility of "lazy" students being carried along by the group. By the same token, however, those students may benefit more from some involvement in an organized project than total involvement in their own, less well-organized effort. In any case, the instructor can gauge each student's involvement in and knowledge of the project from the quality of the written reports. As an additional check, the instructor can have group members evaluate one another's participation and performance.

There are some advantages to allowing students to develop their own projects. They can exercise more creativity and they may become more interested in a project of their own design. Experience has shown me, however, that many students have difficulty with the task of developing a manageable and relevant topic on their own. Providing the structure of a general topic area and allowing students to develop the details within that structure seems to be a good compromise.

Naturally there are some pitfalls necessary in assigning such a project. Meetings with the individuals or groups are necessary to ensure that they are on the right track. What follows is a list of the problems I have encountered most frequently:

1. *Relevance*—"I'd like to look at ads in travel magazines." Why? "I don't know, it just seemed kind of interesting."

2. *What's a medium?*—Some students will want to study graffiti and other less traditional "media." Obviously some limits need to be set.

3. *Poor definitions*—A student once used a category called *Foul Language* and defined it as "words offensive to one's modesty." The obvious question is whose modesty? Such problems can be minimized by requiring students to submit the definitions of their categories for approval in advance.

4. *Lack of findings*—Students become very upset and think that their projects have failed when they don't find what they were looking for. "I'm trying to prove that rock music has lots of drug references but I'm not finding any." Students need to be told, many times it seems, that their job is to find what is there rather than to prove a point. This is actually one of the more frustrating, yet joyous, parts of the project. When students finally realize that getting a negative answer to a question is just as informative as getting a positive answer their facial expressions are a joy to behold.

5. *Examples used as proof*—A student once turned in a 13-page paper. Ten pages of it were descriptions of two scenes from a single episode of one soap opera. She, and others, had missed the point of trying to quantify their observations. What matters are the messages that adolescents get over and over and not just one example that "proves" a point. A related problem is that students may try to use their own record collections as a representative sample of rock music. I try to encourage them to get a broader sampling, such as the top 100 songs.

6. *How many categories?*—Students will want to know exactly how many categories to use and how much observation to do. There are no hard-and-fast rules, and the best number of categories will be different for each project. As a general guideline, there should be enough categories so that the person can capture most of the instances observed but not so many that the general picture is lost amid the details. If 50% of the person's observations cannot be classified or are in the category "other," then more or better categories should be developed. The amount of observation will also vary from one project to the next, but there must be enough instances so that a general pattern emerges. I generally tell students that they should try for a minimum of 20 observations per category on the average.

The media project need not be limited to courses in adolescence. Various aspects of the media could readily be studied in relation to topics in child development, adulthood, social psychology, and psychology of women courses. The exact issues examined will change, but the principles of operationally defining categories, counting instances, and maintaining relevance to course content apply universally. In addition to increasing students' interest in the course, such projects can facilitate their understanding of the specific topic area addressed, give them experience conducting a particular type of research (content analysis), and give them experience in answering questions for themselves in an objective manner. Students who complete such projects should, in the future, be less swayed by other people's subjective statements about the media and the world in general. Perhaps when they hear someone say that rock music is all about sex they will challenge by asking "What do you mean by rock music and how are you defining sexy?"

SECTION VII
DEVELOPMENTAL – ADULT AND AGING

Despite students' claims to the contrary, Paul Panek demonstrated that his students held generally negative attitudes toward aging. Students gave three terms or words that came to mind when they heard the expression "old person." The instructor's summary of the results included students' evaluation of whether the response was positive, negative, or neutral. Students responded with disbelief at their negative attitudes.

As a class exercise, Randall Wight had students adopt the roles of elderly individuals by designing costumes to simulate the physical constraints and appearance of advancing age. While engaging in everyday activities, students observed their own and others' reactions to their condition and behavior. Students reported that the exercise was educational and that it fostered empathy with senior adults.

Stephen Fried described five learning activities for use in courses on aging. The activities included knowledge of aging, aging as portrayed on birthday cards, and old age as represented on television. These activities helped increase students' awareness of their feelings toward aging.

Kathleen Dillon and Sara Goodman selected and reviewed 25 learning exercises for use in courses on aging. The authors' goals were to increase students' motivation, involvement, and satisfaction, to reinforce and clarify concepts covered in reading and lectures, and to combat aging stereotypes. The exercises were organized into the biology, psychology, and sociology of aging. The authors reported successful use of all of the exercises.

A Classroom Technique for Demonstrating Negative Attitudes Toward Aging

Paul E. Panek
Eastern Illinois University

Negative attitudes toward the aging process and older adults, by all age groups, have been well documented in the literature. In fact, Butler (1969) coined the term "ageism" to refer to this phenomenon. Though the literature clearly indicates negative attitudes toward aging and older adults undergraduate students in Adulthood and Aging classes often find it difficult to accept these findings. Students often suggest society's attitudes toward aging have changed significantly in the past few years and the aging process is no longer viewed as negative.

During the past few semesters I have utilized a classroom technique/demonstration that effectively demonstrates to the students the generally negative attitudes toward aging in an apparently relevant and enjoyable manner. This technique involves the use of a number of student investigators and overall class participation. This technique/demonstration, as well as an actual example of its use will be detailed in four phases as follows:

Phase 1 (Selection of Student Researchers).

During the first week of class (Psychology of Adulthood and Aging) the instructor asked for individuals who would like to volunteer to conduct a project relevant to the course material. In the example used in this paper, six students from a class with approximately seventy students enrolled volunteered to participate.

Phase 2 (Data Collection).

Student researchers were each instructed to ask five individuals the "three terms/words that come to mind when they hear the term *old person*." Further, each researcher was instructed to prepare an overall list of responses and a frequency count of each responses after interviewing their five participants.

Phase 3 (Data Presentation).

Student researchers individually presented their findings on the board to the class. Class members openly discussed each response to determine the connotation of that response: positive (e.g. wisdom), negative (e.g., senile), or neutral (e.g., easy to please). These connotations were placed on the board next to

the response and were based on a majority vote of the entire class after open classroom discussion.

Phase 4 (Data Summarization and Discussion).

The instructor presented an overall summary table by frequency of response, of the findings of the student researchers, to the class. An actual summary from last semester's course is presented below. Each response is followed by the frequency reported and the class judgment of positive (P), negative (N) or neutral (O).

old ideas, old fashioned 3 (O)	respect 2 (P)
easy to please 1 (O)	senile 3 (N)
slower paced 4 (N)	humorous 1 (N)
routine, set in ways 2 (N)	trauma 1 (N)
wise, wisdom, knowledge 11 (P)	nursing home 3 (N)
restless 1 (N)	hot 1 (O)
loving, considerate 5 (P)	old 3 (N)
physical deterioration 26 (N)	sad, depressed 1 (N)
retirement 4 (O)	sedentary 4 (N)
senior citizen 2 (N)	crabby 1 (N)
grandparents 7 (P)	mature 2 (P)
fossil 1 (N)	total = 89

As shown, the 89 scorable responses were obtained by the students and they could be classified into the 23 categories above. Of these categories, four (17%) were neutral, five (22%) were positive and fourteen (61%) were negative.

A similar pattern was observed for frequency of response. That is nine responses (10%) were neutral, twenty-seven (30%) were positive, and fifty-three (60%) were negative.

I have found this classroom method/technique to be quite effective in demonstrating the negative attitudes toward aging. There appears to be two major themes in the discussion following the presentation of these data. The first theme centers around what can be described as "disbelief." That is, we really never believed the attitudes toward aging were still so negative, especially in a supposedly enlightened group, i.e., college students. Another major theme of the discussion revolves around the differentiation between "saying" and "doing," in terms of people's attitudes and beliefs. For instance, students report that they are not biased toward older adults, but their actual behavior indicates otherwise.

In addition to accomplishing this primary goal, a number of secondary benefits are derived from this procedure. These include increased classroom discussion/participation, and illustrating some of the issues discussed in the section on research methodology, e.g., sampling problems.

Reference

Butler, R. N. Age-ism: Another form of bigotry. *The Gerontologist*, 1969, *14*, 243-249.

Fostering Insight Into Personal Conceptions of the Elderly: A Simulation Exercise

Randall D. Wight
Ouachita Baptist University

As a class exercise, Human Development students adopted the roles of elderly individuals by designing costumes to simulate the physical constraints and appearance of advancing age. Then, while engaging in everyday activities, they observed the reactions of themselves and others to their condition and behavior. This activity allowed students to examine their personal conceptions of the elderly. Students reported that the exercise was educational and that it fostered empathy with senior adults.

Research indicates that although the public may believe myths about aging (National Council on Aging, 1975), psychology students believe fewer aging misconceptions (Moeller, 1982; Panek, 1982). Moreover, the study of aging may counter students' initial misconceptions (Mueller, 1982). Learning experiences that require personal involvement enhance student understanding (Dillon & Goodman, 1980; Dullaert, 1977; Evans, 1981). Evans (1981) reported that such experiences during the study of aging are associated with more positive course evaluations, increased student motivation, and higher ratings of the educational value of the course. Fried (1988) presented an exercise in which students described their self-concept of personal aging. I developed a simulation assignment that encourages students to examine and experience their personal conceptions of the elderly.

Simulation is a useful and inexpensive tool for communicating the experiential component of complex roles and relationships (Claiborn & Lemberg, 1974).

Aging simulations described in the literature have focused solely on psychomotor changes (Evans, 1981) or physical disabilities (Hulicka & Whitbourne, cited in Dillon & Goodman, 1980). The exercise described herein differs from earlier aging simulations in that students adopted a role and observed their and others' responses while engaging in everyday activities.

Method

Sixty-one students in two Human Development classes devised costumes that approximated the appearance and experience of the elderly.[1] Suggested techniques for accomplishing these goals included the wearing of earplugs (to reduce hearing), the removal or addition of eyewear (to impair vision), the wrapping of joints with elastic bandages (to create stiffness), and the application of latex to skin (to produce wrinkles). The Drama Department provided helpful guidance regarding make-up, hair color, and clothing. Instructions for the costume were deliberately vague to allow students a broad range of possibilities for expressing themselves. The only limitation placed on the costume was that it should create the illusion of age for the participant and casual observer. Although five to seven students in each class reported that they were ineffective in portraying the illusion of age to others, most students reported success.

The exercise required 5 consecutive hours of role-playing during which the students were to appear and behave as senior adults. No more than two students in costume were permitted to conduct the simulation together. For safety reasons, students arranged to be driven by an unimpaired friend. Students' favorite settings for the exercise included business districts, department stores, shopping malls, and restaurants. A written summary describing the costume, events and experiences that occurred while role-playing, and insights kindled during and after the simulation completed the assignment. The summaries were due two thirds of the way into the semester and before a class discussion of aging. Each student submitted two photographs with the summary, one taken before and one taken after the costume was in place, in order to prevent fabrication of the written reports.

In a typical simulation, the student prepared the costume, shopped in a mall or department store, ate lunch or dinner shopped again, and then returned home. The assignment's instructions directed students to observe the manner in which individuals responded as the simulation transpired. Repeatedly, the spark that ignited student insight was social interaction. Students perceived attitudes in the behavior of others that they identified as attitudes they held and often exhibited toward the elderly.

Two common reports illustrate this point. Often when ordering a meal, the waiter or waitress spoke to the student in a loud "motherese." This occurrence disconcerted students and prompted them to recall occasions when they had behaved in similar fashion. An equally disconcerting event was movement in a crowd. Students saw themselves in the impatient, sometimes rude behavior of individuals who jostled past them. These realizations appeared to make students uncomfortable and led many to consider senior adults and their circumstances more carefully.

Results and Discussion

The semester-end course evaluation included a question about the simulation. Students evaluated the educational value of the exercise on a scale ranging from *poor* (1) through *average* (5) to *great* (10). The mean rating was 8.75 (SD = 1.67). This evaluation indicates that students considered the exercise to be a useful instructional tool. Students could also write open-ended comments about the simulation. Of the 24 students who commented, 17 (70.8%) stated that the exercise increased their knowledge of and empathy with the elderly. The following comments were typical: "The study helped me identify with old people"; "It stimulated thought and compassion in me"; "It taught me more about aging than anyone or anything could have. " Although six people either found the task

difficult or did not enjoy it, four of the six stated that the exercise was educational.

An unexpected result suggests that students' assumptions about aging constrained the insights they gained. Based on their written reports, only four of the students portrayed the elderly as active individuals not isolated from society. Although two students simulated adventurous, fun-loving, sports-car-driving women, most students depicted pain-ridden, lonely people (e.g., bums, bag ladies, or decrepit individuals). Similarly, Moeller (1982) and Panek (1982) demonstrated that although psychology students hold a limited number of myths about aging, the myths they do hold include the characterization of the elderly as lonely, isolated, and inflexible. Our class discussion focused on contrasting this predominant simulation portrayal with the fact that senior adults often lead active, fulfilling lives. Demand characteristics of the assignment may have prompted the decrepit portrayals. I do not view this possibility as a limitation of the exercise but as a strength. In the future, I will continue to allow this discrepancy to arise naturally and use it to stimulate class discussion.

Indeed, I suspect that this activity fosters not only insight into the elderly, but also insight into the students' conception of the elderly. The most striking aspect of the exercise is what students learn about themselves. A common theme in student reports is the discovery of personal insensitivity toward elderly individuals and their circumstances. No simulation can age youth. This exercise appears to foster a turning from careless insensitivity to thoughtful consideration through the juxtaposition of social interaction and personal memory. Future research can explore the relationship between students' cognitive misconceptions and personal awareness of senior adults' lives and circumstances. Whether students learn anything about the actual experiences of the elderly also requires exploration. Meanwhile, we should encourage students to acquire information about aging and to develop insight into their conceptions of it. The simulation described here offers a striking way to foster such insight.

References

Claiborn, W. L., & Lemberg, R. W. (1974). A simulated mental hospital as an undergraduate teaching device. *Teaching of Psychology, 1*, 38-40.

Dillon, K. M. H., & Goodman, S. (1980). Think old: Twenty-five classroom exercises for courses in aging. *Teaching of Psychology, 7*, 96-99.

Dullaert, J. (1977) . Teaching psychology of the aged: Six obstacles to learning. *Teaching of Psychology, 4*, 68-72.

Evans, J. D. (1981). Personal involvement projects in the psychology of aging: Some examples and an empirical assessment. *Teaching of Psychology, 8*, 230-233.

---

[1] I offer nontraditional students the choice of completing a simulation or an alternative project and am indebted to Sandra M. Powers for suggesting some possibilities. For example, a student may interview an older family member to discuss various aspects of childhood and adulthood, including attitudes, goals, and life satisfaction.

Fried, S. B. (1988). Learning activities for understanding aging. *Teaching of Psychology, 15,* 160-162.

Moeller, T. G. (1982). Does taking developmental psychology affect students' reactions to aging? *Teaching of Psychology, 9,* 95-99.

National Council on Aging. (1975). *The myths and reality of aging in America.* Washington, DC: Author.

Panek, P. E. (1982). Do beginning psychology of aging students believe 10 common myths of aging? *Teaching of Psychology, 9,* 104-105.

Notes

1. An abridged version of this article was presented at the annual meeting of the American Psychological Association, Atlanta, GA, August 1988.
2. I thank Randolph A. Smith for his helpful comments on a draft of this article.

Learning Activities for Understanding Aging

Stephen B. Fried
Park College

This article describes five learning activities for use in courses on aging. The activities concern knowledge of aging, aging stereo types, personal feelings about aging, aging as portrayed on birthday cards, and old age as represented on television. These activities may help increase awareness of feelings toward aging.

Learning activities used in psychology courses may provide students the opportunity to explore their personal beliefs about the elderly and the process of human aging (Moeller, 1982). Dillon and Goodman (1980) and Evans (1981) described examples of classroom exercises and personal involvement projects (e.g., interviews, questionnaires, and simulations) that may be useful in helping students analyze their own beliefs about aging. I developed five additional learning activities for use in undergraduate courses.

The first activity, based on current demographic information about the elderly (Fowles, 1986), is a 15-item questionnaire. I have given this instrument, The Knowledge of the Elderly Quiz, to students in courses on adult development and aging and social psychology (see appendix A). The goal of this activity is to highlight students' knowledge of demographic data about the aged. After completing the instrument, students are given the key explaining each correct response (see appendix B). I have used this quiz both as a handout to be completed in class and as an out-of-class computer assignment. (A software program for the quiz is available for use with Apple IIe computer.)

I call the second activity The Aging Stereotype Game. This exercise provides an opportunity for students to explore common stereotypes about the elderly. The class is divided into groups of four to seven. Each group develops a list of 15 to 20 negative stereotypes and a list of a similar number of positive stereotypes about the elderly. I give examples of negative and positive stereotypes (e.g., "All old people are senile," and "All of the elderly are wise"). At this point, each group chooses a scribe to write down the stereotypes that are generated through group discussion. After all groups have completed their lists, scribes read each group's list to the entire class. Finally, I lead a discussion that prompts students to identify common themes from the different lists and to examine their own beliefs.

A third activity, What Will I Be Like When I Am Seventy-Five?, focuses on both self-concept and perceptions of personal aging. Students write a paragraph to answer each of the following questions:

1. Which of your current behaviors will be similar and which ones will be different when you are 75?
2. In what ways will you look like you do now and in what ways will your appearance be different?
3. What do you think your eyesight, hearing, and physical strength will be like at age 75?
4. What might you like about being 75 years old?
5. What do you prefer about being your present age compared to being 75 years old?
6. Is it difficult to imagine yourself at 75? Why or why not?

When students finish answering these questions, I pair each student with another and they discuss their answers. I use this activity in conjunction with a lecture on stability and change in adulthood.

A fourth activity is called Happy Birthday Old One. It is designed to investigate attitudes about age as reflected in birthday cards (Dillon & Jones, 1981; Huyck & Duchon, 1986). Students look at the birthday cards in a greeting card shop. (I suggest that students obtain permission of the store manager.) Each student analyzes 20 cards for adults that describe the intended recipient of the card. For each card examined, students complete a form that addresses the following: a general visual description of the card, words on the cover, words on the inside, and any additional content. During the class session in which this activity is reported, I divide students into small groups and ask them to discuss their feelings with their peers. Finally, each group shares its results with the entire class.

A fifth learning experience is called The Elderly and the Tube. The goal of this activity is to examine popular culture's messages about the elderly. Students view 10 hr of television over a 2 or 3 week period. Each student watches 5 different 1-hr dramas and 10½-hr situation comedies. After viewing each program, students fill out the appropriate portion of an activity sheet indicating the name of the show, the type of show (e.g., comedy or drama), ages of continuing characters (children; adolescents; young adults, 20 to 35; middle aged, 35 to 50; mature adults, 50 to 65; or older adults, 65 or over), intergenerational themes, themes involving older adults, and any intergenerational conflicts. After completing this activity, students prepare a two-page summary of their observations and their own personal reactions. Students discuss their findings in class, and I compare their results to published research on similar topics (Atchley, 1985; Harris & Feinberg, 1977; Petersen, 1973).

These five activities can be used in a variety of psychology courses (e.g., adult development and aging, developmental, social, or general). I hope that these exercises will be useful to readers and encourage them to develop their own experiential activities to help students better understand aging and the aged.

References

Atchley, R. C. (1985). *Social forces in later life* (4th ed.). Belmont CA: Wadsworth.

Dillon, K. M. H., & Goodman, S. (1980). Think old: Twenty-five classroom exercises for courses in aging. *Teaching of Psychology, 7,* 96-99.

Dillon, K. M. H., & Jones, B. S. (1981). Attitudes toward aging portrayed by birthday cards. *International Journal of Aging and Human Development, 13,* 79-84.

Evans, J. D. (1981). Personal involvement projects in the psychology of aging: Some examples and an empirical assessment. *Teaching of Psychology, 8,* 230-233.

Fowles, D. G. (1986). *A profile of older Americans: 1986.* Washington, DC: American Association of Retired Persons.

Harris, A. J., & Feinberg, J. F. (1977). Television and aging: Is what you see what you get? *The Gerontologist, 17,* 464-467.

Huyck, M. H., & Duchon, J. (1986). Over the miles: Coping, communicating, and commiserating through age-theme greeting cards. In L. Nahernow, K. A. McClusky-Fawcett, & P. E. McGee (Eds.), *Humor and aging* (pp. 139-159). Orlando, FL: Academic.

Moeller, T. G. (1982). Does taking developmental psychology affect students' reactions to aging? *Teaching of Psychology, 9,* 95-99.

Petersen, M. (1973). The visibility and image of old people on television. *Journalism Quarterly, 50,* 569-573.

Notes

1. The activities described in this article were developed under the auspices of the Missouri Geriatric Education Center funded by the Bureau of Health Professions, Health Resources, and Health Services Administration.
2. I thank Marie Croker, Dick Dalton, Kathy Ehrig, Kurt Fried, Cindy MacQuarrie, Jack Mulligan, Dick Noback, Dorothy Van Bouven, Marc Weinstein, and Lee Willoughby for their assistance.

Appendix A
Knowledge of the Elderly Quiz

Place a check indicating your agreement or disagreement to each of the following statements:

	Agree	Disagree
1. About one in eight Americans is 65 years of age or older.	____	____
2. The most common health problem among the elderly is arthritis.	____	____
3. The state with the highest percentage of elderly residents of the total state population is New York.	____	____
4. Older men are twice as likely to be married as are older women.	____	____

5. About one third of eld-
    erly Blacks live below the
    poverty line.   ____   ____
6. Older men have a higher
    poverty rate than older
    women.   ____   ____
7. The education level of
    the older population has
    been steadily decreasing.   ____   ____
8. Half of all older women
    are widows.   ____   ____
9. Thirty percent of the
    elderly have diabetes.   ____   ____
10. The growth of the older
    population will slow
    down in the 1990s due to
    the small number of
    births during the Great
    Depression.   ____   ____
11. By the year 2030, the
    elderly may comprise
    over one fifth of the U.S.
    population.   ____   ____
12. About 75% of the aged
    have significant hearing
    impairments.   ____   ____
13. A female child born in
    1984 could expect to live
    about 75 years.   ____   ____
14. There are about 150 aged
    women for every 100
    aged men.   ____   ____
15. Most aged parents are in
    the presence of an adult
    child at least once a
    week.   ____   ____

Appendix B
Key: Knowledge of the Elderly Quiz

1. The correct response is agree. In 1985, those 65 years or older comprised 12% of the population.
2. The correct response is agree. Arthritis was the most frequent chronic condition for 53% of those sampled in 1984.
3. The correct response is disagree. Florida has the higher percentage of elderly residents. In 1985, aged persons comprised 18% of the total population of that state.
4. The correct response is agree. In 1985, 77% of aged men, compared to 40% of women, were married.
5. The correct answer is agree. In 1985, about one third (32%) of elderly Blacks were poor.
6. The correct answer is disagree. In 1985, older women had a higher rate of poverty (16%) than did older men (8%).
7. The correct answer is disagree. For the older population, the level of education has been steadily increasing. The median educational level increased from 8.7 years to 11.7 years for aged persons between 1970 and 1985. In

addition, the percentage who finished high school increased from 28% to 48%.
8. The correct response is agree. In 1985, 51% of all women were widows.
9. The correct r esponse is disagree. In 1984, 10% of the aged had diabetes.
10. The correct response is agree. There was a relatively small number of babies born during the Depression.
11. The correct response is agree. By 2030, the aged may well be 21% of the total population.
12. The correct response is disagree. According to data collected in 1984, 40% of the non institutionalized elderly had hearing impairments.
13. The correct response is agree. If a female child was born in 1984, she could expect to live 74.7 years.
14. The correct response is agree. In 1985, there were 147 older women for every 100 men.
15. The correct response is agree. A study conducted in 1975 found that 77% of older parents had seen one of their children during the previous week.

Think Old: Twenty-five Classroom Exercises For Courses in Aging

Kathleen M. Hynek Dillon
and Sara Goodman
Western New England College

Use of this annotated resource guide surely will increase student learning through participation, and may also change attitudes.

As the number of old and very old increases in our population, so does the need for those involved in services for the aged. Although the need is increasing, interest in working with the aged is not. Butler (1975) discusses the reluctance of psychotherapists to work with the aged, known as the YAVIS syndrome—the tendency to treat only Young, Attractive, Verbal, Intelligent, and Successful clientele. In one study of psychiatrists reviewed by Butler, less than 2% of psychiatric time (or less than one hour per week) was spent with elderly patients even though those over age 65 have by far the highest occurrence of new cases of psychopathology. Using data from a questionnaire responded to by 69 graduate students in social work, law, and medicine, Geiger (1978) demonstrated that the YAVIS syndrome is being perpetuated among future professionals. Although many students believed that there were more old people in this country than there actually are (from 44-53 million compared to the actual 22 million), not one person registered a first choice for working with the elderly in their future career. Out of the four age categories, 74% of social work students chose the old as third or fourth preference, and 88% of medical students considered working with old people only as a last resort.

Both Butler and Geiger blame this attitude in part on the failure of the educational system to offer or require courses and experience in working with the aged. As Developmental Psychology finally comes of age with the realization that life does not end in adolescence, the number of courses of at least an elective nature in adulthood and aging is beginning to increase. Many students who elect to take these courses, however, will not be of the age cohort on which the courses focus, and many students will probably bring with them ageism and gerontophobic attitudes from our culture. It becomes the task of the educator then to find ways to bridge the cohort gap in the most stimulating manner possible.

Six hundred fourteen colleges and universities responded to a questionnaire sponsored by the American Psychological Association in order to determine the kinds of programs offered in Psychology. "In talks with students and faculty members, and in our questionnaires to departments, one area emerged as uniquely important in teaching psychology—student involvement in learning activities. It is a widely shared belief in psychology that students learn most when they are active in learning situations" (Kulik *et al.*, p. 206).

The 25 learning exercises we have selected and will review here have the potential to increase student motivation, involvement, and satisfaction, to reinforce and clarify concepts covered in reading and lectures, and to combat aging stereotypes while increasing empathy and understanding. The exercises come from many sources including research studies, course outlines, and popular magazines. Some of the references were intended as classroom exercises; others were not, but any necessary modification is suggested in the summaries. We have arbitrarily divided the exercises into three related categories— the Biology of Aging, the Psychology of Aging, and the Sociology of Aging, although many exercises fit into more than one area. Where possible the summaries were written using words of the authors to describe the intent of the exercise. In the case where a reference would be unavailable from a journal or textbook, we have included an address where it may be obtained.

All of these exercises have been used successfully by one or both of us in either our courses in Adulthood and Aging, Psychosocial Perspectives on Aging, Death and Dying, Developmental Psychology, and Introductory Psychology, or in workshops given by us to staff of long term care facilities for the aged. You will undoubtedly need to personally validate the use of these exercises because success will depend on many factors such as the specific expertise and background of the teacher, the nature of the course, and the type of students enrolled. We do not endorse the use of these exercises as research tools (although some have been used for this purpose) nor do we recommend that these exercises be used in lieu of lectures and reading material; they are intended to complement, not substitute for, traditional learning material.

We hope you find these exercises as helpful and interesting as we have, and that you will be rewarded with many students who become interested in a career in aging

Biology of Aging

1. Palmore, E. Facts on aging: A short quiz. *Gerontologist*, 1977, *17*, 315-320.

A 25-item true-false quiz designed by the author to stimulate group discussions, measure and compare different groups' level of information on aging, identify the most frequently held misconceptions about aging, and indirectly measure bias toward the aging. Palmore also provides comparative data for undergraduate students, graduate students, and faculty.

2. Vickery, D. M. How long will you live? *Family Health*, January 1979, 29-32. (Also in Vickery, D. M. *Life plan for your health*. Cambridge, MA: Addison Wesley, 1979.)

Illustrates how your habits and health history affect the probability of good health and how these factors can be used to estimate your life expectancy (assuming you do not suffer from a serious chronic condition). This test includes not only the more obvious variables as exercise, weight, diet, smoking and drinking habits, but also the use of seat belts, contraceptives, and the Holmes Scale for Stress.

3. Shore, H. Designing a training program for understanding sensory losses in aging. *Gerontologist*, 1976, *16*, 157-165.

Stimulation exercises that review visual, auditory, tactile, olfactory, gustatory, and kinesthetic losses sometimes associated with aging. These exercises provide a useful method for gaining insight and understanding of the difficulties of coping with distorted environmental feedback resulting from sensory losses in order for those working with the elderly to enhance their functioning, independence, and satisfaction.

4. Hulicka, I. M., & Whitbourne, S. K. Teaching undergraduate courses in adult development and aging. Preconvention Workshop, American Psychological Association, Toronto, August 27, 1978. (Obtain from the author, State University of New York College, Buffalo, NY 14627)

Simulation exercises of physical disabilities which affect many older people, including paralysis of fingers and limbs, coordination problems, loss of voice, and constant itching; also role playing exercises of various experiences the aged may encounter in our society. These exercises are designed to foster insight into the difficulties encountered by a handicapped person, and to increase awareness of the experiences of the aged.

5. Farquhar, J. W. Test your heart attack and stroke potential. *Family Circle*, October 23, 1978, 100; 104; 110.

Calculates your risk of heart attack (the leading cause of death) and stroke (the third leading cause of death, but the first in overall costs) by scoring you on such related variables as smoking habits, body weight, physical activity and stress. This article not only tests your potential, but also provides you with a ten step plan to reduce the risk.

6. 60+ and physically fit: Suggested exercises for older people. Hartford, CT: Connecticut Department on Aging's Physical Fitness Committee, (90 Washington St., Room 3123, Hartford, CT 06115), 1977.

Provides simple exercises for both ambulatory and non ambulatory aged to prevent or combat physiological losses that appear to result more from inactivity than from old age. The committee recommends that the exercises be discussed with a physician to decide which would be the most beneficial. Students could try and then discuss the benefits of a regular program of these exercises. A discussion of DeVries' (1977) studies with young men experiencing decreased activity in the form of three weeks of bed rest with resulting losses in physiological functioning similar to those found in the aged might be of interest to the younger student here.

Psychology of Aging

7. Kastenbaum, R. Age: Getting there ahead of time. *Psychology Today*, December, 1971, 52-54; 82-84.

Stimulation and discussion exercises designed for young persons to pre-experience themselves as old, including trying to work at a pace faster than their normal tempo, and being placed in an environment that makes one feel disregarded and ineffective.

8. Pops, O., Godwin, J., Tolone, W. L., & Walsh, R. H. Is there sex after 40? *Psychology Today*, June 1977, 54-56; 87.

Provides questions for students to answer anonymously about their parents' sexual activity and known statistics to compare. Usually students are much more conservative in their estimates than facts warrant. Discussion might follow concerning sexual stereotypes of the aged, and their effects on the aged themselves.

9. Wechsler, D. *Wechsler Adult Intelligence Scale*. New York: The Psychological Corporation, 1955.

Two exercises to provide comparative data for the concepts of fluid intelligence (that which is presumed to increase, plateau, and then decline) and crystallized intelligence (that which is presumed to grow throughout the developmental cycle). The digit symbol test taps fluid intelligence whereas the vocabulary test represents crystallized intelligence. To avoid contaminating the validity of this test we recommend you substitute your own symbols and vocabulary words for these exercises.

10. Albert, W. C., & Zarit, S. H. Income and health care of the aging. In S. H. Zarit (ed.). *Readings in aging and death: Contemporary perspectives.* New York: Harper and Row, 1977.
Schaubaum G. Winning the money game. *NTRA* [National Retired Teachers Association] *Journal*, November-December 1978, 14-16.

First article provides a plan to figure an estimated minimum monthly benefit for an older person living alone including food, housing, utilities, clothing, and medical costs. Students could first figure what they would need for a minimum, then compare this figure to minimum Social Security allotments to become conscious of difficulties of living on a minimum income. Second article plans your retirement income, taking inflation into account to see if you will have enough money to live on when you retire, and if not, how to make adjustments now before it is too late. Students could work on a hypothetical problem or use their own parents' income and savings.

11. Bellak, L., & Bellak, S. S. *The Senior Apperception Technique* (S.A.T.). Larchmont, NY: C. P. S, Inc, 1973. (Obtain from publisher, P.O. Box 83, zip 10538.)

Sixteen pictures providing stimuli which permit ascription of themes of loneliness, illness, and other vicissitudes or reflections of happy sentiments such as joy in grandchildren, or ambiguous stimuli which could be interpreted as either happy or as a reflection of difficulties. Students could be shown pictures and asked to discuss what kinds of themes might be elicited

12. Neale, R. E. Threats to my old age. (Can be obtained from the author, 606 W. 122nd St., New York, NY 10027)

A sometimes difficult exercise asking participants to decide personally what would be the major threats of loss of their body, self, and social environment, and major threats of restraint to their body, self, and social environment as they age.

13. Alpaugh, P., & Haney, M. *Counseling the older adult. A training manual.* Los Angeles: University of Southern California Press, 1978. (Ethel Percy Andrus Gerontology Center, University Park, Los Angeles, CA 90007.)

A workbook providing many informational and skill exercises related to communication skills necessary for knowing and helping the older adult.

14. Neugarten, B. I., Havighurst, R. J., & Tobin, S. S. The measurement of life satisfaction. *Gerontology*, 1961, *16*, 134-143.

Neugarten, B. I. Grow old along with me, the best is yet to be. *Psychology Today*, December 1971, 45-46; 48; 79, 81.

The first article provides a 20-item measure of life satisfaction designed as part of a larger research study of psychological and social factors involved in aging. The second article discusses four major personality types and their likelihood of feeling satisfied with life. Although the life satisfaction scale is primarily designed for those over 65, students could be asked to take the scale and see how to predict which style of aging they thought they would be most likely to adopt and to see if indeed those with the integrated style, for example, were the most likely to have had the highest scores on the life satisfaction scale.

15. Hartford, M. E. Self inventory for planning to maximize my potential in aging. In B. O'Brien. *Aging: Today's research and you. A lecture series.* Los Angeles: University of Southern California Press, 1978. (Obtain from Ethel Percy Andrus Gerontology Center, University Park, Los Angeles, CA 90007.)

Asks you to reflect upon things you enjoyed or considered important first as a child, then a youth, then in young adulthood (and middle years and older, if appropriate), then to look over the lists for common ideas, activities, ambitions, interests, and relationships. Finally, you are asked to examine how your current life fulfills these dreams and expectations and what you can do in the future to accomplish these goals.

16. Neale, R. E. *The art of dying.* New York: Harper and Row, 1971.

Book of reflective exercises and ideas designed to help you explore yourself and your attitudes toward dying.

Sociology of Aging

17. Hartman, A. Diagrammatic assessment of family relationships. *Social Casework*, October 1978, 465-476.

Acknowledging the importance of the family, this article discusses two methods to diagrammatically assess family relationships, and suggests how these techniques can be used as tools in the life review process found helpful in organizing and putting into perspective the past events in the life of an older person and in assessing ongoing family relationships. Students could then diagram their own family relationships, or that of a hypothetical family. Students could also discuss other tools for assisting in a life review process.

18. Coons, D. H., & Bykowski, J. *Brookside Manor: A gerontological simulation.* Ann Arbor, MI: Institute of Gerontology, 1975. (520 East Liberty, Ann Arbor, MI 48108.)

A simulation exercise illustrating the sometimes conflicting needs of staff and patients in long term care facilities for the aged.

19. Metzelaar, L. *A collection of cartoons: A way of experiencing practices in a treatment setting.* Ann Arbor, MI: Institute of Gerontology, 1975. (See address above.)

Thirty eight cartoons designed as discussion aids for staff of long term care facilities for the aged to explore negative attitudes toward the aged as portrayed in non-therapeutic practices by staff. These cartoons provide a good backdrop for students to discuss the potential for physical and psychological abuses in such facilities.

20. Hickey, T. H., Rakowski, W., Kafer, R., & Lachman, M. Aging opinion survey: Developmental data. Paper presented at the annual meeting of the Gerontological Society, Dallas, TX, November 1978. (Rudolph Kafer, S-110 Human Development, University Park, PA 16802.)

Separately measures attitudes toward aging of friends and known others, attitudes toward one's own aging, and attitudes toward aging people in general, using a Likert scale response to 45 statements.

21. Davies, L. Attitudes toward old age and aging as shown by humor. *Gerontologist*, 1977, *17*, 220-226.
Palmore, E. Attitudes toward aging as shown by humor. *Gerontologist*, 1971, *3*, 181-186.
Richman, J. The foolishness and wisdom of age: Attitudes toward the elderly as reflected in jokes. *Gerontologist*, 1977, *17*, 210-219.

Three sources of many jokes about aging and the aged. Class can discuss the intent and meaning of the joke, whether it is based on stereotypes and whether this type of humor should be discouraged. Students can also be asked to find and contribute their own examples.

22. *The myth and reality of aging in America.* Washington, DC: National Council on Aging, 1975. (1828 L St. NW, Suite 504, zip 20036.)

Provides data showing that a recent Harris poll found that most TV watchers feel that TV presents a fair picture of older people, but that TV commercials do not necessarily. Ask your class to find examples of TV shows and commercials or magazine material and to analyze what role the older person is playing in the example.

23. Cautela, J. R., & Wisocki, P. A. The use of imagery in the modification of attitudes toward the elderly: A preliminary report. *Journal of Psychology*, 1969, *73*, 193-199.

Participants are asked to imagine a specific scene read to them in which an elderly man comes to their aid in a crisis situation. Empirical data are provided to show that the use of this imagery task showed a positive increase in attitudes toward the aged.

24. LaMonica, E. L. The aging process: Positive attitudinal development through an existential approach. Paper presented at the American Psychological Association meetings, Toronto, 1978. (Obtain from the author, Department of Nursing Education, Teachers College, Columbia University, New York, NY.)

A personal learning experience conducted in a group setting in which participants are asked to imagine themselves to be the protaganist in a parable about living, growing, and dying. Participants are then asked to share their reactions and feelings.

25. Kogan, N. A sentence completion procedure for assessing attitudes toward old people. *Journal of Gerontology*, 1959, *14*, 355-363.

Provides a projective technique of eliciting attitudes toward old people compared to attitudes toward people in general. Twenty-five pairs of incomplete statements (one of each pair being distinguished only by the presence of the modifier "old") are given. Give half of your class the list without the modifier "old" and half the list with the modifier "old" and compare responses.

References

Butler, R. N. *Why survive? Being old in America.* New York: Harper and Row, 1975.

DeVries, H. A. Physiology of exercise and aging. In S. H. Zarit (ed.). *Readings in aging and death: Contemporary perspectives.* New York: Harper and Row, 1977.

Geiger, D. L. Note: How future professionals view the elderly: A comparative analysis of social work, law, and medical students perceptions. *Gerontologist*, 1978, *18*, 591-594.

Kulik, J. A., Brown, D. R., Vesterwig, R. E., & Wright, J. *Undergraduate education in psychology.* Washington, DC: American Psychological Association, 1973.

SECTION VIII
DEVELOPMENTAL – LIFE SPAN

Starting the Semester

Russell Walls developed a technique to "break the ice" and introduce some fundamental issues in the first classes of a developmental psychology course. The technique consisted of a group exercise on day one and a film on day two. In one exercise, students organized themselves into groups of five students each and learned each others names. In addition the instructor assigned each group to a developmental stage, and for that stage, students had to list as many developmental principles as possible. The showing of the film on the second day helped to illustrate the contributions and limitations of naturalistic observation and experimental investigation. Students' evaluation of the exercises used the categories: positive, ho-hum, or negative. The results revealed very few ho-hum responses.

Arnold LeUnes gave his students a list of 24 items on the first day of class; the students were to be prepared to discuss the items on the third day of class. The instructor designed the assignment to (a) get students into the library and (b) acquaint them with a range of developmental issues. Examples of questions were, "What book did John Watson write in 1928 pertaining to child development?" and "Who is the editor of the *American Journal of Mental Deficiency?*" The author pointed out that one byproduct of the assignment was to "plant seeds of awareness," and he noted that the technique was adaptable to many other courses.

Emphasizing Writing Assignments

Susan Beers developed a writing-across-the-curriculum portfolio that allowed students flexibility in their writing and encouraged their response to the available information in developmental psychology. To help structure students' work, the author identified clear guidelines for the portfolio and required that it be handed in twice during the semester as well as at the end of the semester. The article contained a description of the student portfolio performance. The author reported that she and the students found the portfolio assignment a welcome change from traditional writing assignments. The author also identified several suggested dangers.

Chris Boyatzis used Maya Angelou's (1969) *I Know Why the Caged Bird Sings* to illustrate many child development topics; development of self-concept and self-esteem, ego resilience, industry versus inferiority, effects of abuse, parenting styles, sibling and friendship relations, gender issues, cognitive development, puberty, and identity formation in adolescence. Students reacted very positively to the book and to a paper in which they analyzed Angelou's development using theory and research from the course.

Ellen Junn designed an exercise to examine several developmental issues. Students wrote, but did not necessarily send, semiautobiographical personal letters to their parents and a future or current child. Students' responses were overwhelmingly positive and suggested several beneficial outcomes. The author also described recommendations for instructors.

Kathleen Galotti asked students to choose different developmental psychologists and to read as much of that person's published work as was feasible. Students wrote papers describing the psychologists' works, focusing on the question, "How has this person's work developed?" The author described students' reactions and made suggestions for implementation.

Incorporating Field Experience

Kathleen McCluskey-Fawcett and Patricia Green had about half of their students participate in 50 hr of community service settings for children and families; the rest chose to write three papers. Although there were no significant differences between the two groups on overall course satisfaction, results also indicated that students found the community service to be a valuable experience for understanding course material and achieving other personal and educational goals. The authors identified techniques to incorporate such fieldwork into very large classes.

Samuel Saxon and Michael Holt found that about two-thirds of their students elected an option to work as volunteers for 2-4 hr per week in a community developmental facility. The option was in lieu of one-fourth class time and material. Students generally evaluated the volunteer experience favorably. The class also performed significantly higher on the final exam than a previous class that had not had the volunteer option.

Instigating Miscellaneous Techniques

Marsha Walton designed a project to help students (a) apply the theory and research they studied and (b) develop basic interviewing skills. Students interviewed individuals from different phases of the life cycle and wrote a paper discussing their subjects' lives in terms of major developmental psychology concepts. The article described how the instructor prepared the students for the project, how the instructor evaluated them, and some potential problems.

Anne Bryan reported on seven discussion topics for developmental psychology. The topics focused on problems that students might encounter in their lives and promoted application of course material. Students enrolled in a large developmental psychology class gave favorable ratings to the use of this technique.

Thomas Moeller used classroom debates to teach students about controversial issues and to help them improve their thinking and oral communications skills. The results of evaluation revealed that students thought the debates were a positive learning experience. The author discussed problems with the technique and proposed some solutions.

Steven Pulos designed an activity to counteract the view that there is an inevitable, major decline in physical performance with increasing age. The activity also illustrated how life-span changes in physical performance can be influenced by psychological factors. The instructor explored students' misconceptions through class discussion.

Marsha Walton developed a group exercise to help students understand how science can and cannot be used to resolve questions of practical importance in developmental psychology. Students with similar value preferences worked together on a project that required them to compile research and theory covered during the term. They compared their work to that of groups with different value preferences. The author concluded that the exercise seemed to promote a better appreciation of the contributions and limitations of empirical data and theory for answering practical questions.

Using Videotapes

Gregory Harper and John Silvestro developed and used videotaped programs on parents child rearing strategies. Each of the eight programs dealt with a different child or adolescent developmental issue and a discussion of such themes as parental discipline, sex role development, and parental views regarding their child's education. A guide accompanied each tape to assist students in summarizing and interpreting the tapes content. The results of student evaluation led the author to conclude that the students had gained increased empathy toward parents and placed a positive value on instructional use of the tapes.

Because of difficulty in obtaining live examples of a variety of developmental behaviors, Mark Grabe and Lila Tabor substituted structured videotaped experiences in a weekly discussion/laboratory meeting. The tapes illustrated both the affective and cognitive domains. Moreover assignments required students to evaluate and explain the principles of behavior depicted in the tapes. Students who viewed the tapes (versus those who did not) reported that the class was more interesting, attended laboratory sessions more regularly, and performed higher on exams. The technique also demonstrated the possibility of evaluating students explanations of samples of behavior.

1. STARTING THE SEMESTER

Taking the "Ho-Hum" Out of the First Two Days of Developmental Psychology

Russell E. Walls
Appalachian State University

With the approach of each new semester I always find myself trying to decide the best way to "break the ice" and get things off on a positive note. I have recently developed a method for my introductory developmental classes that seems to accomplish this aim, while at the same time introducing the students to some fundamental issues in developmental psychology. I have used the method with five recent developmental classes with very encouraging results. The response has been so positive that I want to share the procedures involved and present a sample of the students' reactions.

The First Day. I begin by giving a brief overview of the course requirements and then divide the students into six small groups with six to seven students per group. The first five minutes is allotted for a round-robin name game to facilitate personalization of each group. The name game begins by having someone in the circle state his first name. The person to his left repeats the name and then gives his own; the third person repeats the first two names and gives his name, and so on around the circle. The procedure is reversed at the end of the circle in order to give a second exposure to all the names. Generally, everyone seems highly motivated to remember the names, and the procedure is carried out in a spirited manner.

Following the name game I state the major purpose of the groups. Each group is assigned one of six developmental stages (prenatal, birth, infancy, early childhood, middle childhood, adolescence) and asked to see how many developmental principles or laws characteristic of that period they can reach through small group discussion. One member of each group volunteers to record their findings. Before the groups begin discussion, I give a few illustrations of what I mean by a developmental principle (i.e. "We get 23 chromosomes from the ovum and 23 from the sperm." or "The average age for one word sentences is about 12 months."). Once the task is clear to everyone the groups are turned loose for about fifteen minutes of brainstorming. I then call a halt to the discussion so that each group can share their list with the whole class. During this time I encourage the class to be on guard for any serious omissions or faulty principles. I also use this final twenty minute period to briefly introduce some interesting topics we will be studying during the semester. For example, I usually allude to Le Boyer's techniques in *Birth Without Violence* (1975) during the presentation of the principles from the birth group, and to Burton White's work (1973) on the origins of competence during the presentation by the infancy group. The rapid-fire pace of this period results in most of the students leaving with a high level of enthusiasm about the prospects of studying developmental psychology.

The Second Day. The second day combines a short presentation contrasting naturalistic observation and experimentation with showing the film, "The Child Watchers," which provides an excellent cross section of developmental research. There is a fairly natural transition between the first and second day since most of the principles reported by the small groups are based on naturalistic observation. I begin my presentation on a positive note by emphasizing they are already aware of many of the issues studied by developmental psychologists as evidenced by their lists of principles. I suggest, however, that their lists lack the kind of sophistication made possible by empirical studies, and that one major goal for the course is to provide a richness of detail to fill their existing framework. I then contrast naturalistic observation and experimentation by defining and giving examples of each and pointing out some advantages and disadvantages of each. I give special emphasis to Willems and Raush's argument (1969) that naturalistic observation is propadeutic to experimentation, suggesting that naturalistic observation provides leads to be followed up by experimentation. I further emphasize that without such experimentation it would be difficult or impossible to isolate causal variables. My final emphasis is on the use of age as a major independent variable in developmental psychology. I ask them to look for examples of such experiments while they view the film, "The Child Watchers." In fact, they are told that I will ask them to write out two examples of experiments which used age as the independent variable, once the film is over. During the course of the 25 minute film I alert them to each example of such experiments just prior to its presentation. After the film there is a brief period for discussion and questions. They then write out their choice of experiments, which concludes the class period.

Student Evaluation of the Method. At the beginning of the third period I ask the students to evaluate the first two days. They evaluate (a) the small group exercise, (b) the film, and (c) their overall opinion of the first two days. For each of the three questions they indicate their opinion by circling one of the following three words: positive, ho-hum, or negative. In each case they are also asked to briefly explain their choices.

Results suggest that the method outlined in this paper serves as an effective ice-breaker for students in developmental psychology. This claim is supported by the fact that 98% of the students indicated a positive response for their overall opinion of the two days. The small group exercise was rated "positive" by 82% and the film by 94%. The written explanations are also quite encouraging. A sample of the opinions follows:

Enjoyed it very much. It relaxed me and made me feel comfortable in a class with complete strangers.

I wish all learning classes could be like this.

I feel you brought the subject matter across in a different manner from all the other courses I've been to Instead of beginning the first few days with lectures and facts, you enticed us to think and become aware of the course. I thought your introduction was different and motivating.

A very definite total learning experience. I learned more in two days than I learn in some classes in an entire semester.

The first two days were great! I knew after the first class meeting I would enjoy the class.

So far I've really gotten into it! I'm taking 11 hours of psych and this class is definitely the most exciting part of that I like the repeated requests for student contributions to class.

I thought the first two days were very interesting and the time flew by. I was thinking about cutting the 3rd day, but I did not want to miss anything.

Although a substantial majority (82%) indicated a positive response to the small group exercise, it had the lowest relative evaluation of the three areas sampled. The most frequent explanation given by those few who felt "ho-hum" about the small group exercise was that they were tired of such procedures because of overuse in previous classes. Personal shyness was the next most frequent reason given. The explanation given by the one negative respondent was that a single person had led the group. Neither of the other ratings showed any negative responses.

My overall feeling, based especially on the students' written explanations for their responses, is that the factor most responsible for the success of the outlined method is the involvement of the students in direct participation. My personal enthusiasm was also emphasized as an important factor. A part of the effectiveness of the method may also be due to the Hawthorne Effect. Evidence for this is implicitly suggested by numerous students who emphasized that other classes typically begin with a factually oriented lecture. Whatever the reasons may be for the success of the technique I have described, my major hope in sharing it is that it might provide an incentive for change for anyone who is experiencing dissatisfaction with his introduction to developmental psychology. As one student succinctly concluded in explaining his overall positive, "It sure takes the 'ho-hum' out of the first few days of class!"

References

Leboyer, F. *Birth without violence.* New York: Knopf, 1975.

White B. L. & Watts, J. C. *Experience and environment: Major influences on the development of the young child* (Vol. 1). Englewood Cliffs, NJ: Prentice Hall, 1973.

Willems, E. P., & Raush, H. L. (Eds.). *Naturalistic viewpoints in psychological research.* New York: Holt, Rinehart & Winston, 1969.

The Developmental Psychology Library Search: Can a Nonsense Assignment Make Sense?

Arnold D. LeUnes
Texas A & M University

It is obvious that the creation of a positive learning environment is essential in getting one's point across in any subject matter area. Further, getting the attention of the subjects to be taught is conducive to effective learning. In an attempt to accomplish both of these goals, a library assignment was created for a junior-level course in developmental psychology. The students were handed a list of 24 questions on the first day of class to be completed and discussed on the third day. The assignment was designed to: (a) get the students into the library, and (b) acquaint them with the subjective reflections and objective data that make up the rather huge area of our discipline known as developmental psychology. In the process, it was hoped that the assignment would arouse some interest on the part of the students in selected aspects of the area, would alert them to topics to be covered during the term, and would provide a basis for understanding of the overlap and interrelationships within the area.

Initial student reaction was subdued but polite humor. "You've got to be kidding" type responses were occasionally heard and often sensed. Some feeling that there might be some method to the professor's madness was equally sensed. In any case, the 70 students left with the feeling that they would give it the old college try.

If there is in fact some sense to the assignment, I believed that it could serve as an attention-getter in my class in developmental psychology. It could also be adapted to fit a variety of topic areas within psychology.

A sample of the 24 questions/statements and a brief rationale for them are as follows:

1. *Name eight educational/psychological journals that deal with studies on development of children.* Though the list is somewhat endless and the rationale reasonably self-evident, it was maintained that little student exposure to these materials had been required in earlier courses.

2. *Name four journals that deal exclusively with mental retardation.* Familiarity with journals in retardation was deemed useful for several reasons. One, of course, is the prevalence of retardation. Second, the class make-up (primarily Psychology, Education, Pre-Medicine, and Physical Therapy majors) was such that the topic was judged to be of considerable interest.

3. *What book did John Watson write in 1928 pertaining to child development?* This was an opportunity to discuss one of the most influential historical figures in psychology. Further, it created an opening for a discussion of his not-so-popular 1928 dissertation on child rearing.

4. *Name the presidents of the United States who were first-born children.* This one served as a means for introducing birth-order effects into the developmental menu.

5. *How would Dr. Spock handle the problem of the toddler who won't stay in the crib?* Some mention of the Spock influence on child-rearing practices is warranted, and this provides an introduction to his ideas.

6. *Who is the editor of the American Journal of Mental Deficiency?* This was just another device for creating an awareness of the literature on mental retardation. It could well be the first time that many have ever taken the time to read about such things as editorial policy and other matters pertinent to the publication of a professional journal.

7. *Reference: Archives of General Psychiatry, 1972, 27, 711. What topic is discussed?* This is an advertisement for a leading anti-anxiety drug. It serves as an introduction to the use of prescription drugs with young people, particularly but not exclusively the hyperactive child.

8. *What famous developmental psychologist is listed on page 616 of the Manhattan phone book, 1972-73?* This was an attempt to see if the name of Haim Ginott was easily recognized. The opportunity to elaborate on his ideas about children was most welcomed.

9. *Name two fictional books on childhood schizophrenia and/or childhood autism.* This was designed to alert the students to the topic of behavioral disorders of children.

10. *How many children did Sigmund Freud have? How tall was he?* An awareness of Freud as a person was the intent of these questions. They also led to lengthy discussion of his contributions to our

understanding of behavior, with particular emphasis on childhood concerns.

11. *Who is Gloria Strauss?* This was a fun question in that the answer was as near as the students' elbows, for Strauss was one of the authors of the course text (Liebert, Poulos, and Strauss, 1974).

It is obvious that there is substantial topical overlap among the various questions. This is intentional and serves to highlight the interrelationships that exist in developmental psychology.

Though no objective data were gathered with respect to the success of the assignment, it seemed to be an educationally profitable venture. It may be that a fair assessment of its success would be hard to make in that its purpose was to plant seeds of awareness in the minds of unsophisticated subjects (with regard to expertise in developmental psychology, at least). As any teacher can testify, whether or not one is planting ideas in the minds of his students is an argumentative and elusive question.

Finally, there is nothing magic about the sample questions presented here. They could be easily altered to fit other subject matter areas within psychology. This exercise is intended to serve only as a general model for the development of alternative assignments for classroom use. Its apparent success in the present case leads me to believe that it is applicable in a broader context.

Reference

Liebert, R. Poulos, R., & Strauss, G. *Developmental psychology.* Englewood Cliffs, NJ: Prentice Hall, 1974.

2. EMPHASIZING WRITING ASSIGNMENTS

Use of a Portfolio Writing Assignment in a Course on Developmental Psychology

Susan E. Beers
Sweet Briar College

The writing-across-the-curriculum movement has made college teachers aware of their shared responsibility to help students develop writing skills, and thus has inspired many of us to include writing in the courses we teach. The challenge is to develop ways to integrate writing assignments into a course in such a way that they enrich course content and help students with writing, but do not place an unreasonable workload on the teacher or students.

I found myself faced with this challenge anew in planning the writing assignments for my course in life span develop mental psychology for the spring of 1984. This course enrolled 26 students, primarily sophomores and juniors. I wanted students to write often, and to have the opportunity to have their writing commented on. I wanted them to do some reading from original sources. But my typical assignments, a term paper or three short papers on topics that I would suggest, seemed inappropriate, given my goals for this course. I wanted to ensure that students had the opportunity to respond to each phase of the life span; I did not want to construct an assignment that would force some to become "childhood experts" and some "adolescence experts," for example. I also wanted students to have the opportunity to take an eclectic approach: I did not necessarily want some to become "cognitive developmental experts" and others "social developmental experts." In short, I wanted an assignment that would allow students a good deal of freedom and flexibility in their writing, and one that would encourage them to respond to the wealth of information in developmental psychology with an independent investment that would go beyond typical assignments given by a teacher.

NATURE OF THE PORTFOLIO

After a good deal of reflection, I decided to construct "the portfolio assignment." The instructions to the students, as written in the course outline, were as follows:

You will be required to complete 10-15 (typewritten) pages of writing for this course. The specific writing assignments that you choose to undertake will vary from person to person. In class we will work on autobiographical essays, and outside of class we will have exercises, observations, and possibly interviews to conduct. Any of these might be written up in 2 or 3 pages for the portfolio. The end of each chapter of your text includes a list of books to read, and the library subscribes to *Child Development* and the *Journal of Experimental Child Psychology*. In your portfolio I will expect to see a summary of at least one piece of outside reading, and a discussion of its relevance. You might also consider writing short stories or poems related to what we are learning in class.

Portfolios will be turned in twice during the course of the semester, and at the end of the semester. Each time I will expect around 5 pages of "completed" work, and whatever drafts you would like me to comment on. For example, when you first turn in your portfolio it might contain (a) a 3-page portion of your autobiography and discussion of text material that is relevant to your experience (typed); (b) a 2-page write-up of a class exercise and its relevance to course material (typed); (c) a draft of a short story related to infancy; and (d) some notes on a journal article that you read. I would comment on, and grade (a) and (b), and comment on (c) and (d). The next time portfolios are due you might include (c) or (d) rewritten and typed for grading, and other material that you have been working on.

The portfolio comprised 40% of a student's course grade; exams comprised 60% of the grade.

I had several concerns in making such an open-ended assignment. I feared that some students would not be able to structure their writing independently, that they would not write enough, or that they would write inappropriate (e.g., purely personal) essays. I was also concerned about grading fairly and consistently, given the variety of material I anticipated receiving.

I instituted two strategies to guard against the realization of these fears. I planned class meetings to include some activities that could be written up as portfolio essays, and mentioned the portfolios to students when these exercises occurred. The second strategy was the way that I responded to the portfolios. I graded each portfolio as a whole each of the three times it was turned in. As well as commenting briefly on each essay, I wrote a general letter to each student describing the strengths and weaknesses of her portfolio. There, I commented on the quantity as well as the quality of the student's work. Students who were writing too little were encouraged to write more, and the occasional student who wrote a purely personal essay was encouraged to attempt theoretical analyses. Grading and responding to the portfolio as a whole also had the decided advantage of allowing me to point out the student's strongest essay, and compare it with weaker ones. Thus, I was almost always able to say something positive while indicating areas that needed improvement.

Grading itself proved to be less of a worry than I had expected. I found that I responded to all essays essentially with the same criteria. First, I looked for a complete account of the topic the student was writing about, be it a personal experience, class exercise, or report of outside reading. Then I looked for an interpretation or response to that description. It seemed to me that my comments by and large enabled students to grasp the "rules of this game," to understand the need to write at a conceptual and theoretical level. Very personal essays and creative writing were counted toward the page requirement, but were not graded.

STUDENT PORTFOLIO PERFORMANCE

What types of materials did I find myself reading, and how were they distributed throughout the semester? Of course, the writing each student accomplished at each point in the semester varied greatly. The shortest portfolio that was turned in at any one time was 1 page long; the longest was 8 pages. The average number of pages per student, how ever, remained fairly constant, averaging 4.04, 4.75, and 4.88 pages each time the portfolios were turned in. Most students were able to monitor the amount of work successfully.

The papers were brief, averaging 1.71, 2.04, and 1.95 pages at each of the three times that the portfolios were turned in. Although a few students did write several essays on a single topic, this was rare. Perhaps my instructions to the students discouraged them from developing sustained arguments or exploring a single topic in depth.

The types of writing included in the portfolios may be described in six categories: summaries of reading (journal articles or books), general essays based on course material but not referring directly to outside reading, essays based on specific class exercises, autobiographical essays (including those about relatives and friends), creative writing, and rough drafts. The proportion of students who included each of these types of writing each time the portfolios were turned in is presented in Table 1.
The two most frequent types of writing were summaries of journal articles or books, and autobiographical essays. I was impressed that most

students went beyond the minimum requirement of reporting one piece of "outside" reading, as it had been my experience that students were reluctant to read original sources. The proportion of students including autobiographical essays probably varied according to the topics that were covered before the portfolios were turned in each time: infancy for the first period, childhood for the second, and adolescence and adulthood for the third. The largest number of rough drafts were turned in the first time portfolios were due. Whereas this probably reflected students' insecurities about just what was appropriate, it also gave me an impression of students' writing and thinking early in the semester.

Table 1. Proportion of Students Including Six Categories of Writing in Their Portfolios

Type	Report Number		
	1	2	3
Summary of reading	.46	.50	.69
General essay	.19	.23	.19
Class exercise	.46	.15	.35
Autobiographical	.58	.65	.35
Creative writing	.08	.08	.23
Rough draft	.23	.08	.00

EVALUATION

At the end of the semester students completed a questionnaire concerning the portfolio assignment. Due to the end of the semester "crunch," only 17 of the 26 students returned the questionnaire, and thus one must interpret the results with caution. Students responded to three questions on a 5-point scale: Please evaluate the overall utility of the portfolio assignment for this course (1 = *not at all useful*, 5 = *very useful*); Did you feel you were given enough information concerning the types of writing that might be included in the portfolio? (1 = *definitely no*, 5 = *definitely yes*); Did you feel the grading standards for the portfolio were clear? (same scale). They were also asked to list the three major strengths and weaknesses of the portfolio assignment.

The majority of the students found the assignment to be quite useful, 93% rating it a 4 or 5 (*M* = 4.43). Students would have liked more clarity, however, in terms of the content and grading standards of the portfolio; 28% rated the clarity of the assignment itself as average or below (*M* = 4.09), and 46% rated it average or below in terms of clarity of grading standards (*M* = 3.59).

Given the perceived lack of clarity, it is surprising that so many of the students found the assignment useful. When students listed weaknesses of the assignment, clarity and grading were often mentioned. Three major strengths were mentioned, however, that apparently outweighed these disadvantages. Students mentioned that they appreciated the freedom to write about topics they chose themselves; several mentioned that they did not feel the "pressure" one does when a term paper is assigned. Many mentioned that they enjoyed doing the outside reading, and "picking their own articles." And several mentioned that they enjoyed having the opportunity to relate what they were learning to their own experiences. Entwistle and Ramsden (1982) have found that freedom, intrinsic motivation, and perceived self-relevance are related to a "deep approach" to studying course content.

In all, both the students and I found portfolio writing to be a nice change from the writing assignments one typically encounters. It deepened and broadened students' involvement in course material. Although one cannot be sure if writing itself improved, I suspect that doing a lot of writing and receiving comments on it in a relatively non threatening context does set the stage for improvement. The portfolio assignment was a good deal of work for the teacher, but no more so than having students engage in other types of writing. And the variety of the work made it enjoyable to read and respond to.

Although I am pleased with the outcome of this assignment, I will make some changes when I use it again. Of course, I will attempt to make the assignment itself and my grading standards clearer to students; this should not be difficult as I myself am more confident about the assignment than I was at its inception. I will also make it clear that longer, sustained pieces of work are appropriate for the portfolio. The portfolio assignment seems uniquely appropriate for life span developmental psychology, and might not be as appropriate for other courses, or courses taught from a different approach than my own. But extensive teacher commentary on writing, and assignments that allow for freedom, flexibility, and personal integration of course material might be incorporated in any course that includes writing.

Reference

Entwistle, N. J., & Ramsden, P. (1982). *Understanding student learning.* New York: Nichols.

Notes

1. This work was supported in part by a Sweet Briar College Faculty Grant.
2. The author thanks the students in Psychology 104, Spring, 1984 for their assistance and support.

Let the Caged Bird Sing: Using Literature to Teach Developmental Psychology

Chris J. Boyatzis
California State University-Fullerton

Reading lists of developmental psychology courses are replete with scientific theory and research. Narrative material from literature can supplement this theory and research by elucidating psychological concepts with real-life examples, while deepening students' appreciation for the complexity and diversity of development. In several courses I have used Maya Angelou's (1969) I Know Why the Caged Bird Sings, which is highly effective at illustrating many child development topics: development of self-concept and self-esteem, ego resilience, industry versus inferiority, effects of abuse, parenting styles, sibling and friendship relations, gender issues, cognitive development, puberty, and identity formation in adolescence. Students react very positively to the book and to a paper in which they analyze Angelou's development using theory and research from the course.

The benefit of using narrative in literature to teach psychological concepts has received empirical confirmation (e.g., Fernald, 1987; Gorman, 1984; Levine, 1983; Ramirez, 1991; Williams & Kolupke, 1986). For several years, I have used literature in my child development courses to help students elucidate the broader psychological issues treated in theory and research. Although literature alone is not adequate, it complements psychology and is compatible with theory and research. Literature's value is precisely that it uses personal, subjective experiences. Stories vivify theories, which students often find too abstract, as well as "humanize the stark quantitative findings of psychological research" (Grant, 1987, p. 86). Literature is also important because it can depict diversity in development, especially cultural diversity. It can help students appreciate broad, complex influences (e.g., culture, social class, geography, and historical era) as well as universal or culturally specific factors.

I have used Angelou's (1969) remarkable childhood autobiography, *I Know Why the Caged Bird Sings*, in my sophomore- and junior-level developmental psychology classes to illustrate topics we study via scientific research and theory. Year after year, students claim that this book is one of the most valuable educational and personal experiences in the course. The book recounts Angelou's childhood from the preschool through adolescent years. The first half of the book spans her early and middle childhood and offers examples of many topics: a sense of industry versus inferiority, the development of self-concept and self-esteem, the impact of abuse, the growth of logic and concrete operational thought, child-rearing styles and family relations, gender issues, friendship and the "society of children," and the effects of different environments on development. The second half of the book is a compelling history of the challenges of puberty and identity formation in adolescence; it illustrates family issues, functions of the peer group, emergence of formal operational thought, formation of a sexual identity, exploration of vocational interests, and, ultimately, parenthood.

Students write a paper following instructions to "discuss how Angelou's childhood experiences exemplify two or three aspects or topics of development. Use course materials (text, supplementary readings, class notes, films, handouts) to build a framework of theory and research to analyze Angelou's development." In short, students make connections between the general and the particular: They use the course to explain Angelou's development and use Angelou's experiences to illustrate the course. Students cite course materials in their paper and use quotes and passages from Angelou's book to illustrate their ideas.

Many students focus on the topics of self-esteem and resilience. Angelou's book is, among other things, a case study of resilience (Werner, 1984). In fact, one student said the book "corresponded so well to work on resiliency, it seemed as if Angelou read the research before writing her story." Other popular topics students choose are friendship and sibling relations, parent-child relations, gender issues, and cultural and ethnic influences on development. Six to eight pages is an appropriate length for the assignment.

I have used the Angelou book as a final assignment and also as an integrated one throughout the course. Although both formats have been successful, the course-ending assignment has been most effective at synthesizing course material. One student wrote, "the book and paper was a marvelous way to bring together concepts we discussed all semester," and another said it was "a powerful culmination of the course." Toward the end of the semester, students have several weeks to read the book, select materials to use in their analyses, and write their papers. After students finish their papers, we spend one or two classes discussing the book and their analyses.

I have used this assignment in classes as small as 12 and as large as 41 students. The paper is usually worth 25% of the student's grade. Students' papers tend to differ primarily in their thoroughness and accuracy in using course materials to analyze Angelou's development. However, the overall quality of most papers is impressive; the papers are typically more insightful than students' other papers or essay exams perhaps because, as many students claim, the book makes the course topics seem "real." Also encouraging is the fact that, despite having read nearly 200 of these Angelou papers, I frequently encounter truly original connections between Angelou's childhood and course materials.

The assignment develops students' ability to integrate course materials and helps them understand the complex issues of race, gender, and social class in development. One student wrote that the assignment helped her "integrate culture, resiliency, and development in a child 4 years old to junior high." Many others have said the assignment "makes the abstract concrete," and one wrote that it allowed her to "bounce back and forth between the personal and scientific." The Angelou assignment enhances understanding of development, as the high ratings (*M* = 4.4 of 5) in Table 1 demonstrate.

Table 1. Student Responses to the Statement "Rate the Angelou book and assignment in terms of its educational value to you."

	Rating					
	Excellent	Very Good	Good	Fair	Poor	Total
Number	94	29	11	2	1	137
Percentage	69	21	8	1	1	100

Note. The sample consists of students enrolled in six courses.

Angelou's childhood account is such a powerful psychological journey for the reader than I am confident students remember much about development because of this book. The potency of the assignment is captured in students' comments. One wrote "I will remember the book and assignment for a very long time," and another said the assignment was "the most rewarding and beneficial I've had in college."

In *The Call of Stories*, Robert Coles (1989) presented an elegant argument for the use of narrative in teaching, especially in the sciences, because as "theorists we lose sight of human particularity" (p. 21). Vitz (1990) asserted that stories are a popular means of communication in all cultures; educators should attend to this "narrative need . . . [and] work with human nature rather than against it" (pp. 716-717). I concur. In addition to scientific psychology, teachers might offer students stories that will help them understand development. These stories, like Angelou's, also should possess the personal and spiritual resonance to bring students to worlds beyond their own.

References

Angelou, M. (1969) *I know why the caged bird sings.* New York: Bantam.

Coles, R. (1989). *The call of stones: Teaching and the moral Imagination.* Boston: Houghton Mifflin.

Fernald, L. D. (1987). Of windmills and rope dancing: The instructional value of narrative structures. *Teaching of Psychology, 14,* 214-216.

Gorman, M. E. (1984). Using the *Eden Express* to teach introductory psychology. *Teaching of Psychology, 11 ,* 39-40.

Grant, L. (1987). Psychology and literature: A survey of courses. *Teaching of Psychology, 14,* 86-88.

Levine, R. V. (1983). An interdisciplinary course studying psychological issues through literature. *Teaching of Psychology, 10,* 214-216.

Ramirez, J. V. (1991, November). *Using ethnic literature to teach about children's development.* Paper presented at the annual meeting of the American Educational Research Association, San Jose.

Vitz, P. (1990). The use of stories in moral development. *American Psychologist, 45,* 709-720.

Werner, E. E. (1984, November). Resilient children. *Young Children,* pp. 68-72.

Williams, K. G., & Kolupke, J. (1986). Psychology and literature: An interdisciplinary approach to the liberal curriculum. *Teaching of Psychology, 13,* 59-61.

Notes

1. Portions of this article were presented at the 4th annual conference on the Teaching of Psychology, Springfield, MA, March 1989.
2. I thank former colleagues at Wheelock College for introducing me to Angelou's book and my students for their rich insights about Angelou's development. I also thank Ruth L. Ault, anonymous reviewers, and Robin Jarrell for their comments on an earlier version.

"Dear Mom and Dad": Using Personal Letters to Enhance Students' Understanding of Developmental Issues

Ellen N. Junn
California State University, San Bernardino

An exercise designed to address a number of developmental issues by requiring students to write semiautobiographical personal letters is described. Student responses were overwhelmingly positive and suggest a number of beneficial outcomes. Recommendations for instructors are provided.

When teaching courses on human development, I am invariably struck by the implicit, sometimes faulty, assumptions and analyses that students often rely on when confronted with developmental issues. First, the typical college student possesses only vague knowledge about children and their development. Second, students' perceptions of themselves as potential parents are often characterized by idealism and a false sense of having complete control over a child's developmental progress. At some levels, this sense of optimism is probably important and healthy for anyone caring for children, but it does not account for the many factors that interact in complex ways to affect development (Belsky, Lerner, & Spanier, 1980). Third, in courses dealing with human development, students often use their personal experiences as the sole criterion for evaluating research. For instance, when presented with a controversial topic, such as moral development, students often engage in heated debate over research findings, basing their arguments on nothing more than their own anecdotal experiences.

In an effort to address these issues, I designed a written exercise involving the writing of two semiautobiographical personal letters. A letter-writing assignment was chosen because it seemed particularly amenable to addressing a variety of developmental issues, and it is an innovative approach that has been used successfully by several researchers for purposes such as enhancing students' critical reading skills (Chamberlain & Burrough, 1985; Keller, 1982). This article describes the assignment, students' reactions to it, and the benefits of this technique.

The Assignment

Seventeen students enrolled in an upper division psychology course on parenting and family relations were given a detailed handout explaining the assignment. Students were told that the purpose of the assignment was to provide them with an opportunity to discuss various issues in developmental psychology from a personal, concrete perspective. Students were also told to draw from or incorporate relevant research in this assignment. Students were required to write two personal letters: (a) one to a future or actual child (son, daughter, or both) on the occasion of the child's 18th birthday and (b) one to both of the students' parents. In the handout, the instructor guaranteed confidentiality and assured students that the letters were not designed to demand disclosures of private or emotional family events. Instead, students were told to address a number of specific questions in each letter to the degree they felt most comfortable.

In the first letter to their child, students were told to cover the following areas: (a) When or why did you decide to have this child? (b) What specific qualities do you think are most important for a mother/father to have, and why? (c) What qualities do you personally possess that may help make you a successful parent? What qualities do you possess that may interfere with your ability to be a good parent? (d) Describe the qualities you hope your child will possess, and why. In doing so, address each of the following developmental areas and mention something specific you could do as a parent to foster growth in these areas: discipline, intellectual development, social and emotional development, sex-role development, moral development, and personality development. For this section, students were encouraged to use their knowledge of relevant research and theory in formulating concrete and reasonable ways of translating research findings into productive parenting practices with children. (e) Mention what you wish for your child in the future, and pass on any words of wisdom you might have acquired.

In the letter addressed to both of their parents, students were to cover four related areas: (a) Describe your general feelings about your present life and values and try to assess how much impact your parents had on you. (b) Describe three of the most important strengths of your mother and your father. Do you share these qualities? (c) Everyone has certain shortcomings; briefly describe a weakness or something that you would like to have changed in your parents. Do you share any of these qualities? (d) Given the following areas (discipline, intellectual development, social and emotional development, moral development, sex-role development, and personality development), choose one or two areas in which your mother and your father had the most influence on you, and explain how or why. (e) Thank your mother and father for something special.

Finally, in an optional third letter, students were told that they could send the instructions for the first letter (letter to your child) to their own mother or father and have them write the letter with the student in mind. In turn, students and parents could then exchange letters with one another.

Student Feedback

At the end of the course, 16 of the 17 students completed an anonymous questionnaire concerning their reactions to the assignment. Ratings for three questions were made on a 7-point scale, ranging from *strongly disagree* (1) to *strongly agree* (7). Student response to the assignment was very positive. The mean rating students gave for the value of the assignment in integrating course material with personal experience was 6.4 (*SD* = .73). Students also agreed that the assignment was relevant to the course (*M* = 6.1, SD = 1.15). Moreover, when asked how they felt about the exercise in general, almost all of the students (88%) felt either moderately or very positive about the assignment (*M* = 6.4, *SD* = .89); only two students (12%) felt neutral about the assignment. In fact, when polled on whether the assignment promoted learning, every student responded in the affirmative.

Several themes emerged from students' open-ended comments. Students were enthusiastic about the exercise, and some wrote the following statements: "it was a fantastic exercise, " "loved everything about it, " "invaluable," "it was like a rock thrown into still water—ripple effect—really made me think," and "it was very interesting, fun, and insightful. " Students also agreed that they profited from this exercise, and one wrote that the assignment "has made it easier to relate to the issues in class. " All students wrote that the exercise gave them valuable insights into their feelings about a whole range of issues—everything from simply sorting out feelings associated with the possibility of becoming a parent someday, to being flooded with special childhood memories, to renewing often unexpressed feelings of deep warmth and appreciation for their parents or children, and to gaining new insights into themselves and their parents. However, not all of the emotions associated with doing the exercise were positive. Two students wrote that the assignment was "difficult" or "stressful" because suppressed, sometimes hurtful childhood memories surfaced. These same students also stated that the exercise was nonetheless "very beneficial" and helped them sort out and express their feelings to their parents in a direct and constructive way. When asked if they intended to deliver the letter to their adult child someday, 75% of the students responded "yes," and the remaining 25% were unsure. The students who planned to give the letters to their children hoped that the letter would promote "insights" and "open closer communication" channels between parent and child. The responses for delivering their parent letters were more mixed: 63% responded "yes," 25% said "no," and 12% were unsure. The reason for not sending the letter to their parents was that these students were either "embarrassed" or "didn't want to hurt them. " On the other hand, the primary reason cited for sending the letter to their parents was summed up by one student who stated, "I wanted to affirm [my parents] for their efforts and impact on my life. " One student intended to try the optional third letter at a later date. Another student even intended to get her fiance to complete the assignment as well.

Finally, students were told that although the exercise was of a more personal nature, their performance on the assignment would be evaluated objectively in terms of how completely they addressed all parts of the letters and, in particular, how well they demonstrated an ability to integrate and incorporate developmental research and theory with their personal experiences. Because this assignment was the smaller of two writing assignments for the course and because I was not certain of how students would respond to the assignment, I began by allocating this exercise a relatively small number of points (25 out of total of 325 points for the entire course). Student performance was evaluated by scoring each of the five parts of both letters as deserving anywhere from 0 to 6 points, depending on the specific area being addressed. Thus, in the first letter addressed to the students' child, the maximum number of points assigned for sections (a) through (e) were 1, 2, 2, 6, 1 points, respectively, with a maximum of 12 points for this first letter. The maximum number of points allocated for sections (a) through (e) in the second letter addressed to students' parents were 1, 4, 2, 3, 1, respectively, for a maximum of 11 points. An additional 2 points were allotted for overall clarity, writing style, and neatness. Students who completely addressed all areas of the letters and who clearly integrated research data and theory to support their conclusions were awarded the maximum number of points. The scores for the class ranged from 25 to 9, with a class average of 19.6 ($SD = 4.9$).

Discussion

This exercise achieved at least three objectives cited at the beginning of the article. First, in order to perform well on this assignment, students had to possess and display knowledge about children and their development.

Second, in completing the exercise, students became acutely aware of their implicit, often very unrealistic notions and attitudes regarding child development and parenting issues. For example, many students wrote the following comments: "It was astounding! It really made me reflect on my values and get a realistic view of parenting." "It made me think about what I expect of my children and it made me realize and reevaluate my expectations. I learned that my expectations for my children have to grow with them." "I learned that I had expectations for my future child that I never realized before." Upon returning the papers to students, I opened the discussion with the observation that although students expressed a general awareness that their expectations were often implicit and unrealistic, it was nonetheless highly instructive to contrast the tone of their letters to their child with the tone of the letters to their parents. Hence, the letters students addressed to their child were overwhelmingly positive, joyous, and replete with good intentions, whereas the letters to their parents were much more down-to earth, concrete, and realistic in tone. Part of the reason for this difference is the fact that in writing to a future child, students often relied on their wishes and hopes for an "ideal" child as a future parent; whereas in writing to an actual parent, students resorted to writing about their concrete childhood experiences in a matter-of-fact, sometimes brutally honest manner without acknowledging the possibility that their parents once nursed or still possess similar idealistic expectations and hopes for them as children. This led to a fruitful discussion of the impact of expectations on development and the pitfalls of making attributions based on information that is related to the self versus related to another individual (e.g., Jones & Nisbett, 1972; Nisbett & Ross, 1980). This awareness or egotism (e.g., Synder, Stephan, & Rosenfield, 1976) was cited by several students who wrote, "It let me come to terms with my children and what I want for them in their lives. I want them to know that I wasn't perfect and that I don't expect perfection from them." Another student expressed similar sentiments by writing, "It made you think of your past and future. Writing to my future child made me really think about how I was as a son. It also made me think about what to do if my children turn out like me."

Third, and perhaps most important, this exercise was designed to promote students' ability to understand, apply, and integrate current research and theory with their own lives in a productive and potentially useful way. Judging from the quality of the class discussions and the written comments of students, this assignment appears to have had some real impact in this area. For instance, one student wrote, "Most of us are always busy with our lives and trying to be a good mom or dad. But we don't sit down and think to learn about the research and theory out there that could be beneficial to us. " Another student wrote, "This [assignment] really made me evaluate *how* to instill those qualities in my own child someday by becoming more aware of research. " Finally, another student wrote, "By understanding the research, I learned that parenthood [and development] are very complex issues. " All of these statements indicate that students are consciously and actively attempting to relate developmental research and theory to understand and perhaps even guide their own everyday experiences.

A similar letter-writing technique was discussed by Keller (1982) and Chamberlain and Burrough (1985). However, their methods were designed to enhance students' critical reading skills, and students were asked to critique a journal article in the form of a letter to a parent or a close friend. Thus, their students' letters were impersonal and not autobiographical. Other instructors have personalized assignments by having students keep journals or diaries (Baldwin, 1977; Hart, 1972; Hettich, 1976, 1980; Miller, 1979; Nin, 1969-1981; Ranier, 1978) or by presenting students with fictional or "live" case studies (Beckman, 1972; Gilliland, 1982; Graham & Cline, 1980; Hoover, 1980; McManus, 1986). However, all of these methods have various problems: Student journals tend to be difficult and time-consuming for instructors to monitor and evaluate; case studies are often limited in reflecting the complexities of real-life situations; and "live" case studies require instructors and students to arrange actual meetings with a "live" subject (see Graham & Cline, 1980, Hettich, 1980, McManus, 1986, for more on these points). My letter-writing technique is simple, straightforward, and avoids many of the pitfalls of the just mentioned methods, yet it permits students to reap many of the rewards.

For example, in my letter-writing technique and others like it students are able to integrate abstract course concepts with their everyday lives (see Graham & Cline, 1980; Keller, 1982; Lott, 1978, for similar results), and this may stimulate critical thinking skills (Chamberlain & Burrough, 1985; Graham & Cline, 1980; Hettich, 1976, 1980; Keller, 1982). As other investigators have noted, one reason techniques such as these may be successful is that students enjoy the opportunity to express their own views and relate what they are learning to their own experiences (Beers, 1985; McKeachie, Lin, Moffett, & Daugherty, 1978; Polyson, 1985). In addition, techniques that rely on concrete or personal information increase student interest and motivation and may enhance retention of course information (Beckman, 1972; Beers, 1985; Hart, 1972; Kulik, Brown, Vestewig, & Wright, 1973; McManus, 1986). Furthermore, participants engaged in exercises that draw on personal experience also report greater self-understanding and personal growth (Baldwin, 1977; Jung, 1972; McManus, 1986; Miller, 1979; Milner, 1967; Nin, 1969-1981; Rogers, 1969). Other benefits include reducing plagiarism (Keller, 1982) and improving communication and writing skills (Beers, 1985; Blevins-Knabe, 1987; Britton, Burgess, Martin, McLeod, & Rosen, 1975; Staton, 1980).

Clearly, this personal letter-writing technique suggests many beneficial outcomes for student learning and represents a simple, engaging, and worthwhile assignment in the eyes of students. Instructors who wish to use this technique might heed a number of suggestions. Provide a detailed handout outlining the assignment's purpose and requirements and discuss these in class. In more intensive personal techniques, others have noted the need for instructors to demonstrate high levels of flexibility, sensitivity, and respect, particularly for the student who may find writing about personal experiences difficult (Polyson, 1985; Vande Kemp, 1981) . Problems of this kind can probably be avoided if the instructor prepares well, remains flexible, and stresses that the assignment is meant to deepen understanding of developmental phenomena without being painful or intrusive. Evaluation of students' performance on this exercise is not difficult. Instructors could easily amend the exercise to incorporate more points. Instructors should also provide warm, meaningful, supportive, and sensitive feedback to students concerning their letters. An additional suggestion is to include comments on a separate page and avoid marking the original letter, because many students may wish to deliver their letters someday. Finally, this exercise can be a springboard for rich discussions involving a host of important topics, including the complexities of developmental interaction as well as other more specific empirical, theoretical, and methodological issues.

References

Baldwin, C. (1977) . *One to one: Self-understanding through journal writing.* New York: Evans.

Beckman, M. D. (1972). Evaluating the case method. *Educational Forum, 36,* 489-497.

Beers, S. E. (1985). Use of a portfolio writing assignment in a course on developmental psychology. *Teaching of Psychology, 12,* 94-96.

Belsky, J., Lerner, R. M., & Spanier, G. B. (1980) . *The child in the family.* Reading, MA: Addison-Wesley.

Blevins-Knabe, B. (1987). Writing to learn while learning to write. *Teaching of Psychology, 14,* 239-241.

Britton, J., Burgess, T., Martin, N., McLeod, A., & Rosen, N. (1975). *The development of writing abilities* (11-18). London: Macmillan.

Chamberlain, K., & Burrough, S. (1985). Techniques for teaching critical reading. *Teaching of Psychology, 12*, 213-215.

Gilliland, K. (1982) . Use of drama students as "clients" in teaching abnormal psychology. *Teaching of Psychology, 9*, 120- 121.

Graham, P. T., & Cline, P. C. (1980). The case method: A basic teaching approach. *Theory Into Practice, 19*, 112-116.

Hart, N. I. (1972). Using the personal journal in literature teaching. *Reading Improvement, 9*, 87-89.

Hettich, P. (1976). The journal: An autobiographical approach to learning. *Teaching of Psychology, 3*, 60-63.

Hettich, P. (1980). The journal revisited. *Teaching of Psychology, 7*, 105-106.

Hoover, K. A. (1980). Analyzing reality: The case method. In K. A. Hoover (Ed.), *College teaching today: A handbook for postsecondary instruction* (pp. 199-223). Boston: Allyn & Bacon.

Jones, E. E., & Nisbett, R. E. (1972). The actor and the observer: Divergent perceptions of the causes of behavior. In E. E. Jones, D. E. Kanouse, H. H. Kelley, R. E. Nisbett, S. Valins, & B. Weiner (Eds.), *Attribution: Perceiving the causes of behavior* (pp. 79-94). Morristown, NJ: General Learning Press.

Jung, J. (1972). Autobiographies of college students as a teaching and research tool in the study of personality development. *American Psychologist, 27*, 779-783.

Keller, R. A. (1982). Teaching from the journals. *Teaching Sociology, 9*, 407-409

Kulik, J. A., Brown, D. R., Vestewig, R. E., & Wright, J. (1973). *Undergraduate education in psychology.* Washington, DC: American Psychological Association.

Lott, J . (1978) . Improving reading in the social studies: Classroom journals. *Social Education, 42*(1), 15-17.

McKeachie, W. J., Lin, Y-G., Moffett, M. M., & Daugherty, M. (1978). Effective teaching: Facilitative vs. directive style. *Teaching of Psychology, 5*, 193-194.

McManus, J. L. (1986). "Live" case study/journal recording adolescent psychology. *Teaching of Psychology, 13*, 70-74.

Miller, S. U. (1979). Keeping a psychological journal. *Gifted Child Quarterly, 23*, 168-175.

Milner, M. (1967). *On not being able to paint.* New York: International Universities Press.

Nin, A. (1969-1981). *The diary* (Vols. I-VII). New York: Harcourt Brace Jovanovich.

Nisbett, R. E., & Ross, L. (1980). *Human inference: Strategies and shortcomings of social judgment.* Engelwood Cliffs, NJ: PrenticeHall.

Polyson, J. (1985). Students' peak experiences: A written exercise. *Teaching of Psychology, 12*, 211-213.

Ranier, T. (1978). *The new diary.* Los Angeles: Tarcher.

Rogers, C. R. (1969). *Freedom to learn.* Columbus, OH: Merrill.

Snyder, M. L., Stephan, W. G., & Rosenfield, D. (1976). Egotism and attribution. *Journal of Personality and Social Psychology, 35*, 656-666.

Staton, J. (1980). Writing and counseling: Using a dialogue journal. *Language Arts, 57*, 514-519.

Vande Kemp, H. (1981). Teaching psychology of the family: An experiential approach and a working bibliography. *Teaching of Psychology, 8*, 152-156.

Describing the Development of a Developmental Psychologist: An Alternative Term Paper Assignment

Kathleen M. Galotti
Carleton College

Each student taking a sophomore/junior level course in developmental psychology is asked to choose a different developmental psychologist and to read as much of that person's published work as is feasible. Students are encouraged to select articles that range over different research areas and different years of publication. They then write a paper describing the target psychologist's work, focusing on the question, "How has this person's work developed?"

The assignment is intended to address a number of goals, including the following: (a) to acquaint students with primary literature in developmental psychology, (b) to provoke critical thinking about the concept of development, and (c) to recognize that the progress of an academic career is seldom linear or preordained. Student reaction and implementation suggestions are discussed.

A sophomore/junior level course in psychology typically attracts some students who have little background in psychology beyond the introductory course or sequence. The assignment described in this article grew out of my experience in developmental psychology with freshman and sophomore students who lacked the skills necessary to circumscribe a workable topic when asked to "write a term paper on any topic of your choosing." In addition, I wanted students to define and refine their own conceptions of development and see that entities other than infants and children (e.g., careers) also undergo development.

Introductory psychology is a prerequisite for the course for which this project was designed. It covers development from the prenatal period through adolescence. The assignment is made the first week of a 10-week term and is due during the eighth week. The initial assignment sheet includes some suggestions for psychologists whose work would be appropriate, with the suggestions grouped by the general area (social or cognitive) and the period of development (infancy, preschool, middle childhood, or adolescence) with which the psychologist is typically associated. Students are invited to consider other psychologists not on the list, but to check on the local availability of appropriate published work.

Students prepare a paper based on the work of a recently or currently active developmental psychologist. The "development" that students need to come to terms with is twofold: (a) some aspect of development, as their target psychologist describes it; and (b) the development of their target psychologist's ideas and research program. Students are also required to assess the reaction of other psychologists to the work of their target person. From their exploration of their target person's work and other's reactions, students evaluate their target person's contribution to the field. Hence, the assignment forces students to move beyond a simple enumeration of publications to a more reflective evaluation of what constitutes development and how to assess a contributor's impact on the field.

Students have 1 week from the time the assignment is given to submit requests for a target developmental psychologist. During the second week, each student is assigned a different target. I make sure that all targets are reasonable ones and that each student has a different target. Students are then directed to *Psychological Abstracts* to prepare a list of their target psychologist's published journal articles. By the third week, students submit a bibliography of their target person's published journal articles together with a list of books, chapters in edited volumes, or other materials, if they plan to include them. Students select 7 to 12 published works, covering a range of years and topics, which are available in our library or a neighboring one. Students indicate in their bibliographies which sources will contribute to the final paper and provide some justification for the selection. This bibliography encourages students to begin working early in the term and to make some organizational decisions. It also provides me with information to make recommendations and suggest supplementary material.

After reading the collection of articles by the target person, students are asked to find two or three reaction pieces to their person's work. Students are advised to use the *Science Citation Index* and *Social Science Citation Index* to locate sources. In the ideal case, these reaction pieces consist of published replies directly addressing some aspect of the target person's work. Often no such pieces exist or are readily available. In those cases, students are advised to choose articles written by other psychologists working in the same area, to compare the approaches adopted by the other psychologists to that of the target psychologist, and to evaluate the work's standing in the field.

This assignment was developed to meet several goals. Listed from specific to general, these are: (a) to teach beginning psychology majors to use bibliographic resources, such as *Psychological Abstracts* and the *Science* or *Social Science Citation Index*, and to offer students practice in conducting literature searches; (b) to introduce students to primary literature in the field; (c) to have students gain knowledge of an area of developmental psychology of their choosing; (d) to offer students practice in recognizing and reconciling different points of view within an area of research; (e) to provoke students to think critically as they construct definitions of *development*, distinguishing between this concept and related ones, such as change, growth, expansion, or focusing; and (fl to demonstrate that the progress of an academic career is seldom linear or inevitable.

The assignment's relation to the first four goals is self-evident, so I discuss the latter two. Students start to find the assignment a real challenge after they complete the reading and begin organizing their papers. Many confront a stumbling block at this point: There is much more than one could say than will fit into a paper of reasonable length. Thus, some organizing principles must be discovered or invented. My suggestion to students undergoing this uncertainty is to question their own definitions of development and to sketch out ways in which their definitions apply to the work of their target psychologist. Those sketches often precipitate a redefinition of development; they also help guide the student in deciding what material to highlight and what themes to use in organizing the other material.

The last goal, demonstrating the nonlinearity of most careers, has apparently struck an important chord for some students, especially those seeking academic careers. They report finding it both liberating and exhilarating to find that some prominent developmental psychologist started a career in an area of research often very different from the one in which prominence was eventually achieved. This finding, students suggested, makes it easier to contemplate one's own prospective career: If renowned Psychologist X had no well-marked road map to begin a career, maybe the student, lacking a detailed plan for the next 20 years, could also someday establish a significant research program.

Student reaction to the assignment has been positive since its inception 4 years ago. One hundred eighteen students took the course during those years, and 84 of those returned course evaluations asking them to assess the value of the assignment on a scale ranging from *outstanding* (6) to *very poor* (1). The modal rating was 4, with 77% of the students rating the assignment a 4, 5, or 6. Some students complained about the constraints of the assignment, stating a preference for a topic-based rather than person-based assignment. My informal assessment is that this assignment works best for talented and/or diligent students; procrastinators of average ability encounter difficulty and express less enjoyment of the assignment (and less comprehension of the goals).

I look forward to receiving this set of papers every year. Usually, two or three students choose target psychologists with whom I am not familiar, and their papers help broaden my knowledge. Students who write about people more familiar to me often uncover less well-known papers and make interesting inferences about how that work has fit in with or shaped other and better known work. Some students have shown a remarkable level of energy, some wrote to (and one student arranged for a telephone interview with) their target person. (In every case, the psychologists have been gracious, often flattered, and always helpful.) Finally, some students have found this exercise to be extremely valuable when thinking about graduate work and in targeting potential graduate advisers. Being very familiar with a developmental psychologist's work, students are able to make more informed decisions about whether that person would be someone with whom they would like to work.

Several implementation details of the assignment have evolved over the years. None is intrinsic to the assignment, but all have proven useful. First, I require each student in the class to choose a different target psychologist. This procedure promotes quick selection of targets by everyone (all the good targets are perceived to be taken early) and enhances my willingness to encourage collaboration among students working on psychologists from similar areas. Second, I limit papers to 20 pages of double-spaced text, not including title page, abstract, references, or tables and figures. The papers could become quite long (in earlier years, when I did not impose limits, papers of 35 to 40 pages were not uncommon), with much unnecessary prose. I have tried different limits and found 20 pages to be stringent but manageable. Third, because the paper is challenging to organize and write, I keep copies of successful papers. Once all targets are assigned, I choose from my files a few papers about psychologists who are not current targets and place those papers on closed reserve. I always put more than one example on reserve to illustrate that there is no single recipe for organizing the material. Fourth, I try to organize voluntary working groups for students to share ideas about defining development, applying definitions to published works, planning possible modes of organization, and other common concerns. These working groups meet informally outside of class, and I try to include at least one advanced psychology major in each group. Fifth, I encourage all students, but particularly those who have not taken courses in data analysis and research methods, to consult with me in office hours if they encounter problems comprehending the methods and results sections of journal articles. Sixth, I arrange with the Carleton College library staff to provide appropriate bibliographic instruction to students who need it. If most students in the class have never conducted literature searches, I invite the librarians to class to describe skills and strategies of searches.

Students have chosen a variety of target psychologists over the years. Some examples of the most popular targets are: Diana Baumrind, Jay Belsky, Jeanne Block, Micki Chi, Carol Dweck, David Elkind, Rochel Gelman, Carol Gilligan, Susan Harter, Martin Hoffman, James Marcia, Robert Selman, and Eliot Turiel. Some especially prolific psychologists (e.g., Jean Piaget) have proven much more challenging, and I generally steer students to other targets.

I am pleased with the way this assignment meets my goals. The assignment is a very demanding one. At the same time, if given the appropriate levels of structure and support, students generally find it a rewarding one. From my perspective as an instructor, it is gratifying to see that an assignment to consider the development of a developmental psychologist sometimes promotes students' own intellectual and career development.

Notes

I thank Lloyd Komatsu, Joseph Palladino, and three anonymous reviewers for comments on an earlier draft.

3. INCORPORATING FIELD EXPERIENCE

Using Community Service to Teach Developmental Psychology

Kathleen McCluskey-Fawcett
Patricia Green
University of Kansas

Students in two large sections of developmental psychology participated in community service settings for children and families. They also encountered the social issues facing children in contemporary America. About half of the students (293 of 567) chose to work 50 hr as volunteers; the rest chose to write three papers. Although no significant differences were found between the two groups on overall satisfaction with the course, evaluation of these options suggested that students found the community service to be a valuable experience for understanding course material and achieving other personal and educational goals. Techniques to incorporate such fieldwork into very large classes are presented.

In large undergraduate courses, psychology students rarely have direct experience with the phenomena and populations they study. Students' ability to understand theory, research, and application may be hindered by this lack of personal involvement with the material (Junn, 1989; Linn & Jako, in press). Furthermore, when students confront material that is difficult to comprehend, they may become apathetic, denying or minimizing the issues. For example, we have frequently observed victim blaming and personal distancing when topics such as child abuse, adolescent pregnancy, and poverty are covered in class. Instructors of small classes can incorporate experiences such as in-class demonstrations, field trips, or fieldwork that provide direct access to children. The success of fieldwork in teaching general psychology and child psychology has been previously reported. Benefits include increased performance in final exams (Saxon & Holt, 1974; Sugar & Livosky, 1988), positive attitude changes (Fox, Lopuch, & Fisher, 1984), integration of theory and practice (Fernald et al., 1982), and high student satisfaction (Sherman, 1982). All of the reports of the efficacy of fieldwork, however, are based on a small number of participating students, from 3 (Sherman, 1982) to 44 (Saxon & Holt, 1974). In some reports, students were carefully screened before being allowed to participate (Fernald et al., 1982; Sherman, 1982). To incorporate hands-on experience into very large sections of students with varying backgrounds and abilities can be daunting for an instructor. This article describes how this can be accomplished in an efficient, feasible manner.

For the past several years, we have taught sections of developmental psychology to approximately 300 students. To allow students direct contact with children, we developed opportunities for work in community settings that serve children and families. Many students have not had sufficient experience outside the classroom to help them clarify their career objectives or to determine their areas of interest. This option allowed students to explore a social service setting in-depth. Moreover, fieldwork exposes students to the notion of public service. Most colleges and universities espouse the development of social and civic responsibility, yet traditional curricula hinder this. Finally, we wanted students to confront a wider variety of issues concerning children in contemporary society than is typically experienced through readings and lectures.

Course Requirements

Approximately 600 students were enrolled in two sections of an upper division course in developmental psychology. The course is required for a major in psychology, and approximately half of the students were majors. The rest were in liberal arts, sciences, and professional schools. A traditional lecture format was used. All students were required to do written assignments and to take periodic multiple-choice exams and a cumulative final. Students were given two options to fulfill the writing requirement. One option was to write three 5-page papers, one for each of three age periods: infancy, childhood, and adolescence. These highly structured assignments included child observations, journal critiques, and book reviews designed to help students develop analytical skills and the ability to read and write critically. Each project was worth a maximum of 35 points, totaling

105 points. They also took three exams and a comprehensive final.

The community service option required students to perform 50 hr of service in settings relevant to the course, which gives students adequate time to learn the responsibilities, provides maximum benefit to the children served, and makes likely a breadth of practical experiences. This option required students to read approximately 100 pages of assigned material relevant to their site, to keep a daily journal, and to submit a written summary of their work. Students were excused from or could drop one of the three exams.

Students were given a list of approved agencies willing to accept volunteers. Seven supervisors from the sites that could accommodate 15 or more students attended a class session early in the semester to describe their agencies and answer questions. Descriptions and contacts for participating small agencies were provided, and students made their own arrangements with these agencies. Each student and the agency supervisor signed a contract that specified the student's expected duties; the instructors, the agency, and the student all kept copies. When students completed their work, the supervisor evaluated their performance on six matters, such as "The student completed all duties outlined in the contract in a way that was maximally useful to the agency—*totally* = 15 points, *mostly* = 10 points, *somewhat* = 5 points, and *not really* = 0 points." This evaluation was worth a maximum of 80 points in the first semester in which this option was used. It was reduced to 57 points in the second semester because supervisors tended to give the full credit, creating grade inflation.

Students wrote their daily observations of child behavior down the left column of lined paper. In the right column, they filled in material from the lecture, textbook, and reading list that corresponded to each of the daily observations. The grading criteria specified for the students were detailed observations (12 points) and incorporation of course material (*textbook* = 11, *lecture* = 10, and *extra readings* = 10), totaling 43 points. By scanning both columns, it was relatively easy to assess the students' performance.

In the final written summary, students answered six requests: Describe the setting (7 points), relate five things you observed to the material from the textbook and lecture (15 points), relate five things you observed to the extra readings (15 points), describe what you gained from the experience (6 points), describe what the agency gained from having you (6 points), and describe what you did or did not learn from this experience (6 points)—for a total of 55 points. Specifying points in advance made grading relatively easy. The three parts of the volunteer project were worth a total of 155 points. All three parts were submitted to the instructor at the completion of the community service work. Each midterm exam was worth 50 points; the cumulative final was worth 120 points. The total number of points a student could earn in either option was 375.

Evaluation

Of the 567 students who completed these two sections, 293 chose the volunteer option. The primary sites were Head Start, local elementary schools, a transitional care group home for chemically dependent women and their children, a homeless shelter, and Special Olympics.

Students evaluated the course anonymously on a 16-item questionnaire. Timing of the administration differed for the two sections. Section 1 students were sent the questionnaire 4 months after completing the course. Section 2 students completed the evaluation during the last day of class. In Section 1, 110 students returned the form (62 chose the community service option; 48 chose the written paper option). In Section 2, 237 completed the form (130 chose community service; 107 chose the written paper).

Five questions assessed the effectiveness of the course using a 5-point scale. A 2 x 2 (Section 1 vs. Section 2 x Community Service Option vs. Written Paper Option) multivariate analysis of variance was computed for these five questions. Only the main effect of section was significant (Pillai's value = .047), $F(5, 338) = 3.36$, $p = .006$. Subsequent univariate tests were all significant. The means, standard deviations, and F ratios are displayed in Table 1. The section differences are most likely due to the timing of the evaluation. Section 2 students were in the midst of preparing for final exams for this and other courses and may have been anxious and feeling oppressed, whereas Section 1 students were assessed 4 months after completing the course and may have had the perspective of temporal distance.

Four questions assessing the community service project suggested fairly strong satisfaction with the experience. Percentages in the two sections were comparable and we combined them. A majority of respondents agreed or strongly agreed that (a) the volunteer work had increased their learning of text (60%); (b) the volunteer work had increased their learning the lecture material (60%); (c) the community service option was a valuable learning experience (94%); and (d) because of this experience, they planned to do more community service in the future (79%). Section 1 students were asked if they were currently doing volunteer work. Twenty-three of the 62 respondents reported they were, and 2 were employed by the site at which they had volunteered. Students in both sections indicated that the experience was valuable for future professional and personal goals: (a) job applications (84%), (b) graduate or professional school applications (64%), (c) being a parent (75%), and (d) other types of volunteer work (73%). Students who did not select this option were asked why. The majority (75%) reported they would have liked to but did not have the time. All students were asked if the volunteer option should be offered in this course in the future; 330 of 347 respondents said yes.

Table 1. Student Evaluation of the Course

	Section 1[a]		Section 2[b]		
Question	M	SD	M	SD	F(1, 342)
I learned a lot.	1.62	.85	1.90	.72	10.04*
My interest in psychology increased.	2.00	.82	2.38	.92	14.36*
I am interested in taking another course in psychology.	2.09	.92	2.42	.96	10.59*
I would recommend this instructor to other students.	1.43	.87	1.75	.93	9.54*
I would take another course from this instructor if it was appropriate to my interests.	1.49	.95	1.82	1.02	9.02*

Note. Responses ranged from *strongly agree* (1) to *strongly disagree* (5).
[a]$N = 110.$ [b]$N = 237.$
*$p < .001.$

Discussion

The personal impact of this experience on the students appears to have been considerable. Students' written work and comments on the follow-up evaluation provide evidence that the direct exposure to children was very beneficial in understanding the course content. For example, one student wrote, "Instead of just reading about a child being egocentric, I was actually able to see it take place." For several, this experience helped to clarify their educational and career goals: "I have been considering a career as a counselor for young people, and this experience has made me realize that I could really enjoy it." This work seemed especially valuable in raising the students' awareness of the many difficulties that face children and families in contemporary American society. One woman wrote, "I'd never really been exposed to people living in poverty or fighting to be free of drugs before. I just couldn't believe it at first." Others were affected at a personal level. One woman related her acute discomfort upon leaving a temporary homeless shelter after her volunteer work was completed for the day. She saw two of the residents on the street, who asked her where she was going. In her journal she wrote, "For the first time in my life, I felt truly ashamed saying 'I am going home.'"

Another important benefit of this service work can be the positive effect on the community, reducing the occasional tensions between any university campus and the surrounding community. Students performed over 14,000 hr of community service, and the responses from the volunteer sites were overwhelmingly positive. All of the sites have requested volunteers in the future and many contacted us to express their disappointment that this course is only offered once a year. Students also reported feeling more integrated into the community rather than being merely campus residents.

Using this technique in very large classes requires a fair amount of preparation (about 20 hr the first semester and 10 hr in subsequent semesters) and the enthusiastic assistance of graduate teaching assistants or graders (a .50 FTE assistant was needed). Establishing good working relationships with community agencies is essential. We used 15 to 20 sites, working most closely with the 7 largest. Some students made their own arrangements. Instructors need to assess carefully the liability issues involved in placing students in agencies with children. Sugar and Livosky (1988) discussed this issue in clear detail. Of the 293 volunteers, we have received only one minor complaint concerning a student's attitude. After a brief conversation with the student, the issue was resolved. Despite the costs of planning and grading, the benefits of exposing students to social problems that affect children and families in our society can be obtained even in large classes.

References

Fernald, C. D., Tedeschi, R. G., Siegfried, W. D., Gilmore, D. C., Grimsley, D. L., & Chipley, B. (1982). Designing and managing an undergraduate practicum course in psychology. *Teaching of Psychology, 9*, 155-160.

Fox, R. A., Lopuch, W. R., & Fisher, E. (1984). Using volunteer work to teach undergraduates about exceptional children. *Teaching of Psychology, 11*, 113-115.

Junn, E. N . (1989). "Dear Mom and Dad" Using personal letters to enhance students' understanding of developmental issues. *Teaching of Psychology, 16*, 135-139.

Linn, P. L., & Jako, K. C. (in press). Alternating currents Integrating study and work in the undergraduate curriculum. *Journal of Excellence in College Training.*

Saxon, S. A., & Holt, M. M. (1974). Field placements as an adjunct experience for developmental psychology students. *Teaching of Psychology, 1*, 82-83.

Sherman, A. R. (1982). Psychology fieldwork A catalyst for advancing knowledge and academic skills. *Teaching of Psychology, 9*, 82-85.

Sugar, J., & Livosky, M. (1988). Enriching child psychology courses with a preschool journal option. *Teaching of Psychology, 15*, 93-95.

Field Placements as an Adjunct Experience for Developmental Psychology Students

Samuel A. Saxon and Michael M. Holt
Marquette University of Alabama in Birmingham

Although large scale independent study may be impractical for large universities, faculties are being increasingly inundated by internal and external needs to alter their curricula format. In psychology, various individuals (e.g. Diamond, 1972) have demonstrated that certain academic subjects can be made more relevant and interesting. Bijou (1968) felt that developmental psychology in particular must become more relevant to community needs in order to remain a funded area of study. Regardless of the source or nature of the directives, there does appear to be a strong *Zeitgeist* urging us to make education more relevant to student and community needs.

In response to these needs a decision was made to alter the structure of a developmental psychology course at the University of Alabama in Birmingham. The students (*N*=67) in the Winter quarter of 1974 were relieved of one-fourth of the textbook and anthology readings as well as one-fourth of the class lecture and discussion time. They were given an option of completing one of three types of individual projects in lieu of this "freed-from-class" time. One option, an applied project, was to work as volunteers for 2-4 hours per week in one of several different types of community developmental facilities. The students were provided with a list and description of consenting agencies, a project contract, and two questionnaires. One questionnaire was used by the student to evaluate his experiences at the facility and the other was used by facility personnel in evaluating the student.

Because a previous developmental psychology course (Fall, 1973) had taken the same final content examination that the present class would take, the opportunity existed for determining if less in-class work and the addition of field placement experiences would have a detrimental effect on their general knowledge of developmental psychology. It was assumed that the final content examination in Developmental Psychology had a moderate degree of content validity.

Forty-four students opted for the "applied" field placement projects. Note 1 lists the facilities and number of students participating in their programs. Although students frequently consulted with the instructors about their projects, no attempt was made by the instructors to either program student activities or to evaluate the student's activities directly. The instructors' policy was to let the students become involved in the agencies' programs to the extent that the students desired and the agencies permitted. During the last week of classes the evaluations completed by the agencies and students were collected.

Evaluation. The results of the agencies' evaluations of the students revealed that 96% of the students were participants in the ongoing program with 19% listed as occasional participants and 77% listed as active participants. Students participated in the evaluation (13%), the care (43%) and the treatment (43%) of the agencies' clients. In terms of having fulfilled their project contracts, the agencies indicated that 93% of the students either fulfilled or went beyond (67%) the level of promptness, dependability and time involvements specified in the project contracts. The agencies also reported that 83% of the students seemed to appreciate and profit from the feedback that was given to them concerning their work. The other 17% of the students were working in situations where they were given either minimal or no feedback. In terms of placements being helpful to the agencies, 93% of the students were seen as very helpful workers and during the quarter showed increasing amounts of interest in their work. Although some agencies felt that more than 10 weeks' involvement would be necessary for the student to gain ail he could have, 70% reported that the time was sufficient for the students to gain detailed knowledge of their programs, clients and techniques. All 15 agencies involved reported being either interested or very interested in continuing this kind of field placement.

Generally the students' evaluations of their experiences were in agreement with how the agencies had evaluated them. One hundred percent of the students felt that their presence was appreciated and 91% of them reported that the agencies went out of their way to make them feel comfortable and accepted. All but one student felt that sufficient feedback was given to them to make their experience a meaningful and learning one. Additionally, 91% of the students reported being given the flexibility to participate in the way and to the extent that they wished. Although one student stated that the experience was not very beneficial to him, 95% felt that it was a very useful activity which they appreciated being given the opportunity to do. Also, 98% of the students reported that the experience had added greatly to their knowledge of human growth and development, and 61% of them felt that it also significantly altered their attitude toward this content area of psychology. Although the questionnaire did not allow for expressing the direction of attitudinal change, it was assumed to be positive.

The present class also did significantly better than the previous class on the final examination. The final examination consisted of 75 multiple-choice test items which, by and large, sampled the students' recall of factual information from the text. The present class, which had access to the individual projects, obtained a mean raw score of 51 with a standard deviation of 6.7. Compared with the previous class, which obtained a mean raw score of 44 with a standard deviation of 6.7, this resulted in a T-score of 3.75 ($p < .05$).

Although one can only speculate as to why the substitution of individual projects enhanced the students' performance on the final examination, it did appear to do so. The important thing was that permitting students to work independently doing what they reported was relevant and interesting to them did not interfere with their performance in the class.

In summary, both students and agencies responded in a manner that suggests both community and student needs can be met without sacrificing what is felt to be academically necessary for students. The implications that this approach has for undergraduate education in the applied psychology areas are numerous. It is hoped that others who have not yet begun to add such an option to similar courses will take the time and effort to do so. Recent data which suggest that the largest proportion of undergraduate psychology majors do not go to graduate school but instead take psychology-related jobs (Thornton, 1974) should make us keenly aware of our need (or obligation?) to expose our graduates to field experiences

References

Bijou, S. W. Ages, stages and the naturalization of human development. *American Psychologist*, 1968, *23*, 419-429.

Diamond, N. J. Improving the undergraduate lecture class by use of student led discussion groups. *American Psychologist*, 1972, 27, 978-981 .

Thornton, G. L. The BA degree in psychology in the state colleges: Where do graduates go? What do they do? *Teaching Psychology Newsletter*, 1974, February, 5-6.

Note

Kind appreciation is expressed to those agencies and the personnel in those agencies where our students were placed, for their time and effort in having made this a successful and meaningful experience: Center for Developmental and Learning Disorders, Division of Child Development (10 students), Head Start (7); Center for Developmental and Learning Disorders, Nursing's Infant Stimulation Lab (5); Center for Developmental and Learning Disorders, Division of Psychology (4); United Cerebral Palsy Center (4); Jackson School of Hope (3); Charlanne School for the Physically Handicapped (2); Freedom House (2); Alabama Boys Industrial School (1); Big Brothers of Greater Birmingham (1); EPIC Program (1); Family Court (1); Five Points South YMCA (1); Juvenile Court (1); Psychiatric Unit University Hospital (1); (Total: 44)

4. INSTIGATING MISCELLANEOUS TECHNIQUES

Interviewing Across the Life Span: A Project for an Adult Development Course

Marsha D. Walton
Rhodes College

A project for an adult development course is described. The project helps students apply the theory and research they study and develop basic interviewing steins. Students interview Individuals from different phases of the life cycle and write a paper discussing their subjects' lives in terms of major developmental psychology concepts. This article describes how the students are prepared for the project and how they are evaluated. Some potential problems are discussed.

Courses on adult or life-span development are now offered to undergraduates in many psychology departments. One advantage of this addition to psychology curricula is its potential for helping "put the person back together." Unlike the separate courses students take on learning, perception, social, and abnormal behavior, the adult development course challenges students to under stand how all of these psychological processes function together for individuals in complex social settings. Many teachers have recognized the need for helping students achieve this understanding. Mueller (1985) developed an assignment that required students to integrate course concepts in the analysis of an individual whose biography or autobiography they read. Some authors of developmental psychology textbooks attempt to overcome this problem of disintegration of the individual by including detailed life histories (e.g., Newman & Newman, 1976) or by stressing the holistic nature of development (e.g., Van Hoose & Worth, 1982). This article describes an interview project designed to help students achieve an integrated sense of human development.

The primary purpose of the project is to encourage students to apply developmental theory and research to the understanding of individual lives. Students use the constructs and vocabulary of the theories they have studied in discussing the development of individuals at various life stages. They compare their interview subjects to the populations described in the research they read throughout the term.

Another purpose of the project is to develop interviewing skills. Students are expected to establish rapport with subjects and to ask appropriate questions that will lead to an understanding of the persons' current life circumstances, history and goals, self-perceptions, and world views Although teaching techniques have been designed to help graduate students, clinicians, and personnel directors develop interviewing skills (e.g., Benjamin, 1987; Cormier & Cormier, 1985; Sommers-Flanagan & Means, 1987), little attention has been paid to teaching undergraduates to conduct interviews. Development of interviewing skills is an appropriate part of an undergraduate psychology program because it Improves students' preparation for most careers and for further study.

Description of the Assignment

Students are required to interview five individuals from different phases of the life cycle. Their goal is to achieve an understanding of each person's development. Students prepare questions for these interviews with the help of the instructor and classmates. Each interview lasts from 1 to 2 hr and is recorded on a cassette audiotape. In a final paper, students discuss their five individual subjects' lives in the context of developmental theory and research.

Preparing Students

Throughout the term, seven class sessions are devoted to preparing students for completing their interview projects. The first class is a lecture/discussion on basic interviewing skills. The material includes ways of establishing rapport, different kinds of questions, common interviewer mistakes (e.g., talking too much and asking leading questions), and potential problems (e.g., subjects who ramble and touchy topics) .

Early in the term, students submit a set of interview questions that are organized topically and arranged in approximately the order they will be asked. A class session is spent examining these questions. Students identify questions that may presume the values or beliefs of the interviewer (e.g., "How has religion shaped your life?") and revise them accordingly (e.g., "What role has religion played in your life?"). Questions that require only yes or no answers are also revised (e.g., "Have you tried to rear your children the same way your parents reared you?" can be changed to "What things about the way your parents reared you have you tried to do the same with your children? What have you tried to do differently. Class members discuss the implications of the order in which questions are asked. For example, if students ask more open-ended questions first, they often discover how the interview subject defines the issues. Questions that are more narrowly focused tend to impose the interviewer's framework if they are asked at the beginning of the interview. After this class session, students prepare their final set of questions and begin to conduct their interviews.

In five sessions, interspersed throughout the term, individuals from different phases of the life cycle are interviewed in class. Selecting interviewees who are well-adjusted, open individuals, who will comfortably reveal fairly personal information about their development helps assure the success of these classes. Although it is a little difficult to find adolescents who meet these criteria, it is easy to find individuals of other age groups who will speak freely and allow a class of college students to ask them questions about their lives.

In the first of the five sessions, the instructor takes primary responsibility for conducting the interview, although students are encouraged to ask questions. As the term progresses, students take more and more responsibility for conducting the in-class interviews. During these interviews, the instructor records the questions and makes notes of questions that will be commented on later. About 50 to 60 min of class time is used for the interview. After the guest leaves, the class uses the remaining time to analyze the interview. Students identify effective and ineffective questions, and they consider points in the interview where follow-up questions were needed and where the subject or interviewer seemed uncomfortable. This analysis helps the students revise their interview questions and improve their technique.

Evaluating Student Performance

The interview project constitutes 25% of the student's term grade (15% is based on evaluation of the final paper and 10% on evaluation of the tapes of the interviews). The criteria for evaluating the final paper are: (a) the number of distinct theoretical concepts and research findings the student uses appropriately in the discussion of the individuals interviewed, (b) the effectiveness with which the student integrates material from the course and from other coursework in a coherent discussion, and (c) the depth of understanding and insight the student achieves about the individuals studied.

There are several logistical problems to overcome in evaluating the tapes of the interviews. I have found it very effective to allow students to do part of the

work. Each student submits recordings of all five interviews, along with an index that identifies: (a) the tape that demonstrates the best opening, or "warm-up," including the student's explanation to the subject of the purpose of the interview; (b) the 5-min sequence the student believes demonstrates the ability to ask good follow-up questions; (c) the 5-min segment the student believes demonstrates the best overall interviewing; and (d) the interview that the student believes includes the best closing. In addition, the instructor selects one 5-min segment to be evaluated. Students are asked to have the tape ready to play the sections to be evaluated. The five segments are weighed equally in determining the interview grade. The evaluation requires about ½ hr per student.

Student Evaluations of the Assignment

In final course evaluations, students rated the value, difficulty, and fairness of each course assignment on a 7-point scale. They also rated the value of lectures and class discussion. Table 1 presents these ratings pooled over two terms. (Between-subjects multivariate analyses of variance [MANOVAs] comparing the two terms showed no significant year effects or interactions on the variables considered here.) A within-subjects MANOVA comparing the interview project to the average of the oral presentation and reaction papers showed that the interview project was rated more difficult, $F(1, 23) = 19.9$, $p < .001$, about equally fair, $F(1, 24) = 1.2$, $p > .1$, and more valuable, $F(1, 23) = 9.3$, $p < .01$. Students' assessment of the value of the interview project was not significantly different from the value of the lectures or discussions, $F(1, 23) = 3.6$, $p = .07$.

Students ($N = 25$) were asked to indicate how much class time and course credit should be given to each class activity and assignment. One student recommended that the interview project be given less class time, and one student recommended that it be given less course credit.

Potential Costs and Benefits

This project poses several logistical hurdles and some ethical concerns. For class sizes greater than 10 or 15, the time required for supervision and evaluation may be excessive. Some of this pressure can be alleviated by giving students the option of collaborating. Students may, in fact, benefit more from the project if they collaborate, because they will learn from discussing the interviews with one another.

Freshmen or sophomores may have difficulty finding interview subjects because they do not know people in town at the various life stages. Juniors and seniors have not usually had this problem. Many students use vacation time to interview people from their home towns.

Table 1. Student Ratings of Difficulty. Fairness. and Value of Course Activities

Course Activity	Difficulty		Fairness		Value	
	M	SD	M	SD	M	SD
Lectures					4.62	1.53
Class Discussion					4.21	1.50
Reaction Papers	3.17	1.04	4.72	1.40	4.25	1.48
Oral Presentations	4.33	1.44	4.36	1.41	3.92	1.54
Interview Project	4.50	1.44	4.40	1.50	5.08	1.27

Note. Ratings were made on a 7-point scale, with higher numbers indicating more of the quality labeled. Ratings are the unweighted averages form two terms, $N = 25$.

One of the goals of this project is to make students more sensitive to issues of confidentiality and ethical responsibility in research and therapeutic interviewing. The importance of informing subjects about how the tapes will be used and of honoring promises about confidentiality is stressed. Class time was spent discussing ethical issues such as an individual's right to privacy and the possibility that the interview experience will have a lasting impact on the subject's life. At the end of the interviews, subjects should not feel that their lives have been evaluated negatively. The student's responsibility to commun-icate respect for the subject and interest in the forces that influenced the subject's development are stressed. All interviews should end with subjects' talking about some satisfying aspect of their lives. Considerable attention is focused on these ethical issues because of a concern that some harm might be done by an insensitive and unskillful student doing this project. So far, there have been no serious problems resulting from student negligence or insensitivity.

At the conclusion of the project, the five in-class interview subjects are invited to a class party. This party always elicits interesting conversation and seems to evoke spontaneous discussions about problems such as separating cohort from maturation effects.

The benefits of this project to students are at least commensurate with the amount of work required of the instructor to supervise and evaluate it. Students bring to the assignment concepts they have learned in previous coursework in other disciplines as well as psychology. Several students commented on final course evaluations that this was the first time they felt as though "things are coming together." They are capable of integrating ideas, and they usually find the task challenging and enjoyable.

References

Benjamin, A. (1987). *The helping interview: With case illustrations.* Boston: Houghton Mifflin.

Cormier, W. H., & Cormier, L. S. (1985). *Interviewing strategies for helpers: Fundamental skills and cognitive behavioral interventions.* Monterey, CA: Brooks/Cole.

Mueller, S. C. (1985). Persons in the personality theory course: Student papers based on biographies. *Teaching of Psychology, 12,* 74-78.

Newman, B. M., & Newman, P. R. (1976). *Development through life: A case study approach.* Homewood, IL: Dorsey.

Sommers-Flanagan, J., & Means, J. R. (1987). Thou shalt not ask questions: An approach to teaching interviewing skills. *Teaching of Psychology, 14,* 164-166.

Van Hoose, W. H., & Worth, M. R. (1982). *Adulthood in the life cycle.* Dubuque, IA: Brown.

Discussion Topics for Developmental Psychology

Anne J. Bryan
University of Minnesota-Duluth

Seven discussion topics for developmental psychology are presented. The topics focus on problems that students might encounter in their lives and are intended to promote application of course material. Students enrolled in a large developmental psychology class gave favorable ratings to the use of this technique.

This article describes seven group discussion topics created for use in a life-span developmental psychology course. I prepared these exercises to meet one of my goals for students in the course: to apply what they are learning to themselves and the people they know. These exercises correspond to seven of the nine life stages described by Newman and Newman (1984) in their version of Erikson's psychosocial theory. The exercises are not peculiar to psychosocial theory, however, and could be used with any approach to a life-span course or in other developmental psychology courses.

These exercises are very effective in generating discussion in small and large classes. Students often comment that they have experienced similar situations to those described in the exercises or know someone who has. I deliberately select topics that focus on "real" problems that students might encounter in order to increase the likelihood that they will apply what they are learning in the classroom. Each topic covers specific developmental issues either directly or as a lead-in to lecture or further discussion. These issues are listed after the description of each discussion topic. The absence of topics concerning middle and later adulthood is not due to lack of interest, but to lack of time in a quarter system.

Infancy

You are the parent of a 9-month-old child. When your child was born, you decided to take a year off work to be a full-time parent and primary caregiver. You will be going back to work in 3 months, and your child will be cared for by someone else. You want to figure out a way to minimize the problem of separation anxiety for you and your child and continue to build a sense of trust in your child. As a group, come up with a way to minimize separation anxiety and facilitate trust.

Development issues take into account development and evidence of social attachment, including separation and stranger anxiety, trust between primary caregiver and infant, the impact on infant development of parents working outside the home, and issues related to day care.

Toddlerhood

You work in the state welfare department in children's services. You are given a case to investigate and discover the following information:

Child's name: John　　Age: 3 years, 5 months

Parent Information:

Mother: Mary　　Father: George

Age: 34　　Age: 37

Occupation: Homemaker　　Occuation: Engineer

Education: high school　　Education: bachelor's degree

Intake Report on Child

Physical condition. There are numerous bruises on back, shoulders, face, head, and arms. Scar tissue appears on left arm between elbow and shoulder, probably resulting from a burn. X-rays indicate healed fracture of right forearm.

Interview with child. The child is extremely withdrawn. He keeps arms crossed in front of him and head down. He does not make eye contact. He responds to verbal requests with silence or the response, "I can't." Attempts to touch the child were stopped as his response was further withdrawal, shaking his head, and crying. He did not respond to questions about his injuries.

Interview with mother. She appeared nervous (i.e., shifted frequently in the chair, stammered when speaking, little eye contact). When questioned about child's injuries, she stated that he was very clumsy and was always falling down. When questioned about the burn scar, she responded that he ran into an electric space heater when he was 2½ years old. When asked how she felt about the child, she said she loves him but, "He's so clumsy, I think he might be retarded." She went on to complain briefly about how hard it was to keep the house clean and to take care of John. She mentioned her husband's frequent absences from home.

Interview with father. The father appeared to be relaxed and at ease. He began interview by asking case worker why the welfare department was doing this to his family. When questioned about child's injuries, both present and past, he said he wasn't there when they happened, but his wife told him the child was accident-prone. When asked whether he had ever seen his wife hit the child, he replied, "Of course not; that's ridiculous."

Attempt to define John's developmental problems and how they might have come about. What would your recommendation be in this case: Remove the child from the home and have him placed in a foster home or leave him in the custody of the parents? In either case, what recommendations would you make to the caregivers in order to help promote John's development?

The primary issue is child abuse, including detection, reporting, and treatment. Additional issues are cumulative aspects of development, relating trust in infancy to autonomy in toddlerhood, and the strength of social attachment, including Harlow and Harlow's (1969) research on social attachment.

Early School Age

You are the parent of a 5-year-old child named Susie. Susie began kindergarten this past year. It is May and her teachers have called you in to tell you they think Susie should repeat kindergarten. The teachers have based this decision on the fact that Susie, a pleasant child (no trouble in the classroom), is very shy with other children, does not seem to be very eager to learn, is slow to start her work, and often doesn't complete assignments in the allotted time. Susie has good language skills and is of above average intelligence, but her teachers believe that she is not ready for first grade. The task for your group is to make this decision: keep Susie in kindergarten for a second year or have her move on to first grade. Also make recommendations about how to help Susie developmentally.

The problem of cumulative failure (being promoted to first grade without the skills needed to master the curriculum) versus public failure (being kept back in kindergarten while classmates move on) are two relevant issues in this scenario. Other issues include the child beginning to take initiative in the learning process, recognizing when a child is developmentally ready for learning, and making decisions in the best interest of the child.

Middle School Age

Billy and Chris are 12 and 10 years old, respectively. They are brothers and the oldest in a family of four children. Although Billy is older, Chris is larger and stronger. Although Billy is more successful in school than Chris, he is having some developmental problems. He is very quick-tempered and gets upset easily. He picks on his two younger sisters (8 and 5 years old), especially the 8-year-old. He gets in fights with Chris, but because he is smaller, Billy stops fighting quickly, usually crying and appealing to his parents to intervene. When both boys were younger they were involved in team sports. Billy recently quit team sports, but Chris has continued and done well. What developmental problems do you see here with Billy, and what recommendations would you make to his parents?

Developmental issues include sibling rivalry, first-born versus later-born children, the development of a sense of industry in middle school age, and parenting strategies.

Early Adolescence

Your 14-year-old daughter has become a problem recently. She has always been a good student, helpful around the house, active in sports activities, and has always shown good judgment in making decisions. Since last summer, she has become a part of a peer group. Although the peer group is made up of basically good kids, lately they and your daughter have been getting into some trouble. They were caught drinking beer one evening in a public park. On several occasions your daughter has arrived home later then she was supposed to, and at least twice in the last 3 weeks, she has not been where she was supposed to be (she told you one thing, but did something else).

This peer group is very important to your daughter. Her best friend since grade school is also a member of this group. She tells you that she knows that many of the things they do are wrong, but she doesn't feel that she can tell them what to do. She's afraid they won't like her anymore. As a group, decide what you could do to help your daughter.

The major issue in this example is peer pressure, including conflicts between personal and peer values and beliefs, and practical ways for teenagers to deal with peer pressure.

Later Adolescence

Your 21-year-old son is still living at home. He has a job at a local fast-food restaurant and makes enough money to pay for his car and to provide his own spending money. He does not contribute to household expenses or his own clothing. He was a B student in high school and does not want to work in the restaurant as a career, but he is not sure what he wants to do. He spends most of his free time with his friends from high school who are still in town. Although you do not object to your son living with you and he is helpful around the house, you are concerned that he is delaying making some important choices. As a group, arrive at some conclusions about his current development and what you would do about your son.

The development issues of identity, autonomy from parents, and career choice are addressed in this example.

Early Adulthood

A couple in their late 20s is planning to get married. Neither of them has been married before, and they have been together for 5 years. He has a house which he has been paying on for 6 years. They will live in this house when they are married. He also owns his own car and a truck. She owns her own small business which she started before she met him. She also owns her own car. They both have individual pension plans. Shortly before the wedding, he suggested that they draw up a premarital agreement so that, in the event of a divorce, a property settlement would be easier. He wants the contract to specify that what each owned prior to the marriage would remain his or her individual property in the event of a divorce.

Both are feeling the stress of wedding preparations, and they are not in total agreement on the specifics of the contract. She doesn't think that they need a contract. She also believes that having children could alter their living and financial conditions (i.e., she might sell her business to stay home with the children). Discuss this situation in relation to development in early adulthood and decide what advice you would give this couple.

Developmental issues included in this example are trust as related to intimacy, identity, and the purpose and usefulness of premarital contracts.

I used these exercises in a life-span developmental psychology course during spring quarter of 1987. Course enrollment was 308, and the class met 5 days a week. On the course evaluation form, students were asked to rate these exercises on their usefulness in learning to apply the material and in getting them to attend class. (Thirty points out of 305 total points were awarded for participation in these exercises; class participation days were not announced in advance.) Students rated these items on a 5-point scale ranging from *unsatisfactory* (1) to *excellent* (5). Two hundred students completed the course evaluation form.

On the usefulness of the exercises in learning to apply the material, the mean rating was 3.48 (mode = 3; range = 1 to 5). On their usefulness in getting students to attend class, the mean rating was 4.00 (mode = 5; range = 1 to 5). Attendance averaged 226 (range = 153 to 290) students per day over the 10 weeks of the quarter (excluding exam days). Mean attendance on days with group discussions was 243 (range = 193 to 290). The majority of students indicated that the exercises were more useful in getting them to attend class than they were in learning to apply the material, but ratings on both uses were good. Based on my experience, I encourage other teachers to try this approach in their classes.

References

Harlow, H. F., & Harlow, M. K. (1969). Effects of various mother-infant relationships on rhesus monkey behaviors. In B. M. Foss (Ed.), *Determinants of infant behaviour* (pp. 15-36). London: Methuen.

Newman, B., & Newman, P. (1984). *Development through life: A psychosocial approach.* Homewood, IL: Dorsey.

Using Classroom Debates in Teaching Developmental Psychology

Thomas G. Moeller
Mary Washington College

Classroom debates have been used in a developmental psychology course in order to teach students about controversial issues and to help them improve their thinking and oral communications skills. Specific procedures and policies for the debates are described. Evaluation indicates that students consider the debates to be a positive learning experience. Problems with the technique are discussed and some possible solutions proposed.

Undergraduate courses in psychology may serve a number of valid purposes. One of these is to teach students something about the "facts" of psychology-the purposes, methods, theories, principles, and empirical findings of the discipline. However, another valid purpose of psychology courses is to help students develop their ability to think and communicate, both orally and in writing. Indeed, Lunneborg and Wilson (1985) recently found that graduated psychology majors considered the development of thinking/analytic skills to be one of the most valuable aspects of their psychology training.

One technique that I have found to be successful in fulfilling both of these purposes is the classroom debate. For the past two semesters, students in my course on the developmental psychology of infancy and childhood have participated in one formal debate on some controversial issue in developmental psychology. In order to make their presentations, students must learn the basic arguments and supporting evidence for both sides of an issue, while practicing the thinking and communications skills involved in a debate.

PROCEDURES AND POLICIES

Toward the beginning of the semester, students are presented with a handout that discusses the rationale for the debates, lists the topics and the readings, and describes the procedures and grading policies to be followed. Examples of topics are: "Resolved: Children should be able to live their lives without interference from parents"; "Resolved: Standardized IQ tests are biased against black and other minority children";

"Resolved: Attending day-care centers during the first 3 years of life is psychologically damaging to children"; and "Resolved: Behavioral differences between boys and girls are due to biology and not to environment." Students are asked to rank the topics in terms of their preferences. Although I take these preferences into account, I also try to arrange teams so as to equalize academic ability across groups by considering students' grades on the first examination and my subjective impression of their academic ability and verbal facility.

I have adopted a formal debate procedure in which one team argues the affirmative position and the other advocates the negative viewpoint. Each side gives two constructive speeches (in which members present the major arguments and supporting evidence for their own position) and two rebuttal speeches (in which they attempt to refute the arguments of the other team). Although I try to assign four students to each team, sometimes a team only has two or three members; in such cases, each team decides which student(s) will give more than one speech. Because the teams must know the opposing arguments in order to develop an effective rebuttal, they are told that they must prepare for both sides of the issue. Approximately 1 week before the debate, the teams flip a coin and the winning team chooses whether to argue the affirmative or the negative position.

Beginning with the affirmative side, teams alternate constructive speeches, with the order being reversed during the rebuttal phase. Because the class period is 50 min, each of the eight speeches is limited to 5 min A 5-min intermission (during which teams review their strategy) occurs between the constructive and rebuttal phases. A member of the class keeps time and gives a nonverbal signal when the speaker has 1 min remaining. When time is up, the timekeeper says, "Stop," and the debater must stop at the end of the sentence .

Reference material for the debate is culled from books and journals and placed on reserve in the college library, and students are limited to using only those sources that I supply. (I attempt to find material that presents good arguments for both sides of the issue.) In addition, however, students are encouraged to incorporate into their debates anything that they have learned in the course. In this way I hope to encourage them to integrate their course work and outside reading.

There are a number of reasons for limiting the sources that students use. First, the major purposes of the debates are to help students apply new material to what they have already learned, to think critically about what they read, and to understand the complexity of making judgments about psychological research. In other words, my main goal is to help students learn to deal cognitively with the body of information they have, rather than to teach them how to find more information. Furthermore, because I have also read the sources, I can better judge how well students have used their material than if they consulted sources with which I am not familiar.

After students have had a chance to read the material and to think about the issues, I meet with each team separately. During these meetings I clarify procedural questions, discuss psychological issues that I want the team to consider, and describe general tactical possibilities. I especially point out that the team should emphasize psychological issues such as adequate definitions of terms and concepts, the methodological adequacy of the research cited in the reference material, the empirical evidence that supports the team's position, and the extent to which the team's arguments are consistent with well-documented psychological principles.

In addition to oral presentations, I also require a 250-word paper in which students must tell whether and why they agree with the affirmative or negative position taken in one of the class debates in which they did not participate. The purpose of this requirement is to encourage students to attend class and pay attention to the other debates.

It is helpful to specify in the course syllabus the due-dates for the various aspects of the debates. Thus, I include on the syllabus the dates for each of the debates, as well as the deadlines for team meetings with me and for submitting the written papers. I occasionally give teams time in class to work on the debate.

GRADING

Students receive both an individual and a team grade on their oral presentations, as well as a grade on their written paper. The individual grade is based on the student's own performance in the debate and reflects technical effectiveness (e.g., diction, eye contact), insight into psychology (e.g., ability to use empirical data accurately), and overall effectiveness (a global estimate of the student's value to the team). Of these, degree of demonstrated psychological insight is weighted most heavily. The team grade is the same for all members of the team and is based on the

group's preparation, organization of the presentations, extent to which the team clearly articulates the major arguments for its position, use of appropriate supporting evidence, effectiveness at countering the opposition's arguments, and degree of psychological insight. The individual oral presentation grade and the grade on the written paper account for 60% of the student's overall debate grade; the remaining 40% is based on the team grade.

I have developed a special scoring form for making notes on students' performance during the debate. A class member takes notes (of which I later make a copy) concerning the content of the debate. Following each debate, I write out an evaluation of each team, make copies of it, and give students a copy of their individual evaluation along with a copy of their team's evaluation. I also keep one copy of each for my records.

EVALUATION AND CONCLUSIONS

Classroom debates were held during the fall of 1984 and the spring of 1985. At the end of each semester a formal assessment of the debates was conducted. Students were asked to rate, on a scale from 1 to 10, how valuable a learning experience they found the debates to be, both as a participant and as a member of the audience. They were also encouraged to make written comments regarding their perception of the debates.

From the point of view of being a participant, the mean rating was 7.34 with a standard deviation of 2.07, suggesting that students found the debates to be a valuable learning experience. A number of students reported that classroom debates were a new experience. One said: "I had never participated in a debate before, and now, looking back on it, it was kind of exciting!" Many students expressed an initial apprehension about the debates, which appeared to reflect anxiety about presenting oral arguments in front of the class. However, most students reported that their initial fears dissipated and that they found the debate to be worthwhile. Said another student: "I never debated before, so it was a learning experience. It helped me to see both sides [of] an argument. It also helped me to critically analyze articles." Nevertheless, it should be acknowledged that a small minority of students (one or two per semester) found the debate unproductive. Said one student: "Debates, in general . . . don't help me to learn, but only help to make me frustrated, nervous, and upset."

The mean rating of the value of the debates from the perspective of being an observer was 7.28 with a standard deviation of 1.82, suggesting that students found listening to the debates to be as valuable as participating in them. Some students pointed out that listening to the debates was a more relaxed form of learning than was participating in them. Other students found it interesting to observe intellectual arguments among peers. One student commented: "It really makes me think, because both sides were convincing and I learned how to evaluate major evidence to make my decisions." Some students mentioned that the debates either provided them with new information and arguments or reminded them of things that they had forgotten. However, few students reported that their own position on a topic had been changed as a result of the debates.

My impression is that debates are a valuable tool for teaching both thinking and content, but that certain problems limit their overall effectiveness. As mentioned previously, some students express initial anxiety over the debates. I have tried to assuage students' anxiety by providing very explicit information about my expectations, by meeting with each team separately, and by using only three grading categories (fail, pass, and high-pass); even so, some students find the debates unproductive. A second problem is that a 50-min period is too short to accommodate eight speeches and an intermission; a 75-min period would be better. In the fixture, with my 50-min period, I plan to shorten the format to two constructive speeches and one rebuttal per team. A third problem is that developing topics, finding appropriate readings, developing procedural details, writing the handouts, meeting the students, and writing detailed evaluations all require a great amount of time and energy. Finally, the grading is problematic. Assessing oral presentations is more difficult than grading written work, and I am still wrestling with the issue of how best to integrate individual performance with team performance. Despite these difficulties, my overall experience with debates has been positive. I will continue to use them as worthwhile activities for most of my students.

Reference

Lunneborg, P. W., & Wilson, V. M. (1985). Would you major in psychology again? *Teaching of Psychology, 12*, 17-20.

Illustrating Life-Span Development in Physical Competence

Steven Pulos
University of Northern Colorado

Many undergraduates have the misconception that there is an inevitable major decline in physical performance with increasing age. This article describes an activity to counteract this misconception and to illustrate how life-span changes in physical performance can be influenced by psychological factors. Students are asked to predict developmental changes in championship times for an athletic event— the 1-km bicycle time trial. Next, they are presented with the actual results and asked to rate their surprise at the discrepancy between their predictions and the actual results. Students' misconceptions are explored in a follow-up class discussion.

Most textbooks on life-span human development cover changes in physical performance. Typically, they present physical ability as declining during adulthood. Occasionally, a small space describes how the "decline" can be influenced by experience and activity. Unfortunately, such passages appear to have little impact on students, who frequently minimize or forget the role of volitional activity in physical development and underestimate capabilities of physically competent older adults in a number of different areas (Pulos, 1991).

The classroom activity described herein was designed to reduce students' misconceptions about the development of physical competence. The activity is based on the correction of misconceptions through guided group discussion (Nussbaum & Haroni-Dagan, 1981). Briefly, this technique involves (a) presenting a task to elicit misconceptions, (b) presenting the students with their misconceptions, (c) presenting the correct answer, and (d) discussing the results and implications with guidance from the instructor.

Procedure

To demonstrate life-span development in physical competence, students are asked to predict speeds of national winners of the 1-km bicycle time trial.

Predictions are made for regular intervals between adolescence and the late 60s.

First, students are given a description of a 1-km time trial. Then, they are told that each participant sets off alone, and the one who covers 1 km in the shortest time is the winner. They are also told that this event is considered an intense form of track racing. To help students conceptualize 1 km, a familiar 1-km distance on campus is identified. They also could be told that 1 km is about as long as 17½ football fields or that it is .621 of a mile.

Students are given a table listing age intervals from adolescence to the 60s. The winning time for 30-year-olds at the U.S. Masters Championship is printed next to the appropriate age groups. Students are asked to predict the winning times far the other age intervals and enter these times in the table. Responses from each student are collected and tabulated; medians and ranges are then written on the chalkboard.

Next, students are shown actual results from the national championships (Clapper, 1990; Fuller, 1990; Gindling, 1990); annual results are usually published in *Winning* and *VeloNews*. The intervals and times for the 1990 championships were 17-18 years, 1:10.85; 20s 1:09.38; 30-34, 1:13.40; 35-39, 1:13.52; 40-44, 1:18.32; 45-49, 1:17.29; 50-54, 1:21.39; 55-59, 1:26.62; and 60+, 1:30.58. Students are then asked to rate their surprise at seeing the discrepancy between the actual results and their estimates on a 7-point Likert scale . The median ratings are then presented to the class. Students discuss their observations and possible reasons for them. To consolidate the lesson further, students are presented vignettes of physically fit and active individuals over the age of 40 from a book titled *Over the Hill but Not Out to Lunch*! (Kahn, 1986). The activity can serve as a basis for discussing the influence of personality and motivational factors on physical competence and other aspects of life-span development.

Evaluation

Twenty-two students in a developmental psychology class participated in the activity after they had read the discussion of physical development in their textbook (Sugarman, 1986). All times used in the activity were from the 1990 U.S. Masters Championship, except the times for late adolescence, which were from Junior Championship, and the times for the 20s, which came from the U. S. National Track Championships.

Students greatly overestimated the speed of athletes in their teens and 20s and greatly underestimated the speed of athletes in their 50s and 60s. The median estimate of the 60 year-olds' performance exceeded the actual performance by over 600%, with some students exceeding the actual performance by more than 1000%! The discrepancy between expected and actual time first exceeded 100% for athletes in the 45- to 49-year-old category. In contrast, the median estimated time for cyclists in their late teens and 20s was half the actual times.

Using a scale ranging from *no surprise* (1) to *extreme surprise* (7), students evaluated their surprise at seeing the discrepancy between actual results and their estimates. The median rating for the class was just under 6, with a range from 4 to 7. Apparently, they were quite surprised at their poor estimates.

Students' participation in the discussion was enthusiastic and lively. The most frequent topics mentioned in the discussion were the lack of personal experience with physically fit older individuals and the image of older individuals depicted in the media. The discussion also covered other misconceptions, including those about cognitive decline during adulthood.

The instructor may wish to discuss the limits of this activity. First, the instructor may point out that this activity was based on healthy individuals and that the effect of life style on physical decline may be less dramatic in individuals with illness or injury. Second, the results are based on a cross-sectional design, but similar results are found with longitudinal studies (e.g., Pollock, Foster, Knapp, Rod, & Schmidt, 1987). Third, the instructor may wish to point out that although the example is based on a sample of dedicated amateur athletes, the decline in fitness among normal healthy adults can be partially reversed by lifestyle and exercise (Posner, Gorman, & Windsor-Landsberg, 1992).

The instructor also may wish to use the activity to explore with the students issues in human development. For example, the activity can highlight how secular trends could change developmental trends. Because activity level and aging appear to make equal contributions to physical performance (Katch & McArdle, 1988), an increase in activity level in the general population could alter the rate of decline in physical performance.

Helping students to confront their misconceptions appears to hold promise for enhancing learning. Activities based on this technique could be used to counteract students' misconceptions in many areas of psychology.

References

Clapper, B. (1990). Medal haul for Hegg, Eickhoff at track nationals. *VeloNews, 19*(13), 20-22.

Fuller, A. (1990). Masters national becomes cycling who's who. *VeloNews, 19* (14), 25, 48.

Gindling, D. (1990). Seven gold medals for Grieco. *VeloNews, 19*(15), 39-40.

Kahn, L. (1986). *Over the hill but not out to lunch!* Bolinas, CA: Shelter.

Katch, F. I., & McArdle, W. D. (1988). *Nutrition, weight control and exercise* (3rd ed.). Philadelphia: Lea & Febiger.

Nussbaum, J., & Haroni-Dagan, N. (1981). Changes in children's perception and alternative frameworks about the earth as a cosmic body resulting from a series of auto-tutorials. Unpublished manuscript, Israel Science Teaching Centre, The Hebrew University of Jerusalem.

Pollock, M. L., Foster, C., Knapp, D., Rod, J. L., & Schmidt, D. H. (1987). Effects of age, training and competition on aerobic capacity and body composition of master athletes. *Journal of Applied Physiology, 63*, 725-731.

Posner, J. D., Gorman, K. M., & Windsor-Landsberg, L. (1992). Low to moderate intensity endurance training in healthy older adults. *Journal of the American Geriatrics Society, 40*(1), 1-7.

Pulos, S. (1991, April). *An activity for illustrating life-span development in physical competence.* Paper presented at the Rocky Mountain Psychological Association, Denver.

Sugarman, L. (1986). *Life-span development: Concepts, theories and interventions.* London: Methuen.

Note

I thank the students who participated in the activity for their enthusiasm and encouragement and Jeanne Ormrod, Leah Smith, Janie Meford, and Charlotte Pulos for their helpful comments on a draft of this article.

Science and Values: Addressing Practical Issues in Developmental Psychology

Marsha D. Walton
Rhodes College

This article describes a group exercise to help students understand how science can and cannot be used to resolve questions of practical importance in developmental psychology. Students with similar value preferences work together on a project that requires them to compile research and theory covered during the term. They then compare their work to that of groups with different value preferences. The exercise seems to promote a better appreciation of the contributions and limitations of empirical data and theory for answering practical questions.

Developmental psychology is a course taken by a number of nonmajors who are preparing for careers in education or health care or those who are interested in learning more about children in anticipation of parenthood. My experience suggests that most of these students, and many psychology majors as well, expect to find answers to a number of practical questions about child care and childrearing in the developmental psychology course. By the end of a semester, many students tend to be frustrated by the realization that developmental psychology rarely provides clear answers to the kind of questions they find most important. I believe that the source of this frustration is an inability to distinguish empirical questions from questions of value. Helping students to make this distinction will not only reduce their frustration with the developmental psychology course, but will also make an important contribution to their intellectual development.

I tried several techniques for helping students to develop a better understanding of the role that empirical data can play in forming decisions about childrearing. For example, when students ask questions like, "So how long should a child be allowed to keep a transitional object?" or "What is the best method for disciplining a temperamentally 'difficult child?' " I tried to get them to design a research study that would provide answers to their questions. I allow students to work in groups, and find that some of them do catch on to the idea that questions about optimal development involve issues of value that cannot be satisfactorily answered by science alone. However, many students do not come to this conclusion and find the project extremely frustrating. I believe that the

315

project described later is more effective in promoting this insight. In addition, it requires students to compile research evidence and to use theoretical constructs in a group exercise. I use it at the end of a semester when students have acquired a substantial knowledge base in developmental psychology.

Each student is asked to answer both of the following questions: "Which is more important, the development of individual uniqueness and independence or the development of the ability to relate to and get along with others?" and "Which is more important, the development of emotional security or the development of cognitive and intellectual skills?" No discussion is allowed until every student has made a choice. No one is allowed to equivocate, and all students must sign their choices. Once the choices are made, class members are given an opportunity to justify their preferences, which always results in a lively discussion. Students quickly recognize this as the kind of discussion where participants are rarely convinced to change their views. "This is like trying to justify your religion," one student commented.

After a few minutes of discussion, I present two or three "case histories" or scenarios where the two sets of values conflict. For example, I will describe in detail a child who is a loner, ignored or rejected by the other children, and writes remarkable poetry and short stories mostly on the theme of loneliness. Students consider whether the parents and teacher of this child should intervene, and is so, to what extent.

For the following class, students are asked to study Garbarino (1982), which includes a clear presentation of Bronfenbrenner's (1979) systems approach to the study of development. Other readings or a lecture might be substituted for this reading assignment. When they arrive for the class, students are assigned to one of four groups with classmates whose responses to the two initial questions were the same as their own. (In the 3 years that I have used this exercise, students have always divided themselves fairly evenly, with the "ability to relate/intellectual development" group somewhat less popular than the other three.) Students must work in their groups and come to a consensus on a response to two questions: "Describe the five most important characteristics of a *microsystem* that you consider necessary for optimizing human development," and "Describe the five most important characteristics of an *exosystem you* consider necessary for optimizing human development."(Students will be familiar with the terms microsystem and exosystem from their reading assignment. Briefly, microsystem is Bronfenbrenner's term for the setting in which individuals experience their daily lives and the interactions that constitute that experience. The exosystem is the cultural, economic, and political reality that affects the developing indi-

vidual indirectly.) For each characteristic, the groups are encouraged to note relevant research evidence.

I recommend that the groups begin their work by listing all the characteristics that members consider important, then pare the list to five through discussion. Each group submits its final choices, and I prepare a handout that facilitates comparison of the conclusions according to the group members' value preferences. Although all four groups usually agree on some things (e.g., the importance of good nutrition and health care), there are interesting differences between the choices of the different groups. For example, the "individual uniqueness/emotional security" group may stress the importance of an intense relationship with a primary caregiver, arguing for at-home mothering, and mentioning the importance of unconditional love. The "relate to others/cognitive skills" group, on the other hand, is more likely to talk about high-quality day care, and the contributions of an extended family or friendship group to the microsystem. In a final class session, each group is given time to justify its choices and to ask questions about the choices made by the other groups.

As described, this exercise takes 3 class hr. I did it in 2 hr by limiting the initial discussion of the values conflicts and by not presenting the "values conflict scenarios." When I did this, I had some groups make arrangements to meet after class to complete their discussion or to achieve consensus. When I used three class sessions, the third was my final class of the semester. The discussion leads comfortably into a "summing up what you have learned" closing lecture, which I deliver in the last 20 min.

In the process of coming to a group consensus about the most critical aspects of a healthy environment for human development, students are usually impressed with how much they have learned about development and with how much of the research and theory is relevant to their important questions. (Many of them have previously complained that the developmental theory and empirical research I emphasized in the course were not relevant to practical issues.) The experience of comparing the different choices of the four groups encourages the realization that science can inform such choices but it cannot make them. If students leave my class with that insight and none other, I believe that developmental psychology has served them well.

References

Bronfenbrenner, A. (1979). *The ecology of human development.* Cambridge, MA: Harvard University Press.

Garbarino, J. (1982). Sociocultural risk: Dangers to competence. In C. B. Kopp & J. B. Krakow (Eds.), *The child: Development in a social context* (pp. 630-685). Reading, MA: Addison-Wesley.

5. USING VIDEOTAPES

Use of Videocassette Parent Interviews in Teaching Developmental Psychology

Gregory F. Harper
John R. Silvestro
Fredonia State University College

In this instructional improvement project, eight videocassette programs were produced that focused on the child rearing strategies of parents. They were 25 to 30 minutes in length and were produced by the Instructional Resources Center of SUNY-Fredonia, either in the participating parents' homes or in the College's television studio.

The eight programs each deal with a different child or adolescent developmental concern or a particular family structural component characteristic. The goal in selecting these situations was to have sufficient diversity so that the undergraduate and graduate viewing audience would have exposure to a wide range of parenting perspectives. It was hoped that by viewing many of the programs, students preparing for careers (where interaction with parents is an expressed or implicit requirement) would gain a greater awareness of the diversity of parent perspectives on child rearing.

Each videocassette program includes a discussion of some general child development theme, such as styles of parental discipline, sex role development, and parental views on their children's education. The degree of depth on these themes varied, depending upon the degree of parental interest and the relevance of a theme to the particular family situation. In addition to developmental themes, the interviewers concentrated on the special interests of each group of parent participants. Thus, for example, in the program on the effects of divorce on children the bulk of the interview centers on such issues as child custody arrangements, the explanation of the divorce to the children, and short- and long-term reactions of children to the divorce.

Accompanying the eight videocassettes is an observation guide, produced by the project directors, to assist students in summarizing and interpreting the content of each program. This guide includes an approximate one to two page discussion on the underlying child development issues relevant to each program, followed by a series of six to eight discussion questions based upon the specific content of the particular program. The use of the observation guides allows students to become more actively involved in the intended learning process.

An important element of the project is evaluation. The videocassette programs are yielding student evaluative data for each course in which they are employed. As the evaluative data accumulate over several semesters, modifications in the use of the programs will be made. Also the publication of articles and the presentation of papers related to the project will be accomplished as soon as sufficient evaluative data become available.

Project Background and Rationale. Both of us have had extensive experience in teaching courses in the area of child and adolescent development. As a result of our experience, we were acutely aware of the relative lack of understanding which most undergraduate students possessed about the parenting role. Perhaps as a result of lingering adolescent egocentrism, many students naively assumed that all parents behaved, or should behave, as their own parents did and do. As a result, we believed that students required greater exposure to a variety of parents. Ideally it would have been valuable for students to go out into the community and interview parents, but logistically, this would have been a prohibitive task. It was then decided that the production of videocassette interviews would be an effective alternative way of educating large numbers of students about parents. They would also provide the greatest degree of instructional flexibility, as they could be utilized in a variety of courses relating to child development. Another feature was the fact that they could provide a standardized stimulus for the analysis of varying parenting strategies.

Having decided to proceed with the production of the programs, we quickly realized that to accomplish our goals and to produce programs of high technical quality, we would have to obtain financial support from sources external to our academic department and local campus. Thus, application for an Improvement of Undergraduate Instruction grant from the State University of New York was a necessity.

Project Design. The overall objective of the project was to improve the undergraduate instruction of teacher education students as well as students in the helping professions who plan to work with children and adolescents. The project sought to improve undergraduates' knowledge of and understanding of parents and parents' viewpoints on child rearing and child development. The following specific objectives were sought in the project:

1. Students will become more familiar with the overall concerns of parents in raising children and to parental expectations of children's school learning experiences.
2. Students will become more sensitive to differences in parental viewpoints on child development which are related to variations in parental socio-economic backgrounds.
3. Students will become more cognizant of the important parental and home influences on children, both advantageous and detrimental, which affect learning and development
4. Students will be able to observe how parents of children with "special" developmental characteristics (e.g., gifted. handicapped) feel about their children and the professionals who interact with their children
5. Students after viewing the videocassettes, will be more likely to actively seek parental assistance and advice when they later assume professional positions which involve working with children.

Project Activities. Upon notification of the grant award, but prior to program production, we developed detailed interview protocols for all of the selected parent participants. Each protocol was individually tailored to the unique family structure characteristics and to the unique developmental characteristics of the children within each family. Although the interview protocols insured a degree of structure for the parent interview sessions, they did not preclude the use of spontaneous questions by the interviewers during the program production sessions.

Four of the interviews were conducted in the homes of the parent participants: items numbered 4, 5, 6, and 7 in the list below. Production of the in-home programs proved to be difficult and time consuming. Problems with lighting, camera position, and sound were more numerous than they were for in-studio productions. The in-home productions probably contributed to greater program realism, but we concluded in retrospect that they were not worth their effort in terms of final program quality. Thus, the last four programs (items 1, 2, 3, and 8, below) were produced in the campus color television studio. We were accompanied in their production sessions by a television director, two camera operators, and a sound operator. The television director also played a significant role in the final editing of the eight programs and in the production of the introductory program segments.

Materials Developed. A total of eight 25 to 30 minute color videocassette programs along with a 19 page observation guide were produced. The eight videocassette programs are as follows:

1. The Expectant Parents. Interview with a young couple expecting their first child and their plans for child rearing.
2. The Adopted Child. Interview with a couple who recently adopted an infant. They describe the adoption process and the special concerns of adopting parents.
3. The Traditional Family. Interview with a couple with strong lower-middle class ethnic values, which influence their child rearing strategies.
4. The Large Family. Interview with the parents of eight children ranging in age from 9 to 25 They describe the unique difficulties of their parenting task.
5. Effects of Divorce for Children. Interview with a young mother of two daughters reveals the reaction of children to divorce and the effect of a "joint custody" arrangement.
6. Guiding Adolescent Growth Interview with parents of four adolescents that includes an examination of adolescent sexuality, drug use, discipline, and moral development.
7. The Gifted Child Interview with parents of a gifted nine year old boy reveals the developmental pattern and societal response to giftedness.
8. The Handicapped Child. Interview with parents of a young child with a chronic lung problem and developmental delay reveals their ordeal with doctors and other professionals during the course of their son's hospitalization and later rehabilitation

The observation guide that was produced includes a one to two page narrative about the relevance of the child rearing concern featured in each program along with six to eight study questions per program. The observation guide is a bound publication which includes material on all eight videocassette programs.

Implementation of Program. As indicated earlier, the videocassette programs that were produced were implemented within one month of their completion. One of us (JRS) integrated five of the videocassettes into his summer school course of Developmental Psychology. Students in this class were shown the programs during class time, then discussion and questions concerning each program ensued. Students were requested to answer, in writing, the questions appropriate to each program from the observation guide, and to give their responses to the instructor at the next class meeting. Student responses were limited to two typed pages, in order to encourage clarity and brevity in writing. They were evaluated on a scale of 1 to 10, and were returned to students one day after submission.

The other author (GFH) has utilized virtually all of the videocassettes into three undergraduate courses.

Four tapes are usually shown in Developmental Psychology: "The Expectant Parent" in conjunction with discussions of prenatal development; "The Traditional Family," or the "Effects of Divorce on Children" in conjunction with discussions of socialization factors. "The Adopted Child" is used in the discussion of the nature/nurture controversy, and "Guiding Adolescent Growth" is used to illustrate adolescent development. The tapes relating to gifted and handicapped children are used in the courses Learning and Behavior Disorders and Developmental Disabilities to illustrate the effects of family factors on the development of exceptional children.

In each case, students complete the questions pertaining to the tape in the study guide. These are graded and returned and are used as a basis for class discussion of the issues raised in the tapes. This pertains to another value of these videocassettes. Virtually all students see each tape shown, so they provide a common core of experience to which reference can be made in lectures and discussions and to which students can refer when writing essay or exam questions. They are far more successful in this regard than are assigned readings for this purpose.

In addition to the expectations listed above, we hoped that individuals viewing these tapes and utilizing the study guide learn to be careful and intelligent listeners: able to abstract from a conversation important ideas and themes, and able to relate these to knowledge gained elsewhere. The latter point is central, for students frequently fail to grasp the relevance of course content without illustration. Finally, it is hoped that some viewers are led to objectify and analyze their own experience with parents and to recognize both the unique and common aspects of this relationship.

Evaluation Techniques and Results. There are two sources of evaluation of this project. The first consists of written assignments accompanying the study guide. These are evaluated in terms of their accuracy adequacy and in the case of inferential or implication/application type questions, their relationship to course content. Although students are free to speculate on certain questions, answers are expected to integrate information presented in the text or class discussions. This is largely a subjective source of project evaluation, but it is clear that student responses are uniformly good, with the average grade equaling a B + equivalent.

The second source of project evaluation is a survey distributed at the end of the semester to all course participants ($N = 211$). Results are summarized below. Each question is followed by the mean and the standard deviation (in parentheses). The scale was from 1, strongly agree, to 5, strongly disagree.

1. The interviews in this series helped me to better understand the parents' point of view in child development. 1.90 (.62)

2. The interviews helped me to better understand certain concepts in the course. 2.34 (82)
3. As a result of viewing these interviews, I would be more likely to seek information from the parents of children I will teach. 2.00 (.83)
4. As a result of viewing these interviews I better understood child development. 2.37 (.83)
5. As a result of viewing these interviews I better understand the contribution of parents to child development. 1.78 (.63)
6. These interviews should become a permanent part of the course. 1.97 (.85)
7. I would have learned as much listening to a lecture on the topic of parental influences on child development as I did by viewing these tapes. 3.42 (.98)
8. I have a better appreciation for the difficulties faced by parents as a result of viewing these tapes. 2.11 (.80)
9. The study guide was useful in viewing these observations. 1.76 (.77)

As can be seen, students generally agree that the objectives of the tape series are largely met. Answers to questions 1 and 8 indicate increased empathy with parents. Responses to questions 2, 4 and 5 indicate that students appreciate the illustrative nature of the interviews. The response to question 3 indicates that students better appreciate the information parents can provide to teachers. Answers to questions 6, 7, and 9 suggest a positive value placed on the tapes as a means of instruction and on the study guide as a useful adjunct.

Other considerations in evaluating this project clearly favor its implementation. Once the videocassettes are developed they are easily and simply integrated with course content. Because the tapes are on campus problems with scheduling and rental costs are eliminated. On the Fredonia campus playback equipment is readily available or the cassettes are shown over closed circuit television. The nature of the cassette is itself an advantage. They are easily reproduced inexpensive easy to store and not generally subject to the same deterioration as film, for example. The cost of implementation and operation of the tapes and of the project generally are virtually nil, and continued implementation is highly likely.

Summary and Conclusions. In the judgment of the authors this has been a most rewarding project. Project products and the outcomes of their implementation have directly and simply accomplished the major objectives established by the authors. There is no doubt that the project resulted in a clear benefit to students and in a general improvement of the instruction in the courses where it has been implemented.

Reflecting on our personal involvement, the production of this series of tapes has been educational for us as well. It has broadened our expertise in media production and uses made us aware of the uses and limitations of this media, and has suggested other uses for the medium of television in instruction. The use of the videocassettes in class has afforded us an opportunity to share experiences with our students and to update our curricula to accommodate the information presented .

Generally, it has been a most rewarding experience for all involved.

Note

This paper is adapted from a presentation at the Annual Convention of the American Psychological Association, Washington, DC, 1981.

The Use of Videotaped Material in the Instruction And Evaluation of Developmental Psychology Students

Mark Grabe and Lila Tabor
University of North Dakota

One of the major problems involved in the teaching of large psychology courses is to provide "real life" examples of the behaviors under discussion. This is particularly evident in developmental psychology courses where several factors combine to increase the difficulties of securing appropriate samples of human behavior. First, universities of even moderate size may instruct several hundred students in a course of this type each semester. There may not be sufficient numbers of willing subjects within the desired age categories to meet the needs of this many students. Secondly, repeated use of available subject populations invites the displeasure of host agencies (e.g., day care centers) and if carried to an extreme may violate an ethical responsibility to the subjects. Finally, there are certain potential observational experiences which for reasons of timing or practicality cannot be provided on a regular schedule (e.g., a newborn infant).

Our solution to these difficulties has been to substitute carefully structured videotaped experiences for the existing activities of a weekly discussion/laboratory meeting. There are, of course, circumstances in which video experiences cannot equal the impact of interaction with a human subject, but intuitively video experiences seem to have certain advantages. Taped presentations can guarantee that students will be exposed to situations and behaviors that the instructor expects them to see, can have repeated opportunities to view behaviors that present conceptual difficulty, will have relatively similar experiences, and will be allowed to view behavior occurring in normally inaccessible settings (e.g., newborn nursery).

Although the use of videotapes as a substitute for live interaction is certainly not unique (e.g., Silvestro, 1979), the evaluation of videotaped instruction in higher education has generally been ignored. For instance, Campeau (1971) reports that virtually no quality research exists systematically demonstrating that videotaped experiences influence cognitive achievements. Thus, in addition to providing readers with a specific model for utilizing videotapes, we intend to provide empirical support for the value of expending instructional resources in this manner.

The approach employed in this study proposes that videotapes be utilized in a rather unique way. Our philosophy in structuring the video presentations was to put students into a situation which allowed them to organize their own impressions about a given type of behavior. In other words, our intent was not to produce carefully orchestrated "canned" lectures complete with appropriate demonstrations. This type of experience is already inexpensively available through the many existing educational films. Our belief was that commercial films do not lend themselves to the development of an appreciation for the diversity and complexity of actual behavior. Viewers may develop the false impression that children of a given age will respond to a given experimental situation with exactly the same "textbook" response. As an alternative, the tapes developed for this study sought to provide broader and less externally organized samples of behavior which could provide the basis for discussion and analysis within small-group discussion sections.

This paper will focus primarily on attempts to evaluate the effectiveness of the proposed use of videotapes. It was expected that tape presentations would result in demonstrated advantages in both the affective and cognitive domains when compared with a traditional discussion approach. Particular benefits were expected when students were required to demonstrate their ability to evaluate actual samples of behavior and explain the principles of behavior involved.

Method. The subjects in this study were 249 undergraduates taking either of two lecture sections of the introductory course in developmental psychology. Each lecture section was instructed by a different faculty member. Two graduate teaching assistants (GTA), each in charge of four discussion/laboratory sections, were assigned to each faculty member Each GTA taught two sections using the tape and two sections using the traditional discussion formats.

All discussion/laboratory groups covered the same 11 topical areas. The content to be discussed in each area was specified in a detailed lesson plan given the GTAs at a weekly planning meeting. In both the tape and traditional sections, the GTAs first presented a brief overview of the week's topic. In the tape sections, the students then viewed and discussed the contents of the corresponding tape. The discussion was partly based on questions provided by the GTA and partly based on comments or issues volunteered by the students. GTAs in the traditional sections described the behavior depicted on the tapes verbally and then also engaged the class in a discussion of the material. As a concrete example of a typical discussion/laboratory session, the unit on moral development first required the GTAs to present a brief outline of Kohl berg's stage theory. Students in the tape sections then viewed a tape of children responding to moral dilemma problems. Students in the traditional sections were verbally presented with responses typical of the stages of moral development. Both treatment groups then responded to questions from the GTA and were encouraged to provide their own comments.

Variables assessing both affective reactions and cognitive performance were gathered from all students'. Affective variables included the proportion of weekly discussion/laboratory sessions attended and responses to a five item questionnaire evaluating the student's response to discussion/laboratory experiences (see Table 1 for items). The student's knowledge was evaluated utilizing both a ten item multiple choice examination included as part of the course final and a special lab practical examination. This lab final required students to read short-answer type questions and then to respond on the basis of their interpretation of taped material they were shown in the testing situation. The short-answer items were weighted according to the complexity of response that each required. The taped test material not only repeated some behaviors shown in class but also included some novel examples. Items also required both the identification of specific types of behavior with a descriptive term and the explanation of the factors responsible for a given type of behavior.

All analyses assumed a fixed effects model with Lecturer, Lab Instructor (within Lecturer), and Method of Instruction as the main effects. With the exception of a MANOVA applied to the affective questionnaire scores, the dependent variables were analyzed using an ANOVA procedure. While Lecturer and Lab Instructor did reach significance in several analyses, these variables are not of primary interest to this study and will not be reported.

Table 1. Mean Questionnaire Item Ratings for Tape and Traditional Students

Item	Tape	Traditional
1. Generally, I felt the labs were interesting/stimulating.	2.38	2.82*
2. I found the labs helpful in deriving practical insights.	2.13	2.61*
3. The concrete examples used in labs contributed to my theoretical understanding of child development.	2.05	2.49*
4. The labs were helpful in preparing for tests.	2.88	2.99
5. The labs could be dropped without detracting from the overall quality of the course.	3.41	3.05*

Students responded on a 5-point scale (1 = strongly agree, 5 = strongly disagree). Items marked with an asterisk produced a significant difference.

Results. Students assigned to the tape sections were found to attend the class at a significantly higher rate, $F(1, 238) = 4.87$, $p < .05$. Mean rate of attendance for the tape and traditional sections were .82 and .76 respectively.

Results obtained from the five item affective questionnaire were first analyzed using a multivariate analysis of variance. A significant difference was indicated (F approximation of the Hotelling-Lawley Trace $(5, 241) = 5.85$, $p < .001$). Univariate MANOVAs indicated significant differences for all but item 4 (see Table 1). All mean differences indicate more positive reactions within the tape sections.

Analysis of the totals from the 10 item multiple choice final produced a significant method effect, $F(1, 245) = 6.14$, $p < 01$. Students attending the recitation sessions employing tapes averaged 6.83 correct responses and the control students averaged 6.27 correct responses.

The lab practical test consisted of 10 short answer items scored according to a strict answer key. The items varied in point value depending upon the complexity of the response required. A coefficient alpha (Nunnally, 1967) value of .60 indicated that this examination had adequate reliability. Student performance was analyzed utilizing composite scores and on an item by item basis. The item by item analyses were performed to gain some insight into the types of questions which might be sensitive to the method of instruction .

Total exam performance was found to vary significantly between the two methods of instruction, $F(1, 233) = 9.33$, $p < .01$. Mean exam performance was 19.4 in the tape sections and 17.3 in the control sections. Four items also produced significant differences favoring the tape based method of instruction. These items included a question requiring the identification of a basic developmental phenomenon (metamemory) seen in the tape sections, identification of a basic developmental phenomenon (conservation) viewed in other forms in the tape sections, an item requiring students to explain why children could solve a problem in one situation but not in a variation of that situation (object permanence problem) and finally an item requiring an explanation of the difference in two children's responses to a moral dilemma problem. Thus, students who had viewed the tapes showed superiority on several item types.

A final analysis was suggested by the significant difference in attendance. The tapes may have produced superior performance on the lab practical test because students were able to learn better from the concrete visual examples, but the students in the tape sections may also have learned more because they came to class more frequently. In order to investigate these possibilities, an R^2 improvement regression technique (Kerlinger & Pedhazur, 1973) was employed. This procedure allows the user to determine if a given variable accounts for a significant change in the variability of the dependent variable after the impact of other variables has been removed. Variables were entered into the regression equation in the following order: score from the lecture final, lab attendance, and method of instruction. Scores on the lecture final, a measure of ability, accounted for 22% of the variability in lab performance. Lab attendance augmented this value by 5% and method of instruction accounted for an additional 2%. The contribution of instructional method was significant, $F(1, 239) = 6.90$, $p < .05$. Although the impact of method was not large, the difference between methods of instruction could not be accounted for entirely by the difference in rate of attendance.

Discussion. This study makes two contributions. First, in a relatively sound experimental manner, this research has demonstrated the affective and cognitive advantages of employing videotapes to provide examples of relevant human behavior. Students exposed to the videotapes found the course to be more interesting and meaningful, attended the laboratory sessions more regularly and performed better on both the traditional multiple choice and experimental lab practical evaluations of their acquired knowledge. Further analysis suggested that the tapes had an impact on learning beyond the important motivational function of encouraging a higher rate of discussion/laboratory attendance. While the differences among the means were not always substantial, the research reported here offers a relatively optimistic opinion regarding the instructional value of videotapes. Those interested in further research in this relatively unexplored area would be wise to impose greater control over the exact procedures utilized in the instructional settings.

The second important contribution of this study is that it demonstrated the possibility of evaluating a student's ability to explain actual samples of behavior. Whereas the instrument employed in this study was rather crude, future research might focus on the types of items which could be most profitably presented in this manner. An obvious problem to be considered is the limited amount of information that can be gathered in a given amount of time. As a general suggestion it might be argued that as a science of behavior, psychology should be taught and evaluated in a manner more directly utilizing samples of the content it seeks to explain.

References

Campeau, P. Selective review of the results of research on the use of audiovisual media to teach adults. ERIC Document EDO66923, 1971.

Kerlinger, F., & Pedhazur, E. *Multiple regression in behavioral research.* New York: Holt, Rinehart & Winston, 1973.

Nunnally, J. *Psychometric theory.* New York: McGraw-Hill, 1967.

Silvestro, J. Use of video-cassette summaries of childhood in teaching developmental psychology. *Teaching of Psychology*, 1979, 6, 171-l72.

Notes

1. Missing data from some subjects requires that less than 249 subjects be used in some analyses.
2. This research was partially supported by a Local Course Improvement Grant SER 7900363 from the National Science Foundation. The authors take full responsibility for the contents of the paper.

Table - Volume 2

Articles	Topics												
	1	2	3	4	5	6	7	8	9	10	11	12	13
Physiological-Comparative													
Preparing for Exams													
Ackil					P								
Teaching Neuroanatomy, Neurophysiology, and Neuropharmacology													
Daniels					P								
Wilson & Marcus					P								
Hamilton & Knox	S				P								
Solomon, Cooper, & Pomerleau					P								
Klosterhalfen					P								
Schumacher					P								
Wellman					P								
Teaching Hemispheric Laterality													
Kemble, Filipi, & Gravlin	S				P								
Morris	S				P								
Introducing Reaction Time as a Measure of Neural Activity													
Harcum	S				P								
Rozin, & Jonides	S				P								
Teaching Comparative Psychology													
Batsell					P		S						
Batsell					P								
Brown					P		S						
Kemble					P								
Perception													
Acquiring Demonstrations													
Benjamin	S					P							
Wagor						P							
Teaching About Illusions													
Corey						P							
Cowan						P							
Klopfer & Doherty	S					P							
Kunkel	S					P							
Solomon	S					P							
Jacobs	S					P							
Teaching Color Vision													
Mershon						P							
Beins	S					P							
Teaching Sensation													
Mason						P							
Batson					S	P							
Teaching Various Concepts in Perception													
Goodwin						P							
Kozub	S					P							
Lumsden						P							
Terborg						P							

	1	2	3	4	5	6	7	8	9	10	11	12	13
Learning													
Introducing Learning													
Olsen						P							
Rocklin						P							
Using Animals to Teach Learning													
Owren & Scheuneman						P							
Hunt & Shields						P							
Plant	S					P							
Solomon & Morse						P							
Nallan & Bentley						P							
Ackil & Ward						P							
Rowland, Jordan, & Olson						P							
Teaching Classical Conditioning													
Cogan & Cogan	S					P							
Gibb	S					P							
Sparrow & Fernald	S					P							
Vernoy	S					P							
Kohn & Kalat	S					P							
Teaching Operant Conditioning													
Chrisler						P							
Hodge & Nelson						P							
Tauber						P							
Teaching Biological Aspects of Learning													
Kemble & Phillips						P							
Kling						P							
Cognitive													
Olsen	S			S	S	P		S					S
Hassebrock			S		S	P	S	S	S	S	S		
Shaffer	S					P							
Terry	S					P							
Gronlund & Lewandowsky	S					P							
Miserandino	S					P							
Chaffin & Herrmann	S					P							
Larsen	S					P							
Thieman						P							
Smith	S					P							
Katz						P							
Schoen						P							
Developmental - Child													
Instigating Miscellaneous Techniques													
Hardwick	S	S	S	S	S	S	S	S	P	S	S	S	S
Miller	S								P				
Dollinger & Brown									P				
Balch									P				
Allen			S						P				
Sugar & Livosky									P				
Incorporating Piagetian Concepts													
Harper	S								P				
Holbrook	S								P				

	1	2	3	4	5	6	7	8	9	10	11	12	13
Ormrod & Carter									P				
Promoting the Study of Exceptional Children													
Fox, Lopuch, & Fisher									P				
Vacc & Pace									P				
McCallum									P				
Using Videotapes													
Trnavsky & Willey									P				
Silvestro									P				
Poole									P				
Developmental - Adolescent													
Wlodkowski									P				
Schwanenflugel									P				
McManus									P	S	S		
Charlesworth & Slate									P				
McManus									P				
Toner									P				
Ward									P				
Developmental - Adult and Aging													
Panek									P				
Wight									P				
Fried									P				
Dillon & Goodman									P				
Developmental - Life Span													
Starting the Semester													
Walls	S		S						P	S			S
LeUnes			S	S	S	S	S		P	S	S	S	S
Emphasizing Writing Assignments													
Beers	S						S	S	P	S			S
Boyatzis									P	S	S	S	S
Junn									P				
Galotti			S	S	S	S	S		P	S	S	S	S
Incorporating Field Experience													
McCluskey-Fawcett & Green	S								P	S	S		
Saxon & Holt	S								P	S	S		
Instigating Miscellaneous Techniques													
Walton									P		S		
Bryan									P		S		
Moeller	S		S	S	S	S	S	S	P	S	S	S	S
Pulos									P				
Walton			S						P	S	S	S	S
Using Videotapes													
Harper & Silvestro									P		S	S	S
Grabe & Tabor									P		S	S	S

1 Introductory	8 Cognition
2 Statistics	9 Developmental
3 Research Methods	10 Personality
4 History	11 Abnormal
5 Physiological-Comparative	12 Clinical-Counseling
6 Perception	13 Social
7 Learning	

P = Primary   S = Secondary

Appendix - Volume 2

Physiological-Comparative

Preparing for Exams
   Ackil, 1986, *13*, 91.

Teaching Neuroanatomy, Neurophysiology, and Neuropharmacology
   Daniels, 1979, *6*, 175-177.
   Wilson & Marcus, 1992, *19*, 223-225.
   Hamilton & Knox, 1985, *12*, 153-156.
   Solomon, Cooper, & Pomerleau, 1988, *15*, 46-47.
   Klosterhalfen, 1981, *8*, 242-243.
   Schumacher, 1982, *9*, 239-241.
   Wellman, 1984, *11*, 115-116.

Teaching Hemispheric Laterality
   Kemble, Filipi, & Gravlin, 1985, *12*, 81-83.
   Morris, 1991, *18*, 226-228.

Introducing Reaction Time as a Measure of Neural Activity
   Harcum, 1988, *15*, 208-209.
   Rozin & Jonides, 1977, *4*, 91-94.

Teaching Comparative Psychology
   Batsell, 1991, *18*, 229-231.
   Batsell, 1993, *20*, 228-230.
   Brown, 1989, *16*, 131-132.
   Kemble, 1983, *10*, 109-110.

Perception

Acquiring Demonstrations
   Benjamin, 1976, *3*, 37-39.
   Wagor, 1990, *17*, 253-255.

Teaching About Illusions
   Corey, 1989, *16*, 139-140
   Cowan, 1974, *1*, 80-82.
   Klopfer & Doherty, 1992, *19*, 37-40.
   Kunkel, 1993, *20*, 178-180.
   Solomon, 1980, *7*, 3-8.
   Jacobs, 1985, *12*, 169-170.

Teaching Color Vision
   Mershon, 1980, *7*, 183-184.
   Beins, 1983, *10*, 113-114.

Teaching Sensation
   Mason, 1981, *8*, 117-119.
   Batson, 1990, *17*, 110-112.

Teaching Various Concepts in Perception
   Goodwin, 1988, *15*, 104-105.
   Kozub, 1991, *18*, 180-181.
   Lumsden, 1976, *3*, 143-144.
   Terborg, 1990, *17*, 243-245.

Learning

Introducing Learning
   Olsen, 1981, *8*, 177-178.
   Rocklin, 1987, *14*, 228-229.

Using Animals to Teach Learning
   Owren & Scheuneman, 1993, *20*, 226-228.
   Hunt & Shields, 1978, *5*, 210-211.
   Plant, 1980, *7*, 109.
   Solomon & Morse, 1981, *8*, 111-112.
   Nallan & Bentley, 1990, *17*, 249-251.
   Ackil & Ward, 1982, *9*, 107-108.
   Rowland, Jordan, & Olson, 1984, *11*, 45-46.

Teaching Classical Conditioning
   Cogan & Cogan, 1984, *11*, 170-171.
   Gibb, 1983, *10*, 112-113.
   Sparrow & Fernald, 1989, *16*, 204-206.
   Vernoy, 1987, *14*, 176-177.
   Kohn & Kalat, 1992, *19*, 100-102.

Teaching Operant Conditioning
   Chrisler, 1988, *15*, 135-137.
   Hodge & Nelson, 1991, *18*, 239-241.
   Tauber, 1988, *15*, 152-153.

Teaching Biological Aspects of Learning
   Kemble & Phillips, 1980, *8*, 246-247.
   Kling, 1981, *8*, 166-169.

Cognitive

   Olsen, 1981, *8*, 107-108.
   Hassebrock, 1990, *17*, 251-252.
   Shaffer, 1982, *9*, 116-117.
   Terry, 1984, *11*, 111-112.
   Gronlund & Lewandowsky, 1992, *19*, 158-160.
   Miserandino, 1991, *18*, 169-171.
   Chaffin & Herrmann, 1983, *10*, 105-107.
   Larsen, 1991, *18*, 238-239.
   Thieman, 1984, *11*, 101-102.
   Smith, 1985, *12*, 156-158.

Katz, 1979, *6*, 173-175.
Schoen, 1988, *15*, 95-97.

Toner, 1978, *5*, 218-219.
Ward, 1985, *12*, 87-89.

Developmental - Child

Instigating Miscellaneous Techniques
    Hardwick, 1983, *10*, 174-175.
    Miller, 1988, *15*, 147-148.
    Dollinger & Brown, 1979, *6*, 180-181.
    Balch, 1986, *13*, 140-142.
    Allen, 1979, *6*, 119-121.
    Sugar & Livosky, 1988, *15*, 93-95.

Incorporating Piagetian Concepts
    Harper, 1979, *6*, 58-59.
    Holbrook, 1992, *19*, 169-170.
    Ormrod & Carter, 1985, *12*, 216-219.

Promoting the Study of Exceptional Children
    Fox, Lopuch, & Fisher, 1984, *11*, 113-115.
    Vacc & Pace, 1983, *10*, 107-108.
    McCallum, 1979, *6*, 118-119.

Using Videotapes
    Trnavsky & Willey, 1984, *11*, 169-170.
    Silvestro, 1979, *6*, 171-172.
    Poole, 1986, *13*, 212-214.

Developmental - Adolescent

Wlodkowski, 1975, *2*, 129-130.
Schwanenflugel, 1987, *14*, 167-168.
McManus, 1986, *13*, 92-93.
Charlesworth & Slate, 1986, *13*, 215-217.
McManus, 1986, *13*, 70-74.

Developmental - Adult and Aging

Panek, 1984, *11*, 173-174.
Wight, 1989, *16*, 216-218.
Fried, 1988, *15*, 160-162.
Dillon & Goodman, 1980, *7*, 96-99.

Developmental - Life Span

Starting the Semester
    Walls, 1978, *5*, 158- 159.
    LeUnes, 1977, *4*, 86.

Emphasizing Writing Assignments
    Beers, 1985, *12*, 94-96.
    Boyatzis, 1992, *19*, 221-222.
    Junn, 1989, *16*, 135-139.
    Galotti, 1989, *16*, 18-20.

Incorporating Field Experience
    McCluskey-Fawcett & Green, 1992, *19*, 150-152.
    Saxon & Holt, 1974, *1*, 82-83.

Instigating Miscellaneous Techniques
    Walton, 1988, *15*, 198-200.
    Bryan, 1988, *15*, 42-44.
    Moeller, 1985, *12*, 207-209.
    Pulos, 1993, *20*, 244-245.
    Walton, 1987, *14*, 50-51.

Using Videotapes
    Harper & Silvestro, 1983, *10*, 239-241.
    Grabe & Tabor, 1981, *8*, 115-117.